UNDERSTANDING
THE NEOLITHIC OF
NORTH-WESTERN
EUROPE

Understanding the Neolithic of North-Western Europe

Edited by

Mark Edmonds & Colin Richards

1998

Glasgow

Cruithne Press

1998

© Contributors

Cruithne Press
197 Great Western Road
Glasgow G4 9EB
Great Britain

British Library Catalouging in Publication Data

A catalouge record for this book is available
from the British Library

ISBN 1 873448 05 8

Set in Palatino by ╓ᵃᶻᶻ Cornets
Printed and bound by Bookcraft, Midsomer Norton, Somerset

CONTENTS

This volume brings together a large number of papers that explore a wide variety of themes concerning the Neolithic of north-western Europe. Many of these papers were prepared for a conference held in Glasgow in September 1992, others were specially invited to allow a wide representation of the diversity of approaches currently being applied in western Europe.

For the conference a series of 'themes' were introduced in order to provide an overall structure to the proceedings. However, during the conference it became apparent that such a structuring process was inadequate. Not only did individual scholars from different countries present accounts of the Neolithic grounded in specific academic traditions but the division of papers into clearly defined themes created false divisions that were consistently breached. Rather than attempting to apply a similar structure to this book, we have decided to allow the papers to exercise their true diversity and have imposed no thematic divisions. In this respect the sequence of contributions deliberately juxtaposes differences in theme and approach with region and chronology and the reader is encouraged to move beyond their normal sphere of interest.

It is a consequence of this diversity that has influenced the title of this volume. Understanding is contingent and by including a large number of contributions displaying a range of gender, age, nationality, and academic position we hope to show how such differentiation creates a multiplicity of such 'understandings'. Regardless of interpretative framework, much of the material evidence discussed in these papers is new and in many cases research is still underway. In this respect this book is, hopefully, informative and useful at many levels of research.

It remains for us to thank the many people who were originally involved in the conference. We apologise for the lateness of this volume for which we take full responsibility. In this regard we thank the contributors for their patience. Finally we would like to thank Ross Samson for his great efforts in getting this huge collection of papers into the public domain.

Mark Edmonds and Colin Richards

What's in a Name: the Mesolithic, the Neolithic, and Social Change at the Mesolithic-Neolithic Transition

Marek Zvelebil

THE EPISTEMOLOGY OF THE LATE STONE AGE

When *prehistorians* first defined the Mesolithic and Neolithic at the end of the last century, they could hardly have expected that these concepts would come to mean so many different things to so few people. The Victorian social scientists introduced these terms as chronological entities, as periods, the import of which was clear: they were chronological markers along the great road of progress from the primitive condition of man to 'the blessings of civilisation' (Lubbock 1865:487–488; Morgan 1881).

The Neolithic was originally defined by Sir John Lubbock in 1865 to distinguish the New Stone Age from the Old, where Neolithic man was contemporary with modern fauna, lived at least partly by cultivation and animal husbandry, and enjoyed technological advances such as the use of polished stone and pottery (Lubbock 1865:2–3, 192, 234–5, 247–8, 445, see also Clark 1981). The subsequent consolidation of this 'Neolithic package' and its transformation into a type of society defined primarily by its mode of subsistence – agriculture – in the works of Gordon Childe (1925; 1963) is recounted elsewhere in this volume by Pluciennik.

This transition had at least two important consequences. The shift in meaning for the Neolithic from explicitly chronological (and implicitly

social evolutionary) to explicitly social was gradual, allowing the Neolithic to retain its chronological significance, with the result that any
co-existence of Mesolithic and Neolithic societies would challenge the
implicit chronological position retained by the Neolithic. Second, even
though the Neolithic came to be defined by the introduction of farming, it was the presence of more easily recognisable technological attributes, pottery and polished stone tools, which retained their significance as primary archaeological signatures of the Neolithic. This led to
the tendency to see any Stone Age societies in Europe which used pottery and polished stone tools as food producing (i.a. Ammerman and
Cavalli-Sforza 1984), even though this is not the case (Zvelebil 1986b).
In eastern Europe, the Neolithic continues to be defined on technological grounds, irrespective of the prevailing means of subsistence,
and in apparent contrast to the Marxist ideology which predominated
there until recently.

The Mesolithic experienced a somewhat different evolution. It arose
as an alternative to nothing: to a hiatus which was thought to exist
between the Palaeolithic and Neolithic (de Mortlilet 1883, see Clark
1981). As a chronological period, the Mesolithic was first introduced
by Westropp in 1872, and then again by Brown in 1893, to denote flint
assemblages intermediate between the Palaeolithic and Neolithic; but
it did not gain a measure of acceptance until the 1930s. When Childe
finally recognised the existence of the Mesolithic period in the second
edition of the *Dawn of European Civilisation* (1947), he felt obliged to
emphasise the chronological rather than socio-economic content of the
period. In the Soviet Union, the concept of the Mesolithic was not fully
recognised until more recently (Mongait 1959, Gurina 1966; Matyushin
1976), while in Mediterranean Europe, the post-glacial hunter-gatherers remain tagged on to the end of the Palaeolithic as 'Epipalaeolithic'
to this day.

The reasons for the reluctance to accept the Mesolithic as a social
'epoch' equal to the Palaeolithic and the Neolithic lay in its noncon-
formity with the prevailing social evolutionary views (Clark 1980).
Until the more recent excavation of wetland sites both in western and
eastern Europe (Clark 1954; Coles, J. and Lawson 1987; Coles, B. 1992)
the Mesolithic was regarded as a period of decline, not of progress,
whose diminutive stone tools – microlithis – neatly symbolised the ir-
relevance of the period (Clark 1978:3). As Evans (1975:90) put it, as
recently as 1975: 'There is nothing of the brilliance of the upper Palaeolithic hunters living as they were in the stimulating landscape of the
Ice Age, nor anything of the vital urgency with which later farming

communities were to settle and cultivate the landscape of western Europe and the British Isles.'

The shift from the evolutionary to historical and anthropological perspectives in 1920s and 1930s, which discredited the notion of absolute stages in the development of mankind, served to reinforce the chronological status of the Mesolithic, without any further elucidation of the social or economic connotations. This is implicit in the careful definition of the Mesolithic by Grahame Clark (1936: xiv) in 1936: 'In employing this term, nothing more is implied than that the Mesolithic flourished in the main between the Palaeolithic and Neolithic civilisations in point of time; it may be emphasised that it is not intended to suggest an evolutionary stage between the two.'

Ironically, while Childe was refusing to recognise the Mesolithic as anything other than a chronological stop-gap term because it did not fit the evolutionary and Marxist ideas about the 'vital stages in human progress' (1935), Clark arrived at the same position as a result of rejecting these views (1936; 1980).

Subsequent attempts to re-define the Mesolithic as a period with social and economic content of its own, and more recently as a form of society broadly encompassing prehistoric hunter-gatherers with a degree of social and economic complexity have been neither generally acknowledged, nor accepted (Clark 1980; Binford 1968; Mellars 1981; Newell 1984; Dolukhanov 1979; Kozlowski and Kozlowski 1978; 1986; Price 1986; Price and Gebauer 1991; Zvelebil 1986a; 1986b; Zvelebil and Dolukhanov 1991).

At the same time, various cultural, social and economic associations crept in to attach vague meaning to the period, and in this way the socio-economic content of both the Mesolithic and Neolithic were subtly altered. Notwithstanding the development of economic and culture historical archaeology, the Mesolithic retained its status of post-glacial, but pre-Neolithic hunter-gatherer societies by a sort of grudging consensus, (i.e. Mellars 1981; Zvelebil 1986c), while the Neolithic came to stand for Stone Age farming societies, and more specifically, village-based agro-pastoral farmers (Dennell 1983; Barker 1985; Whittle 1985; Lewthwaite 1986), whose roots – cultural or genetic – extend ultimately to the Near East (Childe 1925; 1957; Piggot 1965; Ammerman and Cavalli-Sforza 1984; Renfrew 1987; Hodder 1990). Mesolithic hunter-gatherers and Neolithic farmers came to be defined, primarily, by their mode of subsistence, and to a large extent they still are. On the basis of ethnographic analogies, such hunter-gatherer societies tend to be regarded as mobile groups with low population densities, simple social and economic organisation, while the Neolithic farmers are inevitably viewed as sedentary, village-based groups with limited mobility and evolved symbolic, social and economic structure. This remains the predominant view among most archaeologists, despite the evidence to the contrary (see, for example, Rowley-Conwy 1983; Price 1985 on sedentism among the Mesolithic hunter-gatherers and Barker 1985; Whittle 1985; Bogucki 1988 on mobility among the Neolithic farmers), and despite the recent reappraisal of modern hunter-gatherer societies (Lee and DeVore 1968; Leacock and Lee 1982; Ingold et al. 1988; etc.).

As a result of such cognitive sedimentation by default, the disparity inherent in the original concepts of the Mesolithic and the Neolithic grew into a major rift, pitting the early post-glacial hunter-gatherers against Neolithic farming societies as two typological extremes. As Pluciennik notes in this volume, we are saddled with 'the implicit assumption that there is some essential difference, beyond that of subsistence, between farming and non-farming societies – whatever the variability within either'. This assumption is often made by the economically and socially oriented archaeologists alike: a fact, re-cognised by Bradley (1984: 11) in his comment on the perceived poverty of social life among the Mesolithic hunter-gatherers: 'in liter-ature as a whole, successful farmers have social relations with one another, while hunter-gatherers have ecological relationships with hazelnuts.' Here, the link between the mode of subsistence and social life is made explicit. This link is retained by Thomas (1988: 64, emphasis mine), for example: 'The expansion of the Neolithic at the end of the fourth millennium bc was a consequence both of a major change in the structuring of *agricultural* social relations and of the willingness of indigenous populations to adopt innovations. . . . Instead of the isolated elements of an alien lifestyle, a whole structure of ideas could now be transmitted which contained within it the blue-print for a particular set of social relationships.'

In adopting this framework, Thomas follows in a long line of social evolutionary and Marxist thinking (i.e. Morgan 1877; Engels 1884; Childe 1935; Meillassoux 1972; Godelier 1977; Bloch 1975; Friedman and Rowlands 1978; Bender 1990) which explicitly links subsistence and society, mode of production and relations of production, economy and social complexity to create societal types. At the same time, the ethnographic record and its anthropological interpretation reveals the wide-ranging differences between and within the two societal types nominally called hunter-gatherers and subsistence farmers.

[4]

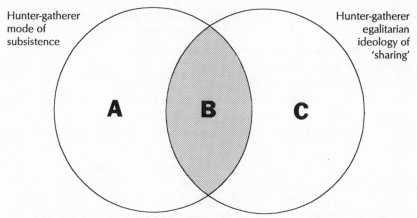

Hunter-gatherer mode of subsistence

Hunter-gatherer egalitarian ideology of 'sharing'

A Hunter-gatherer groups with hunter-gatherer 'mode of subsistence': hunting, fishing, gathering but with non-egalitarian ideology allowing for some inequalities and ranking.

B Hunter-gatherer groups with 'mode of production': based on hunting, fishing and gathering and egalitarian ideology and sharing.

C Hunter-gatherer groups with some farming but with ideology of sharing, who perceive themselves as hunter-gatherers.

Figure 1. Mode of production and mode of subsistence in hunter-gatherer societies.

MODERN HUNTER-GATHERERS: THE DEBATE IN CONTEMPORARY ANTHROPOLOGY

In recent years anthropology has seen a debate which calls into question the very existence of hunter-gatherers as a discrete social type and hunting and gathering as a self-contained way of life (Bender and Morris 1988; Wilmsen and Denbow 1990; Solway and Lee 1990; Lee 1992; Kent 1992). This is a logical outcome of the re-evaluation, originating in the 1960s, of normative and cultural evolutionary views of hunter-gatherers as uniformly egalitarian, mobile and culturally simple (Steward 1936; 1955; White 1959; Service 1962), which were replaced by the recognition of cultural diversity and organisational flexibility among hunter-gatherer societies (Lee and DeVore 1968; Sahlins 1974). This recognition called into question what it means to be a hunter-gatherer.[1]

The current debate includes those who, while recognising the cultural variability and flexibility of hunter-gatherers, argue that they share common traits that define them as a group (Lee 1992; Solvay and Lee 1990; Bettinger 1991; Kent 1992; 1993; Ingold 1983; 1988; Woodburn 1982; 1988; Bird-David 1992a; 1992b). In summary, hunter-gatherers are economically dependent on hunting, fishing and gathering. Their social relations are typically defined by their relationship to resources provided by the environment and by their personal skill in using them. Prestige and status are dependent on personal ability, rather than on land or resource ownership. Ecological relations are dominant and set limits to exploitation, social relations are selective in specifying how the environment is utilised. Hunter-gatherers maintain the practice of sharing, embedded in resources owned communally, 'ownership' conferring the right to distribute food in return for social prestige.

Within this hunter-gatherer 'mode of production' (Ingold 1988), or 'band society' (Lee 1990; 1992), the practice of sharing plays a key role. As Lee notes, the remarkable organisational principle of such societies is their 'ability to reproduce themselves while limiting the accumulation of wealth and power . . . by powerful social mechanisms known as leveling devices' (1992: 39–40). Sharing is perhaps the most powerful of these mechanisms, but as Kent argues, it is so only within the context of an ideology which is intolerant of private possessions (except personal gear), status differences, and social hierarchies (1993; see also Lee 1990). Such societies are characterised by kinship structures (Bird-David 1988: 26; Woodburn 1980: 105) as the major organising device for the sharing of goods. As such, sharing 'solidifies and reinforces the all-important social relationships by equalizing otherwise unequal situations' (Kent 1993: 498). Bird-David (1988; 1990; 1992a; 1992b) and Ingold (1980; 1983; 1988) link the egalitarian ideology to the broader hunter-gatherer world-view: for Bird-David, most hunter-gatherers perceive themselves as 'children of the forest' (1992: 29), of the 'giving environment' (1990: 189), which in turn legitimates their generalised reciprocity for immediate consumption as among siblings (1990: 192) and allows them to 'engage with their natural environment as with sharing partners' (1992: 30). As a part of this ideology, groups such as the Naiken do not distinguish between gathering and planting of crops, although they are engaged in both (Bird-David 1992: 39). Ingold draws the distinction between hunting-gathering as a mode of subsistence and mode of production, where the 'essence of hunting and gathering as production lies in the intentional control of procurement behaviour by the self-conscious human object' (1988: 273). While the mode of subsistence includes labour, the technology and the targeted resources, the mode of production is specified by the social relations of production and the associated ideology (Fig. 1). Among hunter-gatherers, these typically include open access to resources, sexual division of labour and sharing. Unlike Bird-David,

Figure 2. Table of attributes of complexity in hunter-gatherer societies.

Technological complexity	Economic complexity	Social complexity	Symbolic complexity
Anthropological signatures	Anthropological signatures	Anthropological signatures	Anthropological signatures
Increased labour investment in tool production	'Logistic' procurement of resources (see text)	Emergence of leaders (chiefs, 'big men', etc.)	Elaboration of kinship relationships
Use of capture facilities	more sedentary existence	elaboration of decision hierarchies	elaboration of alliances
use of multi-component tools and of stages in tool production	use of storage	development of inter-regional alliances	formalisation of group membership
increase in tool maintenance and advance preparation	delayed return on labour investment	ceremonial enhancement of social reciprocity, and of economic decisions	elaboration of ritual
	some claims to ownership of resources	formalisation of group membership	
	management of morphologically wild plants and animals through selective cull, taming and environmental intervention	development of banking system to convert short-term surplus into wealth	
		expansion of trading networks, especially in exchange of prestige goods	
Ethnographic example	Ethnographic example	Ethnographic example	Ethnographic example
Eskimoes	Ainu of Hokkaido and Sakhalin	Haida and Kwakiutl of NW coast of America	Australian Aborigines in W and N Australia
Archaeological signatures	Archaeological signatures	Archaeological signatures	Archaeological signatures
tool curation (reworking and mending of tools)	storage facilities (such as pits and pots)	social ranking in mortuary evidence	elaboration of ritual on rock art and portable items
use of capture facilities	specialised exploitation camps	presence of ascribed (inherited) status	
increase in the range of techniques for tool production (such as polishing)	residential sites and evidence of sedentism	elaboration of ritual	
production of specialised tools	evidence for selective cull and taming of animals	increase in prestige goods circulation	
development of multi-component tools (such as microlithic technology)			

however, Ingold sees the underlying ideology of hunter-gatherers in terms of appropriation of resources (1988: 277; 1983: 555), but emphasises the practice of sharing as the determinant 'social relations of the hunter-gatherer mode of production' (1988: 283).

Then there are those who stress the relative complexity of some hunter-gatherer societies, without removing them, however, from the general category of hunter-gatherers (King 1978; Ames 1981; Price and Brown 1985; Marquard 1988; Palsson 1988; etc.). The salient features of complex hunter-gatherers include specialised use of resources, storage, investment in complex technology, delayed return, ownership of resources, increased sedentism, higher population densities, greater social ranking and erosion of egalitarian ideology (Hayden 1981; Gould 1982; Testart 1982; 1984; Woodburn 1982; 1988 and refs above). The identification of complexity among modern hunter-gatherers is usually related to particular case studies, and covers a wide range of attributes, not all of which are shared by any single society: consequently we have relative degrees of complexity with different organisational implications (Fig. 2).

The distinction developed by Woodburn (1982; 1988)[2] between the immediate and delayed return hunter-gatherers has a special relevance to archaeology. An immediate-return system is oriented toward procuring food for immediate consumption using simple technology by groups with an ideology oriented to sharing and to the present, where 'distinctions – other than those between the sexes – of wealth, power and status are systematically eliminated' (1988: 34), while delayed return systems activities are more diachronically oriented, and in which people hold rights over four types of assets (Woodburn 1988: 32):

(1) 'valuable technical facilities used in production': boats, nets, weirs, pit-traps, beehives, etc. which act as delayed return facilities and which require a considerable labour investment (see also Hayden 1981; Testart 1982; 1984; Torrence 1983; Zvelebil 1984; 1986);

(2) 'processed and stored food and materials usually in fixed dwellings' (see also Testart 1982; 1984; Rowley-Conwy and Zvelebil 1989);

(3) 'wild products which have themselves been improved or increased by human labour' (see also Higgs 1972; Hunn and Williams 1982; Lourandos 1985; Zvelebil 1994);

(4) 'assets in the form of rights held by men over their female kin who are then bestowed in marriage on other men.'

These assets, according to Woodburn (1988: 34) are distributed on the basis of contractual bonds based on kinship and affinity, in a society where the development of social ranking is incipient, or at least implicit through the relaxation of egalitarian levelling mechanisms. The advance of Woodburn's analysis over earlier similar work lies in the explicit link he makes between the specific forms of social organisation and ideology and the archaeologically identifiable aspects of technology and material culture in general, within the general category of hunter-gatherers. Woodburn goes on to argue that hunter-gatherers with delayed-return systems tend to become farmers more easily than the immediate-return foragers, while the latter tend to become more marginalised and 'encapsulated' by farming societies: hence the prevalence of immediate return, 'simple' hunter-gatherers in the ethnographic present.

In contrast, there are those who emphasise the historical perspective and regard the present hunter-gatherers as products of their own (modern) history. Many egalitarian, 'simple' foragers are seen as the product of resistance to 'encapsulation' by farming societies (Schrire 1984; Bender and Morris 1988; Pedersen and Waehle 1988; Headland and Reid 1989) or as a result of alternating foraging and farming lifestyles (Griffin 1984; Denbow 1984; Gordon 1984; Wilmsen and Denbow 1990). The very existence of hunter-gatherers as a distinct and cohesive unit is questioned (Schrire 1984; Bender and Morris 1988; Wilmsen and Denbow 1990), which undermines the use of modern hunter-gatherers as an analogue for prehistoric hunter-gatherer societies (Bender and Morris 1988; Wilmsen and Denbow 1990). Such 'integrationist' (Bird-David 1988; 1990) or 'revisionist' (Shott 1992; Solvay and Lee 1990; Lee 1992) arguments create serious problems of extrapolation between anthropological and archaeological knowledge (Shott 1992). They also add another interpretation to the history of modern hunter-gatherers, so that they can now be a product of one (or more) among several historical forces: encapsulation (Woodburn 1988), isolation arising from environmental degradation of habitat (Sahlins 1974; Lee 1969; 1992), survival of egalitarian hunter-gatherers ideologically incompatible with shift to food production (Kent 1992; Bird-David 1992; 1990) and 'reverse' transition to hunting and gathering (Schrire 1984; Wilmsen and Denbow 1990; Bender and Morris 1988); (Fig. 3).[3]

The studies by Headland and Reid (1989), Wilmsen and Denbow (1990) as well as other 'integrationists' have demonstrated another matter of great significance: the existence of long-lasting and historically evolving relationships between foragers and farmers. As a part of these relationships, carried on within the structural context of an agricultural frontier, many hunter-gatherers became part-time farmers

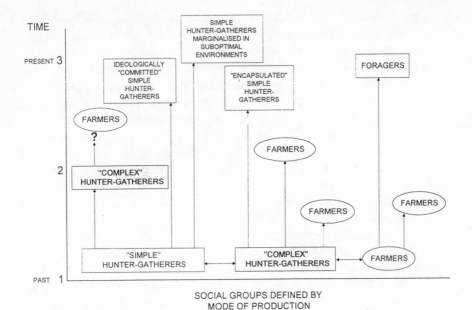

Figure 3. Socio-economic developments among hunter-gatherer and farming societies through time.

through the possession of livestock, through intermittent and op-
portunist cultivation of plants, or by working as hired labour in the
fields of their farming neighbours (Lee 1969; Kent 1992; Lee 1992;
Woodburn 1988; Bird-David 1992; Blurton-Jones et al. 1992). Despite
the long duration of such foraging-farming subsistence arrangements,
extending over at least several hundred and possibly two thousand
years (Wilsen and Denbow 1990; Lee 1992; Kent 1992; Bailey et al.
1989, Pedersen and Waehle 1988; Hill et al. 1987; Woodburn 1988;
Headland and Reidhead 1989; etc.) the hunter-gatherer communities
appear to have retained their egalitarian ideology of sharing.

Even allowing for the possibility of changes in social structure and
ideology in response to the forager-farmer contacts (which may have
led to the reinforcement of egalitarian ideology according to some, i.e.
Woodburn 1988) the general conclusion which can be drawn from this
is that shifts in subsistence practices are not necessarily co-eval with
changes in social structure and ideology, and that hunter-gatherers can
engage in farming while retaining their cultural identity (Lee 1992;
Leacock and Lee 1982; Kent 1992: 56). In Ingold's (1988) terms, the
hunter-gatherer mode of production – predicated on the egalitarian
ideology and sharing – can last beyond the hunter-gatherer mode of

subsistence, defined by the practice of hunting and gathering (Fig. 1).

At the same time, hunter-gatherer societies vary in their degree of egalitarianism and they may practise both immediate and delayed return strategies (Flanagan 1989; Kent 1993; Bird-David 1992; Woodburn 1988; Lee and DeVore 1968). Bender (1978; 1981; 1985; 1990), Hayden (1990), Aldenderfer (1993) and others have shown how the potential for inequality, implicit in the ability to control marital alliances, exchange and ritual developed into more formalised social competition through the circulation of valuables and ritual feasting and led to increased social ranking and social inequalities. Others have advanced arguments explaining the development of social ranking as a consequence of sedentism, population increase, storage and delayed return (Price and Brown 1985; Halstead and O'Shea 1982; Rowley-Conwy and Zvelebil 1989). In both cases, these social changes occurred within the hunting-gathering mode of subsistence. Yet in abandoning the egalitarian ideology, such societies would cease to operate within the hunter-gatherer mode of production (Ingold 1988): the incongruence between hunting-gathering as a means of subsistence and hunting-gathering as ideology is exposed once again, but in this instance the ideology has changed towards inequality and social ranking, while the mode of subsistence remained the same (Fig. 1).

IMPLICATIONS FOR THE MESOLITHIC

Against this anthropological background, the interpretation of the post-glacial hunter-gatherer societies in Europe remains inadequate. Conference volumes reflecting the broad spectrum of research (Kozlowski 1973; Gramsch 1981; Bonsall 1989; Vermeersch and Van Peer 1990) show continuing preoccupation with issues of lithic typology, chronology and culture history (Price 1986; Edmonds 1991), although the number of contributions addressing issues of social complexity and subsistence strategies has been rising (Neeley and Clark 1990). Most of this research operates within a traditional framework marked by (1) a normative concept of archaeological culture as a signature for ethnic groups, and (2) a normative concept of Mesolithic hunter-gatherers as mobile hunters with little social elaboration or organisational complexity.

Some workers have attempted to re-interpret the Mesolithic hunter-gatherers as more sedentary, socio-economically complex societies (Tringham 1971; Rowley-Conwy 1983; Price 1985; Zvelebil 1986b; 1992; Zvelebil and Dolukhanov 1991; Madsen 1987; Larsson 1990; Nygaard

1989), particularly within the coastal and lacustrine zones of temperate Europe. Although this reconstruction has been to some degree successful, it has generated further debate as to what is meant by complexity (Price and Brown 1985; Gebauer and Price 1991) and a consequent reaction against seeing the Mesolithic societies as too complex.

Within this context, the recent debate in anthropology helps to elucidate the relationship between the social and techno-economic domains, leading to the following conclusions. Although economic and technological elaboration has broadly consonant analogues in social elaboration (i.e. Woodburn 1988), hunter-gatherer modes of subsistence and their mode of production are not always co-eval, allowing for social elaboration to occur which goes beyond the hunter-gatherer mode of production, and elements of farming to be incorporated within its mode of production, without the abandonment of egalitarian ideology.

We have to allow for a similar range of variation to have existed among the post-glacial hunter-gatherers in Europe (Rowley-Conwy 1986); in fact, 'complex' hunter-gatherers may have been more widespread in the prehistoric past than they are in the ethno-historic sample if Woodburn is correct (1988) (Fig. 3). As Gamble noted, 'complex' foragers are a product of 'history, rather than just simple ecological opportunity' (Gamble 1991: 5); and in this case, history might have favoured the shift to farming among the 'complex', but not among the 'simple' foragers. In general, however, the recent debate in anthropology shows that a change from egalitarian to non-egalitarian, from simple to complex hunter-gatherers, and to farming/pastoral groups (and in reverse, see Layton 1991) follows historical trajectories of dynamically interacting forces, which, in addition, are structured and prioritised according to the researcher's own ideology and paradigmatic preference.

SOCIAL LIFE IN NEOLITHIC NORTHERN TEMPERATE EUROPE: SOME CURRENT VIEWS

Even if we accept the parity of broadly economic definitions for both periods (i.e. hunter-gatherers versus farmers), the sources for the interpretation of the Neolithic are rather different from those for the Mesolithic. Many reconstructions of the Neolithic lifestyle, particularly those related to technology, subsistence, settlement pattern and land use, rely on the ethno-history of European peasantry for direct historical analogies (Clark 1952; Higgs 1972; 1975; Barker 1985; Halstead 1981; Zvelebil 1981; etc.). This seems reasonable on the assumption of some cultural continuity and similar ecological conditions operating in an area bound by a common historical trajectory. It also reinforces the view of 'farmers our ancestors' : a view which traces the roots of European society to the Neolithic but not earlier, and which is responsible for subtle prejudices in our treatment of the Mesolithic and the Neolithic (Zvelebil 1996).

The social life of the Neolithic people, however, is more often than not interpreted by analogies from extra-European contexts, either directly (i.e. Renfrew 1976; Williams and Dowson 1993) or by recourse to anthropologists whose generalisations are based on societies outside Europe (i.e. Meillassoux 1972; Bradley 1984; Renfrew and Shennan 1982; Thomas 1987; 1990). Partly, this is due to the recognition that the Neolithic past was radically different from the more recent ethno-historical European contexts, and therefore no useful local analogues exist to explain structures such as megalithic monuments or Linear Pottery Ware (henceforth LBK) long-houses. Partly, this reflects two different schools of thought, broadly 'processual' and 'post-proces-sual,' focussing on two different aspects of the Neolithic. The two approaches are difficult to reconcile (i.e. compare Thomas 1991 and Bogucki 1988). We are either presented with autonomous and adaptive farming communities whose practical skill and common sense laid the foundation for European civilisation, or with compulsive megalith-builders who lived only for the ancestors, and who may have had social relations with each other, but only when dead.

This duality of approach is reflected in interpretations of the Neo-lithic social structure and social system (term. as in Hodder 1982; compare Bogucki 1988 and Thomas 1990). It is broadly agreed that the early Neolithic was an egalitarian and communally oriented society: 'In the early Neolithic there is no evidence for other than egalitarian social relations, whether one looks at the Bandkeramik of central Europe (Sherratt 1976) or the early megalith building societies of the west (Renfrew 1973)' (Shennan 1982: 10, see also Hodder 1990; Thomas 1987; 1990; Bogucki 1988; Whittle 1988; Coudart 1987; 1991; Shanks and Tilley 1982; van de Velde 1979); which was nevertheless subject to some social differentiation, arising from social competition (Bradley 1984) and internal contradictions (Thomas 1987; 1990). Lewis-Williams and Dawson (1993) go so far as to postulate three different strata of society in terms of the access to megalithic monuments and of the control over the associated ritual.

[13]

The structure underlying this form of social organisation is said to be based on the relations of production embedded in kinship (Renfrew 1976; Sherratt 1984; Thomas 1987; Bogucki 1988), the cult of the ancestors (Thomas 1987; Hodder 1900; etc.), and the cognitive distinction between the tame and the wild as an instrument of acculturation (Hodder 1990; Thomas 1990). In such a 'lineage mode of production' (Thomas 1987), social relations are determined and structured through kinship, whether fictitious or real, which is traced back to a founding ancestor. Ancestors are perceived as active in the mediation between the spirit world and the physical one, and as a source of legitimate possession of land, resources and labour; they play a powerful role in the social and biological reproduction of the lineage. The exchange of women through marriage and of prestige items as bride wealth bring production and reproduction under the control of elder males. Although ostensibly egalitarian (absence of institutionalised social hierarchies, inherited statuses), the structure supports the reproduction of the social power of the elders as a group, and creates conditions for competition in which social ranking may develop further through the monopoly over the practice of ritual and its interpretation (Bender 1990; Aldenderfer 1993).

Thomas (1987) regards the early Neolithic LBK, and by implication (1991: 13; 1988: 64) other early Neolithic groups in north-western Europe, as 'characteristic lineage society' (1987: 413). This view is broadly in agreement with other workers (Hodder 1984; Sherratt 1990). The social relations of such societies are linked to a specific agricultural mode of subsistence by, for example, Thomas (1987: 414) and Sherratt (1990): hoe-assisted horticulture in which labour was at a premium. Whether this social system was subsequently transformed by the introduction of the plough-assisted agro-pastoral farming or whether profound structural changes preceded its introduction remains a matter of continuing debate (Neustupný 1967; Sherratt 1981; Thomas 1987; 1991; Boujot and Cassen 1993).

On account of the ancestors, megalithic burials and other monumental structures played a central role in the social life of the Neolithic communities. Several major threads run through the vast literature on the subject: they served as focal places for the expression and renegotiation of social power (Sherratt 1990; Hodder 1984; Williams and Dowson 1993), for the 'building up of genealogical memory founded on the cult of ancestors' (Boujot and Cassen 1993), for the articulation of the Neolithic symbolic identity (Sherratt 1990; Hodder 1990; Thomas 1991), as a means of legitimation of territorial claims of corporate descent groups (Chapman 1981), as 'houses of the dead' – a symbolic transformation which facilitated the adoption of farming by the Mesolithic hunter-gatherers (Hodder 1990; Sherratt 1990), who then, as farmers, proceeded to use them as territorial markers of their own in competition with the more established farming communities (Renfrew 1976), or with each other (Bogucki 1988).

At the core of this social structure and embedded within its material manifestations, lie cognitive and ideological perceptions, which, according to Thomas, 'express a fundamental division of the universe into the wild and the tame which creates the Neolithic world' (1990: 13). This basic categorical division is elaborated and linked to other, interlocking binary oppositions, such as inside/outside, women/men, culture/nature, etc. and then played out in the burial and ritual contexts of the Neolithic 'as a means of imposing a certain conceptual scheme upon the world' (Thomas 1991: 182)

SOCIAL CHANGE AT THE TRANSITION?

In producing this summary of social life during the early Neolithic, I have glossed over regional differences and collated, perhaps unfairly, different points of view. Contributions to this volume will show the variety of views bearing upon the topic. I argue, however, that most workers would agree that the themes highlighted above provide a social definition of the Neolithic, to act as an analogue to, or a replacement of, the economic definition (i.e. Bradley 1984; Thomas 1988; 1991; Lewis-Williams and Dowson 1993). But can this really be so? Can this be the 'integrated conceptual and classificatory system', which caused 'a wholesale transformation of social relations' (Thomas 1991: 181, 13)?

For Thomas, the Neolithic is underpinned by a cognitive system of thought and as a cultural tradition is predicated on 'a fundamental division of the universe into the wild and the tame' (1991: 13; 1988: 64). Yet Hodder (1990) has argued persuasively that the origins of agriculture were embedded within an older social and cultural code, which reflected symbolic and conceptual domestication of the natural environment by the post-glacial and even Palaeolithic hunter-gatherers. In the early Holocene, the social and symbolic domestication was extended to the domestication of food resources, thus producing the 'origins of agriculture' (1990: 291). In doing so, Hodder uncouples chronologically the social, economic and ideological facets of domestication, and gives chronological precedence to the taming of the wild over the domestication of food resources. If this is so, either social or conceptual domestication must be dropped as hallmarks of the Neolithic society.

It could be argued that the key distinction lies not in this process of such long duration, but in the specific metaphor employed in its articulation: the development of household/*domus* as the focus of social organisation, production and ideology, reflected in the elaboration of domestic architecture, in the appropriation of the dead through burial within or near dwellings, and in other symbols of controlling the wild within the *domus*. As Lepenski Vir, Skateholm, Vedbaek, Sarnate, Lake Lubans sites and other settlements of the late Mesolithic show, even these particular traits were present in the late Mesolithic (though not everywhere) within the broader context of interference with the environment and local food resources which could be easily described as 'taming' (Welinder 1989; Zvelebil 1994; and in press; Mithen 1990; Dennell 1983; Bogucki 1988). On the other hand, as Thomas (1991) himself has recognised, early Neolithic farmers made an extensive use of wild food resources, and '*domus*/household' is anything but emphasised in the early Neolithic of Britain. We are thus left with the question whether the hunter-gatherers of the Mesolithic recognised their world in terms of the tame and the wild, irrespective of their subsistence activities (i.e. Bird-Nurit 1990). If we are to treat the archaeological evidence evenly (and not use 'context' as an excuse to promote our paradigmatic prejudices), then some hunter-gatherers of late Mesolithic Europe – in parts of southern Scandinavia, eastern Baltic or Britain, for example, were as cognizant of the tame/wild dichotomy as the societies of the early Neolithic (see below p. 20).

One feature which sets the Neolithic societies so much apart is the use of monumental burial architecture, the principal archaeological signature for the existence of ancestor cult in the Neolithic. Thomas (1991: 182) notes that the use of such monuments was fundamental to the Neolithic way of life and that their construction was in many regions the first act of 'Neolithisation'. This does not seem to be the case even in the Neolithic Britain ('there is often a time-lag between the beginning of agricultural settlement and the appearance of formal burial areas' Bradley 1984: 17), while on the continent, the picture varies from the pre-agricultural use of megalithic structures in Brittany (Scarre 1992: 129) to the enduring lack of monumental burials in the Neolithic of central and eastern Europe. Ancestral cults are not always symbolised by monumental burials. But even if we accept monumental burial as a signature of the developing strength of the cult of the ancestors, it would appear that the development of the cult is only partly co-eval with other features of the Neolithic – agriculture, tame/wild dichotomy – and in most areas, it was consequent upon the adoption of agro-pastoral farming (Madsen 1982; Whittle 1988; Bogucki 1988; Sherratt 1990; Scarre 1992). Rather than being an essential part of the Neolithic, it is more likely that monumental burials were employed to emphasise links with ancestral lineages principally in situations of social stress and competition for resources, while in other situations, these links might have been permitted to lapse (Bradley 1984; Renfrew 1976; Chapman 1981).

Finally, we arrive at the consideration of organisation of the Neolithic society as a whole. The consensus seems to be that it should be seen as broadly egalitarian and based on a 'lineage mode of production'. This stands in contrast to the arguments advanced for social (as well as economic) complexity among late Mesolithic hunter-gatherers of the preceding period in southern Scandinavia (Price 1985; Price and Gebauer 1992; Larsson 1990; Zvelebil 1992), and north-eastern Europe (O'Shea and Zvelebil 1984; Dolukhanov 1986; Zvelebil and Dolukhanov 1991). Is this merely a sloppy use of the same terminology, a reflection of paradigmatic prejudice, or a major social change, widespread enough to justify the contention that the Neolithic is a coherent social or ideological phenomenon?

To address this question, let us briefly consider social aspects of three areas of temperate Europe at the time of the Mesolithic-Neolithic transition (as conventionally defined). In the loess areas of central Europe – in Bohemia, Saxony, southern Poland – an intrusive LBK culture replaced local Mesolithic groups in the mid-fifth millennium bc. The change was very rapid with little or no contact evident between the two populations, even though the hunter-gatherers survived for longer in the surrounding upland areas (Vencl 1986). The spread of the LBK is now a classic example of farming colonisation and replacement of local foragers.

Even though this picture may alter as the implications of enormous geomorphological changes, which obscured the archaeological record of the Mesolithic and Neolithic begin to sink in (Neustupný 1987; Kuna 1990; Beneš in press), the Mesolithic record of central Europe will probably continue to support our current reconstruction of mobile, organisationally simple and socially undifferentiated hunter-gatherer societies (Vencl 1986; Kozlowski and Kozlowski 1986; Tringham 1971): the evidence which may be speculatively linked to egalitarian hunter-gatherers of the ethno-historical past, and to Ingold's 'mode of production' (Yellen 1978; Ingold 1988; see Fig. 3).

The fate of these foragers is still completely unknown, unless, and contrary to all our expectations, they adopted the knowledge of farming practices from the Körös groups in the Panonnian plain and rapidly transformed it into LBK cultural traditions: a scenario not impossible in view of recent cases of such transformations (i.e. Ehret 1988; Hall 1987). Alternatively, they were 'absorbed' by farming colonists advancing from the area of present-day Hungary. While Bogucki (1988) argues that the LBK and its derivatives were essentially egalitarian, cognatic, bilateral, and exogamous in their social relations, Thomas (1987) sees the same societies as controlled by male elders in lineage-based descent groups (not necessarily unilinear). The major, but so far unresolved, issue is whether in the early Neolithic kinsmen were aggregated into corporations through a perceived descent from a common ancestor (Thomas 1988; Sherratt 1982), or whether the early Neolithic groups were laterally organised into household-based kin groups with little linkage across generations (Bogucki 1988). Interestingly, Bogucki (1988) argues that the well-known fissioning and rapid dispersal of the LBK groups had a dual function of a conflict avoidance mechanism and risk reduction of crop failure. Such patterns of dispersal would have been possible only in the relative paucity of the local hunter-gatherer settlement, which would otherwise stand in the way of the rapid LBK expansion. The relative mobility of the LBK households (Neustupný 1987; Bogucki 1988) encouraged the continuation of egalitarian social structure of the LBK. So, we seem to have both continuity and difference across a rapid replacement of foraging by farming groups: continuity in egalitarian social relations and the presumed bilaterality of kinship ties,[4] difference in the possible lineage organisation of society and in the development of the *domus*/household ideology (Hodder 1990).

In southern Scandinavia and the adjacent coastal regions of the North European Plain agro-pastoral farming was adopted fairly rapidly between ca 3300 and 3000 bc (Fig. 4). This was preceded by about 1000 years of contact between foragers and farmers, despite which farming was not adopted (Zvelebil & Rowley-Conwy 1984; 1986). Most authorities agree that we are dealing with the adoption of farming by local groups, with little or no immigration from the more established farming groups further south (see Madsen 1987 for a review; Solberg 1989 for a contrary view).

The Ertebølle/Ellerberk foragers of the coastal southern Baltic regions present the best case of social and economic complexity among the Mesolithic hunter-gatherers; (Larsson 1990; Bogucki 1987; Rowley-

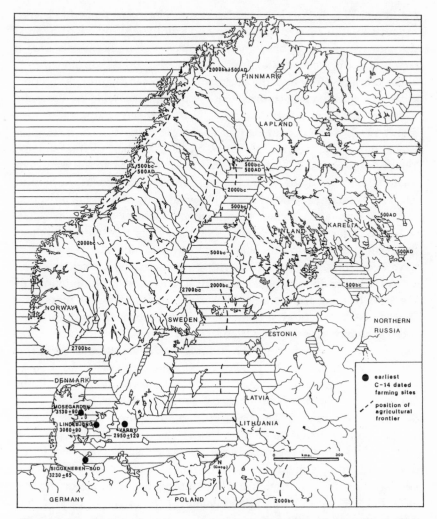

Figure 4. Introduction of agro-pastoral farming into northern Europe. The position of agricultural frontier indicates boundary between the substitution and consolidation phases (Zvelebil and Rowley-Conway 1984; 1986).

Conwy 1983; Rowley-Conwy and Zvelebil 1989; Zvelebil 1992; Price 1985; Price and Gebauer 1992). The logistic and specialised procurement of resources, the investment in mass capture facilities and other labour-intensive technology, the evidence for food processing and storage, and the indications of 'management' of both woodland and its resources (Welinder 1989; Zvelebil 1993; in press; Mithen 1990) all support the notion of a delayed-return system operating here. According to Woodburn (1988), such a system should be embedded within social relations based on kinship and affinity, and operated by men through the exchange of women and other (material) assets within a cognitive framework where the egalitarian ideology was in abeyance.

The social system and the social structure of the Ertebølle hunter-gatherers does seem to confirm these expectations. While the Ertebølle is still regarded as a 'band society' (Newell and Constandse-Westermann 1990), there is evidence for status differentiation (Constandse-Westermann and Newell 1989; Larsson 1990; Clark and Neeley 1987; 1990; Meiklejohn and Zvelebil 1990), linked, perhaps, to the control of 'material assets': food resources and exotic artefacts (O'Shea and Zvelebil 1984; Price and Gebauer 1992). Differences in limb laterisation between men and women at cemeteries such as Skateholm (Constandse-Westermann and Newell 1989) suggests that women gained their status through means other than physical labour, one such may have been through association with high status men. Hodder (1990: 180–181) found that symbolic activity emphasised the dominance of the male, hunting and trading: the '*agrios*', with little or no traces of the '*domus*'. All this would support the delayed-return, male-dominated social structure presented by Woodburn. Yet there are indications that the situation was more complex. Judging by the variation in the grave goods, females gained high status, and signatures of *domus*/household, other than elaborate domestic architecture (Hodder 1990), do in fact occur in the Ertebølle contexts. Formalised burials of dogs at Skateholm (Larsson 1990) – the only domesticated animal in that society – suggest that its members made the distinction between the tame and the wild. In summary, the Ertebølle society was most likely organised along similar lines as 'complex' hunter-gatherers in the ethnographic record: it retained the hunter-gatherer mode of subsistence, but was socially too differentiated for the 'mode of production' (Fig. 1).

The adoption of agro-pastoral farming is co-eval with cultural changes which define the Funnel Beaker (TRB) culture. Despite marked changes in subsistence, settlement pattern and material culture, the social organisation and social system show remarkable continuity. The TRB communities continue to be regarded as broadly egalitarian and structured on descent-linked lineal kinship relations (Bogucki 1988; Thomas 1987) with the role of the ancestors increasingly emphasised though monumental burial, though not from the start, but as a consequence of the growing need for a territorial definition by foragers turned farmers with a dispersed pattern of settlement

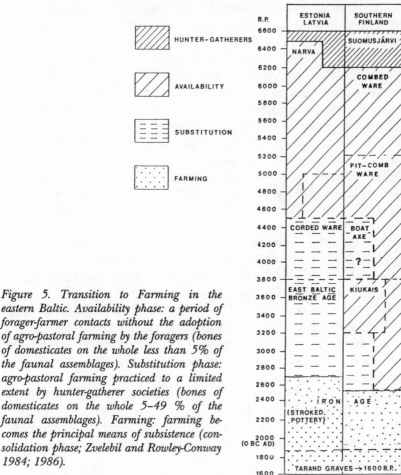

Figure 5. Transition to Farming in the eastern Baltic. Availability phase: a period of forager-farmer contacts without the adoption of agro-pastoral farming by the foragers (bones of domesticates on the whole less than 5% of the faunal assemblages). Substitution phase: agro-pastoral farming practiced to a limited extent by hunter-gatherer societies (bones of domesticates on the whole 5–49 % of the faunal assemblages). Farming: farming becomes the principal means of subsistence (consolidation phase; Zvelebil and Rowley-Conway 1984; 1986).

(Bogucki 1988: 185–190). Certain major features of the TRB burial practices in Poland and Denmark can be traced to the preceding local Mesolithic (Solberg 1989 with refs). Bogucki contrasts this social system with the household-centred, kin-set systems attributed to the later Neolithic of the loess belt (Lengyel, etc.) and locates the roots of the TRB social organisation in the preceding foraging communities. In summary, then, the rapid substitution of foraging by agro-pastoral farming in southern Scandinavia was marked by the continuity and development of existing social structures, rather than by an import of new social relations or ideology.[5]

Finally, in the eastern Baltic and adjacent areas of Russia and southern Finland, agro-pastoral farming was adopted at a very slow rate (Figs 4, 5) over some 2000 years (Zvelebil 1981; 1993; Dolukhanov 1979; Zvelebil and Dolukhanov 1991; Janik in press). Despite the presence of small numbers of domesticates on archaeological sites from ca 2500 bc, and despite a major cultural change marked by the Corded Ware horizon ca 2500–1800 bc, the decisive shift to agro-pastoral economy occurred between 1200 and 700 bc, attested by the shift in the location of major settlements away from wetland and shore-line locations to areas with lighter, arable soils (Zvelebil 1981; 1985), by the rise in the presence of domesticates (Paaver 1961; Zvelebil 1985; 1990) and by the abandonment of symbolism associated with hunting and gathering (Gurina 1956; Hallstrom 1960; Helskong 1985; Tilley 1991) in favour of agricultural symbols (Zvelebil 1991; 1992; 1993). As in the western Baltic, from about 6000 bc, the coastal and lacustrine zones of north-eastern Europe were settled by hunter-gatherer communities of increasing organisational complexity, marked by the use of formalised burial grounds – cemeteries, status differentiation, and increasing residential permanence (Vankina 1970; Rimantiene 1992; Loze 1971; Dolukhanov 1979; 1986; Zvelebil 1981; 1987; 1992; Zvelebil and Dolukhanov 1991). Later, from ca 4000 bc, the development of pottery decoration, the association of burial with settlement, the elaboration of household architecture, all noted by Hodder as the expressions of the *domus*/household, gradually develop within the context of a 'complex' hunter-gatherer society, which, at the same time, retained continuity in wild animal symbolism (Zvelebil 1993; Carpelan 1975). It is only in the course of the second millennium bc that decorative elaboration on pottery and wild animal symbolism decline and eventually disappear, and are replaced by other forms of symbolic expression in the context of an agro-pastoral Iron Age during the first millennium bc.

I have summarised an overall trend and ignored regional variation in both time and space (cf. Janik in press). But we are dealing with a large area and it is the overall trend that is pertinent here. In my opinion, this shows that the 'economic' (presence of domesticates and cultigens) and 'social' (specific ideology and social relations) criteria of the Neolithic are not synchronous. Neither the presence of ceramics from ca 4500 bc (the signature for the start of the Neolithic among our eastern European colleagues), nor of domesticates from ca 2500 bc usher in the Neolithic in its economic (Zvelebil and Rowley-Conwy 1984) or social (Thomas 1988; 1991) sense. While the indicators of social elaboration and of the '*domus*' occur from ca 6000 and 4000 bc respectively, the adoption of agro-pastoral farming does not take place until the end of the second millennium bc. In between there was a society based principally on hunting and gathering for subsistence, yet making some, occasional use of domesticates and possibly cultigens from about 2500 bc (Rimantiene 1990; Vuorela and Lempiainen 1988). In terms of the current discussion of modern hunter-gatherers, the eastern Baltic groups of the later period (2500–700 bc) do not seem to possess either exclusive reliance on hunting-gathering (Fig. 1a) or an egalitarian ideology (Fig. 1b, c) and thus are outside both the mode of production and the mode of subsistence for hunter-gatherers; yet they are principally reliant on hunting and gathering. The socio-economic structure of this society should be regarded as following its own historical trajectory, where the process of agricultural 'transition' became a way of life, and as such remained suspended between our traditional notions of the Mesolithic and the Neolithic (Janik in press, Zvelebil 1993). The subsequent development of a farming society occurred in the context of technology and the trade/exchange relations of the Iron Age; circumstances which encouraged the development of farming (Zvelebil 1985). In a sense, then, there was no Neolithic in the eastern Baltic.

CONCLUSIONS

In this essay I have tried to show that our perceptions of the Mesolithic and the Neolithic as a society are inadequate. Among modern hunter-gatherers, the mode of subsistence does not correspond to the 'mode of production', the latter embedded in egalitarian, sharing social relations. Mesolithic society, as defined by hunting and gathering, also ranged in social organisation from 'simple', 'egalitarian' to 'complex' and 'socially differentiated', from a band-level kinship group to, apparently, lineage-based descent groups.

Similarly in the Neolithic, defined by its farming subsistence, a combination of traits which has been presented as an 'ideological package' (Thomas 1988; 1991) seems to occur individually with time-lags in between, while the transformations in the social relations of production this package should have initiated[6] are implicit already in the organisational complexity of the late Mesolithic in the circum-Baltic area. Consequently, there seems to be a considerable continuity in social organisation across the economically defined Mesolithic-Neolithic transition.

It becomes clear, then, that the subsistence strategies, dichotomised into hunting-gathering and farming, are not exclusively correlated with any specific form of social organisation or ideology, although there are clear relationships and inter-linked constraints (i.e. Woodburn 1988; Bender 1990). It then becomes a moot point whether the Neolithic and the Mesolithic should be socially or economically defined, especially if this division is a conceptual product of our own Western society.

As a historical process, created and understood through the operation of several time scales, the Mesolithic is of necessity a polythetic phenomenon, signified by a number of traits, not all of which have to be present to define the Mesolithic. Thus the older chronological boundary of the period, the supposedly rapid break between the Pleistocene and the Post-glacial, looks now more likely as a gradual transition (Dennell 1983). Correspondingly, the change from the Upper Palaeolithic to the Mesolithic has been more gradual then previously thought, with some 'Mesolithic' attributes, such as microliths, occurring in the late Upper Palaeolithic, while other traditions, such as the Epigravettian, persisted in some areas into the Holocene with their Palaeolithic features intact. At the more recent end of the period, polished stone tools and ceramics, the 'hallmarks of the Neolithic', are common in otherwise 'Mesolithic' contexts, i.e. those marked by microlithic technology and wild fauna. Finally, management of plant and animal resources, analogous in some ways to the agro-pastoral farming of the Neolithic, is now coming to be recognised in some Mesolithic contexts (Dennell 1983; Barker 1985; Bogucki 1988; Zvelebil 1986; 1994). There is a large amount of variability, then, among the early post-glacial cultures in Europe, and only some fit the original view of the Mesolithic as defined chronologically.

At the same time, as a historical process, the Mesolithic has to maintain a unique coherence which sets it apart from other historical phenomena, such as the Neolithic or Industrial Revolution. In this sense, the Mesolithic was given a coherent role as a process of adaptation to post-glacial conditions by hunter-gatherers societies. While some features of the Mesolithic, such as the development of stone axe technology or the shift in subsistence strategies to greater reliance on fish, fowl and plant food can be explained in those terms, others, such as microlithisation, or greater sedentism cannot. The Mesolithic was historically contingent on the existence of the Upper Palaeolithic societies in Europe, historically constrained by Stone Age technology, and historically situated on a peninsular extension of Asian land-mass close to the origin of agro-pastoral farming. Within these conditions, hunter-gatherer societies in some parts of Europe developed social structures and resource management strategies of their own, akin in complexity and perhaps even productivity to those of the Neolithic farmers, yet distinct from the latter because they remained integrated in a hunter-gatherer society in terms of socio-economic relations: they retained either their hunter-gatherer mode of subsistence or their mode of production (Ingold 1988). The course of this indigenous development was altered with the introduction of agro-pastoral farming; yet in some areas this did not engender an immediate transformation of social relations or change in ideology. The Mesolithic as a coherent historical process, then, can be described only as a process of transformation of *hunter-gathering* societies of the late Upper Palaeolithic, unfolding as a response to a set of historical circumstances: the onset of post-glacial conditions, the advances in Stone Age technology, the elaboration of symbolic complexity, and the contact with the early farming societies of the eastern Mediterranean.

By contrast, the Neolithic came to stand for Stone Age farming societies and, more specifically, village-based agro-pastoral farmers (Childe 1925; 1957; Piggott 1965; Dennell 1983; Barker 1985; Whittle 1985; Lewthwaite 1986). Thomas (1991) redefined the Neolithic as a polythetic historical phenomenon, which 'should not be expected to comprise the same elements at different times and places, even if it maintains an identity by constituting a linked sequence of events and transformations' (1990: 12). The linked sequence of events, the identity of the Neolithic, is seen here as a 'wholesale transformation of social relations which results from adopting an integrated cultural system' (1990: 13), embedded within an 'integrated conceptual and classificatory system, something "to think with" ' (1990: 181), an ideology. While this cogent definition of the Neolithic places a welcome emphasis on the historical and polythetic nature of the phenomenon as a process, not a period, its coherence is at least as vague as that of the Mesolithic. As I have tried to show, any attempt to specify the social transformations of the Neolithic will reveal their divergent nature (compare, for example, the Balkan, central and north-western European Neolithic; Thomas 1987; Hodder 1990; Bogucki 1988), while the broader elements of the ideology of the Neolithic – the tame/wild distinction, the cult of the ancestors – can be found already in the Mesolithic. Similarly, technological traits regarded as Neolithic, such as polished stone tools, ceramics, are found in otherwise 'Mesolithic', i.e. hunting-gathering societies, while many 'Neolithic' groups are now found to have been more mobile and engaged in more hunting-gathering than hitherto acknowledged (Thomas 1991; Bogucki 1988).

The polythetic classification exposes a major overlap between our notions of the Mesolithic and the Neolithic, confirming at once the historicity of the two processes and showing that if the Mesolithic and the Neolithic is about two different views of the world (Thomas 1988), it was not their view, but ours. The diffusion and consolidation of agro-pastoral farming, whether by cultural diffusion or migration, appears as the only unifying phenomenon in the linked sequence of events which is denoted by the Neolithic. In that sense, the Neolithic *is the process of agricultural transition*, the process of becoming a farming society within the historical scenario of the Stone Age.

ACKNOWLEDGEMENTS

This paper has been written during my tenure as a fellow at the Netherlands Institute for Advanced Studies in Social Sciences and Humanities (NIAS). I would like to thank Douglas Lewis, Mayke de Jong and Sally Wyatt for reading and commenting on the earlier draft of this paper and to the staff at the Netherlands Institute for Advanced Studies for providing general research support.

NOTES

1. Throughout this essay, I use hunter-gatherers as a general term synonymous with foragers, gatherer-hunters, and hunter-fisher-gatherers. Some other authors give foragers a specific meaning, i.e. Binford (1981) distinguishes between foragers and collectors on the grounds of their organisational complexity; Ingold (1988) makes a distinction between foraging and hunting-gathering in terms of intentionality.

2. See also Testart (1982; 1984) for a similar concept of *collecteurs* and *stockeurs* and Binford (1981; 1983) for the distinction between foragers and collectors.

3. While some foraging communities probably did absorb displaced farmers, the notion that modern egalitarian foragers are principally impoverished farmers turned foragers, on the scale advocated by Schrire (1982), and Wilmsen and Denbow (1990) cannot be supported either historically (Kent 1992; Solvay and Lee 1990; Lee 1992; etc.) or anthropologically. As Woodburn noted, the ideology of sharing and of egalitarianism in such societies functions as an institution with elaborate sanctions and levelling mechanisms reflecting its historical depth, and thus cannot be treated as a product of a recent historical breakdown (1988: 62; Kent 1992). Moreover, The 'communal relations of production' (Lee 1990), the ideology of sharing as a social institution maintained through sanctions and social control (Woodburn 1988; Flanagan 1989; Lee 1992; Boehm 1993), is geographically so widespread and extant in such different historical contexts, that it cannot be regarded as an outcome of a single historical process: the shift to foraging by farmers in distress (Lee 1990; 1992).

4. Bilaterality is preferred over unilineal systems in conditions of low population density to ensure the reproductive success of the individual and the group. Bogucki (1988) believes that population densities sufficient to promote unilineal systems were not reached until the Bronze Age.

5. One thing that demands explanation is the delay in the adoption of farming by the Ertebølle communities, even though Woodburn has argued for an early acceptance of farming by the delayed-return hunter-gatherers (1988: 57–8). Hodder argues that the acceptance of farming was blocked for the Ertebølle as long as the metaphor of the *domus* remained central to the farming way of life. As soon as agriculture was 'made more compatible with Ertebølle principles' (1990: 182) by a shift in central Europe away from the '*domus*', farming was adopted in southern Scandinavia. It seems to me that the reorganisation of the settlement pattern in central Europe, which underlies much of Hodder's argument, can be better explained as a consequence of the removal of frontier conditions which obtained during the early Neolithic (i.e. Bogucki 1988), while some other changes he describes, i.e. in pottery decoration, can be taken as signatures of local foragers adopting farming and not as a prior condition for such adoption. The delay in the adoption of farming by the Ertebølle was probably due to their relative economic affluence, the organisational complexity of their culture and, perhaps, to their self-perception as hunter-gatherers (Zvelebil 1986; Price & Gebauer 1992; Zvelebil 1992).

6. Apart from his paper on social relations in the LBK and the middle Neolithic (Thomas 1987), Thomas does not specify what this change in social relations should be. He merely states that it has occurred and that it was profound (1988; 1991). In absence of a more specific explanation, and bearing in mind his view of the Neolithic as a widespread and ideologically uniform transformation (1988: 63, 64; 1991: 13 but note apparent self-contradiction 1988: 62; 1990: 12), his description of the LBK social relations is taken to apply broadly to the First Neolithic of the North European Plain, Britain, and Denmark (Thomas 1987: 418–19; 1988: 63, 64; 1991: 13).

7. This impression may be created as much by our modern perceptions of the hunter-gatherer and farming past, by the intervening post-depositional processes and by the variable preservation rates of the archaeological record as by the real differences which may have separated Mesolithic and Neolithic communities.

BIBLIOGRAPHY

Aldenderfer, M. 1993. Ritual, hierarchy, and change in foraging societies. *Journal of Anthropological Archaeology* 12 (1): 15.

Ames, K. M. 1981. The evolution of social ranking on the northwest coast of North America. *American Antiquity* 46 (4): 789–805.

Ammerman, A. J. & Cavalli-Sforza, L. L. 1984. *The Neolithic Transition and the Genetics of Populations in Europe.* New Jersey: Princeton University Press.

Barker, G. 1985. *Prehistoric Farming in Europe.* Cambridge: Cambridge University Press.

Barker, G. & Gamble, C. (eds) 1985: *Beyond Domestication in Prehistoric Europe: Investigations in Subsistence Archaeology and Social Complexity.* London: Academic Press.

Bender, B. 1978. Gatherer-hunter to farmer: a social perspective. *World Archaeology* 10: 204–223.

Bender, B. 1981. Gatherer-hunter intensification. In Sheridan, A. & Bailey, G. (eds), *Economic Archaeology: Towards an Integration of Ecological and Social Approaches,* pp. 148–157. Oxford: British Archaeological Reports (International Series 96).

Bender, B. 1985. Emergent tribal formations in the American midcontinent. *American Antiquity* 50: 52–62.

Bender, B. 1990. The dynamics of nonhierarchical societies. In Upham, S. (ed.), *The Evolution of Political Systems*, pp. 247–264. Cambridge: Cambridge University Press.

Bender, B. & Morris, B. 1988. Twenty years of history, evolution and social change in gatherer-hunter studies. In Ingold, T., Riches, D. & Woodburn, J. (eds), *Hunters and Gatherers*, vol. 1, 4–13. Oxford: Berg.

Beneš, J. in press. Erosion and accumulation processes in the late holocene of Bohemia, in relation to prehistoric and mediaeval landscape occupation. In Kuna, M. & Venclová, V. (eds), *Whither Archaeology? A volume dedicated to E. Neustupný*.

Bettinger, R. L. 1991. *Hunter-Gatherers: Archaeological and Evolutionary Theory*. New York: Plenum Press.

Binford, L. R. 1968. Post-Pleistocene adaptations. In Binford, S. & Binford, L. (eds), *New Perspectives in Archaeology*, pp. 313–341. Chicago: Aldine.

Binford, L. R. 1980. Willow smoke and dogs' tails: hunter-gatherer settlement system and archaeological site formation. *American Antiquity* 45 (1): 4–20.

Binford, L. R. 1980. *Working at Archaeology*. New York: Academic Press.

Bird-David N. H. 1988. Hunters and gatherers and outsiders. In Ingold, T., Riches, D. & Woodburn, J. (eds), *Hunters and Gatherers*, vol. 1, *History, evolution and social change*, pp. 17–72. Oxford: Berg.

Bird-David, N. 1990. The giving environment: another perspective on the economic system of gatherer-hunters. *Current Anthropology* 31 (2): 189–196.

Bird-David, N. 1992a. Beyond 'the hunting and gathering mode of subsistence': culture-sensitive observations on the Nayaka and other modern hunter-gatherers. *Man* (n.s.) 27: 19–44.

Bird-David, N. 1992b. Beyond 'the original affluent society': a culturalist reformation. *Current Anthropology* 33 (1): 25–47.

Bloch, M. 1983. *Marxism and Anthropology*. Oxford: Oxford University Press.

Blurton-Jones, N. G., Lars C. Smith, J., O'Connell, F., Hawkes, K. & Kamuzora, C. L. 1992. Demography in the Hadza, an increasing and high density population of Savanna foragers. *American Journal of Physical Anthropology* 89: 159–181.

Boehm, C. 1993. Egalitarian behavior and reverse dominance hierarchy. *Current Anthropology* 34 (3): 227–254.

Bogucki, P. 1987. The establishment of agrarian communities on the North European Plain. *Current Anthropology* 1: 1–13.

Bogucki, P. I. 1988. *Forest Farmers and Stockherders: Early Agriculture and its Consequences in North-Central Europe*. Cambridge: Cambridge University Press.

Bonsall, C. (ed.) 1989. *The Mesolithic in Europe*. Edinburgh: John Donald.

Boujot, C. & Cassen, S. 1993. A pattern of evolution for the Neolithic funerary structure of the west of France. *Antiquity* 67: 477–491.

Bradley, R. 1984. *The Social Foundations of Prehistoric Britain: Themes and Variations in the Archaeology of Power*. London: Longman.

Brown, A. 1893. On the continuity of the Neolithic and Palaeolithic periods. *Journal of the Royal Anthropological Institute* 22: 66–98.

Chapman, R. 1981. The emergence of formal disposal areas and the 'problem' of megalithic tombs in prehistoric Europe. In Chapman, R., Kinnes, I. & Randsborg, K. (eds), *The Archaeology of Death*, pp. 71–81. Cambridge: Cambridge University Press.

Carpelan, C. 1975. Alg-och Björnhuvudföremål Från Europas Nordliga Delar. *Finskt Museum* 82: 5–67.

Childe, V. G. 1925. *The Dawn of European Civilisation*. London: Kegan Paul.

Childe, V. G. 1935. Changing methods and aims in prehistory. *Proc. Prehist. Soc.* 1: 1–15.

Childe, V. G. 1947. *The Dawn of European Civilisation*. 4th edn., London: Kegan Paul.

Childe, V. G. 1957. *The Dawn of European Civilisation*. 6th edn., London: Kegan Paul.

Clark, J. G. D. 1936. *The Mesolithic Settlement of Northern Europe*. Cambridge: Cambridge University Press.

Clark, J. G. D. 1952. *Prehistoric Europe. The Economic Basis*. London: Methuen.

Clark, J. G. D. 1954. *Excavations at Star Carr Mesolithic Site at Seamer, near Scarborough, Yorkshire*. Cambridge: Cambridge University Press.

Clark, J. G. D. 1978. Neothermal Orientations. In P. Mellars (ed.), *The Early Postglacial Settlement of Northern Europe*, pp. 1–11. London: Duckworth.

Clark, G. 1980. *Mesolithic Prelude: The Palaeolithic-Neolithic Transition in Old World Prehistory*. Edinburgh: Edinburgh University Press.

Clark, G. A. & Neeley, M. 1987. Social differentiation in European Mesolithic burial data. In Rowley-Conwy, P., Zvelebil, M. & Blankholm, H. P. (eds), *Mesolithic Northwest Europe, Recent Trends*, pp. 121–130. Sheffield: University of Sheffield Press.

Coles, B. (ed.) 1992. *The Wetland Revolution in Prehistory*. Exeter: University of Exeter Press.

Coles, J. M. & Lawson, A. J. (eds) 1987. *European Wetlands in Prehistory*. Oxford: Clarendon Press.

Constandse-Westermann T. S. & Newell, R. R. 1989. Limb laterisation and social stratification in western Mesolithic societies. In Herskovitz, I. (ed.), *People and Culture in Change*, pp. 405–434. Oxford: British Archaeological Reports (International Series 508).

Coudart, A. 1987. Tradition, uniformity and variability in the architecture of the Danubian Neolithic. In Rulf, J. (ed.), *Bylany Seminar, (1987) Libice, Czechoslovakia*, pp. 199–223.

Coudart, A. 1991. Social structure and relationships in prehistoric small-scale sedentary societies: the Bandkeramik Neolithic groups. In S. Gregg (ed.), *Between Bands and States: Sedentism, Subsistence, and Interaction in Small-Scale Societies*, pp. 1–15. Carbondale: Center for Archaeological Investigations, Southern Illinois University.

Denbow, J. 1984. Prehistoric hunters and foragers of the Kalahari: the evidence for 1500 years of interaction. In Schrire, C. (ed.), *Past and Present in Hunter-Gatherer Studies*. London: Academic Press.

Dennell, R. 1983. *European Economic Prehistory*. London: Academic Press.

Dolukhanov, P. M. 1979. *Ecology and Economy in Neolithic Eastern Europe*. London: Duckworth.

Dolukhanov, P. M. 1993. Foraging and farming groups in north-eastern and north-western Europe: identity and interaction. In Chapman, J. & Dolukhanov, P. (ed.), *Cultural Transformations and Interactions in Eastern Europe*, pp. 122–145. Avebury: Aldershot.

Edmonds, M. 1991. A review of *The Mesolithic in Europe* by Clive Bonsall (ed.). *Proceedings of the Prehistoric Society* 57 (2): 219–221.

Ehret, C. 1988. Language change and the material correlates of language and ethnic shift. *Antiquity* 62: 564–574.

Engels, F. 1884 [1972]. *The Origin of the Family, Private Property and the State.* New York: Pathfinder Press.

Evans, J. C. 1975 [1990]. *The Environment of Early Man in the British Isles.* London: Duckworth.

Flanagan, J. G. 1989. Hierarchy in simple 'egalitarian' societies. *Annual Anthropological Review* 18: 245–266.

Friedman, J. & Rowlands, M. (eds) 1978. *The Evolution of Social Systems.* London: Duckworth.

Gebauer, A. B. & Price, T. D. (eds) 1992. *Transitions to Agriculture in Prehistory.* Madison: Prehistory Press.

Godelier, M. 1977. *Perspectives in Marxist Anthropology.* Cambridge: Cambridge University Press.

Gordon, R. 1984. The !Kung in the Kalahari exchange: an ethnohistorical perspective. In Schrire, C. (ed.), *Past and Present in Hunter-Gatherer Studies,* pp. 195–224, London: Academic Press.

Gould, R. 1982. To have and have not: the ecology of sharing among hunter-gatherers. In Williams, N. & Hunn, E. (eds), *Resource Managers: North American and Australian Hunter-Gatherers,* pp. 69–93. Boulder, CO: Westview.

Gramsch, B. (ed.) 1981. *Veröffentlichungen: Des Museums für ur- und Frühgeschichte Potsdam.* Berlin: VEB Deutscher Verlag der Wissenschaften.

Griffin, P. B. 1984. Forager resource and land use in the humid tropics: The Agta of northeastern Luzon, the Philippines. In Schrire, C. (ed.), *Past and Present in Hunter Gatherer Societies,* pp. 95–121. New York: Academic Press.

Gurina, N. N. 1956. *Oleneostrovski Mogilnik.* (Materialy i Issledovaniya po Arkheologii USSSR 47).

Gurina, I. I. (ed.) 1966. *Sources of Ancient Culture (Mesolithic epoch).* (Materialy i Issledovaniya po Arkheologii USSSR 126).

Halstead, P. 1981. Counting sheep in Neolithic and Bronze Age Greece. In Hodder, I., Isaac, G. & Hammond, N. (eds), *Pattern of the Past: Studies in Honour of David Clarke,* 307–339. Cambridge: Cambridge University Press.

Halstead, P. & O'Shea, J. 1982. A friend in need is a friend indeed: social storage and the origins of social ranking. In Renfrew, C. & Shennan, S. (eds), *Ranking, Resource and Exchange: Aspects of the Archaeology of Early European Society,* pp. 92–99. Cambridge: Cambridge University Press.

Hayden, B. 1981. Research and development in the Stone Age: technological transitions among hunter-gatherers. *Current Anthropology* 22: 519–548.

Hayden B. 1990. Nimrods, piscators, pluckers, and planters: the emergence of food production. *Journal of Anthropological Archaeology* 9: 31–69.

Headland, T. & Reid, L. 1989. Hunter-gatherers and their neighbours from prehistory to the present. *Current Anthropology* 30: 43–66.

Helskog, K. 1985. Boats and meaning: a study of change and continuity in the Alta fjord, arctic Norway, from 4200 to 500 years BC. *Journal of Anthropological Archaeology* 4: 177–205.

Higgs, E. (ed.) 1972. *Papers in Economic Prehistory.* Cambridge: Cambridge University Press.

Higgs, E. (ed.) 1975. *Palaeoeconomy.* Cambridge: Cambridge University Press.

Hill, K., Kaplan, H., Hawkes, K. & Hurtado, A. 1987. Foraging decisions among hunter-gatherers: new data and implications for optimal foraging models. *Ethology and Sociobiology* 8: 1–36.

Hodder, I. 1982. The identification and interpretation of ranking in pre-history: a contextual perspective. In Renfrew, C. & Shennan, S. (eds), *Ranking, Resource and Exchange*, pp. 150–154. Cambridge: Cambridge University Press.

Hodder, I. 1984. Burials, houses, women and men in the European Neolithic. In Miller, D. & Tilley, C. (eds), *Ideology, Power and Prehistory*, 51–68. Cambridge: Cambridge University Press.

Hodder, I. 1990. *The Domestication of Europe*. Oxford: Blackwell.

Ingold, I. 1980. *Hunters, Pastoralists, Ranchers*. Cambridge: Cambridge University Press.

Ingold, T. 1983. The significance of storage in hunting societies. *Man* 18: 553–571.

Ingold, T. 1988. Notes on the foraging mode of production. In Ingold T., Riches, D. and Woodburn, V. (eds), *Hunters and Gatherers*, vol. 1: *History, Evolution and Social Change*, pp. 269–285. Oxford: Berg.

Ingold, T., Riches, D. & Woodburn, J. (eds) 1988. *Hunters and Gatherers*. Oxford: Berg.

Janik, L. in press. The appearance of food producing societies in the south-eastern Baltic region. In Zvelebil, M., Dennell, R. & Domanska, L. (eds), *Agricultural Frontier and the Transition to Farming in the Baltic*. Sheffield Academic Press: Sheffield.

Johnson, A. W. & Earle, T. 1987. *The Evolution of Human Societies*. Stanford: Stanford University Press.

Kent, S. 1992. The current forager controversy: real versus ideal views of hunter-gatherers. *Man* (n.s.) 27: 45–70.

Kent, S. 1993. Sharing in an egalitarian Kalahari community. *Man* (n.s.) 28: 479–514.

King, T. H. 1978. Don't that beat the band? nonegalitarian political organization in prehistoric central California. In Redman, C. L., Langhorne, T. Jr., Berman, M. J., Versaggi, N. M., Curtin, E. V., Wanser, J. C. (eds), *Beyond Subsistence and Dating*, pp. 225–248. New York: Academic Press.

Kozlowski, S. K. (ed.) 1973. *The Mesolithic in Europe*. Warsaw: Warsaw University Press.

Kozlowski, J. K. & Kozlowski, S. K. 1986. Foragers of central Europe and their acculturation. In Zvelebil, M. (ed.), *Hunters in Transition*, pp. 95–108. Cambridge: Cambridge University Press.

Kuna, M. 1991. The structuring of prehistoric landscape. *Antiquity* 65: 332–347.

Larsson, L. 1990. Dogs in fraction – symbols in action. In Vermeersch, P. M. & Van Peer, P. (ed.), *Contributions to the Mesolithic in Europe*, pp. 153–160. Leuven: Leuven University Press.

Leacock, E. & Lee, R. 1982. *Politics and History in Band Societies*. Cambridge: Cambridge University Press.

Lee, R. 1969. *The !Kung San*. New York: Cambridge University Press.

Lee, R. B. 1990. Primitive communism and the origin of social inequality. In Upham, S. (ed.), *The Evolution of Political Systems*, pp. 225–246. Cambridge: Cambridge University Press.

Lee, R. B. 1992. Art, science, or politics? The crisis in hunter-gatherer studies. *American Anthropology* 94 (1): 31–54.

Lee, R. B. & DeVore, I. 1968. Problems in the study of hunters and gatherers. In Lee, R. & DeVore, I. (eds), *Man the Hunter*, pp. 3–13. Chicago: Aldine.

Lewis-Williams, J. D. & Dowson, T. A. 1993. On vision and power in the Neolithic: evidence from the decorated monuments. *Current Anthropology* 34 (1): 55–65.

Lewthwaite, J. 1986. The transition to food production: a Mediterranean perspective. In Zvelebil, M. (ed.), *Hunters in Transition*, pp. 53–66. Cambridge: Cambridge University Press.

Lourandos, H. 1985. Intensification and Australian prehistory. In Price, T. D. & Brown, J. A. (eds), *Prehistoric Hunter-Gatherers: The Emergence of Cultural Complexity*, pp. 385–423. Orlando: Academic Press.

Loze, I. A. 1979. *Pozdnii Neolit i Rannaya Bronza Lubanskoi Ravniny*. Riga: Zinatne.

Lubbock, J. 1865. *Pre-historic Times*. London: Williams & Norgate.

Madsen, T. 1982. Settlement systems of early agricultural societies in east Jutland, Denmark: a regional study of change. *Journal of Anthropological Archaeology* 1: 197–236.

Madsen, T. 1986. Where did all the hunters go? an assessment of an epoch-making episode, Danish prehistory. *Journal of Danish Archaeology* 5: 229–247.

Marquard, W. 1988. Politics and production among the Calusa of south Florida. In Ingold, T., Riches, D. & Woodburn, J. (eds), *Hunters and Gatherers*, vol. 1, pp. 161–188. Oxford: Berg.

Matyushin, G. I. 1976. *Mezolit Yuzhnogo Urala*. Moscow: Nauka.

Meiklejohn, C. & Zvelebil, M. 1991. Health status of European populations at the agricultural transition and the implications for the adoption of farming. In Bush, H. & Zvelebil, M. (eds), *Health in Past Societies: Biocultural Interpretations of Human Skeletal Remains in Archaeological Contexts*, pp. 129–145. Oxford: British Archaeological Reports (International Series 567).

Meillassoux, C. 1972. From production to reproduction. *Economy and Society* 1: 93–105.

Mellars, P. 1981. Towards a definition of the Mesolithic. *Mesolithic Miscellany* 2 (2): 13–16.

Mithen, S. 1990. *Thoughtful Foragers: A Study of Prehistoric Decision Making*. Cambridge: Cambridge University Press.

Mongait, A. 1959. *Archaeology in the USSR*. Moscow (Pelican Edition, London, 1961).

Morgan, H. L. 1877 [1964]. *Ancient Society*. (Reprinted 1964 by Harvard University Press, Cambridge, Mass.)

Morgan, H. L. 1881 [1965]. *Houses and House-Life of the American Aborigines*. (Reprinted 1965 by University of Chicago Press, Chicago.)

de Mortillet, G. 1883. *Le Préhistorique Antiquité de l'Homme*. Paris.

Neeley M. P. & Clark G. A. 1990. Measuring social complexity in the European Mesolithic. In Vermeersch, P. M. & Van Peer, P. (eds), *Contributions to the Mesolithic in Europe*, pp. 127–138. Leuven: Leuven University Press.

Neustupný, E. 1967. *K. Počátkům Patriarchátu ve Střední Evropě*. Praha: Academia.

Neustupný, E. 1985. K Holocénu Komořnského Jezera, On the Holocene period in the Komořany Lake area. *Památky Archeologické* 74: 9–70.

Neustupný, E. 1987. Comments on the establishment of agrarian communities on the North European plain by P. Bogucki. *Current Anthropology* 28 (1): 14–16.

Newell, R. 1984. On the Mesolithic contribution to the social evolution of western European society. In Bintliff, J. (ed.), *European Social Evolution:*

Archaeological Perspectives, pp. 69–82. Bradford: Bradford University Press.

Nygaard, S. E. 1989. The Stone Age of northern Scandinavia: a review. *Journal of World Prehistory* 3 (1): 72–116.

O'Shea, J. & Zvelebil, M. 1984. Oleneostrovskii Mogilnik: reconstructing social and economic organisation of prehistoric hunter-fishers in northern Russia. *Journal of Anthropological Archaeology* 3: 1–40.

Paaver, K. C. 1965. *Formirovaniye Teriofauny i Izmenchivost Mlekopytayushchikh Pribaltiki v Goltsene*. Tartu: Akademiya Nauk Estonskoii SSR.

Palsson, G. 1988. Hunters and gatherers of the sea. In Ingold, T., Riches, D. & Woodburn, J. (eds), *Hunters and Gatherers*, vol. 1, pp. 189–204. Oxford: Berg.

Pederson, J. & Waehle, E. 1988. The complexities of residential organisation among Efe and the Bamcombi. In Ingold, T., Riches, D. & Woodburn, J. (eds), *Hunters and Gatherers*, vol. 1, pp. 75–90. Oxford: Berg.

Piggott, S. 1965. *Ancient Europe*. Edinburgh: Edinburgh University Press.

Price, T. D. 1985. Affluent foragers of Mesolithic southern Scandinavia. In Price, T. D. & Brown, J. A. (eds), *Prehistoric Hunter-Gatherers: The Emergence of Cultural Complexity*, pp. 341–360. Orlando: Academic Press.

Price, T. D. & Brown, J. A. (eds) 1985. *Prehistoric Hunter-Gatherers: The Emergence of Cultural Complexity*. Orlando: Academic Press.

Price, T. D. & Gebauer, A. B. 1992. The final frontier: foragers to farmers in southern Scandinavia. In Gebauer, A. B. & Price, T. D. (eds), *Transitions to Agriculture in Prehistory*, pp. 97–115. Madison, Wisconsin: Prehistory Press.

Renfrew, C. 1973. Monuments, mobilisation and social organisation in Neolithic Wessex. In Renfrew, C. (ed.), *The Explanation of Culture Change*, pp. 539–558. London: Duckworth.

Renfrew, C. 1976. Megaliths, territories and populations. In de Laet, S. J. (ed.) *Acculturation and Continuity in Atlantic Europe*, pp. 198–220. Brugge: De Tempel.

Renfrew, C. 1987. *Archaeology and Language. The Puzzle of Indo-European Origins*. London: Jonathan Cape.

Renfrew, C. & Shennan, S. (eds) 1982. *Ranking, Resource and Exchange: Aspects of the Archaeology of Early European Society*. Cambridge: Cambridge University Press.

Rimantien, R. 1992. Neolithic hunter-gatherers at Sventoji in Lithuania. *Antiquity* 66: 367–376.

Rowley-Conwy, P. 1983. Sedentary hunters: the Ertebølle example. In Bailey, G. (ed.), *Hunter-gatherer Economy in Prehistory: a European Perspective*, pp. 111–126. Cambridge: Cambridge University Press.

Rowley-Conwy, P. 1986. Between cave painters and crop planters: aspects of the temperate European Mesolithic. In Zvelebil, M. (ed.), *Hunters in Transition*, pp. 17–32. Cambridge: Cambridge University Press.

Rowley-Conwy, P. & Zvelebil, M. 1989. Saving it for later: storage by prehistoric hunter-gatherers in Europe. In Halstead, P. and O'Shea, J. (eds), *Bad Year Economics*, pp. 40–56. Cambridge: Cambridge University Press.

Sahlins, M. 1974. *Stone Age Economics*. Chicago: Aldine.

Scarre, C. 1992. The early Neolithic of western France and megalithic origins in Atlantic Europe. *Oxford Journal of Archaeology* 11 (2): 121–154.

Schrire, C. (ed.) 1984. *Past and Present in Hunter Gatherer Studies*. Orlando, FL: Academic Press.

Service, E. 1962. *Primitive Social Organization*. New York: Random House.

Shanks, M. & Tilley, C. Y. 1982. Ideology, symbolic power and ritual communication: a reinterpretation of Neolithic mortuary practices. In Hodder, I. (ed.), *Symbolic and Structural Archaeology*, pp. 129–154. Cambridge: Cambridge University Press.

Shennan, S. 1982. The emergence of hierarchical structure. In Renfrew, C. & Shennan, S. (eds), *Ranking, Resource and Exchange: Aspects of the Archaeology of Early European Society*, pp. 9–12. Cambridge: Cambridge University Press.

Sherratt, A. G. 1976. Resources, technology and trade, an essay in early European metallurgy. In Sieveking, G., Longworth, I. J. & Wilson, K. E. (eds), *Problems in Economic and Social Archaeology*, pp. 557–581. London: Duckworth.

Sherratt, A. G. 1981. Plough and pastoralism: aspects of the secondary products revolution. In Hodder, I., Isaac, G. & Hammond, N. (eds), *Pattern of the Past: Studies in honour of David Clarke*, pp. 261–305. Cambridge: Cambridge University Press.

Sherratt, A. 1982. Mobile resources: settlement and exchange in early agricultural Europe. In Renfrew, C. & Shennan, S. (eds), *Ranking, Resources and Exchange: Aspects of the Archaeology of Early European Society*, pp. 13–26. Cambridge: Cambridge University Press.

Sherratt, A. G. 1984. Social evolution: Europe in the later Neolithic and Copper Ages. In Bintliff, J. (ed.), *European Social Evolution*, pp. 123–134. Bradford: University of Bradford Press.

Sherratt, A. 1990. The genesis of megaliths: monumentality, ethnicity and social complexity in Neolithic north-west Europe. *World Archaeology* 22 (2): 148–167.

Shott, M. J. 1992. On recent trends in the anthropology of foragers: Kalahari revisionism and its archaeological implications. *Man* (n.s.) 27: 843–871.

Solberg, B. 1989. The Neolithic transition in southern Scandinavia: internal development or migration? *Oxford Journal of Archaeology* 8 (3): 261–296.

Solway, J. S. & Lee, R. B. 1990. Foragers, genuine or spurious? *Current Anthropology* 31 (2): 109–145.

Steward, J. 1936. The economic and social basis of primitive bands. In Lowie, R. (ed.), *Essays in Anthropology in Honour of Alfred Louis Kroeber*, pp. 331–350. Berkeley: University of California Press.

Steward, J. 1955. *Theory of Culture Change*. Urbana: University of Illinois Press.

Testart, A. 1982. *Les Chasseurs-Cueilleurs ou L'Origine des Inégalités*. Paris: Société d'Ethnographie.

Thomas, J. 1987. Relations of production and social change in the Neolithic of north-west Europe. *Man* (n.s.) 22: 405–430.

Thomas, J. 1988. Neolithic explanations revisited: the Mesolithic-Neolithic transition in Britain and south Scandinavia. *Proceedings of the Prehistoric Society* 54: 59–66.

Thomas, J. 1991. *Rethinking the Neolithic*. Cambridge: Cambridge Univ. Press.

Tilley, C. 1991. *Material Culture and Text: The Art of Ambiguity*. London: Routledge.

Torrence, R. 1983. Time budgeting and hunter-gatherer technology. In Bailey, G. (ed.), *Hunter-Gatherer Economy in Prehistory: A European Perspective*, pp. 11–22. Cambridge: Cambridge University Press.

Tringham, R. 1971. *Hunters, Fishers and Farmers of Eastern Europe 6000–3000 BC*. London: Hutchinson.

Vankina, L. V. 1970. *Torfyanikovaya Stoyanka Sarnate*. Riga: 'Zinatne'.

Vencl, S. 1986. The role of hunting-gathering populations in the transition to farming: a central-European perspective. In Zvelebil, M. (ed.), *Hunters in Transition*, pp. 43–51. Cambridge: Cambridge University Press.

Vermeersch, P. M. and Van Peer, P. (eds) 1990. *Contributions to the Mesolithic in Europe*. Leuven: Leuven University Press.

van de Velde, P. 1979. *On Bandkeramik Social Structure an Analysis of Pot Decoration and Hut Distributions from the Central European Neolithic Communities of Elsloo and Heinheim*. The Hague: Leiden University Press (Analecta Praehistorica Leidensia).

Vuorela, I. & Lempiainen, T. 1988. Archaeobotany of the oldest cereal grain find in Finland. *Annales Botanici Fennici* 25: 33–45.

Welinder, S. 1989. Mesolithic forest clearance in Scandinavia. In Bonsall, C. (ed.), *The Mesolithic in Europe*, pp. 362–377. Edinburgh: John Donald Publishers.

Westropp, H. M. 1872. *Pre-historic Phases*. London.

White, L. 1959. *The Evolution of Culture*. New York: McGraw-Hill.

Whittle, A. 1985. *Neolithic Europe: A Survey*. Cambridge: Cambridge University Press.

Whittle, A. 1988. *Problems in Neolithic Archaeology*. Cambridge: Cambridge University Press.

Williams, N. M. & Hunn, E. S. (eds) 1982. *Resource Managers: North American and Australian Hunter-Gatherers*. Colorado: Westview.

Wilmsen, E. N. & Denbow, J. R. 1990. Paradigmatic history of San-speaking peoples and current attempts at revision. *Current Anthropology* 31 (5): 489–524.

Woodburn, J. 1982. Egalitarian societies. *Man* (n.s.) 17: 431–51.

Woodburn, J. 1988. African hunter-gatherer social organization: is it best understood as a product of encapsulation? In Ingold, T, Riches, D. & Woodburn, J. (eds), *Hunters and Gatherers*, vol. 1, pp. 31–64. Oxford: Berg.

Yellen, J. 1977. *Archaeological Approaches to the Present*. New York: Academic Press.

Zvelebil, M. 1981. *From Forager to Farmer in the Boreal Zone*. Oxford: British Archaeological Reports (International Series 115).

Zvelebil, M. 1984. Clues to recent human evolution from specialised technologies? *Nature* 307: 314–315.

Zvelebil, M. 1985. Iron age transformations in Northern Russia and the northeast Baltic. In, Barker, G. & Gamble, C. (eds), *Beyond Domestication in Prehistoric Europe*, pp. 147–180.

Zvelebil, M. 1986a. Mesolithic prelude and Neolithic revolution. In Zvelebil, M. (ed.), *Hunters in Transition*, pp. 5–15. Cambridge: Cambridge University Press.

Zvelebil, M. 1986b. Mesolithic societies and the transition to farming: problems of time, scale and organisation. In Zvelebil, M. (ed.), *Hunters in Transition*, pp. 167–187. Cambridge: Cambridge University Press.

Zvelebil, M. (ed.) 1986c. *Hunters in Transition. Mesolithic Societies of Temperate Eurasia and their Transition to Farming*. Cambridge: Cambridge University Press.

Zvelebil, M. 1987. Wetland settlements in eastern Europe. In Coles, J. M. & Lawson, A. J. (eds), *European Wetlands in Prehistory*, pp. 94–117. Oxford: Clarendon.

Zvelebil, M. 1992. Prehistoric hunter-fishers in northern Europe. *La Recherche* 246: 982–990.

Zvelebil, M. 1992. Les chasseurs pécheurs de la Scandinavie préhistorique. *La Recherche* 246.

Zvelebil, M. 1993. Hunters or farmers? The Neolithic and Bronze Age societies of north-east Europe. In Chapman, J. & Dolukhanov, P. (eds), *Cultural Transformation and Interactions in Eastern Europe*, pp. 146–172. Aldershot: Avebury.

Zvelebil, M. 1994. Plant use in the Mesolithic and the implications for the transition to farming. *Proceedings of Prehistoric Society* 60.

Zvelebil, M. & Rowley-Conwy, P. 1986. Foragers and farmers in Atlantic Europe. In Zvelebil, M. (ed.), *Hunters in Transition*, pp. 67–93. Cambridge: Cambridge University Press.

Zvelebil, M. & Dolukhanov, P. 1991. Transition to farming in eastern and northern Europe. *Journal of World Prehistory* 5 (3): 233–278.

Zvelebil, M. 1996. Farmers our ancestors, In Jones, S., Gamble, C. & Graves, P. (eds), *European Communities: Archaeology and the Construction of Cultural Identity*. London: Routledge.

Zvelebil, M. in press. Hunting, gathering or husbandry? Management of food resources by the late Mesolithic communities of temperate Europe. In Dampana, D. (ed.), *Before Farming*. Philadelphia: The University Museum Publications, University of Pennsylvania (Masca research papers in science and archaeology).

2

Towards a Regional Geography of the Neolithic

Julian Thomas

It *could be argued* that in the past decade the major successes of Neolithic studies have been those accounts which focus upon the local and specific details of social practice, architecture, and the use and deposition of material culture (e.g. Barrett, Bradley and Green 1991; Edmonds 1992; Richards 1992). Implicit or explicit in these approaches has been an understanding that grander historical processes only become comprehensible when they are considered in terms of the ways in which they were lived through and experienced. In other words, much recent writing in prehistoric studies has attempted to resist the totalisation which was evident both in 'processual' archaeology, and in some approaches inspired by structural Marxism. Strathern (1991: i-xxv) effectively demonstrates the drawbacks of too generalised an approach by drawing an analogy with fractal graphics. At whatever scale we look at the fractal pattern, she points out, the detail looks very much the same. Seeing more of the pattern does not necessarily make a greater amount of information available to us. Similarly, when we are concerned with human beings it is not the case that more and more information accrues as we look at greater and greater aggregates of persons, so that the outcome of an analysis at a larger scale is not necessarily more 'complex': one is simply placed in the position of saying less about more. The potential descriptive information at any scale of analysis is effectively inexhaustible, and what we choose to say can only ever constitute a partial account. We could write a monograph on a single pottery vessel, and still find that there were observations which we had left out.

The 'jeweller's-eye view' has been particularly beneficial in promoting a desire to be more attentive to the archaeological evidence. However, the suggestion made by the organisers of the Glasgow conference that we should address broader and larger-scale issues is a timely one. Even if we wish to write about past social processes 'from the bottom up', it is essential that from time to time we take stock of how we conceive broader historical trajectories, so that we do not find ourselves placing detailed research into grand structures which are by now moribund. Thus there is something to be said for tacking back and forth between a consideration of global processes and of their local manifestations (Geertz 1983; Marcus and Fischer 1986: chapter 4). In this spirit, I should like to offer in this paper some thoughts concerning the character of regional variability in the British Neolithic, for the most part by considering the wider European context of its inception. That is to say, I argue that we should address variations in Neolithic material culture by first considering the character of the Neolithic as a broader cultural phenomenon.

CULTURE HISTORY AND CULTURE PROCESS

I take as my starting point Stuart Piggott's book, *Neolithic Cultures of the British Isles* (1954). Piggott's achievement was to present a vivid picture of a series of geographically and culturally distinctive communities, and he did this through the medium of a *narrative* of cultural change. Piggott saw all of these groups as cultural entities, whole in themselves yet possessing an overall unity, brought about through a sequence of events of contact and migration. Each of these changes is intelligible in terms of what came before it, so that in order to understand any part of the overall pattern, we have to trace the whole back to its origin in the transition from the Mesolithic to the Neolithic. For Piggott, this transition was a fundamental watershed. In his account, regional variability and cultural identity go hand in hand. Thus the primary Neolithic presence in the British Isles was represented by the Windmill Hill culture, an entity defined on the basis of a range of field monuments and artefact types (earthen long barrows, causewayed enclosures, flint mines, round-based pottery and a range of chipped stone tools including leaf-shaped arrowheads) (ibid.: 17). All of these innovations were taken as being intrusive to Britain, and the Windmill

Hill culture was thought of as having arrived as an entirely formed and non-experimental whole. Since no direct parallel for the Windmill Hill complex was known on the continent, Piggott suggested that its origin must lie somewhere between Belgium and Brittany, in an area which had at that time seen little archaeological fieldwork. From a base or heartland established in southern central England, the Windmill Hill culture expanded northwards into Yorkshire, across the Pennines, and toward the head of the Irish Sea (ibid.: 102). Initially, there was little interaction between these incoming groups, with their entirely novel material equipment, and the indigenous Mesolithic population. However, the short (pre-radiocarbon) chronology of the work allowed Piggott to hypothesise 'secondary Neolithic' cultures emerging in the later part of the period (ibid.: 315). These were the outcome of a fusion of incoming settlers from Scandinavia, bringing with them the practice of decorating ceramics with cord impressions (manifested in Peterborough Wares), and surviving forest hunters. In Gordon Childe's (1940) variant of this account, these secondary Neolithic folk retained their habitual mobility, specialising as traders and opening up the stone axe sources in the west of Britain.

While Piggott's book is a landmark in cataloguing the range of cultural manifestations of the British Neolithic, it is clearly an example of the culture-historic approach to prehistory that suffered heavy criticism in the 1960s. Indeed, Piggott's text is littered with the 'backwaters', 'Dead Seas' and 'flowing streams' of what Lewis Binford (1965: 205) would later characterise as the 'aquatic' conception of culture. The essence of Binford's criticism was that culture history depended upon the notion that artefacts were the outcome of shared norms of behaviour, templates held in the human mind. If this was the case, then the significance of material culture lay not in the artefacts themselves but in the heads of long-dead people. Archaeological investigation would then necessarily be limited to either the speculation of 'palaeopsychology' or dry, descriptive typologising (Binford 1972: 104). Moreover, culture history was particularistic, seeing sequences of change as the chance outcome of migrations, meetings, fusions and individual psychological dispositions (Binford 1989: 51). In the form most fully articulated by Gordon Childe (1942: 16), culture history presumed that individuals grew up inculcated into a particular cultural milieu, steeped in particular ways of doing things, and were unlikely ever to cast off the dead hand of tradition.

Over the past century, one of the principal trends in archaeological thought has arguably been the emergence of a greater and greater conceptual distance between groups of people and the material and other culture which they have at their disposal. Thus Kossinna saw a virtual identity between a material assemblage and a racial group, Childe considered cultures to represent 'peoples' in less specific terms, and Binford insisted that culture was not shared by groups of people, but participated in. Culture for him represented a set of strategies which individuals or groups might adopt in order to cope with changing environmental circumstances (Binford 1973: 228). Culture could be used or discarded at will. On the positive side, this meant that culture was no longer assumed to be homogeneous and equally shared by all members of a community, but this was offset by a functionalism which saw those individuals as participating mutually in a project of group survival.

It is arguable whether such an adaptive conception of culture had much impact upon the study of regional variability in Neolithic Britain. David Clarke's Beaker corpus, for instance, used a complex methodology to define a series of Beaker sub-groups, and then reverted to culture history, explaining them as separate invading communities from the continent (Clarke 1970). In the case of Colin Renfrew's (1973a; 1973b; 1976; 1979) studies of monuments and population dynamics there is actually rather little concern with geographical diversity. For Renfrew, the regions of Neolithic Britain became the *territories* of population groups. The variability of material culture and architecture was of interest to him in substantiating local sequences of change (e.g. Renfrew 1979: 207), but on an inter-regional level the differences were clearly considered to be superficial. Beneath the froth of pottery styles and tomb types lay more fundamental processes of social change, which were essentially similar in each area as well as directly comparable with Polynesia (Renfrew 1973b: 170–83). Renfrew's assumption was that in each part of Neolithic north-western Europe, rising population levels led to an increased stress on resources, and thus to the emergence of territorialism. Each individual egalitarian tribal society would choose to signify its indissoluble relationship to its land by constructing a funerary monument, which in some way made reference to the continuous occupation of a place by a given group, down through the generations. As time went on, further rises in population made more labour available for monument construction, but this took the form of large centralised structures rather than small dispersed ones (Renfrew 1973a). The process of population rise thus went hand in hand with one of political centralisation, as clans or lineages merged together to form chiefdoms.

CULTURE, IDENTITY, AND REGIONALITY

Seemingly, neither Piggott's culture history nor a processual approach to cultural dynamics provides us with the resources for a satisfactory account of regional diversity, even if there are elements of each which are helpful. I will argue that some fruitful avenues are opened up by recent writings in social anthropology, human geography, and philosophy, all of which return us to the question of culture and its spatiality. We could begin by noting Rosaldo's (1989: 45) observation that:

> if ethnography once imagined it could describe discrete cultures, it now contends with boundaries that crisscross over a field at once fluid and saturated with power.

In other words, neither the geographical region nor the human population which inhabits it can be considered as given, stable or bounded (Duncan 1989). Rather, localities, regionalisations, and identities should be seen as produced by human beings operating within networks of power and knowledge which are themselves historically constituted. Culture, and cultural identity, are both the outcome of this process and the media through which it is carried forward. Culture, whether mental or material, is a form of knowledge. This knowledge can be transmitted from one person to another, some of it verbally or in written form, yet much of it is acquired practically rather than discursively. If we consider for the sake of argument a traditional art style, it is clear that there is a continuum between the specific motifs and subjects which will be transmitted from person to person explicitly, and the skills of brushwork and execution which are learned through the inculcation of habit. Yet there is no hard and fast line between these extremes. To use Hubert Dreyfus' (1991: 18) example, people in different parts of the world habitually stand at different distances from each other to converse. Thus when we meet people from other countries they can either appear to invade our personal space or seem (literally) 'stand-offish' and remote. This behaviour is not biologically programmed, nor is it ever made explicit in a code of rules. Instead, persons gradually acquire a skilled understanding of how to cope with their own immediate social circumstances. It is rarely the case that even the most complex of social situations are underlain by highly structured and rigid cultural patterns. Instead, a fluid web of stray pieces of information and unconsidered habits form a basis for human practices which are spontaneous and improvisational (Rosaldo 1989: 92; Bourdieu 1977).

[41]

Nor should 'knowledge' be thought of in Cartesian terms as being composed of abstract pieces of information held within human brain-cases. On the contrary, cultural knowledge is a means of engaging with the world, of 'getting on with things'. It is often quite difficult to bring particular ways of coping with things to mind in the abstract, even if in the concrete context we can carry them out 'without thinking about it'. Consequently, material culture should not be seen as a terminal outcome of cultural processes, but as a constituent element in the reproduction of knowledge. Just as Binford indicated, this know-ledge is unevenly distributed within society, but the reasons for this are not exclusively concerned with functional, group survival require-ments. Nobody knows everything about their own culture (Lindstrom 1990: xi), and thus in geographical terms culture is heterogeneous. Cultural knowledge is not inert; it is open to interpretation, and to manipulation by persons who wish to advance particular sectional interests. It can be deployed by individuals in a variety of contexts in which authority and power are at stake. The acquisition of knowledge provides positions from which to act, and from which to speak with authority. Thus the reproduction of social relationships will generally involve procedures which regulate access to particular forms of cul-tural learning.

Communities may have a whole series of spheres of cultural know-ledge, from pottery manufacture and decoration, to folklore and myth, to the initiation rites of secret societies. Because of their differential en-gagement in all of these different practices, individuals perceive the cultural whole which surrounds them in different ways. That is to say, their understanding is positioned. Moreover, it is through their differ-ential access to cultural knowledge that individuals come to develop their personal sense of selfhood. Consequently, public meanings and interpretations will always be negotiated and contested, and will be the outcome of a continual struggle. This will include ethnic or group identity, for this too is not a given. As Clifford (1988: 9) points out, identity is 'not an archaic survival but an ongoing process'. Personal identity may involve a variety of ways of presenting oneself, which are deployed according to context. *Individuals* gain their sense of selfhood by linking together significant memories into autobiography, and similarly the identity of a group is negotiated by bringing particular past events to notice, and by presenting innovations as relevant and acceptable. So communities will always be recreating and re-telling their own histories. Social memory, that which is referenced in this process, is not a fixed and immutable tradition, but involves an active recreation of the past in the present (Barth 1987; Connerton 1989). Thus the cultural character of the group or groups of people occupying a given region is not fixed by biology or environment. It may be something which is volatile, always open to question and redefinition, as different aspects of the past are dredged back up or tactfully passed over, and new developments adopted or rejected accordingly.

The consequence of this train of thought is that geographical regions should not be thought of as determining cultural character. Rather, they represent contexts in which particular stocks of cultural knowledge are available, and in which particular personal and group identities are produced and reproduced (Thrift 1991). Cultural knowledge and learning will also tend to be stratified. As with language, it will be essential to use a given set of learned cultural conventions in order to communicate and be heard, and to have a social identity. As we have noted, many cultural codes are adopted and deployed at a practical rather than discursive level of consciousness, made use of in social life without reflection. Yet it is also possible to adopt or discard particular aspects of culture in a strategic manner, perhaps in order to employ them in expressing an overt message. In this manner, cultural knowledge can move from the realm of the habitual to the discursive. One may unthinkingly comb one's hair in a particular way for years before deciding that this hairstyle represents a statement of individuality. There is consequently no hard and fast line between these two extremes of the discursive and the non-discursive. Convention, custom and tradition become subject to evaluation and reassessment as a result of the unfolding of personal life projects, conditioned by historical circumstances.

THE CONTEXT OF THE MESOLITHIC-NEOLITHIC TRANSITION

Using this perspective it may be possible to reconsider the circumstances which generated cultural diversity in Neolithic Britain. In doing this it is necessary to bow to Piggott's wisdom in seeing subsequent developments as underwritten by the character of the introduction of the Neolithic to Britain, and, I would add, questioning precisely what the Neolithic represented by this time. This requires us to bring together three areas of interest which are often unfortunately held apart as separate debates, namely, the nature of social change in fourth millennium bc (uncalibrated) Europe, the British Mesolithic-Neolithic transition, and the question of regional systems. However, it should be emphasised that what is being presented here is in no way a general model for the Mesolithic-Neolithic transition or the adoption of agriculture in the Old World. Rather, what is at issue is a very specific conjuncture in European prehistory. I have argued elsewhere that the origin of the British Neolithic lies in a fundamental transformation of Neolithic society in continental north-western Europe (Thomas 1988), and I would like to develop that argument somewhat here, by drawing on some of the more recent literature on these issues. In passing, it is necessary to stress that the Neolithic should not be thought of as a static entity which can be held constant across time and space (e.g. Zvelebil 1989). The term itself is a product of archaeological thinking, which can too often solidify into some kind of reified entity (Thomas 1993a). If we are to use the word 'Neolithic' to describe an historical phenomenon at all, it must be a series of interactions which differed across time and space, and which possessed no underlying homogeneity so much as an entanglement through chains of causality.

It is widely recognised that following a very rapid expansion across the loess country of central Europe by Bandkeramik groups, the further spread of the Neolithic way of life was halted, and a lengthy period of stasis set in. This period saw settlement nucleation, regionalisation of material culture, and possibly enhanced social conflict documented by enclosed settlements (Starling 1985; Coudart 1991). Two areas break with this general pattern, however, and demonstrate evidence of considerable cultural innovation. Firstly, in north-western France, the incursion of Epibandkeramik groups into new areas may have involved continued population movement or perhaps the adoption of Bandkeramik-related material culture by native communities (Sherratt 1990: 152). This area also saw more complex combinations of cultural traditions starting to emerge (Roussot-Larroque and Burnez 1992). Secondly, the eastern part of the North European Plain saw the emergence of the earliest TRB (Sarnowo, Rosenhof and Siggeneben-Süd) in the period after 3600 bc (4500 BC) (Midgeley 1992: chapter 5). Interestingly, the comparison of two of Midgeley's maps (1992: figs 6 and 67 – combined here as my Fig. 1) makes the point that this cultural innovation took place *on the periphery* of the areas occupied by the Bandkeramik and post-Bandkeramik groups. Importantly, both of these developments have been considered in terms of interactions between incoming agricultural groups and local foragers (Kinnes 1984; Midgeley 1985; 1992). It is consequently possible to argue that in the period following the decline of the Bandkeramik as a unified cultural entity, new forms of cultural and social organisation were emerging in the interstitial zones where farmers and foragers were in habitual

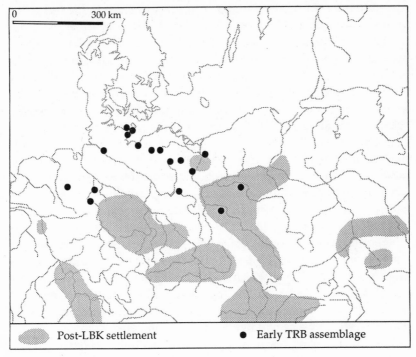

Figure 1. The relationship between the earliest TRB assemblages and the distribution of post-Bandkeramik assemblages (after Midgeley 1992: figs 6 and 67).

contact with each other. In Britain, southern Scandinavia, much of the Alpine foreland and the western part of the North European Plain, however, the emergence of the Neolithic came rather later, and there is a growing acceptance that it involves the adoption of a new way of life on the part of indigenous groups. These changes, which took place in the late fourth millennium bc (ca 4000 BC), are frequently seen in terms of some resource crisis afflicting hunting and gathering groups, and forcing them to take up agriculture (e.g. Zvelebil and Rowley-Conwy 1984). What I suggest is that this period also saw a social transformation amongst established, post-Bandkeramik argriculturalists, which was at least as significant as that overtaking the foraging groups. Moreover, the overall pattern of change across north-western Europe may have as much to do with incipient conflicts *internal* to Neolithic society as with the economic problems of Mesolithic groups.

Thus we may not be dealing simply with a transfer of cultural traits from one kind of group to another, but with a two-way interaction, in which the assimilation of aspects of Mesolithic social organisation served to resolve growing structural incompatibilities in the temperate Neolithic. The particular features which might be considered in this light include mobility, the significance of a seasonal round, the importance of fixed points within a landscape, and the development of relatively exogamous relations between communities. This period saw a general decline, if not disappearance, of the massive domestic architecture that characterised the Bandkeramik and its successors (Kinnes 1985: 25). In the Meuse valley, to give an example, Wansleben and Verhart (1990: 399) have noted an expansion of settlement onto the sandy soils in the Michelsberg phase, and the emergence of an overall settlement structure much more similar to that of the Mesolithic than those of the Bandkeramik or Rössen. We might link this development with the emergence of a more mobile lifestyle, either connected with economic change or as a means of obviating the conflicts and disputes inherent in village co-residence. I will argue that these social changes were facilitated by a very broad process of cultural change. In consequence the 'Neolithic' which came to be established in Britain bore very little resemblance to the 'Neolithic' which had been imposed upon central Europe over a millennium earlier. Problems of interpretation arise where we play down the distinction between the two on the grounds that they represent manifestations of a more fundamental and underlying process, such as the expansion of agriculture. As I have hoped to demonstrate (Thomas 1991), in the British context the adoption of domesticated resources was a comparatively minor element amongst widespread changes which overtook indigenous society at this time. At the scale of analysis indulged in here, the character of the British first Neolithic is comprehensible in the context of a broader cultural transformation, which we can now consider.

THE 'WESTERN NEOLITHIC' RECONSIDERED

The notion of a second phase of western European Neolithic settlement was discussed by Childe amongst others under the rubric of the 'Western Neolithic' (Childe 1925: 287). While he saw this development in terms of a second wave of migrants, originating in Lagozza and Cortaillod and moving north and west, the concept does express the understanding that the late fourth millennium bc saw the emergence of a *different kind* of Neolithic, not simply at the margins, but even in the heartlands of Bandkeramik settlement in the west. This replaced a situation in which the distinction between Mesolithic and Neolithic communities had been relatively clear-cut. In the mid-fourth millennium bc (ca 4500 BC), a series of cultural groups had existed which drew almost exclusively upon the heritage of the Bandkeramik, making use of artefact style in such a way as to express a series of regional identities: Rössen, Lengyel, and the various elements of the Cerny complex (Louwe-Kooijmans 1976: 242). Contact with foraging groups extending across the North European Plain and into Scandinavia is documented by finds of shaft-hole adzes, post-Bandkeramik sherds, bone combs and T-shaped antler axes well beyond their main distribution (Fischer 1982; Gebauer & Price 1990). Evidently, groups like the Ertebølle, Ellerbeck, early Wistka, and Swifterbant for some centuries formed a kind of 'penumbra' around the heartland of agricultural settlement. Each of the groups of foragers demonstrated an ability to assimilate aspects of Neolithic cultural apparatus in the form of pottery or livestock (de Roever 1979; Louwe-Kooijmans 1987; Rowley-Conwy 1981; Cyrek, Grygel & Nowak 1986). 'Precocious' finds of domestic species are also known from Breton, Irish and central Swiss Mesolithic contexts (Bender 1985: 23; Woodman and O'Brien 1993: 33; Sakellaridis 1979: 183). This process of piecemeal adoption of cultural innovations by Mesolithic communities may date back to the first incursions of the Bandkeramik into the west, if we accept the hypothesis that the users of La Hoguette Wares were indigenous foragers (Gronenborn 1990: 178). The initial contacts between agriculturalists and gatherer-hunters have sometimes been interpreted in economic terms as involving a form of mutualism, whereby grain or animal products might be exchanged for services including the hunting down of pests (Gregg 1991). Whether or not this is the case, the relationship between foragers and farmers gives little indication of being balanced in *cultural* terms. For while the Bandkeramik and its successors do show signs of cultural change, this seems to have taken place within a closed symbolic universe. The localisation of traditions of ceramic band infill, and the eventual emergence of local cultural entities like Cerny and the Rössen, can be seen as elaborations upon the prototypes of Bandkeramik material culture. Mesolithic cultural forms do not seem to have been integrated into the Bandkeramik tradition – perhaps an indication of a deep conservatism involved in the maintenance of cultural unity over a long time (Coudart 1991: 404). The cultural exchange between Bandkeramik groups and Mesolithic bands appears to have been essenti-ally one-way, at least as far as its material consequences are concerned.

What sets apart the cultural changes that took place in north-western Europe from around 3200 bc (4000 BC) onwards is the opening up of a much broader range of contacts, between groups sharing quite different cultural traditions. From this time onwards, the eclectic tendencies already present in Brittany and the earliest TRB areas became more widespread. Putting it another way, a series of *separate* symbolic systems were being referenced in the creation of something new. The emergence of the northern Chasséen, the Michelsberg, Chasséo-Michelsberg, Hazendonk II, Cortaillod, Pfyn, the earlier Neolithic of Britain and the primary TRB of Scandinavia, Holland, and southern Germany did not draw *solely* upon elements found in the post-Bandkeramik. So in addition, we have a variety of elements drawn from the southern Chasséen (whose heritage might ultimately be traced back to the Cardial, and a very different 'way of being Neolithic') (Phillips 1982: 55), from the Breton early Neolithic, from the TRB eastern group, and from the Mesolithic groups. As far as the latter are concerned, there is a categorical distinction to be made between the opportunistic 'borrowing' of elements of Neolithic culture which we have just mentioned, and the wholesale transformation of indigenous ways of life in the period after 3200 bc. The indigenous populations of Atlantic Europe were not the passive recipients of a cultural package which had been formulated elsewhere. If we accept that the changes taking place at this point were not exclusively the products of the adoption of agriculture, we should not expect them to flow according to any 'wave of advance' (Ammerman & Cavalli-Sforza 1971) from south-east to north-west. It is thus not the case that the Atlantic Mesolithic communities slavishly transformed themselves into Bandkeramik-style agriculturalists. Rather, they were themselves instrumental in these changes, through becoming meshed into social relationships with formally 'Neolithic' groups. Thus it was not merely what was on offer to Mesolithic groups that was different, but the character of their engagement with Neolithic cultural knowledge.

This should not be taken to imply that the period was one of cultural homogeneity in north-western Europe. Clearly, we can distinguish between the material culture assemblages of the different groups mentioned, even if they tend to merge into one another to some degree (Louwe-Kooijmans 1980; Burkill 1983: 55). But what is suggested is that widespread social changes had resulted in a greater interchange of information between groups, with the effect of making available a much broader pool of cultural knowledge which could be drawn upon in the establishment of regional and local identities. So innovations that had hitherto been restricted in their distribution began to appear over much wider areas. Yet in those areas they might be deployed and combined in wholly novel ways. A case in point would be the development of earthen long mounds, recently addressed again by Ian Kinnes (1992). Allowing for the ambiguity of the Polish evidence (Kinnes 1992: 131; Midgeley 1985), this could be argued to be a roughly synchronous development in Britain, Denmark, and the North European Plain. In each of the areas of emergence the monuments draw in *different* (and locally meaningful) ways upon a pool of traits which might hark back to Breton long mounds (Boujot & Cassen 1992), megalithic communal burial (Scarre 1992), Mesolithic extended burial (Midgeley 1985), and long-house architecture (Hodder 1984). It would obviously be a mistake to seek a single geographical point of origin for such a phenomenon, but the very fact that such diverse elements can be involved is distinctive of a particular juncture in European prehistory.

One point which has been made repeatedly is that funerary monuments in general emerge around the peripheries of the initial zone of Bandkeramik settlement in this later phase of development (Powell 1969; Renfrew 1973b; Hodder 1984; Sherratt 1990). The reasons for this have been suggested to have been involved with territorialism (resulting from constraints on further settlement expansion) or with the absence of timber long-houses as a settlement focus. While what follows is not intended as a global interpretation of the phenomenon, it may be that one determinant of the location of funerary monuments lies in the different character of the change to a Neolithic way of life in different parts of Europe. On the loess of central Europe, Bandkeramik groups arrived as colonisers, having initially very little contact with local foragers and gatherers. The landscape they entered would have been little known to them, and they would have proceeded to name and interpret the places which they encountered in terms of their own cosmology and way of life. But in Britain, Scandinavia, and the North European Plain, there was a continuity of population. The people who had lived in these areas for generations were adopting new ways. *Their* landscape was not anonymous, but would have been the landscape of hunters and gatherers, intimately known by people who had moved through it over the centuries, and deeply bound up with their stories, myths and meanings. Megalithic tombs and earthen long barrows, as well as other monuments like standing stones, were a means of transforming this nomadic understanding of place through a physical intervention, introducing new meanings to the land (Thomas 1993b). This discontinuity was required in order to disrupt or transform existing traditions of the understanding of place. As Tilley (1994) points out, Neolithic monuments are often located in direct juxtaposition with conspicuous landscape features: ridges, rocks, and mountains. If we can suggest that these natural features were the key points in a Mesolithic perception of space and place, monument-building would represent a rewriting or appropriation of their significance. In the intermediate area of Brittany, where some kind of interaction is envisaged between Neolithic and Mesolithic groups, the early monuments might be seen as the outcome of accommodation and negotiation between the two populations. For while the architecture of long mounds, and the very idea of monuments as a transformation of place, may in a general sense derive from post-Bandkeramik long-houses (Hodder 1984), a concern with complex treatments of the remains of the dead was more characteristic of the Breton and Scandinavian Mesolithic groups (Kirk 1991; Larsson 1990: 285).

THE PRODUCTION OF REGIONALITY

Turning to Britain, it may be misleading to talk about the 'introduction of the Neolithic' rather than to say that the indigenous population became involved in a series of complex interactions which resulted in the emergence of a new way of life in north-western Europe. It remains to indicate precisely what this 'new kind of Neolithic' might involve. In David Clarke's terms (1978: 311), we could think of the 'Western Neolithic' (if we want to use that term) as a polythetic cultural entity, composed of a range of forms of cultural knowledge and media for their transmission, which might occur in various combinations, and none of which was present in all geographical areas. So while agricultural production was central to the Bandkeramik as a way of life, and while agricultural knowledge might be an element in the cultural whole, the extent to which north-western European Neolithic communities were agricultural would vary. Similarly, I do not think that a single and uniform set of social relations is implied. This is not to suggest that an understanding of the social relations of production is unimportant in this period, but rather that the Neolithic cultural repertoire might facilitate the establishment and reproduction of a range of different sets of social relationships. For want of a better description, I would suggest that what emerged in the late fourth millennium was an heterogeneous network of power-knowledge relations. These were condensed in and expressed through a set of material cultural products. This materiality is one of the key aspects of the phenomenon.

The artefacts and structures that represent the material trace of the

Neolithic are not merely the terminal products of cultural processes which were primarily cerebral in character. On the contrary, material culture will have been the medium through which ideas were both transmitted and continually brought to mind. The Neolithic was, amongst other things, a technology of memory which was inserted into social life, constantly reminding people of particular aspects of past history, and projecting them forward into future contexts of social interaction. Many of the innovations of the period were thus in some way connected with the *performative* aspects of social relationships, and served to establish repeated patterns of activity. New foods, of domesticated character, might now be eaten at particular times, and pottery technology served to ensure that they were eaten in particular ways. Similarly, monumental tombs introduced reminders of the ancestral dead into the habitual space of a community, which might themselves provide locations for rituals and feasting which involved the bringing to mind of the past.

I think that we can argue that this Neolithic cultural system involved two opposed organisational principles, which underscored subsequent developments (to return to my theme of regional diversity). On the one hand there was the facilitation of interaction *between* social groups. We can see this in the increased importance of exchange late in the fourth millennium bc, evidenced both by the more intensive exploitation of a wider range of flint and stone sources (e.g. Bogucki 1987: 10; de Grooth 1991) and the wider range of exchange goods. We can also see it in the decline of firm social boundaries expressed through material culture difference. Clearly, there are still regional and group identities, but the greater emphasis on undecorated pottery and widespread similarities in basic stone-working traditions may indicate the ability of artefacts to circulate between social contexts. As against this, there is an emphasis upon division, restriction, and regulation *within* communities. This is evident in megalithic architecture, where despite the conspicuous nature of the monuments in the landscape, the character of the chamber area implies restricted access and even exclusion (Kinnes 1992: 81). Similarly, many of the artefacts now in circulation, while widespread geographically, may be restricted in their contexts of use and deposition, as Andrew Herne (1988) has suggested with the initial use of pottery in the British Isles.

Indigenous populations in Britain, as much as established colonisers on the continent, were instrumental in bringing together a range of cultural practices, producing a series of variations on a more widespread theme. Contemporary cultural groupings on the continent should thus be seen as equivalents rather than points of origin for the British Neolithic. From the earliest, local communities in different parts of Britain drew on the potential provided by a horizon of intensive interaction and exchange of ideas in quite different ways. Thus, for instance, particular areas of coastal Wales demonstrate preferences for either portal dolmens or simple, polygonally chambered passage tombs, presumably at least partly based upon the differing degrees of chamber access involved (Lynch 1976: 75). However, as the third millennium progressed, a greater degree of regional diversity developed (Bradley 1984a: 59), and I would argue that this process was the consequence of local conflicts of interpretation and power struggles, played out through unique improvisations on the basis of available cultural materials. One common theme, however, lies in a series of elaborations upon the theme of restriction of space, restriction of knowledge, and greater division within culture and society.

Thus we can recognise a series of parallel developments in monumental architecture were not simply increases in scale, in line with political centralisation; they were designed to physically restrict access to knowledge and its performance (Thomas 1990). In several areas there is increased emphasis upon the forecourt area of megalithic tombs, placing congregations of the living in relation to the remains of the dead. The chamber area itself might become more remote, enclosed, and separate. The greater control over bodily movement through a variety of forms of monument indicates a greater degree of restriction in the way that they might be experienced, and thereby the way in which their significance was understood. These requirements resulted in very distinctive monumental forms, but most often they represent the outcome of either physical addition to or design elaboration upon a more simple prototype. In the case of causewayed enclosures, the increased complexity, enhanced monumentality, changes of function and individuality of form which became more marked through the earlier third millennium are more unequivocally linked with local power struggles, to judge by the evidence of armed conflict at Hambledon Hill and Crickley Hill (Mercer 1980; Dixon 1988). A very similar process can be recognised with the emergence of cursus monuments in the early third millennium bc. The cursus takes aspects of the long barrow tradition and long mortuary enclosures, by now familiar monumental forms, and re-presents them. As Richard Bradley (1983) has demonstrated, cursus monuments may refer back to these earlier structures in a number of ways – elaborating upon their shape, mimicking their outward appearance, aligning upon them, or incorporating them into their fabric. It is as if the long mound tradition had become a metaphor which was being manipulated in various ways in order to produce something which actually broke with the past: a long enclosure which lays down a spatially restricted path across or between significant locations in the landscape.

Changes in ceramic design can be considered in similar terms. The plain ware assemblages of late fourth millennium Britain support general comparison if not specific parallels with contemporary continental material (Herne 1988: 25). The decorated styles which emerged after 3000 bc (3800 BC) do not. While these can be divided into distinctive regional traditions (Whitehawk, Mildenhall, Windmill Hill, etc.), these tend to overlap and merge somewhat, and diagnostic features may not be present throughout whole assemblages. By contrast, the range of decorative traits present in assemblages from different features within given sites may vary markedly. What I take this to mean is that while the established style zones demonstrate regional preferences in decoration, this variation is *isochrestic* rather than *iconic*, a by-product of other classification procedures rather than an assertion of ethnic identity (Wiessner 1983; Sackett 1986). Instead, pottery decoration is active at a smaller spatial scale, used to draw attention to the different character of various practices, locations, and classes of person. In this respect, I suggest that the significance of pottery decoration in Neolithic Britain contrasts with that amongst the earlier, post-Bandkeramik groups on the continent: it referenced more localised and even personalised concerns.

In the course of the third millennium bc, this same emphasis on the contextual significance of ceramic variability can be recognised in the emergence of parallel material traditions with distinctive associations and depositional locations. Generally speaking, the geographical distributions of these styles overlap one another. Thus one has Unstan and Grooved Ware in Orkney; Peterborough and Grooved Ware in southern Britain (Thorpe & Richards 1984); Carrowkeel, Sandhills and the various other decorated bowl styles in northern and eastern Ireland (Herity 1982); and the parallel case of Kerogou, Conguel, and Seine/Oise/Marne-related wares in Brittany (L'Helgouach 1965). In each case, we might choose to interpret the separate assemblages in terms of either distinct social practices or the existence of sub-groups within a society. What might be wrong would be to see them as functional equivalents in each area, rather than as local solutions to specific requirements and social tensions. It seems likely that in each of these areas the proliferation of material forms can be connected with the

[53]

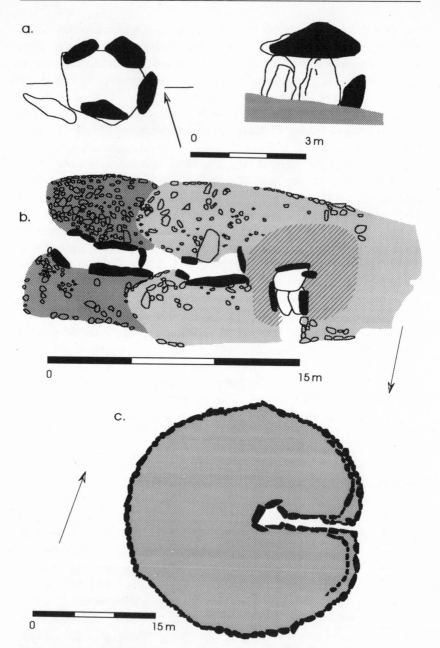

Figure 2. The development of chambered tombs in Anglesey, northern Wales. a. Simple passage tomb, Bodowyr (after Lynch); b. Simple passage tomb incorporated into a two-phase long cairn, Trefignath (after Smith); c. Complex passage tomb, Bryn Celli Ddu (after Hemp).

emergence of multiple forms or resources of social authority. Elsewhere (Thomas 1996), I suggest that in the case of mainland Britain, authority may have become contextually specific, that a series of spatially and temporally segregated arenas allowed particular persons to act in particular ways. These arenas of practice (henge monuments, funerals, feasts, acts of deliberate deposition in pits, rivers, bogs, and caves) were both marked by and constituted through specific combinations of artefacts and materials.

However, while all of these local cultural processes worked to create greater and greater regional distinctiveness, a contradictory pattern can also be discerned. The novel and distinctive character of some of the local products of cultural *bricolage* had the effect of making them suitable subjects for emulation or referencing in distant regions. Thus particular structures or artefacts may be the outcome of recognised sequences of development in one area, before appearing abruptly in another (Bradley 1984b: 12). Presumably, it was the exotic or locally specific character of these things which marked them out as desirable exchange goods or as tokens of contact with far-away places. It is for this reason that one can distinguish an early phase in the development of Grooved Ware in Orkney (MacSween 1992: 267), prior to its more widespread use in 'special' contexts in other parts of the British Isles. Another good example would be the megalithic architecture of northern Wales (Fig. 2). Here simple passage tombs occur, and were in some cases modified and enlarged through structural additions (e.g. Trefignath: Smith & Lynch 1987). Later, larger and more complex passage tombs like Bryn Celli Ddu, Barclodiad y Gawres, and perhaps the Gop cairn were constructed. These are evidently related to the passage tombs of eastern Ireland, where a sequence of structural elaboration over time has recently been outlined by Alison Sheridan (1986). In Sheridan's terms, these are all rather developed types of tomb, indicating something of a rupture with the local architectural sequence. In an area where cultural meanings were clearly volatile, and social conflicts played out through the construction, destruction, alteration, and replacement of monuments, this importation of an exotic form and its equally exotic connotations was a further way in which sectional interests might be advanced: material evidence of long-distance contact.

The regions of Neolithic Britain were thus definable but interlinked contexts of interaction, in which individual and group identities were negotiated on the basis of sectional readings of past events and surviving cultural products. Within these regions, particular stocks of

[55]

cultural knowledge were available, yet individual social actors would have been differentially placed in relation to these. The way in which material culture was directly engaged in the production of personal and group identities, rather than merely reflecting more metaphysical processes, should perhaps encourage us to believe that we can address questions of identity and regionality using archaeological evidence. For both personal and group identities are historical phenomena: they are constructed in a material world rather than being in any sense pre-given. Understanding these processes depends upon understanding the cultural heritage that people had at their disposal to drawn upon and to re-present. In the case of Neolithic Britain, this was a heritage which had emerged from a very specific set of historical circumstances.

REFERENCES

Ammerman, A. J. and Cavalli-Sforza, L. L. 1971. Measuring the rate of spread of early farming in Europe. *Man* 6: 674–688.

Barrett, J. C., Bradley, R. J. and Green, M. 1991. *Landscape, Monuments and Society: The Prehistory of Cranborne Chase*. Cambridge: Cambridge University Press.

Barth, F. 1987. *Cosmologies in the Making: A Generative Approach to Cultural Variation in Inner New Guinea*. Cambridge: Cambridge University Press.

Bender, B. 1985. Prehistoric developments in the American midcontinent and in Brittany, northwest France. In Price, T. D. and Brown, J. A. (eds), *Prehistoric Hunter-Gatherers: The Emergence of Complexity*, pp. 21–58. San Diego: Academic Press.

Binford, L. R. 1965. Archaeological systematics and the study of culture process. *American Antiquity* 31: 203–210.

Binford, L. R. 1972. Culture history versus cultural process: a debate in American archaeology. In Leone, M. P. (ed.), *Contemporary Archaeology*, pp. 102–107. Carbondale: Southern Illinois University Press.

Binford, L. R. 1973. Interassemblage variability – the Mousterian and the 'functional' argument. In Renfrew, C. (ed.), *The Explanation of Culture Change*, pp. 227–254. London: Duckworth.

Binford, L. R. 1989. The 'New Archaeology', then and now. In Lamberg-Karlovsky, C. C. (ed.), *Archaeological Thought in America*, pp. 50–62. Cambridge: Cambridge University Press.

Bogucki, P. 1987. The establishment of agrarian communities on the North European Plain. *Current Anthropology* 28: 1–24.

Boujot, C. and Cassen, S. 1992. Le development des premieres architectures funeraires monumentales en France occidentale. In Le Roux, C. T. (ed.), *Paysans et Bâtisseurs: L'Emergence du Néolithique Atlantique et les Origines du Mégalithisme*, pp. 195–211. Vannes: (Revue Archéologique de l'Ouest, supplément 5).

Bourdieu, P. 1977. *Outline of a Theory of Practice*. Cambridge: Cambridge University Press.

Bradley, R. J. 1983. The bank barrows and related monuments of Dorset in the light of recent fieldwork. *Proceedings of the Dorset Natural History and Archaeological Society* 105: 15–20.

Bradley, R. J. 1984a. *The Social Foundations of Prehistoric Britain*. London: Longman.

Bradley, R. J. 1984b. Regional systems in Neolithic Britain. In Bradley, R. J. and Gardiner, J. (eds), *Neolithic Studies: A Review of Some Current Research*, pp. 5–14. Oxford: British Archaeological Reports.

Burkill, M. 1983. The middle Neolithic of the Paris basin and north-east France. In Scarre, C. (ed.), *Ancient France*, pp. 34–61. Edinburgh: Edinburgh University Press.

Childe, V. G. 1925. *The Dawn of European Civilisation*. London: Routledge and Kegan Paul.

Childe, V. G. 1940. *Prehistoric Communities of the British Isles*. London: Chambers.

Childe, V. G. 1942. *What Happened in History*. Harmondsworth: Penguin.

Clarke, D. L. 1970. *Beaker Pottery of Great Britain and Ireland*. Cambridge: Cambridge University Press.

Clarke, D. L. 1978. *Analytical Archaeology* (second edition). London: Methuen.

Clifford, J. 1988. *The Predicament of Culture: Twentieth-Century Ethnography, Literature, and Art*. Cambridge, Massachusetts: Harvard University Press.

Connerton, P. 1989. *How Societies Remember*. Cambridge: Cambridge University Press.

Coudart, A. 1991. Social structure and relationships in prehistoric small-scale societies: the Bandkeramik groups in Neolithic Europe. In Gregg, S. A. (ed.), *Between Bands and States*, pp. 395–420. Carbondale: Southern Illinois University Press.

Cyrek, K., Grygel, R. and Nowak, K. 1986. The basis for distinguishing the ceramic Neolithic in the Polish lowlands. In Malinowski, T. (ed.), *Problems of the Stone Age in Pomerania*, pp. 95–126. Warsaw: Warsaw University Press.

Dixon, P. 1988. The Neolithic settlements on Crickley Hill. In Burgess, C., Topping, P., Mordant, C. and Maddison, M. (eds), *Enclosures and Defenses in the Neolithic of Western Europe*, pp. 75–88. Oxford: British Archaeological Reports (International Series 403).

Dreyfus, H. L. 1991. *Being-in-the-World: A Commentary on Heidegger's Being and Time, Division 1*. Cambridge, Massachusetts: Massachusetts Institute of Technology Press.

Duncan, S. S. 1989. What is a locality? In Peet, R. and Thrift, N. (eds), *New Models in Geography: The Political-Economy Perspective*, vol. 2, pp. 221–252. London: Unwin Hyman.

Edmonds, M. 1992. 'Their use is wholly unknown'. In Sharples, N. and Sheridan, A. (eds), *Vessels for the Ancestors: Essays on the Neolithic of Britain and Ireland*, pp. 179–193. Edinburgh: Edinburgh University Press.

Fischer, A. 1982. Trade in Danubian shafthole axes and introduction of Neolithic economy in Denmark. *Journal of Danish Archaeology* 1: 7–12.

Gebauer, A. B. and Price, T. .D. 1990. The end of the Mesolithic in eastern Denmark: a preliminary report on the Saltbaek Vig project. In Vermeersch, P. M. and van Peer, P. (eds), *Contributions to the Mesolithic in Europe*, pp. 259–280. Leuven: Leuven University Press.

Geertz, C. 1983. *Local Knowledge*. New York: Basic Books.

Gregg, S. A. 1991. Indirect food production: mutualism and the archaeological visibility of cultivation. In Gregg, S. A. (ed.), *Between Bands and States*, pp. 203–215. Carbondale: Southern Illinois University Press.

Gronenborn, D. 1990. Mesolithic-Neolithic interactions – the lithic industry of the earliest Bandkeramik site at Friedberg-Bruchenbrüken, Wetteraukreis (West Germany). In Vermeersch, P. M. and van Peer, P. (eds), *Contributions to the Mesolithic in Europe*, pp. 173–182. Leuven: Leuven University Press.

de Grooth, M. E. Th. 1991. Socio-economic aspects of Neolithic flint mining: a preliminary study. *Helinium* 31: 153–189.

Herity, M. 1982. Irish decorated Neolithic pottery. *Proceedings of the Royal Irish Academy* 82c: 247–404.

Herne, A. 1988. A time and a place for the Grimston bowl. In Barrett, J. C. and Kinnes, I. A. (eds), *The Archaeology of Context in the Neolithic and Bronze Age: Recent Trends*, pp. 2–29. Sheffield: Department of Archaeology and Prehistory.

Hodder, I. R. 1984. Burials, houses, women and men in the European Neolithic. In Miller, D. and Tilley, C. (eds), *Ideology, Power and Prehistory*, pp. 51–68. Cambridge: Cambridge University Press.

Kinnes, I. A. 1984. Microliths and megaliths: monumental origins on the Atlantic fringe. In Burrenhult, G. (ed.), *The Archaeology of Carrowmore*, pp. 367–370. Stockholm.

Kinnes, I. A. 1985. Circumstance not context: the Neolithic of Scotland as seen from outside. *Proceedings of the Society of Antiquaries of Scotland* 115: 115–157.

Kinnes, I. A. 1992. *Non-Megalithic Long Barrows and Allied Structures in the British Neolithic*. London: British Museum.

Kirk, T. 1991. Structure, agency and power relations *chez les derniers chasseurs-cueilleurs* of northwest France. In Preucel, R. W. (ed.), *Processual and Post-processual Archaeologies*, pp. 108–125. Carbondale: Southern Illinois University Press.

Larsson, L. 1990. The Mesolithic of southern Scandinavia. *Journal of World Prehistory* 4: 257–309.

L'Helgouach, J. 1965. *Les Sépultures Mégalithiques en Armorique (Dolmens à Couloir et Allées Couvertes)*. Rennes: Laboratoire d'Anthropologie Préhistorique.

Lindstrom, L. 1990. *Knowledge and Power in a South Pacific Society*. Washington: Smithsonian Institution Press.

Louwe-Kooijmans, L. P. 1976. Local developments within a borderland. *Oudheidkundige Mededelingen* 57: 226–297.

Louwe-Kooijmans, L. P. 1980. De midden-neolitische vondelsgroep van Het Vormer bij Wijchen en het cultuurpatroon rond de Zuidelijke Noordzee circa 3000 v. Chr. *Oudheidkundige Mededelingen* 61: 116–208.

Louwe-Kooijmans, L. P. 1987. Neolithic settlement and subsistence in the wetlands of the Rhine/Meuse delta of the Netherlands. In Coles, J. and Lawson, A. (eds), *European Wetlands in Prehistory*, pp. 227–251. Oxford: Clarendon.

Lynch, F. 1976. Towards a chronology of megalithic tombs in Wales. In Boon, G. C. and Lewis, J. M. (eds), *Welsh Antiquity*, pp. 63–79. Cardiff: National Museum of Wales.

MacSween, A. 1992. Orcadian Grooved Ware. In Sharples, N. and Sheridan, A. (eds), *Vessels for the Ancestors: Essays on the Neolithic of Britain and Ireland*, pp. 259–271. Edinburgh: Edinburgh University Press.

Marcus, G. E. and Fisher, M. J. 1986. *Anthropology as Cultural Critique: An Experimental Moment in the Human Sciences.* Chicago: Chicago University Press.

Mercer, R. 1980. *Hambledon Hill: A Neolithic Landscape.* Edinburgh: Edinburgh University Press.

Midgeley, M. 1985. *The Origin and Function of the Earthen Long Barrows of Northern Europe.* Oxford: British Archaeological Reports (British Ser. 259).

Midgeley, M. 1992. *T.R.B. Culture: The First Farmers of the North European Plain.* Edinburgh: Edinburgh University Press.

Phillips, P. 1982. *The Middle Neolithic in Southern France.* Oxford: British Archaeological Reports (British Series 142).

Piggott, S. 1954. *The Neolithic Cultures of the British Isles.* Cambridge: Cambridge University Press.

Powell, T. G. E. 1969. The Neolithic in the west of Europe and megalithic sepulture: some points and problems. In Powell, T. G. E., Corcoran, J. W. X. P., Lynch, F. and Scott, J. G. (eds), *Megalithic Enquiries in the West of Britain,* pp. 247–72. Liverpool: Liverpool University Press.

Renfrew, C. 1973a. Monuments, mobilisation and social organisation in Neolithic Wessex. In Renfrew, C. (ed.), *The Explanation of Culture Change,* pp. 539–558. London: Duckworth.

Renfrew, C. 1973b. *Before Civilisation: The Radiocarbon Revolution and Prehistoric Europe.* London: Jonathan Cape.

Renfrew, C. 1976. Megaliths, territories and populations. In De Laet, S. J. (ed.), *Acculturation and Continuity in Atlantic Europe,* pp. 198–220. Bruges: De Tempel.

Renfrew, C. 1979. *Investigations in Orkney.* London: Society of Antiquaries.

Richards, C. 1992. Doorways into another world: the Orkney-Cromarty chambered tombs. In Sharples, N. and Sheridan, A. (eds), *Vessels for the Ancestors: Essays on the Neolithic of Britain and Ireland,* pp. 62–76. Edinburgh: Edinburgh University Press.

de Roever, J. P. 1979. The pottery from Swifterbant – Dutch Ertebølle? *Helenium* 19: 13–36.

Rosaldo, R. 1989. *Culture and Truth: The Remaking of Social Analysis.* Boston: Beacon Press.

Roussot-Larroque, J. and Burnez, C. 1992. Aux sources du Neolithique Atlantique: le Cardial, le 'Danubien', et les autres . . . In Le Roux, C. T. (ed.), *Paysans et Bâtisseurs: L'Emergence du Néolithique Atlantique et les Origines du Mégalithisme,* pp. 127–38. Vannes: Revue Archéologique de l'Ouest, supplément 5.

Rowley-Conwy, P. 1981. Mesolithic Danish bacon: permanent and temporary sites in the Danish Mesolithic. In Sheridan, A. and Bailey, G. (eds), *Economic Archaeology,* pp. 51–55. Oxford: British Archaeological Reports (British Series 96).

Sackett, J. R. 1986. Isochrestism and style: a clarification. *Journal of Anthropological Archaeology* 5: 266–277.

Sakellaridis, M. 1979. *The Mesolithic and Neolithic of the Swiss Area.* Oxford: British Archaeological Reports.

Scarre, C. 1992. The early Neolithic of western France and megalithic origins in Atlantic Europe. *Oxford Journal of Archaeology* 11: 121–154.

Sheridan, A. 1986. Megaliths and megalomania: an account, and interpretation, of the development of passage graves in Ireland. *Journal of Irish Archaeology* 3: 17–30.

Sherratt, A. G. 1990. The genesis of megaliths: monumentality, ethnicity and social complexity in Neolithic north-west Europe. *World Archaeology* 22: 147–168.

Smith, C. A. and Lynch, F. 1987. *Trefignath and Din Dryfol*. Cardiff: Cambrian Archaeological Association.

Starling, N. 1985. Colonisation and succession: the earlier Neolithic of central Europe. *Proceedings of the Prehistoric Society* 51: 41–58.

Strathern, M. 1991. *Partial Connections*. Savage: Rowman and Littlefield.

Thomas, J. S. 1988. Neolithic explanations revisited: the Mesolithic-Neolithic transition in Britain and south Scandinavia. *Proceedings of the Prehistoric Society* 54: 59–66.

Thomas, J. S. 1990. Monuments from the inside: the case of the Irish megalithic tombs. *World Archaeology* 22: 168–178.

Thomas, J. S. 1991. *Rethinking the Neolithic*. Cambridge: Cambridge University Press.

Thomas, J. S. 1993a. Discourse, totalisation and 'the Neolithic'. In Tilley, C. (ed.), *Interpretative Archaeology*, pp. 357–394. London: Berg.

Thomas, J. S. 1993b. The politics of vision and the archaeologies of landscape. In Bender, B. (ed.), *Landscape: Politics and Perspectives*, pp. 19–48. London: Berg.

Thomas, J. S. 1996. *Time, Culture and Identity*. London: Routledge.

Thorpe, I. J. and Richards, C. C. 1984. The decline of ritual authority and the introduction of Beakers into Britain. In Bradley, R. J. and Gardiner, J. (eds), *Neolithic Studies: A Review of Some Current Research*, pp. 67–84. Oxford: British Archaeological Reports (British Series 133).

Thrift, N. 1991. For a new regional geography 2. *Progress in Human Geography* 15: 456–465.

Tilley, C. 1994. *A Phenomenology of Landscape*. London: Berg.

Wansleben, M and Verhart, L. B. M. 1990. Meuse valley project: the transition from the Mesolithic to the Neolithic in the Dutch Meuse valley. In Vermeersch, P. M. and van Peer, P. (eds), *Contributions to the Mesolithic in Europe*, pp. 389–342. Leuven: Leuven University Press.

Wiessner, P. 1983. Style and social information in Kalahari San projectile points. *American Antiquity* 48, 253–76.

Woodman, P. C. and O'Brien, M. 1993. Excavations at Ferriter's Cove, Co. Kerry: an interim statement. In Shee Twohig, E. and Ronayne, M. (eds), *Past Perceptions: The Prehistoric Archaeology of South-West Ireland*, pp. 25–34. Cork: Cork University Press.

Zvelebil, M. 1989. On the transition to farming in Europe, or what was spreading with the Neolithic: a reply to Ammerman. *Antiquity* 63: 379–383.

Zvelebil, M. and Rowley-Conwy, P. 1984. Transition to farming in northern Europe: a gatherer-hunter perspective. *Norwegian Archaeological Review* 17: 104–27.

3

Deconstructing 'the Neolithic' in the Mesolithic-Neolithic Transition

Mark Pluciennik

The division of history into periods is not a fact, but a necessary hypothesis or tool of thought, valid in so far as it is illuminating, and dependent for its validity on interpretation.

– Carr (1987 [1961]: 60)

Words and concepts are historic entities. What I want to look at in this paper are the bundles of associations of some archaeological terms, to consider their history, and to discuss some of the implications. This draws on work relating specifically to the Mesolithic – Neolithic transition, and reviews how societies pertaining to both have been perceived or defined in relation to, or in opposition to, each other.

Archaeologists dealing with the transition have often accepted an oversimplified division between hunting and gathering and agricultural societies. There has been a failure to consider the enormous potential variability, in terms of subsistence, economy, social organisation and settlement pattern *within* farming societies. One reason for this has been the conceptual and academic division between approaches to hunter-gatherers and to farmers, with an over-emphasis on environmental adaptation and optimal foraging approaches within studies of the former groups. In this way the divide between the prehistoric periods of Mesolithic and Neolithic has been maintained, following the tradition of Childe's early emphasis on food-production, and a revolutionary relationship with the environment, as the defining trait of the Neolithic. Those dealing with the transition, from both sides of the divide, have found it easier to classify the other as a mono-lithic entity. In recent years there has been an increased emphasis on the analytical difficulties of separating the 'social' from the 'cultural' or the 'economic'. While this should have highlighted problems of attempting to classify societies on any of these grounds, in relation to the transition we are still prone to lumping, rather than splitting. I argue that potential variability is much greater within both Mesolithic and Neolithic societies than current ethnography and archaeology suggest. Bearing this in mind, a conscious effort to work within an historical, or historical anthropological, paradigm may be a more pro-ductive approach.

THE HISTORICAL BACKGROUND

The terms Palaeolithic, Mesolithic and Neolithic were all first coined in the second half of the nineteenth century. From the beginning, the terms encompassed both a technological and chronological component but were also partly distinguished by other, often faunal, associations. In France in 1872, Gabriel De Mortillet, used site types to subdivide the 'Old Stone Age', but also dealt with the Neolithic. His Robenhausian, named after the Swiss type site, was characterised by polished stone axes, barbed and tanged arrowheads, dolmens and menhirs, pottery, domestic animals and agriculture: this appears to be the first sugges-tion of a Neolithic package in Europe. In the English-speaking world, the association of archaeological traits as a Neolithic package was first made apparently by Grafton Elliot Smith around 1915.[1]

By 1921 Miles Burkitt (who was to become Graham Clark's teacher) wrote that the Neolithic culture consisted of: 'Agriculture. The domest-ication of animals. The manufacture of pottery. The polishing of stone implements . . .' (Burkitt 1921: 157). This position can be compared with that of Gordon Childe, probably the most influential archaeolog-ist writing in English about the Neolithic in the middle years of this century. For him, *The Dawn of European Civilisation* (1925) *was* the Neo-lithic. In *Social Evolution* (1963: 32–33), he wrote that:

> in 1925, adopting an idea advanced by Elliot Smith ten years earlier, from the three current criteria (polishing of stone, or modern fauna, or domestic animals and cultivated plants), I selected 'food-production' as distinguishing the Neolithic from the earlier Palaeolithic and Mesolithic.

What did this do to concepts of the earlier stages? The apparently marked differences in material culture between the Palaeolithic and Mesolithic on the one hand, and the Neolithic on the other, seemed to support a revolutionary view of the Neolithic. This was perhaps especially true for Childe, for whom the Mesolithic was a retrograde period in relation to the upper Palaeolithic too. As he put it: 'By contrast to what had passed away, the Mesolithic societies leave an impression of extreme poverty,' (1964: 50–51).

By the 1960s, the terms Mesolithic (or Epipalaeolithic), and Neolithic, stood as shorthand for a whole series of subsistence, technological and social correlates. Archaeological models for Mesolithic societies utilised a partial, ethnographically derived stereotype of hunter-gatherers, drawn mostly from tropical or extreme environments such as the Kalahari or the Arctic: they were mobile and egalitarian, while farmers were more sedentary, with at least potential social differentiation. Hunter-gatherers were in some sense 'primitive', poor and had a correspondingly scanty material culture. Hunter-gatherer sites were ephemeral or opportunistic, as in the use of caves; but farmers were capable of building houses and hamlets, and producing tells and villages. Hunter-gatherers were linked with nature and the wild, farmers with culture. The former were at the mercy of the environment, the latter in charge of it.

More generally these 'primitive' societies, were considered ahistoric and uncultured. Claude Lévi-Strauss (1976) had influenced many people with his idea of 'hot' and 'cold' societies: those with history, and therefore dynamic; and those without. Further, Lévi-Strauss (among others) continued to equate distance in space with remoteness in time. Travelling in Brazil among hunter-gatherers, he felt he was 'sharing the existence of communities whose poverty was the price . . . for my being able to go back thousands of years in time' (1989 [1955]: 493). Explicitly, Lévi-Strauss ' (1972 [1962]: 256) claimed that history and ethnography were complementary, in the sense that:

> one of them unfurls the range of human societies in time, the other in space . . . the historian strives to reconstruct the picture of vanished societies as they were at the point which for them corresponded to the present, while the ethnographer does his best to reconstruct the historical stages which temporally preceded their existing form.

Such views as these helped to promote and maintain the border between hunter-gatherers and farmers, the Mesolithic and the Neolithic, the passive and the active. They were grounded in imperialist and social evolutionary politics (Fabian 1983; Kuper 1988; Bowler 1992; Gamble 1992; Jones 1992; Murray 1992), and were also associated with modernist ideals. Zygmunt Bauman (1992: note 6, p. xxvi) points out that:

> The modern perspective 'denied coevality' to any form of life different from its own; it construed the Other as 'living in another time'. [It] ... seems to be a variant of a more general expedient: construing the Other (defining the Other) in a way that a priori decides its inferior . . . transient and . . . illegitimate status. In an age of the forward march of reason-guided progress, describing the Other as outdated, backward, obsolete, primitive, and altogether 'pre-', was equivalent to such a decision.

The pervasiveness of such views can be seen, paradoxically, even in the work of archaeologists who had done much to stimulate interest in the Mesolithic. As late as 1980, Grahame Clark described the Mesolithic as an 'essential *prelude* to fundamental advances in the development of culture' (Clark 1980: 7; my emphasis). He ascribed importance to the Mesolithic not necessarily in its own right, but in the light of what came after: 'it is now perceived to be of crucial significance for understanding the course of prehistory, and not least for explaining the rise and spread of the Neolithic societies that laid the foundations of the diverse civilisations of mankind' (ibid.: 5).

As members of farming societies ourselves, there has perhaps been an (over) emphasis on the absolute and essential difference of hunter-gatherers, and on their distance from us economically, practically, conceptually and socially – and by implication temporally. In a subtle restatement of *ex oriente lux* views, the Neolithic was seen as important – a revolutionary step – because it led to us. The roots of European culture were traced back to the 'great civilisations' of the east (based on farming) or the (farming) societies of Greece or Rome. Indeed, the only comparable politically coloured perception of rupture or revolution coinciding with the boundary between archaeological periods in Europe may be that between the Iron Age and Roman. In this case the connotations are of incompatible oppositions between barbarians and civilised societies, chiefs and emperors, and warriors and proto-capitalists (Cumberpatch pers. comm.). Connections with, or origins in the hunter-gatherer societies of Eurasia have not been so much denied as ignored, at least by Europeans. Few claim hunter-gatherers as their ancestors (Zvelebil 1992). The 1960s also saw reactions against such normative views of hunter-gatherers and the division between the Mesolithic and Neolithic. In a famous paper delivered in 1966 Marshall Sahlins (1968: 85) pointed out that: 'Archaeologists and ethnologists had become Neolithic revolutionaries, and in their enthusiasm for the revolution found serious shortcomings in the Old (Stone Age) Regime. Scholars extolled a Neolithic Great Leap Forward.'

Sahlins' comments symbolise part of, or the start of, a major shift in attitudes towards hunter-gatherers. But in the same volume others were 'pre-defining' hunter-gatherers as necessarily 'primitive'; for example Murdock (1968), specifically excluded sedentary and socially complex groups, often associated with rich aquatic resources, from the discussion (p. 15): 'The Indians of the North Pacific coast, for example, seem to me to fall well beyond the range of cultural variation of any known hunting and gathering people.'

However there were also empirical reasons that supported an upgrading of prehistoric hunter-gatherers both socially, materially and historically. There were new finds, particularly in northern Europe, of Mesolithic cemeteries, and evidence of apparent social differentiation. Waterlogged sites with elaborate material culture preserved in organic media demonstrated the general bias of the archaeological record and the danger of judging societies to be materially 'poor' or necessarily 'simple' solely on that basis. Re-analysis of the evidence for site seasonality was used (e.g. Rowley-Conwy 1983) to suggest partial or total sedentism. There was the recognition of great actual or potential variability and complexity. In the 1980s there were many attempts, by both anthropologists and archaeologists, to define the concept of complex hunter-gatherers and to find the correlates of such complexity in the past (Testart 1982; Rowley-Conwy 1983; Price and Brown 1985, for example: see also Zvelebil 1986a: 7–8). The ethnographically recorded hunter-gatherers of the temperate zones (e.g. the Ainu and Kwakiutl), who had been excluded by classifications such as those of Murdock (see above), were seen as a more satisfying analogy for communities in Mesolithic Europe. This emphasis must itself be seen as both a reflection of and contribution to the changed political and intellectual climate of the time. This upgrading of Mesolithic hunter-gatherers led to difficulty in maintaining the boundary (archaeologically and academically) between the two concepts and periods. As Zvelebil (1986b: 168) put it:

> If the postglacial hunters of the temperate zone can really be characterised by logistic, rather than residential mobility, storage, intensive resource-use strategies, non-egalitarian social organisation and the use of pottery, polished stone and other technological innovations traditionally associated with the Neolithic, what is left of the difference between the Mesolithic and the Neolithic?

In Zvelebil's own terms the answer would seem to be clear: viz, economic reliance on domesticates and cultigens. The differences in the ways the periods were conceptualised were increasingly under attack at the same time. In 1984 Richard Bradley (1984: 11) had complained that: 'in the literature as a whole, successful farmers have social relations with one another, while hunter-gatherers have ecological relations with hazelnuts.' A year later Barbara Bender (1985: 21) attacked both Lévi-Strauss's notion of 'hot' and 'cold' societies, and its assumed congruence with the divide between the Neolithic and the Palaeolithic-Mesolithic. Three years later Julian Thomas (1988: 59) was to re-iterate the same point, adding that: 'the Mesolithic-Neolithic transition represents not merely a change of lifestyle, but also a point at which our perception of the past changes. It is the boundary between two models of man [sic].'

Mark Edmonds (pers. comm.) has suggested that the interpretation of 'exotic' materials also reflects this academic boundary, with their occurrence at hunter-gatherer sites being treated as a sign of mobility, but at farming sites as evidence for trade. There is undoubtedly a change in vocabulary in the literature, from 'interaction' to 'trade', but it is entangled in a more complex way with the language of the 'two models' noted above. There is plenty of evidence for the increasing long-distance movement of materials, over hundreds of kilometres in Europe, from the beginning of the Upper Palaeolithic (Gamble 1986a: 331–338). 'Interaction' is certainly seen as one possible mechanism of movement, but the distribution patterns suggest to Gamble that 'raw material residues can be used to monitor aspects of regional adaptation and the variable demographic arrangement of personnel in the environment' (ibid.: 336). In southern Britain, Care (1979; 1982) has suggested late Mesolithic exchange of lithic raw material and the continuation of these exchange networks in the Neolithic. Exchange is also evidenced between the Ertebølle of southern Scandinavia and the TRB communities to the south (Fischer 1982). What seems likely is that there was intra-community variation in mobility in both the Mesolithic and Neolithic periods, and that it is the investigation of this variation, and its links to groups and roles, which may help us understand other changes across the Mesolithic-Neolithic boundary.

Over the last three decades there has been a changed political atmosphere, seen in the attitudes towards hunter-gatherers and, more generally, the indigenous people of colonised lands. This has led to a revised status both for modern-day indigenes (i.e. those who cannot claim a white, western European descent), and for past societies, including hunter-gatherers (at least, by many in liberal political and intellectual circles). Such changes can be observed in the growing acceptance and power of native land rights movements, and in approaches to and political uses of archaeology and history (e.g. McDonald et al. 1991; Gathercole & Lowenthal 1989; Layton 1989a; 1989b). These changes can also be followed in the broader cultural sphere in America, for example. Films such as *Soldier Blue* (1970) and contemporaneous books such as *Bury My Heart at Wounded Knee* can be seen as part of this process of reappraisal, as expressions of colonial guilt, and attempts to rewrite history (cf. Olson 1979: 405–415). This process continues today as seen in mainstream films such as *Dances with Wolves* (1990), which present a sympathetic, albeit sentimental, view of Native Americans.

Thus I want to suggest that a combination of reasons, related to the political and intellectual climate, have influenced archaeological (and anthropological) attitudes towards the transition to farming in the last decade or so. One of the most notable products in archaeology has been Zvelebil's edited volume (1986), which, as a sign of the times, was intentionally titled 'Hunters in Transition'. It consciously adopted a 'hunter-gatherer position' from which to explore the process (and perhaps less successfully the 'meaning') of the transition. This reappraisal of hunter-gatherers in relation to the transition derived from different sources than the ecologically based approach of the Higgs School of palaeoeconomy at Cambridge. But by arguing for gradual change, rather than discontinuity, in human-animal relationships vis-à-vis domestication, palaeoeconomists and those preferring ecologically driven models of change (e.g. Gamble 1986b) also contributed to the rethinking of the boundary.

In contrast, I think it is fair to say that the 'context' of the term Neolithic has not undergone any such revolutionary revision, with the exception of a few recent works to be discussed below (Hodder 1990; Thomas 1991; Armit & Finlayson 1992). There has been a general acceptance that farmers can often be sufficiently characterised simply as farmers, thus reproducing the implicit *essential* difference between agriculturalists and hunter-gatherers (cf. Bender 1985: 21).

CURRENT MODELS

The availability model for the transition to farming suggested by Zvelebil and Rowley-Conwy (1984; 1986; Zvelebil 1986a; 1986b) has been both productive and provocative. They drew on work by Alexander (1977; 1978) and Dennell (1985) to treat the transition as a process occurring in space and time, rather than as an event – 'the arrival of the Neolithic' – which informed so many previous views. They conceived of the frontier between farming and hunting-gathering societies as a zone, which could be characterised in different ways at different times and places. It also placed the emphasis on the members of Mesolithic societies as active participants in the process of transition. They thus injected space, time and regional variability into the transition, compared with many earlier works which treated the Neolithic as an instantaneous phenomenon – which was thus either present or was not.

The model has been widely referred to, and if some of the quantitative definitions of the three phases (Zvelebil 1986a: fig. 3, p. 12) are not taken too rigidly, is broad enough to allow social relations or anthropological approaches to be explored within its framework (e.g. Zvelebil in press). However, there are two general problems which stem from the desire of the authors to provide a model of a wholly general nature, which, despite the injection of time into the transition, produces a peculiarly ahistorical framework. Firstly, despite Zvelebil's (1986b) contention that Mesolithic subsistence strategies can be seen as alternatives to Near Eastern domestication and farming, the transition is basically seen as a one-way process: societies are defined within it according to the stage they have reached towards a pre-defined end (i.e. farming). This presents particular difficulties in areas such as north-eastern Europe. Here, as Dennell (1992) recently pointed out, the so-called substitution phase sometimes lasts for two millennia. In this case it is stretching the model very thinly, and beyond its usefulness, to argue that those societies should be said to be in a process of transition to farming, rather than being considered in their own right.

A second problem derives from the fact that the model holds both the general process and the end result as constant, despite the huge spread in space and time which any talk of a transition to the Neolithic or farming in Europe involves. However, once reached, the Neolithic is treated as a static and unchanging phenomenon (cf. Thomas 1993: 369). Thus Zvelebil (1989: 382) has recently called for: '(a), a clear definition of what constitutes a Neolithic society; (b), agreement on how to identify it in the archaeological record; (c), clear and commonly agreed definition of traits which would allow us to evaluate the contributions of indigenous and the immigrant populations in its formation.'

At present, work on the transition to the Neolithic, in one classification, may be said to fall broadly into two groups, here characterised as the 'Neolithic as economy' and the 'Neolithic as ideology' views. The first, in the tradition described above, sees the Neolithic as synonymous and synchronous with the introduction of farming, although these may take into account, to varying degrees, regional differences which may affect the rate, nature and causes of agricultural adoption. Often implicit in this view is the assumption that there is some essential difference, beyond that of subsistence, between farming and non-farming societies – whatever the variability within either. This is at its most obvious in work by those such as Gebauer & Price, who prefer a global, processual view. Thus, for them (1992: 1):

> the transition to farming involves much more than simple herding and cultivation. It also entails major, long-term changes in the structure and organization of the societies that adopt this new way of life, as well as a totally new relationship with the environment. Such a dramatic shift in the trajectory of cultural evolution demands understanding.

In this group may be placed authors such as Bogucki (1988: 1), for whom: 'The expansion of food production as an economic strategy across Europe . . . marked the most radical transformation of prehistoric society . . . since the retreat of the last glaciation.' Similarly, for Whittle (1988: 99): 'The beginning of the Neolithic is defined by an economic shift of key importance.' For Zvelebil and Rowley-Conwy too, the beginning of the Neolithic is primarily an economic phenomenon. In their paper (1984), in which they introduced their availability – substitution – consolidation model, they stress that 'the key concept is competition between two mutually incompatible ways of life' (ibid.: 105). Although the authors argue that there had been a concentration by researchers on the 'biological and economic rather than social aspects of the transition' (ibid.: 105), their own suggestion is that it was economic stress which may have led to the initial adoption of agricultural resources. This view of environmental change producing territorial and/or subsistence stress within northern Europe is broadly followed by others such as Whittle (1985: 125), Barker (1985: 235), Larsson (1986), and Bogucki (1988).

Within this economic view of the Neolithic, a variety of causes, singly or in combination, has been proposed for its adoption (or expansion). Perhaps naturally enough, given the perception of the Neolithic as primarily economic, many have seen the impetus to change deriving from pressures on the indigenous (or source) economies, whether this be due to environmental factors or, for example, population pressure. Others have preferred to emphasise the social (e.g. Bender 1978; Jennbert 1985). Long lists of reasons which may be invoked for agricultural adoption and spread have been published (e.g. Zvelebil 1986b; Gebauer & Price 1992: 6). But for all these authors the economic shift is the source of the perceived difference between the Mesolithic and the Neolithic, and hence defines it.

The second group of views might in one way be defined as those who are more interested in the Neolithic as an 'ideology', a 'way of thinking' or 'lifestyle' (Thomas 1991). The Neolithic is seen as representing an (emic) conceptual difference. If the economic differences between the Mesolithic and Neolithic are not denied, then their importance is downplayed (on the surface, at least).

Hodder's may be considered the more radical approach, and will be considered first. Hodder (1990) approaches the spread of the Neolithic in an initially traditional way, *via* the origins of farming in the Near East. Rather than using the mainstream theories, however, he draws on the work of Jacques Cauvin (1972; 1978), who emphasised the social changes which can be seen to precede the recognition of farming in the Near East. 'Put simply it seemed possible to argue that the process of domestication – the control of the wild – is a metaphor and mechanism for the control of society' (Hodder 1990: 12). In this sense domestication may come conceptually before agriculture as it is generally understood. But this too is seen as part of a much longer process, related to closer control over environments by Palaeolithic populations. The actual point at which agriculture or 'the Neolithic' can be said to be present is unproblematic for Hodder (1990: 291): 'The same [Mesolithic] idea of controlling the wild was 'simply' extended to plants and animals . . . Plants and animals were separated from the wild, brought in and controlled within the cultural sphere, dominated in order to enhance social prestige by defining the cultural against the wild.'

It is implicit in this argument that there is no particular reason to tie these concepts to agriculture, of which the physical resources (cereals, domestic animals) are purely contingent, epiphenomenal expressions. Thus the Neolithic as a conceptual and structuring process can be pushed back into the Epipalaeolithic or Mesolithic. The Neolithic, or the process of domestication, is a lived metaphor, evident in, but also objectified by and transformed through, material and symbolic practices. Hodder makes it possible to disengage the concept of the Neolithic from the traditional archaeological signifiers. Instead, he particularly uses the idea of the *domus* and the *agrios*. The former refers to the concept of the home or household, including both practical activities and symbolic connotations. The latter is associated with the wild, the outside, and the unsocial. Hodder suggests ways in which these two spheres could be used as metaphors to structure and transform society.

Hodder's consideration of the transition in southern Scandinavia, for example, emphasises that it was, eventually, symbolic and conceptual compatibility that allowed the adoption of 'the Neolithic' by Ertebølle groups from the TRB societies to the south. While not rejecting other factors – environmental, technological and economic – which may have played their part in both the rejection and adoption of agriculture, Hodder points out that in central Europe the *domus* appears to be connected in part at least to agriculture. He then notes changes in central Europe around 3300 bc, including economic, settlement and social practices, and a new emphasis on burial ritual (ibid.: 182):

> This shift allowed or was associated with a changed social and economic system in which dispersed settlement, exchange, defence, and warring increasingly formed the basis of authority structures and in which the agrios could increasingly be used to play a central role. Soon after this transformation in central Europe, agriculture is adopted in southern Scandinavia. It is as if the inhabitants of Ertebølle sites were unable to adopt agriculture until transformations had taken place within central European society which made agriculture more compatible with Ertebølle principles.

Stimulating though this might be, Hodder's return to structuralism has not overcome all the problems associated with such an approach, most notably the 'loss of agency'. A close reading reveals a peculiar kind of 'evolutionary structuralism' in which an hypostasized structure (of the Neolithic) resides in the medium of people, rather than being produced by their agency. This 'Neolithic structure' bides its time on the North European Plain, maintaining its identity through instances of agricultural community practices, until it can join with a like-minded structure in the Ertebølle communities and begin to reproduce and spread once more. On the other hand Hodder has largely overcome the second major criticism of classical structuralism, its ahistoricity. By dealing with structure as metaphor, he manages to retain both plasticity and potential transformations in meaning, while retaining some sort of structural identity across time and space. The difficulty here is the balance between treating that identity as a meaningful and continuous entity ('the Neolithic'), while maintaining that particular instances are contingent and specific in their meanings.

This is a challenging view of the significance and meaning of the Neolithic. It is ambitious, in that it argues for both a long-term and long-distance view of the Neolithic – as an historical process – without sacrificing the specificity of particular case studies, which can be seen as historically particular transformations or appropriations of an underlying structure or metaphor. Nevertheless, it also presents problems both in its own terms, and for those who prefer to deal with the Neolithic as an over-ridingly economic phenomenon.

Firstly, if the Neolithic is treated as a metaphor of the social or cultural versus the wild, and for the relationship between smaller groups (such as the 'household') and the larger social entity, it is not clear why this metaphor should be limited to a particular time or place. It would seem possible to argue for the potential presence of this metaphor among virtually all prehistoric societies, even if its mode of expression may have varied. In other words, the metaphorical structure may be seen everywhere and at all times, and the 'Neolithic' reduced to a problem of style, or form of expression, rather than content, which raises questions about its validity or use as an archaeological concept. At times it is hard to see exactly how the underlying structure of Hodder's Neolithic is more than the old culture: nature dichotomy revisited – or re-clothed.

Perhaps more interestingly, Hodder's ideas raise again the problem of diffusion. Even if it was not (necessarily) physical objects (domesticates and cultigens) which were spreading, but (loosely speaking) concepts – structures, categories, ways of thinking, seeing, and ultimately doing, this does not do away with the problem of innovation, adoption and appropriation by people. Hodder's work demonstrates the tensions between (or the 'fault' inherent in) structuralist views of society and notions of agency. What exactly does Hodder's notion of 'conceptual compatibility' (between farming and hunting-gathering societies in northern Europe and southern Scandinavia) mean in practice? Ethnography and anthropology suggest that people re-categorise new resources and transform ideas. Assimilation, acceptance or rejection is an active matter of social context and attitude (cf. Torrence & van der Leeuw 1989), rather than depending upon some passive and abstract structural or conceptual compatibility.

Julian Thomas (1988; 1991) takes a slightly different approach. Although he recognises marked regional differences in the early Neolithic, throughout northern Europe (1988: 64):

> The expansion of the Neolithic at the end of the fourth millennium bc was a consequence both of a major change in the structuring of agricultural social relations and of the willingness of indigenous populations to adopt innovations . . . the speed with which the transition was achieved must be recognized as the product of abrupt changes in what was on offer to foraging populations.

Thomas is still a 'Neolithic revolutionary', to use Sahlins' term, though he would place the locus of this revolution in the sphere of ideology and social relations. He (1991: 12) specifically attacks those views which *always* define the Neolithic as farming: 'At one point in space and time it might indeed have been primarily an economic phenomenon, at another it might have constituted an ideology.'

This rightly questions the existence of an 'essential' Neolithic at all; indeed, whether it is possible (or desirable) to talk of the 'Neolithic', so defined, as an entity. Thomas argues that there was a rapid and synchronous spread of the Neolithic in northern Europe, which occurred because of the coherence of the new 'ideological package' available. 'Instead of the isolated elements of an alien lifestyle, a whole structure of ideas could now be transmitted which contained within it the blueprint of a particular set of social relationships' (1988: 64); and again: 'the Neolithic . . . is the wholesale transformation of social relations which results from adopting an integrated cultural system . . . It is the recognition of the symbolic potential of these elements to express a fundamental division of the universe into the wild and the tame which creates the Neolithic world '(1991: 13)

The reasons why an 'integrated cultural system' should be adopted, rather than parts of or transformations of other social, conceptual and material entities, are part of the problematic of diffusion. Note, too, the use of the term 'tame', in which the economic characterisation of the Neolithic reappears, and the culture: nature dichotomy is reintroduced.

There are several implications for this approach. The first is that it tends to play down the role of Mesolithic populations, who are characterised as willing but inevitable receptors of the complete package of the new 'Neolithic ideology'. For Thomas, the Neolithic is the beginning of history, which can be inscribed on the *tabula rasa* of the Mesolithic: the time of a new 'people without history'. Yet this is despite the fact that much of his discussion of the early Neolithic (1991: 14–25) might be argued to be evidence of continuity with the preceding Mesolithic, as well as change.

Secondly, by emphasising the coherence of the 'Neolithic lifestyle', the autonomy and distinctiveness of the Neolithic period is maintained. The corollary is that, for Thomas, it is emphatically *not* 'the adoption of the odd Neolithic trait or innovation into a Mesolithic lifestyle which represents the onset of the Neolithic' (1991: 13). The 'Neolithic package' lives on, even if the wrapping has changed, and this too can be seen as a closure, ensuring that 'future debate takes place within his own discourse, and that the words . . . maintain the meanings which he chooses to attribute to them' (Thomas 1993: 369). Thirdly, the ability of the Mesolithic communities to resist, transform or partially or selectively appropriate novel ideas or resources is denied: there is more than a hint of determinism about the proposed schema. While Thomas asserts variability in the Neolithic with one hand (see also Thomas 1993: 390), it is taken away with the other. Finally, at the same time as he has become more insistent that 'social relations' must be seen as a major part of any definition of the Neolithic, Thomas has become more reluctant to specify what those social relations might be (cf. Thomas 1987).

One recent publication which does address many of these problems is that by Ian Armit and Bill Finlayson (1992). Arguing against the general application of the model proposed by Zvelebil and Rowley-Conwy (1984), they begin by noting differences in the archaeological record for the transition between two areas, western Scotland and southern Scandinavia. In terms of environment and potential ecological productivity these two areas may be considered similar. Armit & Finlayson point out that in the western Scottish case patterns of mobility, resource exploitation and lithic technology, for example, may be seen as part of a continuum spanning the period from the Mesolithic until the first millenium BC (ibid.: 670). By contrast, in southern Scandinavia the difference between 'Mesolithic' and 'Neolithic' societies can be seen as more abrupt. Within Scotland there are marked contrasts which perhaps represent the differential appropriation of 'Neolithic'

elements within different Mesolithic regional traditions, and this variability may be seen elsewhere in Europe. They (ibid.: 674) conclude:

> To Mesolithic groups, the elements which comprise our
> archaeological picture of the Neolithic would have represented
> a set of potentials. Material symbols associated with agri-
> culture or derived from agricultural communities provided a
> range of new means of symbolic expression for Mesolithic
> groups. Pre-existing internal power negotiations within Meso-
> lithic populations could develop through the absorption and
> manipulation of such material symbols and could imbue them
> with new, socially relevant and culturally-specific meaning.

Armit and Finalyson's paper is important because it outlines an
historical and contextual approach to meanings of 'the Neolithic'. It is
limited neither to the economy, nor ideology, nor structure, while not
excluding the fact that elements of these may well be important for
particular interpretations of particular transitions. However, to concentrate solely on the potential for 'symbolic expression' of material
items is again to emphasise one aspect of practice over another; the
meanings of changes in the ways that the material world and practices
are recursively structured matters for interpretation.

DISCUSSION

In any model there is a danger of subsuming variability and simplify-
ing complexity. On a European scale it is important to note that the
inception of the so-called Neolithic extends over at least 3000 radiocarbon years. This figure can be more than doubled if parts of north-
eastern Europe are included. Geographically the spread from Franchthi
in Greece to northern Europe is more than 2000 miles. This huge span
in time and space should warn us that it is dangerous to define the
Neolithic in any way except on the most minimal grounds, especially
in terms of a unifying process. Equally, we need to explore our concepts
of both the Mesolithic *and* the Neolithic. It is not a question of what
was on offer for once and for all time, as though it were an unchanging
and unified package, of which equally similar hunter-gatherers could
accept whole or part, but could not avoid receiving in the end.

Attempts have already been made to 'deconstruct' the package
elsewhere in Europe by pointing out not only that the 'elements'
spread at different rates, but also that 'what was on offer' may have
varied over time and space (Lewthwaite 1981; 1986). I would agree

with Julian Thomas that there are many different Neolithics. These would also include many types of farming, even should one wish to adopt that as the definition of the Neolithic. Recognising this variability, Zvelebil (pers. comm.) has recently suggested that the whole of the Neolithic period can in some ways be considered as that of the transition to fully agro-pastoral communities.

There are a variety of themes that underlie considerations, whether general or specific, of transitions to the Neolithic. One of them is the old question of whether there are any necessary correlates between forms of subsistence, and other analytical categories, such as social structure (cf. Bender 1985: 23). Does it make sense to speak of 'Mesolithic' societies with agricultural resources, in the same way as Hodder has suggested that we can have 'Neolithic' concepts before agriculture? This is not a new problem. For example, since 1980 Ingold (1986: 218) has argued that the Kwakiutl on the north-western coast of America, though relying on wild resources, could be viewed as farmers, in terms of their ideology. The whole question of just what is different about hunter-gatherers compared to societies with other forms of subsistence has a long history within anthropology. In archaeology it has been discussed less, but rather accepted as self-evident. This has been due partly to seemingly easier access to subsistence data, rather than evidence for kinship systems or social ethics such as sharing, for example. It is notable that one anthropological classification which has been adopted and pursued by archaeologists is that relating to subsistence. This is the suggestion by Woodburn (1980; 1982) of classifying societies through the notion of delayed-return and immediate-return economies. This has fed into the ensuing debate about storage and hunter-gatherer complexity (e.g. Ingold 1982; 1983; Testart 1982; 1988).

This determination to emphasise differences between hunter-gatherers and agriculturalists may also be seen in the pervasive use, implicit or explicit, of the culture: nature dichotomy, which is still often used as a metonym for farmers: hunters – as though the latter had no culture to speak of until the Neolithic came along. Both the associations, implications and universal existence of this dichotomy have been questioned (MacCormack & Strathern 1980; Moreland 1990 for example) and its use in archaeological narratives needs to be carefully appraised.

Finally, there are more general problems, concerning the way in which we, and others, conceptualise societies, transitions and change. Madsen (1986), in considering the transition in southern Scandinavia, rightly emphasised the problem of temporal resolution in discussing transitions, which partly arises from our own periodisation of history or prehistory. Archaeologists often deal with the long term – which is seen as advantageous in some circumstances. But the record is generally discontinuous, as well as partial in other ways, leaving archaeologists to grapple with the problem of inference, or of producing a narrative describing the path from one state (of the archaeological record) to another. There is a tension between notions of process, and notions of history.

I suggest that, regarding the so-called Mesolithic – Neolithic transition, it is not enough simply to substitute the unqualified word 'farming', for example, for Neolithic, and 'hunter-gatherers' for Mesolithic. There are at least three particular areas within the transition which need to be critically examined. The first is the tendency, at least by those from the hunter-gatherer side of the fence, to treat farming itself as an unproblematic term for a way of life. Neolithic farming is still often typified by reference to sedentary agro-pastoralism. It clearly need not have been so.

Secondly, there is still the hegemony of subsistence as the defining feature of the Neolithic, although this may be only one aspect of change which, for historical and political reasons, we may have tended to overemphasise. Thus, for example, Marxist claims that the economy is determinant in the last instance have influenced many archaeologists and anthropologists, as has the Marxist emphasis on production and labour generally (see however, Baudrillard 1988a; 1988b). There have also been empirical and historical reasons for privileging subsistence and/or the economy in regard to the transition: for these were spheres of activity which left material traces in the archaeological record (e.g. faunal remains), and were therefore deemed to be (archaeologically) relatively accessible.

Thirdly, although with hindsight we may talk of societies 'in transition to farming', history could have been otherwise. To treat Mesolithic societies as 'pre-Neolithic' societies in a processual sense is a mistake (e.g. 1970s arguments about societies 'pre-adapted' to farming), just as it is to see the Neolithic as inevitably radical. I would emphasise again that from the Mesolithic point of view, there must have been many different perceptions of, and ways of encountering, what we call the Neolithic. Those perceptions *may* have been in terms of potential for productivity, as many have argued or assumed, but may also (or rather) have been in terms of new categories, or new resources – cultural, material, ideological or social (cf. Armit & Finlayson 1992).

Thus it is argued that even if we wish to see the transition as process, rather than history, it should perhaps be in terms of changing scales and intensities of social interaction, and the differential appropriation and manipulation of novel resources (conceptual or material). The elements of what has been termed 'the Neolithic' can be treated as offering additional potential for such manipulation within existing social (and other) strategies, as well as participating in the construction of new practices and identities. In Denmark, Fischer (1982: 11) points to Ertebølle imitations of TRB objects. In southern Scandinavia and elsewhere in northern and western Europe the presence of ceramics and rare domesticates in Mesolithic contexts is widespread (de Roever 1979; Hibbs 1983; Price 1981; Scarre 1983). In Britain Thomas suggests that the earlier Neolithic may have been characterised by mobility and wide dependence on wild foods, in which cattle were regarded as symbolic, rather than economic capital (1991: 22–28). It must be remembered, however, that it is the general archaeological visibility of 'the Neolithic' – i.e. ceramics, polished stone and morphologically recognisable domesticates and cultigens, which led to the characterisation of the Neolithic package and the period as a whole in the first place. Such (archaeological) symbols may sometimes represent different media, rather than changed practices. Equally, each of these categories of 'Neolithic' material have been shown to occur, singly or in conjunction, in contexts which would not otherwise be described as such.

It is a peculiarity of work dealing with the transition, that it takes place within, and is an expression of, the radical divide which is *inevitably* seen between hunter-gatherers and agriculturalists. It is often pointed out that generalisation is possible regarding the transition because, eventually, in Europe, virtually all people do subsist by farming. Therefore, it is argued, we *must* be able to characterise the transition in terms of a general process of 'transition to farming'. It is striking that few, if any, archaeologists would expect to treat the 'transition to metal-working', for example, in such a fashion, although all peoples in Europe do use metals. Clearly, what both these scenarios have in common is the spread of new resources, techniques and ideas. In both cases new material cultures have been taken to signify new people (as have, in other cases, new styles of pottery, for example). Similarly, the beginning of metal-working has been linked to changes in social relations, even if not necessarily in such a radical way as 'farming' has been.

I want to suggest that the 'Neolithic', far from (necessarily or invariably) being either a revolution or a package, may be 'just another' case of diffusion, but one which has been made special by our privileging of subsistence and economy as a classification within archaeology, and of 'the farming way of life' in general. The Mesolithic-Neolithic transition may be considered on the one hand as part of a wider problematic of change, diffusion and interaction. What will distinguish it as a subject of discourse will, paradoxically, derive from an insistence on the historicity and particularity of specific instances. The emphasis on an historical anthropological approach allows for the contextual reconceptualisation of what it may be that divides or links various instances of the Mesolithic-Neolithic transition, or of the Neolithic.

A broadening of the sort of approach suggested by Armit & Finlayson (1992) can comprehend both the variability and similarity which we may wish to see in 'the Neolithic' at various scales and at various times. Most importantly, it allows us to introduce notions of history into the Mesolithic, as well as the Neolithic, as a way of overcoming the conceptual and academic barriers of the 'two models' within the transition. Regional traditions of practice, and changes within them, cross-cut the Mesolithic-Neolithic boundary in many areas of Europe, particularly in the north and west. Nor need this sort of analysis and interpretation be confined to 'material symbols associated with agriculture'; patterns of movement of people and materials, and changes in practices preceding the arrival of 'the Neolithic' may help us imagine new ways of approaching 'Mesolithic' perceptions of 'the Neolithic' – and vice versa. What is more likely to stimulate archaeological imaginations in these ways is the sort of historical anthropology exemplified by Sahlins (1985) and N. Thomas (1991).

While the terms 'Mesolithic' and 'Neolithic' will continue to offer a useful shorthand *within* regions limited in time as well as space, the value of their content diminishes rapidly as the scale of application is expanded. We should attempt to treat the transition itself as an historically variable entity, and one in which perceptions of 'the Neolithic' were equally variable, partial, historically determined and different to each other – as are our own constructions of the phenomenon. In that case 'the Neolithic' and the transition should be recognised to refer to different phenomena at different times and in different places. Exploring these differences may be more productive than seeking generalisations in which 'the Neolithic' is forced to cover all cases for all time.

NOTE

1 I have been unable to trace this in Elliot Smith's published works of this period.

ACKNOWLEDGMENTS

I am grateful to Mark Edmonds, Paul Halstead, Louise Martin and Marek Zvelebil for their comments and criticisms of earlier drafts of this paper.

REFERENCES

Alexander, J. 1977. The frontier concept in prehistory: the end of the moving frontier. In Megaw, J. (ed.), *Hunters, Gatherers and First Farmers Beyond Europe*, pp. 25–40. Leicester: Leicester University Press.

Alexander, J. 1978. Frontier studies and the earliest farmers in Europe. In Green, D. & Spriggs, M. (eds), *Social Organisation and Settlement*, pp. 13–29. Oxford: British Archaeological Reports (Int. Ser. 47).

Armit, I. & Finlayson, W. 1992. Hunter-gatherers transformed: the transition to agriculture in northern and western Europe. *Antiquity* 66: 664–676

Barker, G. 1985. *Prehistoric Farming in Europe*. Cambridge: Cambridge University Press.

Baudrillard, J. 1988a. For a critique of the political economy of the sign. In Poster, M. (ed.), pp. 57–97.

Baudrillard, J. 1988b. The mirror of production. In Poster, M. (ed.), pp. 98–118.

Bauman, Z. 1992. *Intimations of Postmodernity*. London: Routledge.

Bender, B. 1978. Gatherer-hunter to farmer: a social perspective. *World Archaeology* 10 (2): 203–222.

Bender, B. 1985. Prehistoric developments in the American Midcontinent and in Brittany, northwest France. In Price, T. & Brown, J. (eds), pp. 21–57.

Bogucki, P. 1988. *Forest Farmers and Stockherders*. Cambridge: Cambridge University Press.

Bourdieu, P. 1977. *Outline of a Theory of Practice*. Cambridge: Cambridge University Press.

Bowler, P. 1992. From 'savage' to 'primitive': Victorian evolutionism and the interpretation of marginalized peoples. *Antiquity* 66: 721–729

Bradley, R. 1984. *The Social Foundations of Prehistoric Britain*. Harlow: Longman.

Brown, D. 1970. *Bury My Heart at Wounded Knee, An Indian History of the American West*. New York: Holt, Rinehart & Winston.

Burkitt, M. 1921. *Prehistory*. London: Cambridge University Press.

Care, V. 1979. The production and distribution of Mesolithic axes in southern England. *Proceedings of the Prehistoric Society* 45: 93–102.

Care, V. 1982. The collection and distribution of lithic materials during the Mesolithic and Neolithic in southern England. *Oxford Journal of Archaeology* 1: 269–285.

Carr, E. 1987. *What is History?* (Second edition). London: Penguin Books.

Cauvin, J. 1972. *Religions Néolithiques de Syro-Palestine*. Saint-Andrée-de-Cruzières. Quoted in Hodder (1989).

Cauvin, J. 1978. *Les premiers villages de Syrie-Palestine du IXème au VIIème millénaire*. Lyon. Quoted in Hodder (1989).

Childe, V. 1925. *The Dawn of European Civilisation*. London: Kegan Paul.

Childe, V. 1963. *Social Evolution*. Harmondsworth: Penguin Books.

Childe, V. 1964. *What Happened in History* (Revised edition). London: Penguin Books.

Clark, G. 1980. *Mesolithic Prelude*. Edinburgh: University Press.

Costner, K. (dir) 1990. *Dances with Wolves* (US).

Dennell, R. 1985. The hunter-gatherer/agricultural frontier in prehistoric temperate Europe. In Green, S. & Perlman, S. (eds), *The Archaeology of Frontiers and Boundaries*, pp. 113–140. New York: Academic Press.

Dennell, R. 1992. Paper given at the conference 'Transition to Farming in the Baltic', Poland.

Fabian, J. 1983. *Time and the Other: How Anthropology Makes its Object*. New York: Columbia University Press.

Fischer, A. 1982. Trade in Danubian shaft-hole axes and the introduction of Neolithic economy in Denmark. *Journal of Danish Archaeology* 1: 7–12

Gamble, C. 1986a. *The Palaeolithic Settlement of Europe*. Cambridge: Cambridge University Press.

Gamble, C. 1986b. The Mesolithic sandwich: ecological approaches and the archaeological record of the early postglacial. In Zvelebil, M. (ed.), pp. 33–42.

Gamble, C. 1992. Archaeology, history and the uttermost ends of the earth – Tasmania, Tierra del Fuego and the Cape. *Antiquity* 66: 712–720.

Gathercole, P. & Lowenthal, D. (eds) 1989. *The Politics of the Past*. London: Unwin Hyman.

Hibbs, J. 1983. The Neolithic of Brittany and Normandy. In Scarre, C. (ed.), *Ancient France. Neolithic Societies and their landscapes 6000 – 2000 bc*, pp. 271–323. Edinburgh: Edinburgh University Press.

Hodder, I. 1989. 'The domestication of society.' Paper given at the conference 'Critical Approaches in Archaeology: Material Life, Meaning, and Power', Portugal.

Hodder, I. 1990. *The Domestication of Europe*. Oxford: Blackwell.

Ingold, T. 1982. Comment on Testart 1982. *Current Anthropology* 23: 531–532.

Ingold, T. 1983. The significance of storage in hunting societies. *Man* 18: 553–571.

Ingold, T. 1986. *The Appropriation of Nature. Essays on Human Ecology and Social Relations*. Manchester: Manchester University Press.

Jennbert, K. 1985. Neolithisation – a Scanian perspective. *Journal of Danish Archaeology* 4: 196–197.

Jones, R. 1992. Philosophical time travellers. *Antiquity* 66: 744–757.

Kuper, A. 1988. *The Invention of Primitive Society*. London: Routledge.

Larsson, M. 1986. Neolithization in Scania – a Funnel Beaker perspective. *Journal of Danish Archaeology* 5: 244–247.

Layton, R. (ed.) 1989a. *Conflict in the Archaeology of Living Traditions*. London: Unwin Hyman.

Layton, R. (ed.) 1989b. *Who Needs the Past? Indigenous Values and Archaeology*. London: Unwin Hyman.

Lee, R. & DeVore, I. (eds) 1968. *Man the Hunter*. Chicago: Aldine Press.

Lévi-Strauss, C. 1972 [1962]. *The Savage Mind*. London: Weidenfeld & Nicholson.

Lévi-Strauss, C. 1976. The scope of anthropology. In *Structural Anthropology*, vol. 2, pp. 3–32. (Translated by Monique Layton.) New York: Basic Books.

Lévi-Strauss, C. 1989 [1955]. *Tristes Tropiques*. London: Pan Books.

Lewthwaite, J. 1981. Ambiguous first impressions: a survey of recent work on the early Neolithic of the west Mediterranean. *Journal of Mediterranean Archaeology and Anthropology* 1: 292–307.

Lewthwaite, J. 1986. The transition to food production: a Mediterranean perspective. In Zvelebil, M. (ed.), pp. 53–66.

MacCormack, C. & Strathern, M. (eds) 1980. *Nature, Culture and Gender*. Cambridge: Cambridge University Press.

McDonald, J., Zimmerman, L., McDonald, A., William Tall Bull and Ted Rising Sun 1991. The Northern Cheyenne outbreak of 1879: using oral history and archaeology as tools of resistance. In McGuire, R. & Paynter, R. (eds), *The Archaeology of Inequality*, pp. 64–78. Oxford: Blackwell.

Madsen, T. 1986. Where did all the hunters go? *Journal of Danish Archaeology* 5: 229–239.

Moreland, J. 1990. From the primeval to the paved: environment, perception, and structural history. *Scottish Archaeological Review* 7: 14–23.

Murdock, G. 1968. The current status of the world's hunting and gathering peoples. In Lee, R. & DeVore, I. (eds), pp. 13–20.

Murray, T. 1992. Tasmania and the constitution of 'the dawn of humanity'. *Antiquity* 66: 730–743.

Nelson, R. (director) 1970. *Soldier Blue* (US).

Olson, J. 1979. *The Ethnic Dimension in American History*. New York: St. Martin's Press.

Poster, M. (ed.) 1988. *Jean Baudrillard: Selected Writings*. Oxford: Polity Press.

Price, T. 1981. Swifterbant, Oost Flevoland, Netherlands: Excavations at the river dune sites S21–S24, 1976. *Palaeohistoria* 23: 75–104.

Price, T. & Brown, J. (eds) 1985. *Prehistoric Hunter-Gatherers. The Emergence of Cultural Complexity*. London: Academic Press.

Price, T. & Gebauer, A. 1992. Foragers to farmers: an introduction. In Price, T. & Gebauer, A. (eds), *Transitions to Agriculture in Prehistory*, pp. 1–10. Madison: Prehistory Press (Monographs in World Archaeology 4).

de Roever, J. 1979. The pottery from Swifterbant – Dutch Ertebølle? *Helinium* 19: 13–36

Rowley-Conwy, P. 1983. Sedentary hunters: the Ertebølle example. In Bailey, G., (ed.), *Hunter-gatherer Economy in Prehistory: A European Perspective*, pp. 111–126. Cambridge: Cambridge University Press.

Sahlins, M. 1968. Notes on the original affluent society. In Lee, R. & DeVore, I. (eds), pp. 85–89.

Sahlins, M. 1985. *Islands of History*. New York: Tavistock Press.

Scarre, C. 1983. The Neolithic of west-central France. In Scarre, C. (ed.), *Ancient France. Neolithic Societies and their Landscapes 6000 – 2000 bc*, pp. 223–270. Edinburgh: Edinburgh University Press.

Testart, A. 1982. The significance of food storage among hunter-gatherers: residence patterns, population densities and social inequalities. *Current Anthropology* 23: 523–537.

Testart, A. 1988. Some major problems in the social anthropology of hunter-gatherers. *Current Anthropology* 29: 1–31 and 489–491.

Thomas, J. 1987. Relations of production and social change in the Neolithic of north-west Europe. *Man* 22: 405–430.

Thomas, J. 1988. Neolithic explanations revisited: the Mesolithic-Neolithic transition in Britain and southern Scandinavia. *Proceedings of the Pre-*

historic Society 54: 59–66.

Thomas, J. 1991. *Rethinking the Neolithic*. Cambridge: Cambridge University Press.

Thomas, J. 1993. Discourse, totalization and 'The Neolithic'. In Tilley, C. (ed.), *Interpretative Archaeology*, pp. 357–394. Providence: Berg Publishers.

Thomas, N. 1991. *Entangled Objects: Exchange, material culture, and colonialism in the Pacific*. Cambridge (Mass.): Harvard University Press.

Torrence, R. & van der Leeuw, S. (eds) 1989. *What's New?* London: Unwin Hyman.

Whittle, A. 1985. *Neolithic Europe. A survey*. Cambridge: Cambridge University Press.

Whittle, A. 1988. *Problems in Neolithic archaeology*. Cambridge: Cambridge University Press.

Woodburn, J. 1980. Hunters and gatherers today and reconstruction of the past. In Gellner, E. (ed.), *Soviet and Western Anthropology*, pp. 95–117. London: Duckworth.

Woodburn, J. 1982. Egalitarian societies. *Man* 17: 431–451.

Zvelebil, M. (ed.) 1986. *Hunters in Transition*. Cambridge: Cambridge University Press.

Zvelebil, M. 1986a. Mesolithic prelude and Neolithic revolution. In Zvelebil M. (ed.), pp. 5–15.

Zvelebil, M. 1986b. Mesolithic societies and the transition to farming: problems of time, scale and organisation. In Zvelebil M. (ed.), pp. 167–188.

Zvelebil, M. 1989. On the transition to farming in Europe, or what was spreading with the Neolithic: a reply to Ammerman (1989). *Antiquity* 63: 379–383.

Zvelebil, M. 1992. Farmers, our ancestors and the identity of Europe. Paper delivered at 'Theoretical Archaeology Group' conference, Southampton.

Zvelebil, M. (in press). 'Agricultural frontier and the transition to farming in the circum-Baltic area.' Paper given at the conference 'Transition to Farming in the Baltic', Poland.

Zvelebil, M. & Rowley-Conwy, P. 1984. Transition to farming in northern Europe: A Hunter-Gatherer perspective. *Norwegian Archaeological Review* 17(2): 104–128.

Zvelebil, M. & Rowley-Conwy, P. 1986. Foragers and farmers in Atlantic Europe. In Zvelebil, M. (ed.), pp. 67–93.

4

The Domus: *Some Problems Reconsidered*

Ian Hodder

As *we came to the top* of the mound in the heat of midday, we blinked at the dark trench cut down perhaps 15 metres. The ladder leaning against the section seemed dangerously vertical. Gradually our eyes became accustomed to a remarkable sight – on the section wall facing us, the house walls which had been cut through seemed to rise the full height of the mound. Closer inspection identified floors and infill deposits at different levels within the gigantically tall houses, and the walls themselves had clearly been built by building later walls on earlier walls. And yet the continuity in the use of space was quite remarkable. At another point on the mound, a street had been sectioned which again seemed to have continued in use, endlessly resurfaced, from the bottom to the top of the mound. We had come to visit the aceramic Neolithic tell at Asiklihöyük on the eastern edge of the Konya Plain in central Turkey. What we had seen stretched credulity beyond its limits. What type of social system could produce such rigid continuities over such long periods? Surely in any society of which we are aware today households expand and contract in size, they create new alliances and have changing needs, and all this variation is expressed in the changing size and form of buildings? There seemed to be no building 'phases' on the site, at least if the one sounding was anything to go by. The mound was built from single houses, continuously reused and relived in through long periods of time.

I will return to the issue of continuity throughout this paper, but the initial point I wish to make about the Asiklihöyük experience concerns our implicit assumptions about the relationship between architecture and society. The reason I found the tall houses difficult to cope with was because I saw houses as reflections or expressions, however active, of social form or social process. Thus the house should ebb and flow with the changing fortunes of social units defined, at the house level, primarily in terms of kinship. I came to see later that this privileging of the social against the material was an underlying problem, both in my writing about the *domus* (Hodder 1990) and in much archaeological discussion of the social meanings of built forms. Perhaps the Asikli houses did not 'represent' or 'express' social units, but formed those units. Perhaps it was residence in the house which defined the social group. Perhaps the houses stayed the same, built on top of earlier houses, because social groups defined themselves in relation to a fixed form – if the house did not remain the same there would be no basis for the social group.

Recent preliminary work at Çatalhöyük has confirmed the general impression of houses built on top of each other, using the same walls, over long periods of time during the ceramic Neolithic. Here there is more variation, with midden or courtyard areas later built upon and earlier houses being transformed in form and function. And yet surviving sections at the site in places show continuous walls rising fifteen metres. In south-eastern Europe, Tringham (1991) has suggested an overall trend during the Neolithic and Chalcolithic. Houses are initially placed directly over earlier houses, but gradually through time they are placed to the side and other strategies concerned with continuity are used. For example, Tringham suggests that the burning of houses is often intentional and can be seen as a cleansing or ritual closure. Bailey (1990) has noted that the replacement of houses in the fourth millennium tells in Bulgaria is inversely proportional to the frequencies of house models. It is as if continuities created by the physical reuse of houses can also be dealt with by the handing on of heirlooms and by rituals of closure and renewal.

No-one living on the upper levels of Asikli or Çatal would have been able to see the tall houses with their continuous walls reaching to the bottom of the mounds. The continuity of walls is visible only after the event to the surgical archaeologist. The tall walls are presumably an unintended consequence of a set of practices which concern the rebuilding of later walls on earlier walls and the retention of house forms. The functions of rooms may well have changed through time, and initial work at Çatalhöyük has provided some evidence of this. The main aim was thus not functional but architectural continuity. The practices which reused walls and inserted new floors on rubble and in-fill materials within those walls were creating a continuity with the past. In reconstructing the building, the practices constructed a history. Within the continual walls things changed, events occurred, artefacts were passed on, rituals took place. But all these events were markers physically channelled into one sequence, written into a history.

The research question underlying the use of the term '*domus*' is why do houses (or in north-western Europe their tomb equivalents) play such a central role in the archaeology of the earlier Neolithic in Europe and the Near East? Why are houses often large or elaborate and why are the domestic ceramics often decorated? The first part of an adequate answer to such questions is to understand the house as a 'seamless web' (Latour 1988) linking the material and the cultural. The practices that produced the continuous walls at Asikli and Çatal were part of the economic production and social reproduction of a group which also passed on artefacts, held rituals, and buried ancestors beneath floors. The term *domus* attempts to capture the dual nature of the house as material and economic on the one hand and social and ideational on the other. The *domus* was both metaphor and mechanism.

The second part of an adequate answer concerns the specific ways in which histories were created in the rebuilding of houses and in the practices and rituals of continuity with which they were surrounded. In the earlier Neolithic, burials occur under floors in the Near East and at sites such as Lepenski Vir in south-eastern Europe. This, and the examples given above, indicates the importance of creating a specific history based on individual houses. All this creates a long term group with its own memory and practices. The art and sculpture at Çatal-höyük are inward-looking. There is little evidence of decoration on the outside of houses, which are closely crammed into the settlement with 'courtyard' areas used as large refuse pits. The art in the houses would have been difficult to see from the outside since entry is through the roof at the farthest end of the house. There are also many differences between the art and sculpture found in the different houses at Çatal-höyük. It remains to be seen whether the same differences between practices in individual houses are retained through time. But it seems possible that the consequence was the identity of a small house-using group, with its own culture and its own history.

Given this, what are the 'objective conditions' within which the *domus* was reproduced? The term 'objective conditions' is here taken from Bourdieu (1977) and refers to the 'world out there' to which individual actors have to accommodate. It includes both material and economic factors and the social relations in which such factors are embedded. Certainly intensive hunting and gathering and early agriculture involve increased inputs of labour and greater dependence between individuals as they jointly invest in clearings, fields, artefacts from which a return is delayed. It becomes necessary to hold the group together over longer periods of time. But there is not, in this description, any a priori reason why the house should become the focus of joint labour and its continuities the focus of longer-term dependencies between people. Certainly, early agriculture involved the need to create histories, but why through the medium of the house?

Part of the answer to such questions might involve a consideration of one aspect of the objective conditions – that is the particular technologies involved in early agriculture in the Near East. The early cereals required intensive joint labour in harvesting, threshing, winnowing, sieving. Grinding stones and ovens occur on early sites and while it is not certain that the earliest sites saw bread being made, cereal grinding and baking may have been involved. Land cannot have been a major limiting factor at this time, and so the main problem would have been the relations between people and their labour – could adequate labour be brought together at the right moments and over considerable spans of time so that individuals could depend on obtaining a return from labour? At least parts of the production process which transformed cereals into food, such as grinding and cooking, would have been well suited to be undertaken in the house, and since the size of group involved in joint labour in early agriculture could have been small, the domestic unit was appropriate.

It would be of interest to compare the role of the house in other areas of indigenous agricultural development to see if the type of technologies involved had an impact on the role of the house. In the central Americas, maize does not require threshing and it was often not ground into flour. The domestic context may have been able to play different roles in different areas. Similarly, domestication in the Near East comes to involve animals which have to be separated from wild herds. In this practice of separation and tending away from the wild, an opposition is set up between domestic and wild which may reinforce the importance of the domestic unit and of the house as metaphor.

The practices of early agriculture also involve storage – at least of seed grain and grain or flour for consumption. Storage pits occur in early Holocene sites, often in or near houses. Certainly the house provides a convenient and well-guarded location for the separation and identification of goods 'owned' by productive units. Reproduction too becomes of major concern where limits to growth are provided by labour rather than land, and certainly the household is well suited as a location for the rearing and nurturing of children.

I have argued that early agriculture, at least of the type found in the Near East, involved a suite of practices which were appropriately centred in the house. I am not arguing for necessary or materialist relations, since none of the practices has to be located in the house. I will mention below other factors which made the house the centre of group production and reproduction. But agriculture which largely functions at the domestic scale is likely to encourage an emphasis on the house, and as agriculture intensifies the organisation of production may become less house centred – and indeed in Europe later in the Neolithic, the importance of the house appears to decline with the introduction of the exploitation of the plough and secondary animal products (Hodder 1990). Thus it was in small-scale agriculture in the earlier Neolithic, involving intensive food preparation and separation of domestic from wild animals, involving storage and where labour rather than land was the main limiting constraint, that the house became an appropriate location for economic as well as social and cultural processes.

The main problem was how to form and hold together small groups over the long term, without coercion and without modern technologies of power. How was it possible to 'bind' people together? In part the answer to this is just that people were bound together by their joint investment in agricultural labour. But even in small communities there are those at times fully involved in reproduction while others grow old or are too young to work in the fields and so on. How can this group as a whole come to see itself as a 'bound' group? And if Bender (1978) is right in arguing for social differentiation at early phases, the problem for individual units of production and reproduction was to enhance their own unit at the expense of others, through exchange, increased production, ritual superiority and the like. In a competitive process the aim was to bind people in a small local group into a common strategy.

The house was an appropriate practical location for the binding of people and for the creation of a common history. The joint project of house building and rebuilding, the activities framed within its historical walls, the rituals specific to each house, the heirlooms passed down from the ancestors buried beneath the walls: all these practices created a frame within which people were bound, literally and by ritual ties and historical associations – a common past. People came to be bound between the walls, metaphorically domesticated as they also had to become practically domesticated. The walls at Asikli and Çatal had to remain the same because it was the historical associations of those bound within them that created a group continuous through time.

Perhaps more can be said about the particular social forms which clung so rigidly to the *domus* as a primary generating principle. In a somewhat evolutionary vein, Lévi-Strauss (1983; 1987; 1991) has defined house societies which have a specific form of social organisation. They have a type of social structure which is a hybrid or transition between kin-based and class-based societies. As well as kinship, other factors such as wealth, power and status begin to be important in the formation of social groups. Lévi-Strauss' distinction between elementary and complex structures is here being blurred. Elementary structures of kinship have positive marriage rules which specify the category of kin from which a spouse must be taken, and so choice of spouse is based on kinship alone. There are thus networks of marriage exchange which give coherence and solidarity to society. In complex systems, on the other hand, non-kinship factors such as wealth, power and class determine choice of spouse. Social integration is now provided by political and economic institutions. House societies still see the world in kinship terms but economic and political considerations come to play an increasingly important role.

It is not necessary to embrace the evolutionary implications of Lévi-Strauss' model to see the potential importance of the idea that 'the house' can provide the basis for non-kinship relations and even for the construction of kinship groupings. In a recent volume devoted to a consideration of Lévi-Strauss' hypothesis (Carsten and Hugh-Jones 1994), examples are provided of house societies without marked stratification. The main criteria of house societies are rather continuity and the passing on of wealth. Lévi-Strauss argues that the house is a grouping which endures through time. Continuity is produced by the succession and replacement of humans but also by passing on fixed or movable property and by handing down special names and titles. In many of the cases discussed in Carsten and Hugh-Jones (ibid.) ritualistic property and heirlooms are important in creating continuity, as is the right to make and use ceremonial ornaments. These sacred regalia or ritual roles which are passed down are likely to vary from house to house as part of the attempt to maintain separate rights and identities (cf. Barth 1987).

One of the most distinctive aspects of the elaborately painted and sculpted houses at Çatalhöyük is their variability. The layout of each house shows some uniformity but the scenes and sculptures vary considerably. Little work has yet been completed on whether houses retain styles of ornamentation over time, but certainly some plaster reliefs, such as the facing leopards, were frequently resurfaced. In some cases there is evidence of replastering walls up to 50 times. Together with the evidence for the reuse of walls, the overall emphasis on continuity of distinct houses is apparent. I have already noted that Tringham makes the same emphasis for south-eastern Europe. As yet we do not know the kinship relations between those who used the same house over many generations, although analysis of the bones from beneath the floors at Asikli and Çatal may provide some information in this regard. But it certainly seems possible that social relations in these sites were not based solely or primarily on kinship. The importance of the continuity of the physical building and the centrality of ritual at Çatalhöyük imply that practical and ritual processes may have formed the basis of the house group. It is also possible that the increasingly intensive use of domesticated resources was associated with shifts in size of the smaller-scale units of production and changes in the division of labour within those units. Even if such realigned groupings were based on kinship, the formation of new kinship relations as the basis of the house group may have been underpinned by other factors, practical and ritual.

I have noted that, at least in Europe, the importance of the house declines in the later periods of the Neolithic (Hodder 1990) and so it is tempting to agree with Lévi-Strauss' evolutionary stage of house societies between elementary and complex forms of social structure. Certainly in the late Neolithic, new forms of power based on exchange rather than descent and gradually leading to greater centralisation of political focus imply a breakdown of the continuity model. However, house societies occur in a variety of different social contexts (Carsten & Hugh-Jones 1994), and they lead to very different social forms after the earlier Neolithic in Europe and the Near East. Perhaps all we can say with some security is that initially in the Near East and south-eastern Europe, houses are inward looking and continuities through time are rigidly adhered to. But through time, burial increasingly occurs outside the house, ceramics which are passed between houses are decorated, and more and more emphasis is placed on the facades or entrances of houses – the going in and the coming out (Hodder 1990). The importance of the house ultimately declines as relationships between groups and their political coordination increase. The house societies of the Near East and Europe thus play a particular role in the development from kinship-based societies to those for which kinship may still have been central but in which other dimensions of power came to be significant.

So far I have argued that the *domus* involved an economic, social and cultural emphasis on the house and its continuity through time. I have further suggested that it was reproduced because it was an appropriate practical and symbolic model in a certain set of 'objective conditions' which included the practices of a particular form of early agriculture and social relations based on kinship in the domestic unit but increasingly expanding to include other forms of power. Thus from the Near East and south-eastern Europe to the Bandkeramik of central Europe, and even to Orkney where houses and tombs of a local style look so like each other, the house occurs as central because it is appropriate to the particular set of conditions set up by early European agriculture. Wherever early European agriculture develops in the context of small-scale social units, so the house is a central social and symbolic focus as well the basis for the organisation of production. Everywhere, people are domesticated through the practices and meanings of the house.

As already mentioned, the house model may be appropriate to a given set of conditions but those conditions do not determine the use of that model. Thus as well as considering the objective conditions it is also necessary to evaluate the loose historical ties between groups in Neolithic Europe and the Near East to see the spread of a specific idea. I have argued (Hodder 1990) for historical connections between different parts of Europe and for the spread of particular aspects of the *domus* over large areas. For example, many of the ceramic traits and symbolism of houses (e.g. use of bucrania) occur in Anatolia and south-eastern Europe. In central Europe a particular emphasis on long linear houses with elaborate entrances develops and shows historical continuities with the linear tombs of north-western Europe.

The objective conditions within which house societies developed in the Neolithic are sufficient to explain neither the durability and reproduction of the general emphasis on houses nor the specific forms that the houses took. It is also necessary, therefore, to consider the historical development of a set of structuring principles embedded within houses, their uses and symbolic meanings. In the most general terms these principles concern the house as creating continuities between past and present, in all realms – economic, social and ritual. A linked idea is that by being embedded within a social group with long-term memory within a house, individuals became 'domesticated'. In more specific terms the principles concern, for example, the importance of cleansing the house with fire at the ends of periods of use. Such deliberate burning is as common in the Neolithic of south-eastern Europe as it is in the burial mounds of north-western Europe. It should be clear from what I have already argued in this paper that these structuring principles are not just 'ideas' in peoples' heads. They may not have been always consciously expressed, and they are as much engrained in practices as they are symbolically meaningful.

I wish to suggest three reasons for the durability and reproduction of these structuring principles beyond their appropriateness in a given set of conditions. The first is that the principles lasted for millennia and survived translation into numerous contexts because they were very general and simply defined. The very generality and simplicity of the principles meant that they could be applied in a variety of different contexts. We would thus expect to see the same principles reappearing wherever loose historical ties existed between groups and provided the medium for the transmission of change. Thus the emphasis on the continuity of the house could be translated into any small-scale society which was attempting to intensify domestic production and create its own history, whether it was hunter-fisher-gatherer (Lepenski Vir) or full farming (Çatalhöyük). It could be applied in dense villages in south-eastern Europe and Anatolia and in the scattered homesteads of the Bandkeramik. It could be translated into houses for the dead in societies with more dispersed and less permanent settlement in north-western Europe, where houses themselves were not long term enough to provide a focus for the handing on of rights and duties. But if the *domus* endured for millennia partly because it was general and simple, how can we explain the disconnected reappearance of the same principles without apparent historical connection? For example, I have already mentioned the Orkney evidence. Here houses and tombs and henges were built with common forms and with common principles (such as the importance of square stone-lined hearths). The emphasis on the house is certainly there, but its particular manifestation seems independent and distinctive. Another example of the presumably disconnected appearance of similar traits in similar conditions is provided by the evidence for female breasts on house walls in Turkey and southern central Europe. The examples from Çatalhöyük claimed by

Mellaart (1967) are supported by clay figurines with naked breasts in domestic contexts. The examples from Lake Constance are more clearly breasts and are associated with a wooden building with other painted clay reliefs (Arnold 1993). The latter are dated to the Pfyn culture. The enormous spans of time and space with which we are here dealing suggest that something other than the diffusion of traits is involved.

It is often the case that general principles are transformed locally and cannot be explained by direct borrowing. Unless it is argued that some psychological predisposition is triggered by the same objective conditions some other mechanism must be found. It may be appropriate to consider general principles reproduced in myth and folklore. Thus the general principle gets passed on in a non-material form and 'resurfaces' in the material record in often different guises, each a local translation of the general into the particular. The loose historical associations which reproduce the *domus* thus occur at the level of general myth rather than solely in terms of the borrowing of specific practices.

The second reason for the long-term durability of the house model of and for society in Neolithic Europe and the Near East is that it has an internal logic. By this I do not mean that the *domus* principles determined the direction of cultural change for millennia. Rather, I mean that social change had to be made sense of in terms of existing principles or their transformation. Another way to say the same thing is that we live in narratives (Ricoeur 1984; Hodder 1993). The story of our lives has to unfold, it has to have a certain coherence, the different parts fitting together into a whole which is continually being rewritten. The building of house walls on earlier walls, the burning or closing off in order to end a period of use, the blocking of megalithic burial monuments are all acts which create narrative relations, beginning and ending, constructing histories within a particular frame of walls, contesting stories. Thus the *domus* endured not simply because it could be widely applied in different contexts but because as it was applied in different situations the new had to relate to the old within a narrative. For example, at the site of Haçilar in Turkey in the sixth millennium the earlier importance of symbolism within the house appears to decline as relations between houses and wider community relations increase in importance. The elaborate symbolism is now transferred from houses to domestic ceramics, still related to the house but more visible and mobile and able to be used in the relations between houses. In central Europe, the same process is dealt with in a different but equally logical way. Here, houses become trapezoidal, and facades, entrances and outer walls become more elaborate, as relations between houses become more important. In each case, after the event, and with long-term hindsight, the principles seem to unfold with an inexorable logic. But the sense of 'logic' is only experienced as the coherence of a narrative linking past and present. It is the narrative character of human lived experience that creates the apparent temporal structures of the archaeologist's long-term gaze.

The third reason for the durability of the *domus* principles concerns the integration of idea and practice outlined earlier. As I have described it, the emphasis on the continuity of the house was embedded within a series of practices. These practices were partly economic, involving the long-term investment of labour, the grinding and cooking of foods. But they were also social, involving relations with ancestors, the passing down of artefacts, rights and privileges and the control of esoteric knowledge. And they were also ritual, involving rites of closure and renewal. In all these practical activities the group was reproduced. But all that reproduction was framed or bound within the physical walls of the house. In a very practical way the events which took place in the house were 'caught' within a sequence – at Asikli a hermetically closed sequence, constructing a time-space continuum lasting centuries or even millennia. The materiality of the house was used to construct a series of practices which, even if only because they were 'framed', told a narrative of continuity.

Now, it has been widely recognised, from Pitt-Rivers to Bourdieu and Giddens that most practices are not discursively available. In other words, we may know what to do and be aware of the effectiveness of our actions but be less able to describe and explain them verbally. As Bourdieu demonstrates, the implicit nature of practices does not mean that they are any the less organised or socially meaningful. The principles are there, within the practices, even if we cannot describe them. It is this taken-for-granted character of practices which contributes to their durability. The principles of most practices are not brought out for conscious discussion except when contradictions or conflict emerge. For the most part, the principles remain undiscussed, the background to our daily lives, the residues of past consciousness.

The emphasis on principles embodied and practically embedded might be seen as contradicting the inference made above that the *domus* principles were handed down in myth. Certainly I would argue that the disconnected appearance throughout the European Neolithic of different versions of the same idea about the centrality and continuity of the house suggests that the idea may have been passed on in non-material form, at least in some instances. But the conscious use of the principles in mythical narratives does not contradict their practical embeddedness. Ricoeur (1984) argues for a dialectical interaction between told and lived narratives, between stories we tell about our-selves and our practical experience of time. In local contexts in the European Neolithic these spoken and lived narratives could take on a particular form, embedded within local myths and local traditions of practice. Another way to make the same point is to note that myth-telling is itself a practice in which general principles are used im-plicitly and explicitly. The principles might at different times be re-produced in different domains of practice (myth, burial, the house it-self, etc.), appearing and reappearing in the archaeological record depending on the survivability of domains. Thus the durability of the *domus* principle was aided both by the general nature of the told stories about the continuity of the house and by the implicit nature of the practices which embodied those principles.

I have suggested how house societies in Europe might have been re-produced. On the one hand, the longevity of a set of objective material and social conditions provided the context for the long-term use and dissemination of house-centred practices and metaphors. But in answering the question 'why did these particular material and social conditions last so long?' we have to consider the dialectical relations between the 'conditions' and the actions which produced them. Thus, on the other hand, a set of generative principles for action, based on the house, had enormous longevity because of their appropriateness to the 'conditions' which they produced, but also because they were general and simple, made narrative sense and were embedded in implicit practices.

MEGALITHS AS THE CREATION OF HISTORY

I wish now to look at the linear tombs of northern Europe and the British Isles in order to explore the way in which the general house principles, and especially the continuity of the house, were translated into a particular form of practices suited to a particular set of economic and social conditions within the general frame set by small-scale mixed farming of European domesticates. As with the houses of south-eastern Europe and the Near East I will argue that a 'house' of people was created through the construction and experience of a common history.

As Kinnes (1992) has demonstrated for the long barrows of the

British Neolithic, the tombs were often used for a series of activities spread over a long time. In some cases the burial use of megaliths was relatively brief (as at West Kennet and Hazleton North – Saville 1990). For the wood-chambered tombs such as Haddenham the numbers of burials are relatively small and the sequence of activities long (Hodder and Shand 1988). A brief summary of the sequence of activities at Haddenham will indicate the extent to which people participated in the project in different ways at different times, creating an overall narrative and building a common historical experience and memory.

A site was chosen, on a late Mesolithic settlement, and an orientation. Pre-mortuary structure activities took place. A large tree, an oak, was chosen, cut and specialist expertise used to split it longitudinally into planks up to 8 metres long. The wood was carried to the site, some of it several tons in weight, requiring joint labour. Turf was stripped from the burial area and mounded as the big uprights were set in the ground. The wooden chamber was built and the earth heaped up around it in an organised way, different soil being placed in different parts of the mound and the turf being carefully stacked. Over the years, as people died, the roof of the chamber was lifted off and the bodies placed inside. Sometimes their flesh and the sinews holding the bones together were cut. People stopped using the tomb and closed off the facade with a bank of earth which was added to as pots were deposited as offerings at the front. The last time the roof of the chamber was taken off, the big uprights were cut down and the front of the chamber filled with turf and small wood. The roof was replaced and the turf set alight. The whole thing burned very slowly and was then covered by an extension to the mound. Even then the use of the site was not finished. Burials were added over the years into the top of the mound.

I have outlined the sequence of activities at Haddenham because over many years many people would have been involved in different aspects of a common project. Although the uses of the tomb changed through time, persons with different skills (how to orient a tomb, how to split wood, how to deflesh a corpse) were involved and at times larger mobilisation of labour was needed. People came together to carry out activities at the tomb and were thus caught in a joint project. They had a common history. The tomb itself framed a set of activities through which people were channelled. How they were channelled changed through time as the narrative changed. Indeed the use of the tomb can be seen as involving a continual tension. On the one hand there is the communal nature of the mound building and the open area in front of the facade. On the other hand, and apparently contradicted by the funnel entrance leading up to the tomb, there is no entry into the chamber from the front; access is blocked and few people are buried in the tomb. The communal group seems to be in dialectical tension with limited access to the tomb itself. The narrative history was thus a contested one, but even in the dialectic a common history was created. A continuity through time had been constructed.

Perhaps another way in which continuity was emphasised can be seen in the mounding of earth and turf which is such a distinctive aspect of the Haddenham sequence, associated with its more communal phases. In particular, as part of the ending of the use of the chamber, turf was stacked in the entrance area and on top of the dismantled posts. This act, associated with the controlled burning of the chamber at the end of its use, and associated with the mounding of earth and pot deposition in front of the facade, can be interpreted as linked to the idea of burial and renewal. The link with burning reinforces the emphasis on ending, cleansing and thus renewal. Even if renewal is not part of the interpretation of these rituals, the formal and elaborated acts of closure certainly suggest a concern with continuity.

An overall emphasis on continuity in the use of tombs in northern Europe has been suggested by Gramsch (1993; 1995). In particular he has documented the widespread occurrence of the placing of tombs on houses or in relation to domestic debris. Such evidence strengthens the link to the *domus*, but it also emphasises the creation of history – the construction of links to the past. The association of burial with domestic discard may also have helped to create liminality through inversion – the sacred linked with the dangers and impurities of dirt. Life would thus be constructed out of death and decay. But it is my main concern here to emphasise the social construction of a common if contested history.

Gramsch notes the recurrent phenomenon of barrows erected upon layers of cultural material consisting of charcoal, sherds, flint and bone tools, animal bones etc. but often also incorporating features such as pits, ditches, hearths and post-holes and in some cases clear buildings. It is possible that such material is connected with ritual or construction use of the site prior to or during the building of the tomb. It has at times been suggested that the domestic material under barrows was intentionally dumped as part of ritual. Gramsch argues for a domestic interpretation of the pre-mound activity for a number of reasons. First, some of the cultural layers are very extensive, spreading well beyond the grave area (e.g. at Lindebjerg, Wollschow and Wartin). Second, the composition of materials in the cultural layers is very similar to that from settlements not associated with barrows. The material includes hearths, and types of flint and pottery found frequently on settlements. Wall daub, clay discs and bowls are found in the cultural layers but rarely with purely ritual features. In Denmark, beakers involved in facade rituals or placed in the graves are decorated more elaborately than sherds from both settlements and cultural layers beneath barrows. Third, in several cases (e.g. Bjornshølm and Mosegarden) the structures below the mounds indicate an occupation more substantial than short-lived ritual activities, including several huts, fireplaces, activity areas and dump areas.

It would be possible to argue that the tombs were placed over houses and settlements not because of an emphasis on continuity but simply because the abandoned settlements offered cleared and unwanted land for tomb building. That some greater intentionality is involved is suggested by the high frequency of such placements and by their sometimes deliberate nature. For example, in several tombs in Kujavia rubbish is heaped over the graves, and in some cases in Denmark the graves are sited very precisely in relation to earlier buildings.

Large stone and wood tombs are associated in northern and western Europe with different types of economy. But in general terms the associated settlement patterns do not include large bounded, permanent sites with dense concentrations of large houses. Farming communities which lived away from the rich loess lands of central Europe may have been rather more mobile or dispersed and small scale. The overall objective conditions that sustained the use of megalithic tombs over the long term included dispersed settlement in which houses themselves could not function to provide a focus for continuity. But a 'house' of people could be constructed in the joint practices repeated over time at large, stable tombs.

But given the variety of economies within which megaliths functioned it is necessary to consider other factors too that sustained the longevity of their use. Bell (1992) has noted the ways in which ritual practices embody social relations and meanings. Certainly the practical construction of the tombs involved bodily participation between people who thus became tied to each other through their joint labour. Richards (1990) has described for Orkney the parallels between houses, tombs and henges, and shown the way in which bodily movement and orientation in each referred to the other monument types. The repetition of similar practices in different domains would have underlined the emphasis on continuity. Certainly too, the practices at many tombs must have involved a distinction between communal events at the entrances and the experience of exclusion and separation in relation to the activities inside the burial chamber. Thus long-term relations are constructed, but so are the social divisions contained within them.

The durability of the tomb practices may have in part derived from their implicit, taken-for-granted nature. However, death rituals are likely to have occurred less frequently than many practices associated with houses. Even if annual or more frequent offerings were made at the tombs, the activities there are likely to have involved more conscious effort to reconstruct sequences of events and performance. There may have been debate about what was the 'right' thing to do. The implications of this are that the tombs offered more opportunities than the houses for the manipulation and conscious framing of the structures of bodily experience.

That manipulation worked within a narrative constructed around the sequence of events at the tombs, which would have had both specific and general components – specific to the history of that particular tomb and general in relation to other widely found narratives and myths on which the particular made comment. Andrén (1993) has shown in a very different context the way in which burial practices can 'tell a story' or be embedded in myth. Some of the components of these narratives may have concerned continuity and renewal. Whatever their content, they may have provided the bridge between infrequent practices at the tombs. But the embedding of ritual practices in myth or narrative produced another realm of practice in which general ideas could be retold and transformed over the long term.

CONCLUSION

In discussing Neolithic houses in Europe and the Near East it is unhelpful to separate too rigidly economic, social and ritual factors. Rather, the houses are a context, a locale (Giddens 1984), in which economic, social and ideological resources are mobilised in strategies focussed on creating a long-term small-scale 'house' of people. These different resources are thoroughly interwoven within practices. They form a seamless web (Latour 1988).

I have argued that the *domus* or house was an appropriate context for practices concerned with creating long-term continuities within small-scale units depending largely on domestic production. Where houses themselves were not stable enough themselves to provide the fixity for the group, as they had been at Asiklihöyük, other strategies were followed such as the building of new houses near earlier ones in small clusters (as in the Bandkeramik cultures of the Rhineland) and such as the construction of tombs, sometimes over houses and settlements. The objective conditions in which house societies could develop in Europe and the Near East lasted a long time and this partly explains the longevity of the importance of the house in the archaeological record.

But lest our seamless web be broken and a materialism introduced, we should also ask why the objective conditions were themselves reproduced over such a long period. The answer to this question concerns the structuring principles through which the objective conditions were reproduced. These structuring principles concerned practices dealing with the continuity of the house, its boundedness, the burning and other rituals associated with closure, the importance of entrances, and so on. The reproduction of such general principles across enormous expanses of space and time has been understood in this paper in relation to three factors beyond the continuity of objective conditions.

First, the structuring principles were general and simple and could thus be applied in a variety of different specific contexts. As part of their generality they could occur in more than one domain. As a result they might exist in myth even if not present in any archaeologically recognisable material. Second, the general and simple principles were understood within a narrative structure. New developments had to be made coherent within an existing framework, or the framework had to be rewritten in order to accommodate change. As a result, sequences of cultural change involving the house appear to 'unfold' with a certain internal 'logic'. Third, the principles were embedded in practices which were generally implicit and thus were continued as part of the unacknowledged conditions of action. Where the practices were largely ritual in nature, the greater opportunity for manipulation by dominant groups may have led to a further reason for the conservative retention of tradition over the long term.

REFERENCES

Andrén, A. 1993. Doors to other worlds. *Journal of European Archaeology* 1: 33–56.

Arnold, B. 1993. Lake Constance yields breast reliefs. *Archaeology* 46 (2): 23.

Bailey, D. 1990. The living house: signifying continuity. In Samson, R. (ed.), *The Social Archaeology of Houses*, pp. 17–48. Edinburgh: Edinburgh University Press.

Barth, F. 1987. *Cosmologies in the Making*. Cambridge: Cambridge University Press.

Bell, C. 1992. *Ritual Theory, Ritual Practice*. Oxford: Oxford University Press.

Bender, B. 1978. Gatherer-hunter to farmer: a social perspective. *World Archaeology* 10: 204–222.

Bourdieu, P. 1977. *Outline of a Theory of Practice*. Cambridge: Cambridge University Press.

Carsten, J. & Hugh-Jones, S 1994. *About the House: Lévi-Strauss and beyond*. Cambridge: Cambridge University Press.

Giddens, A. 1984. *The Constitution of Society: an Outline of the Theory of Structuration*. Cambridge: Polity Press.

Gramsch, A. 1993. Death and Continuity. Unpublished MPhil dissertation, Department of Archaeology, University of Cambridge.

Gramsch, A. 1995. Death and continuity. *Journal of European Archaeology* 3.1: 71–90.

Hodder, I. 1990. *The Domestication of Europe*. Oxford: Blackwell.

Hodder, I. 1993. The narrative and rhetoric of material culture sequences. *World Archaeology* 25: 268–282.

Hodder, I. & Shand, P. 1988. The Haddenham long barrow: an interim statement. *Antiquity* 62: 349–353.

Kinnes, I. 1992. *Non-megalithic Long Barrows and Allied Structures in the British Neolithic*. London: British Museum (Occasional Paper 52).

Latour, B. 1988. 'The prince' for machines as well as for machinations. In Elliott, B. (ed), *Technology and Social Process*, pp. 20–43. Edinburgh: Edinburgh University Press.

Lévi-Strauss, C. 1983. *The Way of the Masks*. London: Jonathan Cape.

Lévi-Strauss, C. 1987. *Anthropology and Myth*. Oxford: Blackwell.

Lévi-Strauss, C. 1991. Maison. *Dictionnaire de l'Ethnologie et de L'Anthropologie*. Paris: Presses Universitaires de France.

Mellaart, J. 1967. *Catal Huyuk*. London: Thames and Hudson.

Richards, C. 1990. The late Neolithic house in Orkney. In Samson, R. (ed.), *The Social Archaeology of Houses*, pp. 111–124. Edinburgh: Edinburgh University Press.

Ricoeur, P. 1984. *Time and Narrative*. Chicago: University of Chicago Press.

Saville, A. 1990. *Hazleton North. Gloucestershire*. (English Heritage Archaeological Report 13).

Tringham, R. 1991. Households with faces. In Gero, J. and Conkey, M. (eds), *Engendering Archaeology*. Blackwell, Oxford.

5

Constructs of Death in the Early Neolithic of the Paris Basin

Trevor Kirk

This *paper reflects* upon the dissolution of death as a unitary theme within contemporary archaeological thought. Through a consideration of the physical and ideational constructs of death generated during the early Neolithic of the Paris basin, it will be argued that meanings and interpretations of death may be disseminated throughout the fabric of social existence. Whilst not to be found everywhere, social action upon the human body pervaded many aspects of Neolithic life. In enclosures, settlements, and cemeteries, the human body was deposited in association with diverse material symbols in the creation of a plethora of contextual settings which became the subject of readings and interpretations by people located within successive historical, social, and cultural settings. Death was encountered, categorised, and known through embodied experience (Shanks 1992: 1), through the historically located event of experiencing structured arrangements of space, place, and material culture through the medium of the sentient human body.

DIALECTICS OF LIFE AND DEATH

Whilst it is true that death comes to all people, the meanings attributed to death are neither universal nor pre-determined. Rather, death and the human body are assigned cultural meaning by the practices and actions in which they are invoked. During the early Neolithic in the Paris basin, the association of the human body with a wide range of places and forms of material culture generated diverse meanings for death and for the body itself. The opposition of death to life represents just one possibility for the creative extension of meaning. For example, identified as other to the living, the dead may be liable to classification as ancestor, spirit, or supernatural power. However, it is the strategic use of such cultural categories in the mediation of relations between the living that is crucial. Dominant symbols (the human body, tombs, pottery) and ideological themes (genealogical priority, ancestral lineage) may be drawn upon in the reproduction or transformation of the social order (Shanks & Tilley 1982). In a very real sense, the dead are not opposed to the living but enjoy a dialectical relation with the same. That is to say, life and death are part of the same categorical system, each category being different from the other, yet each entering into the definition of the other and of the system as a whole.

Mortuary practices are constituted within specific historic and cultural settings. In common with all social constructs they are constituted within and across many different fields of social discourse. To cite a contemporary example, one could not hope to adequately discuss late capitalist class relations exclusively in terms of access to the means of production. Rather, one would need also to consider broader cultural institutions such as teaching establishments, the media, national and local government, religion, and the welfare state. Similarly, in his work on sexuality in the classical world Michel Foucault (1986) discusses diet, the individual's political duties to the city-state, relations within the household, and relations between spouses; in short, a matrix of inter-related practices that were both the context and the underlying substance of the social construction of sexuality at the time.

So too with death and, more specifically, the construction of meanings around the human body and the material culture deposited with it within mortuary structures. This paper will assess the embeddedness of mortuary practice within social strategies for lineage reproduction (for example, exchange, marriage alliance, and the presencing of ancestors) as well as the control of genealogical knowledge, food acquisition and preparation, the engendering of social practice, the structured deposition of material culture, and changing settlement and subsistence patterns. In short, the conceptualisation and material manipulation of death may have constituted a component of that process of domesticating space, time, and social relations which characterises the earlier Neolithic.

LATE BANDKERAMIK AND VILLENEUVE-SAINT-GERMAIN FUNERARY CONTEXTS

The archaeological evidence discussed in this paper is fragmentary and derives from a geographical area loosely centred on the Seine, Aisne, Yonne, and Essonne valleys. Consequently my thoughts and inferences are not concerned with the construction of an overarching meta-narrative for the Neolithic of northern France. Rather, I shall be analysing a patch-work of disparate (even contradictory) rites practised across the Paris basin during the late fifth and early fourth millennia bc. My comments comprise neither generalised models for the whole of northern France, nor are they predicative of what future excavation and research might demonstrate. Rather, places and landscapes will be viewed as historically located creations of local social processes and practices. However, that is not to privilege the specific over the general, the local over the regional. What needs to be retained is the capacity to tack back and forth from the specificity of social practice to the larger regional setting of social, economic, and cultural circumstances and of social change through time.

Death, houses, and gender

Pit graves of late Bandkeramik date comprise the earliest Neolithic funerary contexts in the Paris basin. Many graves are today recovered as isolated structures. Their isolation may reflect a combination of factors including the partial destruction of once large sites (graves are frequently identified during gravel quarrying), the small scale of many rescue excavations, and perhaps even prehistoric reality. However, graves are also frequently associated with long-houses, as at Cuiry-lès-Chaudardes and Cys-la-Commune, Aisne (Agache 1968; Soudsky et al. 1982). Even where graves occur in small cemeteries, as at Charmoy, Yonne (Joly 1970), long-houses are rarely more than tens or at most hundreds of metres distant. A similar pattern may be identified in post-Bandkeramik Villeneuve-Saint-Germain contexts. For example, graves are located near long-houses at La Pente de Croupeton, Jablines (Seine-et-Marne) and Villeneuve-la-Guyard (Yonne), and a cemetery is situated close to three long-houses at Les Réaudins, Balloy (Seine-et-Marne) (Bostyn et al. 1991; Mordant 1991; Prestreau 1992).

Two remarks on the nature of ritual ensue from the observation that graves are frequently located close to long-houses. First, any social practice entails ritualisation to the extent that patterns of routine are evoked (Leach 1966). Action upon human remains represents an aspect of routinised social practice just as is the making of a cup of tea or the production and use of pottery or flint tools. Polarisation of the ritual and the (so-called) domestic is spurious in the sense that it presupposes a qualitative differentiation of forms of social practice. Rather, to take up the instance of burial in the early Neolithic of the Paris basin, components of mortuary practice may have entered into the cultural categories 'house' and 'settlement', and of what it meant to know and experience these structures and places. Second, having postulated a dissemination of ritual throughout the social fabric, some forms of practice are none the less more formally 'ritualised' than others in the sense that access to various forms of knowledge and human experience may be more or less circumscribed or carefully guarded. In the early Neolithic of the Paris basin the dead were clearly incorporated within a space that was also a forum for the day-to-day production, use, discard, and deposition of stone and bone tools, pottery, and foodstuffs. Yet at the same time, access to graves was strictly controlled by their incorporation within or very close to long-houses (either within or adjacent to flanking pits). The dead were therefore incorporated into very specific spatial, social, and cultural contexts. Bodily access to mortuary structures was in some sense controlled by the spatial ordering of graves in relation to long-houses.

It has already been noted that late and post-Bandkeramik cemeteries are invariably located close to long-houses. For example, graves at Charmoy (Yonne) and Les Réaudins, Balloy (Seine-et-Marne) are only 30 metres from the nearest long-house. At Charmoy an explicit spatial separation of houses and graves may be tentatively postulated. Six single inhumations and a small single-cell post-built structure (ca 4,5 x 3,5 m) are divided from one (or two?) long-houses and a further single-cell structure by a 25 m long wooden palisade (Joly 1970). Whilst the absolute sequencing of the graves, long-houses, single-cell structures, and palisade is not fully understood, the spatial patterning of the ensemble is seductive. Whether or not all the elements of the complex are strictly contemporaneous, one is certainly left with the impression that graves and long-houses occupy discrete spaces. Furthermore, that the single-cell structure encloses Grave D and is respected by the remaining graves may even tempt one to envision a mortuary house as part of the funerary complex.

The meaning of death and the human body was clearly not unitary during the early Neolithic. Bodies were deposited in different locations and with different material associations to produce material texts which may have elicited plural, even contradictory, readings. The dead were variously part of and separate from the domain of the living. In lineage societies all relationships, be they economic, social, or political, are determined in the first (and final) instance by kinship (Kahn 1981). The dead, as symbolic if not literal representatives of the lineage ancestry, may therefore have been incorporated into long-houses and the daily round of activities with which they may have been associated (if all long-houses were indeed domestic structures?), as a means of consolidating lineage identity. It is often the case that children were placed closest to long-houses (either in flanking pits or, as at Cuiry-lès-Chaudardes, within the long-house itself). From birth, children take their place within the lineage formation, as offspring, sibling, nephew, or niece. Children are an integral part of the lineage and may not therefore be excluded as an appropriate symbol of lineage identity, irrespective of their lack of personal achievement. Conversely, the deposition of adult bodies may additionally evoke the congealed labour and delayed return of simple farming economies upon which depends the lineage's perpetuation through time (Meillassoux 1978).

Hodder (1990: 107), has proposed that the strong, though not exclusive association of child graves with long-houses may repeat a correlation between settlements, women, and children observed in southeastern Europe. He interprets this pattern in terms of gender associations which relate women to houses, the domestic sphere, and child-rearing. Such an argument defines gender relations in terms of biological sex and reproductive capability. It also assumes that gender relations are about the assignation of social roles, rather than the engendering of the social world, social practices, concepts, and beliefs (Conkey & Gero 1991; 8–9). In my view, an engendered archaeology should seek to investigate the cultural construction of gender as a set of social categories through which people mark out, classify, and know the physical and social world in which they live (Flax 1987: 622–623; Strathern 1980). For example, the often noted correlation between *Spondylus* ornaments and female graves in the Bandkeramik of the Paris basin (Burkill 1983; Hodder 1990: 110), may not simply mark out *Spondylus* as a signifier of femaleness. Rather, the cultural value and meaning of *Spondylus* and the social practices in which it was invoked (the collection of shells, manufacture of ornaments, exchange relations, deposition in graves) may have been in part defined through reference to the engendered concept, female. The engendered construct refers not to the sex of the social actor, but to a classificatory system, through which the world is ordered. The engendered classificatory system meshes with further categorical networks such as domestic/wild, culture/

nature, and human/animal, not in the generation of exact correspondence and difference (for example, male : domestic : culture : : female : wild : nature), but rather in the construction of a symbolic repertoire through which the ambiguities and contradictions of human relations are expressed. Thus, for example, the circulation of *Spondylus* ornaments, perhaps acting to consolidate marital alliance networks, may have been in part viewed as conceptually female in character. Tension between the interests of individuals or groups, for instance new wives and husbands, married initiates, and unmarried juniors, may have been expressed and lived out through the ambiguities and contradictions of symbolic networks and categorical expression (for example, female *Spondylus* references all sides of a range of non-equal relations pertaining between age-sets and genders).

Artefact biography and group genealogy

The grave deposit – the disposition of the body and the form and positioning of material culture – may be an important source of symbolic communication. Material texts are laid out to be read by those who encounter and experience them. Whilst the range of material deposits is not extensive in Bandkeramik graves (ostensibly pottery, *Spondylus* and other seashell ornaments, schist and hard-stone bracelets, and flint and bone tools), the rules governing the arrangement of deposits within graves are complex. Even within the current small sample, apparent structuring principles are contravened at every turn. The dominant east-west orientation of the body placed in a flexed position is counterbalanced by occasional north-south orientations and prone body positions. Bodies may or may not be sprinkled with ochre. Material associations range from nothing, through a few sherds and flint flakes, to elaborate deposits of decorated pots, schist bracelets, shell ornaments, and flint and bone tools. Whilst reflection of the hierarchical structure of Neolithic society may not be ruled out as an explanation for such diversity, I am interested here in the constitution of social systems through social practice rather than an analysis of social roles (Parker Pearson 1982: 100). So, can practices of material inscription and interpretation be detected in the patterning of late and post-Bandkeramik graves in the Paris basin? It is perhaps axiomatic to suggest that pottery, bracelets, shell, flint, and bone tools relate in various ways to the human body and to activities during life (eating, drinking, exchange relations, food processing). However, as Thomas has recently suggested 'The grave assemblage [may have] existed not to reflect the individual's identity in life, but to construct a highly formalised and impoverished kind of identity in death' (1991: 11). That is to say, the coherence of the material text lay in the relation between body and material objects, 'for it would only be through the presence of the body that the whole could be integrated and conceived as a whole' (ibid.). Cultural values may have been internalised and inculcated through their mapping onto a cultural and material landscape (Bourdieu 1977; Moore 1986). But what can be reconstructed of these values, beliefs, and cultural meanings? Contradiction, ambiguity, and dispute over potential meaning is not unlikely, as interest groups jostled to maintain or impose preferred interpretations of material texts which themselves invoke a multiplicity of themes, referents, and issues. Some of these issues, including exchange relations, artefact histories, reproduction of the lineage, genealogical knowledge, food management, and structured deposition, deserve further elaboration.

Exotic non-local items are a repeated, though not invariable, inclusion in late Bandkeramik grave deposits. These include schist and hard-stone bracelets and *Spondylus*, *Cardium*, and *Purpura lapillus* ornaments. It is likely that such artefacts were the subject of circulation and exchange over considerable distances and that Bandkeramik mortuary practices articulated closely with exchange networks. Material objects evolve their own life histories. A schist bracelet, for example, may carry with it and evoke a folk memory of its maker, previous owners, and the social relationships between the various characters, alive and dead, with which the object was associated. Deposition of the schist bracelet in a grave removes the object from circulation. It may no longer contribute to the mediation of human relationships by its passage from one individual to another or by its reciprocal exchange for another item or service. It is possible that knowledge of an object's history may have been limited or guarded. However, by incorporation into a grave deposit, that knowledge may have become subject to even closer control. That is to say, the object became an absent presence within social discourse. A full exegesis of the artefact's biography came to include a personal or folk memory of the final deposition of the object and associated fields of knowledge and understanding of the world, including, for example, the consolidation of lineage identity, the understanding of ancestral history, or the securing of economic and social reproduction.

The immediate sealing of most late and post-Bandkeramik pit graves suggests that mortuary deposits were foci of discrete and possibly short-term events. The general absence of intersecting grave cuts may imply that graves were marked, at least in the short term. However, mortuary deposits appear not to have been invoked in social practice subsequent to their sealing. Opportunities to experience open mortuary structures and associated deposits may therefore have been restricted in time as well as in space. Knowledge of the event and the material incorporated into a grave depended on personal presence or folk memory.

However, patterns of social practice are never absolute. Recent excavations of six Villeneuve-Saint-Germain graves at Villeneuve-la-Guyard suggest that bodies may have been occasionally deposited in graves capped with organic material (Prestreau 1992). This practice, reported also at Elsloo in the Netherlands (Modderman 1975), may pre-empt the timber- and stone-lined/capped graves of some middle Neolithic I (Cerny) contexts, including wooden cists at Passy-sur-Yonne and stone-capped graves at Orville and Malesherbes (Loiret) (Duhamel & Prestreau 1991; Simonin 1991). Open graves/cists may have allowed the viewing of bodies and associated material deposits before final interment. Viewing the formally prepared grave may have heightened or focussed people's awareness of the artefact biographies, social identities, and group genealogies symbolised and embodied by the body and grave deposits. One may also see here a possible root for the stone cist and megalith tradition of the Cerny of the Essonne valley and accessible megalithic chambers in other parts of northern France.

Certain categories of material are repeatedly absent from graves, or are only present in certain circumstances. Chief amongst these are animal bones. Whilst bone points and polissoirs occasionally occur in late Bandkeramik graves, as at Berry-au-Bac (Aisne) (Lasserre & Dubouloz 1982), the association between the dead and animals remains weak before the advent of middle Neolithic I (Cerny) contexts. The principal exception is a single child inhumation incorporated into the lower fill of ditch segment 2 of the Menneville enclosure, a fill which also incorporates a range of articulated animal remains (Coudart & Demoule 1982; Ilett et al., this volume). In certain contexts the human body may have been juxtaposed with novel resources, such as domesticated animals, in an attempt to mediate new ways of looking at, categorising, and understanding the world. Whether or not the human body evoked traditional sets of meanings, it became part of a repertoire of symbols through which people structured and came to know the world at large. During the early Neolithic this process of cognitive mapping took on new form as fresh relationships were negotiated with novel resources (domesticates, pottery), structural forms (long-houses, monuments), and people (the direct resource-productive unit, marriage and exchange networks, and temporary groupings for constructional projects, herding, crop management, and hunting). In short, the human body – as symbol of society and self – was probably invoked in those strategies for the domestication of place, resources, social relationships, and self which characterised the early Neolithic.

The insertion of graves into long-house flanking-pits and enclosure ditches may be part of a broader strategy of incorporation into specific forms of pre-existing context. A double Bandkeramik inhumation at La Pente de Croupeton, Jablines (Seine-et-Marne) was inserted into a pit containing decorated and undecorated sherds, an antler pick, two bone polissoirs, one bone point, one *Cardium* shell, and flint tools including a scraper, sickle blade, and backed knife (Bailloud 1969: 411– 413). The human body may have been just one category of material mobilised in the construction of certain forms of structured deposit drawn upon in the process of categorising and understanding the world (Richards & Thomas 1984). Commemoration of this practice may well be seen in middle Neolithic I (Cerny) contexts at Marolles-sur-Seine and Les Fiefs, Orville (Mordant 1980; Simonin 1991) where pottery was incorporated into grave fills, perhaps recalling the structured deposits with which some Bandkeramik graves had once been associated.

The composition of flanking pit deposits vary widely, and may include pottery, worked flint, animal bone, schist bracelets, daub, and quern-stones. Many of these categories represent novel forms of material culture to Neolithic society and may reference new or elaborated Mesolithic fields of social practice such as storage, the management of domesticated plants and animals, food processing, hunting, and exchange relations. Incorporation of the human body – symbolising the lineage identity and kinship, economic, and exchange relations – may have been a method of inserting society itself into a symbolic microcosm of the world.

LINEAR ENCLOSURES: MIDDLE NEOLITHIC I (CERNY)

Long-houses with Cerny associations are as yet little known in the Paris basin. Consequently, continued association of graves with long-houses cannot be demonstrated. The rite of simple pit-grave inhumation is known to continue, as, for example, at Marolles-sur-Seine, Noyen-sur-Seine, and La Chapelle-Saint-Mesmin (Duday et al. 1990; Mordant 1980). However, Cerny funerary contexts also herald a range of original mortuary practices and monumental forms.

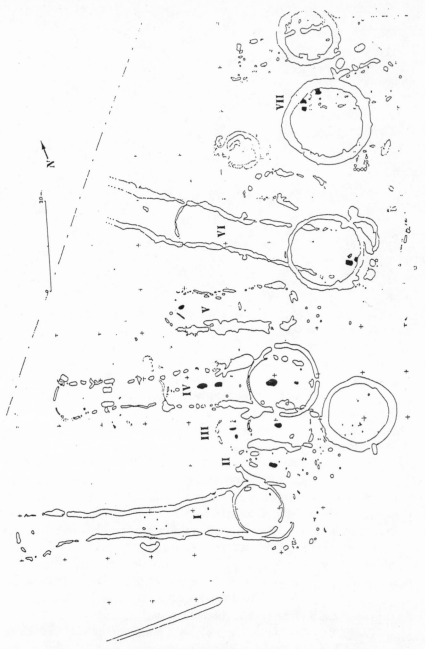

Figure 1. Linear enclosures at Passy-sur-Yonne (secteur Richebourg) (after Duhamel & Prestreau 1991).

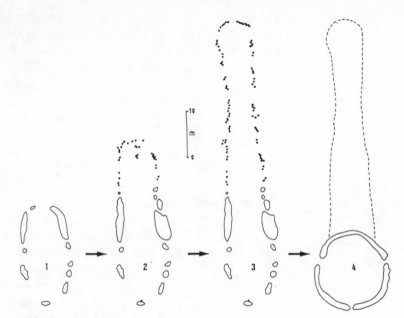

Figure 2. Constructional phases of Monument 4, Passy-sur-Yonne (secteur Richebourg) (after Duhamel & Prestreau 1991).

Aerial photography is currently revealing the presence of linear and trapezoidal enclosures on the valley floors and middle slopes of limestone plateaux throughout the southern Paris basin and Lower Normandy (Duhamel & Prestreau 1991: 113; Jean Desloges, pers. comm.) These monuments are generically known as Passy-style enclosures after the type-site of Passy-sur-Yonne, Yonne (Fig. 1). However, it is clear that such blanket classification masks the diversity of structural forms and social practices represented by these monuments. In this paper the generic term linear enclosures will be used to refer to this disparate collection of monumental forms.

Structural forms vary widely, including trapezoidal, rectangular, oval, and cigar-shaped ditched enclosures. Ditches are in some cases continuous and in others segmented. The western end of certain monuments may have been demarcated by posts rather than by a ditch, as, for example, at Passy-sur-Yonne Monument 4. Some enclosures feature palisading within ditches, as at Passy-sur-Yonne Monument 4, while others do not. Similarly, some monuments at Passy-sur-Yonne may have enclosed a low mound, although again this is an aspect of monument variability rather than a characteristic of all linear enclosures (Duhamel & Prestreau 1991; Mordant 1991). Small wood- or stone-lined cists and deep pit graves are frequently aligned axially, although not all linear enclosures feature a mortuary component. It is the spatial and social context of these single and double inhumations that are of particular interest here. In what range of physical, symbolic, and social contexts were the dead placed? How were funerals, mortuary paraphernalia, and monuments experienced by the living? And how did these experiences relate to processes for the constitution of social relations during the Neolithic?

Projects, tradition, and re-invention

Linear enclosures appear to have been settings for sequences or contemporaneous suites of events. The time-scale of events is currently unknown. However, ditches were frequently recut (Duhamel & Prestreau 1991: 105), enclosures were extended, and, in some cases, ring ditches were placed over eastern terminals (ibid.: 104). Figure 2 illustrates the sequence of construction at Passy-sur-Yonne Monument 4 (secteur Richebourg). Elaboration may be a process of both drawing upon the past and a rethinking of that past. That is to say, monumental texts may have been re-written, thereby redefining their significance within the physical and social landscape and influencing interpretations of the world in line with the interests of particular groups within society (Thomas 1991: 10). At Passy-sur-Yonne graves may have been inserted into monuments as a means of sanctifying each new phase of elaboration and re-writing (see, for example, Phases 1, 2, and 4 of Monument 4). This practice may commemorate or inculcate that which is beyond the monument itself. It may facilitate a presencing of the otherwise absent. In this case the basic rites, material paraphernalia, and knowledges of the Bandkeramik funeral may have been re-invoked. At the same time a matrix of intertextuality is generated as monuments explicitly refer to earlier practices, places, beliefs, and cultural values. Thus, the past is presenced, yet in ways which might render it a technology for rethinking traditional values.

Linear enclosures may have represented a new way of mapping the physical and cognised landscape as the greater exploitation of the limestone plateaux, involving cycles of seasonal pastoralism and/or hunting, began to alter traditional perceptions of the world. The construction of linear monuments and causewayed enclosures, near which linear enclosures are frequently located (Duhamel & Prestreau 1991: 113), achieves an original cognitive mapping and a domestication of space and social order through tradition, memory, and invention. For instance, Bandkeramik funerary rites and a linear ordering of space, perhaps recalling the long-house, may have been re-invoked in novel circumstances within the context of the linear enclosure. The intention may have been to legitimise new strategies for the exploitation of space, time, and resources through reference to traditional concepts or themes, such as the dead as ancestors and as symbols of continuity from past to present.

Activities involving fire may also have been important at linear enclosures. Lenses of ash were deposited within the fill of the ring-ditch of Monument 4 at Passy-sur-Yonne (secteur Richebourg). Deposits of ash were also made in small pits at Passy-sur-Yonne, although the precise relation of pits, enclosures, and graves is uncertain. The cremated remains of a child were also deposited in a pit within Passy-sur-Yonne Monument 6 (Duhamel & Prestreau 1991: 111). In various ways fire, an agent and potent symbol of transformation (Lévi-Strauss 1969), may have metaphorically referenced the rites of passage associated with death (Van Gennep 1960). Rupture of the social fabric by death necessitates a re-negotiation of social position and responsibility. The transformation of society and personal identity from one state to another via a liminal period of instability is mirrored and symbolically represented by the transformation of the body to the state of dry, 'safe' bones, the realm of the dead, via the wetness and 'danger' of bodily decay. The invocation of fire in this process may indicate a need for greater elaboration and ritual management of the passage from life to death. Social stability may have been threatened at this time by expansion into new parts of the landscape, an expansion which increased physical and social distances between reproductive units and co-operative groups. Thus, the safe reproduction of the lineage structure, and not least the passage from living being to ancestor, may have taken on heightened significance.

Monuments and structuration

So far it has been argued that mortuary structures associated with linear enclosures were elements within material complexes, and that these complexes were the material residues of suites of social action. The question remains, how were these complexes experienced, perceived, interpreted, and understood during the Neolithic? I do not claim to recover original meaning. Rather, my comments are in the nature of reflection upon some possibilities of bodily access, sensory perception, interpretation, and understanding (see note 1). It is not unreasonable to suggest that presence during those critical events which gave structure to linear enclosures may have facilitated particular and novel forms of understanding. Experience and participation in the cutting and recutting of ditches, the elongation and amendment of the monumental form, and the deposition of human remains and material culture are clearly crucial events. It is not enough to discuss the subsequent encounter with what we today would call the 'completed monument'. Readings of monuments as texts typically assume that actors interact with and interpret completed monuments. A linear progression of activities is implied. One must first build a monument before one can experience and interpret it. To the contrary, monuments are never really ever completed. Even today we busy ourselves with transforming monuments by, for example, excavation, reconstruction, restoration, and the writing of texts. In addition, the reading of a monument is an ongoing process. It begins during construction, during the deposition of material culture, during actions upon the material world. Archaeologists need to think about monuments less as constructions and more as 'structurations', as building projects caught up in the dialectical and reflexive interaction between self, others, and specific material and historical conditions (Gadamer 1975; Giddens 1979). The physical landscape which we build and, simultaneously, alter, investigate, and interpret cannot be divorced from the process of structuration. From this it follows that monuments, are not constructions which stand apart from the social practices which produce and give meaning to them, but are aspects of the on-going process of structuration itself. Monumental building projects were the medium and outcome of social practice as people drew upon material resources and cultural pre-understandings (Gadamer 1975) to produce potentially novel and competing perceptions and embodiments of the world and the place of society and the self within it.

Monuments may also remain as conspicuous features within prehistoric landscapes in the long-term. They are likely to have been the subject of human experience and interpretation over considerable spans of time. For example, linear enclosures (obviously) circumscribe and order space into a linear structure. It is no longer novel to suggest that experience of the enclosure may therefore have occurred as a linear procession. Post-built 'corridors' leading up to graves within two of the enclosures at Passy-sur-Yonne may have acted as guides to such procession (Duhamel & Prestreau 1991: 105). Large posts at the entrance to Monument 6 (secteur Richebourg) may also have acted as frames directing the approach and thus the reading of the monument. Various architectural elements may therefore have encouraged the adoption of certain bodily postures, avenues of approach to, and views and perspectives of the monument. The material form of the monument may have acted, at least to some extent, in a didactic fashion. Experience and interpretation may have been guided by control exercised over means of access to the monument. In this way specific readings may have been elicited, with the result that experience, perception, and knowledge of the world – in short, aspects of one's subjective being – may have been guided in certain preferred directions.

Technologies of tradition and memory operating in the long-term may also be seen at Les Réaudins, Balloy (Seine-et-Marne) where Ville-neuve-Saint-Germain long-houses and graves were elaborated to incorporate a group of linear enclosures (Fig. 6). That a late Neolithic collective grave was subsequently inserted into Monument 3 (Mordant 1991) may indicate the significance of the location over a period of more than a millennium. Similarly, at Villeneuve-la-Guyard, the site of Villeneuve-Saint-Germain long-houses and graves was elaborated to include successive Cerny and Noyen enclosures (Prestreau 1992). Perhaps significantly, the main group of four long-houses is incorporated within the two concentric enclosures, whilst the principal group of graves lies outside the area selected for subsequent enclosure. The dead may therefore have been extraneous, counter or alien to the sets of meanings mediated at these particular middle Neolithic enclosures. However, not all enclosures mediate the same cultural issues, as human remains have been recovered at other middle Neolithic enclosures. For example, skulls and articulated long bones were incorporated into refuse deposits within the enclosure at Noyen-sur-Seine (Mordant & Mordant 1977: 247–248).

Why did these technologies of tradition and memory develop at this particular juncture in prehistory? The post-Bandkeramik period undoubtedly witnessed changing patterns of settlement and subsistence, but a newly structured landscape – of which monuments were a part – was also created. The evocation of tradition and memory within monuments may therefore have been important in maintaining and legitimating a newly established social and material order. The incorporation of ancestral remains into some of these monuments may have consolidated sentiments of belief, trust, and belonging within this new order.

CEMETERIES AND SÉPULTURES SOUS DALLE

Recent excavations in the Essonne valley have assessed the nature of *sépultures sous dalle* (single and double inhumations sealed beneath large stone slabs) at La Chaise and Les Marsaules, Malesherbes (Loiret) and Les Fiefs, Orville (Loiret) (Richard & Vintrou 1980; Richard et al. 1986; Simonin 1991). At La Chaise, Malesherbes, the *sépulture sous dalle* features one adult female and one adolescent interred in a crouched position with two burins and four blades and is located on the periphery of a cobbled area measuring some 35 metres by 20 metres (Fig. 3). A further Neolithic inhumation, a crouched adult female burial with one polished axe and three blades, lies within ten metres of the *sépulture sous dalle*. The western part of the paved area seals a large pit ca 20 m x 10 m and 1 m deep, excavated into the limestone bedrock. The pit was back-filled, perhaps after a short hiatus, with stone grubbed up from the land-surface, not with the material excavated from the pit. The process of back-filling, possibly occurring during more than one episode, included the incorporation of sherds, flint flakes, charcoal, animal bone, and fragments of sandstone quern (an invocation of the forms of structured deposition associated with Bandkeramik pits?) The paving which overlies the pit is doubled along its extreme southern flank. A series of posts, possibly representing several episodes of activity although generally demarcating a rectilinear space, were inserted into the cobbled surface. A small ash-filled pit is located on the edge of the paved area and a small menhir erected near the *sépulture sous dalle* (Allain 1981; Despriée 1983; Despriée 1986; Richard & Vintrou 1980).

The *sépulture sous dalle* at Les Marsaules, Malesherbes, situated within 500 m of La Chaise, incorporates a male adult interred without material associations in a large pit, back-filled with earth and sealed by a large sandstone slab (Fig. 4) (Richard et al. 1986). The environs of the *sépulture sous dalle* were apparently not elaborated as at La Chaise. At Orville a single *sépulture sous dalle*, an adult interred with a boar's tusk, two projectile points, a retouched blade, and a piece of black mineral, is at the centre of a cemetery of 20 single inhumations (Fig. 5). The other graves, 18 flexed burials and one prone inhumation, vary in 'richness', and include undecorated bowls, polished axes, greenstone pendants, perforated deer teeth, shell beads, projectile points, a quernstone, a flint tranchet, scraper, blades and, flakes. Hearths mark the southern and north-eastern limits of the cemetery. Structured deposits of sandstone blocks, animal remains, and pottery are also part of the complex (Fig. 5) (Simonin 1991).

The digging and back-filling of pits, fire-setting, and the structured deposition of stone, animal bone, and pottery are amongst the suites of social action that can be identified at La Chaise, Les Marsaules, and Orville. As at linear enclosures, the reading or interpretation of

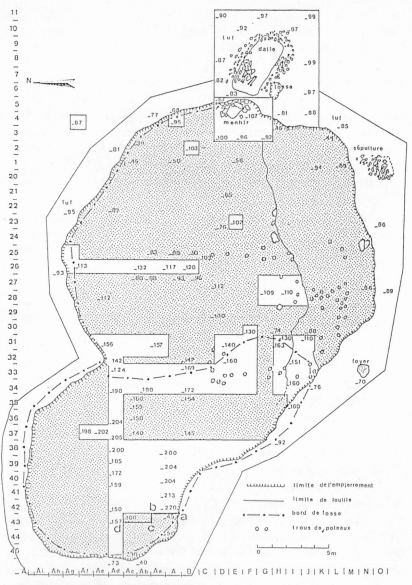

Figure 3. La Chaise, Malesherbes (Loiret). Note the 'sépulture sous dalle', *single inhumation, pit (fosse), paving (empierrement), post holes (trous de poteaux), and hearth (foyer) (after Despriée 1986).*

material space began during the very writing of the material text. That is not to say that I sense any original or intentional authorial meaning. Rather, like any subsequent reader the author is drawn to read mean-

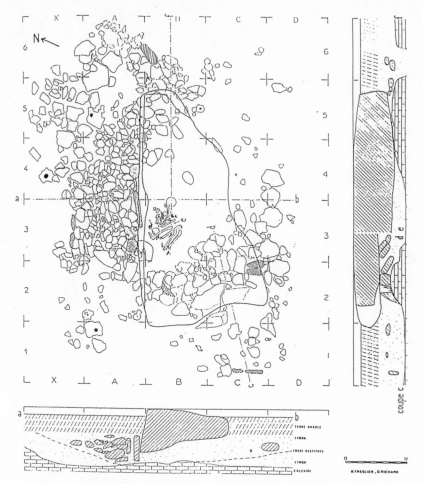

Figure 4. 'Sépulture sous dalle' *at Les Marsaules, Malesherbes (Loiret) (after Richard et al. 1986).*

ing into his or her text in the action of writing. Structuration, that process of simultaneous writing, reading, and transformation, takes on special importance where a manifestation of the material text is so transient that opportunities to read it are severely restricted in time and space.

The spatial organisation of La Chaise and Orville may also implement technologies of tradition and memory. Hearths, alignments of posts, a stone menhir, material deposits, and visible mortuary structures such as the *sépulture sous dalle*: all may have had a mnemonic function in guiding people around sites and in evoking memories, emo-

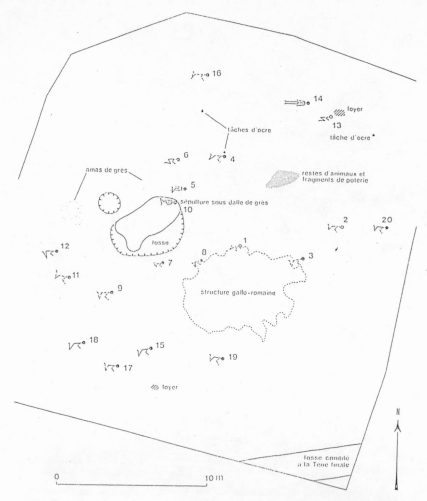

Figure 5. Cerny cemetery and 'sépulture sous dalle' at Les Fiefs, Orville (Loiret) (after Simonin 1991).

tions, and traditional beliefs. As was argued in discussing linear enclosures, these techniques of spatial organisation may have evoked specific forms of understanding of the world and of one's place within it.

ANIMALS IN CERNY MORTUARY CONTEXTS

Earlier remarks on material deposition within late Bandkeramik and Villeneuve-Saint-Germain graves, and especially its status as a material text to be written and read via the sentient body, could also apply to

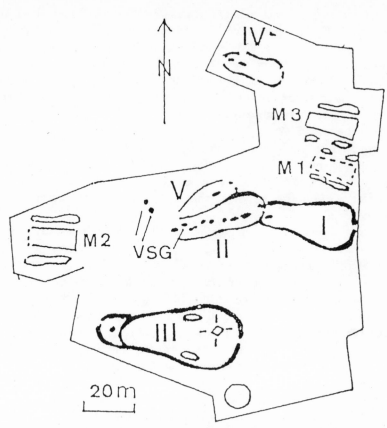

Figure 6. Plan of Les Réaudins, Balloy (Seine-et-Marne) M1-M3, Villeneuve-Saint-Germain long-houses; VSG, Villeneuve-Saint-Germain graves; I-V, linear enclosures; lozenge, Late Neolithic collective inhumation (after Mordant 1991).

the crouched and prone Cerny burials which occur within linear enclosures and cemeteries or as *sépultures sous dalle* and isolated graves. However, one important innovation is the frequent incorporation of animal remains within grave deposits. Significantly, wild animals are the chief referent. For example, boar's tusks are deposited in Grave 10 (the *sépulture sous dalle*) at Orville, Grave 5 (Monument 1) at Les Réaudins, in the grave associated with Monument 13 at Passy-sur-Yonne (secteur Sablonnière), and in a Cerny grave at Noyen-sur-Seine (Duhamel & Prestreau 1991; Mordant 1980; Mordant 1991; Simonin 1991). The bones and talons of birds of prey were recovered from Grave 5 (Monument 1) and Grave 7 (Monument 2) at Les Réaudins (Mordant 1991). Tools manufactured from deer long bones occur at

Noyen-sur-Seine and La Chapelle-Saint-Mesmin (Duday et al. 1990; Mordant 1980) and perforated deer teeth in three graves at Orville (Simonin 1991). Frequent deposition of projectile points, as at Les Réaudins (Grave 3, Monument 1; Grave 7, Monument 2), Graves 10 and 12 at Orville, and seven graves at Passy-sur-Yonne may, along with wild animal remains, reference the hunt and its importance within Cerny subsistence strategies. It has already been noted that expansion beyond the gravel terraces of the Paris basin, a process perhaps begun during the late Bandkeramik and post-Bandkeramik, continued apace according to the distribution of middle Neolithic I (Cerny) material on middle and upper plateaux. Cerny grave deposits may reference the importance of hunting as part of this process of cognitive mapping of the landscape.

At Rots, Calvados, Lower Normandy, a sheep was interred in one of the axial graves of a linear enclosure (Jean Desloges, pers. comm.). This deposit may be a rehearsal of the practice of 'treating as human' those animal resources deemed to be of crucial economic or symbolic importance, thereby sanctifying the animal's position within the subsistence strategies and categorical systems of human society (Bloch & Parry 1982; Thomas 1988: 549). Animals may have been fundamental to societal reproduction either as food resources (although it is unlikely that sheep were a critical food source in the earlier Neolithic) or as components of those conceptual frameworks through which the world is categorised, known, and understood. As part of that package of novel resources through which Neolithic societies re-thought the landscape, social relations, and self, sheep may have been drawn upon as a symbol of changing attitudes towards the world. This process encompassed the domestication of space through monumental construction and the formation and dissolution of transient networks of co-operation and competition in the performance of tasks and projects, including the construction of houses, monuments, and enclosures, food production and processing, exchange, and human reproduction.

CONCLUSION

During the earlier Neolithic of the Paris basin, death and mortuary practice were deeply embedded within the cultural and economic fabric of society. Strategic manipulation of the human body, mortuary deposits, and funerary structures contributed to the reproduction of the lineage formation, not least through conceptual and symbolic links forged between mortuary practice, the control of genealogical knowledge, food production and processing, exchange relations, the structured deposition of material culture, the engendering of social practice, and changing patterns of settlement and subsistence.

The material world is encountered and imbued with meaning through the medium of the sentient human body situated within specific historic fields of social discourse. Every experience brings with it a reading of material texts, an understanding of their place in the social order, and thus a greater understanding of that order and one's place within it. Readings of space may therefore be guided by the structure and form of space itself. In this paper the spatial organisation of funerary contexts has been interpreted as part of a process whereby ambiguity and plurality of meaning were mediated in the struggle between interest groups within Neolithic society.

Also, building and interpretation of the built landscape cannot be separated; they are sides of the same coin, facets of a single process: structuration. The built landscape of Neolithic monuments cannot therefore be considered as constructions, as having beginning and end, as working towards their own completion. Rather, monuments are themselves 'structurations', indissolubly tied to that process of material production and interpretation which is social practice.

ACKNOWLEDGEMENTS

Thanks to Ian Kinnes and Gillian Varndell for stimulating discussions on the relationship between materiality and structuration. My printed thoughts on the subject are, of course, my own responsibility.

NOTE

A textual metaphor today has common currency as an aid to the conceptualisation of human experience and interpretation of the material world. That is to say, both texts and the material world become rapidly divorced from their contexts of production (Ricoeur 1981). Rather, they are read by people located within successive and changing historical and social settings. However, in my view the textual metaphor does not fully capture the essence of human experience in and of the material world. The textual model evokes a linear ordering of both the text and the ways in which it may be read. To the contrary, archaeologists deal with webs and matrices of social practice. People wander across and through material texts via many different trajectories. Neither the text nor human experience of it is strictly linear. People see and touch things, they interpret material culture and space in the construction of a world order and their place within it. Indeed, herein lies a further limitation of the textual metaphor, for it does not adequately express the sentience of that experience which gives rise to interpretation of the material world. Perception and interpretation are grounded in bodily experience; in seeing, hearing, touching, and smelling. The material world has no meaning outside of its dialogical relation with the sentient human agent. The relation is one of dialogue because experience of the material world produces meaning, it illuminates and brings order to that world; yet human subjectivity is also itself re-constituted in this process, as it re-finds its place within a social order under constant renegotiation. The dialogue between subjectivity and materiality is of course historically and socially situated. Experience and interpretation are produced at the interface with an era's historical and contingent fields of discourse and knowledge. It is within the context of one's relations with other people and within fields of power, knowledge, and ideology that the sentient human experience and interpretation of materiality takes place.

BIBLIOGRAPHY

Agache, R. 1968. Circonscription de Nord et Picardie. *Gallia Préhistoire* 11: 267–309.

Allain, J. 1981. Circonscription du Centre. *Gallia Préhistoire* 24: 329–363.

Bailloud, G. 1969. Circonscription de la région parisienne. *Gallia Préhistoire* 12: 401–415.

Bloch, M. & Parry, J. 1982. Introduction: death and the regeneration of life. In Bloch, M., and Parry, J. (eds), *Death and the Regeneration of Life*, pp. 1–44. Cambridge: Cambridge University Press.

Bostyn, F., Hachem, L., & Lanchon, Y. 1991. Le site néolithique de 'la Pente de Croupeton' à Jablines (Seine-et-Marne). Premiers résultats. In *Actes du 15ème Colloque Interrégional sur le Néolithique, Châlons-en-Champagne 1988*, pp. 45–81. Association Régional pour la Protection et l'Etude du Patrimoine Préhistorique.

Bourdieu, P. 1977. *Outline of a Theory of Practice*. Cambridge: Cambridge University Press.

Burkill, M. 1983. The middle Neolithic of the Paris basin and north-eastern France. In Scarre, C. (ed.), *Ancient France*, pp. 34–61. Edinburgh: Edinburgh University Press.

Conkey, M. W. & Gero, J. M. 1991. Tensions, pluralities, and engendering archaeology: an introduction to women and prehistory. In Gero, J. M. & Conkey, M. W. (eds), *Engendering Archaeology. Women and Prehistory*, pp. 3–30. Oxford: Blackwell.

Coudart, A. & Demoule, J.-P. 1982. Le site néolithique et chalcolithique de Menneville. In *Vallée de l'Aisne: Cinq Années de Fouilles Protohistoriques*, pp. 129–147. (Revue Archéologique de Picardie, Numéro Spécial.)

Despriée, J. 1983. Circonscription du Centre. *Gallia Préhistoire* 26: 249–281.

Despriée, J. 1986. Circonscription du Centre. *Gallia Préhistoire* 29: 293–320.

Duday, H., Richard, G., & Verjux, C. 1990. La sépulture double de La Chapelle-Saint-Mesmin (Loiret) dans le cadre du néolithique de la Loire moyenne. In *17ème Colloque Interrégional sur le Néolithique, Vannes 1990. Résumés des communications et présentation des sites visités*, pp. 35–36.

Duhamel, P. & Prestreau, M. 1991. La nécropole monumentale néolithique de Passy dans le contexte de gigantisme-funéraire européen. In *Actes du 14eme Colloque Interrégional sur le Néolithique. La région centre – carrefour d'influences? Blois 1987*, pp. 103–117. (Supplément au Bulletin de la Société Archéologique Scientifique et Littéraire du Vendômois.)

Flax, J. 1987. Postmodernism and gender relations in feminist theory. *Signs: Journal of Women in Culture and Society* 12 (4): 621–643.

Foucault, M. 1986. *The History of Sexuality*, vol. 3. *The Care of the Self*. Harmondsworth: Penguin.

Gadamer, H.-G. 1975. *Truth and Method*. London: Sheed and Ward.

Giddens, A. 1979. *Central Problems in Social Theory. Action, Structure and Contradiction in Social Analysis*. London: MacMillan.

Hodder, I. 1990. *The Domestication of Europe. Structure and Contingency in Neolithic Societies*. Oxford: Blackwell.

Ilett, M. 1983. The early Neolithic of north-eastern France. In Scarre, C. (ed.), *Ancient France*, pp. 6–33. Edinburgh: Edinburgh University Press.

Joly, J. 1970. Circonscription de Bourgogne. *Gallia Préhistoire* 13: 411–458.

Kahn, J. 1981. Marxist anthropology and segmentary societies: a review of the literature. In Kahn, J. & Llobera, J. (eds), *The Anthropology of Pre-Capitalist Societies*, pp. 57–88. London: Macmillan.

Lasserre, M. & Dubouloz, J. 1981. Le site de Berry-au-Bac (La Croix-Maigret) Néolithique-Chalcolithique-Age du Fer. In *Les Fouilles Protohistoriques dans la Vallée de l'Aisne* 9. Paris: Université de Paris I.

Leach, E. 1966. Ritualization in man in relation to conceptual and social development. *Philosophical Transactions of the Royal Society* (series B) 251: 403–408.

Lévi-Strauss, C. 1969. *The Raw and the Cooked*. London: Jonathan Cape.

Meillassoux, C. 1978. 'The economy' in agricultural self-sustaining societies. In Seddon, D. (ed.), *Relations of Production: Marxist Approaches to Economic Anthropology*, pp. 127–157. London: Frank Cass and Co.

Modderman, P. 1975. Elsloo, a Neolithic farming community in the Netherlands. In Bruce-Mitford, R. (ed.), *Recent Archaeological Excavations in Europe*, pp. 260–286. London: Routledge and Kegan Paul.

Moore, H. 1986. *Space, Text and Gender: An Anthropological Study of the Marakwet of Kenya*. Cambridge: Cambridge University Press.

Mordant, D. 1980. Rapports entre le Cerny et les groupes de l'est de la France. In *Préhistoire et Protohistoire en Champagne-Ardenne*, pp. 89–89. Châlons-sur-Marne: Association d'Etudes Préhistoriques et Protohistoriques de Champagne-Ardenne.

Mordant, D. 1991. Le site des Réaudins à Balloy (Seine-et-Marne). Premiers résultats. In *Actes du 15ème Colloque Interrégional sur le Néolithique, Châlons-en-Champagne 1988*, pp. 33–43. Association Régional pour la Protection et l'Etude du Patrimoine Préhistorique.

Parker Pearson, M. 1982. Mortuary practices, society and ideology: an ethno-archaeological study. In Hodder, I. (ed.), *Symbolic and Structural Archaeology*, pp. 99–113. Cambridge: Cambridge University Press.

Prestreau, M. 1992. Le site néolithique et protohistorique des Falaises de Prépoux à Villeneuve-la-Guyard (Yonne). *Gallia Préhistoire* 34: 171–207.

Richard, G., Jagu, D., Girard, C., Guillon, F., & Girard, M. 1986. La sépulture néolithique des 'Marsaules' commune de Malesherbes (Loiret) et les sépultures sous dalle du groupe Essonne-Juine. *Revue Archéologique du Loiret* 12: 16–34.

Richard, G. & Vintrou, J. 1980. Les sépultures néolithiques sous dalles des 'Marsaules' et de 'La Chaise' à Malesherbes (Loiret). *Préhistoire et Protohistoire en Champagne-Ardenne*, pp. 175–181. Châlons-sur-Marne: Association d'Etudes Préhistoriques et Protohistoriques de Champagne-Ardenne.

Richards, C. & Thomas, J. 1984. Ritual activity and structured deposition in later Neolithic Wessex. In Bradley, R. & Gardiner, J. (eds), *Neolithic Studies: A Review of Some Current Research*, pp. 189–218. Oxford: British

Archaeological Reports (British Series 133).

Ricoeur, P. 1981. *Hermeneutics and the Human Sciences*. Cambridge: Cambridge University Press.

Shanks, M. 1992. *Experiencing the Past*. London: Routledge.

Shanks, M. & Tilley, C. 1982. Ideology, symbolic power and ritual communication: a reinterpretation of Neolithic mortuary practices. In Hodder, I. (ed.), *Symbolic and Structural Archaeology*, pp. 129–154. Cambridge: Cambridge University Press.

Simonin, D. 1991. Premières données sur la nécropole des Fiefs à Orville (Loiret) et remarques à propos de la culture de Cerny. In *Actes du 14eme Colloque Interrégional sur le Néolithique. La région centre – carrefour d'influences? Blois 1987*, pp. 53–68. (Supplément au Bulletin de la Société Archéologique Scientifique et Littéraire du Vendômois.)

Soudsky, B., et al. 1982. L'habitat néolithique et chalcolithique de Cuiry-lès-Chaudardes/Les Fontinettes-les-Gravelines (1972–1977). In *Vallée de l'Aisne: Cinq Années de Fouilles Protohistoriques*, pp. 57–119. (Revue Archéologique de Picardie, Numéro Spécial.)

Strathern M. 1980. No nature, no culture: the Hagen case. In MacCormack, C. P. & Strathern, M. (eds), *Nature, Culture and Gender*, pp. 174–222. Cambridge: Cambridge University Press.

Thomas, J. 1988. The social significance of Cotswold-Severn burial practices. *Man* 23: 540–559.

Thomas, J. 1991. Reading the Neolithic. *Anthropology Today* 7 (3): 9–11.

Van Gennep, A. 1960. *The Rites of Passage*. London: Routledge and Kegan Paul.

6

Enclosure and Burial in the Earliest Neolithic of the Aisne Valley

L. Hachem, Y. Guichard, J.-P. Farruggia, J. Dubouloz, and M. Ilett

The aim of this article is to present the results of excavation of a late Bandkeramik site at Menneville (Aisne *département*, north-eastern France), as these provide new information on the nature and possible functions of ditched enclosures of this period.

The late Bandkeramik dates to about 4900 cal. BC and marks the beginning of the Neolithic sequence in this part of the Paris basin, at the western end of early agricultural expansion across temperate Europe. Menneville is the easternmost of eleven late Bandkeramik settlements known from the 60 km stretch of the Aisne valley between the towns of Soissons and Neufchâtel-sur-Aisne (Fig. 1). Seven have been excavated on varying scales, mostly in advance of gravel quarrying, as part of a regional project investigating settlement organisation from the Neolithic through to the late Iron Age (Demoule & Ilett 1985; Ilett et al. 1982; Pion et al. 1990; Plateaux 1990).

As is the case elsewhere in the Bandkeramik world, the sites are multi-phase long-house settlements. So far as one can judge from the three sites that have been totally excavated in the course of the project, these settlements vary in terms of surface area from 1.4 to just over 6 hectares. This variation is more a reflection of the number of phases present on a site. It does not reflect major differences in actual settlement size. Menneville is exceptional in that it is the only settlement in

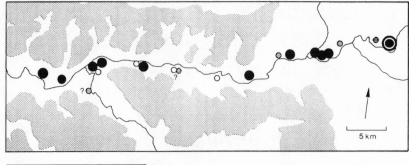

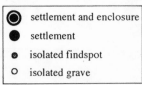

settlement and enclosure
settlement
isolated findspot
isolated grave

Figure 1. Distribution of late Bandkeramik sites in the river Aisne valley, east of Soissons. Shading indicates limestone plateau.

the region to be associated with a ditched enclosure, and the only site which has produced substantial numbers of burials.

The site is located on the first gravel terrace of the river Aisne, just east of the modern village, and overlooks an extensive expanse of flood-plain (Fig. 2). Another late Bandkeramik find spot is recorded just west of the village. The present-day course of the river lies 250 m to the south. Menneville has a long history of research, since two Neolithic graves were discovered during small-scale gravel quarrying in the 1930s. Aerial survey during the dry summer of 1976 revealed a single interrupted ditch, visible in the fields on either side of the early gravel pit, and possible long-houses in the field on the western side (Boureux 1982). A series of relatively small-scale excavations were undertaken by the project between 1976 and 1978, following up the aerial survey (Coudart & Demoule 1982). These confirmed the presence of long-houses belonging to a late Bandkeramik settlement, and indicated that the enclosure ditch was also of Neolithic date, although there was some hesitation about its exact position within the local sequence, which was not fully understood at the time. The ditch also produced two burials.

The real breakthrough came ten years later, with the opportunity to examine the whole of the eastern end of the site, now threatened by gravel extraction. By 1992 this was completely excavated, representing just over a quarter of the site's total surface area. At the same time,

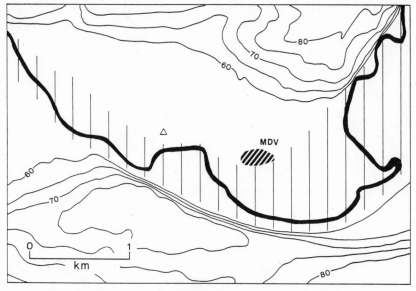

Figure 2. Location of the late Bandkeramik site at Menneville (MDV). Vertical lines: floodplain. Triangle: other late Bandkeramik find spot.

geophysical survey (undertaken by K. Anderson, R.A.A.P., Amsterdam) clarified the layout and extent of the enclosure to the west.

THE ENCLOSURE AND SETTLEMENT

Combining the aerial photographic, resistivity and excavation data, the enclosure is of roughly oval shape, 185 m x 350 m (Fig. 3). Part of the north-western edge disappears under the modern village. The surface enclosed is about 6 hectares, an area that coincides with the maximum size observed for late Bandkeramik settlement sites in the region. On the southern side, the ditch runs along the base of a slight slope, just above the flood-plain. The ditch segments vary in length, depth and profile. A V-shaped profile is quite common, and two relatively deep segments (1.7–2.5 m) show traces of upright posts set into the base of the ditch. One of these segments occupies a strangely isolated position within the enclosure. Two segments on the north-eastern side of the enclosure show signs, in plan if not in section, of re-cutting. The interruptions between ditch segments are usually less than 5 m wide. The 50 m gap in the south-eastern ditch circuit is partly a result of First World War disturbance in this area, and partly a result of enhanced erosion of the slope on the terrace edge. However, neither

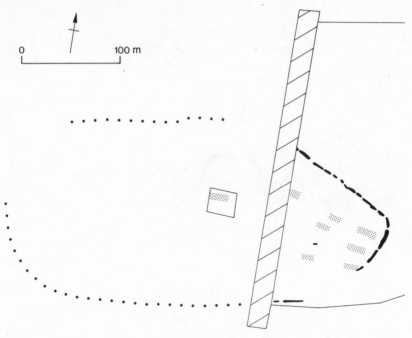

0   100 m

Figure 3. Schematic plan of the Menneville enclosure, showing the main excavated areas on either side of the early gravel pit (hatched). Shading: long-houses. Dotted line: reconstructed ditch circuit in the unexcavated parts of the site, based on aerial photography and geophysical survey.

factor satisfactorily accounts for the total absence here of even the slightest trace of a ditch. If the ditch had existed in this part of the site, it must have been considerably shallower than elsewhere.

Three post-hole alignments within the enclosure possibly indicate a palisade system (Fig. 4). Two are located within a few metres of the ditch, and one of these faces a relatively wide interruption. The third is set further back and is possibly related to the isolated segment of ditch located within the enclosure. Some post-holes could belong to a later, Iron Age settlement, however.

Most ditch sections indicate three main phases of fill. There is generally very little domestic refuse in any of the phases. The most significant aspect is the presence of burials or isolated human bones in six out of fifteen excavated segments. The burials are associated with the first phase of ditch fill, and will be described in more detail below. Decorated sherds from the first two phases of ditch fill date its construction to the late Bandkeramik, and this is confirmed by two radiocarbon dates from animal bone (Ly-1735, 6200 ± 190 uncal. bp; Ly-2324, 6110 ±

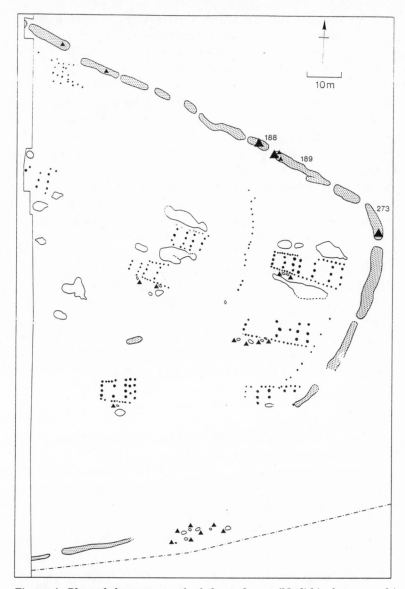

Figure 4. Plan of the eastern end of the enclosure (Neolithic features only). Shading: ditch; small triangles: single burials; large triangles: multiple burials.

140 uncal. bp; Evin et al. 1983: 106). The third, uppermost fill of the ditch contains some post-Bandkeramik Neolithic material, together with a few Iron Age artefacts.

The eight buildings (including the house excavated on the western part of the site) and their associated pits are all located within the enclosure. Extensive areas examined outside the enclosure, to the north and east, produced no trace of Neolithic occupation (Fig. 3). The precise chronological relationship between the enclosure and the long-houses is nevertheless uncertain. The eastern, entrance end of the best preserved building is separated by only 6 m from a substantial segment of ditch (Fig. 4). Just to the south, two more long-houses, poorly preserved, are also close to the ditch, the southernmost ground plan virtually touching the ditch, although the stratigraphic relationship was not visible. As has already been mentioned, the ditch fill contains very little domestic waste, despite the proximity of these buildings. On the grounds of these observations, we can suggest that this part of the enclosure was not in use at precisely the same time as the three long-houses. However, we may well be facing a complex sequence of events, with at least two settlement phases, to judge from the intercutting lateral pits of two other long-houses, and perhaps also different stages in the construction of the enclosure. Another possibility is that the enclosure was built around an abandoned settlement. Detailed ceramic phasing of the settlement has yet to be worked out, and in any case final interpretation of the possible relationships between long-houses and enclosure ditch will have to await the results from the western part of the site, as yet unexcavated on any scale.

THE BURIALS

The eastern and fully excavated part of the site has produced a large number of inhumation burials, representing at least thirty individuals of different ages and both sexes (Farruggia et al. in press). They occur in three different types of location (Fig. 4): just outside the south-eastern edge of the enclosure, within the settlement alongside buildings, and finally in the enclosure ditch.

The graves just outside the enclosure are located next to the apparent gap in the ditch circuit. They form a small group consisting of seven single inhumations. As these burials were found near the southern edge of the excavation, in an area of considerable modern disturbance, it is difficult to evaluate the original size of the group. These are flexed and ochred burials, with the head at the east, facing south. This is the normal position for late Bandkeramik burials in the region (Labriffe 1992). They are accompanied by decorated and undecorated ceramics. Two graves also contain flint artefacts and shell ornaments. There are five adults and two children. The four adults whose sex could be identified are all female. One of the adult graves had clearly been disturbed, and the corpse dismembered in the few months following burial. This had involved pulling off the right foot and both arms from the partially decomposed body.

Five of the seven long-houses on the eastern part of the site are associated with burials. The ten graves are located near the southern side of the buildings, either just outside, or in one case beneath, the southern wall. There are between one and four burials per house. With the exception of an immature male adult, all are children aged between three and seven. As was the case with the group outside the enclosure, the bodies are generally flexed on the left side, with the head at the east, facing south. Almost all the graves contain ochre and ceramic vessels. Other grave-goods include shell ornaments and one bone tool. The sub-adult grave produced no finds, but it had been heavily disturbed by animal burrows.

The ditch segments with burials occur on the northern side of the excavated part of the enclosure. The burials tend to be located near the ends of ditch segments, and all are contained within the first phase of ditch fill. The situation as regards the position, nature and associations of the skeletal remains is relatively complex. A basic distinction can be made between single and multiple inhumations.

The four single burials generally follow the classic pattern observed outside the ditch. The body is in a flexed position with the head at the east, looking south. Ochre is present in these graves. There are some shell or limestone beads, but unlike the graves outside the ditch, there are no ceramic vessels. One burial contains a cattle horn core and rib. All ages are represented, and at least one of the adults is male.

The pattern for the three multiple burials is, in every respect, quite different. Two are in fact double burials and the third contains the remains of seven individuals. One of the double burials occurs in a ditch segment which also contains two single burials. The positions of the skeletons in the multiple burials are unstandardised, not to say chaotic. There are no adults, and the age range is two to eight years, four to six being the most common. Ochre, ornaments and complete ceramic vessels are all absent.

The double grave in segment 273, the best preserved of the multiple burials, is located at the base of the ditch, near the southern end (Fig. 5). Side to side, but head to knees, the bodies are accompanied by fragmentary or complete cattle bones, two antler tools, a number of stones and several large sherds. There is also a scatter of animal bones (including a fragment of skull with horn core) along the base of the

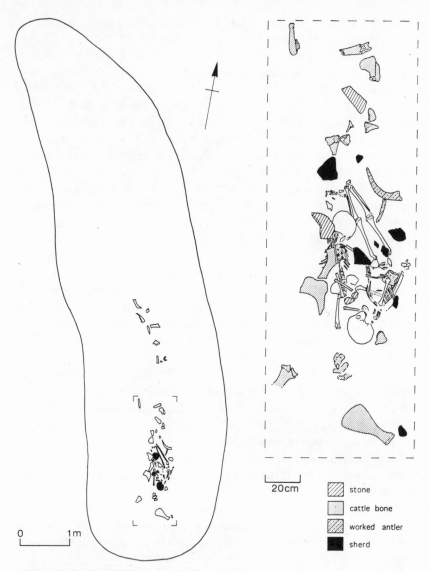

20cm

	stone
	cattle bone
	worked antler
	sherd

0   1m

Figure 5. Double child burial at the base of ditch segment 273 (depth ca 1.10 m).

ditch, outside the immediate area of the burials. The sherds belong to larger vessels than are present in the graves outside the ditch and it seems likely that they were originally deposited as fragments, rather than as complete vessels. The double burial at the north end of ditch segment 189 is stratigraphically later than a single burial at the same end. The skeletons belonging to the double burial are incomplete and

[134]

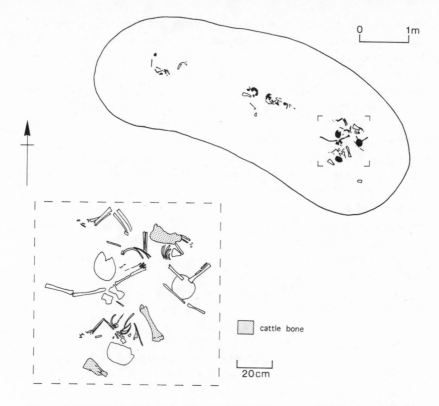

Figure 6. Multiple child burial at the base of ditch segment 188 (depth ca 1.0 m).

disturbed, perhaps due to burrowing. Here again, there are cattle and also caprovine bones.

The seven individuals in the next ditch segment, 188, form three groups, spread out along the whole of the ditch bottom, but all the evidence points to them having being buried together (Fig. 6). They are again associated with cattle and caprovine bones. Only one skeleton is more or less intact, and all seem to have been disturbed to differing degrees by animal burrowing. However, the detailed observations undertaken during excavation suggest that some human interference must have taken place. This could have happened shortly after burial in the ditch. Another possibility is that partially decomposed bodies from elsewhere were reburied in the ditch. In any case, the human bones show neither butchery marks nor traces of gnawing by animals.

The small assemblage of 120 animal bones from the multiple burials bears little resemblance to the faunal material from domestic refuse in the pits alongside long-houses (Desse 1976; Méniel 1984; Hachem

[135]

forthcoming). The material from the long-house pits is extremely fragmentary, with unidentifiable, splintered bones making up about 40% of the total number of fragments. There are no such fragments with the ditch burials. The animal bone fragments here are generally of large size, and their relatively good state of preservation probably reflects rapid circumstances of burial. Butchery marks are present, however, as well as typical fractures for extracting marrow. Another important difference from the settlement refuse is the fact that there are no bones of pig or of wild animals with the multiple burials, leaving aside the few antler tools. Wild animal bones constitute between 5% and 20% of the fauna in settlements from the Aisne valley. All the bones in burial context are of cattle or caprovines. The former are represented by a wide range of anatomical parts, with the exception of the tops of skulls and tails. The caprovine bones, however, are mainly limbs and some of these are articulated. It can be suggested that the selection of bones deposited with the burials reflects two forms of ceremonial behaviour. The cattle bones could be the remains of feasting prior to burial and the caprovine bones meat offerings for the graves.

The middle phase of ditch fill, above the layers containing the burials, is characterised by a similar if smaller assemblage of animal bones. There are also some isolated human bones of both adults and infants in this phase of fill. Perhaps the most significant feature of this phase, however, are three cattle bucrania. Two were found in segment 188, directly above two groups of skeletons, and the other comes from segment 189, slightly to the east of the burials. The bucrania are related, in our opinion, to the earlier child burials.

It is of course impossible to prove whether or not the three multiple burials were part of the same event. Nevertheless, several things point in this direction. The burials occur in a limited part of the ditch circuit. All are contained in a similar layer of ditch fill, composed of a fine grey sediment with flecks of charcoal. The cattle bones from the double burial in ditch segment 273 represent the remains of a minimum of four individuals only (two mature animals and two calves). All the cattle bones from the other multiple burials could, in theory, come from the same four animals. The minimum number of caprovines represented is only four, as well. On these grounds, one can easily envisage the sharing of meat, for consumption and deposition, in a single ceremony. The burials clearly took place in the same manner, with similar animal bone deposits and perhaps also similar commemoration ceremonies involving the placing (or suspension?) of cattle bucrania above the burials at a later date, after temporary disuse of the ditch.

DISCUSSION

Although we are only dealing with a 25% sample of the site, the data presented above are sufficient to underline its significance, both locally and in the broader context of the Bandkeramik culture. No other late Bandkeramik ditched sites are known from the region, despite the intensity of research into Neolithic enclosures, most of which are nearly a thousand years later than Menneville (Dubouloz et al. 1988; 1991). The discovery of a small cemetery adjacent to the settlement could be seen simply as chance. However, fieldwork on some, if not all, late Bandkeramik sites in the Aisne valley has involved the investigation of extensive areas around the settlements, either through trial-trenching or, more often, through routine rescue work in advance of gravel quarrying. Not one of these sites has produced a group of burials at the edge of the settlement. The presence of graves within the settlement is perhaps less exceptional. A number of sites contain apparently isolated adult burials, and the association of child burials with house plans can be seen on three sites other than Menneville. At Cuiry-lès-Chaudardes, the largest and most extensively excavated site, only three out of thirty-two long-houses are involved, and there is only one burial per building. The frequency of child burials alongside houses at Menneville is evidently much higher.

It has become apparent over the last decade or so, at least in the areas that have been subject to large-scale fieldwork, that substantial ditched enclosures are quite a regular feature of the settlement pattern in the loess regions of western central Europe occupied by Bandkeramik populations (Lüning 1988: Abb. 1; Schwellnus 1983: Abb. 15). With its surface area of 6 hectares, Menneville is rather larger than the examples currently known from these regions, where the area enclosed varies from as little as 0.4 to about 4 hectares. Many cover less than 1.5 hectares. Individual ditch segments are generally longer than at Menneville, which of course means that there are fewer interruptions in the ditch circuit. At Rosheim, in Alsace, however, recent excavations have shown that apparently continuous lengths of ditch can in fact be made up of series of inter-cutting short segments (Jeunesse 1992: 51). The large gap apparent in the south-eastern side of the enclosure at Menneville is matched by gaps of similar dimensions in the much smaller enclosure at Darion, in Belgium, although these are backed up by an internal palisade (Cahen et al. 1990: fig. 3). The post settings observed in the base of certain ditch segments at Menneville are also recorded from sites elsewhere (Ihmig 1971).

[137]

Most interpretations of the use of these enclosures mention a range of possibilities, from defensive to social or ceremonial functions. To judge from the variety of the evidence, it seems quite likely that enclosures were built for different purposes at different times. On some sites, as at Menneville, the ditches surround an area with buildings, which has tempted some to stress the defensive aspect (Keeley & Cahen 1989). Other enclosures were built adjacent to settlements or even on abandoned settlement areas. This is clearly the case with the three close-lying Langweiler enclosures on the Aldenhoven plateau, which belong to different phases at the very end of the long sequence of settlement proposed for the Merzbach valley (Stehli 1989: Abb. 11). In many of the loess regions, the decalcified subsoil does not preserve bone. Nevertheless, a small number of enclosures in Germany have produced human bone from the ditches, either in the form of single burials or isolated skeletal remains. Ditch burials include Köln-Lindenthal (Bernhardt 1986: 126) and Schwaigern (Planck 1983). Skeletal remains are also reported from Eilsleben (Kaufmann 1990: 21). The ditch fill of the recently excavated enclosure at Heilbronn-Neckargartach contained remains of at least three individuals, including a child (Schmidgen-Hager 1992: 217). These burials are not apparently associated with selected animal bones. In this respect, the multiple ditch burials at Menneville have no direct parallels for this period, although animal bone deposits accompany graves in a cemetery of the broadly contemporary Hinkelstein group (Driesch 1992).

Combining these scattered data with the evidence from Menneville, there is now little doubt that parts of certain Bandkeramik enclosures were used for funerary ceremonies. The association at Menneville between funerary behaviour and the presence of an enclosure involves not only the content of the ditches, but also the unusually high frequency of child burials on the settlement and the proximity of a small cemetery to the ditch circuit. It is worth repeating here that at Menneville there are no signs of massacre or cannibalism, such as have been occasionally noted in Bandkeramik contexts elsewhere (Wahl & König 1987; Kneipp & Büttner 1988). Throughout the Bandkeramik culture, large inhumation and cremation cemeteries like Elsloo (Modderman 1970) are notoriously rare in comparison with settlement sites. This cannot be entirely dismissed as a preservation or recovery bias. For example, only one cemetery of this kind was discovered on the Aldenhoven plateau, despite the vast scale of fieldwork (Dohrn-Ihmig 1983; Stehli 1989: Abb. 10). This cemetery lies 500 m from contemporary settlement areas. As Modderman (1988: 73) has observed, one can certainly question the representativity of the large cemeteries. In short, the Menneville evidence widens the range of burial practices known for this period, as well as heralding much of later Neolithic developments in the use of ditched enclosures (Bertemes 1991; Burgess et al. 1988).

BIBLIOGRAPHY

Bernardt, G. 1986. Die linearbandkeramische Siedlung von Köln-Lindenthal. *Kölner Jahrbuch für Vor- und Frühgeschichte* 18–19: 7–165.

Bertemes, F. 1991. Untersuchungen zur Funktion der Erdwerke der Michelsberger Kultur im Rahmen der kupferzeitlichen Zivilisation. In Lichardus, J. (ed.), *Die Kupferzeit als Historische Epoche*, pp. 441–464. Bonn: (Saarbrücker Beiträge zur Altertumskunde Band 55).

Boureux, M. 1982. La prospection aerienne dans la vallée de l'Aisne. *Revue Archéologique de Picardie*, numéro spécial: 21–42.

Burgess, C., Topping, P., Mordant, C. & Maddison, M. (eds) 1988. *Enclosures and Defences in the Neolithic of Western Europe*, pp. 209–226. Oxford: British Archaeological Reports (International Series 403).

Cahen, D., Keeley, L. H., Jadin, I. & van Berg, P.-L. 1990. Trois villages fortifiés du Rubané Récent en Hesbaye liègoise. In Cahen, D. & Otte, M. (eds), *Rubané et Cardial*, pp. 125–146. Liège, E.R.A.U.L. 39.

Coudart, A. & Demoule, J.-P. 1982: Le site néolithique et chalcolithique de Menneville. *Revue Archéologique de Picardie*, numéro spécial: 129–147.

Demoule, J.-P. & Ilett, M. 1985: First millennium settlement and society in northern France: a case study from the Aisne valley. In Champion, T. & Megaw, V. (eds), *Settlement and Society: aspects of European Prehistory in the first millennium B.C.*, pp. 193–221. Leicester: University Press.

Desse, J. 1976. La faune du site de Cuiry-lès-Chaudardes: note préliminaire sur le matériel osseux de la campagne de 1973. *Les Fouilles Protohistoriques dans la Vallée de l'Aisne* 4: 187–196.

Dohrn-Ihmig, M. 1983. Das bandkeramische Gräberfeld von Aldenhoven-Niedermerz, Kreis Düren. In *Archäologie in den Rheinischen Lössbörden*, pp. 47–190. Köln: (Rheinische Ausgrabungen 24).

von den Driesch, A. 1992. Die Rolle der Tiere im Grabkult der Kulturgruppen Hinkelstein und Grossgartach. In *Der Tod in der Steinzeit*, pp. 42–49. Darmstadt: Hessisches Landesmuseum.

Dubouloz, J., Lebolloch, M. & Ilett, M. 1988. Middle Neolithic enclosures in the Aisne valley. In Burgess, C., Topping, P., Mordant, C. & Maddison, M. (eds), *Enclosures and Defences in the Neolithic of Western Europe*, pp. 209–226. Oxford: British Archaeological Reports (International Ser. 403).

Dubouloz, J., Mordant, D. & Prestreau, M. 1991. Les enceintes néolithiques du Bassin parisien. In Beeching, A., Binder, D., Blanchet, J.-C., Constantin, C., Dubouloz, J., Martinez, R., Mordant, D., Thévenot, J.-P. & Vaquer, J. (eds), *Identité du Chasséen*, pp. 211–229. Nemours: (Mémoires du Musée de Préhistoire de l'Ile de France 4).

Evin, J., Maréchal, J. & Marien, G. 1983. Lyon natural radiocarbon measurements IX. *Radiocarbon* 25: 59–128.

Farruggia, J.-P., Guichard, Y. & Hachem, L. in press. Les ensembles funéraires rubanés de Menneville 'Derrière le Village'. In *Actes du 18e Colloque Interrégional sur le Néolithique, Dijon 1991.*

Hachem, L. forthcoming. Etude de la faune du site néolithique de Cuiry-lès-Chaudardes. Doctoral thesis, Université de Paris 1.

Ihmig, M. 1971. Ein bandkeramischer Graben mit Einbau bei Langweiler, Kr. Jülich, und die zeitliche Stellung bandkeramischer Gräben im westlichen Verbreitungsgebiet. *Archäologisches Korrespondenzblatt* 1: 23–30.

Ilett, M., Constantin, C., Coudart, A. & Demoule, J.-P. 1982. The late Bandkeramik of the Aisne valley: environment and spatial organization. *Analecta Praehistorica Leidensia* 15: 45–61.

Jeunesse, C. 1992. Du Néolithique ancien à l'Age du Fer, le site du lotissement "Sainte Odile" à Rosheim. In *Il y a 7000 ans, l'Alsace*, pp. 46–69. Zimmersheim: Association pour la Promotion de la Recherche Archéologique en Alsace.

Kaufmann, D. 1990. Ausgrabungen im Bereich linienbandkeramischer Erdwerke bei Eilsleben, Kr. Wanzleben. *Jahresschrift für Mitteldeutsche Vorgeschichte* 73: 15–28.

Keeley, L. H. & Cahen, D. 1989. Early Neolithic forts and villages in NE Belgium: a preliminary report. *Journal of Field Archaeology* 16: 157–176.

Kneipp, J. & Büttner, H. 1988. Anthropophagie in der jüngsten Bandkeramik der Wetterau. *Germania* 66: 490–497.

de Labriffe, P.-A. 1992. Les sépultures de tradition danubienne dans la vallée de l'Aisne (approche synthétique). In *Actes du 11e Colloque Interrégional sur le Néolithique, Mulhouse 1984*, pp. 63–78. Saint-Germain-en-Laye: Interneo.

Lüning, J. 1988. Zur Verbreitung und Datierung bandkeramischer Erdwerke. *Archäologisches Korrespondenzblatt* 18: 155–158.

Méniel, P. 1984. Les faunes du Rubané Récent de Menneville 'Derrière le Village' et de Berry-au-Bac 'La Croix Maigret' (Aisne). *Revue Archéologique de Picardie* 1984: 87–93.

Modderman, P. J. R. 1970. *Linearbandkeramik aus Elsloo und Stein.* (Analecta Praehistorica Leidensia 3.)

Modderman, P. J. R. 1988. The Linear Pottery culture: diversity in uniformity. *Berichten van de Rijksdienst voor het Oudheidkundig Bodemonderzoek* 38: 63–139.

Pion, P., Auxiette, G., Brun, P., Demoule, J.-P. & Pommepuy, C. 1990. De la chefferie à l'état? Territoires et organisation sociale dans la vallée de l'Aisne aux Ages des Métaux (2200–20 av. J.C.). In Fiches, J.-L. & Van der Leeuw, S. (eds), *Archéologie et Espaces*, pp. 183–260. Juan-les-Pins: APDCA.

Planck, D. 1983. Schwaigern. *Fundberichte aus Baden-Württemberg* 8: 146–149.

Plateaux, M. 1990. Approche régionale et différentes échelles d'observation pour l'étude du Néolithique et du Chalcolithique du Nord de la France. In Fiches, J.-L. & Van der Leeuw, S. (eds), *Archéologie et Espaces*, pp. 157–182. Juan-les-Pins: Editions APDCA.

Schmidgen-Hager, E. 1992. Das bandkeramische Erdwerk von Heilbronn-Neckargartach. *Fundberichte aus Baden-Württemberg* 17: 173–291.

Schwellnus, W. 1983. Archäologische Untersuchungen im Rheinischen Braunkohlengebiet 1977–1981. In *Archäologie in den Rheinischen Lössbörden*, pp. 1–31. Köln: (Rheinische Ausgrabungen Band 24).

Stehli, P. 1989. Merzbachtal – Umwelt und Geschichte einer bandkeramischen Siedlungskammer. *Germania* 67: 51–76.

Wahl, J. and König, H. G. 1987. Anthropologisch-traumatologische Untersuchung der menschlichen Skelettreste aus dem bandkeramischen Massengrab bei Talheim, Kr. Heilbronn. *Fundberichte aus Baden-Württemberg* 12: 65–186.

7

Megaliths in Texts

Christopher Tilley

Archaeologists, as is the case in all other disciplines, learn about reality (material remains) through a discourse (set of terms, ways of writing and speaking) that may be said to be in a continual process of structuration. Our discourse structures what and how we think. In turn that which we think and say restructures the discourses we use. Archaeology is a discipline that transforms things into words and speech. The nature of this linguistic transformation of the object into a word into a text and its effects have recently begun to be of some interest and concern in the literature (Evans 1994; Hodder 1989a; 1989b; Thomas 1994; Shanks 1992; Shanks & Tilley 1989; Tilley 1989; 1990; 1994a; 1994b). In this paper I want to discuss the manner in which archaeologists have written and textually transformed a series of stone-built architectural remains, of Neolithic date, into texts. Those remains I refer to, are, of course, megaliths.

The term megalith is a keyword in the archaeological literature concerned with the prehistory of Europe. I want to perform a genealogical analysis of the use of the term in archaeological discourse, investigating the manner in which it has grown, developed, and transformed. The main questions I shall address are: to what ends has the term been employed? Why? Has its meaning shifted through time? To what extent does the term 'capture' the reality of the stone monuments it is used to discuss? Does it illuminate or obfuscate an understanding of the past?

GENEALOGY OF A CONCEPT

As is well known, and indeed repeated constantly in the literature,the term is derived from the Greek *megas*, 'big', and *lithos*, 'stone'. According to Daniel (1958: 14) it was first used to describe stone monuments in Europe and other parts of the world in the period 1840–60. It had its birth, then, at the same time as other keywords in contemporary archaeological discourse such as 'Palaeolithic', 'Neolithic', Bronze Age, and Iron Age. Like them the term was generated during the formative years of the birth of archaeology as a 'scientific' discipline aiming to achieve a systematic and 'objective' study of the past. It is of interest to note that the use of the Greek automatically provides the term with a certain aura of scientificity, part of the technological jargon of a fledgling discipline. Unlike many other archaeological keywords coined around the same time it was not originally used to refer to a putative temporal phase but a specific class of archaeological remains. Today after 150 years of usage the term has a particular and unique resonance in the archaeological consciousness. There is no equivalent 'scientific' term applied to any other specific class of archaeological remains from the prehistoric past in Europe. For example, terms used to describe other widespread types of material remains found over large areas of Europe such as 'cave art', 'beaker', 'barrow', 'cairn', 'midden', 'rock carvings', 'long-house' are quite ordinary everyday words, or the precise terminology varies locally, or is used infrequently. All archaeologists 'know' what the term megalith means and it is used habitually to organise sessions in conference proceedings, in books, university courses, and in reading lists. A term like this one, then, might be claimed to reside at the discursive heart of an archaeology of Europe, which is why it is particularly fascinating to analyse its meanings and usage in texts. A *disciplinary* archaeological consciousness constructed the term to bring order and control to a set of disparate remains. I want to try and make the case that the term has now taken over and structures the archaeological consciousness. The use of it, whether explicitly in texts, or in the mind sets of archaeologists carrying out research, structures what may or may not be said or written about a chunk of the prehistoric past. The term creates a particular form of discourse and, such is its power, there appears to be an inability to reinscribe the past in a fresh manner, despite quite radical changes in theoretical ideas and methods of analysing archaeological information.

The sample of literature used in this analysis consists of sixteen

Table 1. The sample of texts analysed in the survey.

1. James Fergusson (1872), *Rude Stone Monuments*, [532 pp.]
2. Oscar Montelius (1901), *Orienten och Europa*, [252 pp.]
3. T. Eric Peet (1912), *Rough Stone Monuments*, [161 pp.]
4. V. Gordon Childe (1925), *The Dawn of European Civilization*, first edition, parts or all of chapters: 6–9, 13, 18–19, epilogue [76 pp.]
5. Daryll Forde (1930), 'Early cultures of Atlantic Europe', *American Anthropologist*, [82 pp.]
6. Christopher Hawkes (1940), *The Prehistoric Foundations of Europe*, chapter 5 pages 158–199; chapter 6, pages 205–217, [56 pp.]
7. V. Gordon Childe (1957), *The Dawn of European Civilization*, sixth edition, chapters 10: 221–238; 12: 260–270; 13: 277–288; 14; 15: 315–332; 17; 18: 373–81; 19, [109 pp.]
8. Glyn Daniel (1958), *The Megalith Builders of Western Europe*, [136 pp.]
9. Colin Renfrew (1973), *Before Civilization*, chapter 7: 'The enigma of the megaliths', [28 pp.]
10. Colin Renfrew (1976), 'Megaliths, territories and populations', [35 pp.]
11. Robert Chapman (1981), 'The emergence of formal disposal areas and the "problem" of megalithic tombs in prehistoric Europe', [11 pp.]
12. Jarman, M., Bailey, G. and Jarman, H. (1982), *Early European Agriculture*, chapter 7: 'The Megaliths: a problem in palaeoethology', [20 pp.]
13. Ian Hodder (1984), 'Burials, houses, women and men in the European Neolithic', [16 pp.]
14. Roger Joussaume (1985) *Dolmens for the Dead*, [315 pp.]
15. Ian Hodder (1990), *The Domestication of Europe*, chapters 6–9, [131 pp.]
16. Julian Thomas (1991), *Rethinking the Neolithic*, chapters 3, 6–7, [102 pp.]

texts. These include all major published works in the English language specifically devoted to the subject of megaliths (Fergusson 1872; Peet 1912; Daniel 1958), the English translation of Joussaume's *Dolmens for the Dead* (1988), originally published in French in 1985 and Montelius' classic work *Orienten och Europa* (1905). In addition to these books a number of general surveys on the prehistory of Europe published between the 1920s and 1990 were analysed: the first and sixth edition of Childe's *Dawn of European Civilization* (1925 and 1957) and works by Hawkes (1940) and Hodder (1990). A number of papers and book chapters on megaliths published at different dates and representative of different styles of archaeological thinking were also used (Forde 1930; Renfrew 1973; 1976; Chapman 1981; Jarman, Bailey & Jarman 1982; Hodder 1984; Thomas 1991). The sample thus comprises a period of 120 years writing about megaliths and includes examples of work chosen as representative of 'traditional', 'processual', and 'post-pro-

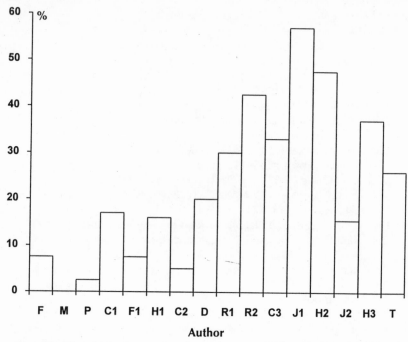

Figure 1. The relative frequencies of generic usage of the terms 'megalith(s)' and 'megalithic' of the texts analysed in relation to author and publication date. F: Fergusson 1872; M: Montelius 1905; P: Peet 1912; C1: Childe 1925; F1: Forde 1930; H1: Hawkes 1940; C2: Childe 1957; D: Daniel 1958; R1: Renfrew 1973; R2: Renfrew 1976; C3: Chapman 1981; J1: Jarman et al. 1982; H2: Hodder 1984; J2: Joussaume 1985; H3: Hodder 1990; T: Thomas 1991.

cessual' archaeology (Table 1).

In these sixteen texts the word 'megalith', the plural 'megaliths' or the derivative term 'megalithic' are employed on no less than 1,648 occasions. In all cases the word has a generic usage. In other words it stands and is used as a classificatory term supposedly replete with meaning in itself. The extent of this generic usage, of course, varies widely from author to author but there is a clear general trend to an increase in the relative frequency of generic usage through time (Fig. 1). The term is rarely used on its own prior to the 1920s and it is interesting to note that the first three books in the sample, all of which are specifically devoted to the subject of megaliths, do not employ the term in their titles. Montelius uses the word on only a few occasions and in his text always inserts it within inverted commas. While Fergusson and Peet use the term infrequently, another equivalent one, 'monument', sometimes qualified with the words 'rough' or 'rude', is

[144]

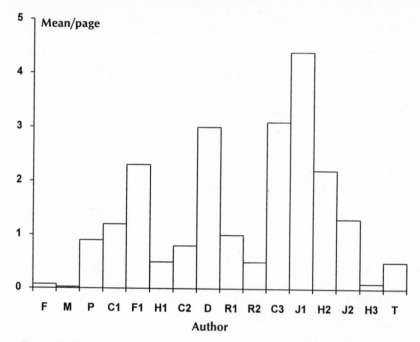

Figure 2. The mean frequency of occurrence of the term megalith/page of text analysed according to author and date of publication. For key see caption to Fig. 1.

clearly more important to them. With the advent of 'processual' archaeological writing (Renfrew 1973; 1976; Chapman 1981; Jarman et al. 1981) generic usage increases significantly, a trend which continues with 'post-processual' works (Hodder 1990; Thomas 1991), although the absolute frequency of usage is in some cases very low. This general trend towards an increase in the frequency of generic use through time indicates the manner in which the term has become relatively unproblematic and has so thoroughly pervaded the archaeological consciousness that its use has become standard practice. Hodder and Thomas deliberately use the word 'monument' very frequently, presumably because it has less clearly defined connotations but in many cases this amounts to a simple synonym for 'megalith' as is the use of another term 'tomb' in their texts. This has clear similarities with the writing style of Fergusson and Peet with their constant references to 'rude stone' and 'rough stone' monuments, except that the rude and the rough have been deleted.

Looking at the absolute frequency of usage, expressed in terms of the mean number of usages of the term per page of text, a slightly

Table 2. Words linked with the term megalith in the sample of analysed texts.

1. **GENERAL** (N = 18)

    ensembles   components   manifestations   aspects   style   feature   character   examples   elements   homology   type   form   complex   phenomenon   intermediate   versions   contexts   'paramegalithic'

2. **SPACE** (N = 14)

    districts   areas   regions   territories   concentration   centre   group   province   seaway   spread   sites   distributions   density   Brittany

3. **TIME** (N = 11)

    times   period   phase   evolution   tradition   series   branch   origins   chronology   facies   epoch

4. **TYPES of MONUMENT** (N = 9)

    circles   huts   passage-tomb   gallery   passage-grave   dolmen   allée   chamber-tomb   gallery-grave

5. **ARCHITECTURE** (N = 35)

    remains   work   monument   chamber   cist   rude   stone   monument   blocks   structure   uprights   construction   galleries   architecture   capstone   building   slabs   walling   wall   slab-cist   extensions   lintel   'table'   sub-megalithic   pillars   stones   chests   facade   vault   passage   'yard'   'fathom'   cubit   roofing-slab   architectural   type   keystones   production

6. **ART** (N = 2)

    art   rude stone art

7. **ARTEFACTS** (N = 3)

    pottery   pendants   axes

8. **DEATH** (N = 18)

    burial-chambers   burial-places   funerary   monuments   grave   tombs   funerary   structures   coffers   grave   chamber   grave   goods   burial   cemeteries   mortuary   practices   collective   tomb   collective   burial   tomb-practice   funeral-practice   funerary   usage   skeleton

9. **RITUAL** (N = 12)

    chamber   sepulchral   architecture   temples   faith   religion   burial   ritual   rituals   rites   cult   sacred   sites   superstition   ideological   megalithicism

10. **PEOPLE** (N = 22)

    people   builders   civilization   populations   building-traders   navigators   building-ancestors   man   settlers   folk   race   culture   civilization   colonization   influence   creativity   diffusion   idea   creativity   occupation   chiefs   aristocracy

11. **WORK OF ARCHAEOLOGISTS** (N = 7)

    'problem'   problem   controversies   antiquities   specialists   studies   literature

different picture arises (Fig. 2). The term is infrequently used in the earliest and latest texts, achieves great significance in the work of 'traditional' archaeologists, in particular those of Forde and Daniel, and enjoys a short renaissance in some 'processual' texts. We seem to have here a growth and dying away of the term, at least in a simple quantitative sense of the frequency of use. However, it is worth noting that the mean frequencies are necessarily artificially depressed in those

Table 3. Some alternative words to associate with the term 'megalithic'.

megalithic	vegetable
megalithic	government
megalithic	hobbies
megalithic	Volvo
megalithic	spaghetti
megalithic	attitude
megalithic	parking space
megalithic	birthing chamber
megalithic	underwear
megalithic	evening
megalithic	brain
megalithic	psychotherapy
megalithic	conversation
megalithic	politician

works discussing a wider range of archaeological evidence than just 'megaliths' such as those by Hodder and Thomas.

As well as occurring on its own the term 'megalith' has always (and necessarily) been consistently linked to others. Taking the sixteen texts as a whole it is employed in combination with 151 other words by the various authors. These can be broken down into a number of general categories (Table 2).

Table 2 might be contextualised by considering it in relation to another alternative one using terms never conventionally associated with 'megaliths' (Table 3). Bearing in mind what the word 'megalith' actually means *big stone*, why is it that we might laugh at 'megalithic' (big stone) vegetable when it is apparently quite normal and unproblematic to refer to big stone evolution, big stone people, big stone territories, big stone rituals, and so forth? The answer is, of course, the deeply metaphorical, yet unrecognised nature, of the entire discourse we use to discuss and describe the past. This emphasises the point that all archaeological texts are primarily *literary constructions* and can be analysed in an analogous manner to literary texts, bracketing aside the questions of truth, falsity, adequacy, or inadequacy in relation to the physical artefact world that are normally asked from the outset.

The concern might rather more pertinently be to do with the manner in which the language itself is structured and mobilised to create meaning and sense. If we examine the frequency of different words connected with the word megalith in terms of author and date (Fig. 3)

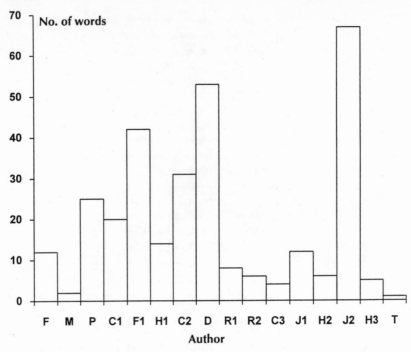

Figure 3. The frequency of different words linked with the term 'megalith' in relation to author and publication date. For key see caption to Figure 1.

and the rank order of usage (Table 4) we see a discourse that is at first extremely restricted, then grows and develops and reaches a florescence up until 1960s, and finally becomes restricted again with advent of so-called 'processual' and 'post-processual' archaeologies. Fergusson (1872) usually confines the word to simply describe sets of architectural remains and the sense intended remains on a more or less literal level. Subsequently metaphorical usage dominates and the meanings of the word become almost infinitely extended to link with radically different terms such as race, region, and culture, although in terms of ranked orders of usage there is remarkable consistency through time with the terms 'monument' and 'tomb' being used more frequently than others. In 'processual' and 'post-processual' accounts, metaphorical extension of sense is mainly restricted to the categories of architecture and death, but is also used to refer to the work of archaeologists themselves. So, at one level, 'processual' and 'post-processual' archaeologies return us to the meanings ascribed at the origins of the discourse, an example of manner in which exactly the same word rather than having a consistency of usage and sense changes its

Table 4. The three most common words used in combination with the term 'megalith' by author and date of publication.

Author	Date	Rank 1 Word	%	Rank 2 Word	%	Rank 3 Word	%	Total %
Fergusson	1872	remains	46	monument	20	art	9	75
Montelius	1905	grave	100	–	–	–	–	100
Peet	1912	monument	36	people	11	area	8	55
Childe	1925	tomb	24	culture	21	builders	14	59
Forde	1930	tomb	20	culture	16	architecture	6	42
Hawkes	1940	tomb	28	religion	20	pass. grave	8	56
Childe	1957	tomb	33	builders	9	culture	8	50
Daniel	1958	tomb	28	monument	15	builders	11	54
Renfrew	1973	tomb	50	construction	10	architect	10	70
Renfrew	1976	tomb	27	monument	18	builders	18	63
Chapman	1981	tomb	86	'problem'	5	'area'	5	96
Jarman	1982	monument	24	tomb	18	area	18	60
Hodder	1984	monument	67	burial	5	problem	5	77
Joussaume	1985	monument	35	building	21	tomb	4	60
Hodder	1990	tomb	40	burial	30	monument	10	80
Thomas	1991	tomb	100	–	–	–	–	100

The words used are ranked according to their order of frequency and the percentages of usage noted for each rank. The percentage of the total number of combinations accounted for the three most commonly used words is also given.

meaning and has different connotations through time in relation to different styles of analysis and understanding.

LITTLE DISCURSIVE TREASURES

As is well known, at a general level an explanatory discourse has moved from a stress on diffusion and megaliths as part of a spatial transmission of culture around the Atlantic seaboards of Europe to a 'processual' emphasis on population and territory to a 'post-processual' concern with symbolism, gender, power relations, and the nature of a megalithic space. The historicity of a megalithic discourse would appear, then, to be characterised by changing interpretations while at any one time generations of archaeologists appear to be in broad agreement as to what megaliths mean and how they may be best understood. Considering the literature at a more fine grained level, despite apparent changes of theoretical orientation, it remains peculiarly restricted and constrained. The same types of statements tend to be repeated over and over again, evidently too good to be lost. To exemplify the point I want to consider one more recent example in some detail.

In 1984 Ian Hodder published 'Burials, houses, women and men in the European Neolithic', the main claims of this article being subsequently repeated in his *The Domestication of Europe* (1990). Part of the explicit authorial position taken in both texts is their representation as a radical break with previous, especially 'processual' discourses on megaliths. Hodder's innovation is to argue that megaliths symbolise or mean houses. In attempting to substantiate this argument he draws eight points of similarity between the form of central European Linearbankeramik long-houses and long mounds on the northern and western European periphery. He reflects on the argument put forward in the 1984 paper in the context of a recent collection of papers (Hodder 1992). He writes that since the initial publication of the paper the idea has been proved more and more plausible to archaeologists citing as evidence of this Sherratt's (1990) adoption of it (Hodder 1992: 21). Now, this idea that tombs might be connected to houses was well known to the 'traditional' archaeologists of the 1920s-50s, who did not emphasise it too much except insofar as it was used to back up a general diffusionistic framework purporting to account for the spread of megaliths from one area of Europe to the next and their work is cited by Hodder. If we were to trace back an initial origin for the idea itself it would have to be to one of the first scientific studies undertaken of megalithic tombs in Sweden by Sven Nilsson. It was one well known to Montelius, a fellow Swede, who used it as the foundation for his interpretation of megaliths in 1905 also arguing that they were derived from house forms. Through the translation of Montelius' work into German it became known more widely in European archaeological circles. Nilsson's book *The Primitive Inhabitants of Scandinavia* was published originally in four parts between 1838–1843 and translated into English in 1868. In it Nilsson systematically compares the ground plans of houses (Eskimo huts in Greenland and North America) with those of Swedish passage graves (Fig. 4). He explicitly draws out seven points of morphological similarity discussing form; proportions; height; size; direction of the long narrow side gallery; the division of the vault into stalls (Nilsson 1868: 139).

Hodder's argument is similarly based on a style of analogical argument adducing morphological similarities. Nilsson (1868: 135) concludes his discussion by stating: 'One cannot but be astonished, when reading the description of our Scandinavian gallery graves, to find it

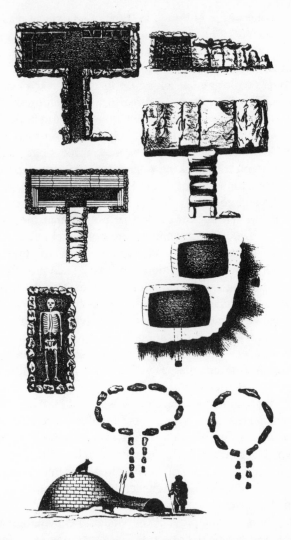

Figure 4. Reproduction of plate XIV from Nilsson's The Primitive Inhabitants of Scandinavia *showing ground plans of Swedish passage graves and a reconstruction diagram of an Eskimo house.*

applicable, almost word for word to the Greenland huts.' He also comments that 'during the years which have elapsed since I first discovered and pointed out this resemblance . . . . I have carefully examined many of the Eskimo huts and found my former statement more and more confirmed' (ibid.: 141). So Hodder in 1984 comes to exactly the same general conclusion as Nilsson did 146 years pre-

[151]

viously, bases his argument on same type of analogical reasoning, and later states, like Nilsson, he is more and more personally convinced of the plausibility of the general position. From antiquarianism to post-processualism a megalithic discourse has turned full circle and returned to its own origins, backing up its claim on the basis of drawing points of formal similarity and reaffirming the power of the argument on the archaeological mind. Of course there are important differences – Hodder compares different classes of archaeological data, Nilsson is involved in drawing ethnographic analogies, Hodder socialises his account by making reference to power relations between men and women and control of the land, while Nilsson does not. But the point of issue here is not whether Hodder's or Nilsson's interpretations are right or wrong, convincing or not, or that the basis for the idea and the mode of argumentation are not novel but formed one of the *earliest* explanatory accounts of megaliths, but why this notion of a connection between tomb and house has had such an evident power over the archaeological imagination. It does not merely reflect a history of ideas in archaeology and the routes by means of which these are filtered between and transformed by individual authors. I want to suggest instead that the implications of this repetition are more profound. 'Good' ideas, such as this one, get recycled, reused, and re-appropriated in different discursive contexts, they are little treasures that cannot be forgotten. But perhaps to be truly innovative it is the forgetting that should be attempted. Nilsson and Hodder and all other writers on megaliths, including myself, inhabit a discourse, a series of largely anonymous and habitual rules and constraints for thinking and writing, that structures, in part, both what can be written and what can actually be thought. Because of the discourse we inhabit, and because it acts largely unconsciously, archaeologists are doomed to repeat it, whether in the form of the spatial structures of their narratives, the types of diagrams they employ, or the modes of explanation adopted.

These are not personal criticisms, they are one of a tradition of thought, an interrogation of a discourse rather than that of an individual who necessarily operates within its terms of reference. What may be said is clearly constrained by a discourse of writing about megaliths in general, a code for producing knowledge which is *out of control* because it is not understood, or even suspected to exist. The implications are that if we are, or want, to write in a radically different manner about megaliths, or indeed anything else from the past, a first requirement would seem to be to attempt to understand exactly what the discourse is that we inhabit and how it operates. There is a need to begin to excavate what determines an archaeological consciousness to think in one way rather than another. The chief point of issue is: given that megaliths *might* be interpreted in so many different ways, why is this clearly not the case? Why do we tend to think about them in such a limited number of ways? What constrains the archaeological imagination? A response that it is because we have arrived at a kernel of truth of the matter and therefore have no alternative but to repeat ourselves, is surely too glib and self-congratulatory to be entertained.

SOME PRINCIPLES OF THE GENRE

1. The grand narrative

All accounts of megaliths are narrative constructions and all the authors considered in the survey in section I above, from Fergusson to Thomas, *assume* that there is something linking these stone monuments together, either at a regional or a European level: battlegrounds, people, ideas, races, chiefs, critical resources, house symbolism, ideology or power. In books about European megaliths the reader follows the author in a journey around a textually constructed continent. The lines of movement in the text between different European nation states are often integral to the argument being made. So with Montelius we embark on a journey that begins in the Orient and ends in Scandinavia. The dolmens and passage graves metaphorically take on the roles of peoples and their journeys. Joussaume's *Dolmens for the Dead*, (this time on a world rather than continental scale) reads like a travel guide with Joussaume himself as personal narrator: 'We cannot leave the Near East without a word about . . .' (p. 258), 'We will not linger over the megalithic monuments of the Balearic islands . . .' (p. 220), 'This journey through the world of dolmens' (p. 295) and so on. The reader, in effect, becomes his anonymous travel companion. The spatial and narrative flow and organisation of Joussaume's, and other texts, is as vital to the message and arguments being made as is the discursive content. They frequently exist in a relation of tension and systematically act so as to deconstruct and undermine each other. Renfrew (1973; 1976) in his 'processual' position claims a series of independent centres for the 'invention' of megaliths. Similarly for Hodder (1984), no necessary connection exists between megaliths in different areas of Europe. Yet the 'routes' taken in their texts to describe and discuss the evidence are exactly the same as in traditional archaeological discourse (Fig. 5). We begin on fringes, in the Aegean or Scandinavia, and go round in a prescribed direction. There is no

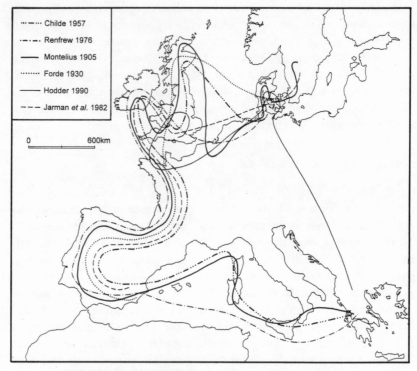

Figure 5. Some megalithic textual journeys around Europe.

logical reason for this. The texts could, on the basis of their theoretical grounding, (independent origins) begin and go anywhere, trace new routes and directions. The fact that they do not do so implies the operation of a powerful subconscious discursive constraint of the 'correct' manner in which to construct an 'acceptable' text.

2. The subsumption of particularity

The notion that what are termed megaliths have nothing whatsoever to do with each other has constantly threatened archaeological discourses about these monuments from the very beginning that the category was first invented. The history of archaeological writing about megaliths is one of a continual definition and redefinition of the terminology. In the early works of Fergusson and Peet stone circles, menhirs, and alignments are all included in the accounts. The category of the megalith is kaleidoscopic and threatens to explode. From Childe onwards the discourse is more restricted revolving around stone chambers. Then what counts as a true megalithic chamber becomes problematic. Time and time again attempts are made to save the discourse and impose unity. The monuments of Sardinia and the Balearic islands get dropped from the discussion by Daniel who distinguishes between 'cyclopean' and 'megalithic' architecture. For Renfrew the Maltese megaliths do not fit the category and become temples instead. There are sometimes queries about how big a stone should be to be a big stone, i.e. a megalith, and whether a rock cut monument can be properly included in the category. Is Newgrange really the same kind of thing as a Pembrokeshire dolmen?

The category 'megalith' unifies what are disparate things. The more archaeologists pay attention to empirical detail the more the analysis shatters the category that it sets out to investigate and that supposedly unifies, but this cannot be accepted. Megaliths are frequently labelled as tombs, but are they? Is a single functional attribution adequate? Might this provide a basis for unification? Renfrew (1973; 1976) both thinks they are, and are not, sometimes referring to 'tombs'. A typical line from Thomas' book reads: 'as with the Cotswold-Severn tombs, then, the passage-grave tradition integrates temporal control into the control of access to the chamber' (Thomas 1991: 45). The totally different tomb morphology of Cotswold-Severn tombs and passage graves is explained as part of a desire to control the movement of the body through space and exercise control over it. Difference is recognised (there are different megalithic 'tombs') but is simultaneously denied in desire to create a narrative structure and an explanatory account that can work with and embrace different categories of monuments. But why should totally different cultural arrangements of stones be forced into same narrative? Why is this natural? Why is it needed? Why might it not be suggested that Cotswold Severn tomb and passage grave have completely different meaning sets and associations? Perhaps this is a failure to think and allow for difference, a desire to tame and domesticate the difference of the past within a single narrative structure. The unthinkable of the archaeological discourse that controls us is to suggest that all megaliths, or different typological groups of megaliths, have nothing whatsoever to do with each other. Difference is, then, the unthinkable. Why? The answer resides in that discursive object of knowledge archaeologists themselves have created, 'megalith', which by its very objectification in discourse as a separate entity leads us to expect we *should* be dealing with a unitary phenomenon.

Not only is there a textual reductionism at work in the manner in which megaliths are operated upon but also a particular manner to illustrate and represent them – generally as small postage stamp line diagrams or line plans set, side by side, for comparative purposes. The illustrations which occur in recent texts are frequently exactly the same as those used by Montelius 90 years or more before. Like the written message, the illustrative message is constrained by the 'right' way to depict these things.

3. An obsession with origins

Hawkes opens his *The Prehistoric Foundations of Europe* (1940: 1) with a quote from Aristotle: 'he who thus considers things in their first growth and origin, whether a State or anything else, will obtain the clearest view of them.' The notion of a single origin is a *leitmotif* running throughout discourses on megaliths, despite assertions to the contrary. We all know that the earlier work of Montelius, Childe, Daniel, and Piggott attempted to trace this origin to the Orient and/ or the Aegean. With the advent of 'processual' and 'post-processual' archaeologies we apparently get a totally different perspective. Renfrew suggests independent centres of development as does Chapman, Hodder stresses local sequences. But this does not in fact result in an abandonment of concern with origins but merely displaces it somewhat. For all his independent centres of development Renfrew still has a single origin in a postulated movement of farmers to an Atlantic facade where the megaliths mushroom up. Hodder's point of origin is in the central European long-house tradition, Jarman's in a pastoralist economy, Thomas' in a need to assert ideological control over populations. What we have here are an origin in movement, an origin in the house, an origin in the economy, an origin in political structure. The theoretical emphasis has of course shifted somewhat, but only in terms of substituting a conceptual or a more geographically diffused 'beginning' for one located rather more precisely, in a geographical sense, in south-eastern Europe.

IV: DISCOURSES THAT DECONSTRUCT

A close examination of all works concerned with megaliths shows that, time and time again, the texts embrace an uneasy agglomeration of contradictory relations, so much so that they deconstruct their own striving for meaning. In *Orienten och Europa* Montelius puts forward the case for an oriental origin of megaliths. He is quite unequivocal on this. He also discusses at length the Scandinavian monuments and puts forward a typological sequence for their development. This is a four phase sequence from simple box like dolmens to gallery graves (Montelius 1905: 183). In so doing he clearly wanted to order the Scandinavian remains into an evolutionary sequence. The implications of this, not lost on other archaeologists, is that here we might have an independent Scandinavian origin, or at the very least an internal development from dolmen to passage grave. Montelius (1905: 187) is unable to even entertain the thought, arguing for separate waves of oriental inspiration introducing first dolmens and later passage graves. Why then does he introduce transitional typological forms between dolmens and passage graves, why all the detail?

In Childe's work there is a systematic tension between wanting to provide a single grand narrative for the megaliths, based on a notion of eastern 'inspiration' and realising that there may be nothing that links them together, that the category is completely vacuous. In the first paragraph of chapter 12 of the 1957 edition of *The Dawn of European Civilization*, entitled 'megalith builders and beaker-folk', he states (1975: 260): 'the diffusion of Oriental culture in Western Europe must have been effected in part by maritime intercourse. And evidence of such intercourse is supposedly afforded by the architecture of groups of tombs.' The significant word here is 'supposedly'. Why should Childe use it at all? He explicitly considers certain features which might be argued to be common factors linking together earlier European prehistoric monuments. First he considers the application of the word 'megalith' to describe the monuments and finds it inadequate because European tombs may be built of big or small stones, or may be cut out of rock. Second, he considers other potential classificatory devices in which archaeologists refer to passage graves, long cists etc. but considers these terms equally arbitrary and useless because there exist such a bewildering variety of forms. Third, he examines whether collective burial might provide a unifying thread but notes that it 'can hardly represent the unifying idea, since collective burial in natural caves was practised even in Mesolithic Palestine' (Childe 1957: 266). Grave goods are of little help either because they differ so radically throughout Europe and the presence of exotic imports or metals, in some cases, does nothing to clarify the situation. So, going systematically through various categorisations and types of archaeological evidence, Childe is forced to acknowledge its particularity and the difference between various 'tomb' types. In so doing he effectively destroys any reason to believe in European Neolithic 'tombs' or megaliths as a unitary archaeological class or entity for which a single explanation might suffice. Yet he is also unable to accept this. Having stressed architectural difference he then denies it: 'No new typology need be attempted here. The architectural agreements cited reveal the megalithic province as a cultural continuum' (Childe 1957: 269). The only 'agreements' Childe, in fact, mentions are 'seemingly arbitrary peculiarities of plan and in accessories such as porthole slabs and fore-courts' (ibid.: 267) yet as he also points out these are only found in a few of the monuments.

It is my suspicion that Childe wanted to accept difference but was unable to do so. The evidence for difference was, and is, overwhelming but Childe inhabited a discourse that would not allow him to accept this as an intellectual possibility, for to do so would be to fall into a terminological and explanatory abyss. This is repeated again and again in the literature. Variability is stressed, recognised, and then almost immediately suppressed. This is also manifested in the obsession with origins, for Renfrew and Hodder the origin of megaliths in different areas is independent, and yet it is not. For Thomas the mega-liths are polysemous texts, and yet they are not, because the same story is encountered in the interpretation of each 'text'.

CONCLUSION

The word, and the discursive object of knowledge, 'megalith' is one that has surfaced through 120 years and more of texts. *Rarity* (repetition) is a primary characteristic of this megalithic discourse. Given that there is so much that might be said or written it is surprising how constrained the discourse appears to be. From the very beginning the value of such a discursive object has questioned and its appearance and use in the literature have created as many problems and confusions as have been solved, yet it continues to be employed and has almost taken on a life of its own. The concept is simultaneously acknowledged as useless and yet it remains so apparently valuable that it cannot be thrown away and must be retained. As the discourse extends and ramifies through time the meaning of the term changes in various ways and its ability to unify that which is disparate collection of archaeological remains weakens, yet the notion of a unity embedded in the concept itself between various stone monuments is so strong that it cannot be denied. It would require a fresh fold in thought, a rethinking of every archaeological assumption. This unthinkable of archaeology recurrently surfaces to deconstruct the texts in which the discursive object is employed, undermining their claim to make sense or meaning of the data. I suppose the question becomes: do we want to

try and think what to us is the unthinkable, that the primary characteristic of these European megaliths is difference rather than sameness?
Could we think there might be as enormous a gulf between a Cotswold-Severn cairn and a portal dolmen, or between a passage grave at
Los Millares and one in Denmark, as between a Beaker and an
Acheulean hand axe? An archaeological discourse on megaliths has
been productive of knowledge and understanding, of texts and
lectures that purport to be representing some prehistoric realities. It
has similarly restrained and restricted thought so that we have an end-
less series of textual repetitions with our knowledge going round in
circles. Discourse has always begun and ended at the monument. An
alternative might be to stop thinking of these monuments as pivotal in
any sense and inscribe them in a discourse which is *topological* in form,
i.e. they become points for discussion amongst many others – non-
privileged sites for discursive articulation. In this short text I have
written the word 'megalith' or 'megalithic' 62 times, excluding the use
of the word in tables and captions! Is it useful for us now to start to
cross the word out in our texts (~~megalith~~), in a classic Derridean move,
and accept that ~~megaliths~~ do not exist, while realising they will almost
certainly continue to do so?

REFERENCES

Chapman, R. 1981. The emergence of formal disposal areas and the 'problem'
of megalithic tombs in prehistoric Europe. In Chapman, R., Kinnes, I. and
Randsborg, K. (eds), *The Archaeology of Death*. Cambridge: Cambridge
University Press.

Childe, V. G. 1925. *The Dawn of European Civilization*. 1st ed., London: Kegan
Paul: London.

Childe, V. G. 1957. *The Dawn of European Civilization*. 6th ed., London:
Routledge and Kegan Paul.

Daniel, G. 1958. *The Megalith Builders of Western Europe*. London: Hutchinson.

Evans, C. 1993. Digging with the pen: novel archaeologies and literary traditions. In Tilley, C. 1993b, pp. 417–448.

Fergusson, J. 1872. *Rude Stone Monuments in All Countries: Their Age and Uses*.
London: John Murray.

Forde, C. D. 1930. Early cultures of Atlantic Europe. *American Anthropologist*
32 (1): 19–100.

Hawkes, C. 1940. *The Prehistoric Foundations of Europe to the Mycenean Age*.
London: Methuen.

Hodder, I. 1984. Burials, houses, women and men in the European Neolithic.
In Miller, D. and Tilley, C. (eds), *Ideology, Power and Prehistory*, pp. 111–
146. Cambridge: Cambridge University Press.

Hodder, I. (ed.) 1989a. *The Meanings of Things*. London: Unwin-Hyman.

Hodder, I. 1989b. Writing archaeology: site reports in context. *Antiquity* 63: 268–274.

Hodder, I. 1990. *The Domestication of Europe*. Oxford: Blackwell.

Hodder, I. 1992. *Theory and Practice in Archaeology*. London: Routledge.

Jarman, M., Bailey, G. and Jarman, H. (eds) 1982. *Early European Agriculture*. Cambridge: Cambridge University Press.

Joussaume, R. 1988. *Dolmens for the Dead*. London: Batsford.

Montelius, O. 1905. Orienten och Europa. *Antiqvarisk Tidskrift für Sverige* 13: 1–252.

Nilsson, S. 1868 [1838–43]. *The Primitive Inhabitants of Scandinavia*. London: Longmans, Green and Co.

Peet, T. 1912. *Rough Stone Monuments and Their Builders*. London: Harper and Brothers.

Renfrew, C. 1973. *Before Civilization*. London: Jonathan Cape.

Renfrew, C. 1976. Megaliths, territories and populations. In de Laet, S. J. (ed.), *Acculturation and Continuity in Atlantic Europe*. Brugge: De Tempel.

Shanks, M. 1992. *Experiencing the Past*. London: Routledge.

Shanks, M. and Tilley, C. 1989. Archaeology into the 1990s. *Norwegian Archaeological Review* 22 (1): 1–12.

Sherratt, A. 1990. The genesis of megaliths. *World Archaeology* 22: 147–67.

Thomas, J. 1991. *Rethinking the Neolithic*. Cambridge: Cambridge University Press.

Thomas, J. 1993. Discourse, totalization and the Neolithic. In Tilley, C. 1993b, pp. 357–394.

Tilley, C. 1989. Discourse and power: the genre of the Cambridge inaugural lecture. In Miller, D., Rowlands, M. and Tilley, C. (eds), *Domination and Resistance*, pp. 41–62. London: Unwin-Hyman.

Tilley, C. 1990. Michel Foucault: towards an archaeology of archaeology. In C. Tilley (ed.), *Reading Material Culture*, pp. 281–347. Oxford: Blackwell.

Tilley, C. 1993a. Interpretation and a poetics of the past. In Tilley, C. 1993b, pp. 1–30.

Tilley, C. (ed.) 1993b. *Interpretative Archaeology*. Oxford: Berg.

Tilley, C. 1993c. Prospecting archaeology. In Tilley, C. 1993b, pp. 395–416.

8

Traditions of Death: Mounded Tombs, Megalithic Art, and Funerary Ideology in Neolithic Western Europe

Chris Scarre

Recent years have seen a resurgence of broad-sweep interpretations of European prehistory which seek to integrate the diversity of European evidence into all-embracing cultural and ideological schemes (e.g. Hodder 1990; Sherratt 1990). At the same time, there has been a sustained emphasis on the analysis of prehistoric ideology in terms of power relations in society. This has very notably been so in the case of mounded tombs – the so-called megalithic tombs or long mounds of western and northern Europe (e.g. Shanks & Tilley 1982; Tilley 1984; Thomas 1990). The purpose of this article is to consider these trends in relation to a series of critical questions. Firstly, how well do the mounded tombs of particular regions such as Brittany fit into these broad-sweep interpretative schemes? Secondly, how far can we attribute developments to the spread of similar ideologies, and what are the likeliest directions of inter-regional contact and ideological interaction? Finally, we must question whether indeed the ideology of these monuments is best seen in terms of power relations in society.

Mounded tombs with stone-built chambers are among the most conspicuous surviving traces of the period of European prehistory which is conventionally labelled the Neolithic. Though many still survive, they were once much more numerous, before accelerated agricultural development of the eighteenth and nineteenth centuries led to their widespread destruction. Built over a period of some 2000 years, these monuments represent an enormous expenditure of communal effort, and mark a radical change in the scale and nature of society. We may no longer believe that it was the wholesale adoption of agriculture by communities at the western and northern margins of Europe which lay immediately behind this phenomenon, but it is abundantly clear that these monuments were the product of societies organised in a new and different way.

One approach to their monumentality is to consider the mounded tomb phenomenon alongside the other conspicuous human-made features of the Neolithic landscape. Of these, the most widespread are the various kinds of enclosure. These had varying functions and can hardly be a regarded as a uniform phenomenon, but as a landscape feature they provide an interesting complement to monumental tombs. This is clearly the case in France. Here, chambered tombs seem to have a distribution in time and space which is mutually exclusive with that of enclosures or substantial settlement sites. Thus in the north-east, collective burial monuments are unknown during the period of Band-keramik long-houses and the period of enclosures which follows; only after the enclosures fall out of use in the later part of the Neolithic do burial monuments start to be built. A similar sequence can be shown in western France (Scarre 1983). The conclusion seems to be that the creation of burial monuments was a way of humanising or cultivating the landscape in circumstances where other types of substantial human-made construction were absent.

If this line of thought has any validity, then it underlines even more strongly the contrast between the pre-Neolithic and the Neolithic: earlier societies felt no need to leave their mark upon the landscape, and generally did not; Neolithic societies, on the other hand, at least in western Europe, were prone to express their attitude to landscape by the construction of substantial houses, enclosures or ritual monuments.

Though of some interest, such an argument suffers from paying insufficient attention to the actual form of monument which was chosen; it treats monument-construction as one manifestation of a more general phenomenon but does not explain why some societies built enclosures, others long-houses, and still others mounded tombs. To approach this aspect of the question it is necessary to move to a greater level of specificity and to consider particular classes of monument and the kinds of meaning which may lie behind their specific morphologies.

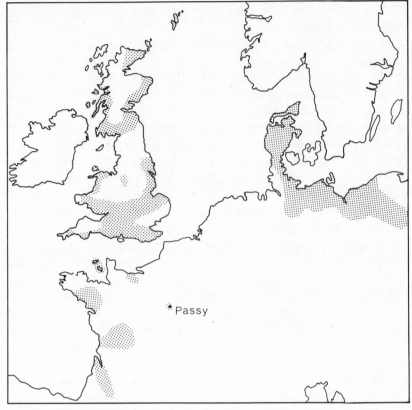

Figure 1. Distribution of Neolithic long mounds in northern and western Europe.

LONG MOUNDS AND THE BRETON SEQUENCE

One class of mounded tomb for which a specific meaning has been suggested is the long mound. They are found along the northern and north-western periphery of the Bandkeramik, from Poland (the so-called Kujavian long mounds), through Denmark to the Hunebedden of the northern Netherlands, the chambered and unchambered long mounds of eastern and southern Britain, and the long mounds of northern and western France (Fig. 1). These regional manifestations are best considered not as a single tradition, but a series of linked traditions in which the principal unifying feature is external morphology, the shape of the long mound itself. The internal arrangements, the burial facility itself, can take a variety of forms, from simple pits and boulder-lined graves (Poland) or timber mortuary houses within or beneath the mound (Denmark, southern Britain) to full-scale megalithic chambers (for example, the Severn-Cotswold group) (Midgeley 1985; Kinnes 1992).

A number of authors have seen the inspiration of the Bandkeramik long-house in the shape of the long mound. According to this view, the long mound was a monumental version of the long-house built by early farming communities who looked to the Bandkeramik in negotiating their internal social strategies (Hodder 1984; 1990; Sherratt 1990). Hodder sees the long mounds of northern Europe and the long-houses of the Bandkeramik as manifestations of the same organising principles of communal effort and the linear ordering of space; both are expressions of the *domus*, a particular form of the domestication of the wild (Hodder 1990: 149–56, 185–9). This conclusion is based on the fact that spatial and temporal distance makes it difficult to derive all long mounds or long tombs from the long-houses of central Europe. The late Neolithic elongated *allées couvertes* of the Paris basin have no close spatial or temporal connection with any other series of long mounds or long-houses. Hence, it must be a principle deeply rooted in society, rather than a straightforward cultural link (Hodder 1990: 154).

The differences between these viewpoints should not be allowed to obscure the basic point behind their argument, that the builders of early long-houses in central Europe and the builders of early long mounds in western and northern Europe were linked together by a common idea. This idea was one which led societies to place especial emphasis on the notion of linearity in their constructions, as the manifestation of a common world view. We may envisage a long-held tradition linking the long mounds to the long-houses.

These large-scale interpretations of the mounded tomb phenomenon do not bestow equal attention on the other early classes of Atlantic monument, such as the circular or oval burial mounds, including the famous passage graves. Since the publication of radiocarbon dates from Ile Gaignog and Barnenez in the 1970s, passage graves have widely been recognised as the earliest of the Breton mounded tombs (L'Helgouach 1979; 1990; L'Helgouach & Le Roux 1986) and a precocious regional development. They were, in addition, geographically separated from the earliest Neolithic of the Paris basin; thus, if there was an axis of contact, it was as likely to run southwards to the Neolithic communities of Mediterranean France than eastwards towards the Paris basin. This north-south axis ties in well with the distribution of megalithic tombs, especially the famous passage graves, along the Atlantic facade of Europe, from Portugal to Scandinavia (Fig. 2).

The early dates obtained from the Breton tombs gave rise to several

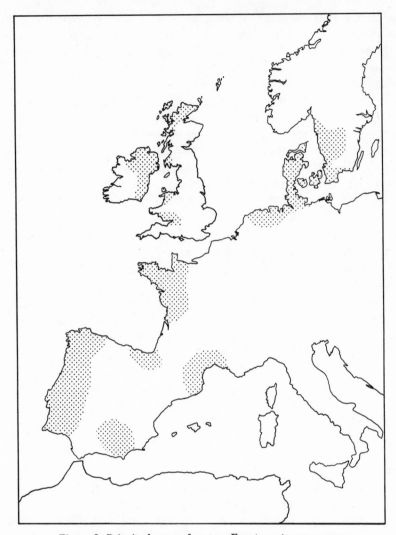

Figure 2. Principal areas of western European passage graves.

hypotheses for megalithic origins in the course of the 1970s, all of which emphasised the Atlantic context. One of the most influential models, put forward by Renfrew, stressed the role of farming advance and its impact on the Mesolithic communities of the Atlantic fringes of Europe. He proposed that megalithic tombs were a response of Atlantic Mesolithic communities to the advance of farming from the east (Renfrew 1976). Humphrey Case argued that Mesolithic burials such as those found at Téviec and Hoëdic off the coast of the Morbihan constituted a likely origin for the tradition of collective burial witnessed in early passage graves (Case 1976). Grahame Clark (1977) suggested that migratory fish were an important factor behind the Atlantic passage grave phenomenon. He observed that certain types of tomb, notably the so-called entrance graves, were often clustered in areas close to rich fishing grounds, as for instance on the Scilly Isles. Furthermore, since spawning of important shoal fish such as hake and mackerel takes place earliest in the southern fishing grounds, and progressively later towards the north, fishermen were able to extend the catching season by moving north during the course of the spawning season, which could extend over three months. Clark argued that if communities of Mesolithic or early Neolithic fishermen operated in a similar way, they would have been brought into contact every year as they followed the northward progress of the annual spawning cycle. This in itself could have provided a mechanism for the dissemination of ideas relating to burial fashions, funerary beliefs, and tomb architecture.

Emphasis on Atlantic links runs counter to views which place more weight on cultural links between central Europe and the Atlantic facade. Brittany presents the further complication of combining two traditions of mounded tomb. On the one hand are the long mounds, seen at their most imposing in the great Carnac mounds such as the Tumulus Saint-Michel, 125 m long, 60 m broad, and 10 m high. On the other hand are the chambered tombs belonging to the passage grave family, often covered by round or oval mounds and appearing to incorporate different principles of design and burial practice in their construction. There are also the Mesolithic collective graves on the small offshore islands of Téviec and Hoëdic (Péquart & Péquart 1954; Péquart et al. 1937). Hodder (1990: 233ff) accepts that, in Brittany at least, there may be an alternative set of factors at play, referring to 'the subtle interlacing of indigenous principles and the Danubian principles of social domination centred on the dramatic idea of linear monumentality'. He accepts the possibility that the principles of the *domus* were prefigured in, and grew out of, Mesolithic Europe. None the less, while paying due regard to these Breton Mesolithic antecedents, Hodder concludes that, as far as early Neolithic monuments are concerned, 'when the tombs were built, it was in a milieu influenced by or in contact with Danubian groups in the Paris Basin constructing linear houses' (Hodder 1990: 235).

Recent work has begun to stress the early nature of the Breton long mounds, suggesting that they may be as old as, if not older than, the regional passage grave tradition. In view of the significance which the broad-brush interpretation of European long mounds has recently attained, this is a claim that demands careful consideration. To be sure of our conclusions, we need to resolve a number of questions about the nature and chronology of the Breton long mounds. Are they all sufficiently similar in form and structure to have derived from a single unified long mound tradition? And are they indeed as early as the earliest passage graves?

Broadly speaking, the early long mounds of Brittany may be divided into three distinct groups: (1) long mounds which cover a series of passage graves arranged side by side, the most famous example of which is Barnenez; (2) the long mounds special to the Carnac area known as 'tumulus carnacéens' or Carnac mounds; and (3) the so-called 'tertres tumulaires' such as the much-discussed monument of Le Manio I (Fig. 3).

The first group differs significantly from the others in structure and design, the long mound element being combined with a number of passage graves. The Barnenez mound on the northern coast of Brittany covers no fewer than eleven burial chambers arranged side by side and reached by long passages (Giot 1987). The cairn is thought to have been built in two phases, beginning with an eastern section containing five chambers, to which an extension with a further six chambers was added not long afterwards. The mound itself is slightly trapezoidal. There are similar monumental ensembles, with rectangular or sub-rectangular mounds, at Ile Gaignog and Ville-Pichard in northern Brittany (Giot 1987; L'Helgouach 1965: fig. 5, p. 26; fig. 14, p. 40). Note that in all three cases long mound and passage graves appear to be integral and contemporary parts of the same monument. This appears to be a northern Breton type, though rounded or oval mounds with two or three chambers are known in southern Brittany and beyond. The dating of the Barnenez-type long mounds is disputed: radiocarbon dates of ca 3800 bc have been obtained from one of the chambers (chamber G: Radiocarbon 13: 215), but other dates range from 3600 bc to 3150 bc (Radiocarbon 13: 214–15; Giot 1990: 32).

Barnenez, then, has early radiocarbon dates which relate both to the long mound and the passage graves. On the other hand, the linearity of the long mound axis is weakened by the presence of the passage graves opening through long passages from one side of the mound. Indeed, this kind of long mound is unlike any other in northern and western Europe. The linearity of the mound may be derived from a central European long-house ideology, but the possibility of a purely local origin must also be born in mind.

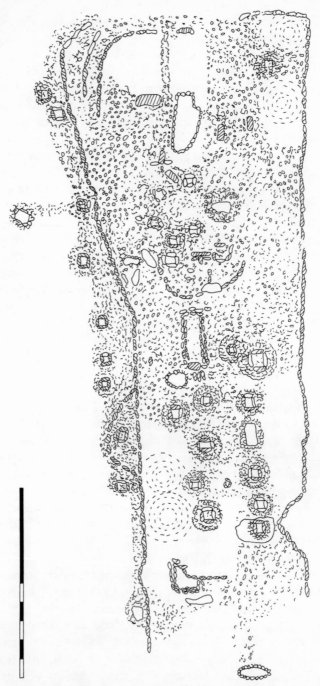

Figure 3. The tertre tumulaire *of Le Manio I at Carnac, Morbihan (after Le Rouzic).*

The form of the Barnenez mound, covering a series of passage graves, sets it clearly apart from the two other categories of early Breton long mound. Of these, it is the second category, the Carnac mounds, which are the most spectacular, distinguished from the *tertres tumulaires* both by their size and by the richness of their grave furnishings. The largest of all the Carnac mounds, the imposing Tumulus Saint-Michel at Carnac, forms a platform large enough to dwarf the Christian chapel built upon it. Excavations in the nineteenth and early twentieth centuries uncovered a number of sealed megalithic chambers beneath the mound, the richest containing 136 beads of jasper and turquoise, nine pendants, and 39 polished stone axes, eleven of jadeite (Le Rouzic 1932). The enclosed chamber at Mané Er-Hroeck nearby was even richer, with no fewer than 106 axes of jadeite, fibrolite and diorite, and 49 callaïs beads (Galles 1863; L'Helgouach 1979: 222). In addition to its sealed megalithic chambers, the Tumulus Saint-Michel has a passage grave at one extremity, but in contrast to the long mounds of the Barnenez type this seems to have been inserted at a later date. The same may be true of the passage graves in the Carnac mounds of Er-Grah and Mané Lud. As regards chronology, there are three conflicting dates from the Tumulus Saint-Michel: 3770 ± 300 bc (Sa-96) from the central chamber, 3030 ± 150 bc (GsY-89) from cist Y, but 6850 ± 300 bc (GsY-90) from cist Z (Coursaget et al. 1962; corrected dates in Giot et al. 1979: 249). It is possibly to rationalise these dates and attribute the first two to stages in the construction of the monument and the third to old wood, but such arguments are hazardous. Only new excavations, or perhaps accelerator dating of the weathered bone fragments now in the Vannes museum, will be able to resolve the question.

These Carnac mounds may be a development of the third type of early Breton long mound, the smaller '*tertres tumulaires*'. The best known of these is Le Manio I, which now lies partly beneath the Kermario stone rows at Carnac (Le Rouzic et al. 1923). This is a small trapezoidal structure, 45 m long and 16m wide at its broader end. It was excavated by Le Rouzic in 1922 and found to contain numerous small cist graves composed of four stone slabs standing on edge. The same year, he excavated a second similar multi-chambered mound at Lann Vras near Le Castellic; charcoal from one of the cists here gave a date of 3075 ± 300 bc (Gif-198 B), but a hearth at the opposite end gave 1980 ± 250 bc (Gif-198 A) (L'Helgouach 1979: 215, 248). The Castellic pottery of which this is the type site has been dated elsewhere to around 3000 bc (L'Helgouach 1990), suggesting that the earlier date may relate to the construction of the mound.

Long mounds related to these *tertres tumulaires* are found outside the Carnac area in central Brittany. At La Grée de Cojoux, hearths beneath such a long mound gave dates of 3710 ±120 bc (Gif-5458), 3630 ±120 bc (Gif-5456), and 3600 ±120 bc (Gif-5457), but these provide only a terminus post quem for the mound itself (Le Roux 1981: 395–99).

Another mound that may be related to this series of *tertres tumulaires* has been revealed by the excavations at Le Petit Mont near Carnac. This large multi-phase monument began as an elongated mound of dark earth. Charcoal from within the dark earth gave a radiocarbon date of 3700 ±70 bc (Gif-6844), but is considered by the excavator to be from earlier occupation on the site (Lecornec 1987: 55). During the second phase of construction, a dry-stone long cairn, slightly trapezoidal in plan, was built partly on top of the earlier mound; this cairn is as yet undated, but must be earlier than ca 3000 bc, when an extension covering two passage graves was built. Neither the mound of dark earth nor the trapezoidal cairn contain any burial structures (ibid.).

What may we conclude from this brief review? Firstly, that there may indeed be some link between the *tertres tumulaires* and the Carnac mounds, although the relative chronology of the two categories remains to be demonstrated. Both are found to have small closed chambers within them, often several in number, which may be interpreted (with due caution) as burial chambers, though the acidic soil conditions mean that little or no bone survives. Furthermore, both Carnac mounds and *tertres tumulaires* are concentrated largely in the southern part of Brittany, and their distribution is focussed on the Gulf of Morbihan. Secondly, that the long mounds covering passage graves of Barnenez type may be entirely unrelated; few in number, the most notable examples are found on the northern coast of Brittany at Barnenez itself and Ile Gaignog. They may thus be more of a northern Breton phenomenon, although examples are also found far to the south in Poitou-Charentes. The passage graves beneath the Barnenez-type mounds have led to them generally being placed within the context of the Atlantic passage graves, rather than the Breton long mounds. We shall discuss the origin of these passage graves below. But let us first consider the ancestry of the other categories of Breton long mound, the '*tumulus carnacéens*', and '*tertres tumulaires*'.

EX ORIENTE LUX?

We have seen above that the *tumulus carnacéens* or Carnac mounds may have been an enlarged and aggrandised variant of the *tertre tumulaire*. At present the suggested sequence from one to the other is based more on an assumed typological sequence than a closely dated series of monuments, but this is not to deny the plausibility of that hypothesis, nor the possibility that they are early in the Breton monument sequence. Furthermore, they may well be related to developments further east. This much is supported by the consistently trapezoidal form of the long mounds, which immediately recalls sites such as Passy in the Paris basin and Les Fouaillages on Jersey.

The site of Passy-sur-Yonne consists of a group of elongated structures on the gravel terrace of the Yonne valley, south of Paris. These were first discovered by aerial photography in the 1950s but were the subject of renewed interest and new aerial photographs in 1978, and then of excavations, which began in 1982 (Duhamel & Prestreau 1991). The cemetery consists of 25–30 monuments, ranging from 20 m to 300 m in length. In most cases the marks visible on the aerial photographs were those of ditches, but some of the structures also incorporated lengths of palisade. Study of the ditch fills suggests that mounds once stood within them, although these have now been ploughed flat. Several of the structures show multiple phases of construction. At Richebourg 4, for example, there were four phases, each of them associated with a single burial in a pit. In each case, the latest phase appears to be a circular monument, sometimes with cremations. Most of the burials are, however, single extended inhumations. The few double burials which have been found all involve children: either an adult plus a child, or two children together. There are no double or multiple burials of adults.

The Passy burials have few grave-goods, though the flint and bone work in general suggest a Cerny association (ca 3800–3500 bc). One grave has a vessel of Grossgartach type (a Rhenish pottery tradition earlier than Cerny, ending ca 3900 bc); another has a square-mouthed vessel with late Cerny decoration (Duhamel & Prestreau 1991: 107, 111). These finds are consistent with a dating in the first half of the fourth millennium bc. The trapezoidal monument of Les Fouaillages (Kinnes 1982) may be contemporary; the dates originally published have now been corrected to 3900 ± 100 bc (BM-1892R), 3950 ± 110 bc (BM-1893R), and 3720 ± 170 bc (BM-1894R) (Kinnes 1992). As so often with chambered tombs, it is not possible to pronounce with complete assurance how these determinations on charcoal relate to the construction and use of the monument.

The significance of the Passy cemetery derives from its position on the edge of the distribution of Bandkeramik farming communities in the Paris basin. It thus provides strong support for the argument which sees the Bandkeramik long-house as the inspiration for the long mound tradition of northern and western Europe. Passy-type mounds are already known in central Normandy at Rots near Caen (Chancerel et al. 1992), and from there it is but a short step to Guernsey and Les Fouaillages. The long mound concept could also have spread down the Loire valley and thence along the coast of southern Brittany to the Carnac region.

How far should we take the logic of this argument? Does the monumentalism of the Breton burial tradition begin with the arrival of Bandkeramik 'linear' ideology? If so, then the long trapezoidal *'tertres tumulaires'*, with small enclosed chambers, are perhaps the likeliest candidates for the earliest Breton burial mounds. They could in time have inspired two separate lines of development, one leading to the massive *'tumulus carnacéens'*, the other to long mounds with multiple passage graves such as Barnenez.

One of the most interesting recent interpretations has been the work of Boujot and Cassen. They argue that the Breton burial monuments develop by stages from the simple pit grave. In their view, the first monumental tombs are the *'tertres tumulaires'* and *'tumulus carnacéens'*, in which the pit grave has become a sealed stone-built cist or chamber. These they consider to have been designed for individual burials. From the long mounds with sealed cists or chambers, the other classes of monument then developed by processes of imitation and adaptation (Boujot & Cassen 1992, 1993). Their diagram (Fig. 4) summarises the proposed scheme. One argument in favour of their scheme is the relative architectural sophistication of the earliest passage graves, such as those at Barnenez with their corbel-vaulted roofs. The mastery of the material evident in these structures would have taken time to develop. This suggests there must have been a pre-passage grave stage in which less complex structures were created, including perhaps the sealed chambers beneath the long mounds (Boujot & Cassen 1992: 198). For this scheme to work, however, it would be necessary to show that the long mounds are earlier than the passage graves by perhaps several centuries. A key part of their argument is rejection of the existing radiocarbon dates of around 3800 bc from passage graves such as Barnenez and Bougon. Instead they would place the *tertres tumulaires* at about that point in the chronology, with the passage graves following three or four centuries later (see Fig. 4).

Whether this is the correct sequence of developments remains an open question. No *tertres tumulaires* or Carnac mounds have yet been

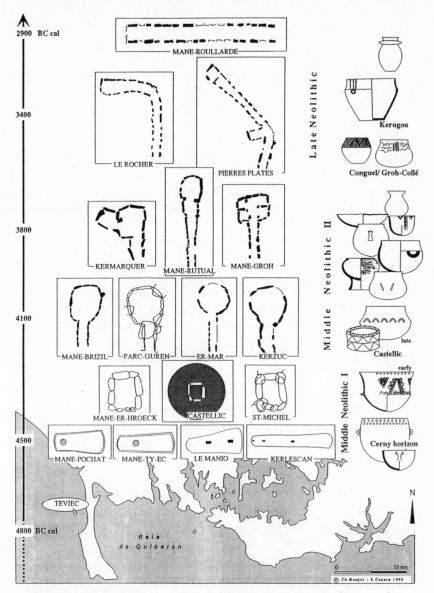

Figure 4. The Boujot-Cassen scheme of Breton monument development, from long mounds to allées couvertes. *(After Boujot & Cassen 1992: fig. 9).*

dated to before 3200 bc. On the other hand, the new radiocarbon evidence from Bougon (Scarre et al. 1993) strengthens the view that the earliest passage graves of north-western France date to around 3800 bc. To this extent, the accepted model which sees passage graves as an early and largely indigenous development of Brittany and other parts of Atlantic Europe is still supported by the latest evidence.

None the less, the argument that a single pervasive ideology, of eastern origin, lay behind these various types of monuments is seductive in its simplicity. Both long mounds and long-houses appear to incorporate a symbolism based on communal structures and linearity. Nor need we limit the concept of linearity to the mound form alone. If such linearity lay behind the construction of the *tertres tumulaires* and Carnac mounds, it may also have been adapted to give rise to Breton passage graves in which the linearity is transferred from mound form to the long axis of passage and chamber (Hodder 1990: 236). At the same time, however, warning bells sound as it brings to mind the grand theories of European prehistory associated with Gordon Childe in the earlier part of this century and above all, the concept of 'the irradiation of European barbarism by Oriental civilization' (Childe 1958).

There may be another way of looking at the question. The theories discussed above have tended to assume that there is a clear choice between the 'long mound theory' and the 'passage grave' theory. The problem in assessing the relative merits of these competing views in the context of north-western France is the interrelatedness of the different monument types. It is not easy to trace a single line of development from one initial monument type. Instead, we have a pattern of cultural interplay between a number of separate and converging traditions. The Breton 'tertres tumulaires' and 'Carnac mounds', with their strong linear emphasis, may indeed be an extension of Bandkeramik ideology. Classic Bandkeramik long-houses are known from the Paris basin, some 400 km to the east of Brittany. But that does not prevent us from concluding that the passage graves fit best into an Atlantic context, and may reflect a different set of contacts and ideologies. Let us therefore consider more closely the arguments for an indigenous Atlantic contribution to the mounded tomb tradition.

First and foremost, collective burial, no part of the Bandkeramik tradition, is present in the local Breton Mesolithic at Téviec and Hoëdic. One of the graves at Téviec, H6, contained remains of no fewer than six individuals, and may have been opened on several occasions to allow a new body to be introduced. After the final burial, stones were placed over the grave, and a hearth built on top of them, perhaps as part of the funerary rites. When the ritual was complete, a pile of larger stones was laid on top to form a small tumulus that contains no fewer than six inhumations (Péquart et al. 1937). The Passy long mounds, on the other hand, contain for the most part only single inhumations. The exceptions, as we have seen, are occasional double burials involving children. Multiple burials of adults are so far unknown at Passy (Duhamel & Prestreau 1991). Single graves are also standard in Bandkeramik cemeteries such as Elsloo (Modderman 1970) or Nitra (Pavúk 1972) and in the scattered burials of the Paris basin Bandkeramik (Ilett 1983). The practice of multiple inhumation is thus either an innovation of the Breton early Neolithic or the continuation of an earlier regional Mesolithic tradition.

A second point is that the long mound/long-house equation replaces an earlier emphasis on chamber form (e.g. L'Helgouach 1965) by a new and equally strong emphasis on mound form. We may accept that the concept of linearity which the long mounds display is derived from Bandkeramik ideology, but we must also recognise that the form and architecture of the burial chambers, whether passage graves or sealed chambers within the mound, is not immediately traceable to a Bandkeramik source. The chambers of the earliest passage graves are often circular in plan; it has been suggested that a local Neolithic round house tradition could be the inspiration (Daniel 1941). At present there is no real evidence for such a tradition. If this were so, however, we would have the curious situation where the long mound form is derived from the Bandkeramik house and the chamber form for passage graves from the local early Neolithic house!

A third and more crucial observation is that mounded tombs are not merely a Breton tradition but are also found in other regions of France and in the British Isles, Portugal, Spain, northern Germany, Poland, and Scandinavia. How does the long mound hypothesis fit with this broader geographical perspective? It may well account for the inception of mounded tomb development in areas adjacent to the Bandkeramik settlement zone, but it is clearly more difficult to use it to explain the Atlantic distribution of mounded tombs in regions far from Bandkeramik settlement, such as Portugal.

ATLANTIC CONNECTIONS: A THREE-PHASE MODEL

The three arguments stated above begin to turn the emphasis away from Breton long mounds, and the long-house/long mound equation, and lead us instead to consider those kinds of mounded tomb, notably passage graves, which appear to have an Atlantic context and origin. What we need here is an explanation which works not only at the regional or local level but also makes sense of the Atlantic tradition of monumental chambered tombs as a whole. Processual explanations which posit parallel processes, such as pressure from expanding agricultural groups, may be discounted since they are unable to account for the precise morphology of individual monuments, still less the clear resemblances between monument development in different areas. What we must look for instead is an explanation couched in terms not of vague general processes but of specific cultural features and stimuli.

Here again, as in the case of the long-house/long mound equation, we may expect ideological orientations to have played a part in structuring the ways in which communities approached the disposal of their dead. We may look for manifestations of this in the form of the burial monument, and perhaps also in the way in which the corpses were treated. A further powerful source of information is the so-called 'megalithic art', the pecked and engraved designs, mostly abstract, with which some of the passage graves were decorated.

Passage graves and megalithic art have a marked Atlantic distribution, suggesting a sharing of ideas or ideologies along coastal maritime routes. Other kinds of evidence support the view that there was maritime contact between Atlantic prehistoric communities, both during the Neolithic and before.

Two good sources of evidence for the scope and extent of Mesolithic and Neolithic contacts are the settlement of offshore islands and the movement of raw materials which can be attributed to a specified source. The material of the burial monuments themselves provides little information, as it is virtually always of local origin. The derivation of the capstone of one of the Bougon chambered tombs in an outcrop of limestone 4 km from the site is fairly typical of the distances involved. The quarry source probably lay within the territory of the community that built the tomb (Mohen 1977). For evidence of contacts between prehistoric communities of western Europe, we must look to smaller and more portable kinds of material. The connections which these reveal may be an indication of the routes along which new ideas and influences, including those concerning burial monuments and their meaning, could have travelled both within and between regions.

In a mainland context, raw materials were probably passed from hand to hand between communities; the long-distance movement of, for example, chocolate-coloured flint from the Holy Cross Mountains of central Poland in the late Upper Palaeolithic (Schild 1976) or of polished stone axes of fine-grained volcanic tuff from Great Langdale in the British Neolithic (Bradley & Edmonds 1993) need not imply that any individual moved more than a few tens of kilometres. Maritime contacts, however, give evidence of travel over rather longer distances during the fourth and third millennia. Thus the Orkney islands must have been settled by sailors from northern Scotland, crossing at least 12 km of open sea, by at least 3500 BC; there are dates of 2800 bc from the small settlement at Knap of Howar (Ritchie 1985). Only a little later than this, around 2500 bc, are the earliest houses at Scord of Brouster on the more remote Shetland Isles, a further 80 km to the north (Whittle et al. 1986). The Scilly Isles off the south-western tip of Britain were probably first settled at about the same time. Polished stone axes of Tievebulliagh porcellanite are relatively common in south-western Scotland, testifying to fairly regular traffic across the straits from northern Ireland during the fourth and third millennia BC (Sheridan 1986a). As far as cross-Channel traffic is concerned, five axes of Breton type A dolerite have been found at locations in southern England (Parlborough, Sussex; Moordown and Shirley, Hants; Priddy, Somerset; and Bredon Hill, Worcestershire) (Le Roux 1990). Radiocarbon dates show that the Plussulien quarries were in operation during the period ca 3300–2400 bc (Giot et al. 1979: 373).

We should expect to find echoes of these maritime contacts in cultural developments in different parts of the Atlantic zone. The difficulty rests in determining what criteria may be accepted as evidence of interaction, and whether external contacts had a significant impact on local developments. We have no wish to resurrect the idea of a single megalithic religion, spread by missionaries (Hawkes 1934: 26; Piggott 1935: 60), nor of a widely disseminated funerary goddess cult (Crawford 1957; Daniel 1941; Fleming 1969). What I would like to suggest, however, is that the development of Atlantic chambered tombs may be divided into three broad stages, each characterised by a different balance of regionally specific and more generally shared features in tomb architecture. A similar scheme has been suggested by Shee Twohig (1993).

The first phase (3800–3300 bc) is marked by considerable regional variation in the form of the earliest monumental tombs. In Brittany the first passage graves may belong to this period, as may the early passage graves at Bougon further south near Poitiers. In the Carnac region, by contrast, the earliest monuments may have been long mounds and menhirs.

Megalithic art in this first phase appears to be restricted to Brittany, and consists of motifs which are schematic but representational, rather than purely abstract as in later phases. Motifs include axes, hafted axes, crooks, and crosses. They are found on menhirs and on simple passage graves (Shee-Twohig 1981: 49–65).

Moving northwards to Ireland, the Carrowmore tombs may also fall within this phase, although we still await confirmation of their chronological status. The early date of ca 3800 bc from tomb 4 is now generally discounted (Burenhult 1980; Caulfield 1983). Simple tombs of the type represented here by, for example, Carrowmore 27 may nevertheless be among the earliest Irish chambered tombs, and constitute another Atlantic regional tradition (Sheridan 1986b: 19).

Phase one in north-western Iberia probably consists of mounds covering simple closed chambers, which Criado Boado and Fabregas Valcarce (1989) have suggested stand at the head of the Galician sequence. This is borne out by a recent critique of radiocarbon dates for the chambered mounds on the Aboboreira plateau in northern Portugal (Da Cruz 1988). In south-western Iberia the earliest monuments may likewise be simple closed chambers (Shee Twohig 1981: 20). Savory (1968: 83, 96) suggests that single burials in slab-lined cists, roofed with rough corbelling and covered by a mound, found in southern Portugal, may precede the first Portuguese passage graves. If these do indeed come before early passage graves such as Poço da Gateira 1 and Anta dos Gorginos 2, with TL dates of ca 4500 BC, they would be very early indeed (Whittle & Arnaud 1975).

To sum up, despite chronological uncertainties this first phase of Atlantic chambered tombs appears to be characterised by (a) monumental construction, whether simply an unchambered earthen cairn (for instance the earliest structure at Petit-Mont, Arzon) or perhaps a long mound with multiple cists (e.g. Le Manio I); (b) smaller mounds covering a simple chamber perhaps generally sealed (Carrowmore, south-western Iberia), and possibly containing multiple inhumations; and maybe also (c) passage graves in some areas of north-western France, such as northern Brittany and Poitou. The overall picture is one of considerable regional variance, but it is still difficult to believe that all of these constitute autonomous local developments; there seems to be a common basis in the development of mortuary-related monuments in the different regions.

The second phase is marked by the *floruit* of the classic passage graves (3300–2800 bc or possibly as late as 2500 bc), which were built in regions as far apart as southern Portugal and Scandinavia. Both tomb architecture and megalithic art show strong inter-regional similarities in this period. In contrast to the preceding period, the principal art motifs are non-representational, consisting of abstract curves, circles, spirals, and meanders, often in closely spaced concentric patterns. In terms of Twohig's classification, this includes the phase 2 art of Brittany, the Fourknocks and Loughcrew styles in Ireland, and the non-Viseu art of Portugal (Shee Twohig 1981: 135–8). This kind of art is represented most spectacularly at Gavrinis, a passage grave on a small island in the Gulf of Morbihan in southern Brittany, where the blocking of the tomb is dated to 2470 ± 80 bc (Gif-5766) (Le Roux 1985). By far the greatest number of examples is to be found however in the passage graves of the Boyne valley, especially Knowth (Eogan 1986). Perhaps in this phase, as Bradley and Chapman suggest (1986), we should see these regions as competing centres of power, imitating and emulating each other's funerary monuments along the Atlantic seaboard of Europe.

The fact that this kind of megalithic art is shared between different regions does not automatically mean that it had been transferred from one place to another. As Shee Twohig (1981: 139) puts it, with due caution, 'The similarities are not strong enough to demonstrate unequivocally that the art was transferred from one area to another but some contact seems likely to have taken place.' Under certain circumstances, identical motifs may be developed by different societies entirely in isolation. This is the alternative possibility presented by recent writers seeking to demonstrate the entoptic nature of the designs involved (Bradley 1989; Lewis-Williams & Dowson 1993; Dronfield 1995, 1996). Entoptic motifs are a universal product of the human psyche in certain altered states of consciousness, such as trances induced by narcotics or other intoxicants. The abstract patterns which are seen in these circumstances are the same irrespective of cultural or social background. If it is accepted that some megalithic art consists of entoptic motifs, then we need not expect to find direct cultural contacts between the regions using this art. Any specific parallels would be indicative not of cultural contact between these regions, but would stem instead from the origin of these motifs in universal characteristics of the human psyche.

This hypothesis must, however, be put in context. Entoptic imagery may indeed provide an explanation for the independent development of similar motifs in different societies. Must we also assume that the use of mind-altering substances and the decision to decorate the walls of tomb chambers with the resulting entoptic motifs were also independent developments? Both are specific social actions which do not depend on the forms of the motifs themselves. A large number of French Neolithic burial chambers have yielded fragments of 'incense-burners' which may well have been used for the inhalation of a narcotic such as opium (Sherratt 1991). Only a small minority of the chambers in which they occur are decorated with engraved designs. Unless we assume that the remainder of these chambers had painted decoration which has since disappeared (Devignes 1992), we must conclude that the decision to use intoxicating substances was separate from the decision to carve these designs on the tomb walls. The decision to inhale and the decision to carve must be clearly distinguished from each other. Hence even if the motifs themselves derive from the universal human psyche, it is still unlikely that the act of reproducing them on tomb walls arose in each of these regions at about the same time merely by chance. A measure of contact in the use of the entoptic motifs seems to be the most probable explanation (Lewis-Williams & Dowson 1993: 61–62).

The third phase, finally, is marked by a return to a greater regional variation in tomb architecture (from ca 2500 bc or a little earlier to ca 2000 bc or even later). In Brittany at this time we find the angled passage graves, V-shaped tombs, side-entrance tombs, and *allées couvertes*; in Portugal, the simple cist graves under low mounds; while in Ireland, the distinctive wedge-tombs often associated with Beaker pottery may belong to this phase (Harbison 1988: 100–102; Woodman 1992).

The inter-regional connections were not entirely broken at this period. The Boyne valley tombs, dated to ca 2500 bc (Sheridan 1986b) lie at the transition from the second to third phase. In analysing the art present in these monuments, O'Sullivan (1986; 1989) distinguishes two separate and successive styles. The first of these is the depictive style, which includes the standard repertory of Irish passage grave geometric motifs and must have been the style in currency when the monuments were built, since some of the motifs were located on the back surfaces of stone which were later hidden within the mound. The second style he labels the plastic style, from its greater exploitation of the three-dimensional qualities of the stones on which it appears; it focusses on decorating the stone as a solid form (O'Sullivan 1989). It also includes several standard passage graves elements together with certain novel motifs. O'Sullivan points to close parallels to this style in the angled passage graves of Brittany, such as Goërem and Les Pierres Plates (Shee Twohig 1981: figs 134–6, 143–8). Certain of these elements are thought within the Breton context to be derived from the earlier 'buckler' motif, which may be anthropomorphic; if so, the Boyne valley plastic style may represent the transfer of derived anthropomorphic imagery to Ireland (O'Sullivan 1986: 81–2). Other Breton tombs of this third phase have what is thought to be more explicit anthropomorphic imagery, including 'necklaces' and paired 'breasts' (e.g. Crec'h Quillé, Tressé, and Kergüntuil: Shee Twohig 1981: figs 8, 149–51, 160).

This three-phase scheme places emphasis on the common patterns in tomb development in the regions concerned. The evidence of the art in particular suggests that there may have been a shared ideology between the different regions. Are we then justified in explaining the mounded tombs of western and northern Europe in terms of twin interacting ideologies, one originating among the communities of the Atlantic facade, the other derived from the Bandkeramik long-house tradition of central Europe? This is certainly the model that the evidence currently appears best to fit. At the same time, individual mounded tombs must be seen in their local context. Contact between communities will have brought new ideas and influences, but the ways in which these were accepted or rejected will have varied. This much is evident in the diversity of the monuments themselves; no two are exactly alike. Each of them is a unique product of a particular community, imbued with a unique set of meanings and significances by the people who built and used it. If the treatment here has concentrated largely on questions at a broader geographical scale, this can only ever be one part of the story.

POWER AND BELIEF IN NEOLITHIC SOCIETY

The discussion above differs in may respects from recent British approaches to chambered tombs by authors such as Thomas and Tilley. They have sought new ways to understand these monuments in terms of how they may have been regarded by the people who built them and by succeeding generations who lived nearby. A regularly repeated theme has been that of power, a preoccupation which betrays these authors' original adherence to the structural Marxist school. In the case of burial chambers enclosed within a mound or accessible only via a narrow passage the idea of exclusion and privileged access has been given prominence. The development of more complex tomb forms has been directly linked to growing social differentiation, in which most of the community were excluded from the tomb itself, and allowed to witness ceremonies only from the outside (Thomas 1990). Similar arguments have been put forward for the Maltese temples (Stoddart et al. 1993).

Lewis-Williams and Dowson (1993) have taken these ideas of power and exclusivity as inferred from tomb layout and have combined them with their own interpretation of non-representational 'megalithic' art as entoptically inspired. According to this view, the motifs copy the form of mental images perceived during altered states of consciousness. They (ibid.: 63) suggest that

> during the Neolithic, an élite increasingly appropriated ecstatic religious experience. Greater social complexity and differentiation may have gone hand in hand with the greater differentiation of ritual roles suggested by more numerous divisions of ritual space. The importance of the boundaries between divisions increased: transition from one social group to another was denied or marked by rites of passage, and the divisions of ritual space (kerbstones, portals and doorways) were marked by entoptic motifs . . . which suggest that certain altered states of consciousness may have played a role in some rites of passage or may have been the exclusive property of the group that enjoyed the right to pass through the divisions.

The trend in the analysis of chambered tombs raised the question of how indeed were they actually used, and whether they played the prominent part in a game of politico-ritual power relations which these authors suggest. Is this a humanising or dehumanising perspective? It is certainly only a partial interpretation for the construction and use of these tombs, and in this respect may be compared with the processual interpretations of the 1970s, which placed great emphasis on the tombs as territorial markers (e.g. Chapman 1981; Renfrew 1976). As was pointed out in response, the hypothesis of territorial marker goes only a little way towards the explaining the tombs as a whole. In the same way, the interpretation which sees the enclosed chamber as a source of power for an elite group must be considered marginal to the full meaning of the tombs in their prehistoric social and ideological context. If indeed they were conceived of primarily as burial places – rather than as raised platforms for rituals in which the burial element was subsidiary rather than central – then they would have been associated with beliefs about death.

Beliefs, like ritual or esoteric knowledge (Helms 1988), are of course a source of power in human societies; they may be manipulated for advantage by individuals or groups. They are not, however, invented merely to mislead and subjugate others. Death is a particularly powerful concept, but its power is in large measure emotional, and consists in the attempt by the living to come to terms with bereavement and with the concept of death itself. There is also a strong connection between funerary practices and what the living community believes happens to a person after death. The notion of a journey is common, as Van Gennep described over eighty years ago in his classic study of rites of passage. The length of mourning is sometimes thought to cover the time which it takes the dead person to reach their final state or resting place (Van Gennep 1960 [1906]).

It should further be noted that the recent analyses which have placed great emphasis on the power of beliefs in rise of social elites have not really addressed the importance of those beliefs themselves in motivating societies to construct tombs and perform burial and post-mortem rituals. These must in part have been the consequence of the particular attitudes of these societies to death and burial; a modern approach focussing predominantly on power relations can only provide a partial interpretation of the role and meaning of the monuments. To the extent that an emotional response to death is an innate human characteristic, power-centred approaches may be considered dehumanising. It is here that the entoptic interpretation of megalithic art displays its greatest explanatory potential, in suggesting that the burial chambers were places giving access, or 'doorways', to the other world or contact with other-worldly beings. Yet here again Lewis-Williams and Dowson immediately stress the social power associated with such access, discussing (1993: 60) it in terms of 'a select group that entered the deep chambers and a deep altered state of consciousness that took them and them alone into the realm of the ancestors, the imagined centre and source of power.' There must, surely, have been more to the symbolism of death and burial than social power alone. In the absence of the legends and myths that went with these tombs, it is difficult to point out exactly where this analysis fails; but we may be sure that the richness of belief went far beyond such a narrow instrumentalist conception of a spirit world manipulated to advantage by a nascent Neolithic elite.

ACKNOWLEDGEMENTS

I wish to thank Ezra Zubrow for reading and commenting on an early version of this article.

REFERENCES

Boujot, C. & Cassen, S. 1992. Le développement des premières architectures funéraires monumentales en France occidentale. In *Paysans et Batisseurs. Actes du 17e Colloque Interrégional sur le Néolithique, Vannes, 1990*, pp. 195–211.

Boujot, C. and Cassen, S. 1993. A pattern of evolution for the Neolithic funerary structures of the west of France. *Antiquity* 67: 477–491.

Bradley, R. 1989. Deaths and entrances: a contextual analysis of megalithic art. *Current Anthropology* 30: 68–75.

Bradley, R. & Chapman, R. 1986. The nature and development of long-distance relations in later Neolithic Britain and Ireland. In Renfrew C. & Cherry, J. (eds), *Peer-Polity Interaction and Socio-political Change*, pp. 127–136. Cambridge: Cambridge University Press.

Bradley, R. & Edmonds, M. 1993. *Interpreting the Axe Trade. Production and Exchange in Neolithic Britain.* Cambridge: Cambridge University Press.

Burenhult, G. 1980. *The Archaeological Excavation at Carrowmore, Co. Sligo, Ireland: excavation seasons 1977–79.* Stockholm: University of Stockholm, Institute of Archaeology (Theses & Papers in North European Archaeology 9).

Case, H. 1976. Acculturation and the earlier Neolithic in western Europe. In de Laet, S. J. (ed.), *Acculturation and Continuity in Atlantic Europe*, pp. 45–58. Brugge: De Tempel.

Caulfield, S. 1983. The Neolithic settlement of north Connaught. In Reeves-Smyth, T. & Hamond, F. (eds), *Landscape Archaeology in Ireland*, pp. 195–215. Oxford: British Archaeological Reports.

Chancerel, A., Desloges, J., Dron, J.-L., & San Juan, G. 1992. Le début du Néolithique en Basse-Normandie. In *Paysans et Batisseurs. Actes du 17e Colloque Interrégional sur le Néolithique, Vannes, 1990*, pp. 153–73.

Chapman, R. 1981. The emergence of formal disposal areas and the ' problem' of megalithic tombs in prehistoric Europe. In Chapman, R., Kinnes, I. and Randsborg, K. (eds), *The Archaeology of Death*, pp. 71–81. Cambridge: Cambridge University Press.

Childe, V. G. 1958. Retrospect. *Antiquity* 32: 69–74.

Clark, J. G. D. 1977. The economic context of dolmens and passage-graves in Sweden. In Markotic, V. (ed.), *Ancient Europe and the Mediterranean*, pp. 35–49. Warminster: Aris & Phillips.

Coursaget, J., Giot, P.-R., & Le Run, J. 1962. A fresh series of radiocarbon dates from France. *Antiquity* 36: 139–141.

Crawford, O. G. S. 1957. *The Eye Goddess.* London: Phoenix House.

Criado Boado, F. & Fabregas Valcarce, F. 1989. The megalithic phenomenon of northwest Spain: main trends. *Antiquity* 63: 682–696.

Da Cruz, D. J. 1988. O megalitismo do norte de Portugal. *Trabalhos de Antropologia e Etnologia* 28: 31–41.

Daniel, G. E. 1941. The dual nature of the megalithic colonisation of prehistoric Europe. *Proceedings of the Prehistoric Society* 7: 1–49.

Daniel, G. E. 1958. *The Megalith Builders of Western Europe.* London.

Devignes, M. 1992. L'art des dolmens peints. *Archéologia*, June 1992: 50–57.

Dronfield, J. 1995. Subjective vision and the source of Irish megalithic art. *Antiquity* 69: 539–549.

Dronfield, J. 1996. Entering alternative realities: cognition, art and architecture in Irish passage tombs. *Cambridge Archaeological Journal* 6.

Duhamel, P. & Prestreau, M. 1991. La nécropole monumentale néolithique de Passy dans le contexte du gigantisme-funéraire européen. In *La Région Centre: Carrefour d'Influences? Actes du 14e Colloque Interrégional sur le Néolithique, Blois 1987*, 103–117.

Eogan, G. 1986. *Knowth and the Passage-Tombs of Ireland.* London: Thames & Hudson.

Fleming, A. 1969. The myth of the mother-goddess. *World Archaeology* 1: 247–261.

Galles, R. 1863. Manné-er-H'roëk. Dolmen découvert sous un tumulus à Locmariaquer. *Bulletin de la Société Polymathique du Morbihan* 1863: 18–33.

Giot, P.-R. 1987. *Barnenez, Carn, Guennoc.* Rennes: Travaux du Laboratoire Anthropologie-Préhistoire-Protohistoire-Quaternaire armoricains.

Giot, P.-R. 1990. Les dates d'utilisation des sépultures mégalithiques. *Bulletin de la Sociéte Archéologique du Finistère* 119: 32–33.

Giot, P.-R., L'Helgouach, J., & Monnier, J.-L. 1979. *Préhistoire de la Bretagne.* Rennes: Ouest-France.

Harbison, P. 1988. *Pre-Christian Ireland. From the First Settlers to the Early Celts.* London: Thames & Hudson.

Hawkes, J. 1934. Aspects of the Neolithic and Chalcolithic periods in western Europe. *Antiquity* 8: 24–42.

Helms, M. W. 1988. *Ulysses' Sail. An Ethnographic Odyssey of Power, Knowledge, and Geographical Distance.* Princeton, N. J.: Princeton University Press.

Hodder, I. 1984. Burials, houses, women and men in the European Neolithic. In Miller, D. & Tilley, C. (eds), *Ideology, Power and Prehistory*, pp. 51–68. Cambridge: Cambridge University Press.

Hodder, I. 1990. *The Domestication of Europe.* Oxford: Basil Blackwell.

Ilett, M. 1983. The early Neolithic of north-eastern France. In Scarre, C. (ed.), *Ancient France 6000–2000 BC: Neolithic Societies and their Landscapes*, pp. 6–33. Edinburgh: Edinburgh University Press.

Kinnes, I. 1982. Les Fouaillages and megalithic origins. *Antiquity* 56: 24–30.

Kinnes, I. 1992. *Non-Megalithic Long Barrows and Allied Structures in the British Neolithic.* London: British Museum (British Museum Occasional Paper 52).

Lecornec, J. 1987. Le complexe mégalithique du Petit Mont à Arzon (Morbihan). *Revue Archéologique de l'Ouest* 4: 37–56.

Le Roux, C.-T. 1981. Circonscription de la Bretagne. *Gallia Préhistoire* 24: 395–423.

Le Roux, C.-T. 1985. New excavations at Gavrinis. *Antiquity* 59: 183–187.

Le Roux, C.-T. 1990. La pétro-archéologie des haches polies armoricaines, 40 ans après. In *La Bretagne et L'Europe Préhistoriques*, pp. 345–353. (Revue Archéologique de l'Ouest, Supplément no. 2).

Le Rouzic, Z. 1932. *Carnac: Fouilles Faites dans la Région. Tumulus du Mont Saint-Michel, 1900–1906.* Vannes.

Le Rouzic, Z., Péquart, S-J., & Péquart, M. 1923. *Carnac: Fouilles Faites dans la Region. Campagne 1922. Tumulus du Crucuny, Tertre du Manio, Tertre du Castellic.* Paris.

Lewis-Williams, J. D. & Dowson, T. A. 1993. On vision and power in the Neolithic: evidence from the decorated monuments. *Current Anthropology* 34: 55–65.

L'Helgouach, J. 1965. *Les sépultures mégalithiques en Armorique.* Rennes: Travaux du Laboratoire d'Anthropologie et de Préhistoire de la Faculté des Sciences.

L'Helgouach, J. 1979. Les groupes humains de V^e au IIIe millénaires. In Giot, P.-R., L'Helgouach, J., & Monnier, J.-L., *Préhistoire de la Bretagne*, pp. 155–320. Rennes: Ouest-France.

L'Helgouach, J. 1990. De l'Ile Carn à La Table des Marchand. In *La Bretagne et L'Europe Préhistoriques*, pp. 89–95. (Revue Archéologique de l'Ouest, Supplément no. 2.)

L'Helgouach, J. & Le Roux, C.-T. 1986. Morphologie et chronologie des grandes architectures de l'Ouest de la France. In Demoule, J.-P. & Guilaine, J. (eds), *Le Néolithique de la France*, pp. 181–191. Paris: Picard.

Midgeley, M. S. 1985. *The Origin and Function of the Earthen Long Barrows of Northern Europe*. Oxford: British Archaeological Reports.

Mohen, J.-P. 1977. Les tumulus de Bougon. Cinq années de recherches (1972–1977). *Bulletin de la Société Historique et Scientifique des Deux-Sèvres*, pp. 1–48.

Modderman, P. J. R. 1970. *Linearbandkeramik aus Elsloo und Stein*. (Analecta Praehistorica Leidensia 3.)

O'Sullivan, M. 1986. Approaches to passage tomb art. *Journal of the Royal Society of Antiquaries of Ireland* 116: 68–83.

O'Sullivan, M. 1989. A stylistic revolution in the megalithic art of the Boyne Valley. *Archaeology Ireland* 3: 138–142.

Pavúk, J. 1972. Neolithisches Gräberfeld in Nitra. *Slovenska Archeologia* 20: 5–105.

Péquart, M., Péquart, S.-J., Boule, M., & Vallois, H. V. 1937. *Téviec: Station nécropole mésolithique du Morbihan*. Paris: (Archives de l'Institut de Paléontologie Humaine 18).

Péquart, M. & Péquart, S.-J. 1954. *Hoëdic. Deuxième station nécropole mésolithique du Morbihan*. Antwerp: De Sikkel.

Piggott, S. 1935. *The Progress of Early Man*. London: Black.

Renfrew, C. 1976. Megaliths, territories and populations. In de Laet, S. J. (ed.), *Acculturation and Continuity in Atlantic Europe*, pp. 198–220. Brugge: De Tempel.

Ritchie, A. 1985. The first settlers. In Renfrew, C. (ed.), *The Prehistory of Orkney*, pp. 36–53. Edinburgh: Edinburgh University Press.

Savory, H. N. 1968. *Spain and Portugal*. London: Thames & Hudson.

Scarre, C. 1983. Settlements and chambered tombs in Neolithic France. *Oxford Journal of Archaeology* 2: 265–278.

Scarre, C., Switsur, V. R., & Mohen, J.-P. 1993. New dates for French passage graves. *Antiquity*.

Schild, R. 1976. The final Palaeolithic settlements of the European plain. *Scientific American* 234: 88–99.

Shanks, M. & Tilley, C. 1982. Ideology, symbolic power and ritual communication: a reinterpretation of Neolithic mortuary practices. In Hodder, I. (ed.), *Symbolic and Structural Archaeology*, pp. 129–154. Cambridge: Cambridge University Press.

Shee Twohig, E. 1981. *The Megalithic Art of Western Europe*. Oxford: Clarendon Press.

Shee Twohig, E. 1993. Megalithic tombs and megalithic art in Atlantic Europe. In Scarre, C. and Healy, F. (eds), *Trade and Exchange in Prehistoric Europe*, pp. 87–99. Oxford: Oxbow Books.

Sheridan, A. 1986a. Porcellanite artefacts: a new survey. *Ulster Journal of Archaeology* 49: 19–32.

Sheridan, A. 1986b. Megaliths and megalomania: an account, and interpretation, of the development of passage tombs in Ireland. *Journal of Irish Archaeology* 3: 17–30.

Sherratt, A. 1990. The genesis of megaliths: monumentality, ethnicity and social complexity in Neolithic north-west Europe. *World Archaeology* 22: 147–167.

Sherratt, A. 1991. Sacred and profane substances: the ritual use of narcotics in later Neolithic Europe. In Garwood, P., Jennings, D., Skeates, R., & Toms, J. (eds), *Sacred and Profane. Proceedings of a Conference on Archaeology, Ritual and Religion, Oxford 1989*, pp. 50–64. Oxford: Oxford University Committee for Archaeology.

Stoddart, S., Bonnano, A., Gouder, T., Malone, C., & Trump, D. 1993. Cult in an island society: prehistoric Malta in the Tarxien period. *Cambridge Archaeological Journal* 3: 3–19.

Thomas, J. 1990. Monuments from the inside: the case of the Irish megalithic tombs. *World Archaeology* 22: 168–178.

Tilley, C. 1984. Ideology and the legitimation of power in the middle Neolithic of southern Sweden. In Miller, D. & Tilley, C. (eds), *Ideology, Power and Prehistory*, pp. 111–146. Cambridge: Cambridge University Press.

Van Gennep, A. 1962. *The Rites of Passage*. London: Routledge & Kegan Paul.

Whittle, A., Keith-Lucas, M., Milles, A., Noddle, B., Rees, S., & Romans, J. C. C. 1986. *Scord of Brouster. An Early Agricultural Settlement on Shetland*. Oxford: Oxford University Committee for Archaeology.

Whittle, E. H. & Arnaud, J. M. 1975. Thermoluminescent dating of Neolithic and Chalcolithic pottery from sites in central Portugal. *Archaeometry* 17: 5–24.

Woodman, P. C. 1992. Filling in the spaces in Irish prehistory. *Antiquity* 66: 295–314.

9

Interpreting Enclosures

Richard Bradley

Il n'y a de création que dans l'imprévisible devenant necessité.

– Pierre Boulez

It comes as something of a surprise to see a corpus of central European enclosures that compares them with the henge monuments of the British Isles (Trnka 1991: 298–9). After all, their distributions may be separated by 900 kilometres and their construction by more than 1500 years. At first sight the comparison seems out of place in an eminently respectable monograph published in Vienna. The strange thing is that similar links have been suggested before, and by scholars with little obvious interest in archaeological theory. Some years ago Behrens (1981) published a paper announcing the discovery of 'the first "Woodhenge" in Middle Europe', and Modderman (1976) wrote another account of Neolithic enclosures on the Continent in which he referred to them collectively as 'the Aveburys and their . . . counterparts'. Although his own site at Heinheim was of about the same age as the first henge monuments (Modderman 1986: 95–6), his essay ranged equally widely. Once again he was quite content to postulate connections extending over fifty generations. We need to explore the circumstances in which such comparisons are possible and must ask ourselves whether there is a context in which such projections are legitimate.

They were made for obvious reasons. Such appeals to distant comparanda usually resulted from the desire to fix the right interpretation of these monuments. Such theories tended to oscillate between their role as domestic sites and an alternative version that saw them as ceremonial centres (Whittle 1988 a). That ambivalence is widespread. It characterised much of the discussion of causewayed enclosures in this country during the 1970s and 80s (Whittle 1977; Mercer 1980: ch. 1), and it can also be traced in the French and German literature (Beeching, Coudart & Lebolloch 1982; Boelicke et al. 1988: 417–26). Indeed, ever since the work of Stuart Piggott in the 1950s there had been a feeling among British prehistorians that if they were to discover the correct interpretation of continental enclosures they would be able to use the same ideas in their own research (cf. Piggott 1954: 17–32).

Yet such an appeal to authority is bound to fail. It depends on the existence of traditions of very great antiquity, but these are wedded to an inadequate conception of material culture, one that treats its categories as closed. The work of recent years has shown quite clearly that material culture cannot be studied in this way. Such research stresses its unstable character, its mutability from one context to another (Shanks & Tilley 1987: ch. 6; Hodder 1991: ch. 7). The self-same elements could be interpreted and reinterpreted through time and space. Thus a portable artefact like an axe might carry quite different connotations according to the ways in which it was obtained and the cultural conditions under which it was used (Bradley & Edmonds 1993). In the same way, pottery styles have lost their neutral character, for they may have played a special role in social transactions in the past (Thomas 1991: ch. 4). Much the same argument applies to earthwork monuments. Thus Julian Thomas talks of 'reading' such monuments (ibid.: ch. 3), and Ian Hodder suggests that Neolithic enclosures had something of the character of texts, to be interpreted by different people in different ways (1988: 69–71).

MONUMENTS AS MATERIAL CULTURE

Discussions of this kind do not go far enough, for they treat distinct kinds of material culture in very much the same fashion. That procedure does not do full justice to the special properties of monumental architecture. This is particularly unfortunate because in north-western Europe earthwork monuments are as much a Neolithic development as domesticated plants and animals (Bradley 1993: ch. 1). Monuments have certain characteristics which make them quite unlike the objects or styles of decoration on which so much discussion has been based.

Monuments are extremely durable, so that some of them form

significant features of the landscape even today. Earthwork enclosures would last for a very long time unless they were levelled deliberately, and that would be difficult to achieve. Thus they might be present in human consciousness whether or not those sites were in active use. They are not like portable artefacts which can be deposited or destroyed; a construction like a megalithic tomb might assume new roles after it had apparently been closed. Such monuments were constantly visible, and in this respect they differ still more radically from other forms of material culture which can be displayed or concealed according to the occasion. Of course there could be restrictions on who was allowed to visit particular monuments, or on when they could be used, but their scale and resistance to decay mean that for many people they would have posed special problems of interpretation.

The second point applies mainly to the larger monuments. Unlike ceramics or lithic artefacts, it seems likely that their production involved a considerable number of workers. Even though we do not know how long it took to build these sites, practical considerations allow us to estimate the approximate size of the labour forces necessary to create them (Abrams 1989). That does not mean that they need have remained accessible to everyone once their construction was finished (Bradley 1993: ch. 3). In any case the very idea of 'completion' may be inappropriate, for some earthworks witnessed so many episodes of renewal and modification that it is probably better to think of them as projects (see, for example, Pryor 1984: 8–12; Whittle 1988 a). It is a familiar argument that the task of building such monuments helped to create a sense of group identity (cf. Hodder 1989: 264–5). The creation of Neolithic enclosures certainly required more people than most productive activities.

Taken together, these distinctive features of earthwork monuments would give them a special place in human experience, and would also tend to provide them with a lengthy history. Ideas about their origin and significance may have changed quite radically, but it would be difficult to remain innocent of their very existence. The fact of their survival meant that they had to be incorporated in any understanding of the world.

That process of thinking about monuments was not straightforward either, for those constructions could not travel: it was the concept of that monument which passed from one cultural setting to another. Kopytoff (1986) suggests that portable artefacts carry their own histories with them, but in the case of an earthwork enclosure only the ideas behind its creation might have moved. This is utterly different from most forms of material culture. Again we need to appreciate the special problems of studying the monumental.

CAUSEWAYED ENCLOSURES

I shall devote most of this paper to the so-called causewayed enclosures as these have the longest history and the widest distribution (the circular enclosures that I mentioned at the outset are a specialised element within that wider tradition of earthwork building; so perhaps are henges). The common elements of that tradition are easy to recognise. They involve a restricted space, encompassed by one or more ditches, which are either close together or separated by areas of open ground. These earthworks are accompanied by internal banks and sometimes by palisades. The distribution of these enclosures is enormous. Examples are known as far north as Sweden and as far south as Languedoc (Larsson 1982; Vaquer 1990: 294–6). They also extend the whole way from Ulster to the Danube (Mallory & Hartwell 1984; Lüning 1988).

The feature that seems to unite these enclosures can be described as segmentation. As their conventional name suggests, the ditches of these enclosures are interrupted at regular intervals, although continuous earthworks may also be found in some of the same cultural contexts. It is a moot point how often the banks had been broken, but at times the earthworks follow the same course as interrupted palisades. On a few sites there was one major entrance flanked by a more considerable earthwork which formed a kind of facade (Evans 1988). Elsewhere a number of separate causeways were enhanced by complicated structures interpreted as gateways (Boelicke 1976).

It is easier to appreciate the stereotyped character of these earthworks than it is to interpret them, but several elements feature prominently in most discussions, and they are worth mentioning here. As Jan Harding suggests (this volume), on sites with several circuits of earthworks the effect is to emphasise the depth of the passage leading from exterior to interior (cf. Hodder 1990: 160). At the same time, the sheer number of breaks in the perimeter also indicates the openness of the site to people from the surrounding area. It may be possible to combine both those ideas with the suggestion that the segmented ground plan expressed the participation of different groups in the creation of the monument.

It is difficult to assess these arguments, and in a way it may not be necessary to do so, for the point that I wish to stress is how that characteristic ground plan was interpreted and reinterpreted in the past itself. I take my cue from a recent paper by Matthew Johnson (1987) in which he argues that one way of incorporating a concept of agency in archaeological research is to contrast local developments with the long-term structures out of which they arise. As he says (Johnson 1987: 206–7; *my emphasis*):

> Agency is a manipulation of an existing structure that is external to the individual . . . and appears to the agent . . . as something to be drawn upon. . . . Such a normative outline is not necessarily a repressive, prescriptive one. While to the social agent it appears to be a coherent set of values, it is one to be drawn upon selectively, *manipulated and even inverted.*

How can this approach illuminate the history of causewayed enclosures? One of the most widespread practices in Neolithic Europe was the building of earthworks with interrupted ditches. At one level this seems to have been a process attended by very strict rules, and that may be why enclosures that were built in different periods and different areas followed virtually the same ground plan (Fig. 1). At the same time, those monuments appear to have been used in radically different ways from one context to another. In this paper I consider a number of permutations of the basic idea of the causewayed enclosure, from the end of the Linearbandkeramik through to the late Neolithic period. I have chosen my examples to cross two important thresholds. They take us from the intensive settlement of the loess to the broad-spectrum economies that developed during subsequent phases. At the same time, they also extend from the core areas of Neolithic Europe towards its margins. By focussing on local transformations of just one form of monument we can define some of the salient features of social life in those regions.

THE 'EVOLUTION' OF MONUMENTS

Before considering this evidence, there is one further problem to discuss. Archaeologists have a rather inflexible idea of the way in which monuments developed. They tend to apply an evolutionary model in which simple constructions give way to more complex creations in an orderly progression. The approach is teleological since the final aim of research is to provide the major types of monument with a credible family tree. A good example is Alison Sheridan's (1986) scheme for the development of Irish passage tombs in which monu-

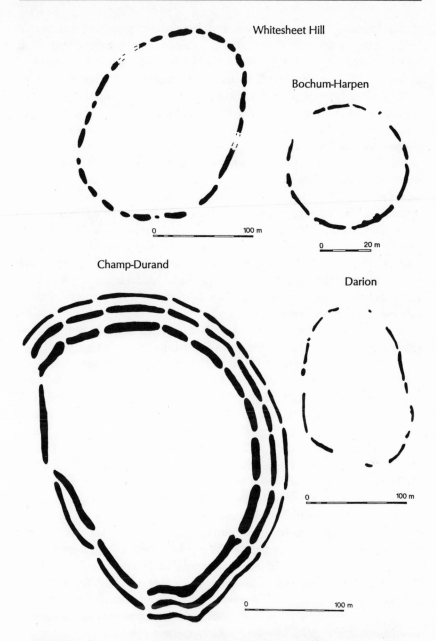

Whitesheet Hill

Bochum-Harpen

0   100 m

0   20 m

Champ-Durand

Darion

0   100 m

0   100 m

Figure 1. Outline plans of four causewayed enclosures illustrating their wide distribution across space and time. Whitesheet Hill, Wessex and Champ-Durand, Poitou both date from the late fourth millennium BC; Bochum-Harpen in north-western Germany belongs to the Rössen culture and Darion, Belgium to the late LBK (drawing by Steve Rippon).

ments become larger over time and consume a growing amount of human energy. The same is true of henges and stone circles, and a still better illustration of this kind of sequence is provided by the Iron Age defended sites of Wessex (Cunliffe 1984). The latter seem to start as palisaded or open settlements. Some were enhanced by the construction of a bank and ditch, and in certain cases this barrier was reinforced by a timber revetment. In time the number of earthworks decreased until the landscape came to be dominated by a series of regularly spaced 'hillforts'. Smaller sites gave way to larger ones, and quite often the enclosed area was considerably augmented. As part of this process, the layout of the internal buildings changed, from an apparently informal use of space to the development of a stricter overall design. Ritual activity also changed its focus, from an initial concern with the boundary to the construction of formal shrines at the heart of the enclosure. Cunliffe's terminology is most revealing. Sites evolved from 'hilltop enclosures' into 'early hillforts', and eventually some of them became the 'developed hillforts' whose interpretation has led to so much discussion.

To some extent my treatment of Neolithic enclosures will also be chronological, but they do not lend themselves to the same kind of narrative structure, for in fact the physical changes that accompanied their construction were very limited indeed. They play less part in this interpretation than the different practices that took place within them. The number of entrances to these enclosures may have increased over time, and the layout of certain sites perhaps attained a rather greater formality. There are also indications that the ditches sometimes changed their form, so that earthworks became easier to maintain. Alasdair Whittle (1977) identified each of these trends from the material that was available twenty years ago, and there is little to add today.

It may help to focus this discussion on a series of thresholds in the use of causewayed enclosures: transformations that mark particularly striking changes in the roles of these monuments. My treatment is thematic rather than strictly chronological, although I shall start with the earliest sites and end with some of the latest. Again we must not suppose that enclosures were created with some ultimate goal in view: that after a long enough period of experiment causewayed enclosures would assume a definitive form. Rather, the same elements were deployed in different configurations from one setting to another according to local inventiveness and the needs of particular interest groups. Instead of masking so much variation in the interests of a straightforward sequence, we should pay more attention to the contexts in which these enclosures were created. We must also understand the ways in which they were changed. There was always a complicated relationship between tradition and invention, and that is precisely why we can never discover the purpose of causewayed enclosures. The approach considered at the beginning of this paper has to be abandoned.

ENCLOSURES, HOUSES, AND SETTLEMENTS

The first threshold is the appearance of enclosures at all. This seems to have taken place late in the Linearbandkeramik and in the period that immediately followed (Lüning 1988). The circumstances are obscure, but one point is not in any dispute. Earthwork enclosures are first found in a domesticated landscape. That is to say, they are found in regions that had already experienced a substantial history of settlement, and they were built near to groups of houses (Boelicke et al. 1988: 417–26).

Their siting follows no obvious rules. They tend to be found towards the limits of the loess and often in areas that were first colonised in the Linearbankeramik. Lawrence Keeley has suggested that some of these enclosures possessed a defensive character and reflect increasing tensions between early farmers and their neighbours (1992: 91–2), but that interpretation ignores the full complexity of the sequence on individual sites. It is the relationship between earthworks and longhouses that offers the most promising line of enquiry. This is characteristically volatile. There are sites at which an enclosure was built in an open space within a larger concentration of houses, but there are other examples where the earthwork could have bounded a group of domestic buildings (Boelicke et al. 1988: 417–26). In each case the important element is that this spatial relationship was by no means fortuitous. An enclosure might be constructed after the houses were abandoned, but where that happened it monumentalised a space that had already been important in the life of the settlement. Similarly, when houses were built beside an existing enclosure they respected the position of its earthworks (Modderman 1959).

Not all these enclosures assumed the regular layout characteristic of later examples, nor did they see such a wide variety of activities. For example, the only features inside the enclosure at Langweiler Site 9 were a small number of pits. It is likely that this area was used for food preparation and for making tools: activities that may already have taken place there before the earthwork was constructed (Kuper et al. 1977). In that case the building of a bank and ditch would merely have provided those activities with an enhanced significance. Moreover the early enclosures formed only part of a wider pattern. A few sites show evidence of craft production (Keeley & Cahen 1989), whilst cemeteries of flat graves can be found in the vicinity (Whittle 1988 b: ch. 5). There is little evidence of structured deposits associated with these earthworks.

As Ian Hodder has noted (1988: 69–71), we may also encounter the opposite sequence. For example, on the famous site of Köln-Lindenthal (Buttler & Haberey 1936) the excavators recognised a whole sequence of ditched enclosures, one of them with a causewayed ditch of classic type. It seems that this did not contain any houses. The strongest evidence of occupation in fact belongs to the final phase of activity when the largest of these earthworks was constructed (Boelicke et al. 1988: 417–26). This was built on a greater scale than any of its predecessors and formed a continuous barrier. Although the site could have become a defended settlement, there is a danger of extending this idea too widely. The first enclosures are often found with groups of domestic buildings, but there is nothing to suggest a uniform pattern of development. Their relationship with one another could be worked out in several different ways.

ENCLOSURES, HOUSES, AND DEPOSITS

Now we can consider a second threshold in the history of causewayed enclosures, for in succeeding phases the links with domestic sites seem to have been less straightforward. This is a period of growing diversity in material culture and we should not be surprised to find it reflected in monumental architecture, but in fact only two basic models can be identified. The first is represented by the circular enclosures referred to at the beginning of this paper (Trnka 1991). Here the principle of the interrupted barrier reached its fullest development. These earthworks had a stereotyped ground plan. They were quite small and generally their entrances were aligned on the cardinal points. The ditches were often supplemented by palisades. There is no evidence that these enclosures contained any houses, but, once again, settlements have been found in the vicinity. Unlike the enclosures described so far, the earthworks in this group can be associated with specialised deposits, including figurines and human remains. Once the characteristic form of these enclosures had been adopted, such sites were built over an appreciable period.

The central European evidence is echoed, but far less strongly, among the earthworks found in the regional groups that developed at the end of the Linearbandkeramik. The key feature was an emphasis on a permeable perimeter. This was particularly obvious at sites like Urmitz where an interrupted palisade existed before any earthworks were built (Boelicke 1976). On some of these sites the causeways in the ditch were enhanced by wooden gateways (Raetzel-Fabian 1991).

There were houses inside some of these enclosures, but with the demise of flat cemeteries certain of these earthworks seem have taken on new roles, and we also find evidence of human remains within their area. For example, at Menneville in northern France an enclosure dating from the Rössen period may have enclosed a settlement (Coudart & Demoule 1982), but in this case the excavation also provided evidence of a series of structured deposits including articulated animal bones and the burials of two children covered by red ochre: a practice that recalls the evidence from older cemeteries. At the same time, the enclosure ditch was broken by a series of causeways and shows the sequence of filling and recutting that becomes increasingly common on later sites. Similar evidence is associated with the Michelsberg phase. A good example is the enclosed settlement at Mairy in the Ardennes (Marolle 1989). This contained a range of unusually large houses, but it also included a series of pits. These had a complex filling and contained articulated animal bones, as well as elaborate artefacts and complete pots. There seems little doubt that they were formal deposits.

There is another development to consider. I have already mentioned the idea that some of the first enclosures may have been used as defensive sites. The same arguments apply to later earthworks, and with rather more reason, for at a number of sites, particularly in eastern France, there are indications that these possessed substantial stone-faced ramparts not unlike the structures created during late prehistory (Nicardot 1974). Again there is a danger of framing the argument too rigidly. Not all these sites are associated with houses, and in some cases they may have been located in marginal areas of the landscape some distance away from the major settlements of this period. Nor can we assume that these earthworks were confined to only one role. For example at Boury in northern France there is evidence that an enclosure with a considerable rampart had been levelled, and yet overlying the remains of its defences there was an extraordinary series of animal burials, ranged symmetrically on either side of a causeway in the ditch (Lombardo, Martinez, & Verret 1984). At a still later stage in the history of this site the same area was used for the deposition of human bones. This sequence is another reminder of how misleading it can be to assume that enclosures had one predominant role and that the range of activities taking place on those sites remained the same over time. At Boury we have an enclosure which had apparently been attacked and destroyed, and yet one of the causeways in its ditch provided the focal point for a series of placed deposits.

ENCLOSURES, DEPOSITS, AND HUMAN REMAINS

That particular sequence is important because it introduces a further threshold in the interpretation of causewayed enclosures. So far I have followed the changing articulation of enclosures and settlement sites, suggesting how some of the later earthworks assumed additional roles after the Linearbandkeramik. Some major enclosures were not occupied until a late stage in their development, while others were never used as settlement sites at all. This is a particular development of the Michelsberg phase, and it is found widely. Some of the recently excavated enclosures are particularly elaborate affairs, with multiple ditches, palisades, and complex entrance structures (Biel 1991). These ditches contain deposits of human and animal bones, whilst similar material can be found in pits within their interior. A well-known example of this practice comes from the type site at Michelsberg itself (Lüning 1967: 113-19, 297-332).

A particular feature of such finds is the discovery of disarticulated human bones in some of these deposits, for this recalls the evidence from other sites of this date (Lichardus 1986). Again there is no uniformity. In northern Germany the distribution of enclosures overlaps with that of megalithic tombs (Raetzel-Fabian 1991), yet in northern France deposits of human bone may be associated with enclosures in regions which seem to be without other kinds of mortuary deposit. In such cases human skull fragments are the commonest find and tend to be associated with the upper levels of the enclosure ditches (Mazingue & Mordant 1982). These sites may also be set apart from the main areas of settlement.

A good example of this transformation of the principle of the causewayed enclosure is provided by a site at Noyen-sur-Seine (Mordant & Mordant 1977). At different times this was enclosed by an interrupted palisade and by a causewayed ditch, but inside the excavated area there were no convincing traces of houses. The excavators recognised local areas of cobbling and also a line of hearths, but their report gives the impression that this was principally a place where artefacts were deposited. Some of these objects had concentrated distributions within the excavated area, including animal bones, quern-stones, pottery, and a group of axe fragments. There were also ceramic figurines and a perforated human skull. Taken together, such finds seem to suggest that by this stage there may have been a wider range of deposits on these sites and perhaps more concern with the relics of the dead.

ENCLOSURES, DEPOSITS, AND SETTLEMENTS

It is no accident that the Michelsberg enclosures were the group that Stuart Piggott (1954: 17–32) compared with those in the British Isles. There are striking similarities in the forms taken by the earthworks and in the character of the associated material, but once again it is quite misleading to select one version of the causewayed enclosure and to suppose that it represents the entire phenomenon. Even 'ceremonial' enclosures did not remain entirely unaltered. The last transformation took place in widely separated areas around the margins of Neolithic Europe. In western France, for instance, we find further earthworks with interrupted ditches, and once again they contain concentrations of human skull fragments and groups of non-local artefacts (Joussaume & Pautreau 1990: 159–61 & 246–90). Here there is one novel development. Some of these sites were eventually rebuilt with considerable stone-walled ramparts and complicated out-works which resemble nothing so much as the defences of Iron Age forts. These sites continued to form a focus for specialised deposits, but the outward appearance of the enclosures was altered completely.

A number of the same observations apply to the enclosures of southern Scandinavia (Madsen 1988). Again these have a very stereo-typed ground plan and seem to have contained intentionally placed deposits of exotic and unusual artefacts. Some of these sites are situated near to mortuary monuments. In Scandinavia there may have been a further transformation, but one which differed in some respects from developments in Atlantic France. A number of Danish sites seem to have seen a final phase of activity as large open settlements after their earthworks had gone out of use. These settlements were more extensive than those of earlier phases. The development of domestic sites in and around existing enclosures may be shared between Denmark and western France, but again the details are different. In the French example they were turned into hillforts, but in Scandinavia their earthworks were superseded as these sites became unenclosed settlements.

It is less of a surprise, then, that occasional sites in the British Isles should show a rather similar sequence, with a late phase of domestic activity in which enclosures were rebuilt with considerable defences. That evidence is already well known and it is not necessary to expand on it here. There are just two points to emphasise. First, where enclosures were provided with defences their period of use was much shorter than that of sites in western France, and some of these earthworks seem to have been attacked and destroyed (Mercer 1980). Secondly, there is evidence of later Neolithic activity on the sites of some causewayed enclosures in Britain, but the associated material has a rather specialised character. It has close counterparts in the secondary levels of other kinds of Neolithic monument (Thomas 1991: fig. 5.9) and it is too soon to say whether any of these finds reflect a similar development to the sequence identified in Denmark. Only the last and rather anomalous enclosures in Britain – earthworks like Flagstones, Stonehenge 1, or the inner ring at Briar Hill – bear any resemblance to the monuments of the late Neolithic.

CONCLUSION

I have considered the first Neolithic enclosures in north-western Europe and the ways in which their roles were transformed from one area and one cultural setting to another. They were changed from specialised enclosures to settlement sites and vice versa. Some of the domestic enclosures provided an arena for specialised deposits, while still other earthworks played a more obvious role in ritual activity and lacked any domestic component at all. Lastly, that entire sequence could be reversed so that ceremonial enclosures could be chosen as the sites for settlements or could even be rebuilt as hillforts. At one level some of these relationships echo wider patterns in Neolithic archaeology. The increasing separation of enclosures from settlement sites comes at a time when houses are harder to find. Again, human remains are more often associated with enclosures as mortuary monuments eclipse the dwellings of the living population. On the other hand, that is to consider the evidence at too large a geographical scale. The most important point is to emphasise the interplay between the conventions that dictated that earthwork enclosures should take the traditional form and the wide range of practices that actually took place within them. The original idea of constructing an enclosure might be modified many times, but the conventions that controlled their building were left largely unaltered.

Of course this account has been selective, but it should be enough to establish one fundamental point. The causewayed enclosure may have taken a predetermined form, but this was adopted in a whole range of different settings. There is no direct relationship between form and function in the way that British prehistorians once supposed. The form of these enclosures was dictated by traditional norms, but the activities that took place in and around these sites were much less stable. It is quite impossible to impose a narrative structure on so much variation and it means very little to talk about the 'evolution' of this kind of monument. The contrast with southern English hillforts could hardly be more obvious.

What of the kinds of long-distance comparison with which I began this paper? I can give two answers to that question. Perhaps it really is possible to think in terms of a very long-lived idea of enclosure in the European Neolithic. It may be that there are points in common between sites of quite different dates in central Europe and the British Isles, but they came about by chance, through the complex process of *bricolage* that characterises the entire history of these monuments. To lay any weight on such resemblances is to overlook the more local character of Neolithic culture after the Linearbandkeramik. Yet not to discuss the problem at all is, if anything, still more misguided, for that loses sight of the power of tradition in ancient societies. It was through the creation and interpretation of traditions such as monument building that people in quite different areas felt themselves to 'be Neolithic'.

REFERENCES

Abrams, E. 1989. Architecture and energy: an evolutionary perspective. In Schiffer, M. (ed.), *Archaeological Method and Theory*, 1, pp. 47–87. Tucson: University of Arizona Press.

Beeching, A., Coudart, A. and Lebolloch, M. 1982. Concevreux (Aisne): Une enceinte chalcolithique et la problématique des 'camps'. In *Vallée de l'Aisne: cinq anneés de fouille protohistoriques*, pp. 149–169. Revue Archéologique de Picardie numéro spécial.

Behrens, H. 1981. The first 'Woodhenge' in Middle Europe. *Antiquity* 55: 172–178.

Biel, J. 1991. Auf den Spuren der Michelsberger Kultur. *Archäologie in Deutschland* 4 (October – December 1991): 26–9.

Boelicke, U. 1976. Das Neolithische Erdwerk Urmitz. *Acta Praehistorica et Archaeologica* 7: 73–121.

Boelicke, U., Van Brandt, D., Lüning, J., Stehli, P. and Zimmerman, A. 1988. *Der bandkeramische Siedlungsplatz Langweiler* 8. Bonn: Habelt.

Bradley, R. 1993. *Altering the Earth: The Origins of Monuments in Britain and Continental Europe*. Edinburgh: Society of Antiquaries of Scotland.

Bradley, R. and Edmonds, M. 1993. *Interpreting the Axe Trade: Production and Exchange in Neolithic Britain*. Cambridge: Cambridge University Press.

Buttler, W. and Haberey, W. 1936. *Die bandkeramische Ansiedlung bei Köln-Lindenthal*. Leipzig: Römisch-Germanisches Kommission.

Coudart, A. and Demoule, J.-P. 1982 Le site néolithique et chalcolithique de Menneville. *Revue Archéologique de Picardie* (numéro spécial), pp. 119–147.

Cunliffe, B. 1984. Iron Age Wessex: continuity and change. In Cunliffe, B. and Miles, D. (eds), *Aspects of the Iron Age in Central Southern Britain*, pp. 12–45. Oxford: Oxford University Committee for Archaeology.

Evans, C. 1988. Acts of enclosure: a consideration of concentrically-organised causewayed enclosures. In Barrett, J. and Kinnes, I. (eds), *The Archaeology of Context in the Neolithic and Bronze Age: Recent Trends*, pp. 85–96. Sheffield: Sheffield University Department of Archaeology and Prehistory.

Hodder, I. 1988. Material culture texts and social change: a theoretical discussion and some archaeological examples. *Procedings of the Prehistoric Society* 54: 67–75.

Hodder, I. 1989. This is not an article about material culture as text. *Journal of Anthropological Archaeology* 8: 250–69.

Hodder, I. 1990: *The Domestication of Europe: Structure and Contingency in Neolithic Societies*. Oxford: Blackwell.

Hodder, I. 1991. *Reading the Past*, 2nd edn. Cambridge: Cambridge University Press.

Johnson, M. 1987. Conceptions of agency in archaeological interpretation. *Journal of Anthropological Archaeology* 8: 189–211.

Joussaume, R. and Pautreau, J.-P. 1990. *Le Préhistoire du Poitou*. Tours: Ouest-France.

Keeley, L. 1992. The introduction of agriculture to the western North European Plain. In Gebauer, A. B. and Price, T. D. (eds), *Transitions to Agriculture in Prehistory*, pp. 81–95. Madison: Prehistory Press.

Keeley, L. and Cahen, D. 1989. Early Neolithic forts and villages in north-east Belgium: a preliminary report. *Journal of Field Archaeology* 16: 157–176.

Kopytoff, I. 1986. The cultural biography of things: commodotisation as process. In Appadurai, A. (ed.) *The Social Life of Things*, pp. 64–91. Cambridge: Cambridge University Press.

Larsson, L. 1982. A causewayed enclosure and a site with Valby pottery at Støvie, Western Scania. *Meddelanden fran Lunds Universitets Historiska Museum 1981–1982*, pp. 65–114.

Lichardus, J. 1986. Le rituel funéraire de la culture de Michelsberg dans la région du Rhin supérieur et moyen. In Demoule, J.-P. and Guiliane, J. (eds), *Le Néolithique en France*, pp. 343–358. Paris: Picard.

Lombardo, J.-C., Martinez, R. and Verret, D. 1984. Le Chasséen de Culfroid à Boury-en-Vexin dans son contexte historique et les apports de la stratigraphie de son fossée. *Revue Archéologique de Picardie* 1.2: 269–292.

Lüning, J. 1967. Die Michelsberg Kultur. Ihre Funde in zeitlicher und räumlicher Gliederung. *Bericht der Römisch-Germanischen Kommission* 48: 1–350.

Lüning, J. 1988. Zur Verbreitung und Datierung bandkeramischer Erdwerk. *Archäologisches Korrespondenzblatt* 18: 155–158.

Madsen, T. 1988. Causewayed camps in south Scandinavia. In Burgess, C., Topping, P., Mordant, C. and Maddison, M. (eds), *Enclosures and Defences in the Neolithic of Western Europe*, pp. 301–336. Oxford: British Archaeological Reports (International Series 403).

Mallory, J. and Hartwell, B. 1984. Donegore. *Current Archaeology* 92: 271–275.

Marolle, C. 1989. Le village Michelsberg des Hautes Chanvières à Mairy (Ardennes). *Gallia Préhistoire* 31: 93–117.

Mazingue, B. and Mordant, D. 1982. Fonctions primaires et secondaires des fosses du site néolithique de Noyen-sur-Seine et les enceintes de la Bassées (Seine-et-Marne). In *Le Néolithique de l'est de la France*, pp. 129–134. Sens: Société Archéologique de Sens.

Mercer, R. 1980. *Hambledon Hill: A Neolithic Landscape*. Edinburgh: Edinburgh University Press.

Modderman, P. 1958. Die bandkeramische Siedlung von Sittard. *Palaeohistoria* 6: 33–120.

Modderman, P. 1976; The Aveburys and their continental counterparts. In Megaw, J. V. S. (ed.), *To Illustrate the Monuments*, pp. 99–106. London: Thames and Hudson.

Modderman, P. 1986. Die neolithische Besiedlung bei Heinheim. *Analecta Praehistorica Leidensia* 19.

Mordant, D. and Mordant, C. 1977. Habitat néolithique de fond de vallée alluviale à Noyen-sur-Seine (Seine-et-Marne): étude archéologique. *Gallia Préhistoire* 20: 229–269.

Nicardot, J.-P. 1974. Structures d'habitats à caractères défensif dans le Centre Est de la France. *Antiquités Nationales* 6: 32–45.

Piggott, S. 1954. *The Neolithic Cultures of the British Isles*. Cambridge: Cambridge University Press.

Pryor, F. 1984. Personalities of Britain: two examples of long-term regional contrast. *Scottish Archaeological Review* 3.1: 8–15.

Raetzel-Fabian, D. 1991. Zwischen Fluchtburg und Kultstätte. *Archaologie in Deutschland* 4 (October – December 1991): 22–25.

Shanks, M. and Tilley, C. 1987. *Re-constructing Archaeology*. Cambridge: Cambridge University Press.

Sheridan, A. 1986. Megaliths and megalomania: an account, and interpretation, of the development of passage tombs in Ireland. *Journal of Irish Archaeology* 3: 17–30.

Thomas, J. 1991. *Rethinking the Neolithic*. Cambridge: Cambridge University Press.

Trnka, G. 1991. *Studien zu mittelneolischen Kreisgrabenanlagen*. Vienna: Österreichischen Akademie der Wissenschaften.

Vaquer, J. 1990. *Le Néolithique en Languedoc Occidental*. Paris: Editions du CNRS.

Whittle, A. 1977. Earlier Neolithic enclosures in north-west Europe. *Proceedings of the Prehistoric Society* 43: 329–348.

Whittle, A. 1988a. Contexts, activities, events – aspects of Neolithic and Copper Age enclosures in central and western Europe. In Burgess, C., Topping, P., Mordant, C., & Maddison, M. (eds), *Enclosures and Defences in the Neolithic of Western Europe*, pp. 1–19. Oxford: British Archaeological Reports (International Series 403).

Whittle, A. 1988b. *Problems in Neolithic Archaeology*. Cambridge: Cambridge University Press.

10

An Architecture of Meaning: the Causewayed Enclosures and Henges of Lowland England

Jan Harding

With the study of the Neolithic in lowland England it often appears that familiar and well-excavated monuments are used as structural 'norms' or fixed archetypes for different classes of site. These outstanding individual discoveries seemingly dominate the way we think about particular parts of our evidence and there is at least a partial failure to supplement our appreciation of individual sites with a more general discussion of monuments. This is an archaeology which is readily obsessed with the descriptive specifics of individual sites while often avoiding the broader themes behind monument design which link spatial properties with processes of cognition and human interaction. Many of our studies, in other words, detach the intrinsic material nature of these sites from meaning and the knowledge and experience of the human subject. There is also little attempt to interpret the wider social implications of specific forms of architecture and spatial layout. That monument design was embedded in power relations and social strategies is often lost in the uniformity of our interpretations: these sites are generally seen as nothing more than mere stages for corporate activity. Given all the straining and scrutinising of excavation reports, it has been too easy to forget that underlying concepts or principles constituted the particular shape, size, and form of sites. Yet, as long as monument construction fails to be regarded as a more general phenomenon these various structural and symbolic traditions will continue to be largely underestimated and we will avoid any consideration of why sites took on certain appearances.

While many accounts describe the various physical features and 'functions' of monuments, they fail to recognise that these cultural transformations of space and time are a meaningful element in social agency. The spatial layout and architectural components which once structured activity are so often downgraded into features which seemingly lack the ability to constrain movement and perception, or create opportunities for individual interaction. Behind many of these approaches has been a tendency to conceptualise monuments as nothing more than flat two-dimensional plans, thus equating prehistoric perception with the analytical process of the archaeologist. As a number of recent studies have noted, this assumes that the builders and users of these sites were not only capable of comprehending the complete spatial panorama of the monuments, but also able to perceive the space and architecture of locales at an external and removed distance (Evans 1985: 83–4; Thomas 1990: 168–9; 1993: 23–5). It establishes a fixed relationship whereby individuals are actually placed outside the three-dimensional realm which would have constrained and structured their experience. However, it is the physical presence of the human body vis-à-vis other people and material culture which actually characterises the spatial experience of individuals, and this relationship is constituted by the movement and positioning of the body in relation to particular configurations of space and time (Carlstein 1981; Giddens 1984; Hillier & Hanson 1984; Pred 1977; Rappoport 1976). Patterns of movement, encounter, and avoidance are orientated by the various architectural components of the monuments – be they ditches, banks, timber settings or standing stones – and these features or physical objects create and order the empty systems of space across which people interact. It is therefore essential that our investigations of monuments rejoin cultural space and social agency by emphasising the specific patterns of movement and encounter which constituted a locales' integrated reality.

It is also apparent that many of our studies tend to separate the spatial transformations which were inherent in the design of the monuments from what would have been their underlying cognitive structure or system of beliefs. Although many of our approaches regard space as culturally defined and articulated, they often fail to emphasise its ideological and cosmological significance. They seem displaced from the cognitive mechanisms that produced the different classes of monument through time and interlaced the subconscious

[205]

thought of their creators. After all, societies change and order their physical environment according to their conceptual or structural schema, and such spatial and temporal planning can be seen as essential to the ideological mapping of the world (Duncan 1976; Kus 1983; Rappoport 1976; Sack 1980; Sayer 1982; Tuan 1974b). Therefore, while the human body is at the centre of the relationship between space, time, and physical positioning, the subjective experience of individuals is defined and guided by the structuring properties and principles which would fill a place with the concepts, codes, and symbols of a societies cognitive image of itself (Bourdieu 1977; Giddens 1979; 1984). The spatial layout and architecture of monuments are not arbitrary creations, or indeed a utilitarian response to biological demands or requirements, but a product of cognitive structures which are negotiated or imposed through social relations. They make visible certain ideal and conceptual concepts and constitute a form of order which is created for social purposes and through which society is constrained and recognised. It is evident, in other words, that just as the material nature of monuments has become detached from the human subject and social action, so it has also been separated from the symbolic universe which would have defined a locales' meanings.

A number of recent studies have emphasised the relationship between cultural space, social agency, and cognitive structure. However, these have generally taken an extremely selective approach to the full range of Neolithic monuments (Barrett 1988; Evans 1988b; Hodder 1984; Richards 1988; Shanks & Tilley 1982; Sharples 1985; Thomas 1988; 1990; 1991). They are almost exclusively concerned with either megalithic tombs or causewayed enclosures and as such, they fail to come to terms with the extensive morphological variability which is evident between different classes of monument. The purpose of this paper is to extend the scope of present research by examining one of these site types – early Neolithic enclosures – alongside the similarly numerous henge monuments. There is little chronological overlap between these two categories of site. Indeed, there is an apparent contemporaneity in the decline of the causewayed enclosures and the emergence of the henge monuments.[1] Important contrasts can also be drawn in terms of the overall design of the two classes of monument. The ditches of causewayed enclosures are regularly segmented, and their shape is often far from circular (cf. Palmer 1976: figs 13–20). Some sites are more or less D-shaped with an open side, or consist of banks and ditches placed across a promontory or an area between streams (Bradley 1986; Darvill 1981; Dixon 1988; Drewett 1977; Evans 1988a;

Musson 1950). Others may have more elaborate plans. For example, both the Trundle and Whitesheet Hill take the form of irregular nine-sided polygons (Curwen 1929; Piggott 1952). In comparison, the perimeters of the (generally smaller) henges are relatively regular and circular in outline.[2] When these sites are considered alongside Neolithic ring ditches, the earliest of which date to between about 2800–2300 bc, it appears that by the middle of the third millennium there was a fundamental transformation in spatial design and monumental architecture which was to dominate later in the Neolithic. I will return to this suggestion after an examination of the layout and design of causewayed enclosures.

ENCOUNTER AND CLASSIFICATION: THE SEGMENTARY AND REPETITIVE STRUCTURE OF CAUSEWAYED ENCLOSURES

While causewayed enclosures vary enormously in size, location, and layout, it is evident that their overall plan illustrates both morphic segmentation and repetition. The circuits of these monuments are generally characterised by irregular sections of fully joined or partially linked ovoid pits which are repeatedly strung together around an oval or circular space. At the same time, with over two-thirds of these monuments the circuits themselves were reproduced to form a multi-ring and generally concentric layout. Their irregular perimeters, in other words, not only illustrate morphological diversity but also spatial fragmentation and duplication, and it is commonly believed that these characteristics reflect excavation by small quarrying gangs working in relative isolation and with a minimal level of co-ordination (Evans 1988b: 88ff; Startin & Bradley 1981: 291; Whittle 1988: 8). In fact, this process of morphic repetition could have important implications for interpreting the potential interaction of individuals and groups at these sites. The reproduction of these characteristic perimeter segments, which sometimes resemble pit alignments rather than causewayed ditches, not only implies the multiplication of perimeter ditches but also that of causeways. This arrangement would clearly inscribe a complex series of spatial and temporal divisions and paths for the orientation of movement. As such, these monuments provided a potentially extensive range of options for experiencing these cultural locales and generating social interaction.

However, the apparent emphasis upon multiple pathways and boundaries at causewayed enclosures can also be illustrated by other notable characteristics of these sites. The relatively large size of the enclosures, and the generally undifferentiated area between their rings, all emphasise the potential for visible movement through and around the ditch segments of these sites. The importance of movement to the spatial organisation of these monuments is also illustrated by the evidence from a number of sites for formal entrances (Avery 1982; Bamford 1985; Connah 1965; Curwen 1934; Dixon 1988; Drewett 1977; Evans 1988a; Hedges & Buckley 1978; Mercer 1980; Smith 1965). Their probable existence is not only indicated by wider than average causeways and timber or hurdle gateways and post settings, but also by the tendency for larger and slightly curving ditches – and in two instances higher bank terminals – on either side of these gaps. These entranceways, often aligned opposite one another, could perhaps represent the elaboration of specific spatial and temporal points along the pathways of individuals and groups. The in-turned ditches, wider causeways, and upright posts or gate structures would have orientated the viewers' attention towards formal entry points, and while crossing these causeways the same characteristics could emphasise the perception of moving across a boundary and leaving one region of space and entering another. Indeed, the slight size of many of the proposed gate structures – particularly at Briar Hill (Bamford 1985: 3, 7, 37) and Haddenham (Evans 1988a: 136) – seems to suggest that these features acted as symbolic markers rather than being of any practical use.

If these entrance-ways illustrate an attempt to orientate human movement, the same can perhaps be said for the construction of banks, usually on the inner side of the ditch segments. This is perhaps most apparent at those enclosures where the earthworks were both considerable in size and only broken opposite major causeways. This is certainly the case at Abingdon (Avery 1982; Bradley 1986), Briar Hill (Bamford 1985), and Offham Hill (Drewett 1977). On the other hand, while the banks at these sites constitute a substantial obstacle, thereby limiting the possibilities for movement, elsewhere their known dimensions could be slight. Moreover, their existence, which is often based upon asymmetrical ditch filling, is speculative and can in fact be questioned at a number of monuments (Curwen 1934; Ross Williamson 1930; Sharples 1986; Wheeler 1943), while at some excavated enclosures there is strong positive evidence against the presence of banks.[3] It is therefore apparent that while some enclosures possessed earthworks of defensible proportions, elsewhere the dumped banks were merely one part of a discontinuous boundary. Along with the ditches, they could illustrate the physical and cognitive orientation of people towards specific points, most notably causeways, within these monuments. The importance of such spatial and architectural manipulation is evident if we consider the general significance which is attached to 'crossing' boundaries in most traditional societies (Eliade 1959: 18, 25; Hillier & Hanson 1984; Hillier et al. 1978). When individuals move across symbolic thresholds they not only leave one region of space and enter another, but also appear to emphasise and often transform their own social identity and relationships. It is perhaps apparent that the replication of discontinuous ditches and thus causeways, along with the existence of wide entrance gaps, could illustrate a concern with the creation of spatial thresholds for the purposes of social classification. These enclosures would, in other words, provide an ideal setting for the creation or reiteration of distinctive identities, whether they were based on age, gender or descent. This possibility assumes added importance when we consider that these monuments could have been the location for regularly scheduled large-scale aggregations of people. This is a theme to which I shall return.

The importance of such processes might well account for another notable characteristic of these monuments. A number of excavations have revealed that within the ditch segments there were often large quantities of differing deposits. Although a significant amount of this material seems to have been dumped, this is not to say that its distribution within the ditches was random (Pryor et al. 1985b: 293; Smith 1971: 111). Moreover, a prominent proportion of these deposits appear to result from more structured and intentional placing, and this material is often found in hollows within the ditch segments or was even placed in bags or on mats (e.g. Mercer 1980: 30; 1988: 94; Pryor et al. 1985b: fig. 13, pl. xxxix b; Smith 1965: 7, 9). These discrete in situ deposits include human and animal burials, human skulls placed along the floor of the ditches, piles of animal bones or antler, finely flaked flint implements, unweathered or complete pots, and an array of chalk objects. It is important to note, however, that many of these in situ deposits seem to have been specifically placed in the terminals of the ditch segments. At Haddenham, for instance, burnt bone was placed on a platform located in a ditch butt-end which flanked the excavated entrance (Evans 1988a: 134–5), and Flagstones had four *in situ* engravings on the sides of the terminals (Woodward 1988). In other words, it is apparent that these deposits were often spatially associated with boundary causeways, especially the possible entrance-ways (Thomas 1991: 65).

If we accept that at least some of the numerous causeways were thresholds between regions of differing social and symbolic importance, the distinct nature and location of these *in situ* artefacts, burials, and bones suggest that they were deposited and experienced as individuals moved through and around the spatially independent but comparable ditch segments. Placing these deposits, each with their own specific connotations, indicates an act of interpretation as individuals passed through spaces or boundaries and constructed their own social narratives (Bradley 1986: 185; Curwen 1934: 102ff; Pryor et al. 1985: 307–8). Along with the spatial layout of the ditch segments, these deposits represent a series of symbolic keys for 'cueing' the appropriate awareness of social segregation and classification. Human burials and bones would be particularly poignant, and this could well account for their frequent occurrence in the ditches.

It is evident from the above that depending on the layout of each enclosure, people could have moved directly through the perimeter circuits, between the segments, or around the circumference of the circuits. However, as Evans (1988b: 92–3) has recently suggested, at a number of sites there are morphological characteristics which suggest the importance of a linear path-structure through to an internal 'deep space'. As already mentioned, at multi-circuit monuments, which do constitute the majority of these enclosures, the banks and ditches are usually concentric in plan, and the major causeways are often aligned opposite one another. Such a layout provides a straight line for movement between some or all of the rings (Figs 1 & 2). Indeed, at Crickley Hill such a path-structure appears to have been formalised by what can only be described as a fenced road which passed through the ditch circuits and headed towards the inner area of the site where there was a concentration of flint and pottery, along with a large number of associated features (Dixon 1988). However, the possible significance of inner enclosures and ditch perimeters is also illustrated by a number of morphological differences which seem to indicate a mutual correspondence between the ditches of the outer circuits which is not shared with the innermost ring(s). The inner circuit pits at a number of sites are considerably shorter, narrower, and shallower than those of the other rings, while this comparison is reversed at an equivalent number of other enclosures. Furthermore, as Evans (1988b: 90, fig. 8.1) notes, a consideration of the overall layout of both Briar Hill and Orsett demonstrates that the inner circuit at both sites had an independent spatial integrity. While the inner ring of the former site had an eccentric setting, the plans of both enclosures seem to illustrate a spatial division into an outer area defined by two closely spaced ditches, and an inner and appreciably smaller enclosure. Indeed, at

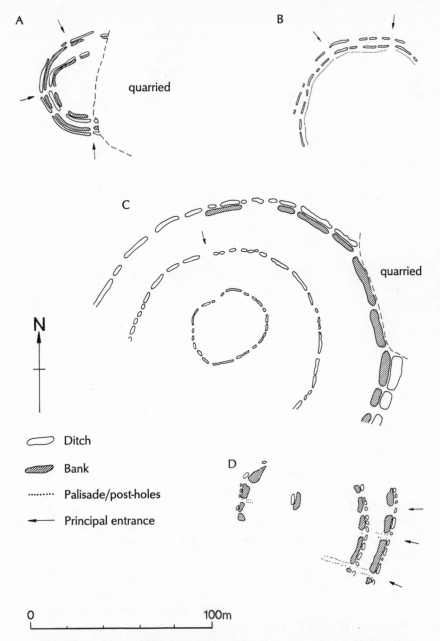

Figure 1. Plans of causewayed enclosures illustrating principal entrances.
A. Offham (after Drewett 1977: fig. 2); B. Orsett (after Hedges & Buckley
1978: fig. 3); C. Windmill Hill (after Smith 1965: fig. 3); D. Crickley Hill
(after Dixon 1988: fig. 4).

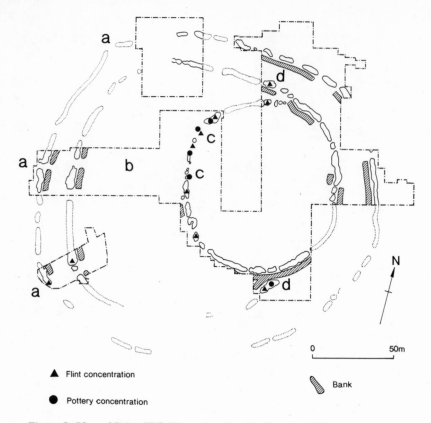

▲ Flint concentration

● Pottery concentration

Bank

0   50m

N

Figure 2. Plan of Briar Hill illustrating the distribution of flint and pottery in the ditches (Bamford 1985).

Whitehawk Camp similar contrasts are perhaps apparent with the differences in spacing between the inner two ditches and the outer two (Curwen 1934: pl. XII). It is therefore possible that an important aspect of the spatial organisation of concentrically planned enclosures is the perceptive and physical orientation of people towards an inner, and in some cases earlier,[4] area of significance.

The extensive excavations at Briar Hill allow a more detailed discussion (Bamford 1985). Despite the unique sequence of complex recutting at the site, it is evident that its overall plan was established at an early stage in the development of the monument (ibid, 39). An examination of the site plan illustrates that there were at least three entrances through the outer and middle ditch (Fig. 2a). These were all on the western side of the enclosure and led through to a large crescent-shaped open space which was bounded on one side by part of the offset inner circuit (Fig. 2b). This layout strongly suggests that people could have passed through the outer two circuits and into the open space which dominates the western part of the enclosure. The orientation of these three entrances also appears to converge on the length of the inner ditch perimeter which had the widest causeways, a number of possible post-holes, and no indications of a bank (Fig. 2c). It is possible, therefore, that individuals could have continued moving through to the inner enclosure. Indeed, the inner circuit pits facing the outer entrances at Briar Hill are exactly those which appear to illustrate the most intense sequence of deposition. They contain by far the greatest numbers of flint, the only large concentrations of early Neolithic pottery, the one worked stone artefact from the site, and the most complex series of recuts. They are also associated with deposits of dumped 'ashy' material (ibid, 133). Taken together, this appears to indicate that movement across the inner boundary was associated with important events of symbolic deposition, and activity within this area is illustrated by the fact that it contained almost all the worked flints which were found in the subsoil of the site (ibid.: fig. 32). Moreover, crossing the outer ditch circuit could have allowed movement around the entire circumference of the site, and the two pit segments which are located where the inner and outer ditches meet also have large concentrations of artefacts and intense recutting (Fig. 2d). These pits would have been passed as people moved around the site, and their location further suggests that the inner enclosure circuit was of special importance.

The example of Briar Hill goes some way to suggesting that concentricity divides the enclosures into successively bounded zones of meaning. The manipulation of space into concentric regions of differing significance could have had the effect of socially dividing the people who moved around the locale, with only some individuals or groups perhaps being allowed to progress through to the inner enclosure. This would present an obvious contrast between the core and periphery of the monument, and such a structured or ranked relationship would be most apparent at those enclosures where the outer ditch and bank are either more or less continuous or of a comparably large size. It is also important to note that surface scraping at some chalk land enclosures would have added to the visual and cognitive impact of the outer perimeters. Furthermore, despite the fact that the narrow gaps between the circuits of some sites clearly restricts the possibility for functional activity, especially if an upcast bank was placed between them, sites with more even ring distributions seem to illustrate that there could have been discrete functional differences between the enclosed regions (Evans 1988b: 90). I have already referred to the far greater quantity of artefacts which were recovered from the inner ditch circuit at Briar Hill, and it is perhaps significant that a similar pattern has been recorded elsewhere (Curwen 1934; Hedges & Buckley 1978; Sharples 1991; Smith 1965; Thomas 1964). At both Abingdon and Hambledon Hill, a greater frequency of human skeletal material and articulated animal bones came from the inner ditch enclosures (Avery 1982; Case 1956; Leeds 1927; 1928; Mercer 1980). At the latter site it has been suggested that these differences perhaps reflect a spatial distinction between areas of possible habitation and those where the dead were exposed (Barrett et al. 1991: 36), while it was similarly concluded that the enclosed area at Abingdon could have had different functions (Bradley 1986: 186). There are also indications at a number of these monuments for differentiated patterns of recutting, the inner circuits being the most frequently re-emphasised in this way. This was certainly the case at Briar Hill, and it is also evident at Abingdon (Bradley & Holgate 1984: 116), Crickley Hill (Dixon 1988: 81), and possibly Windmill Hill (Evans 1988b: fig. 8.1).

The creation and maintenance of a physically and symbolically distinguishable inner region of concentric space may have been an important theme, but it was one which was not developed at every enclosure. Many sites consist of single ditch and bank circuits, and in those cases where more than one circuit was cut, important chronological problems remain. Artefactual and other dating evidence from a number of concentrically planned enclosures suggest that pits in all the circuits could have been open simultaneously. However, this is extremely difficult to substantiate in many cases, especially when it is considered that some segments could have been back-filled immediately after cutting. These problems aside, if social identity was indeed inherent in the physical and depositional history of these monuments, the distinction between those concentric sites with a morphologically distinct inner ring, and the single-circuit enclosures, may refer to the intensity of classification and negotiation between individuals and groups. If we accept the widely held view that early Neolithic society was segmentary in nature, the differences between single and multiple ring sites could represent the level and intensity at which social discourse was generated both within and between these autonomous groups. These differences in layout and design could also refer to the extent to which spatial organisation was manipulated in order to control movement and interaction, and together with the scale of social interaction, this could account for a number of other varying features. There are, after all, contrasting topographic settings for these monuments, differences in bank size and continuity, variations in the layout and frequency of formal entrances, and finally, varying levels of re-cutting, including the fact that the ditches of some enclosures never appear to have been deliberately back-filled.

THE ENCLOSED COSMOS: THE EMERGENCE OF NEW REGIONS OF MEANING

I have suggested that there is general contemporaneity between the appearance of new circular-shaped monuments and a decline in the construction of causewayed enclosures. While there seems to be a seg-mentary and repetitive structure to the architecture of enclosures, the layout of later Neolithic henge monuments illustrate the creation of more regular, continuous, and circular perimeters. However, rather than a sudden transition between these two forms of monument con-struction, the available evidence indicates the gradual appearance of the new perimeter form. It is certainly apparent that some of the cause-wayed enclosures underwent transformations in their design and pos-sible use (Bradley 1984: 34–5; Thomas 1991: 36). At Orsett it was postul-ated that changes in the layout of the excavated entrance, most notably the erection of an additional timber fence, could illustrate an increasing effort to orientate movement through a whole series of structural divi-sions (Hedges & Buckley 1978: 242). A similar, although less marked process is evident at the recently excavated enclosure at Haddenham. In this case, a large causeway was encroached upon by an extension of one of the ditch segments, and a gap in the palisade directly opposite the possible entrance-way was blocked (Evans 1988a: 130). While the numerous perimeter causeways at both of these enclosures appear to suggest that these later structural modifications were not associated with an increasing concern for better defences, the picture elsewhere is somewhat different. The physical extent and time scales of the well-known structural modifications at both Hambledon Hill (Bonney 1961; Mercer 1980; 1988) and Crickley Hill (Dixon 1988) are greater than at both Haddenham and Orsett, and comparable transformations are also apparent at Abingdon and Maiden Castle. It is possible that the deeper and more continuous outer ditch at Abingdon was later in date than the inner circuit (cf. Avery 1982; Bradley 1986), while recent excavation and a number of radiocarbon determinations at Maiden Castle have suggested that the ditch segments of the original inner circuit were joined together and the outer ditch was back-filled (Sharples 1991: 253).

In some cases, therefore, it can be demonstrated that the shift to more continuous and defensive perimeters is secondary to the rather more modest and causewayed phases of construction. While the design of the earlier perimeters seem to emphasise morphic segmentation and repetition, with all the implications for movement and interaction, the later and more continuous perimeters appear to represent a re-working of meaning and strategy. Rather than generating opportunities for social interaction between a number of symbolic and physical boundaries, the spatial organisation of these later enclosures appears to reflect an increased concern with regulating access.

These changes in design and form toward the end of the latter half of the third millennium bc appear to illustrate an emerging emphasis upon the continuity and size of monument boundaries. This is also apparent with Neolithic round barrows. An examination of the radiocarbon determinations from these monuments is equivocal, but it does suggest that round barrows without ditches are actually earlier than the ditched mounds. All the primary context dates from the former group of sites range from 3320 ± 70 bc to 2830 ± 70 bc (Brewster 1984; Hedges et al. 1991a: 127; Jobey 1968: 40; Kinnes 1979: 13; Richards 1986-90: 26-7). Of the four available determinations for ditched round barrows, at least three are decidedly later than this range.[5] Although such a small number of radiocarbon dates certainly limits the conclusions that can be drawn about the development of this monument category, that the associated pottery also seems to indicate a possible chronological distinction between the ditched round barrows and those without ditches. While the excavated primary features and ditch fills of both these types are in fact found with a range of Neolithic pottery styles, the ditch-less group of monuments are usually associated with plain vessels and the ditched mounds with Peterborough Ware (Barrett et al. 1991: 85; Evison 1956: 88-9; Harding & Lee 1987: 181; Kinnes 1979: 65; Manby 1980: 30-1, 42). It seems, in other words, that both the radiocarbon determinations and the pottery suggest that the encircling ditches were not an original feature of these monuments. With a few exceptions, ditched mounds could date from the beginning of the second quarter of the third millennium, and it is noticeable that their appearance generally coincides with the earliest radiocarbon determinations from the Neolithic ring ditches. These range from between 2713 ±102 bc and 2370 ±50 bc (Ambers et al. 1989: 18-9; Barrett et al. 1991: table 2.4; Bradley & Chambers 1988: 279; Fasham 1982: 21; Harding & Lee 1987: 277).

It seems then, that the generally continuous and circular perimeters which characterise many of the henges did in fact develop as an architectural form at the end of the early Neolithic. As such, the emergence of these perimeters – at a time when both the construction of long barrows and causewayed enclosures had declined – indicates the inception of a distinct tradition of demarcating particular forms of cultural space, although the irregular and segmented appearance of certain early henges suggest that the traits of past monument forms continued to be reintroduced (Barrett et al. 1991: fig. 3.18; Richards 1990: fig. 99). These transformations in perimeter design are significant. Circular or slightly ovoid shapes are the most compact two-dimensional figures available to design. They minimise the area of contact between the enclosed region of space and everything outside it (Hillier & Hanson 1984: 17), and the generally continuous ditches and banks of the henge monuments would certainly emphasise the spatial principles of containment and exclusion (Thomas 1991: 46). If many causewayed enclosures appear to compartmentalise space into a complex series of pathways and regions by the creation of segmentary and repetitive boundaries, henge design appears to be more concerned with enclosing and defining areas of space within the wider landscape. These enclosures emphasise the separation and demarcation of that which is enclosed and that which is outside, and between the two it creates a physical and cognitive barrier. Whereas the ditches and banks of the henges are generally broken by only one or two causeways, it is also apparent that their form, when compared to those at many causewayed enclosures, were physically pronounced. Although there is general comparability between enclosures and henges as regards ditch depth, both the ditches and banks of the henges possess a more extensive range of widths (Fig. 3). While this appears to illustrate the visual importance of henge perimeters, a further comparison, between the enclosed area and the overall size of these sites, reiterates this point. It seems that the internal diameters of the henge monuments often represent a lower percentage of their external size than is the case for causewayed enclosures. While the inner enclosure at the multiple circuit sites of the latter category cover a smaller percentage of the overall monument when compared to single ring henges, the enclosed area of multi-circuit henges are generally only between about 30–40% of their external size (Fig. 4). In other words, the perimeters of henges, when compared to causewayed enclosures, tend to cover a greater percentage of the site.

One way of understanding these patterns would be to suggest that the circular perimeters of henges reflect a marked concern with

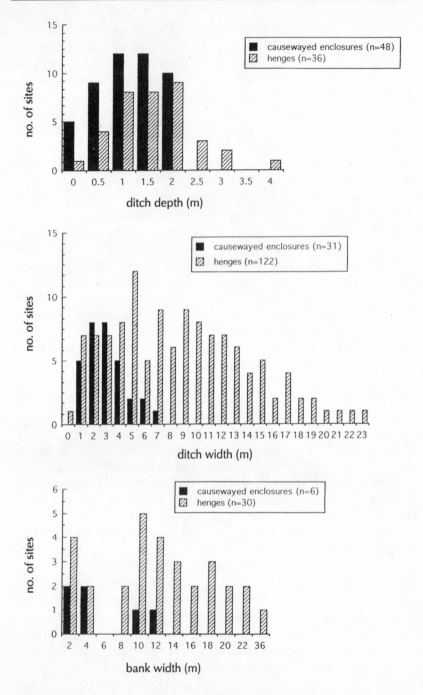

Figure 3. Ditch and bank sizes at causewayed enclosures and henges compared.

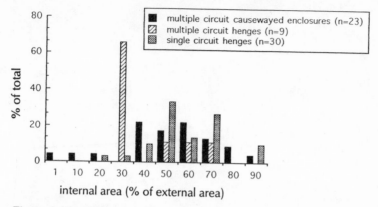

Figure 4. The relationship between the internal and external diameters of cause-wayed enclosures and henges.

controlling the interface and generation of encounter between the enclosed region of space and everything outside it. This also implies that henge entrances assume a significant importance since they are the only means of 'crossing' from the outside world into the enclosed space. Indeed, the causeways are often associated with additional structural features which physically emphasise these spatial thresholds and draw the viewers' attention towards the place of entry into the monuments. Most numerous are the single standing stones located in the entrances of a number of henges, and it seems that timber posts could have served the same purpose at other sites (Gray 1974: 74; Harding & Lee 1987: 261). Variations on this theme can be seen at a number of sites. For example, a grave and two pits placed immediately outside the Yeavering henge were aligned upon the entrances (Harding 1981: fig. 28), while Stonehenge 1 saw the erection of 2 orthostats and 52 timber posts in the north-eastern entrance (Atkinson 1979: 69–72; Burl 1987: fig. 7, 53ff).

Although they are varied in character, many of these features may have drawn upon and reaffirmed the significance that people attached to the crossing of the threshold of these sites. This may have been further enhanced by certain characteristics of the ditches themselves. The ditches which flank the causeways are often physically larger than at any other point around the perimeter and some have squared-off terminal ends. These characteristics again enhance the impression of an abruptly bounded and significant threshold, and at a number of sites it seems that the act of entering or leaving a henge was marked by complex patterns of activity. Indeed, the ditches flanking the cause-

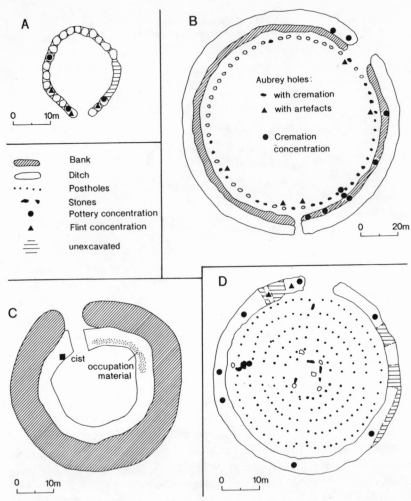

Figure 5. Plans of henges illustrating the location of artefact and bone concentrations. A. Wyke Down (after Barrett et al. 1991); B. Stonehenge I (after Burl 1987); C. Gorsey Bigbury (after Harding & Lee 1987); D. Mount Pleasant IV (after Wainwright 1979).

ways were often the only part of the site where deposits were deliberately placed (Barnatt 1990: 27; Burl 1987: fig. 8, 60, 72, 97; Harding 1981: 108; Shand unpublished).

The visual impression created by many henge perimeters emphasises the interior of these monuments as a defined region within which certain activities could be undertaken. Attention would have been focussed upon the enclosed space as individuals or groups moved across the causeways and into this area. Once this physical and symbolic 'crossing' was complete, the common location of the ditch on the inside of the bank would be visually noted, and this could only add to the perceived importance of the central area. Such a perimeter layout would orientate the viewers' gaze inwards, and at a number of sites the large size of many associated banks would have either completely restricted the view of the outside world or limited it to the rising and probably less immediate features of topography. However, the importance of the enclosed space was also emphasised by a series of associated features (Thomas 1991: 46). Individual or groups of pits and postholes are frequently found in the central area of henge interiors, as are rectangular or circular orthostatic structures. There are also timber circles, stone circles, and pit circles, and these features often tend to be concentric with the inner edge of the enclosure ditch. These components divide the naturally undifferentiated circular area of these monuments into a series of spaces, creating more complex patterns of spatial distinction and classification. It is apparent that these features would have drawn attention to a particular part of the central space, and it seems that the movement of individuals or groups around these features were often associated with acts of deposition (Barnatt 1990: 38; Burl 1987: 125; Harding 1981: 97, 109–11, figs 18–21). These various internal features also created patterns of differentiated visibility, and in a number of cases they encompassed the entire enclosed area, thus adding to the hiddenness of the interior space (Thomas 1991: 48).

The implications of a bounded circular design goes beyond the simple practical control of the interface between contrasting regions of space. The circle historically appears to represent wholeness and harmony, its form symbolically emphasising cyclical space and time (Sack 1980; Tuan 1974a; 1974b). It is certainly apparent that the act of visually following or moving around the outline of this shape would eventually return a viewers' perception to the original point of departure without necessarily repeating any part of the spatial experience. The cyclical nature of such a physical and mental journey could therefore be interpreted as a spatial metaphor for the repetitive and recurring qualities of society and the perceived cosmos. In this sense, the occupants would perhaps experience and reiterate the established qualities and relationships of social life as they moved around the locale, and the importance of circular pathways has been recognised at a number of the complex timber circles which have been found within henge monuments and the larger Wessex enclosures (Pollard 1992: 222–3, figs 7 & 8; Thomas 1991: 51–2, fig. 3.9).

These themes may have been drawn upon or reaffirmed in a variety of ways. At specific spatial and temporal junctures in the movement of individuals and groups, acts of deliberate deposition could emphasise certain aspects of the perceived social narrative. It is evident that artefacts and bone remains are generally found in the half of the site nearest the entrance (Fig. 5). Such a pattern of deposition certainly seems to be evident at the recently excavated Wyke Down, and it is the entrance end of the site which had some of the deepest pits and larger pockets of recutting (cf. Barrett et al. 1991: 96–101). Such a pattern is also strikingly apparent with the deposition associated with the ditch, bank, and Aubrey Holes of Stonehenge I. The distribution of the series of secondary cremations, placed burials, and artefacts all emphasise the eastern area of the site around and between the two unaligned entrances, while the western half of the site is more or less barren of deposits (Burl 1987: 98ff, fig. 8). Similarly, at Gorsey Bigbury a disturbed cist, with two individuals and a number of associated artefacts, was found in the bottom of the ditch near the causeway, and at the other side of this gap a substantial deposit of what was interpreted as occupation material overlay the primary silting (Harding & Lee 1987: 261). A slightly different pattern of deposition is evident at Mount Pleasant IV with the numbers of primary and secondary artefacts increasing clockwise around the perimeter (Wainwright 1979: 10ff). However, it is again evident that the largest number of deposits are associated with a section of the ditch near the single causeway.

CONCLUDING REMARKS

While causewayed enclosures and henges were both places of social aggregation their varying 'qualities' reflect something of the specific nature of interaction at these sites. The architectural and spatial characteristics of these sites refer to a series of potential contrasts and relationships concerning rights of access, movement, and the orientation of the human subject. I have suggested that the basic architectural and depositional repertoires of causewayed enclosures appear to have been structured by a tradition of segmentation which intentionally multiplied symbolic and physical boundaries, thus compartmentalising space into distinct and hierarchical regions. This tradition was expressed at the micro level, in the form of the enclosure ditches, and at the macro level, through the concentric layout of the perimeters of many sites. These spatial patterns of discontinuous morphic repetition could manifest the separate identities of kin-based or 'segmented' groups with the defined stretches of each circuit associated with the digging activities of particular lineages (Evans 1988b: 89; Startin & Bradley 1981: 293). If so, the contribution and usage of separate groups would be emphasised, the great feats of construction passing into the social memory of the wider community and recounted to illustrate the prestigious history of specific lineages. At the same time, the varying levels of recutting at the enclosures could reflect the changing ability of these groups to maintain their status at important social gatherings.

However, it is equally apparent that the enclosures of the early Neolithic represent a spatial and social contradiction (Evans 1988b: 92). By providing multiple paths of access across the boundaries, these locales would also serve to represent the symbolic integration of politically autonomous groups. This seems to suggest that the bringing together of people during various acts and rites was an important concern. The communities which were scattered throughout the landscape during the early Neolithic would not have existed in isolation from each other, and indeed, the reproductive capacity of each of these groups must have depended upon the establishment of wider contacts. It is possible, therefore, that the construction of the enclosures served to institutionalise inter-group relations, integrating a number of lineages into a larger corporate structure. These monuments could have been the location for regularly scheduled large-scale aggregations of people, perhaps at times of resource abundance. It certainly seems that many of the enclosures encompassed distinct areas of contemporary settlement, and it is also apparent that at least some of the sites could have potentially been associated with plentiful supplies of seasonal grazing (Barker & Webley 1978). These locales could have served as arenas for a multiplicity of activities and events through which the participating lineages may have formalised and reinforced various social alliances and institutions. The generation of social encounter was, in other words, essential to their existence and this might be represented by the partial continuity of monument interior and spatial exterior.

The physical division of these enclosures might therefore relate to both the social segregation and integration of groups. Such an interpretation could well account for the highly structured re-cutting which often maintained the original ditches of the monuments. The complex evidence for ditch cleaning and maintenance seems to indicate the successive reproduction or transformation of the enclosures' spatial layout, and thus symbolic meaning, with any reinstatement of the existing earthwork being only one part of this process (Bamford 1985: 39, 133; Evans 1988b: 89). Old ditch designs are sometimes exactly preserved, while elsewhere the layout of both earlier and later phases of construction are intermingled until they appear physically inextricable, thereby creating an 'eternal present' where the physical traces of successive events are all similarly interwoven. These activities would effectively emphasise the contribution of individual groups while also symbolically representing the long-term links and alliances which had been established between each. Along with the intentional deposition of artefacts and bone in the ditch segments, these events were undertaken and experienced as people moved through and around the spatially independent but comparable ditch segments, and the layout of the enclosures thus emphasised a specific tradition of ritually formalised movement. At many enclosures individuals could have generally been orientated upon 'back' regions of space which were physically and symbolically 'deep' or hidden within concentric zones of differing meaning. In other words, the perception and experience of people would constantly be focussed upon their sequential and lineal positioning between symbolic boundaries. These borders provided spatial and temporal 'cues' for the bracketing of experience, enabling the readers of these monumental 'texts' to define relevant meanings and generate social interaction and classification.

By contrast, the spatial and architectural patterns of the henge monuments reflect a different tradition in the 'positioning' of the human body and social encounter. They represent a more compact form, their continuous perimeters enclosing a single inner area of ideologically charged space. That henge perimeters are often larger, more imposing and less permeable than those of causewayed enclosures, with smaller and less manageable internal spaces, not only suggests a greater regulation of access but also the increasing control of events. The architecture of these monuments seems to have been employed to orientate the movement and perception of individuals across the enclosing border and into an inner region. Compared to the causewayed enclosures there was little emphasis upon the social 'journey' from the constituted reality of the outside landscape to the representative or symbolic world of the inner 'deep space', although the defining boundary of these monuments were physically stressed. Rather, social classification now revolved around a distinction between the excluded 'outsiders' and the privileged 'occupants'. In other words, individuals moved within a dominant symbolic and often physically imposing perimeter instead of between a number of boundaries. Acting in such a way, the monuments perhaps emphasise an 'authoritative' form of constraint which orientated movement and restrained interaction;

their architecture could have restricted face-to-face interaction by controlling the accessibility and interface of the enclosed regions of space.

It is therefore evident that instead of generating social encounters henges limit them, and this perhaps suggests that participation within these social arenas might have been more exclusive and regulated. However, the significance of these relatively continuous, regular, and circular perimeters can be illustrated in other ways. It is apparent that the final form of the causewayed enclosures was a product of discontinuous phases of construction, recutting, and rebuilding. In other words, as monuments they should be perceived as the product of continuous events rather than a finished cognitive construct (Evans 1988b: 89; Thomas 1991: 39, 52). On the other hand, the more continuous and generally larger ditches and banks of the henge monuments could represent a greater level of preconceived design. Rather than an 'emergent' spatial and architectural form which illustrates periodic refurbishment in response to changing social reality, these sites appear to represent the imposition of a fixed 'reading' of space, meaning, and social classification. Such an interpretation certainly seems to be supported if we consider the structural sequence of the henges. While some of these early monuments underwent ditch maintenance or modification (Atkinson et al. 1951: 43ff; Barrett et al. 1991: 92, 96; Richards 1990: 129, 269), it is evident that by at least the beginning of the second millennium the history of structural activity had generally altered. With the exception of the partial back-filling of the encircling ditches at some henges there is no evidence for the substantial modification of the existing perimeters. These monuments could, therefore, illustrate a greater level of formal design and preconceived intention, with the actual structural modification of locales now becoming less important. This suggests that the inscription of meaning was seen to be increasingly permanent, the abstract or elementary principles of tradition establishing a lasting spatial and temporal 'text' within the landscape.

NOTES

1. The evidence from a number of causewayed enclosures seems to indicate that the last of these sites were constructed by about 2400 bc (Hedges et al. 1991b: 228; Woodward 1988: 269; Hedges & Buckley 1978: appendix II; Hedges et al. 1992: 142-3; Smith 1974: 135). The first henge monuments appear to slightly overlap with this period, the available determinations falling between 2500-2100 bc (Evans 1984: 28; Richards 1990: 129, 259; Barrett et al. 1991: 96).

2. For the purposes of this paper the four large Wessex enclosures of Avebury, Durrington Walls, Mount Pleasant, and Marden are excluded from consideration.

These monuments stand out by reason of their giant size, irregular outline, and unusual internal and entrance characteristics (Wainwright 1989).

3. This was certainly the case at the massive single-circuit site of Haddenham (Evans 1988a), the middle ditch at Orsett (Hedges & Buckley 1978), the outer and second ring at Whitehawk Camp (Curwen 1934), the proposed original enclosure at Windmill Hill (Whittle 1990), and finally, the inner spiral arm at Briar Hill (Bamford 1985).

4. The available evidence from a number of enclosures appears to suggest that the inner circuits could possibly be earlier than the other rings (Abingdon, Avery 1982: 12, 24; Bradley 1986: 186: Briar Hill, Bamford 1985: 39; Offham Hill. Drewett 1977: 211: Orsett, Hedges & Buckley 1978: 259, Appendix 2: Windmill Hill, Whittle 1990: 28). If these inner circuits were indeed the result of primary phases, this would again illustrate their significance to the overall layout of the enclosures. However, the evidence is tentative and it should be noted that the inner ring at Crickley Hill was in fact probably late in date, although it must be noted that this site is unusual in both its location and layout (Dixon 1988).

5. Charcoal from the bottom of the inner concentric ditch at Aldwincle 1 produced a determination of 2610 ± 70 bc (HAR-1411) and the primary cremation from Low Farm 3 was dated to 2270 ± 180 bc (HAR-4302) (Jackson 1977). Moreover, the burnt timber structure at Grindale 1 was dated to 2560 ± 90 bc and 2520 ± 120 bc (HAR-266-7), and this was covered by freshly cut chalk rubble which appears to have come from the digging of an outer oval ditch (Manby 1980: 45-6).

BIBLIOGRAPHY

Ambers, J., Mathews, K., & Bowman, S. 1989. British Museum natural radiocarbon measurements XXI. *Radiocarbon* 31: 15–32.

Atkinson, R. J. C. 1979. *Stonehenge: Archaeology and Interpretation*. London: Penguin Press.

Atkinson, R. J. C., Piggott, C. M., Sandars, N. K. 1951. *Excavations at Dorchester, Oxon*. Oxford: Department of Antiquities, Ashmolean Museum.

Avery, M. 1982. The Neolithic Causewayed Enclosure, Abingdon. In Case, H. J & Whittle, A. W. R. (eds), *Settlement Patterns in the Oxford Region: excavations at the Abingdon Causewayed Enclosure and other Sites*, pp. 10–50. London: Council for British Archaeology (Research Report No. 44).

Bamford, H. M. 1985. *Briar Hill Excavation 1974–1978*. Northampton Development Corporation (Archaeological Monograph, No. 3).

Barker, G. W. & Webley, D. 1978. Causewayed camps and early Neolithic economies in central southern England. *Proceedings of the Prehistoric Society* 44: 161–186.

Barnatt, J. 1990. *The Henges, Stone Circles and Ringcairns of the Peak District*. Sheffield: University of Sheffield (Archaeological Monograph 1).

Barrett, J. C. 1988. The living, the dead, and the ancestors: Neolithic and early Bronze Age mortuary practices. In Barrett, J. C. & Kinnes, I. A. (eds), *The Archaeology of Context in the Neolithic and Bronze Age: Recent Trends*, pp. 30–41. Sheffield: Department of Archaeology and Prehistory.

Barrett, J. C., Bradley, R. J., & Green, M. 1991. *Landscape, Monuments and Society. The Prehistory of Cranborne Chase*. Cambridge: Cambridge University Press.

Bonney, D. 1961. Notes on excavations, 1960. *Proceedings of the Prehistoric Society* 27: 344.

Bourdieu, P. 1977. *Outline of a Theory of Practice*. Cambridge: Cambridge University Press.

Bradley, R. J. 1984. *The Social Foundations of Prehistoric Britain*. London: Longman.

Bradley, R. J. 1986. A reinterpretation of the Abingdon causewayed enclosure. *Oxoniensia* 51: 183–7.

Bradley, R. J. & Chambers, R. A. 1988. A new study of the cursus complex at Dorchester on Thames. *Oxford Journal of Archaeology* 7: 271–290.

Bradley, R. J. & Holgate, R. 1984. The Neolithic sequence in the upper Thames valley. In Bradley, R. J. & Gardiner, J. (eds), *Neolithic Studies. A Review of Some Current Research*, pp. 107–135. Oxford: British Archaeological Reports (British Series 133).

Brewster, A. 1984. *The Excavations of Whitegrounds, Burythorpe*. Wintringham: John Gett.

Burl, H. A. W. 1987. *The Stonehenge People*. London: Dent & Sons.

Carlstein, T. 1981. The sociology of structuration in time and space: a time-geographic assessment of Giddens's theory. *Swedish Geographic Yearbook*, 41–57.

Case, H. J. 1956. The Neolithic causewayed camp at Abingdon, Berks. *Antiquaries Journal* 36: 11–30.

Connah, G. 1965. Excavations at Knap Hill, Alton Priors, 1961. *Wiltshire Archaeological Magazine* 60: 1–23.

Curwen, E. C. 1929. Excavations in the Trundle, Goodwood, 1928. *Sussex Archaeological Collections* 70: 32–85.

Curwen, E. C. 1934. Excavations in Whitehawk Neolithic camp, Brighton, 1932–3. *Antiquaries Journal* 14: 99–133.

Darvill, T. C. 1981. Excavations at the Peak Camp, Cowley: an interim note. *Glevensis* 15: 52–56.

Dixon, P. 1988. The Neolithic settlements on Crickley Hill. In Burgess, C., Topping, P., Mordant, C. & Maddison, M. (eds), *Enclosures and Defences in the Neolithic of Western Europe*, pp. 75–87. Oxford: British Archaeological Reports (International Series 403 i).

Drewett, P. 1977. The excavation of a Neolithic causewayed enclosure on Offham Hill, East Sussex, 1976. *Proceedings of the Prehistoric Society* 43: 201–241.

Duncan, J. S. 1976. Landscape and the communication of social identity. In Rappoport, A. (ed.), *The Mutual Interaction of People and their Built Environment*, pp. 391–400. The Hague: Mouton Publishers.

Eliade, M. 1959. *The Sacred and the Profane*. New York: Harcourt, Brace & World.

Evans, C. 1985. Tradition and the cultural landscape: an archaeology of place. *Archaeological Review from Cambridge* 4: 80–94.

Evans, C. 1988a. Excavations at Haddenham, Cambridgeshire: a 'planned' enclosure and its regional affinities. In Burgess, C., Topping, P., Mordant, C. & Maddison, M. (eds), *Enclosures and Defences in the Neolithic of Western Europe*, pp. 127–148. Oxford: British Archaeological Reports (International Series 403 i).

Evans, C. 1988b. Acts of enclosure: a consideration of concentrically-organised causewayed enclosures. In Barrett, J. C. & Kinnes, I. A. (eds), *The Archaeology of Context in the Neolithic and Bronze Age: Recent Trends*, pp. 85–96. Sheffield: Department of Archaeology and Prehistory.

Evans, J. G. 1984. Stonehenge – the environment in the late Neolithic and

Early Bronze Age and a Beaker-Age burial. *Wiltshire Archaeological and Natural History Magazine* 78: 7–30.

Evison, V. I. 1956. An Anglo-Saxon cemetery at Holborough, Kent. *Archaeologia Cantiana* 70: 84–141.

Fasham, P. J. 1982. The excavation of four ring-ditches in central Hampshire. *Proceedings of the Hampshire Field Club Archaeological Society* 38: 19–56.

Giddens, A. 1979. *Central Problems in Social Theory*. London: Macmillan Press.

Giddens, A. 1984. *The Constitution of Society*. London: Polity Press.

Gray, M. 1974. The Devil's Quoits, Stanton Harcourt, Oxon. *Oxoniensia* 39: 96–97.

Harding, A. F. 1981. Excavations in the prehistoric ritual complex near Milfield, Northumberland. *Proceedings of the Prehistoric Society* 47: 87–135.

Harding, A. F. & Lee, G. E. 1987. *Henge Monuments and Related Sites of Great Britain. Air Photographic Evidence and Catalogue*. Oxford: British Archaeological Reports (British Series 175).

Hedges, J. D. & Buckley, D. G. 1978. Excavations at a Neolithic Causewayed Enclosure, Orsett, Essex, 1975. *Proceedings of the Prehistoric Society* 44: 219–308.

Hedges, R. E. M., Housley, R. A., Bronk, C. R., & Van Klinken, G. J. 1991a. Radiocarbon dates from the Oxford AMS System: Archaeometry datelist 12. *Archaeometry* 33: 279–296.

Hedges, R. E. M. et al. 1991b. Radiocarbon dates from the Oxford AMS System: Archaeometry datelist 13. *Archaeometry* 33: 279–296.

Hedges, R. E. M. et al. 1992. Radiocarbon dates from the Oxford AMS System: Archaeometry datelist 14. *Archaeometry* 34: 141–159.

Hillier, B. & Hanson, J. 1984. *The Social Logic of Space*. Cambridge: Cambridge University Press.

Hillier, B., Leaman, A., Stansall, P., & Bedford, M. 1978. Space syntax. In Green, D., Haselgrove, C., & Spriggs, M. (eds), *Social Organisation and Settlement*, part 2, pp. 343–381. Oxford: British Archaeological Reports (International Series 47 ii).

Hodder, I. 1984. Burials, houses, women and men in the European Neolithic. In Miller, D. & Tilley, C. (eds), *Ideology, Power and Prehistory*. Cambridge: Cambridge University Press.

Jackson, D. A. 1977. A radiocarbon date from the Aldwincle mortuary enclosure. *Northamptonshire Archaeology* 12: 183.

Jobey, G. 1968. Excavations of cairns at Chatton Sandyford, Northumberland. *Archaeologia Aeliana* 46: 5–50.

Kinnes, I. A. 1979. *Round Barrows and Ring-ditches in the British Neolithic*. London: British Museum (Occasional Paper 7).

Kus, S. M. 1983. The social representation of space: dimensioning the cosmological and quotidian. In Moore, J. A. & Keene, A. S. (eds), *Archaeological Hammers and Theories*, pp. 277–298. New York: Academic Press.

Leeds, E. T. 1927. A Neolithic site at Abingdon, Berks. *Antiquaries Journal* 7: 438–464.

Leeds, E. T. 1928. A Neolithic site at Abingdon, Berks. (second report). *Antiquaries Journal* 8: 461–77.

Manby, T. G. 1980. Excavation of barrows at Grindale and Boynton, East Yorkshire, 1972. *Yorkshire Archaeological Journal* 52: 19–47.

Mercer, R. J. 1980. *Hambledon Hill. A Neolithic Landscape*. Edinburgh: Edinburgh University Press.

Mercer, R. J. 1988. Hambledon Hill, Dorset, England. In Burgess, C., Topping, P., Mordant, C. & Maddison, M. (eds), *Enclosures and Defences in the Neolithic of Western Europe*, pp. 89–106. Oxford: British Archaeological Reports (International Series 403 i).

Musson, R. 1950. An excavation at Combe Hill Camp Eastbourne August 1949. *Sussex Archaeological Collections* 89: 105–115.

Palmer, R. 1976. Interrupted Ditch Enclosures in Britain: the use of Aerial Photography for Comparative Studies. *Proceedings of the Prehistoric Society* 42: 161–186.

Piggott, S. 1952. The Neolithic camp on Whitesheet Hill, Kilmington Parish. *Wiltshire Archaeological Magazine* 54: 404–410.

Pollard, J. 1992. The Sanctuary, Overton Hill, Wiltshire: a re-examination. *Proceedings of the Prehistoric Society* 58: 213–226.

Pred, A. 1977. The choreography of existence: comments on Hägerstrand's time-geography and its usefulness. *Economic Geography* 53: 207–221.

Pryor, F., French, C., Taylor, M. 1985. An interim report on excavations at Etton, Maxey, Cambridgeshire, 1982–1984. *Antiquaries Journal* 65: 275–311.

Rappoport, A. 1976. Sociocultural aspects of man-environment studies. In Rappoport, A. (ed.), *The Mutual Interaction of People and their Built Environment*, pp. 7–35. The Hague: Mouton Publishers.

Richards, C. C. 1988. Altered images: a re-examination of Neolithic mortuary practices in Orkney. In Barrett, J. C. & Kinnes, I. A. (eds), *The Archaeology of Context in the Neolithic and Bronze Age: Recent Trends*, pp. 42–56. Sheffield: Department of Archaeology and Prehistory.

Richards, J. 1986–90. Death and the past environment. The results of work on barrows on the Berkshire Downs. *Berkshire Archaeological Journal* 73: 1–42.

Richards, J. 1990. *The Stonehenge Environs Project*. London: English Heritage (Archaeological Report No. 16) (Historic Buildings and Monuments Commission for England).

Ross Williamson, R. P. 1930. Excavations in Whitehawk Neolithic Camp, near Brighton. *Sussex Archaeological Collections* 71: 57–87.

Sack, R. D. 1980. *Conceptions of Space in Social Thought*. London: Macmillan Press.

Sayer, R. A. 1982. Misconceptions of space in social thought. *Transactions of the Institute of British Geographers* 7: 494–503.

Shanks, M. & Tilley, C. 1982. Ideology, symbolic power and ritual communication: a reinterpretation of Neolithic mortuary practices. In Hodder, I. (ed.), *Symbolic and Structural Archaeology*, pp. 129–154. Cambridge: Cambridge University Press.

Shand, P. unpublished. Excavation of Corporation Farm, Abingdon. Undergraduate dissertation, University of Reading.

Sharples, N. M. 1985. Individual and community: the changing role of megaliths in the Orcadian Neolithic. *Proceedings of the Prehistoric Society* 51: 59–74.

Sharples, N. M. 1986. Maiden Castle 1985: an interim report. *Proceedings of the Dorset Natural History and Archaeological Society* 107: 111–120.

Sharples, N. M. 1991. *Maiden Castle. Excavations and Field Survey 1985–6*. London: English Heritage (Archaeological Report No. 19) (Historic Buildings and Monuments Commission for England).

Smith, I. F. 1965. *Windmill Hill and Avebury – Excavations by Alexander Keiller 1925–39*. Oxford: Clarendon Press.

Smith, I. F. 1971. Causewayed enclosures. In Simpson, D. D. A. (ed.), *Economy and Settlement in Neolithic and Early Bronze Age Britain and Europe*, pp. 89–112. Leicester: Leicester University Press.

Smith, I. F. 1974. The Neolithic. In Renfrew, C. (ed.), *British Prehistory. A New Outline*, pp. 100–136. London: Gerald Duckworth.

Startin, W. & Bradley, R. J. 1981. Some notes on work organisation and society in prehistoric Wessex. In Ruggles, C. & Whittle, A. W. R. (eds), *Astronomy and Society during the Period 4000–1500 BC*, pp. 289–296. Oxford: British Archaeological Reports (British Series 88).

Thomas, J. S. 1988. The social significance of Cotswold-Severn burial rites. *Man* 23: 540–559.

Thomas, J. S. 1990. Monuments from the inside: the case of the Irish megalithic tombs. *World Archaeology* 22: 168–178.

Thomas, J. S. 1991. *Rethinking the Neolithic*. Cambridge: Cambridge University Press.

Thomas, J. S. 1993. The politics of vision and the archaeologies of landscape. In Bender, B. (ed.), *Landscape: Politics and Perspectives*, pp. 19–48. Oxford: Berg.

Thomas, N. 1964. The Neolithic causewayed camp at Robin Hood's Ball, Shrewton. *Wiltshire Archaeological Magazine* 59: 1–27.

Tuan, Yi-Fu. 1974a. *Topophilia: a Study of Environmental Perception, Attitudes, and Values*. Englewood Cliffs: Prentice-Hall.

Tuan, Yi-Fu. 1974b. Space and place: humanistic perspective. *Progress in Geography* 6: 211–252.

Wainwright, G. J. 1979. *Mount Pleasant, Dorset: Excavations 1970–1971*. London: Society of Antiquaries (Research Report 37).

Wainwright, G. J. 1989. *The Henge Monuments*. London: Thames & Hudson.

Wheeler, R. E. M. 1943. *Maiden Castle, Dorset*. London: Society of Antiquaries.

Whittle, A. W. R. 1988. Contexts, activities, events – aspects of Neolithic and Copper Age enclosures in central and western Europe. In Burgess, C., Topping, P., Mordant, C. & Maddision, M. (eds), *Enclosures and Defences in the Neolithic of Western Europe*, pp. 1–19. Oxford: British Archaeological Reports (International Series 403 i).

Whittle, A. W. R. 1990. A pre-enclosure burial at Windmill Hill, Wiltshire. *Oxford Journal of Archaeology* 9: 25–28.

Woodward, P. J. 1988. Pictures of the Neolithic: discoveries from the Flagstones House excavations, Dorchester, Dorset. *Antiquity* 62: 266–274.

11

Windmill Hill Causewayed Enclosure: the Harmony of Symbols

Alasdair Whittle and Joshua Pollard

Over the decades, the Neolithic has been many things to those who study it: a chronology, a technology, a culture, an economy, a population, a social system, an ideology, and now a conceptual scheme. Of particular importance amongst recent, rapid changes in approach to the period can be signalled the new general emphasis on values and symbolism, the firm espousal of acculturation to explain the beginnings of the period, and the role envisaged for monuments as creators (rather than just symptoms) of novel attitudes to place and identity (from a much longer list, see Hodder 1990; Thomas 1991; Kinnes 1988; Sherratt 1990; Bradley 1993). But while many new ideas are attractive individually, there remains a serious lack of integration of all relevant aspects, which results in contradictory characterisations of the Neolithic.

For example, most authors assume on theoretical grounds that hunter-gatherers needed to be (semi-)sedentary and (semi-)complex, as well as ubiquitous, before adopting 'Neolithic' ways, even when the archaeological evidence is often for sparse, mobile populations. Thus Patton (1993: 37 & 64) uses the scrappy and sparse Breton shell middens as evidence for 'large, settled coastal communities' (contrast Whittle 1990a). As well as the need for better characterisation of the varying Mesolithic presence from region to region, much more theoretical attention also needs to be given to the possibilities of change amongst mobile hunter-gatherers. There is plenty of ethnographic evidence to suggest the receptiveness of mobile hunter-gatherers to new ideas and techniques from outside and their conceptual flexibility in resource procurement (Bird-David 1992; Kent 1992; cf. Ashbee 1982). This need is all the greater since early Neolithic populations in southern Britain are themselves increasingly – and reasonably – characterised as 'relatively' mobile (e.g. Ford 1987; Thomas 1991). As another contrasting example, the *domus*: *agrios* opposition of Hodder (1990) really only makes sense in terms of a rather unsophisticated late Mesolithic, in which the simple concept of 'the wild' is acceptable without further discussion. Other detailed considerations of hunter-gatherers, however, give rather more weight to such questions as attitudes to sharing within a framework of working with nature than to categorical pronouncements on wild and tame (e.g. Ingold 1986). Thus, the basic idea of native acculturation is expressed in both over-complex and over-simple models, both of which conflict with the available archaeological evidence.

With monuments, the contradictions are both theoretical and empirical. Monuments are increasingly being seen as part of the way in which mobile dispersed populations could be encouraged to embrace new concepts of community, identity, and adherence to chosen places, and to accept the routines and constraints of more settled life and of agriculture. They are increasingly bound into the spiritual cosmologies of the Neolithic, via ancestors and myths of origin, ideas which could have been both fundamental and powerful. But there is still a strong tendency in various theoretical stances, both processualist and post-processualist, to read into monuments preconceived notions of social difference and competition, generally seen as working within bounded communities. There are, therefore, simultaneous roles envisaged of conflicting character: on the one hand working towards integration and on the other towards control. This is not to claim that contradiction of this kind could never happen, but to point out the generally unstated theoretical conflict, which is usually avoided by talking as though the monuments themselves acted, without specifying the identity and relationships of those people who actually conceived, built, used, and were influenced by monuments of various kinds.

These questions also raise practical considerations of the early Neolithic milieu. In a wider review of the Mesolithic/Neolithic transition across Europe, Dennell (1984) has suggested that the availability of mates among native populations would have been one way for young men of Neolithic communities to avoid the constraints imposed by their elders. The issue goes wider still than mate choice and marriage eligibility. Now that settlement mobility is favoured in the early Neolithic on the evidence of several large research projects in southern Britain (French 1990; Woodward 1991; Sharples 1991; Barrett et al. 1991; Whittle 1993), how can one envisage the maintenance of tight social control, without instant disputes and fissioning? The continued availability of social space must have allowed people simply to turn their backs on coercion. On top of all this, these kinds of fractured hypotheses briefly reviewed above are too often applied 'from the top down', without sufficient regard for the detail of individual sites and regions (Shanks 1990: 295).

The Windmill Hill causewayed enclosure belongs to the end of the first period (Whittle 1993) of the Neolithic in its area, the upper Kennet valley and surrounding downland in northern Wiltshire. This paper raises many of the questions discussed above and attempts to show how better integration of approach can be achieved, working with the regional context and site detail on the one hand and with different preconceptions of social relations and values on the other. Work is well advanced on a final report, where most detail will be presented. The paper does not offer a neat 'hermeneutic circle' (Hodder 1992), more perhaps a still tangled knot.

The site was first excavated in the 1920s. Keiller explored some 75 per cent of the inner ditch and about half of the inner interior, over 25 per cent of the middle ditch and about 6 per cent of the outer ditch. In bringing his work to publication, Isobel Smith (1965) made five small cuttings. As part of a wider, regional programme, six further cuttings were dug (by A. W.) in 1988, with the specific aims of recovering dating and environmental samples (Whittle 1993). The post-excavation analysis has involved considerable work on the Keiller archive (Pollard 1993) in an attempt to relate the 1988 results to earlier research; Smith's classic account (1965), to which the reader is referred for basic description, is rather generalised.

Windmill Hill only makes sense in a regional context, not as a site on its own, but we do not know fully what the regional context was. Past research and the current project suggest some possibilities. The site is part of what appears to be a cluster of monuments. There are over twenty long barrows and chambered tombs in the area. It is very unlikely that all were built at the same time, and the radiocarbon evidence suggests that construction was spread over local phases B and C (Windmill Hill itself belonging to C: Whittle 1993: table 2; Table 1 here). Nor is it likely that all these monuments had the same character. Although some emphasise the human dead in large quantities, such as West Kennet and perhaps Millbarrow (Piggott 1962; Whittle 1994),

Table 1. Outline summary of phases in the Neolithic of the Avebury area.

Phase	BP uncal range
A	5450–5150
B	5150–4850
C	4850–4550
D	4550–4250
E	4250–3950
F	3950–3650

	CAL BC range at 1	Environment and subsistence
A	4354/4245–3999/3826	Woodland. First clearances?
B	3999/3826–3698/3542	Scattered small clearances in woodland. Animal husbandry
C	3698/3542–3361/3109	More clearances, in mosaic pattern. Some plough cultivation and cereals. Animal husbandry; some herding beyond area?
D	3361/3109–2916/2782	Trend to more scrub or woodland again
E	2916/2782–2564/2457	Renewed clearances
F	2564/2457–2133/1959	Trend to open country, though timber still available. Cultivation. Pigs.

	Settlement	Monuments
A	?	?
B	Dispersed. Small pit groups	Simple barrows, shrines?
C	Dispersed, with ? local nucleation, small sites, pit groups, lithic scatters	More elaborate and larger barrows (? lineages), sacred enclosures towards end of C
D	Uncertain, density as in A and B?	? Simple circles, ? start of West Kennet Avenue
E	Small sites and pit groups, larger lithic scatters	Development of Avebury, sanctuary Silbury at E/F border
F	More permanent or marked habitation areas?	Palisade enclosures, Beaker burials

others probably contained few human remains, such as Easton Down (Whittle et al. 1993), or none at all, such as Horslip, South Street, and Beckhampton Road long barrows (Ashbee et al. 1979). The cult of the dead may have developed through phases B and C, and could have emphasised principles of ancestry, but other monuments could as well have had significance as shrines to mythical ancestors, whose actual remains would be of no importance. The startling innovation of Windmill Hill (and other enclosures at Knap Hill and probably Rybury) thus came after perhaps centuries of varied shrines and tombs.

This raises further questions of beginnings and of settlement. One model for the development of Neolithic activity in the area is by secondary infill, by whatever population was involved, since there is little evidence (as also now around Stonehenge, in Cranborne Chase, and on the Dorset Ridgeway) for an established late Mesolithic presence in the area (Whittle 1990a). If settlement mobility is to be read from the lithic scatters and pit clusters identified in the area, there seems no compelling reason to confine the early Neolithic population to the upper Kennet alone. The environmental evidence from monuments suggests a mosaic of clearances, perhaps of modest size (Evans, Limbrey et al. 1993; Whittle 1993; Whittle et al. 1993), which lasted for varying periods of time. A wider population, using the middle and lower Kennet and the surrounding Vales for example, could have regarded the upper Kennet as either a home range or as a special core associated with the ancestors, or both. The population density could have been rather low. Before Windmill Hill, the Neolithic was probably still in the process of initial establishment.

It is unlikely that the idea of such an enclosure was invented at Windmill Hill itself, since there are so many other comparable sites in Britain and on the continent. That idea might have been part of culturally transferred memory of earlier enclosures, going back ultimately to LBK enclosures on the continent (Whittle 1977) or, perhaps more probably, an element in a repertoire of appropriate ways of doing things shared between Neolithic communities over broad areas of western Europe as part of the process of becoming fully Neolithic (Bradley & Chapman 1984; Thomas 1991). In either case, there is much that we do not understand about the process by which a general idea was put into local practice. Who was responsible for the first move? We do not know why one particular location was chosen, but the enclosure was preceded by occupation and burial on Windmill Hill, and the setting was one of woodland or scrub according to both soil and molluscan evidence (Whittle 1990b; Whittle 1993). By contrast, the long barrows and chambered tombs appear to have been set in or on the edges of localised clearings. The contrast may well have been deliberate, and it has been suggested elsewhere that the motive was to contain potentially dangerous ritual in an out-of-the-way location (Sharples 1991: 255). An alternative is to envisage an opposition in which the ancestors and the dead were made present in the clearances of the living, while the rituals celebrating – among other things – the social relations of the living were set further afield from daily spheres, to enhance their specialness rather than to contain their potential danger.

The construction of the site could have had an event-like character, recognised at the time as special and remembered as such long after (Whittle 1988). It remains unclear whether all three circuits were exactly contemporaneous. The evidence of joining sherds from different circuits (Smith 1965: 14) is ambiguous, and the radiocarbon dates are insufficiently precise (Whittle 1993: table 1). There are differences between the circuits, including the fact that only the outer circuit definitely had an accompanying bank and many divergences in the nature of depositions in the respective ditches, but layout will be assumed here to have been unitary. Construction, even if spread over a number of years, could have brought larger numbers of people together than for the construction of shrines and tombs. For a different task, the setting up of the great menhir in the Morbihan, it was estimated that over 3000 people would have had to be present (Hornsey 1987), but there are no similar constructional parameters here to enable specific guesses. Nevertheless, the successful laying out of the enclosure should be seen as one its most significant aspects, since a sizeable work-force, drawn from a wider population roundabout, must have been in agreement. Given the context, it is difficult to see this task as carried out under duress or coercion. It is far easier to envisage beliefs and attitudes which stressed cohesion and cooperation, even if the overall task was split into smaller operations with gangs working on individual ditch segments. One might invoke the hunter-gatherer ethic of sharing, and suppose it still active among mobile herders and sporadic horticulturalists (or 'vicarious farmers' (Kent 1992: 60)).

Primary use of the site may have lasted only for a few generations. Again the radiocarbon dates are too imprecise, though they are compatible with this claim. The duration of primary silting should have been short by analogy with modern observations of the filling of chalk-cut features (Bell 1990). Most depositions are contained within the primary and lower secondary fills of the ditch segments. After construction, the quantity of depositions suggests, again in an unquantifiable way, that a considerable number of people were involved in the initial use of the site.

Neither aspect, however, explains why circumstances changed to produce this new kind of site, here or elsewhere. One kind of answer would be to invoke, perhaps rather crudely, more people in the landscape or in relevant social groupings, thus giving – in functionalist style – an integrative role to the enclosure. There is as yet no in-dependent evidence for more people in this region. This also fails to explain why and how individuals became participants in the construc-tion and use of the enclosure (cf. Shennan 1993). Another answer is to invoke the continued process of becoming Neolithic, of individuals and groupings consciously adopting, or being influenced by others to adopt, new attitudes to locality, labour, descent, identity, and a place in the scheme of things both human and supernatural, cultural and natural. Although necessarily it comes from after the construction of the enclosure, the evidence for the primary use of the site provides the best material for a fuller answer of this kind.

The layout of the enclosure is distinctive. The outer earthwork, over 350 m in maximum diameter, sprawls off the hill. The middle and inner circuits may have lacked formal banks. The inner circuit is in-dented, presumably deliberately, and the middle circuit has alterna-tions of shorter and longer segments; in both there could have been some succession from initial pits to redefined or longer segments. We assume that these features were deliberate. Though perception of the monument might have been very different to Neolithic eyes, it is tempting from our map-like perception of the site to see in the layout a symbolism of inclusion and exclusion, of multiple access and yet re-striction and bounding. Such is the scale of the site, however, that it is difficult to see how use of it could in fact have been tightly controlled. Once again, a communal dimension is raised, and the monument can be seen as an act of self-definition and communal integration at a wider scale than previously attempted in tombs or shrines.

Depositions within the site appear to have reinforced the symbolism of the layout, by marking off the different circuits and emphasising boundaries and points of entry and transition. In general, activity appears to have been intensive. Bones, flints, and sherds are profuse, and quern fragments, rubbers, pounders, and bone and chalk artefacts are not uncommon. The Keiller archive allows some quantification. Often the biggest totals for flints and sherds are from tertiary contexts but these must have been originally present near the ditches. There is some evidence from the interior of the inner circuit for occupation spreads or middens in the form of varying flint densities recovered by Keiller. Some, indeed much, of this material, particularly the surface material, could be the result of occupation, and to maintenance tools like querns and pounders can be added concentrations of charcoal. Similar concentrations of material have not turned up elsewhere (and one can add the southern flank of Windmill Hill too), and it becomes perverse to exclude the site from the distribution of population in the area, especially if the general pattern was one of small, shifting camps and short-term bases. Occupation should not therefore be excluded, but it may not have been a major aspect of the primary use of the site (cf. Bradley 1993: 90), which certainly involved activities of a special kind.

Individual adult human bones and human infant and animal burials in the ditches are one obvious manifestation of special activity. It is also evident from analysis of both Keiller's and the 1988 results that there was considerable pattern in the deposition of all classes of material, and that deposition was a consciously motivated and formal affair. There is not the space here to do more than sketch some of the main points, and it is convenient to concentrate primarily on animal bone, which is the most striking of the materials deposited. It may be claimed that much of this in the primary and lower secondary fills of the ditches had been deliberately selected, some perhaps after transformations in middens or elsewhere, and that it was deliberately placed, along with other material, in significant locations in and around the ditch circuits.

Most material occurs along the centre of silting in the ditches, but little of its disposition appears to be the result of casual dumping, the action of gravity or scavenging. It can be argued that in some cases animal bone left over from meals or feasts had gone straight into the ditches. In the primary fills of the inner ditch segments, and to a lesser extent in those of the middle ditch, there were discrete groups of animal bone; in the outer ditch there were both groups and spreads of bone. These deposits, however, were regularly accompanied by low numbers of artefacts, including sherds (not representing whole pots), flints, querns, and other rubbing stones, and so on, and were often set in a matrix of charcoal-rich soil. The accompanying artefacts do not suggest that the bone was the direct residue of meals or feasts, and the accompanying dark soil suggests derivation from some other kind of deposit. In the interior of the inner enclosure excavated by Keiller, there is evidence (already noted above) in the form of varying flint distributions for the possible existence of middens. One can suggest that at least some of the bone which ended in the ditches was deposited first in some such location. The animal bone varies in condition and completeness (full study by Caroline Grigson of weathering and fragmentation is not yet finished). Many bones appear partly weathered, and many are broken. The spreads and groups of bone

POSSIBLE ACTIVITIES AND SYMBOLIC REFERENCES

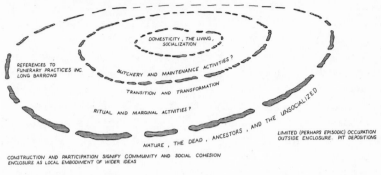

DOMESTICITY, THE LIVING, SOCIALIZATION

REFERENCES TO FUNERARY PRACTICES INC. LONG BARROWS

BUTCHERY AND MAINTENANCE ACTIVITIES?

TRANSITION AND TRANSFORMATION

RITUAL AND MARGINAL ACTIVITIES?

NATURE, THE DEAD, ANCESTORS, AND THE UNSOCIALIZED

LIMITED (PERHAPS EPISODIC) OCCUPATION OUTSIDE ENCLOSURE. PIT DEPOSITIONS

CONSTRUCTION AND PARTICIPATION SIGNIFY COMMUNITY AND SOCIAL COHESION ENCLOSURE AS LOCAL EMBODIMENT OF WIDER IDEAS

DEPOSITS IN THE DITCHES

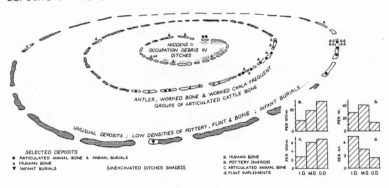

MIDDENS & OCCUPATION DEBRIS IN DITCHES

ANTLER, WORKED BONE & WORKED CHALK FREQUENT
GROUPS OF ARTICULATED CATTLE BONE

INFANT BURIALS...

UNUSUAL DEPOSITS; LOW DENSITIES OF POTTERY, FLINT & BONE

SELECTED DEPOSITS
● ARTICULATED ANIMAL BONE & ANIMAL BURIALS
▲ HUMAN BONE
▼ INFANT BURIALS   (UNEXCAVATED DITCHES SHADED)

a. HUMAN BONE
b. POTTERY (SHERDS)
c. ARTICULATED ANIMAL BONE
d. FLINT IMPLEMENTS

I.D M.D O.D

THE MONUMENT AND ITS SETTING

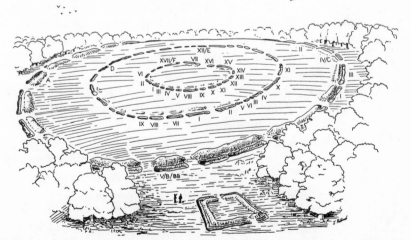

Figure 1. The layout of the Windmill Hill causewayed enclosure, from the east, with deposits, activities, and symbolic references of its primary phase (by Joshua Pollard).

[239]

rarely consist of the remains of only one individual. It is usual to find parts of more than one animal and more than one species. In one series of deposits in the inner ditch (Trench F, 1988), cattle bone (as elsewhere) was in the majority, but there were also bones of pig, sheep/goat, and dog. The cattle were represented by skull fragments, ribs, vertebrae, a pelvis, and feet bones, and there were pig scapulae, vertebrae, and a mandible. Remains of the other species were sporadic. A human femur was inserted into the shaft of a cattle humerus. This must show deliberate association, and other mixings and juxtapositions may have been either deliberate or the result of shared transformations in middens.

As well as the evidence for transformation and selection, there are many indications that animal bones and other material were deliberately placed. Bone groups in segment terminals appear to emphasise major entrances between segments. There were repeated depositions in ID VII and MD II, for example, in each case on the right hand of the causeway as one progresses towards the interior. The two segments of ID VII produced the largest concentration of Windmill Hill ware, 95 vessels in total (Smith 1965: 5). There were also flint tools, worked sarsen, and worked chalk pieces in quantity. The majority of the finds derived from a dark, humic, and charcoal-rich soil overlying the primary fill. Both the character of the fill and the quantity of finds suggest that it was back-filled with material immediately after the primary fill had accumulated. This event could correspond with the deposition of substantial bone groups, including articulated joints, on top of the primary rubble in ID XVI, on the eastern side of the causeway in question. Some of the opposing segments flanking major causeways have markedly different finds assemblages. For example, while ID VII had around 120 sherds per metre of primary fill, the opposing segments ID XV and XVI produced an average of only 14 sherds per metre. ID VII produced five pieces of worked chalk (two from the primary fill and three unstratified); there was one chalk ball from ID XVI and one incised piece from the refill of ID XV.

The treatment of cattle skulls and horn cores is particularly interesting. Proportionately more came from the middle circuit than the inner or outer circuits. In 10 out of 11 instances where the context is reconstructable, skulls occurred against causeways, and always with other cattle bone. Deliberate placing can be inferred in most instances, both through positioning and sets of associations. In layer 3 of ID XVI and layer 4 of MD IB, crania had been placed upright, within bone groups (in the latter case including another cleft cattle skull), facing the adjoining causeways. A substantial portion of cranium from the eastern terminal of ID II was found with three horn cores, one being of *Bos primigenius*. Three cattle skulls and two odd horn cores from the southern end of MD XA were found close to the skeleton of a dog. Other associations between skulls and horn cores occurred in the base of ID XVII, layer 4 of MD VIII, layer 4 of MD XIA, and Trench A. Other associations of cattle horn cores can be noted. A sarsen pounder from the primary fill of ID VIII was ringed by three horn cores. Horn cores were also found with the skeleton of a puppy in the northern terminal of MD XB, and with a leaf arrowhead in the secondary fill of the southern half of the same ditch.

Another sense of spatial order comes from the mapping of inter-circuit patterning. Each of the three circuits possessed its own depositional character. For example, the most numerous bone groups come from the inner ditch, but virtually all the groups of articulated animal bone were of cattle, and came from the middle and outer ditches. Human bone was more common in the outer ditch than in the middle and inner. There were more sherds and worked flints in the inner and middle ditches than in the outer, though implements formed a higher proportion of the lithic assemblage from the outer ditch than from the other circuits. Differences in detail can be noted, such as the occurrence of leaf arrowheads in the lowest ditch fills only in the inner ditch, and the greatest frequency of scrapers and axe fragments in the outer ditch.

It is important here to try to understand the frequency with which depositions were made. If the duration of primary use was two or three generations, the picture is perhaps one of single depositions repeated at intervals and probably occurring at different points in the circuit at any one time. It is likely that the first depositions were neither as formalised nor as abundant in material as those from a little later in the primary sequence, and this may suggest some development from an initial emphasis on the physical demarcation of space to its reinforcement with depositions. The overall sense of order is the result of conformity to a sense of what was appropriate in different parts of the site, but it is hard to envisage tight rules for or control over each and every act of deposition. The size of audience, if and when one was present, may also have been limited by the layout of the ditch segments. Just as in the restricted spaces of chambered tombs, comparatively few people would have been able to witness directly the detail of what was being deposited.

So far it has been suggested that the enclosure was constructed towards the end of an opening period of the regional Neolithic (in local phase C), in an area still relatively little settled. Local contrasts can be drawn between the scale of clearance associated with the shrines and tombs which precede the enclosure and that detectable around the enclosure itself. The embodiment of the general idea of enclosure was a stunning novelty locally, and both its construction and its careful layout may have constituted a powerful symbol of inclusion and exclusion, conveying a strong sense of cohesion and identity to its prime users. The enclosure was in use for at least two or three generations, and witnessed a succession of acts of deposition, at intervals, which were so arranged within and around the ditch circuits as to create a strong sense of spatial order. Further consideration of the possible meanings of these depositions may offer better understanding of the nature of the enclosure.

The things deposited in the ditches were varied. As well as the artefacts of different kinds and the remains of animals and humans already mentioned, there were plant remains, though these too may have been accidental inclusions from midden deposits elsewhere. At a simple level, this range of material can evoke a number of different spheres of Neolithic life: subsistence; consumption; and relations with neighbours and ancestors. The location of the site may reflect a deliberate choice of a wild, natural setting, and the symbolism of the site layout may suggest a concern with group solidarity. The combination of possible meanings and references is equally important. The overwhelming impression is a concern for the deposition of animal bone, accompanied by other signifiers of domesticity, but this was framed also by references to specific groups of social actors including those from a wider world than the purely local stage, and through selected bones and deposits of the deceased was further highlighted by the presence of death. The practice of deposition in individual segments might suggest, as hinted at above, rituals carried out by small groups, such as households, kin groups, and age or gender sets, but even if this was the case, the opposition between opposing segments shows that depositions did not take place in isolation. In spatial terms, the inner parts of the site might be seen to stress the domestic, the living, the socialised, and the adult spheres, while the outer circuit could be seen to present aspects of nature, the dead, and the unsocialised.

We can also consider metonymic and metaphoric codes. In Leach's terms (1976: fig. 1), a metonym is a sign, offering part for the whole, while a metaphor is an arbitrary (but consistently used) symbol. It has been argued above that few of the ditch deposits are direct residues from immediately antecedent activities. Through transformation and selection, some deposits may have acted as a metonym for feasting and its possible connotations of successful subsistence and social gatherings. As Leach has pointed out (1976: 16), the same material can be used both metonymically and metaphorically, and apparently separate acts can be linked to the same ritual cycle (Leach 1976: 27). Thus here, cattle bone, the prominent material in the various groups and spreads, could have carried metaphoric associations. Animals in general could have served as tokens of gender, identity, and descent. Cattle skulls have been found in long barrows, for example. At Fussell's Lodge, there was a skull placed in the proximal end of the mortuary deposit, adjacent to the bones of two women (Ashbee 1966). Locally, there was a skull in an axial position near the north-eastern end of the Beckhampton long barrow (Ashbee et al. 1979: fig. 14). In the fill of the pre-enclosure grave of an adult man at Windmill Hill (Whittle 1990b) there were pig bones. It might be suggested therefore that there was some association between women and cattle and between pigs and men. On a wider scale, it has also been suggested that archery was a male activity (Edmonds & Thomas 1987), and that axes too were principally associated with men (Bradley & Edmonds 1993). Neither arrowheads nor axes were abundant at Windmill Hill, the latter anyway occurring more in secondary than in primary contexts.

Despite these suggestions, there is insufficient comparative evidence from other contexts for metaphoric codes to be broken, and we must remain with a broad range of possibilities only. None the less, it is also possible that the transformation and selection of animal bone deliberately mimics the treatment of human bone in the extended burial rites documented in barrows and chambered tombs. Whatever the case may be with issues of gender, it may be legitimate to claim a metaphoric link between animals and people, related to identity and descent. Speculating further, it may be noted that Eliade (1968: 43–7) has observed the frequency of myths to do with origins and human guilt at domesticating the natural world. Could at least some of the Windmill Hill deposits be seen as part of propitiatory rites arising out of the process of becoming Neolithic?

The unresolved speculation about metaphoric codes is important, because, quite apart from the problems of chronological imprecision and extent of excavation so often associated with sites of this kind, it indicates that there is a level of meaning which is very hard, if not impossible to penetrate. We may have to fall back on more general characterisations of the site as a celebration of domesticity, as a harmony of symbols, in the newly created and still consolidating Neolithic world.

This in turn is important for proper appreciation of the sequence. One of the most striking features of the depositions at Windmill Hill is the sheer variety of form and content. Whilst parallels may be drawn with contemporary depositional practices in pits and long barrows, the heterogeneous character of those at Windmill Hill could be taken to indicate the participation of a diverse range of practitioners, in a more open social discourse than that associated with funerary monuments. The ceramic evidence from the enclosure also suggests a range of users or participants (Cleal 1992: 303). It has been common for prehistorians to invoke models of development based on competition and unequal social relations (Friedman & Rowlands 1977; Patton 1993: 66; Bradley 1993: 16). There is no need to envisage a happy Neolithic Arcadia; the human bones with missile points in them are counter to that notion. But the scale and locus of difference are important. Too often models of prehistoric development mimic present-day social difference within communities. The important locus of difference in the earlier part of the Neolithic may rather have been between communities, and the evidence increasingly suggests scattered populations dispersed over broad areas, on whom tight social control could hardly be imposed. Without excluding the possibility that lineages or other groupings jostled for position, it is far more likely on the basis of both the context and the details of the Windmill Hill site that the enclosure was part of the process of creating a 'conceptual community' (Gellner 1988: 58; cf. Liversage 1992: 88; Sharples 1992: 324-6). That feasting has been used competitively in strategies of lineage or clan dominance (Friedman & Rowlands 1977; Hayden & Gargett 1990: 14-15) should not entail that it is always so used. In the context under discussion here, consolidation of a new way of life and new attitudes was the principal theme. The enclosure had a role in the creation of a 'participatory community' (Gellner 1988: 152). For Gellner (1988: 55), 'loyalty to concepts makes possible loyalty to community', and a concept 'encapsulates and communicates and authorizes a shared way of classifying, valuing, a shared range of social and natural expectations and obligations.' Solidarity and cohesion were probably more important goals at Windmill Hill than competition and differentiation.

Finally, the primary use of the enclosure was not continued indefinitely. If the creation and use of the enclosure are to be explained by reference to competition and differentiation, then at this point we must have recourse to 'collapse' models of various kinds. In the model offered here, there was a long process of transition from Mesolithic to

Neolithic, and Windmill Hill belongs to its latter part. Rather than a swift shift from Mesolithic 'accumulators' (Hayden 1990), the transition may involve a longer and slower shift in attitudes among people adept at procurement (Bird-David 1992: 40), but for whom something more than technical adaptability was required to become Neolithic. Once such a mind-shift was achieved, the particular circumstances in which the enclosure came into being must have changed, and in a sense the full Neolithic began thereafter (cf. Bradley 1993: chapter 1). Perhaps this is in the end a functionalist explanation of one particular enclosure, but it can only be offered with full attention to context and meaning.

ACKNOWLEDGEMENTS

We must thank all those involved in preparing the final report on Windmill Hill and especially Caroline Grigson for her work on the animal bones. We are grateful to Francis Pryor, Andrew Sherratt, and Mark Edmonds for comments on earlier drafts. Permission to excavate was granted by the Department of the Environment, and the 1988 field-work was supported by The British Academy, The Society of Antiquaries, The Prehistoric Society, The Wiltshire Archaeological and Natural History Society, and UWCC. Access was granted by The National Trust and English Heritage, to whom grateful thanks are expressed.

BIBLIOGRAPHY

Ashbee, P. 1966. Fussell's Lodge long barrow excavations, 1957. *Archaeologia* 100: 1–80.

Ashbee, P. 1982. A reconsideration of the British Neolithic. *Antiquity* 56: 134–138.

Ashbee, P., Smith, I. F., & Evans, J. G. 1979. Excavation of three long barrows near Avebury, Wiltshire. *Proceedings of the Prehistoric Society* 45: 207–300.

Barrett, J., Bradley, R. and Green, M. 1991. *Landscape, Monuments and Society. The Prehistory of Cranborne Chase.* Cambridge: Cambridge University Press.

Bell, M. 1990. Sedimentation rates in the primary fills of chalk-cut features. In Robinson, D. E. (ed.), *Experiment and Reconstruction in Environmental Archaeology*, pp. 237–248. Oxford: Oxbow Books.

Bird-David, N. 1992. Beyond 'the hunting and gathering mode of subsistence': culture-sensitive observations on the Nayaka and other modern hunter-gatherers. *Man* 27: 19–44.

Bradley, R. 1993. *Altering the Earth.* Edinburgh: Society of Antiquaries of Scotland.

Bradley, R. J. & Chapman, R. C. 1984. Passage graves in the European Neolithic: a theory of convergent evolution. In Burenhult, G. (ed.), *The Archaeology of Carrowmore*, pp. 348–356. Stockholm: Institute of Archaeology.

Bradley, R. & Edmonds, M. 1993. *Interpreting the Axe Trade*. Cambridge: Cambridge University Press.

Cleal, R. 1992. Significant form: ceramic styles in the earlier Neolithic of southern England. In Sharples, N. and Sheridan, A. (eds), *Vessels for the Ancestors*, pp. 322–331. Edinburgh: Edinburgh University Press.

Dennell, R. 1984. The expansion of exogenous-based economies across Europe: the Balkans and central Europe. In DeAtley, S. P. and Findlow, F. J. (eds), *Exploring the Limits: Frontiers and Boundaries in Prehistory*, pp. 93–115. Oxford: British Archaeological Reports.

Edmonds, M. R. & Thomas, J. S. 1987. The Archers: an everyday story of country folk. In Brown, A. & Edmonds, M. R. (eds), *Lithic Analysis and Later British Prehistory*, pp. 187–199. Oxford: British Archaeological Reports.

Eliade, M. 1968. *Myths, Dreams and Mysteries* (first published 1957). London: Collins.

Evans, J. G., Limbrey, S., Máté, I., & Mount, R. 1993. An environmental history of the upper Kennet valley, Wiltshire, for the last 10,000 years. *Proceedings of the Prehistoric Society* 59: 139–195.

Ford, S. 1987. Chronological and functional aspects of flint assemblages. In Brown, A. and Edmonds, M. R. (eds), *Lithic Analysis and Later British Prehistory*, pp. 67–86. Oxford: British Archaeological Reports.

French, C. A. I. 1990. Neolithic soils, middens and alluvium in the lower Welland valley. *Oxford Journal of Archaeology* 9: 305–311.

Friedman, J. & Rowlands, M. J. 1977. Notes towards an epigenetic model for the evolution of civilisation. In Friedman, J. & Rowlands, M. J. (eds), *The Evolution of Social Systems*, pp. 201–276. London: Duckworth.

Gellner, E. 1988. *Plough, Sword and Book. The Structure of Human History*. London: Collins Harvill.

Hayden, B. 1990. Nimrods, piscators, pluckers and planters: the emergence of food production. *Journal of Anthropological Archaeology* 9: 31–69.

Hayden, B. & Gargett, R. 1990. Big man, big heart? A Mesoamerican view of the emergence of complex society. *Ancient Mesoamerica* 1: 3–20.

Hodder, I. 1990. *The Domestication of Europe*. Oxford: Blackwell.

Hodder, I. 1992. The Haddenham causewayed enclosure – a hermeneutic circle. In Hodder, I. (ed.), *Theory and Practice in Archaeology*, pp. 213–240. London and New York: Routledge.

Hornsey, R. 1987. The Grand Menhir Brisé: megalithic success or failure? *Oxford Journal of Archaeology* 6: 185–217.

Ingold, T. 1986. *The Appropriation of Nature*. Manchester: Manchester University Press.

Kent, S. 1992. The current forager controversy: real versus ideal views of hunter-gatherers. *Man* 27: 45–70.

Kinnes, I. 1988. The cattleship Potemkin: the First Neolithic in Britain. In Barrett, J. C. & Kinnes, I. (eds), *The Archaeology of Context in the Neolithic and Bronze Age: Recent Trends*, pp. 2–8. Sheffield: University of Sheffield, Department of Archaeology and Prehistory.

Leach, E. 1976. *Culture and Communication. The Logic by which Symbols are Connected*. Cambridge: Cambridge University Press.

Liversage, D. 1992. *Barkaer. Long Barrows and Settlements*. Copenhagen: Akademisk Forlag.

Patton, M. 1993. *Statements in Stone. Monuments and Society in Neolithic Brittany*. London and New York: Routledge.

Piggott, S. 1962. *The West Kennet Long Barrow. Excavations 1955–56*. London: Her Majesty's Stationery Office.

Pollard, J. 1993. Traditions of Deposition in Neolithic Wessex. Unpublished Ph.D. thesis, University of Wales College of Cardiff.

Shanks, M. 1990. Conclusion. Reading the signs: responses to archaeology after structuralism. In Bapty, I. & Yates, T. (eds), *Archaeology after Structuralism*, pp. 294–310. London: Routledge.

Sharples, N. M. 1991. *Maiden Castle: Excavations and Field Survey 1985–86*. London: English Heritage.

Sharples, N. 1992. Aspects of regionalisation in the Scottish Neolithic. In Sharples, N. and Sheridan, A. (eds), *Vessels for the Ancestors*, pp. 322–331. Edinburgh: Edinburgh University Press.

Shennan, S. 1993. After social evolution: a new archaeological agenda? In Yoffee, N. and Sherratt, A. (eds), *Archaeological Theory: Who Sets the Agenda?*, pp. 53–59. Cambridge: Cambridge University Press.

Sherratt, A. 1990. The genesis of megaliths: ethnicity and social complexity in Neolithic northwest Europe. *World Archaeology* 22: 147–167.

Smith, I. F. 1965. *Windmill Hill and Avebury*. Oxford: Clarendon Press.

Thomas, J. 1991. *Rethinking the Neolithic*. Cambridge: Cambridge University Press.

Whittle, A. 1977. Earlier Neolithic enclosures in north-west Europe. *Proceedings of the Prehistoric Society* 43: 329–348.

Whittle, A. 1988. Contexts, activities, events – aspects of Neolithic and Copper Age enclosures in central and western Europe. In Burgess, C., Topping, P., Mordant, C., & Maddison, M. (eds), *Enclosures and Defences in the Neolithic of Western Europe*, pp. 1–19. Oxford: British Archaeological Reports.

Whittle, A. 1990a. A model for the Mesolithic-Neolithic transition in the upper Kennet valley, north Wiltshire. *Proceedings of the Prehistoric Society* 56: 101–110.

Whittle, A. 1990b. A pre-enclosure burial at Windmill Hill, Wiltshire. *Oxford Journal of Archaeology* 9: 25–28.

Whittle, A. 1993. The Neolithic of the Avebury area: sequence, environment, settlement and monuments. *Oxford Journal of Archaeology* 12: 29–53.

Whittle, A. 1994. Excavations at Millbarrow chambered tomb, Winterbourne Monkton, north Wiltshire. *Wiltshire Archaeological and Natural History Magazine* 87: 1–53.

Whittle, A., Rouse, A., & Evans, J. G. 1993. A Neolithic downland monument in its environment: excavations at the Easton Down long barrow, Bishops Cannings, north Wiltshire. *Proceedings of the Prehistoric Society* 59: 197–239.

Woodward, P. J. 1991. *The South Dorset Ridgeway. Survey and Excavations 1977–84*. Dorchester: Dorset Natural History and Archaeology Society.

12

Sermons in Stone: Identity, Value, and Stone Tools in Later Neolithic Britain

Mark Edmonds

It *has long been* a commonplace that, later in the Neolithic, Britain witnessed a series of profound developments in the character of material and social life. From Piggott's 'secondary cultures' to the chiefdoms, core areas, and peer polities of more recent literature, it has been acknowledged that the latter half of the third millennium bc saw changes in a variety of social practices (Bradley 1984; Darvill 1987; Piggott 1954; Renfrew 1973). Although their character and timing may vary from one part of the country to another, these changes include developments in the nature of funerary rites and ceremonial, and in the character and diversity of artefact assemblages. It is in the later Neolithic that we see a shift of emphasis towards single burial in many areas and a gradual diminution of the importance attached to traditions of collective burial that had persisted for many generations. The period also saw changes in the character and context of ceremonial practices, indicated by the emergence of monuments such as henges and other stone and timber arangements.

Important developments can also be identified in material culture repertoires, with a marked increase in inter-assemblage variability. From the mid-third millennium onwards, a wider range of artefacts were produced, used, circulated, and deposited, and it is at this juncture that we find a wealth of evidence for the movement of both objects and ideas over considerable distances. Taken together, these changing material traditions appear to reflect a marked increase in regional heterogeneity when compared to the earlier Neolithic period. It is these changes in material culture repertoires which form the focus for this paper. In particular, I want to use the changing character of stone tool assemblages to consider the value of prestige goods models for our understanding of the period.

INTER-ASSEMBLAGE VARIABILITY AND PRESTIGE GOODS

The starting point for this discussion is Richard Bradley's (1982; 1984) analysis of inter-assemblage variability. Drawing on data from a number of areas, he makes an important contrast between earlier and later Neolithic artefact assemblages in terms of their character and diversity. While far from standardised, earlier lithic assemblages tend to be characterised by a relatively restricted range of retouched artefacts alongside blades, narrow flakes, and their respective cores. This situation changes towards the middle of the third millennium bc, with a marked increase in the range of what he terms 'complex' artefacts – objects singled out on the basis of their form, context, investment in production and/or raw materials. These include elaborate axes, arrowheads and knives, carved stone balls and mace-heads.

Together with jet items, bone pins, boars' tusks, and carved chalk objects, some of these artefacts occur as exotica in areas remote from their sources and many seem to have been accorded a measure of special treatment. Examples have been recovered from burials, hoards, and other contexts where they appear to have been deposited with some formality (Kinnes 1979; Manby 1988), and it seems that a series of subtle conventions may have guided their combination with Peterborough and Grooved Wares in these settings (Thomas 1991). Others have been recovered as surface finds and in many areas frequencies tend to increase with proximity to ceremonial monuments.

How are we to understand these developments? The character and context of these artefacts suggests that some, at least, were accorded significance as tokens of value, and one of the more persistent arguments has been that they reflect the development of *prestige-goods systems*. These models start from the idea that dominant or elite groups within a society may create and maintain their position by controlling the production, circulation, and consumption of status items or symbolic resources in ranked or restricted spheres. Originally applied in an archaeological context to capture the character of contacts between states and tribal societies (Frankenstein & Rowlands 1978), these models have subsequently been re-cast to encompass relations between societies that were structured along broadly similar lines (Renfrew & Cherry 1986). In this case, it is argued that elites in different regional settings may engage in socially restricted exchanges with each other in order to obtain objects that they may subsequently deploy as status items. These objects mark wider connections and alliances, and are at the same time sufficiently restricted in their social distribution to serve as important media in local networks of gift exchange.

It is easy to understand why these models have enjoyed a measure of popularity. They appear to make sense of some of the data, in particular, the movement of objects and even ideas from one part of Britain to another. More importantly, they emphasise that the political relations that are built on such a basis are often fluid, competitive, and unstable. The significance or exclusive character of particular status items can be easily undermined through emulation, and through changes in the conditions under which they are acquired and used by different sections within society. Control over production may be difficult to maintain, and new networks of alliance and exchange may create different conditions for the acquisition of important wealth items.

This perspective finds its clearest expression in Bradley's (1984) account of the changing character of Neolithic ceramics. Following the sequence from early undecorated vessels through to Peterborough and Grooved wares and beyond, he suggests that each category was initially highly specialised and associated with a restricted range of practices and people. Drawing on the work of Miller (1985), he argues that the passage of time saw these status items become objects of competition and emulation by others. As a result, their special status or significance was gradually undermined, creating the need for innovation and for the definition of new and exclusive categories of decorated vessel. Crucial to this argument is the idea that the later Neolithic was also a time at which the social geography of Britain began to resolve itself into a series of regional systems or *core areas*. The development of distinct regional systems created the conditions under which the circulation of status items – particularly exotica – could emerge as one of the principal media through which political authority was negotiated and maintained.

These ideas are undoubtedly useful. As Mary Helms (1988) has shown, the manipulation of objects and ideas derived from distant sources or from different regimes of value may create a variety of potentials for the negotiation of political authority. Having said that, such models place a series of constraints upon our understanding of

the conditions under which artefacts may have been produced, circulated, and deposited during the later Neolithic. As a result, we may
be some way from capturing the rather more varied ways in which
traditions of production and consumption were caught up in the
broader process of social life and social change.

We can begin by asking whether our models of regionality really do
justice to the data. There can be no doubt that the later Neolithic
periods did see a marked increase in regional heterogeneity, reflecting
differences in the emphases that were placed upon particular forms of
social practice from one part of Britain to another. Distinctions can be
drawn between regions according to varying degrees of emphasis
placed upon ancestral rites, the control of public ceremonies and the
supernatural, or the celebration of particular individuals through portable artefacts and funerary rites (Bradley 1984; Thorpe & Richards
1984). Equally, several studies have suggested the existence of 'style
zones', regional clusters characterised by a high degree of similarity in
the form or decorative traits of particular categories of artefact. These
regional clusters and differences of emphasis are important. Yet in
many models it appears that we are dealing with a series of discrete
totalities – distinct systems with clearly defined geographic boundaries. In some accounts, these regional systems are understood as
emergent chiefdoms (Darvill 1987; Renfrew 1973). In others, the details
of social structure are left unspecified, but one is still left with models
which presuppose the existence of geographically and socially distinct
entities, signalling their ethnicity or regional identity through material
culture with shared traits.

These models can be questioned on empirical and theoretical
grounds. Close inspection of ceramic 'style zones' suggests that whilst
it may be useful to retain a concept of regional traditions, there is a
considerable degree of blurring between areas (Thomas 1991). Similar
problems are encountered with stone tools (Green 1980), and field
research and aerial reconnaissance continue to undermine the integrity
of assumed geographic boundaries. There are also problems with the
application of broad social evolutionary models which envisage the
steady rise to dominance of regional chiefdoms. As Richards (this
volume) points out, the data can be interpreted rather differently and
even if we accept that some groups may have achieved a measure of
hereditary political authority, we must also allow that those structures
may have varied from one area and from one time to another. Rather
than a simple, linear progression towards increasing social complexity,
the material changes of the later Neolithic (encompassing twenty-five

to thirty generations) may indicate a rather more fluid and complex process. Networks of kinship, affiliation, corporate identity, and political authority may have shifted across generations, and these shifts would have had important consequences for the configuration of the social landscape (Barrett 1994). It is this complexity and fluidity that many of our models fail to capture. Rather than distinct totalities, we may be dealing with a series of dynamic local traditions which often lacked such clear boundaries, which were, in fact, connected or overlapped at a variety of different scales of spatial and temporal resolution (Barth 1987).

These ideas have a series of implications for our understanding of the conditions under which stone tools were produced, used, and circulated. To begin with, it may be unhelpful to assume that regional traditions of making and using particular categories of artefact were *necessarily* caught up in the presentation of ethnicity. As Thomas (this volume) notes in relation to ceramic traditions: 'while established style zones demonstrate regional preferences in decoration, this variation is isochrestic rather than iconic, a by-product of other classification procedures rather than an assertion of ethnic identity.' Although they may have played specialised roles, the later Neolithic sequence may reflect the emergence of different classes of ceramics for different social practices, rather than the simple succession of categories of elite paraphernalia. By extension, it may be simplistic to conclude that an apparent increase in the visibility of objects derived from distant sources was entirely a product of direct, long-distance communication between different regional elites. Competition for certain status items or symbolic resources was probably important, as were networks of contact and alliance between communities and broader kin-groups. However, we again set overly rigid limits if we assume that such connections were simply caught up in arguments over prestige and political authority at a regional level. In other words, it may be better to envisage the passage of objects and ideas through rather more complex webs of communication and exchange (Bradley & Edmonds 1993). Just as these networks may have changed in their character and complexity from one generation to another, so the purposes that were served by the circulation of particular artefacts may have varied over time and according to context.

One response to these suggestions might be that this blurring and intra-regional variability is simply a function of time depth. Given current problems with the chronology of ceramic traditions, this remains something of an open question, and it is clear that some 'complex' artefacts, laurel leaves for example, were produced from an earlier stage than others, such as mace-heads. However, regularities in the contexts and patterns of combination of these artefacts suggest the operation of structured classification schemes and dispositions. These are as difficult to ignore as they are to explain, and they require us to consider the rather more varied purposes that may have been served through the production and consumption of portable artefacts. Similar concerns have recently been addressed by anthropologists, and a number of studies have shown how seemingly mundane traditions of making and using tools and other material items may play an intimate and subtle role in social reproduction (Battaglia 1990; Govoroff 1993; Lemmonier 1992). In many small-scale societies, social identities are often tied to the possession and use of things, and the circulation of material culture may contribute in a variety of ways to the routine classification of people and to the negotiation of social relations (N. Thomas 1991).

Two recent studies provide examples which are particularly relevant here. Amongst Australian Aboriginal groups in Western Arnhem Land, the classification, procurement, and use of stone is intimately bound up with ideas about the activities and identities of ancestral beings. Raw materials may be regarded as the residues of dreamtime activities or even as the remains of ancestral beings, and they may be classified according to their spiritual or totemic qualities (Taçon 1991). These traditional associations and values are acknowledged as people acquire and use stone, and thus they serve as some of the media through which concepts of place, kinship, and even age and gender are reproduced. Work in Irian Jaya has also shown how the timing and spacing of stone tool procurement and use may be keyed into broader concepts of kinship and personal identity. In this case, even qualities such as colour, lustre, elegance, and balance during use are caught up in the routine process through which certain tools come to stand for particular people or properties of people (Pétrequin & Pétrequin 1994). It is these varied qualities and biographic associations that may be drawn upon when certain tools are exchanged between communities and between particular age grades. Neither of these cases can be treated as direct analogues, but they do remind us that our tendency to regard lithic technology as hardware may set unnecessary limits on our understanding. Even routine traditions of procuring, making, and using things may have social, political, and even spiritual qualities, and it is with these varied potentials in mind that we should consider the traditions of stone-working that emerged in the later Neolithic.

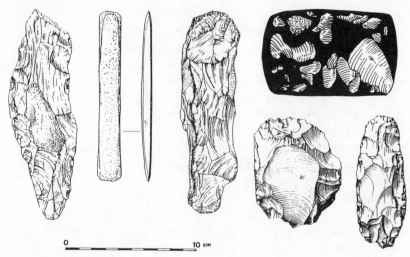

Figure 1. Selected later Neolithic artefacts: crudely flaked picks, polished chisel and knife, 'Levallois' style core, and flaked chisel/fabricator.

WORKING STONE IN LATER NEOLITHIC BRITAIN

The inventories of later Neolithic assemblages reveal evidence for a rich variety of retouched tools and for an equally varied range of technological repertoires. In place of the emphasis upon narrow flakes and blades that had prevailed earlier in the Neolithic, the later phases of the period saw the production of a wider range of core forms, reflecting a diversity of approaches to flake production. In many cases, the form of cores reflects a relative decrease in the level of concern exercised in the preparation of platforms and in the controlled removal of more or less standardised flakes or blades. Multi-platform cores are often larger than earlier Neolithic cores, and flakes tend to be broader, thicker, and more irregular than before.

Alongside these patterns we find evidence for the working of cores with rather different characteristics. These range from large, split nodules, some of which may have been related to bifacial tool production, through to more consistent forms such as discoidal or levallois-style tortoise cores. The latter reflect the controlled and extensive preparation of stone for the removal of distinctive broad flakes. Some may have served as blanks for the production of arrowheads, and in the case of larger cores, may have been a point of departure in the production of elaborate knives. This more formal pattern of core reduction was highly structured and of a different order to the produc-

Figure 2. Flaked flint knives.

tion of broad and irregular flakes on many multi-platform cores. These patterns have their clearest expression in central, southern, and eastern Britain, areas with long histories of investigation which are also relatively rich in raw materials. It may be unwise to assume that northern and western parts of the country witnessed precisely the same trajectories of technological development, not least because of differences in raw material conditions. However, these areas do contain evidence for broad similarities in the character and treatment of retouched tools, and it is to those that we can now turn.

A similar degree of complexity can be detected in retouched tools. For example, there is a marked increase in the range of crude core and flake tools, including picks, rod-like implements, and smaller bifacially flaked pieces. Many of these tools lack any clear or consistent definition of form and reflect a high degree of expediency and variability in production and use. Few show signs that consistent flaking routines were followed, and there often seems to have been little concern with the avoidance of errors and miss-hits during production. Earlier Neolithic parallels for some of these artefacts are generally restricted to mines and quarries, but by the latter part of the period, their distribution is far more widespread.

In keeping with the trend away from narrow flakes and blades, this increase in the frequency and distribution of large, crude artefacts accords with the idea that a high degree of routine, perhaps seasonal, mobility was no longer as important as it had been during the earlier Neolithic (Edmonds 1987). In other words, a move away from portable and adaptable tools, and the more profligate use of stone, might be expected in circumstances where routine movement over considerable distances was no longer a paramount concern. These changes are difficult to interpret, but they may indicate that for some regions at least, the later Neolithic saw shifts in the emphasis placed upon different spheres of economic activity, and in the character of the ties that bound people to particular places. While the roll-call of settlement probably continued to be shaped by close kinship ties, cultivation may have assumed a greater degree of importance, and this may have had consequences for the duration of residential sites. Equally, while transhumance probably remained important, there may have been a reduction in the scale or geographic range of routine activities associated with the husbandry of animals. These suggestions find some support in the evidence that we have for the character and distribution of later Neolithic flint scatters in a number of areas (e.g. Gardiner 1984; Holgate 1988; Richards 1990). Problems of palimpsests aside, these are often larger than their earlier Neolithic counterparts, and they are found in a wider range of settings. These changes in the scale and distribution of scatters are open to a number of interpretations, but in the wake of recent large-scale surveys, it is clear that we need to move beyond the placement of dots on maps. Using forms of technological analysis that are often restricted to excavated assemblages, it may be useful to look in more detail at what these scatters represent in terms of the changing character and distribution of stone-working activities across the landscape as a whole.

Like the bulk of the flakes made on multi-platform cores, implements such as crude picks and irregular bifacial tools were probably produced and used in the context of a variety of activities, then discarded with little formality. Some would have been particularly well suited to tasks such as digging, either in the context of exploiting surface deposits of stone or during cultivation. The production and use of these tools was probably unrestricted in both practical and social terms, and there is little empirical evidence to suggest that such items were commonly drawn upon as objects of social discourse. Yet, like the variations in core reduction procedures noted above, the character and context of these artefacts can be contrasted with other categories of stone tool, where it seems that subtle conventions may have played a part in shaping patterns of production and consumption. These include plano-convex, discoidal, and polished knives, finely flaked and polished chisels, axes and adzes of flint and stone, elaborate arrowheads, decorated coarse stone tools, carved stone balls, and mace-heads. It is difficult to explain the appearance of all of these forms as products of a change in mobility patterns, or as reflections of subtle changes in the character of subsistence. In the absence of such generalisations, we have to ask why it is that the later Neolithic witnessed a significant increase in the range of stone artefacts being produced.

The possibility that other themes may have attended the production, use, and deposition of these items finds support in the details of their character and context. To begin with, it is clear that our fascination with exotica and prestige goods has directed attention away from the fact that many of these artefacts are found rather closer to their (geological) homes. Despite problems with the characterisation of flint, this is likely to be the case for many unifacial, bifacial, and polished knives, and may also apply to many elaborate flint axes, arrowheads and carved stone balls (Manby 1988; Pierpoint 1980). Examples can be found in each of these categories where the distances involved may be sufficient to warrant the use of the term exotica. However, these are exceptions to the more common occurrence of artefacts within their regional source areas.

Further detail is provided where we have evidence for the character and context of production. Taken together, these categories of artefact include examples that probably took anything from several minutes to several days to produce. While investment in production cannot be taken as a definitive index against which to assess value or symbolic content, this variation may indicate that the significance attached to different categories may have been equally varied. For certain artefacts, the context of production remains unrecognised. Many carved stone balls can be traced back to broad geological sources, but there is generally little or no evidence for the conditions under which they were actually produced (Marshall 1977). A similar problem applies to mace-heads, although in this case a number appear to have been made from materials that had already seen use as a sources for stone axes. The same limitations apply to a variety of flint artefacts where, again, characterisation problems limit us to talking in terms of general source areas. In these cases, however, the evidence of flint scatters is revealing. Many tools appear to have been made in a wide variety of contexts; across scatters and between different categories of site. Yet evidence from a number of regional surveys suggests that some forms and epsiodes of core working and tool production may have been rather more restricted in spatial and perhaps social terms.

This was not an entirely new phenomenon. During the earlier Neolithic, axes of both flint and stone had already taken on a significance as both practical tools and as media for exchange (Bradley & Edmonds 1993). Major sources tended to be set apart from settlement contexts, and the timing and spacing of procurement and production may have been keyed into the roles that axes played as tokens of identity and value (Edmonds 1994). Parallels for this situation can be found at later Neolithic sources such as Grimes Graves and perhaps at locations along the coastline running south from Flamborough Head in Yorkshire. In the former case at least, it seems that, as for earlier generations, the procurement and production of certain tools was an event involving movement away from an immediate settlement context. Grimes Graves witnessed the production of a range of artefacts, including axes, chisels, and discoidal knives, and there is little evidence for permanent settlement in the immediate area. This pattern is not so clear in areas such as the Yorkshire coast, but even here, production may sometimes have been divided into two stages, with initial working on the coast and finishing inland (Durden, pers. comm.). Such patterns might be expected where raw materials were concentrated only in these locations. However, this is not entirely the case, and we should therefore allow that sociological as well as practical concerns were addressed by restricting production to specific places and perhaps to specific times. Despite the lengths of time over which these sources were used, the character of sites such as Grimes Graves suggests that major mines and outcrops were contexts in which members of different communities might come into close contact with each other on a periodic basis.

Similar distinctions may have been drawn at rather tighter scales of spatial resolution. Surveys in a number of areas have shown that distinctive categories of both artefacts and debitage may occur as clusters within broader spreads of later Neolithic material. Here again, there is a potential for blurring caused by palimpsests of activity and by different forms of deposition. But in some cases it seems that specialised core reduction and the production of artefacts such as arrowheads and discoidal knives may have been concentrated in specific areas within settlements (Manby 1974; Richards 1990). Whether these clusters represent specialised workshops or rather less proscribed – perhaps communal – working areas remains impossible to judge, but these patterns do suggest the existence of conventions which shaped the contexts in which certain categories of tool could be made. What is interesting is that these conventions often seem to have applied to artefacts that can also be differentiated in terms of their immediate appearance. Just as the period saw a proliferation of artefact classes, so it also witnessed an increased concern with elaboration and form. Flaked and ground or polished chisels occur more widely and in greater numbers

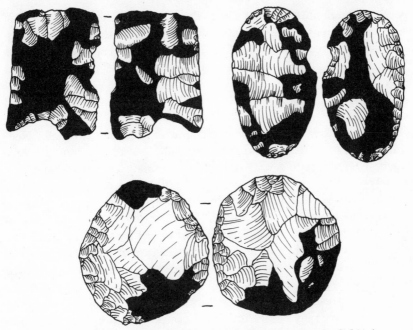

Figure 3. Polished edge flint knives (shading indicates area of polishing).

than before, as do a variety of knives, from laurel leaves through to discoidal and plano-convex forms. Some of these knives display parallel scars; others bear traces of grinding and polishing on their edges or over their entire surfaces – a practice taken to its logical conclusion with the rectangular knife found with a burial at Duggleby Howe and the similar form from Aldro 57 (Kinnes et al. 1983; Manby 1974).

The elaboration of tools or the creation of a distinctive appearance through flaking and/or grinding is manifest in many areas and on a variety of classes of artefact. Other examples include ripple-flaked arrowheads, one of a range of projectile points which are widespread in their geographic distribution (Green 1980). Axes, too, display a concern with similar themes. Specialised forms have long been recognised (Manby 1979) and it is possible that some of these were made as much to be displayed as to be used. By extension, many major stone sources continued in use during the later Neolithic and in flint rich areas, axes were often made on material that seems to have been selected because of its distinctive appearance. Examples made on orange, red, and banded or mottled flint have been recognised in a variety of contexts in eastern Britain, from East Anglia to Southern Scotland, and the use of distinctive pieces of flint for axe production has also been noted in southern England (Gardiner 1990). These are trends and differences of emphasis rather than black and white patterns, but they suggest a concern with the recognisability of tools, and thus perhaps with the roles those artefacts played as part of a technology of social classification.

TOKENS OF IDENTITY AND VALUE

It should already be clear that the character and context of later Neolithic stone tools resists simple generalisations. Procurement and production was probably undertaken for a variety of reasons and at a variety of different spatial, temporal, and social scales. Ranging in character from daily, household, and unrestricted patterns of working through to more specialised events surrounded by conventions and proscriptions, each probably contributed in its own way to the satisfaction of practical demands and the reproduction of social categories. It seems inappropriate to conclude that these patterns can be subsumed within models which place an almost exclusive emphasis upon the concept of prestige goods. Indeed, in the sorts of small-scale societies with which we may be dealing, it is not uncommon to find that traditions of production and consumption are keyed into a complex web of discourses, only some of which have direct implications for broader structures of political authority. To this list can be added concepts of age and gender, of kinship and descent, and other bonds of affiliation and obligation. Already present in the context of day-to-day patterns of use, these concepts are often intertwined, and they may be drawn upon in different ways at different times. Their proper deployment in various forms of ceremonial – from rites of passage to various forms of competitive activity – may be crucial for the manner in which those events are conducted and understood.

The technological traditions of the later Neolithic suggest that this was a time at which stone tools, together with other categories of material culture, were drawn upon to sustain a wider range of ideas about people, place, and practice than they had in earlier times. Questions of personal prestige and political authority may well have been important, but these traditions were also caught up in the reproduction of more localised categories and relations. Like the production and use of many tools, the learning of basic stoneworking techniques may have been relatively open. Many flakes and other tools were probably made and used as needs arose, and their disposal may have only rarely been an occasion for comment. Practised and taken on board at a household and community level, basic skills in the making

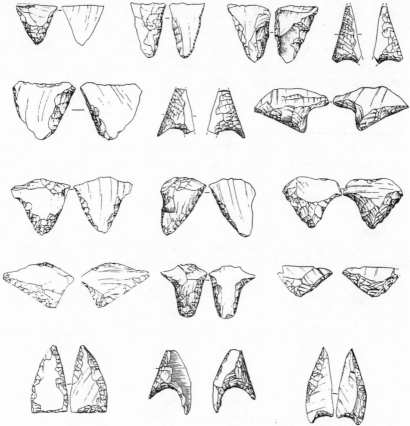

Figure 4. Later Neolithic arrowheads (after Clark 1935).

and using of many tools may have contributed in a largely routine way to the reproduction of broad age and gender categories. Taught by older members of the community, children may have become accustomed to acquiring and working stone in particular places and in particular ways. The acquisition of knowledge about sources and of technical skills in production and use may have been media through which their progression towards maturity was quietly acknowledged.

In certain cases, this sense of progression may have been brought into sharper focus. The demarcation of places and times at which certain tools could be made may have been linked to the more active negotiation of varied rites of passage, and even to the reproduction of ties between people drawn from different communities. Within individual settlements, it is possible that some demarcated working areas reflect the existence of skilled stone-workers who operated under some form of local patronage (Manby 1974). This suggestion is interesting but it may be that many 'workshops' simply reflect a close association with the making of specific artefacts and with particular categories of person. This spatial distinction would have had consequences for the ways in which items such as specialised knives and arrowheads took on roles as both practical tools and tokens of identity. At a broader level, it is likely that the procurement of stone and the acquisition of tools was also embedded in a variety of cycles of movement and activity. For example, routines of movement with animals would have constituted a series of pathways along which people from different communities might meet, and through which trading partnerships and barter bonds could be established. By extension, the exploitation of distant or discrete raw material sources would have also involved separation from the wider community. As in earlier times, this would have allowed distinctions to be drawn in terms of who was allowed to attend and participate in these events, as well as providing a context for contact and communication with more distant kin, and perhaps with members of particular age or gender grades. Workshops and discrete sources were also contexts within which rather more specialised working techniques may have been learnt, and it is possible that the acquisition of know-how was itself caught up in the negotiation of rites of passage such as those which marked entry into adulthood. Subsequently practised and perfected in the context of day-to-day tasks, the ability to employ these techniques may have continued to contribute to the routine classification of people.

Once created, the mundane use of many tools may have contributed to social reproduction in a variety of ways. Worn, used, and/or carried on a regular basis, they may have helped to mark the identities of people and the roles that they played within and beyond the boundaries of the community. Thus axes and certain forms of specialised arrowhead may have served as tools and as 'weapons of exclusion' – tokens linked to particular age grades or fraternities (Bradley & Edmonds 1993; Edmonds & Thomas 1987). Other tools may have performed comparable roles, but the relative paucity of well-excavated settlements places limits on our capacity to identify whether or not their use, and the organisation of many day to day tasks, was structured around distinct divisions of labour. In the absence of evidence, it is probably unwise to assume that such hard and fast divisions were manifest in all spheres of practical activity. Distinctions drawn on the basis of themes such as age and gender may have been blurred in daily practice, only coming into sharper focus in more formal circumstances. These problems aside, the application of tools in practical tasks would have strengthened their biographic qualities. Patinated with use and routine handling, knives, scrapers, axes, and other tools would have acquired histories which connected them to specific people. It may have been these histories, as much as broader categoric associations, which were drawn upon when items were exchanged or deposited with some formality.

The vast majority of stone tools probably remained in the hands of those who made and used them, but it is clear that others passed from one hand and from one community to another. Raw materials may have also been the subject of varied transactions, and we should acknowledge that many items may have been distributed as largely alienated commodities. Other forms of transaction, from barter through to more regularised exchanges between trading partners, may have helped to sustain networks of contact and communication that stretched some distance across the social landscape. Woven into these networks were forms of exchange which involved what Annette Weiner (1992) calls 'keeping while giving' – the creation of ties between groups and individuals which persisted long after the transaction had passed. From marriage payments and blood fines through to more competitive forms of prestation, the passage of certain artefacts between people would have sanctioned a variety of ties of affiliation, obligation, and relatedness. This may have taken on a broader political aspect on certain occasions, as particular groups attempted to establish a measure of authority over others. But for much of the time, gift giving was probably tied to the reproduction of links that were rather more horizontal than vertical. Although the purposes served by the circulation of stone tools would have varied according to context, the histories, and biographies of particular items would have been extended as they moved from giver to receiver and from one 'regime of value' to another. Often crucial in these circumstances is the capacity of exchanged objects to 'stand for' specific people or categories, and for the particular sets of relations that their passage has sustained. It may have been these qualities and potentials which contributed to the increased concern with distinctive raw materials, patterns of working or decoration on many later Neolithic stone tools. Acquired in the context of important meetings or ceremonies, and subsequently carried, displayed, and handed on in other transactions, exchanged items would have served as tangible reminders of the past, present, and future order of social relations.

Just as exchanged objects can be said to have duration, or the capa-

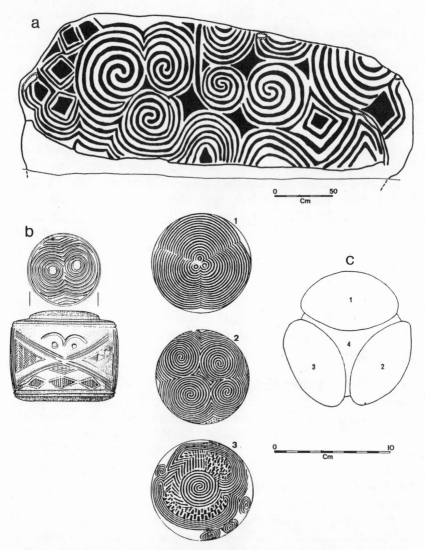

Figure 5. A. carving from Newgrange, Boyne valley; B. carved chalk drum from Folkton, Yorkshire; C. carved stone ball from Towie, Aberdeenshire.

city to project social relations into the future, so certain artefacts may have drawn attention to the ties that stretched across generations. Passed down from one generation to another, their acquisition and display may have helped to define the position of individuals within networks of descent, and may even have sanctioned the inheritance of certain forms of local authority. In these cases at least, the patina of

[264]

handling and service that they carried may have lent itself to the evocation of ideas concerning continuity across generations. Such a role has been suggested for many carved stone balls (Marshall 1977). Largely restricted in their distribution to north-eastern Scotland and the Orkney Isles, carved stone balls were decorated in a variety of ways, but some bear incised carvings which have their closest parallels on Grooved Ware and in Passage Grave art (Edmonds 1992). Given these decorative connections, some of these enigmatic artefacts may have been cult objects – items which made reference to distant forces and connections, which were displayed and handled in the context of important ceremonies. Handed down over time, their acquisition may have sanctioned the right to participate or even officiate at these events.

DEPOSITION AND DEFINITION

In addition to their potential as tokens of identity and value, stone tools may have served a variety of purposes when they were caught up in episodes of formal or intentional deposition. Linked to certain practices, people or properties of people, the deliberate placement of combinations of material in the earth provided a medium through which various ideas could be 'presenced'. Episodes of formal deposition would have been singular events at which a variety of concepts may have been brought into sharp relief, and the ways in which such acts were understood is likely to have varied with context and audience.

Developing out of a tradition that stretched back at least as far as the earlier Neolithic, these acts of interment may have been crucial to the ways in which the cultural and historical associations of particular places were defined. In contexts such as settlements, the cutting and filling of pits may have been junctures at which the links between people and place were given material expression. Drawn from different spheres of day-to-day experience, from middens or from the residues of specific episodes of consumption, these deposits may have helped to sustain the ties that bound particular communities to specific locations. Examples include pits containing varied assemblages of axes, arrowheads, scrapers, and debitage with other categories of material such as antler, boars' tusks, and Peterborough or Grooved Ware, identified on Cranborne Chase, in the environs of Stonehenge and in a variety of settings in Yorkshire (Barrett, Bradley & Green 1991: 84; Manby 1988; Richards 1990). While it is clear that subtle conventions guided the bringing together of these materials and their associations,

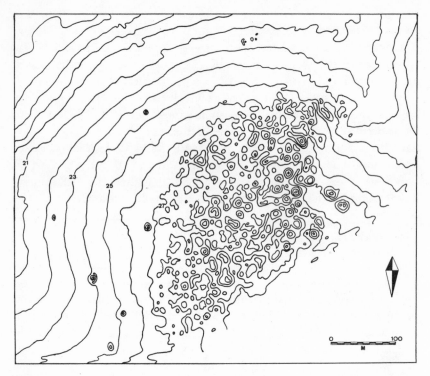

Figure 6. Contour plan of shafts and upcast features at Grimes Graves, East Anglia.

it is perhaps inappropriate to assume that all of these acts addressed either a broad audience or a broad range of issues. More often than not, pits and their contents may have highlighted themes that had their most immediate relevance to the members of a single community or close kin group.

Similar themes can be considered where the fragmentary remains of people were included in pits located in or close to settlement contexts (Thomas 1991). This connection with human remains is interesting, because it reminds us that the biographies, qualities, and perhaps even the powers of the dead may have been addressed in a variety of material and social settings, not just in what we define as funerary contexts. Presencing the dead in a direct and palpable way, these deposits may have also served to reaffirm the historical and genealogical ties that bound particular families to the land in which they lived and worked. Certain episodes of pit deposition may have even been linked to the rites of passage that attended the death of a particular person, and it is worth noting that burial in more formal funerary contexts, such as barrows, may not have been a privelige extended to all. Undertaken by close kin and/or by senior members of the community, artefacts or fragments of artefacts associated with the deceased may have been placed in the ground to both signal and sanction the social transformation of the individual on death. Deposited amongst the living, tools and materials that spoke of aspects of the identity of a person and their ties to others may have been as important as fragments of the body itself.

Knowledge concerning the precise contents of such pits was probably forgotten, confused or otherwise changed with the passage of time, and it is reasonable to suggest that it was at the time of their creation that the redolences and associations of their contents would have been most clearly appreciated. However, given their juxtaposition with contexts in which people lived, these features may have also helped to sustain certain ideas about genealogy and belonging over time. Many pits probably remained visible long after they had been back-filled, either as areas of disturbed ground, or as locations marked by stakes or posts. Encountered on a relatively routine basis by members of particular communities, they may have continued to contribute to the cultural definition of place long after they had been back-filled.

Although the conditions under which they were created and encountered may have been rather more varied, it may be unwise to assume that equally localised issues were not addressed where pits were cut and filled in close proximity to major ceremonial monuments. In certain cases, monuments were already ancient by the time that such acts were undertaken; examples include the Grooved Ware pits identified during excavations on the causewayed enclosure at Etton (Pryor in press). This particular form of re-use may have been part of the process through which the traditional associations of a place came to be augmented or reworked. Yet even here, there is no requirement to assume that these singular acts were *necessarily* undertaken or observed by large numbers of people, or that they had consequences that were recognised across the broader social landscape.

This last point remains important where episodes of pit deposition were broadly contemporary with the construction, use, and re-use of later Neolithic monuments. Pits have been identified in the environs of many later Neolithic ceremonial sites, and the increased frequency of exotica and other complex artefacts in the vicinity of henges and some cursus monuments may reflect the truncation/destruction of similar features by modern cultivation (Barrett, Bradley & Green 1991; Bradley 1984). Here again, the possibility exists that certain acts of deposition may have been linked to funerary rites of passage and to the evocation of ideas regarding the place of specific communities in the landscape. However, given the character of the contexts involved, this is unlikely to have exhausted their purpose. Many ceremonial monuments were locales that saw the periodic aggregation of people drawn from a number of different communities, and we need to consider the rather different potentials that this may have created. Here at least, the tradition of placing certain cultural materials in the earth may have been drawn upon to serve a broader range of interests.

Although sites vary considerably in terms of their scale and longevity, recent years have seen the emergence of a broad (if vague) consensus that many henge monuments were important 'arenas of value'. Often constructed, modified, and used over many generations, these were demarcated contexts within which feasting, funerary rites, dealings with the supernatural, and a variety of socially charged transactions could be undertaken. Many of these transactions or tournaments of value may have been mediated through the passage of tokens of identity and value such as those discussed above. Others may have been marked by the passing on of restricted knowledge; by the movement of a person from one community to another; by the provision of labour, or by offers of support in feuds and other forms of graded conflict. The setting, form, and internal arrangements of individual sites may have played an important part in shaping the physical character of the activities undertaken within their bounds; directing movement and creating varied opportunities for access and vision (Barrett 1994; Thomas 1993). These physical frames would have had consequences for the manner in which those activities were understood both by participants and those who could only stand and watch. The right to enter and participate at certain times may have been socially restricted, and I would follow the suggestion that the activities associated with the periodic construction and use of these sites may have sometimes had consequences for the character and distribution of authority at a regional as well as a local scale.

For both Barrett and Thomas, the deposition of material culture within the confines of these sites is seen as crucial to the ways in which particular monuments, and the activities that they witnessed, were understood by contemporary observers. Both draw attention to the roles these deposits may have played in shaping the meanings of particular places and, while their papers focus primarily on Wessex, one can draw parallels with sites such as Cairnpapple Hill in West Lothian; Llandegai in northern Wales and various monuments in Yorkshire

(Clarke et al. 1985; Houlder 1976; Manby 1974; Pierpoint 1980). Because of their categoric and biographical associations, tools, waste, and other materials may have been placed in the ditches or internal features of particular sites. Some deposits would have been laid down in the course of particular ceremonies; others may reflect the bringing together of residues on the completion of certain rites. Beyond general concepts of fertility, commemoration, renewal, and the supernatural, it is generally difficult to specify the significance that was attached to individual acts of deposition (cf. Pollard 1993; Richards & Thomas 1984). However, it was the links that tools had with particular people or properties of people which probably justified their inclusion. Once established, these deposits would have helped to mould and renew the significance attached to the internal features and boundaries that made up particular sites. Remembered by participants, and encountered as sites were modified or maintained over time, these deposits would have served as potent 'technologies of remembrance'.

These arguments can be extended to encompass the zone beyond the boundaries of many sites. The environs of many later Neolithic monuments probably saw a variety of forms of settlement, and formal deposits of material culture in contexts such as pits are likely to have served an equally varied range of purposes. However, labour estimates for monument construction remind us that these particular areas would have also seen the coming together of large numbers of people on a periodic basis (Startin & Bradley 1981). Embedded in broader routines of economic activity, these aggregations would have been a dramatic departure from more routine patterns of settlement and social encounter. Where ties of kinship and affiliation were normally stretched across the landscape as a whole, junctures such as these would have seen the concentration of kin and relative strangers in a far smaller geographic space.

Under these conditions, we should envisage a rich array of encounters and activities, many of which involved the purposive selection, circulation, and deposition of artefacts, food, and other materials. The conclusion of feasts or episodes of conspicuous consumption may have been marked by the burial of particular artefacts and residues and, like the deliberate disposal of objects in rivers (Bradley 1991), these acts may have sometimes been overtly competitive in character. In the case of the York hoard case, a rich array of flaked and polished artefacts were placed in a narrow pit which was subsequently sealed by gravel. Precise details regarding the original contents and context of this feature are now lost, but the selection of artefacts that survive include a number of elaborate edge-polished axes, serrated blades, laurel leaves, and other knives (Radley 1970). The inventory of this feature can be compared with the Seamer hoard, where a similar range of tools were deposited together with fragments of human bone in the cap of an existing burial mound. Given its immediate context, it is possible this act of deposition was tied to funerary rites of passage. Tools that were given or otherwise linked to a person in life were brought together with fragments of their skull, and their deposition in an existing mound may have contributed a sense of continuity and ancestry for the event. Unlike rivers, reclamation from contexts such as these may have remained a possibility, and we should allow that certain hoards were never intended to be anything other than temporary. However, the deliberate burial of tokens of identity may have often been linked to a variety of discourses – the redefinition of kinship through marriage, the creation or conclusion of other affinities, and the celebration of links between age grades and gender classes which cross-cut the contours of kinship. In each of these cases, the biographies and associations of particular tokens of identity and value may have been drawn upon to shape the significance of these events. Their eventual burial may have served to sanction and project newly established ties into the future.

If the deposition of artefacts or fragments of artefacts in pits was sometimes linked to funerary rites of passage, we must also consider the purposes that were served where materials were selected for burial with the dead. As we have seen, the development of the later Neolithic sees a steady increase in the incidence of individual burials, many of which were laid to rest with a variety of goods (Barrett 1988; Darvill 1987). These developments may suggest an increased concern with the genealogies of the living and the place of people within specific lines of descent and inheritance. We can also note a trend in funerary associations identified by Ian Kinnes, who suggests that the passage of the third millennium saw a marked increase in the range of artefacts buried with people (Kinnes 1979). Although projectile points dominate at an early stage, this gives way to an emphasis on a much wider range of artefacts, including other tools and decorative items. Placed by the mourners around the body, tools (and even waste) may again have served as cues for the interpretation of the dead person, providing material metaphors for their place within a web of social relations. Some tools may have spoken of the links that they may have had with particular spheres of activity, while others referred to specific aspects of their biography. Exotica and other items obtained through exchange may have signalled the existence of ties which stretched beyond the boundaries of kinship.

At the same time, the burial of particular artefacts may have drawn attention to the rights and influence that had been held by a person in life, as means of passing on those rights to particular descendants. The act of placing objects with a body may have also been seen as a form of exchange, in which a mourner established a lasting relationship with the dead. This may have provided an affirmation of close kinship ties where the right to 'give to the dead' was restricted. Yet it would also have provided a medium through which different mourners could demonstrate their own standing as well as their links to the deceased. On occasion, this may have had important consequences amongst the living, where ties of affiliation and the inheritance of various forms of authority may not have been beyond question. Indeed, in cases where a measure of hereditary authority had been established by particular groups, some of these items may have been acquired as tributary gifts from subordinates. Their inclusion may have been undertaken as a reminder of existing obligations, or as an act which marked the end of long-standing relations of authority.

Elements of these processes can be seen at a number of funerary sites across Britain, including Duggleby Howe and Whitegrounds in Yorkshire (Brewster 1984; Kinnes et al. 1983), Liff's Lowe in Derbyshire (Bateman 1848), Dorchester on Thames site 2 (Atkinson et al. 1951), and perhaps at Greenbrae in Aberdeenshire (Kenworthy 1977). The first phase of activity at Whitegrounds saw disarticulated human remains placed in a grave beneath a low cairn. After a time the site was reused, becoming the focus for the articulated burial of a man associated with a calf's jaw, the leg of a pig, a polished jet belt slider, and a distinctive 'Seamer' axe. A radiocarbon detemination on the burial yielded a date of 2570 bc ± 90 (Har-5587). Whether or not there was any continuity of observance between these two phases is unclear. However, the reuse of the site may represent an attempt to draw upon the historical or mythic associations of the place to create a sense of continuity between the past and present order of things. The evidence from Whitegrounds can be compared with that from Liff's Lowe, where again, a single crouched inhumation was interred in a round mound. Here the associations with the body were more varied and included two finely flaked and edge polished axes, lozenge-shaped arrowheads, flint knives, a pottery vessel, a worked boar's tusk, and a decorated antler mace-head. With the exception of the mace-head, all of these items were placed in a group behind the shoulders of the de-

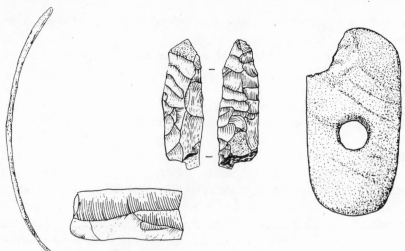

Figure 7. Grave goods from Site 2, Dorchester on Thames.

ceased. Some appear to have seen some use, while others were probably intended for display and may have been given to the corpse at the
time of burial. Here it may be significant that variations can be observed in both the colour and the cortication of the flint artefacts associated with the burial. Such variations are difficult to interpret, but they
suggest the use of materials drawn from different geological sources.

Elements within each of these assemblages may have accrued rather
different histories before they came to be associated with the deceased.
Some may indeed have been gifts to the dead, but others may have
been tokens of identity and value that were made, acquired, displayed,
and/or used during life. Given the potentially varied associations and
stories that these artefacts embodied, we may be doing little justice to
the conditions that determined their inclusion if we simply fall back on
an overly generalised model which emphasises regional authority. At
the moment of burial, the physical context, the spoken word, the
identities of the audience and the choreography of people would no
doubt have had an important influence on the manner in which a
funeral was to be understood. However, the tableau of the body with
its associated goods would have addressed a variety of themes relating to both the categoric and the personal identity of the deceased.

CONCLUSION

The broad purpose of this paper has been to suggest that some of the
assumptions underlying current interpretations of the later Neolithic

in Britain may be open to question. In particular, I have tried show that our dominant concern with prestige goods and structures of regional authority may have limited our understanding of the conditions under which many stone tools were made and used and the purposes that they served. These arguments could be extended to cover other categories of material culture. At the same time, I have tried to suggest that some of our models carry with them a set of assumptions about the constitution and boundedness of small-scale societies which should – at the very least – be open to question.

These arguments should not lead us to throw the baby out with the bathwater. Prestige goods models remain important because of the attention that they draw to the ties between political position and the production and circulation of wealth items. It is simply that they may be insufficient to capture the varied and often mundane ways in which traditions of making and using things were harnessed to the reproduction of rather more localised categories and concerns. By the same token, there is no necessity to step back from the concept of the regional system or the peer polity, to suggest, like certain contemporary politicians, that there is no such thing as society. Rather than take that path, it may be more useful to recast some of our questions and to look again at the constitution of regional traditions, particularly in northern and western parts of the country. The passage of some twenty-five to thirty generations probably saw a variety of changes in the character and configuration of the social landscape, reflecting shifts in the details of social structure and in the scale and orientation of networks of contact and alliance. It is this potential fluidity that our models have often failed to capture.

Taken together, the evidence can be used to suggest that the later Neolithic saw an increasingly wide range of artefacts being drawn upon in the construction of complex social identities and in the moulding of particular concepts of place. At certain times and in certain places, 'vertical' status distinctions were no doubt important. However, the production and consumption of many tools was also linked to the reproduction of localised and context specific concepts of identity and authority and it may have been these links that were emphasised when tools were drawn upon in ceremonial activities, in exchange, and in acts of formal deposition.

Important though it may be, this last point marks the beginning rather than the end of discussion. The particular character and content of these links is often difficult to specify or explore, and it is for that reason that the time may be right to consider something of a change of focus. The excavation of overtly ceremonial contexts will no doubt continue to add much to our understanding, but it may be that it can only take us so far. It may now be timely to place an equal, if not greater emphasis upon the varied day-to-day social practices in which many stone tools were employed, looking in particular at the character of stone tool production and use at both a site and landscape level (e.g. Van Gijn this volume). While this change of focus may not lead us in some inevitable fashion to definitive answers, it may help us to put some flesh on the bones of the arguments presented here.

ACKNOWLEDGEMENTS

This paper was originally presented at the Washington meeting of the American Anthropological Association in 1993. I am grateful to the organisers of that session for their invitation, and to Christine Hastorf for reading the paper in my absence. Since that time, I have benefitted from general and specific discussions with a number of people, particularly John Moreland and Julian Thomas. The conventional rules of responsibility apply.

BIBLIOGRAPHY

Barrett, J. 1994. *Fragments from Antiquity*. Blackwell. Oxford.

Barrett, J. C., Bradley, R. J., & Green, M. 1991. *Landscape, Monuments and Society: The prehistory of Cranborne Chase*. Cambridge: Cambridge University Press.

Barth, F. 1987. *Cosmologies in the Making*. Cambridge: Cambridge University Press.

Battaglia, D. 1990. *On the Bones of the Serpent. Person, memory and mortality in Sabarl Island society*. Chicago and London: Chicago University Press.

Bradley, R. J. 1982. Position and possession: assemblage variation in the British Neolithic. *Oxford Journal of Archaeology* 1: 27–38.

Bradley, R. 1984. *The Social Foundations of Prehistoric Britain: themes and variations in the archaeology of power*. London: Longmans.

Bradley, R. J. 1991. *The Passage of Arms*. Cambridge University Press. Cambridge.

Bradley, R. & Edmonds, M. 1993. *Interpreting the Axe Trade*. Cambridge: Cambridge University Press.

Clarke, D. , Cowie, T., & Foxon, A. 1985. *Symbols of Power at the Time of Stonehenge*. Edinburgh: National Museum of Scotland.

Darvill, T. C. 1987. *Prehistoric Britain*. London: Batsford.

Edmonds, M. R. 1987. Rocks and risk: Problems with lithic procurement strategies. In Brown, A. and Edmonds, M. R. (eds), *Lithic Analysis and Later British Prehistory*, pp. 155–180. Oxford: British Archaeological Reports (162).

Edmonds, M. R. & Thomas, J. S. 1987. The Archers: an everyday story of country folk. In Brown, A. and Edmonds, M. R. (eds), *Lithic Analysis and Later British Prehistory*, pp. 187–199. Oxford: British Archaeological Reports (162).

Edmonds, M. 1992. Their use is wholly unknown. In Sharples, N. & Sheridan, A. (eds), *Vessels for the Ancestors*. Edinburgh: Edinburgh University Press.

Frankenstein, S. & Rowlands, M. 1978. The internal structure and regional context of early Iron Age society in south-west Germany. *Bulletin of the Institute of Archaeology, London* 15: 73–112.

Gardiner, J. 1990. Flint procurement and Neolithic axe production on the South Downs: a reassessment. *Oxford Journal of Archaeology* 9: 119–140.

Green, H. S. 1980. *The Flint Arrowheads of the British Isles*. Oxford: British Archaeological reports (British series 75).

Govoroff, N. C. 1993. The hunter and his gun in Haute-Provence. In Lemmonier, P. (ed.), *Technological Choices*. London: Routledge.

Helms, M. 1988. *Ulysses' Sail*. Princeton, NJ: Princeton University Press.

Holgate, R. 1988 *Neolithic Settlement of the Thames Basin*. Oxford: British Archaeological Reports (194).

Houlder, C. 1976. Stone axes and henge monuments. In Boon, G. & Lewis, J. M. (eds), *Welsh Antiquity*, pp. 56–62. Cardiff: National Museum of Wales.

Kinnes, I. 1979. *Round Barrows and Ring Ditches in the British Neolithic*. London. British Museum.

Kinnes, I., Schadla-Hall, T., Chadwick, P., & Dean, P. 1983. Duggleby Howe reconsidered. *Archaeological Journal* 140: 83–108.

Lemmonier, P. 1992. *Elements for an Anthropology of Technology*. University of Michigan (Anthropological Papers of the Museum of Anthropology 88).

Manby, T. G. 1974. *Grooved Ware Sites in Yorkshire and the North of England*. Oxford: British Archaeological Reports (9).

Manby, T. G. 1979. Typology, materials and distribution of flint and stone axes in Yorkshire. In Clough, T. H. McK. & Cummins, W. A. (eds), *Stone Axe Studies*, pp. 65–81. London: Council for British Archaeology (Research Report 23).

Manby, T. 1988. The Neolithic in eastern Yorkshire. In Manby, T. (ed.), *Archaeology in Eastern Yorkshire*, pp. 35–88. Sheffield: Sheffield University, Department of Archaeology and Prehistory.

Marshall, D. 1977. Carved stone balls. *Proceedings of the Society of Antiquaries of Scotland* 108: 40–72.

Miller, D. 1985. *Artefacts as Categories*. Cambridge University Press. Cambridge.

Petrequin, P. & Petrequin, A. 1993. *Ecologie d'un outil: La hache de pierre en Irian Jaya (Indonésie)*. Paris: CNRS (Monograph du CRA 12).

Pierpoint, S. 1980. *Social Patterns in Yorkshire Prehistory*. Oxford: British Archaeological Reports (74).

Piggott, S. 1954. *The Neolithic Cultures of the British Isles*. Cambridge. Cambridge University Press.

Pollard, J. 1992. The Sanctuary, Overton Hill: A re-examination. *Proceedings of the Prehistoric Society* 58: 213–226.

Pryor, F. in press. *Excavations at Etton Causewayed Enclosure*. London: HMSO (English Heritage Monograph).

Radley, J. 1967. The York hoard of flint tools. *Yorkshire Archaeological Journal* 42: 131–132.

[275]

Renfrew, A. C. 1973. Monuments, mobilisation and social organisation in Neolithic Wessex. In Renfrew, A. C. (ed.), *The Explanation of Culture Change*, pp. 539–558. London: Duckworth.

Renfrew, C. & Cherry, J. (eds) 1986. *Peer Polity Interaction and Sociopolitical Change*. Cambridge: Cambridge University Press.

Richards, C. & Thomas, J. S. 1984. Ritual activity and structured deposition in later Neolithic Wessex. In Bradley, R. J. & Gardiner, J. (eds), *Neolithic Studies*, pp. 189–218. Oxford: British Archaeological Reports (133).

Richards, J. 1990. *The Stonehenge Environs Project*. London: (English Heritage monograph).

Startin, W. & Bradley, R. 1981. Some notes on work organisation and society in prehistoric Wessex. In Ruggles, C. & Whittle, A. (eds), *Astronomy and Society during the Period 4000–1500 BC*. Oxford: British Archaeological Reports (88).

Taçon, P. 1991. The power of stone: symbolic aspects of stone use and tool development in western Arnhem Land, Australia. *Antiquity* 65: 192–207.

Thomas, J. S. 1991. *Rethinking the Neolithic*. Cambridge: Cambridge University Press.

Thomas, N. 1991. *Entangled Objects*. Cambridge, Mass. and London: Harvard University Press.

Thorpe, I. J. & Richards, C. C. 1984 The decline of ritual authority and the introduction of Beakers into Britain. In Bradley, R. J. & Gardiner, J. (eds), *Neolithic Studies*, pp. 67–84. Oxford: British Archaeological Reports (133).

Weiner, A. 1992. *Inalienable Possessions*. Berkeley: University of California Press.

13

From the Raw Material to the Neolithic Stone Axe. Production Processes and Social Context

Pierre Pétrequin, Anne-Marie Pétrequin, Françoise Jeudy, Christian Jeunesse, Jean-Louis Monnier, Jacques Pelegrin, Ivan Praud

In France, studies of cultural technology and, in particular, the technology of stone tools have been highly prized, particularly when compared to published works in English (Pelegrin 1990). Nevertheless, when reading French publications on the production of polished stone blades for Neolithic axes and adzes, it is clear that certain aspects of the production processes (*chaînes operatoires*) tend to be given priority over others. Discussions seldom deal with the total phenomenon. As a function of the technical organisation of research, individual dimensions or aspects of this phenomenon – the polished stone blade – are dissected into smaller (and thus more easily studied) fields. These smaller groups have tended to take the following forms:

> 1. recognition of the conditions of rock choice, by detailed petrographic determination and studies of distribution, but not in their chronological and cultural context, as in the case of the axes made in Brittany (Le Roux 1990) or the Alps (Ricq-de Bouard, Compagnoni et al. 1990); 2. recognition of the exploited mineral outcrops, but not in their chronological, cultural or technical context, as in the case of the Rouergue quarries (Servelle 1991); 3. the study of quarries and mining pits, but

again, not in the cultural or social context, as in the case of Plussulien, a major study of Dolerite type A (Le Roux 1990), as well as most of the excellent studies currently undertaken at flint mines (Desloges 1990; Bostyn & Lanchon 1992); 4. the study of the distribution of a type of rock and its production techniques, without knowing the extraction points, (a frequent procedure, perhaps because geologists themselves often lack interest in the problems that archaeologists wish to address), exemplified by material from the Alps, the Massif Central, Brittany, and the Ardennes, among others (Caspar 1984), 5. typological and chronological studies on polished blades, without using petrographic analysis, with numerous examples in the archaeological literature dedicated to cultural references (Gallay 1977); 6. typological and chronological studies on direct hafting or on antler socket hafting, without reference to the hafted blades or environmental context (Voruz 1984); 7. experimental research on the production of polished blades, without validation by the user or feed-back into the archaeological literature (Piningre 1974) and; 8. theoretical approaches to the use of polished blades, without reference to social, economic or environmental context (Bocquet & Houot 1983).

Each of these procedures is, of course, vital, adding important facets to our understanding of the polished stone tool phenomenon. However, this narrowing of focus can bring with it the assumption that a similar degree of compartmentalisation and specialisation was a feature of the prehistoric past. As a result, we run the risk of forgetting the original goal of our studies, the broader articulation of *chaînes opératoires*, operational links in the production process, across time and space. The process of tool fabrication (Lemonnier 1976), which was essential for both the physical and ideological reproduction of Neolithic societies, is today divided into as many conceptual segments as there are archaeological specialisations.

We accept that the assignment of priority to one aspect of a broader phenomenon can lead to more detailed understandings, and that this analytical procedure is universal in scientific research. Here, however, we want to present an example of a production process in the middle of its study (the development of Neolithic quarries in Plancher-les-Mines, Haute-Saône). In particular, we want to explore some of the connections that can and should be made between fields of research that are often pursued in relative isolation. We hope to show that these different fields can be brought together in a manner which retains all the positive aspects of current research without maintaining the rigid divisions between individual specialisations. As we see it, this strategy offers considerable potential for our understanding of the complex systems within which polished stone axes and adzes were produced, circulated, and used. The approach that we propose is not a new one (Binder & Perlès 1990), but it is based, in our case, on a new experience: the ethno-archaeological study of New Guinea tools in their social and ecological context (Burton 1984; Højlund 1981; Pétrequin & Pétrequin 1990; 1994).

APHANITE POLISHED BLADES: A CENTURY OF RESEARCH

Under the name '*aphanite*', obsolete but consecrated by a century of archaeological studies in eastern France, prehistorians have unconsciously regrouped different types of black rocks from the Viséen geological levels of the Vosges, located along the south-eastern border of the massif (Diethelm 1989). By the end of the last century (Tuefferd 1878), many authors had commented on the abundance of 'aphanite' polished blades in the Montbéliard and Belfort regions (we now put the term in inverted commas because of its inaccuracy). 'Aphanite' is a type of quartz-schist, which was believed to be abundant in the south of the Vosges. The regional production of these tools was clearly demonstrated by the large number of waste flakes, especially in the fortified enclosures of the Belfort gap. During the first half of the century, these finds were numerous and the authors indicated different outcrops of 'aphanite' in the upper valley of the Moselle, in the Thur and Doller valleys, and even in Devonian and Dinantian geological formations in the Belfort and Chagey regions. However, all of these determinations were based upon assumptions, lacking any clear proof that these outcrops were ever exploited in the past.

Subsequent progress in this field was published by Glory (1942). He tried to establish a classification for the polished blades of upper Alsace (blades with an oval cross-section, which are differentiated from blades with a rectangular cross-section). He also insisted on the mineralogical complexity which is hidden by the term 'aphanite'. Glory reserved the name 'aphanite' for what we now call quartz-pelites, clearly different from the schists and greywackes which also have sources in the Vosges. The study of polished blades made from Vosges black rocks was continued by Thévenin (1961). He proposed a typo-chronology, but at a time when the cultural classification of the regional Neolithic was poorly understood. The first petrographic studies suggested that 'aphanite' could be a micaceous quartzite from the Devonian and Dinantian levels in south of the Vosges, without the possibility of precise localisation.

The first broad approach to this phenomenon can be found in the work of Piningre (1974). Although it is far from explicit, it is here that we find an approach which embraces the concept of a series of production processes in a re-evaluation of all the older finds. According to Piningre, small blocks of 'aphanite' were collected from the Vosges streams, then transported up to the Neolithic villages in the Belfort gap, and there knapped and polished. The same author outlined the first chronologies of Vosges black rock tools (although the distinction between these different types of rocks was not clear at all), drew the first distribution maps for eastern France (but the presence of 'aphanite' in lake dwellings of Switzerland was deliberately hidden), and proposed the premise of the circulation of rough-outs and polished blades (in relation to a general phenomenon during the middle Neolithic II, the settlements and fortified enclosures on hilltops). Gallay's research (1977) sums up the situation regarding chronology and indicates a better comprehension of cultural references. But, for him, a polished stone blade is considered only as a part of typological sets – one among others. This point of view is coherent with the methodological choices which were essential for his research.

The first transportation of 'aphanite' blades to Swiss lake settlements was recognised by Willms (1980) during a study of the archaeological lake dwellings in Twann (BE, Switzerland), where the axe collections were subjected to petrological analysis. Drawing on a number of accurate mineralogical studies, Diethelm (1989) proved that the term 'aphanite' encompasses several different petrographical types, whose origin in the Vosges Viséen is probable, but not demonstrated for all. She proposed a clear differentiation between quartz-pelites, nodulous schists, volcanic tuffas, and Alpine Flysch rocks. For archaeological purposes, she proposed to regroup all of these under the term 'black rock', unless samples had been examined in detail by a geologist. She further suggested that the term 'aphanite' should be abandoned. As to the manner in which the raw material for making blades had been procured, Diethelm envisaged nothing more complex than the collection of material from Vosges stream-beds. These issues were taken up again in a synthesis of the Neolithic period from Alsace to Lake

Constance by Jeunesse (1990). Drawing attention to the cultural problems posed by the diffusion of these Vosges black rocks from the Belfort gap to Lake Constance, he also proposed a chronology for that diffusion. This outline of past research demonstrates the specialisations of each archaeologist, the vectors of progress, but also the barriers to the circulation of ideas or to the understanding of the broader phenomenon. Only in the work of Piningre (1974), and later that of Le Roux (1984), are these broader goals addressed. Even in these cases, however, research was constrained by the lack of a well-developed chrono-cultural frame, while the concepts of a chain of production processes, ethno-archaeology, and experimentation were almost completely lacking.

ETHNO-ARCHAEOLOGICAL STUDIES AND THE DISCOVERY OF THE QUARRIES

Since 1984, two of us (A.-M. P. and P. P.) have been interested in the agricultural communities of Irian Jaya (Indonesia), which still use (or did until recently) polished stone tools. The aim of this research was to describe the global phenomena (and the part that polished blades play), propose hypotheses on the conditions under which axes were made, circulated, and used and construct ethno-archeological models (Pétrequin & Pétrequin 1990; 1994). In particular, we focussed on raw material constraints, on the level of technical knowledge and know-how of the producers and the users of axes and adzes, on the social controls of the operation links in production, on the ways of exchange and of diffusion in relation to social distance and to the operating of societies and cultures, and lastly on the indispensable equilibriums between stone tools, the social context, and the state of the environment modified by humans.

Our current research on rocks from the Vosges, particularly on their exploitation and their diffusion, is one of the first contexts in which ethno-archaeological models derived from work on New Guinea have been applied explicitly to the European Neolithic. Such an approach is not without its practical and theoretical problems. However, we are also convinced of its value as a relevant tool for the recognition and understanding of cultural and chronological problems. It seemed to us that now was the right moment to apply this research to a context where models derived from occidental knowledge and experience may be inappropriate. It was also the right moment because of the considerable strength of archaeological documentation in the study

[281]

area. The region had seen detailed study for more than a century, and the chrono-cultural frame was as accurate as it can be on the basis of terrestrial sites. Dendrochronological studies of lake settlements added further strengths. In addition, thousands of polished stone artefacts were readily available, stored in museums or in private collections, and we were able to collaborate with the Laboratory of Petrography, University of Franche-Comté, where two geologists (M. Rossy and N. Morre-Biot) are studying the large series of polished thin sections that are necessary for any systematic study of the origin of the polished blades used in the production of axes or adzes.

Despite the consensus view that small blocks of rock were simply gathered from the river beds (Piningre 1974; Diethelm 1989), the first stage of our field research involved the identification of mining pits and quarries in the south of the Vosges. This was due, in no small part, to observations made in Irian Jaya, where only polished blades which are not produced for use in long distance exchange can be made from pebbles. These are often dry, not very durable, and difficult to knapp. This contrasts with the situation that applies where long-distance exchange is the motivation for procurement. In these cases, it is necessary to have rapid access to plenty of good quality raw materials, which, in cristalline, metamorphic, or volcanic environments, are classically rare geological anomalies (and the criteria of choice considered by blade producers in Irian Jaya are far more detailed than those used by western geologists), in primary or secondary formation, at short distances from undisturbed levels. For the survey of these anomalies, where the rock has good qualities for the production of resilient polished blades, people in Irian Jaya prospect in the river beds, with a hammer-stone in the hand. They test the raw materials, and even try to polish small flakes of the rock to have an idea of the resilience of a cutting-edge. Then, if it looks promising, they walk up-river until they find the primary origin of the raw material.

Applying this ethno-archaeological model of survey was our way to discard most of the streams of the Vosges and their torrential deposits at the entrances of valleys. Soon it appeared that only the river Rahin, a left bank tributary of the Ognon, was carrying along its bed some small quartz-pelites pebbles that are hard and good for knapping (this fact was already reported by Glory 1942 and Piningre 1974). After a two-day survey, it was possible to identify the first primary pelites formations, worked during the Neolithic, in the bed of the Marbranche brook (Figs 1 and 2) in Plancher-les-Mines (Haute-Saône). Later, the systematic survey of the Vosges rivers showed that most of the pelites

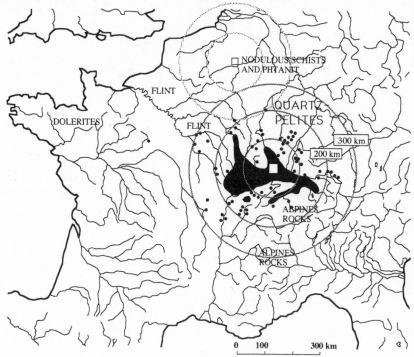

In black: the regions where black rocks represent more than 50% of the polished blades during the middle Neolithic II. The points indicate the sites where the black rock polished blades have been found, but in lower percentages. The distribution of the rocks from the Vosges follows schematically an east-west axis, with heavier concentration toward the valley of the Marne, of the Aar and of the Rhine.

Figure 1. General distribution of the polished blades made of Vosges black rocks between Burgundy and the upper Rhine valley.

rocks, which constitute the continuation of Viséen geological formations in Plancher-les-Mines, were elsewhere heavily modified by tectonics, or were composed of schist facies, unusuable for working stone blades. But other types of rocks, in particular greywackes, were probably worked, at a smaller scale, in the high valley of the river Thur (Wildenstein, Haut-Rhin, 'Herzrunz'). Working with recent geological maps and surveying the alluvial deposits, we were also able to locate other rock formations in the Vosges, worked during the Neolithic: nodulous schists in Sondernach (Haut-Rhin, 'Kummer') and Saint-Amarin (Haut-Rhin) and volcanic tuffas in Bourbach-le-Haut (Haut-Rhin, 'Niederwyhl').

[283]

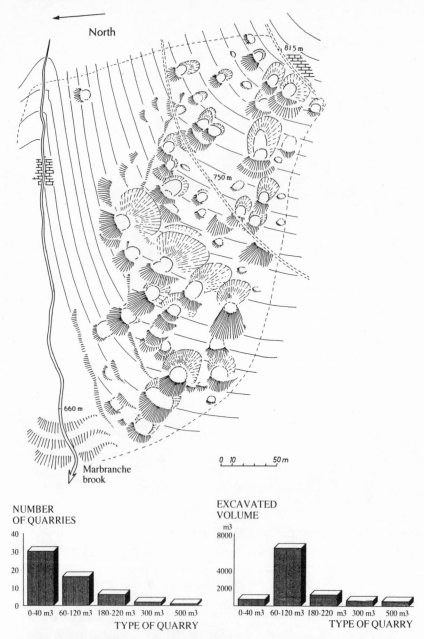

Figure 2. Quarries of the upper Marbranche brook in Plancher-les-Mines (Haute-Saône). At the top of the page, the plan of the quarries. In the bottom left-hand corner, classification of quarries in relation to exploited volume. In the bottom right-hand corner, total volume exploited in the fonction of the dimension of the quarries.

At present, the quarries in Plancher-les-Mines remain the only evidence that we have for Neolithic exploitation for quartz-pelites. In spite of the repetition and intensification of the surveys, the one and only quarry discovered was that which had been located on the second day of survey. What is particularly interesting here is that the quarry in Plancher-les-Mines coincides with an exceptional anomaly in the Viséen formations of the south-eastern border of the Vosges, a correspondence anticipated in the ethno-archaeological models which helped to shape the survey.

DEFINING THE PRODUCTION SEQUENCES

The pelites quarries in Plancher-les-Mines fall into two distinct groups in relation to two prominent outcrops on the slopes of the Marbranche valley. The strata of quartz-pelites, harder than the neighbouring rocks, are set almost upright; in the local topography, they form two long spines, ca 300 m in length and 150 m in width, orientated toward the axis of the slope. The whole of south-eastern slope, where rock has been cracked by the flow of the quaternary glaciers, yields many adjacent quarries. The largest of these are 35m wide, with an exploitation face up to 15 m high (Fig. 2). These quarries are still amazingly well preserved, with their broad terraces of fallen rocks and wasted flakes beneath each open exploitation face. The study of cones of discarded earth allows us to distinguish the units of extraction, which succeed one another along the slope, following the same layer of pelites. Not surprisingly, these units of extraction become larger and larger, before being abandoned. The smallest quarries are located in the beginning of the series and are the oldest ones.

This sequence cannot really be understood as a result of chronological developments in exploitation techniques *per se*. It is more useful to see it as a change in the scale of extraction, with an increased emphasis placed upon trying to reach under the superficial clay and rock deposits to the outcrop itself and creating a working face that is altogether larger. At the end of the sequence of quarry development, it seems that the units of extraction begin to fall from medium sizes to small, as they were during the earlier phases of quarrying. Despite this pattern, it is not possible to think that all rocks of good quality had been exploited, and that changes in the scale of operations reflect the exhaustion of the source. On the contrary, it can be demonstrated that despite the volume of extracted earth (from 40,000 to 80,000 m^3 for the only group of quarries in Haut-Ruisseau, Fig. 2), only half of the initial

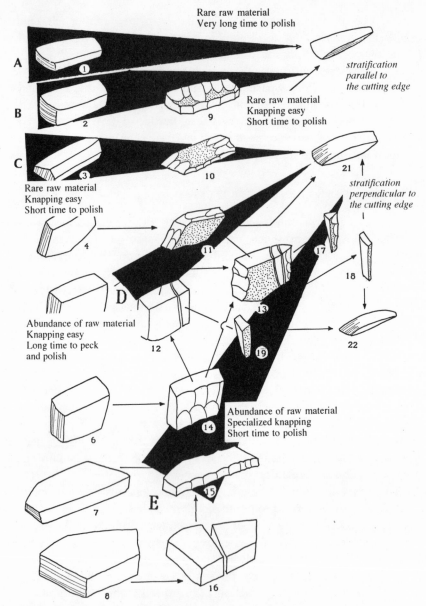

Figure 3. Theoretical manufacturing processes in relation to the type of raw material and levels of technical knowledge at the quarries of Plancher-les-Mines.

stock has been affected by the quarries. The rock, in vertical layers, is covered by one or two meters of fallen stones, where the usable small blocks of rhombohedric form are numerous; the underlying stratas show a cracked facies, which was excavated up to a depth of 1 to 1.5 m, up to the compact rock. This would have been impossible to dig out with the techniques available during the Neolithic.

For us, it was out of the question to carry out archaeological excavations in these quarries, save some basic probing, because the freshness of the evidence seemed sufficient enough to understand the working principles. In addition, the Neolithic deposits were cut by forestry tracks for a distance of almost 800 m. Therefore, ethno-archaeological models were used for determining the theoretical succession of extraction phases (quarry faces and the first test of the blocks, platforms and areas of debitage, and wasted flakes on the cones down-slope); and for choosing sixteen sampling points where all the waste materials have been described and measured (that is to say about 1,900 kg of archaeological material). This quick procedure allowed us to first locate, in the quarries, the potential for the longest blades (these we will discuss later, from the hoards or the graves at two or three days walk from the source); next, to define the stages of production that could have been used to change the raw material into good polished blades (Fig. 3). The quartz-pelites are composed of volcanic ash laminites, deposited on sea-bottoms; they are rocks that can be hammered and pecked or knapped. But if one chooses to knapp the pelites, the parallel or longitudinal removals are more favoured by stratification (laminites of different granulometries) than are the transverse blows. In almost all cases, Neolithic people knapped in the longitudinal direction, that is to say that the future cutting-edge of the polished blade would always be oriented crosswise to the main stratification of the rock. In our attempts to understand the production operations that were followed, we again drew upon our work in Irian Jaya, constructing a series of models of increasing technological complexity. These models of technical 'know-how' were as follows:

a. the direct polishing of small, naturally pre-formed blocks;
b. knapping by longitudinal removal on small blocks whose naturally occuring form was favourable;
c. knapping by transverse removal on small blocks whose naturally occuring form was favourable;
d. the thinning of small blocks by longitudinal and transversal removals;
e. the debitage of longitudinal blades from the edge of a large block, worked as a core.

Among the wasted flakes and remnants of fabrication, we have little evidence for procedures A and B. Procedure C is demonstrated, but the nature of raw material required for it is rare in the quarries. From the first exploitations, the D and E operations, the more complex ones, were privileged because they allowed work with the best quality raw material, here abundant in thick blocks and large slabs of rock. Technique E was much more common and more productive than technique D.

LOCATING THE PRODUCERS

So far there is no trace of permanent settlement in the quarries or in their immediate environs. Moreover, the Plancher-les-Mines valley is located in a mountainous environment, not favourable at all to the cultivation of cereals. This absence of permanent Neolithic settlements appears clearly on the map of all Neolithic finds known in the region of the Belfort gap (Fig. 4). This suggests that the pattern of exploitation in the quarries could have been occasional or even cyclical (annual cycles or more complex social cycles, in relation to the character of exchange). For confirmation of this interpretation, we can turn to the permanent settlement sites discovered in the Haute-Saône plateau, the plateau edges of the Belfort gap, and the loess deposits in upper Alsace. The study of the old collections and the recent surveys show two concentrations of settlements with evidence of quartz-pelite debitage; these quartz-pelites are similar or identical to those of Plancher-les-Mines (Fig. 4, top). The first group of settlements is located one days walk from the quarries, near to rivers, which, from the Vosges, extend to the nearest agricultural land. The second group, at two days walk, coincide with favourable agricultural lands on the Alsace side between Altkirch and Thann. In both cases, the pattern is the same. In the settlements where polished blades were produced, the producers were accustomed to use pelites flakes and blades as everyday tools, as were grattoirs, scrapers, and sickle blades, not to mention occasional tools, instead of flint (Fig. 4, bottom). The producers were also using original chisels out of pelites. The origin of the exploiters is now clear.

THE CHRONOLOGY OF PRODUCTION

Without archaeological artefacts of characteristic typological forms, and without the possibilities of radiocarbon dating in the quarries, questions regarding the chronological development of production could only be addressed in more favourable sites: permanent settle-

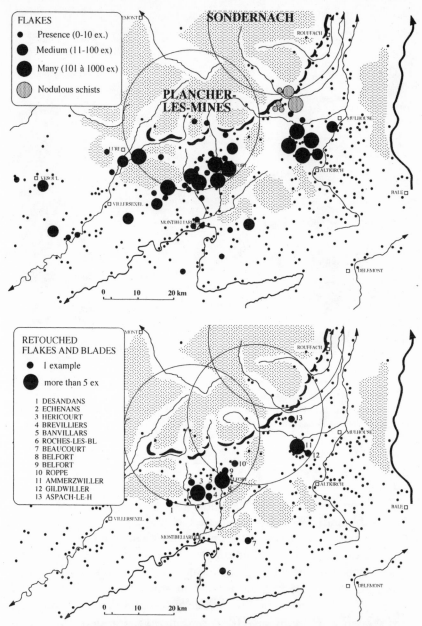

Figure 4. Distribution of settlements in which production of quartz-pelite polished blades occurred in the plateaus from Haute-Saône to Sundgau. Top: rejected raw flakes; bottom: raw flakes and pelite blades used as scrapers, end scrapers or sickle blades. The small black dots indicate all the Neolithic finds known in the region.

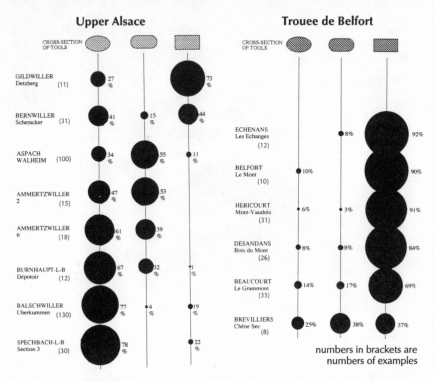

Figure 5. Chronological seriation of producers villages, in relation to the cross-section of polished blades. The modification of techniques (from an oval cross-section and a pecking technique to a rectangular cross-section and a debitage of blades easy to polish) is followed by a geographical shifting of the production areas in the direction of the Plancher-les-Mines quarries.

ments and camp sites in caves with pottery sherds, burials and hoards, and lake settlements dated by dendrochronology. A first study was undertaken on waste flakes from knapping and on the broken polished blades which were discarded in the producers' villages (enclosures in the Montbéliard region and open settlements between Altkirch and Thann). An evolution in the cross-section of blades and blanks was demonstrated. Statistitically, the oval cross-sections were favoured initially, then the intermediate cross-sections, and later the rectangular cross-sections (Fig. 5). Glory (1942) had already hinted at this sequence, and Piningre (1974) recognised it, but only on the basis of a small archaeological sample. However, despite the problems associated with the statistical analysis of large quantities of unstratified artefacts, this pattern of change through time can now be accepted. Moreover, in this region, it can be correlated to the evolution

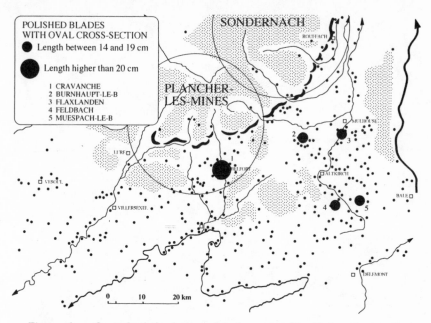

Figure 6 a. Control of the large polished quartz-pelite blades. During the earlier production phase, the large polished blades were rare because of long use. Some examples have been found in graves (continued over).

of polished blades from the Rössen period (oval cross-sections) to Cortaillod (rectangular cross-sections, achieved from long sawn pre-forms) (Furger 1981). These chronological developments were then compared with known cultural attributes. In the case of the upper Alsace, it can be established schematically, from Rössen III to Munzingen (Jeunesse 1990); and, in the case of the Belfort gap and the first limestone plateau, from Rössen III to the Burgundian middle Neolithic, early phase (Pétrequin & Gallay 1981), that is to say, the period from 4600 to 3700 cal. BC.

These chronological changes have implications in the sphere of techniques and chain of manufacturing processes. The polished blades with an oval or intermediate cross-section were made from short and thick blades or small blocks, knapped in the quarries, then shaped by hammering in the settlements. In most cases, this production centred on upper Alsace and, in particular, the region between Altkirch und Thann. The polished blades with an intermediate cross-section were perhaps made under the influence of the diffusion of the triangular Alpine axes or Carnac axes out of pyroxenite (Fig. 6 a) (Le Roux 1984); they were also shaped by hammering and pecking, but polishing

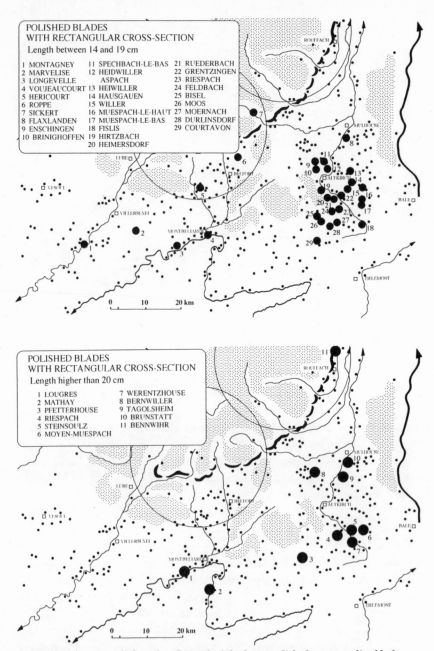

Figure 6 (continued) b and c. Control of the large polished quartz-pelite blades. During the major production period, the large polished blades could have been controlled by the polishers (two days walk from the quarries) rather than by the producers.

represents the longest time investment. In the case of blades with a rectangular cross-section, whose production was, for the most part, located in the Belfort gap and the Haute-Saône plateau, the manufacturing processes privileged the debitage according to the longitudinal axis of pelites blocks, in order to obtain blades that were gauged and thin. At the same time the fabrication of thicker blanks, knapped from small blocks or through the re-use of exhausted blade cores, was a less important process. These operations of pre-forming were almost always done at the quarries, and not in the permanent settlements, as was supposed until now (Piningre 1974).

The patterns outlined above suggest an early phase, centred in upper Alsace (and on the edge of the epicentres of the demographic and cultural progress that took place during the middle Neolithic). Here, the chosen method was the same as one which, traditionally, has been used since the early Neolithic. In the Mulhouse and Altkirch region, this technique of fabrication still seems to be testified during part of the recent phase. This appears to have been followed by a later phase, in the Belfort region, where better advantage was taken of the raw material, with a more difficult knapping technique for long and regular blades (at the moment where the agricultural colonisation increased in the direction of the plateau and the less favourable soils). This opposition between the two groups is also clear from the study of waste flakes in the permanent settlements. In upper Alsace, blanks broken during hammering are numerous. By contrast, waste flakes are far less abundant in the Belfort gap and broken rough-outs are very rare.

THE EVOLUTION OF TECHNICAL KNOW-HOW

Returning to the ethno-archaeological models derived from our work in New Guinea, we were also able to differentiate between production operations in terms of distance to the quarries and the range of exchange networks. It is possible to recognise the modes of production which require a low investment for the acquisition of knowledge and efficient practical experience (Roux & Pelegrin 1989): knapping with a hard striker, or the long process of hammering of pre-forms, obtained by way of thermic shock or violent percussion, or even the long and tedious polishing of roughly shaped blanks. In Irian Jaya, these techniques can be done by all the men, and almost all men practise them, if only for half an hour each day. But in no case is the product of these acts exchanged over any great distance. Above all, the producers are working for their own needs and, incidentally, for the needs of their neighbours. In this case, the opening of quarries or deep mining pits is not always necessary and a good number of pre-forms are shaped from pebbles or from blocks picked up from the surface of the mineral deposits or out-crops.

This situation can be contrasted with more complex techniques, which involve knapping with a soft striker, where production is in the hands of part-time specialists. Periodically, these specialists can deliver large stocks of rough-outs, whose form is so regular that the polishing time is kept short. Here the technical knowledge is well developed. With their part-time specialists, these villages are able to supply (from genuine mining pits and quarries or from very large accumulations of river pebbles next to the outcrops) exchange networks which take the polished blades up to 400 km or more, as the crow flies. In between, there are the villages where all men are part-time specialists in blade production by hammering, particulary from the schists and the crystalline rocks which are not convenient for knapping. For each man, the level of technical knowledge is low, but each of them has excellent know-how and practice. The diffusion of this artefacts resulting from this type of production seldom exceeds 200 km because, in all cases, the shaping of a hammered blade is a lengthy process.

If these data are applied to the evolution of the manufacture/use procedures of quartz-pelites blades in *our* Neolithic, the know-how of the two groups can be seen to change in accordance with chronological and geographical trends (an older phase in upper Alsace, and a more recent phase in the Belfort gap). The approaches appear to be different, though we cannot prejudge the level of technical knowledge. The oval cross-sections (the knapping of thick blades and hammering) could reflect specialised villages with small or medium production for exchange networks which did not privilege the stone blade as a symbolic valuable. Beyond the regional traditions, hammering could have been a slower and less risky technique because the distance to the quarries was two or three days walk. By contrast, the rectangular cross-sections (the knapping of regular blades and thinning of small blocks) could have been the consequence of a shorter distance between the producers and the quarries, for a standardised production, linked to long-distance exchanges, needing a long apprenticeship.

LONG POLISHED BLADES AND SOCIAL COMPETITION

In Irian Jaya, the length of polished blades seems to be correlated with two factors (Pétrequin & Pétrequin 1990; 1994): the situation of the en-

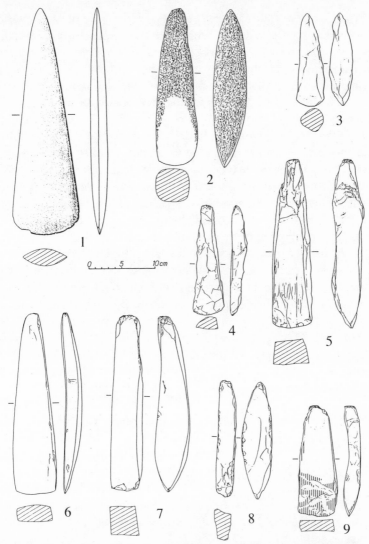

Figure 7. The hoard in Bennwihr (Haut-Rhin). Selection of some blades, from the total 18 pieces found. 1. Brittany type blade in green rock; 2 and 3, greenish volcanic tuffas, knapped preform and pecked rough-out; 4 and 5, nodulous schists, preforms on knapped blades; 6 to 9, quartz-pelites, rough-out in the process of polishing, and polished adzes on blade and on block (drawing: D. Sellet).

vironment modified by people and competition to display social status. For the moment, let us go past the first variable. In egalitarian societies with war leaders, such as the Wano or Dani people, all men try to display their status of accomplished warrior by working with a very heavy stone axe. The largest polished blades are not used by their producers, but by the polishers who make exchanges for their own advantage or for special occasions (marriage payments, blood prices, death compensations). In these regions, heavy axes are used to perform the same work that others can do with lighter stone blades. This fact is not without consequences for the methods of the exploitation of the environment (Pétrequin & Pétrequin 1994). In other societies, where hierarchy clearly appears to the advantage of the lineage, different statuses between men are shown by the length of stone blades, and sometimes even by specific types of rock (Pétrequin & Pétrequin 1994).

If these concepts are transposed to the regional Neolithic, it is not very surprising that the longest quartz-pelites blades were spread over the two days walk radius around the quarries, that is to say, in the areas of the polishers and the managers of the hoards (Fig. 6). In contrast, in the area of the producers' villages, a long blank could testify to prestige, as shown by the previous discoveries in the burials of Mont-Vaudois in Héricourt (Haute-Saône) (Voulot 1897). Likewise, the composition of the hoard in Bennwihr (Haut-Rhin) shows that one has gathered, at three days walk from Plancher-les-Mines, eighteen blades, pre-forms, blanks, or polished blades (Fig. 7). These artefacts come out of different quarries (pelites from Plancher-les-Mines, nodulous schists from the Sondernach and Saint-Amarain region, and Granito-Gneiss from the Saint-Dré area, they also include a long axe blade, of Carnac type, of green rock. If we judge by techniques, this hoard also contains the work of several producers, whose know-how was very different from each other when working the same rock or different rocks. The Bennwihr hoard, as with most of the other hoards in the Sundgau (Werner 1922; Glory 1942) demonstrates preoccupations more or less similar to those suggested by the distribution of the largest polished blades: competition and control for the benefit of a select few. This model runs counter to the general (traditional) concept of *egalitarianism* amongst societies during the Neolithic.

SEGMENTATION OF THE PRODUCTION PROCEDURES AND THE EVOLUTION OF SOCIAL CONTROL

The consequences of these ethno-archaeological models and a new interpretation of previous archaeological discoveries in the Belfort gap has already been presented in detail elsewhere (Pétrequin, Jeudy & Jeunesse, in press). In that discussion, we proposed an interpretation of social control around the Plancher-les-Mines quarries. The conclusions of that discussion can be summarised as follows. During the early phase (end of middle Neolithic I), the villages of the producers were open settlements in valleys (Fig. 8, top), located at one or two days walk from Plancher-les-Mines. The debitage or shaping of thick blades occurred at the quarry and they were then taken to the permanent settlements. Exchanges involving the products were not highly developed; the pelites polished blades had some difficulty competing with Alpine rock productions, which was widespread in Switzerland.

During the following phase (Fig. 8, middle), agricultural colonisation was in progress and the first hill-forts were appearing, during the full development of Kugelbecher cultural groups (Pétrequin & Piningre 1974, Strahm, Jeunesse et al. 1990). The production of pecked blades was intensified, and it is possible to allocate the major part of the upper Alsace production to this period (4500–4200 BC). But already the levels of know-how were beginning to vary between upper Alsace (people there preferred pecking and hammering) and the first producers in the Belfort gap (Frotey-les-Lure and the beginnings of long blades production by knapping).

Around 4200–4000 BC, the exchange networks were controlled by fortified settlements (Fig. 8, bottom). Open villages were becoming rare, and the first burials in barrows or in cists began to appear. Then began the highest production in the quarries in Plancher-les-Mines, with numerous blades which were exchanged as far as Burgundy to the west, and lake Zürich to the east (Fig. 1). Above all, the process of fabrication was turned toward the debitage of long blades and blanks knapped from oblong blocks, regular in form and easy to polish quickly. The largest part of the production was now in the hands of people in the Belfort gap. This technical evolution also involved a pattern of working where almost all risky phases were achieved at the quarries, rather than in the villages. The speed of production then increased, in accordance with a know-how which was increasingly complex. Around the quarries, the geographical space was organised in concentric rings (Fig. 9), where the production of pre-forms (a days walk from the quarries) and the polishing of blanks (two days walk) were becoming distinct operations in different places. In other words, different specialised villages existed in a complementary relation to each other, a situation imposed by the extent of exchange networks.

Up to 3700 BC (Willms 1980; Suter 1987; Gross, Brombacher et al. 1987), quarry production, control of exchange through enclosures, burials with polished blades, and hoards reached their apogee. The

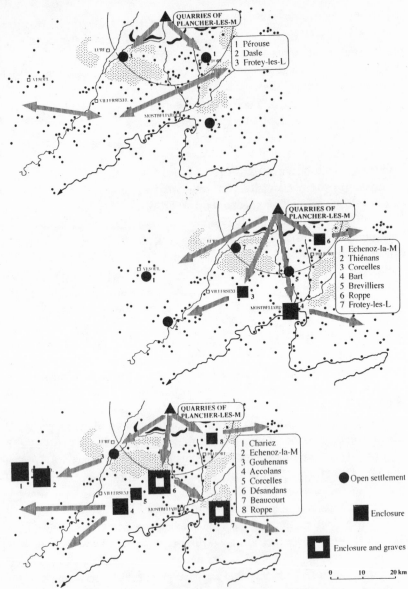

Figure 8. Production in the Belfort gap, from Rössen III to the Burgundian middle Neolithic. Top: during the earliest phase the villages of producers, situated in valleys, were located next to the Plancher-les-Mines quarries. Middle: in the next phase the number of producers' villages increased and were solely concerned with the settlements on the edges of plateaus and the fortified enclosures up to two day's walk from the quarries. Bottom: in the major production period all the settlements were fortified enclosures on hill tops, controlled by two of the biggest villages with monumental burials.

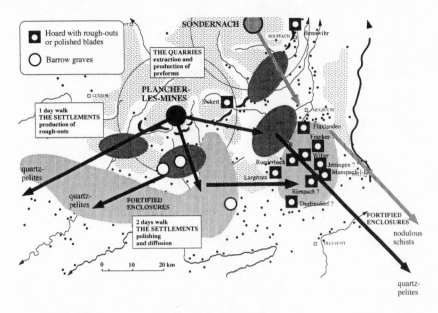

Figure 9. Political control during the major production phase. Two forms of control seem to be in opposition: in the west, control by the pelites knappers, regrouped in fortified villages; in the east, control by the blanks polishers, who hoarded and deposited some of the blades in graves.

same evolution is probably demonstrated by the progressive intensification at the quarry faces in Plancher-les-Mines (Fig. 2), managed by communities which were more and more numerous. Finally, we have to underline the asymmetry of the distribution of quartz-pelites blades around Plancher-les-Mines. This asymmetry, which favoured an axis of exchange schematically oriented east-west, could probably be interpreted in terms of social distance, as suggested by the ethno-archaeological models of New Guinea. If we try to judge by the pottery, the Rössen III and the beginning of Kugelbecher groups, known to the west as far as Chassey (Saône-et-Loire) and eastern Burgundy (Gallay 1977), could have been the phase of the Neolithic where stylistic relationships were the highest on both sides of the Belfort gap. In fact, exchange networks and the diffusion of polished blades could have later benefitted from networks well established several centuries before the maximum production in Plancher-les-Mines. In traditional interpretations, the stone tool could have taken the place of pottery as a symbol, when cultural unity was decaying (Burgundian middle Neolithic, Munzingen, Cortaillod, Pfyn).

FROM ONE QUARRY TO ANOTHER

During the major period of production, at the turn of the fifth and fourth millennium, we still have to establish the connections of distribution between the different quarries in the south-east of the Vosges, in particular between Plancher-les-Mines (quartz-pelites) and the Sondernach Saint-Amarin region (nodulous schists). The typology of the tools suggests that both quarries were more or less active during the same period, as confirmed by the distribution maps (Fig. 9). In the Thann region, some of the villages located near the Vosges were producing blanks out of nodulous schist. Simultaneously, other villages, located at some distance from the Vosges foothills, were working only with quartz-pelites. This division of space coincides, more or less, with a traditional cultural division shown by pottery styles (Jeunesse 1990), with a clear north-south partition of Alsace.

We could distinguish three geographical areas in the distribution of nodulous schist blades around the Belfort gap (Fig. 10, c): in the north, the Bas-Rhin where nodulous schists are predominant; in the centre, the Sundgau, where they are well represented, but not in the majority; in the west, where they show exceptional exchanges, at least during the period of maximum production in Plancher-les-Mines. One cannot exclude the possibility that, at the beginning of the fourth millennium, these geographic divisions reflect the regionalisation of cultural identities.

From 3700 BC, the decrease of the exchange curve in the direction of the Swiss lakes is spectacular. This decrease is correlated with the disintegration of the fortified enclosures, interpreted as central places and social nubs of the exchange networks. The breaking-off of extensive exchanges is a general phenomenon during this period. Later, when long-distance exchange was once again common, the Plancher-les-Mines quarries were not re-exploited to the same extent as they had been earlier. The production in the south-eastern Vosges never exceeded the strictly regional level (Haut-Rhin, Doubs, and Haute-Saône, and, even then, the pelites blades were never numerous). From 3200 BC this trend becomes more marked, with the intensification of cultural movements from the east in the direction of the Saône plains and the Paris basin. Such a cultural colonisation would have increased the diffusion of Alpine polished blades produced in Switzerland (Willms 1980; Furger 1981).

In spite of what has been argued here, many problems still remain with the study of the distribution of quarry products such as those of

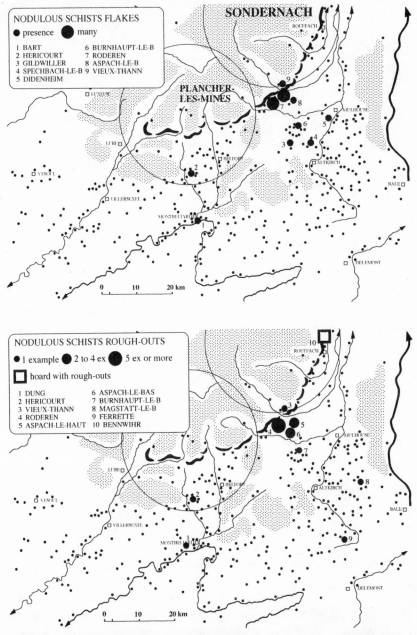

Figure 10 (continued over). The relationships between quarries: a. distribution of nodulous schist flakes from the quarries of the Sondernach region (Haut-Rhin), b. distribution of nodulous schist rough-outs. The frontier between the users of pelites and the users of nodulous schists seems remarkably strong.

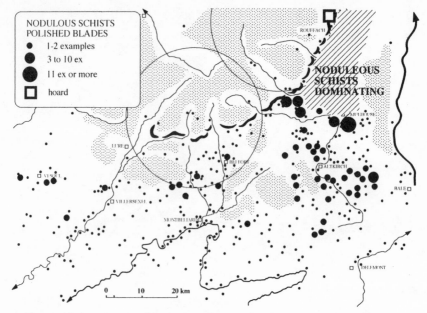

Figure 10 (continued). The relationships between quarries: c. distribution of nodulous schist polished blades. The frontier between the users of pelites and the users of nodulous schists seems remarkably strong.

Plancher-les-Mines. To prove the reality of this distribution, we first have to be sure that no other quarry produced similar or identical products (from a mineralogical point of view). One has to interpret the remote distribution of the black rocks of the Vosges carefully, because there is a risk of confusion in petrographic determination. In Belgium, Caspar (1984) described levels of phtanit, inserted in Revinien schists (Cambrian), and also in the lower levels of the Namurien (upper Carboniferous). These rocks consist of genuine phtanits, but also of nodulous schists, broadly used during the Rubané period (Bakels 1987). From the altered surface of polished blades, it is not easy to recognise these rocks with the naked eye. To differentiate them from the black rocks of the Vosges, we often need accurate analysis, and even a certain caution when the geological criteria are not well defined. In consequence, we need to be wary of the attribution of the polished black rock blades from the northern Paris basin or from Lorraine. In many cases, it is likely that these axes and adzes could have been extracted and shaped in Belgium. Le Roux and Richard (1987) point out that some 'aphanite' polished blades among the hard rock axes from Loiret are typologically similar to blades from the Vosges and would not be problematic if geological identification could confirm their origin. However, this includes a battle-axe with a central perforation which is absolutely unknown in the area of the Vosges and in the east of France. In all probability, this battle-axe, an Atlantic type, could have come from England, where there are also some pelites very similar to those of the Vosges. From the archaeological literature (Vaquer 1990), very little is known about 'petro-silex', volcanic ashes from Rouergue, where Neolithic quarries were recently published by Servelle (1991). From the succinct descriptions of these types of rock, there could be some petrographical similarities to the pelites of the Vosgian Viséen, but the idea has yet to be verified. In fact, the risks of confusion are minor, because the distribution of the blades manufactured from Rouergue 'petro-silex' is only dense in Rouergue, Albigeois, Quercy, and Toulousain, with some examples up to the French Catalonia.

EXPERIMENTAL CONTROL OF A QUARRY

We have already noted the close links between our archaeological research and our ethnographic observations in Irian Jaya. However, we are still in the early stages of a study which will need one or two more years before all the data has been studied. Here it may be more useful to discuss another branch of research which has been important for our work on the quarries in Plancher-les-Mines. We also used experimentation or, more correctly, apprenticeship to test hypotheses derived from archaeological data, albeit with a low-level of know-how. The aim was to open a new quarry by ourselves, keeping in mind the potentials and character of exploitation techniques during the Neolithic.

The first problem was the choice of the tools. In Plancher-les-Mines, a siliceous and acidic environment, no wood or bone implement was preserved, so direct evidence was lacking. Among the potential range of implements discovered elsewhere (limestone mining pits, Neolithic lake settlements, and ethnographic data), we chose and made reproductions of some of the tools which could have been used: a pick-axe from a red deer antler; a furrowing stick made from beech wood; a red deer shoulder blade; a digging stick; hide and so on. Quickly, it appeared that only the antler and beech picks could enable us to dig through the first level of earth and roots; the other tools were not very efficient. At a depth of 0.60 m, the first fallen blocks in the slope appear in clay deposits which are very sticky when wet. This makes it difficult to work during bad weather and rain, and makes it necessary to wash the blocks before knapping. In these heaps of fallen stone, the most efficient form of exploitation is to maintain an overhanging quarry face, first dug out with a pick, then hewed with a long digging stick from the top of the front. Earth and blocks then fall en masse onto hides, bark sheets or baskets which can be carried and emptied on the edge of the earthern terrace of the quarry. The blocks are then selected; those which are considered good for knapping are put into a heap; later they have to be tested with a hammer stone.

The opening of a small quarry (excavated volume: about 10 m^3) required two full days work for ten men, while the blocks were selected, but not knapped. The average number of usable blocks per cubic meter was around 18, after throwing out those which were cracked or not well oriented in relation to the stratification of the rock. The fissured rock itself was reached at a 1.5 m depth. At this point, the profitability of the exploitations is probably about the same as in the fallen blocks of the slope. Here, however, the blocks can be extracted without sticky clays; levers and heavy stone pebbles are then needed for quarrying. The average output of such a quarry was as follows: 1 man per day produced 0.5 m^3 excavated material = 9 blocks, each heavier than one kilogramme, ready for knapping. This output is important, but the quality of the quarried blocks varied in relation to the different strata, and some of them had to be quickly discarded during the process of knapping. It should be noted in preparing our estimates, we did not take into account the time needed for the preparation of the pre-forms and part of the blanks.

In Plancher-les-Mines, a middle-sized quarry has an excavated volume of about 60 to 120 m^3 (Fig. 2), that is to say, 120 to 240 days for one person. Probably during the major phase of production and control by fortified enclosures in the Montbéliard region, the largest quarries had an excavated volume of about 300 to 500 m^3, that is to say, 600 to 1000 days for one person. Such totals for collective effort at the quarries seem important in absolute terms, but it is useful to compare them with the volume of earth and stones moved during the same period of the Neolithic, to build the ramparts of fortified settlements in the region (Pétrequin 1982). Here the values vary from 700 to 2,000 m^3.

In very broad terms, the total effort required for the exploitation of the Haut-Ruisseau quarries in Plancher-les-Mines (Fig. 2) was a minimum of 40,000 m^3 of wasted earth and blocks during the period from 4100 to 3700 BC (the maximum production for exchanges), it represents about 80,000 days work over a period of 400 years. The total investment in time can also be expressed as 200 days work for one person each year. However, this is only if we accept the idea (not proved at all) that the different periods of exploitation are regularly spaced in time. Two hundred work days each year is a minimum value, just to have access to the raw materials, to select and test them. Even if this value had to be doubled, it would always be perfectly reasonable for the large communities, such as those of the fortified enclosures in the Montbéliard area during middle Neolithic II. For example, if we look at Grammont in Beaucourt (T. de Belfort), Bois du Mont in Désandans (Doubs), and Mont-Vaudois in Héricourt (Haute-Saône), these are all large settlements enclosed by ramparts about 260 m in length. If the pelite exploitation from small- or medium-sized quarries did not pose problems in an egalitarian society (during the early and latest phases of exploitation) the management of very high and long working faces could not have been so easy. The regular removal of waste earth, blocks, discarded flakes, and nuclei, with the development of a regular earthern terrace in front of the rock outcrops, could have been a basic condition for regular and permanent production. We find here exactly the same problems of social organisation as those shown by the construction of Neolithic enclosures, where all the different social segments of the community had to contribute jointly to the work. Near the largest Neolithic enclosures, the presence of exceptional barrow burials, built for one body only, lets us suppose that certain forms of hierarchy were in action. It does not seem possible to explain these hierarchies only by the status of blade-knapping specialists (Lichardus, Lichardus et al. 1985).

As for the length of each period of exploitation and the number of people concerned with these expeditions to a low mountain area, no more than twenty would have been in action for the duration of days during the early phase of exploitation. This pattern was probably quite different during the period of maximum production, because the whole face of a quarry seems to have been constantly and regularly worked. The size of the work group could have numbered from thirty to fifty and the length of exploitation might have been one or two weeks, just to clear a large quarry face and remove the earthen waste and fallen blocks accumulated during one or two winters.

EXPERIMENTAL CONTROL OF FABRICATION

From the ethno-archaeological models of New Guinea, we suggested that the average time for the preparation of a blank – out of a knapped support (blade or block) – could be about twenty to fifty minutes. By contrast, the shaping of an axe or an adze from a hammered block can last many hours, or even several tens of hours in the case of especially long axe blades. One of us (J. P.) began a series of experiments with the debitage of Plancher-les-Mines quartz-pelites. In the archaeological data and the waste flakes in the quarries, we first had to recognise the marks of debitage in relation to the type of hammer-stones used for knapping. Secondly, we had to infer the possible operations involved in the shaping of rough-outs, whether from blades or blocks. Then it would be possible to compare the experimentally knapped flakes with the archaeological flakes in Plancher-les-Mines. Thirdly, we had to estimate the level of know-how required for the different techniques (Pelegrin 1991; Roux & Pelegrin 1989).

This experimental research is not yet finished and the results have not been compared with all archaeological data. Nevertheless, a number of general observations can already be made. Firstly, the loss of raw material during the early stages of working is enormous. Only an average of 4 or 5 out of the 18 blocks extracted in each cubic meter can withstand working up to the end of the manufacturing operations. The others are smashed due to weaknesses along pre-existent cracks or the degree of stratification/lamination. The fine-grained pelites, where stratification planes are not perceptible, are fit for knapping to a far greater extent than any other type of pelites. This demontrates that specific rock stratas were probably sought, and followed during the exploitation. In addition, experiment suggests that both methods of knapping and shaping (out of blades or blocks) could have been used jointly. Both testify to the same concern for the profitable utilisation of the raw material. It also seems that debitage with a soft rather than hard hammer is favoured. For that reason, it seems likely that a lot of the large and heavy strikers, made from granite and found in the quarries, were, in fact, used for the quarrying and the fragmentation of slabs of rock, but not for the debitage of blocks and the shaping of rough-outs.

Further observations can also be made regarding levels of accomplishment. For example, the knapping of blanks out of blocks, which were centred and then thinned, could have been within the capacity of all men after some months of apprenticeship (Roux 1991; Roux & Pelegrin 1989). The debitage of blades, even if they are short and thick, already poses some more serious problems of apprenticeship. Knapped blades, 20 cm long or more, need a high-level know-how and could have been the responsibility of specialists (without pre-judging the forms of specialisation). The experimental debitage of the longest blades has not yet been reproduced, perhaps because of the lack of appropriate strikers (for example, very heavy red deer antlers). The average time needed to shape a blank, out of a block or a blade, could be about twenty to sixty minutes, without taking the polishing time into account.

Our general model, which considers the hierarchisation of techniques and know-how for working at the quarry face, has considerable implications for the profitability of ways in which work was organised during periods of exploitation. On the basis of the number of blocks per cubic meter actually extracted, a first calculation indicated 18 polished blades per cubic-meter as a minimum potential production. On the basis of experimental production, the number falls to 4 or 5 potential blades. But, if we choose the debitage from a core, the production of blades will be doubled at least. As for the productivity at Plancher-les-Mines, it seems probable that it could have been about 0.5 to 0.25 m³ per person/day if the knapping of blades at quarries was used for the calculation. From these observations, the total time invested at the site increases notably, not to mention the walking time from the village to the quarries (at least two days trekking for each expedition, and up to six days from the more remote villages, in the region of Altkirch and Vesoul). We know that Plancher-les-Mines is located in the foothills of the Vosges and the altitude of the upper quarries is about 800 m. We have estimated, even schematically, the time investment for periods of exploitation. Now it will be necessary to test, in the field, the hypothesis of long expeditions during the summer months and also the idea that groups may have built shelters or even real houses on the large terraces in front of the quarries, at least during the period of maximum production of quartz-pelites blades. It will also be necessary to estimate more accurately the possible evolution of the techniques from one quarry to another, in the same area of exploitation (Fig. 2). These questions are vitally important, but production at Plancher-les-Mines could be indirectly estimated another way – on the basis of the consumption of pelite polished blades in Neolithic lake villages, whose duration can be measured from dendrochronological dates (as at Twann, NE, Switzerland, for example).

THE EVOLUTION OF SHAFTING AND ENVIRONMENTAL CHANGE

It should be clear that the work undertaken thus far in no way exhausts the subject. However, research shows that many aspects of ancient realities were obscured, consciously or not, in earlier accounts,

[307]

and that the integration of archaeological data with ethno-archaeological models and experimentation has encouraged the development of additional themes.

One of the most obvious themes that can be explored is a calculation of time invested in polishing. During the Neolithic, not all stone blades were polished in the same way or to the same extent. Ethno-archaeological research shows that some agricultural communities take a long time to polish their stone blades, so that these tools become highly prized exchange valuables or social markers. Other groups are content to roughly shape the body and polish the cutting-edge to produce a technically efficient tool which is easy to replace but of lesser value. In this interplay, exchange networks and social functioning have a major role.

Other issues have been identified through work on the relationship between a wide range of variables in Irian Jaya. These include the average length of polished blades, the situation of the modified environment, methods of agricultural exploitation, and the density of the population. For cutting down poles rather than large trees, the prestigious heavy stone axe is not very efficient. This insight is useful for understanding the relationship between ecological and technical factors and may, by extension, give an idea of demographic pressure. Such an approach could easily be applied to the large collections of Neolithic polished stone tools in the lake settlements (Furger 1981).

It may also prove valuable to consider the evolution of shaft types in relation to the length of polished blades, cultural traditions, and patterns of environmental modification. In the case of the quartz-pelites blades, the importance of the adze in relation to the axe has been under-estimated (Piningre 1974), with significant repercussions on the cultural interpretations. During a period of the middle Neolithic II, where the eastern influences of the Paris basin were increasing, it may be worthwhile to describe, and perhaps even understand, the processes which led to the adoption of antler axe shafting in south-eastern Germany (at about 4100 BC). During the same time, people in the Belfort gap prefered to use adze blades ligatured on a cranked shaft and were quarrying in the south of the Vosges in order to supply increasing demands for polished blades for use in clearance. Such a tradition of mining-pit exploitation and direct hafting of the polished blades is also particulary striking in the Paris basin. With the fabrication of a large series of flint blades, knapped and also polished, people tried to solve problems of population increase, social organisation, and the modification of the environment. At this time, in Souabe, a technical choice was made for saving polished stone blades (hafting them in an antler socket), precipitated by the lack of new rough-outs in hard rock. But during the end of the Neolithic (Horgen and Seine-Oise-Marne), the principle of hafting with an antler socket was accepted in all these regions, but with some different cultural adaptations. Finally, if we wish to increase our understanding these processes, it will also be necessary to learn and then experiment with the felling of trees with stone axes or adzes. The few attempts, such as those undertaken in Denmark (Jørgensen 1985), have been too narrowly focussed to allow us to grasp the roles of polished stone blades in the technical and social reproduction of Neolithic societies.

BIBLIOGRAPHY

Bakels, C. 1987. On the adzes of the northwestern Linearbandkeramik. *Analecta Praehistorica Leidensia*, 53–85.

Binder, D. & Perles, C. 1980. Stratégies de gestion des outillages lithiques au Néolithique. *Paléo* 1980: 257–283.

Bocquet, A. & Houot, A. 1982. La vie au Néolithique, Charavines, Un village au bord d'un lac il y a 5000 ans. *Histoire et Archéologie, Les Dossiers* 1984: 64.

Bostyn, F. & Lanchon, Y. (ed.) 1992. *Jablines, Le Haut Château (Seine-et-Marne), Une minière de silex au Néolithique*, Paris: Maison des Sciences de l'Homme (Documents d'Archéologie Française).

Buret, C. & Ricq-de-Bouard, M. 1982. *L'industrie de la 'pierre polie' du Néolithique moyen d'Auvernier (Neuchâtel-Suisse) : les relations entre la matière première et les objets*. Paris: CNRS (Centre de Recherches Archéologiques, Notes internes, 41).

Burton, J. 1984. Axes Makers of the Wahgi, Pre-colonial Industrialists of the Papua New Guinea Highlands. Australian National University, Canberra, Phil. D thesis.

Caspar, J. P. 1984. Fabrication et réaménagement d'herminettes rubanées en phtanite. *Bulletin de la Société Royale Belge de Préhistoire* 95: 47–58.

Desloges, J. 1990. *L'extraction minière de silex au Néolithique et l'exemple de Bretteville-le-Rabet (Calvados)*. Toulouse: Ecole des Hautes Etudes en Sciences Sociales, Mémoire de diplôme.

Diethelm, I. 1989. Aphanit – ein pseudowissenschaftliche Begriff? Eine mineralogisch-petrographisch Bilanz, *Jahrbuch der Schweizerischen Gesellschaft für Ur- und Frügeschichte* 72: 201–214.

Furger, A. R. 1981. *Die Kleinfunde aus den Horgener Schichten, Die neolithischen Ufersiedlungen von Twann*, 13. Bern: Staatlicher Lehrmittelverlag.

Gangi, S. 1989. *Haches polies de Haute-Saône, collection du Musée de Besançon*. Besançon: Faculté des Lettres, Préhistoire, mémoire de maîtrise.

Gallay, A. 1977. *Le Néolithique moyen du Jura et des plaines de la Saône, Contribution à l'étude des relations Chassey-Cortaillod-Michelsberg*. Frauenfeld: Verlag Huber (Antiqua 6, Publications de la Société Suisse de Préhistoire et d'Archéologie).

Glory, A. 1942. *La civilisation du Néolithique en Haute-Alsace*. Strasbourg: Publications de l'Institut des Hautes Etudes Alsaciennes (1).

Gross, E., Brombacher, C. & alii 1987. *Zürich 'Mozartstrasse', Neolithische und bronzezeitliche Ufersiedlungen*, vol. 1. Zürich: Orell Füssli Verlag (Berichte der Zürcher Denkmalpflege, Monographien 4).

Højlund, F. 1981. The function of prestige weapons in the reproduction of New Guinea Highlands societies. *Oral History* 9 (3): 1–25 (Boroko: National Museum and Art Gallery).

Jeudy, F. 1991. *De la roche à la lame de pierre polie néolithique : les minières de pélite de Plancher-les-Mines*, 2 vols. Besançon: Faculté des Lettres, Préhistoire, mémoire de maîtrise, Besançon.

Jeunesse, C. 1990. Le Néolithique alsacien et ses relations avec les régions voisines. In *Die ersten Bauern, Pfahlbaufunde Europas*, 2, pp. 177–194. Zürich: Schweizerisches Landesmuseum Zürich.

Jørgensen S. 1985. *Tree-felling in Draved*. National Museum of Denmark.

Lemonnier, P. 1976. La description des chaînes opératoires : contribution à l'analyse des systèmes techniques. *Technique et Culture* 1: 100– 151.

Le Roux, C. T. 1984. L'implantation néolithique en Bretagne centrale. *Revue Archéologique de l'Ouest* 1: 33–54.

Le Roux, C. T. 1990. La pétro-archéologie des haches armoricaines, 40 ans après. *Revue Archéologique de l'Ouest*, supplément 2, 345–353.

Le Roux, C. J. & Richard, G. 1987. Etude pétrographique des haches polies en roche dure du Loiret et de ses bordures septentrionales. *Actes du 14ème Colloque inter-régional sur le Néolithique*, pp. 159–161. supplément au bulletin de la Société Archéologique Scientifique et Littéraire du Vendômois.

Lichardus J. Lichardus-Itten, M. & alii 1985. *La protohistoire de l'Europe, Le Néolithique et le Chalcolithique*. Paris: Presses Universitaires de France, Nouvelle Clio.

Pelegrin, J. 1991. Aspects de démarche expérimentale en technologie lithique, *25 ans d'études technologiques en préhistoire*, pp. 57–63. Ed. APDCA: (XIème Rencontres Internationales d'Archéologie et d'Histoire d'Antibes, Juan-les-Pins).

Pétrequin, P. 1982. Agriculture néolithique et sédentarisation: le lac de Clairvaux dans son contexte culturel. *Mémoires de la Société d'Emulation du Jura* 1980/1982: 21–46.

Pétrequin, A. M. & Pétrequin, P. 1988. *Le Néolithique des Lacs, Préhistoire des lacs de Chalain et de Clairvaux (4000–2000 av. J.C.)*. Paris: Editions Errance, Collection des Hespérides.

Pétrequin, A. M. & Pétrequin, P. 1990. Haches de Yeleme, herminettes de Mumyeme, La répartition des lames de pierre polie en Irian Jaya central (Indonésie). *Journal de la Société des Océanistes* 91 (2): 95–113.

Pétrequin, P. & Pétrequin, A. M. 1994. *Ecologie d'un outil : la hache de pierre polie en Irian Jaya (Indonésie)*. Paris: CNRS (Monographies du CRA).

Pétrequin, P. & Gallay, A. (ed.) 1984. *Le Néolithique Moyen Bourguignon*. (Archives Suisses d'Anthropologie Générale, 48 (2), numéro spécial, Actes du Colloque de Beffia).

Petrequin, P., Jeudy, F. & Jeunesse, C. in press. Minières néolithiques, échanges de haches et contrôle social du Sud vosgien à la Bourgogne. 18ème Colloque interrégional sur le Néolithique, Dijon, 1991, 31.

Pétrequin, P. & Piningre, J. F. 1974. Elemente der Rössener Kultur in der nördlichen Franche-Comté, *Germania* 49 (1–2): 187–191.

Piningre, J. F. 1974. *Un aspect de l'économie néolithique: le problème de l'aphanite en Franche-Comté et dans les régions limitrophes*. Paris: Les Belles Lettres (Annales Littéraires de l'Université de Besançon).

Ricq-de-Bouard, M., Compagnoni, R. et alii 1990. Les roches alpines dans l'outillage poli néolithique de la France méditerranéenne, Classification, origine, circulation. *Gallia-Préhistoire* 32: 125–149.

Roux, V. 1991. Peut-on interpréter les activités lithiques préhistoriques en termes de durée d'apprentissage? Apport de l'ethnologie et de la psychologie aux études technologiques. *25 ans d'études technologiques en préhistoire*, pp. 47–56. Ed. APDCA (XIème Rencontres Internationales d'Archéologie et d'Histoire d'Antibes, Juan-les-Pins).

Roux, I. & Pelegrin, J. 1989. Taille des perles et spécialisation artisanale. Enquête ethnoarchéologique dans le Gujarat. *Techniques et culture* 14: 23–50.

Schlichtherle, H. 1990. *Siedlungsarchäologie im Alpenvorland, I, Die Sondagen 1973–1978 in der Ufersiedlungen Hornstaad-Hörnle I.* Stuttgart: Konrad Theiss Verlag (Forschungen und Berichte zur Vor-und Frühgeschichte in Baden-Würtemberg 36).

Servelle, C. 1991. L'exploration et l'exploitation sélective du milieu minéral au Néolithique et à l'Age du Bronze : quelques exemples du S.-O. de la France, *Bulletin de la Société Préhistorique Française* 88 (5): 142–144.

Strahm, C., Jeunesse, C. & alii 1990. Wauwil, Bruebach, Entzheim, Strassburg ... Les groupes à 'Kugelbecher' dans le sud de la Plaine du Rhin supérieur (4500–4100 av. J.C.), *Cahiers de l'Association pour la Promotion de la Recherche Archéologique en Alsace*, 6, numéro spécial.

Suter, J. P. 1987. *Zürich 'Kleiner Hafner', Tauchgrabungen 1981–1984*. Bern: Orell Füssli Verlag (Berichte der Zürcher Denkmalpflege, Monographien 3).

Théry, B., Pétrequin, P. & Pétrequin, A. M. 1990. *Langda, L'herminette de pierre polie en Nouvelle Guinée*, Cassette vidéo VHS, 25 mn, réalisateur B. Théry, production JVP Films, CNRS Audiovisuel et CRAVA.

Théry, B., Pétrequin, P. & Pétrequin, A. M. 1991. *Yeleme, La hache de pierre polie en Nouvelle Guinée*, Cassette vidéo VHS, 30 mn, réalisateur B. Théry, production JVP Films, CNRS Audiovisuel et CRAVA.

Tuefferd, P. E. 1878. Notice sur les antiquités préhistoriques des pays de Montbéliard et Belfort. *Mémoires de la Société d'Emulation de Montbéliard* 3 (1): 41 ff.

Thevenin, A. 1961. Contribution à l'étude du Néolithique et du Chalcolithique de la région de Montbéliard et ses régions voisines. Haches et instruments en quartzite micacé. *Bulletin de la Société d'Histoire Naturelle du Pays de Montbéliard* 62–73.

Vaquer, J. 1990. *Le Néolithique en Languedoc occidental*. Paris: Editions du CNRS.

Voulot, F. 1897. Enceinte et vallum funéraire du Mont-Vaudois près Héricourt, *Bulletin de la Société Belfortaine d'Emulation* 16: 275 ff.

Voruz, J. L. 1984. *Outillages osseux et dynamisme industriel dans le Neolithique jurassien*. Lausanne: Bibliothéque Historique Vaudoise (Cahiers d'Archéologie Romande 29).

Werner, L. G. 1922. Les dépôts et cachettes néolithiques du département du Haut-Rhin. *Bulletin de la Société Belfortaine d'Emulation* 38: 116.

Willms, C. 1980. *Die Felsgesteinartefakte der Cortaillod-Schichten, Die neolithischen Ufersiedlungen von Twann*, 9. Bern: Staatlicher Lehrmittelverlag.

14

F*lint Extraction, Axe Offering, and the Value of Cortex*

Elisabeth Rudebeck

In *the presence* of friends and kin, parents confirm the marriage between their children by means of fire, and this is executed by making fire over them with steel and flint. For with fire and flint matrimony must be tied, because these symbols are held to bring more fortune and to be more promising for married life than any other sign, and so recognised and established is this custom as if it had been founded in Greece itself or in Latium. In giving such a merit to fire they [i.e. the Saami] are however not alone, since this custom (. . .) was upheld and accompanied by ceremony in times past by the Romans, the world's most important people. Their intention is to imply, through this symbol of a fire drawn from the flint and again enclosed in the same, a bond or a power of insoluble love. Just as the flint holds a disguised fire within itself, with which it is closely connected and which can be brought to spark by a blow against an object, so also in both sexes a life is hidden, which through the union between spouses comes forward by degrees in the living offspring. But neither do the more civilised Christian peoples in other parts of the Nordic countries want to dispense with fire in the enhancement of their wedding ceremonies. Thus every wedding couple that goes to church to be blessed by the priest will, according to position and descent, have carried before them high candles of varying colours, made with great skill from soft wax and with pieces of silk in different colours hanging from them. These candles are left behind after the ceremony together with valuable offerings, while the candlebearers struggle over the silk pieces in a kind of rage, as if they were valuable prey.

– Olaus Magnus 1555

This quotation from the Swedish bishop and historian Olaus Magnus (Olaus Magnus 1555/1976: 184, my translation) is chosen as an introduction because it brings out some of the issues that have plagued me in preparing this chapter. Without trying to evaluate the ethnographic statements made by Olaus Magnus, I found his description inspiring and suitable as a starting point for a discussion concerning ritual, votive offerings, and the ascription of social value to objects.

After making some short comments on the possible motives and meanings of rituals involving offerings, I will discuss the tradition of offering flint axes during the early Neolithic in southern Scandinavia. My concern will be patterns of change during this period in the tradition of offering axes, and the relation of these changes to possible changes in localities for flint extraction. Finally, I will discuss possible connections between an early Neolithic flint extraction site and a certain type of flint axe within a limited area in the south of Sweden (Fig. 1). Some questions concerning the possibility of identifying social value will be discussed, more precisely the possible significance accorded to the practice of extracting flint and the extracted flint itself (the raw material).

OCCASIONS FOR MAKING OFFERINGS

In my opinion, scholars have too often assumed motives of social prestige and competition, at the cost of other motives, in discussions on prehistoric ritual and votive offering. Important though these issues are, it may be more useful to consider the possibility of more existential motives for executing the rituals which have left traces for archaeologists to meditate upon.

In the ethnographic statement by Olaus Magnus we see that normal fire-making tools, flint and steel, were used in the marriage ritual. Marriage is a symbolic transformation, a *rite de passage*, and it changes

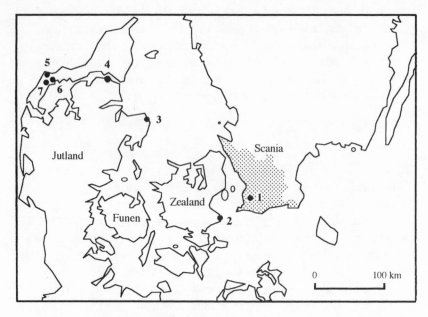

Figure 1. Large flint extraction sites of southern Scandinavia: 1. Kvarnby-Södra Sallerup, 2. Stevns Klint, 3. Fornaes, 4. Aalborg, 5. Bjerre, 6. Hov, 7. Hillerslev. The shaded area in Scania is the administrative district of Malmöhuslän and a couple of parishes outside this district.

a person's social position as well as the personal life and experience of every individual who passes through it. In the life of a human being some transformations, such as birth and death, occur only once whereas others, e.g. marriage and childbirth, may occur several times. Building houses, clearing ground for cultivation or pasture, making journeys to specific places or persons, burying relatives, or extracting particular resources may also be considered to be transformative events, which may provide the motivation for particular rituals. Some of these events happened only once, or just a few times, in the life of an individual, and some probably required initiation that gave access to particular kinds of knowledge or tasks. To the individual and family these events were therefore rare and dramatic, but to society at large they were repetitious and continuous. At this broader level, we may also imagine rare and dramatic events, such as the building and consecration of large-scale monuments, as junctures that may also have provided the motivation for various forms of communal rites.

Beside the rare rites of passage we may add repeated rituals, such as those connected to seasonal, monthly, and daily tasks and actions –

rituals of expiation, thanksgiving or request (Bradley 1990: 37ff). It is possible to imagine rituals at several social levels, from the individual, family, kin-group, lineage or special task groups to the communal and most public level of participation. This applies as much to so-called mundane tasks as it does to more formalised activities or events: for some individuals, the extraction of particular resources may have been a rare event whereas to others it was a routine part of the recurrent events of life. Whatever the case, we may anticipate ritual to have accompanied tasks and events at every frequency level.

If we are to believe Lévi-Strauss (1987: 222 ff), votive offerings serve to introduce a relation between a divinity and people. The establishment of this relation is the prerequisite for subsequent communication. The relation is started by breaking up the 'natural order' of the world, the chain of being, through the handling of objects in particular ways. Different rituals can be assumed to have had different prescribed objects, but according to Lévi-Strauss the typical feature of making offerings is the principle of substitution. This is possible because it is the intention, rather than the material item, that is important. In many cases, the creation of a relationship between people and a divinity is predicated upon the selection, sanctification, and destruction or deposition of an object, animal or person. The transformation of the chosen object from one state to another is the purpose of the ritual and it involves taking objects or living beings out of what could be referred to as a normal context. If we press the transformation concept, we may say that every altering of the environment, of materials, living beings, and social relations may be accompanied by ritual. In other words, similar themes may be relevant for our understanding of activities such as the extraction of raw materials, the making of tools, the burning of pottery, and the melting of ore to extract metal. Whether or not we accept these features involved in making offerings as being universally applicable, the description may serve as an inspiration when we try to give meaning to the archaeological evidence that we have for purposeful or ritualised acts of deposition. It is with these themes in mind that we can begin to investigate the tradition of offering flint axes during the early Neolithic in southern Scandianvia.

THE AXE TYPES

Votive offerings containing flint axes are abundant in southern Scandinavia (Nielsen 1977; Rech 1979; Karsten 1989). Perhaps it would be proper to note that I have chosen to take as a point of departure the interpretation of these finds as votive offerings. I am of course well aware of other interpretative possibilities.

Two types of flint axes dominate during the early Neolithic in southern Scandinavia: the point-butted axe and the thin-butted axe. The point-butted axe is generally considered to be the earliest type of Neolithic polished flint axe in this region and is dated to the earliest phase of the early Neolithic, between 3200 and 2800/2700 bc (uncal.) (Madsen & Petersen 1984: 101). This axe is seen as a transitional type between the unpolished core axe of the Mesolithic Ertebølle culture and the thin-butted axe of the early Neolithic TRB culture (Nielsen 1977: 72; Jennbert 1984: 110). Both the point-butted and the thin-butted axes are, furthermore, divided into several, more or less, local and chronologically significant types, but these will not be considered here. It will suffice to say that the earlier types of thin-butted flint axe (I-III) seem to have a more eastern distribution in southern Scandinavia, while the later types (IV-VI) are more common in the west and north-west, with a more or less even distribution in modern Denmark (Nielsen 1977: figs 7–19 & 35–42).

BIAS AND SOURCE CRITICISM

It is not possible to discuss this period and area without making a few comments regarding the influence of modern political and ad-ministrative boundaries on our interpretations of patterns in pre-history. Eastern Denmark, particularly Zealand, and western Scania seem to have been a closely tied cultural area during the Neolithic. In spite of this, most archaeological research until this day treats these areas separately. There are of course exceptions, such as the work of Nielsen (1977) and Rech (1979) on early Neolithic axes. The difficulty of dealing with very large materials is obviously also a limiting factor. Archaeological interpretations are inevitably biased by these factors. I experienced this bias in an attempt to find published information on the distribution and composition of votive offerings and single finds containing these two axe types in southern Scandinavia. Even though the total number of registered axes of the two types remains a rough estimate, it is clear that the thin-butted form is much more common than the point-butted axe. The estimated number of point-butted axes in southern Scandinavia is somewhere between 1000 and 1100 (Rude-beck 1976; Nielsen 1977; Hernek 1988; Østmo 1988). The distribution of the axe shows a strong concentration in Scania, particularly in the southern and south-western parts of the region. At least 682 of the estimated 1000–1100 axes are found in Scania, whereas 21 axes are registered in Norway, mainly in the south, and 280 axes are found in Denmark (these are only axes with registered find locations), mainly in the eastern part of the country (Nielsen 1977: 69 f).

In Sweden and Norway alone, the number of thin-butted flint axes is probably around 10,000 and there is no reason to believe that the number is any lower in Denmark and northern Germany. In Sweden, the majority of thin-butted axes (probably more than 6000) are found in Scania (Rudebeck 1976). These figures indicate that the acquisition of flint became an increasingly important task in society during the early Neolithic. The extraction of flint, and the production, use, and ritual deposition of the flint axe was made a concern for more and more people during the later part of the early Neolithic. Unfortunately the most recent source on votive offerings and single finds of the axe types in the region only covers western and south-western Scania, the administrative district of Malmöhus (Malmöhuslän) and a few parishes outside of this district (Karsten 1989) (Fig. 1). Other sources (Hernek 1985; 1988) cover both find categories in Scania, but only for point-butted axes. Nielsen (1977) covers both axe types but only votive offerings in Scania and Denmark and not the single finds. This, of course, makes comparisons rather problematic. I have chosen to use the most recent information from Hernek (1985; 1988) and Karsten (1989) and to investigate the distributions in the area covered by Karsten, mainly because this area lies at the heart of the point-butted flint axe distribution. Votive offerings are here taken to be all the published deposits containing two or more axes, or one or more axe(s) of the specific types and one or more axe(s) of another type (or another object) in combination (the vast majority of deposits contains axes of one of the two types only). I will follow Karsten's suggestion and include single finds with wet-ground find contexts as single object offerings (Karsten 1989: 82 ff).

For the point-butted flint axe, following Hernek (1985; 1988), we find 18 votive offerings, containing a total of 65 axes, in Malmöhuslän. Karsten (1989: fig. 4) claims 21 votive offerings in the area (but gives no information as to the composition of the offerings) and 59 single finds from wet ground. In the case of thin-butted axes, Karsten records about 90 votive offerings and 145 single finds from wet ground in the area (ibid.: fig. 5). As there is no information on the composition of the 90 votive offerings, this information had to be taken from Nielsen's investigation (1977) on the 35 votive offerings in the same area, containing 118 thin-butted flint axes.

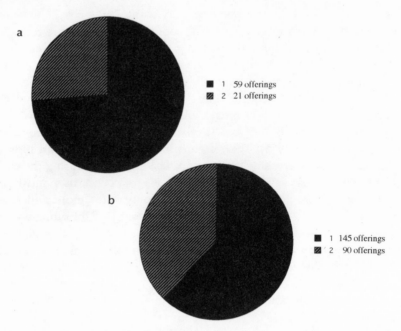

Figure 2. The relationship between offerings with one axe and two or more axes: a. point-butted; b. thin-butted.

PATTERNS IN THE OFFERING OF AXES

If we accept the chronological difference between the two axe types, we find that despite the limited samples involved, both single offerings and offerings of two or more increased with time (Fig. 2 a & b). Within this overall trend, the most significant change is the higher proportion of deposits containing at least two objects in relation to single offerings when it comes to deposits containing thin-butted axes. Further comparisons can also be made. Figures 3a and 3b show the composition of deposits with two or more point-butted axes and those with two or more thin-butted axes in Malmöhuslän only. Thus, apart from single finds, the deposits containing two axes, or rather two objects, are the most common type of formal deposit with point-butted and with thin-butted flint axes. One pattern is clear: a 'normal' offering contained between one and four objects – offerings with more than four objects are rare.

We may also compare the amount and composition of votive offerings with two or more thin-butted axes in Malmöhuslän and Denmark respectively. When comparing information from Nielsen (1977) con-

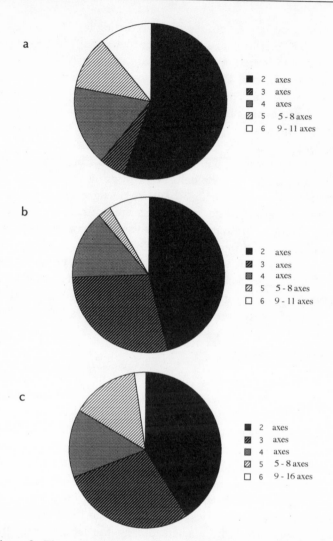

a

	2	axes
	3	axes
	4	axes
	5	5 - 8 axes
	6	9 - 11 axes

b

	2	axes
	3	axes
	4	axes
	5	5 - 8 axes
	6	9 - 11 axes

c

	2	axes
	3	axes
	4	axes
	5	5 - 8 axes
	6	9 - 16 axes

Figure 3. The compositions of various offerings: a. 18 offerings with two or more point-butted axes in Malmöhuslän (Hernek 1985); b. 35 offerings with two or more thin-butted axes in Malmöhuslän (NB this information comes from Nielsen 1977, thus only 35 offerings with this axe are used, whereas the actual number of offerings, according to Karsten 1989, is 90); c. 176 offerings with two or mor thin-butted axes in Denmark (Nielsen 1977).

cerning the composition of 176 offerings with two or more thin-butted axes in present Denmark with the composition of 35 offerings of two or more thin-butted axes in Malmöhuslän, some patterns are distinguishable (Fig. 3 b & c). It is clear that offerings with two to four axes are the most common in both regions. According to Nielsen (1977: figs 35–41, 121–136), medium-sized offerings, that is with five to eight axes, containing thin-butted axes (type I-III) are most frequent in Zealand and Scania (8 out of 11). The medium-sized offerings with the later types (IV-VI) are concentrated in northern Jutland (8 out of 10). The large offerings, with nine to sixteen axes, are even fewer in number and this makes interpretations difficult. One pattern can, however, be identified: of 7 large offerings with identified axes, 6 contained early types and of these 4 are from Zealand, 1 from Scania, and 1 from the island of Gotland in the Baltic. One offering from the island of Funen contained later types. Thus, there are no signs of an increase in the number of very large offerings in this area during the second half of the early Neolithic, rather the opposite seems to be the case. As to the medium-sized offerings we find more of these in Denmark, compared to offerings both with thin-butted and with point-butted axes in Scania. If we also include the axes of types III, IV or VI that were not possible to identify in detail (Nielsen 1977: 99 f), we find that the number of offerings decreases evenly as the number of axes per offering increases.

FLINT SOURCES

The till in southern Scandinavia contains flint of both Senonian (Maastrichtian) and Danian origin. Between 10 and 50% of the stones in the till are flint nodules (Gry & Søndergaard 1958: 5; Olausson 1983: 13). Apart from the extraction of flint from the till there were primary and large secondary sources available (Fig. 1). During the earliest part of the early Neolithic, flint was extracted from the Senonian (Maastrichtian) chalk in the Kvarnby – Södra Sallerup area in southwestern Scania (Olausson et al. 1980; Rudebeck 1986; 1987). The chalk was transported to the area by glaciers during the later part of the Weichselian, probably from the south/south-east (Ringberg 1980). As these blocks are absolutely huge the extraction of flint in the area has the same character as extractions from primary flint sources, with pits and shafts cut into the chalk. To my knowledge, these mines are the earliest in southern Scandinavia, with the earliest dating to around 3100 bc. The extraction of flint from different sources in present-day Denmark commences during the later phase of the early Neolithic and continues during the middle and late Neolithic (Becker & Weisgerber 1980: 456–73).

On the basis of current dates from flint mines in Scania and Jutland we may assume that the southern Scandinavian flint extraction from larger sources was concentrated in south-western Scania during the earliest part of the early Neolithic. During the second half of the early Neolithic, however, flint extraction became more concentrated on the primary sources found in northern Jutland. The large secondary Senonian flint source at Stevns Klint on Zealand may also have been used during this time, although the dates obtained so far indicate extraction during the middle Neolithic (Weisgerber 1980: 473).

ONE AXE, GOOD; TWO AXES, BETTER?

When considering Malmöhuslän we find that about 90% of the offerings containing point-butted axes have one or two axes, while the comparable figure for the thin-butted axe is 70% (Figs 2 & 3). Of the remaining offerings with thin-butted axes, the ones with three axes make up about one third. The composition of offerings with two or more thin-butted axes in Denmark has a similar pattern, except that here the medium-sized offerings with thin-butted axes are more abundant than in Scania. The large votive offerings are very rare and therefore well-founded interpretations are difficult to make. What we do not find, however, is a significant increase in large offerings with late types of thin-butted axes. In fact the earlier types were more often deposited in the large offerings and this may be an argument against increasing competition and social prestige displays, at least in this particular realm, during the course of the early Neolithic. If we dare draw any conclusions from this it may be that there is a positive correlation between the exploitation of large flint sources and the occurrence of medium-sized offerings.

The clear dominance of offerings with one and two axes and the even decrease in the number of low- and medium-sized votive offerings with thin-butted axes may indicate that the tradition of making offerings did not change, at least in its content or meaning. It may be that increasing access to flint axes or to flint sources made the offering of axes less tied to social competition and that this kind of social activity was instead more concentrated around the megalithic tombs and other monuments.

Are we then to interpret the increase in medium-sized offerings as a sign of an increase in the number of people involved in the rituals, i.e. as a more public undertaking? Or did the same social group or groups as before deposit more axes at every instance of deposition, and especially those groups close to the flint sources? Was there a norm among certain social groups that stated 'one axe, good; two axes, better; three axes, even better'? Did such a norm in fact act as an incentive for the intensification of flint extraction? Perhaps there was an increase in particular transformative rituals – and, conversely, a decrease in others – connected to changes in social and/or family life.

CORTEXUAL ARCHAEOLOGY AND THE VALUE OF MINED FLINT

Several axe offerings contain axes that were very long and obviously not intended for every-day utilitarian purposes (Olausson 1982: 28). Other offerings contain flint nodules that were only roughly shaped to resemble axes and these would have been equally unsuitable for use as working tools. Most votive offerings contain axes that 'seem to have been used for different tasks which varied by axe length' (ibid.: 28). This indicates that there was not necessarily any clear divide between a utilitarian and a non-utilitarian example intended for offering. The significance accorded to an axe was in the eye, or in the mind, of the possessor or beholder. Since a basic utilitarian/non-utilitarian dichotomy does not appear to have been employed in the context of offerings in the past, it may be unwise to maintain a similar division in our analyses.

I owe the following idea concerning the appearance of the Neolithic flint axe to my colleague Dr Ulf Säfvestad. Säfvestad had noted that many flint axes of different types had a piece, sometimes a very minute piece, of cortex on the butt. The very minute size of the cortex, quite often less than 1 sq. cm, indicated that it could have been removed easily, had one wished to do so. From the flint knapper Don Crabtree (1967: 9) we learn that

> A toolmaker's criteria for identifying good lithic materials are: texture, lustre, surface character, cortex (rind), colour, transparency, sound, flexibility, sharpness of removed flakes and perhaps most important, the amount of resistance to the necessary force required for detaching a flake.

Crabtree (1967: 24) also states that 'Most materials have a natural surface layer that is sometimes sufficiently distinctive to be useful for identifying places of origin.' It seems evident that to persons familiar with lithic materials, the cortex, or some other original surface, is important both for the identification of quality and of source. Good quality ought to be a factor in the evaluation of both raw materials and finished products. The quality of workmanship of finished tools is another factor that would determine the evaluation. It is also possible that lithic material from particular sources was more valued than that from other sources.

THE SIGN OF THE CORTEX

The flint from the sources of Senonian (Maastrichtian) chalk in the Kvarnby – Södra Sallerup area in south-western Scania has quite good flaking properites (Fig. 1). It is dark grey or black, though often with lighter inclusions, shiny and has a smooth chalky cortex. Due to chalk quarrying, rescue excavations have taken place in the area of Kvarnby – Södra Sallerup between 1977 and 1992. These excavations, altogether covering about eleven hectares, have revealed traces of Neolithic flint extraction. Radiocarbon dates from material from deep shafts and pits in the chalk have yielded dates between 5080 ± 65 BP (Lu-1636) and 4140 ± 60 BP (Lu-2509), i.e. between 3130 and 2190 bc (Rudebeck 1986; 1987). The early Neolithic dates are the more abundant.

Through four test pits in the chalk in the flint extraction area at Kvarnby – Södra Sallerup, it has been possible to investigate the amount and size distribution of flint nodules in the chalk (Fig. 4). Two features are particularly obvious: the nodules are very unevenly distributed within the chalk and the nodule size is on average quite modest. Thus it is hardly possible to interpret the flint extraction site as some kind of 'axe-factory'. Large volumes of clayey till and chalk were removed from the deeper shafts for a very unpredictable yield of nodules. The number of nodules of good quality, i.e. without obvious cracks and irregularities, per cubic meter of chalk varies between about 10 and 106!

If we consider 15 centimeters to be the minimum nodule size for the manufacturing of an axe we find that around 10–15% of the nodules were usable – this is when we count only flat and regular nodules of good quality. Irregular nodules of good quality at sizes over 15 cm length were generally very rare. The flint could, of course, be used for smaller tools and there are several indications that the good quality of the flint and acquisition by mining were both important in the valuation of the raw material and subsequent products.

In order to investigate the possible relation between point-butted axes made from (probably) mined Senonian flint and the suggested 'sign' of the cortex, I investigated a collection of 97 mainly intact (and some reshaped) axes in the surface find collection at the museum in Malmö. For comparison about 100 thin-butted axes were also in-

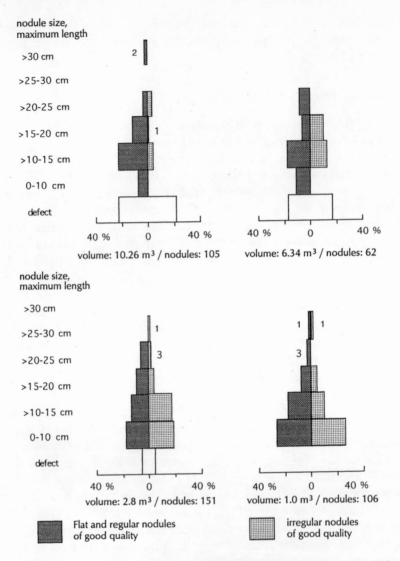

Figure 4. Flint nodule size from four test pits in the chalk at Kvarnby – Södra Sallerup. The numbers 1–3 indicate actual number of nodules. Number of nodules per cubic meter chalk varies between ca 10 and 106.

vestigated. The find locations of the axes were not recorded but it is known that most axes have been found in south-western Scania, in other words fairly close to the flint extraction site at Södra Sallerup. It should be noted that the determination of flint type is only made through visual inspection, and this, of course, does not make it

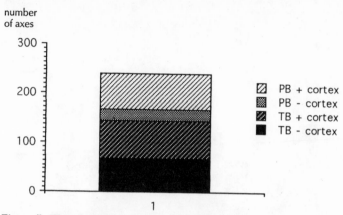

Figure 5. The relationship between point-butted axes with and without cortex to thin-butted axes with and without cortex.

completely reliable. For the purpose of this discussion, however, such a determination is sufficient. In Figure 5 we can see the relationship between point-butted and thin-butted axes with and without cortex of both Senonian and Danian flint. The patterns that emerge are not very clear, but we do find that about 70% of all axes had remains of the cortex or of some other original surface on the finished tool. There was no indication of the polished axes having fewer cortex remains than the unpolished ones.

Of the 97 point-butted axes 54 were made from Senonian flint and 43 were made from Danian flint. Thus, there was only a slight dominance of axes made from possibly mined flint. In Figure 6 we can compare Senonian axes of both point-butted and thin-butted types for the absence or presence and type of cortex (or other original surface). It seems as if cortex is more often present on the point-butted axes and that smooth cortex is also more abundant on this axe. Though the material is scant we may suggest that the 'sign' of the cortex was more important during the time of the point-butted axe and hence during the time of flint extraction in Kvarnby – Södra Sallerup. The axes with eroded cortex offer problems of evaluation as the eroded surface is not sufficient for excluding the possibility of fabrication from mined flint. The erosion of the cortex may in some cases be due to 'post-fabrication' factors.

It may be that flint mining was made a less spectacular event during the course of the early Neolithic and that it became an ordinary task within society. During the earlier phase of the early Neolithic we may anticipate flint mining as being a rare and esoteric event, perhaps a rite

number
of axes

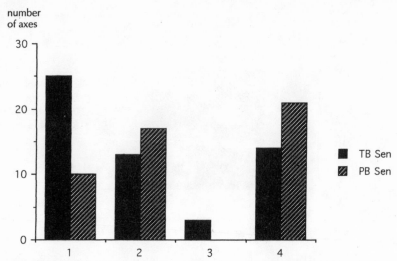

Figure 6. Point-butted and thin-butted Senonian axes compared: 1. absence of cortex, 2. eroded cortex, 3. original patinated flint surface, 4. smooth cortex.

of passage. The mined flint may have been desirable, not only because of the physical qualities of the raw material, but also because of its meaning as a sign of particular events in the social realm. The sign of the cortex may thus have been not only a sign of quality and source in an entirely profane way, but also a sign of the special value attributed to the act of extracting flint for the celebration of social transformations.

ACKNOWLEDGEMENTS

In this paper I have discussed some non-utilitarian aspects of the early Neolithic flint axes and flint extraction in southern Scandinavia. I have left several loose ends and ended up with a heap of questions. Hopefully the reader has found some of these worth reflecting upon. Finally I would like to thank Dr Ulf Säfvestad and Dr Deborah Olausson for discussions and advice and for correcting some of the unavoidable 'Swenglish' formulations.

REFERENCES

Becker, C. J. & Weisgerber, G. 1980. (Notes on the flint mines in Denmark). In Weisgerber, G. (ed.), *5000 Jahre Feuersteinbergbau, Die Suche nach dem Stahl der Steinzeit*, pp. 457–473. Bochum.

Bradley, R. 1990. *The Passage of Arms. An archaeological analysis of prehistoric hoards and votive deposits.* Cambridge: Cambridge University Press.

Crabtree, D. 1967. Notes on experiments in flintknapping: 3. The flint-knapper's raw materials. *Tebiwa* 10 (1): 8–24 (Pocatello).

Gry, H. & Søndergaard, B. 1958. *Flintforekomster i Danmark.* Copenhagen: The Danish National Institute of Building Research and the Academy of Technical Sciences (Progress Report D2).

Hernek, R. 1985. Den spetsnackiga yxan av flinta; typologi, kronologi och ursprung. Unpublished paper at the Lund Institute of Archaeology.

Hernek, R. 1988. Den spetsnackiga yxan av flinta. *Fornvännen* 83 (4): 216–223.

Jennbert, K. 1984. *Den produktiva gåvan; Tradition och innovation i Sydskandinavien för omkring 5 300 år sedan* [The fertile gift. Tradition and innovation in southern Scandinavia some 5 300 years ago]. Lund (with an English summary).

Karsten, P. 1989. Rituella neolitiska fynd i Skåne. In Larsson & Wyszomirska (eds), *Arkeologi och Religion,* pp. 77–86. Lund: University of Lund, Institute of Archaeology (Report 34).

Lévi-Strauss, C. 1987. *Det vilda tänkandet,* 3rd edn. Malmö.

Madsen, T. & Petersen, J. E. 1984. Tidligneolitiske anlæg ved Mosegården; Regionale og kronologiske forskelle i tidligneolitikum. *KUML* 1982–83: 61–120 (with an English summary).

Nielsen, P. O. 1977. Die Flintbeile der frühen Trichterbecherkultur in Dänemark. *Acta Archaeologica* 48: 61–138.

Olaus Magnus 1555 [1976]. *Historia de Gentibus Septentrionalibus. Historia om de Nordiska Folken* [History of the Nordic Peoples, 4th book, 7th chapter, On marriage among the Laplanders confirmed by fire]. Östervåla.

Olausson, D. 1982. Lithic technological analysis of the thin-butted flint axe. *Acta Archaeologica* 53: 1–87.

Olausson, D. 1983. *Flint and Groundstone Axes in the Scanian Neolithic.* Lund: (Scripta Minora, Publication of the Royal Society of Letters at Lund 2).

Rech, M. 1979. *Studien zu Depotfunden der Trichterbecher- und Einzelgrabkultur des Nordens.* Neumünster: (Offa Bücher 39).

Ringberg, B. 1980. Beskrivning till jordartskartan Malmö SO, in: SGU (Swedish Geological Survey), Serie Ae, Nr. 38, Uppsala 1980.

Rudebeck, E. 1976. Flintutvinning och flintdistribution under neolitisk tid i Norden. Unpublished paper at the Lund Institute of Archaeology.

Rudebeck, E. 1986. Ängdala, Flintgruvor från yngre stenåldern S. Sallerup, Utgrävningar 1977 – 1981, Rapport no. 1, Malmö muséer, Stadsantikvariska enheten, Malmö 1986 (with an English summary).

Rudebeck, E. 1987. Flint mining in Sweden during the Neolithic period: new evidence from the Kvarnby – S. Sallerup area. In Sieveking, G. de G. & Newcomer, M. (eds), *The Human Uses of Flint and Chert,* pp. 151–157. Cambridge. Cambridge University Press.

Seitzer Olausson, D., Rudebeck, E., & Säfvestad, U. 1980. Die südschwedischen Feuersteingruben – Ergebnisse und Probleme. In Weisgerber, G. (ed.), *5000 Jahre Feuersteinbergbau. Die Suche nach dem Stahl der Steinzeit,* pp. 183–204. Bochum.

Weisgerber, G. 1980. DK 6 Stevns Klint, Seeland. In Weisgerber, G. (ed.), *5000 Jahre Feuersteinbergbau, Die Suche nach dem Stahl der Steinzeit,* pp. 473ff. Bochum.

Østmo, E. 1988. Etableringen av jordbrukskultur i Østfold i steinalderen, Universitetets Oldsaksamlings Skrifter Ny rekke, Nr. 10, Oslo 1988 (with an English summary).

15

Craft Activities in the Dutch Neolithic: a Lithic Viewpoint

Annelou van Gijn

Placed on the first rung on Hawkes' ladder of inference, technology has traditionally been regarded as the most easily knowable aspect of prehistory. Nowhere is this clearer than in research on lithic assemblages, where many studies have worked from the assumption that a full understanding of stone tools will be gained by examining their role in the business of food procurement. This view, which has its roots in contemporary concepts of technology in western society, remains at the heart of much of our work (Ingold 1990). Most archaeologists have regarded material culture as passively reflecting past behaviour, more specifically past subsistence behaviour. Lately, however, we have begun to acknowledge that the material traditions that we study may have played an active part in the creation and maintenance of the social and ideological structures that existed in the past. Ethnographic studies have demonstrated that while they may have practical roles, objects also have social lives, and that new technologies and objects (innovations) have to be compatible with the actor's vision of the world in order to be accepted. There are always a number of options, equally suitable from a mechanical point of view, and choices are made according to which options can be taken on within the existing technological, social, and ideological system (Lemonnier 1986; 1990).

One aspect of material culture in which I would expect such cultural choices to have been made is the manufacture of various craft articles. It is through their houses, fences, pots, baskets, clothing, and ornaments that people often address a variety of ideas concerning their social identity. Unfortunately, much of the material repertoires of the past have decayed and archaeologists are frequently left with only scatters of flint or pottery sherds. However, it is possible, even with these meagre data, to arrive at statements about the social identity of past communities; it is exactly this, making use of data on flint implements, which I intend to do in this chapter. Although the typology of lithic artefacts has traditionally been used to infer (ethnic) groups, the choice of raw material, the reduction sequence, and the way tools are treated during use can also reveal technological choices indicative of aspects of past social identity. Additionally, traces of use on flint tools provide us with indirect evidence for the practice of craft activities with perishable end products. I would like to suggest in this paper that use-wear analysis of stone tools is potentially a good method for the investigation of technological choices, because it links two (or more) artefact categories and offers us glimpses of various 'chains of operation'.

It has been proposed that the so-called Danubian cultures, i.e. Linearbandkeramic and Rössen farmers whose roots basically lay in the Near East, were not compatible with the so-called Maglemose tradition in the coastal areas of the Netherlands, ultimately descending from the Mesolithic hunter-gatherers in the north. Admittedly, part of the contrast in traditions of material culture may be attributed to a difference in preservation conditions. However, interestingly enough, the two-fold division of the territory of the Netherlands can be traced back to the middle Mesolithic, when Newell (1973) postulated the development of a Rhine basin and a north-western *Kreis*, and possibly even to the late Paleolithic with the division between the Federmesser and the tanged point traditions. The two traditions, in the sense of Braudel's *longue durée*, probably had very different ways of looking at their (natural) surroundings. Examining craft is one possible avenue of research which could shed light on the differences between the various Neolithic cultures, their mutual affinities, and their traditions. A lithic perspective on the craft activities performed, the techniques employed, and the tools involved, may contribute towards a better understanding of the Dutch Neolithic and the societal transformations that took place during this period.

METHODOLOGICAL OUTLINE OF USE-WEAR ANALYSIS

Use-wear analysis of flint artefacts was introduced during the early 1970s as a powerful alternative for paleobotanical and archaeozoological research, to be applied on those sites lacking organic preservation. When introduced, its potential for reconstructing the food economy of past societies was deemed to be considerable. Use-wear analysis clearly was part of the 'battery of new techniques' which flooded archaeology during the 1960s and 1970s (cf. Cross 1983) and expectations of this new method were high. By the mid-1980s, however, the emergence of problems with use-wear analysis led many researchers to doubt whether the method had any value whatsoever. Many of these problems were raised at the Tübingen conference in 1985, which focussed primarily on high-powered microscopy (e.g. Newcomer et al. 1986; Unrath et al. 1986). I believe that, given certain restrictions, the method can be a useful tool. However, it should be considered a strictly archaeological, that is interpretive, procedure instead of a mechanical, objective way of determining the function of prehistoric flint tools (cf. Van Gijn 1990a for a methodological outline).

In the Netherlands, the vast majority of use-wear research has addressed Neolithic flint (Bienenfeld 1986; 1989; Flamman 1990; Van Gijn 1990a; Schreurs 1988; in press). One of the main reasons for this emphasis is the lengthy period during which Neolithisation (in the traditional sense of a dependency on agriculture and animal husbandry and a fully sedentary lifestyle) remained incomplete. After the occupation of the Linearbandkeramic people in southern Limburg, it is not until the period of the Michelsberg culture that agriculture gradually becomes an integral part of the subsistence system in the south-east of the Netherlands. In the western and northern coastal areas, several sites with dates until the middle Bronze Age are known, which can be interpreted as temporarily occupied and used for the exploitation of various wild resources. Due to the fact that animal bones are generally not preserved in the sandy soils of southern and eastern Holland, it is possible that wild resources were exploited here to a larger extent than we presently think. Often these sites are difficult to interpret in terms of their function within a settlement system and use-wear analysis seemed an additional tool to unravel the trajectory towards a fully 'Neolithic' economy (Van Gijn 1990a; Schreurs in press).

Most assemblages were studied by high-power analysis, sometimes also by stereo-microscope (Schreurs in press). It is not the purpose of this paper to give an outline of the method of use-wear analysis of flint implements, but there are a few methodological issues which are of relevance here. First of all, it should be stressed that use-wear analysis is essentially an inductive, experimental discipline. By carrying out various experiments we create a reference collection which defines and circumscribes the limits of our inferences; we can only interpret wear traces with which we are familiar. For the analysis of Paleolithic material this has not caused serious problems, perhaps because the tasks for which flint tools were used turned out to be relatively straightforward, involving only one contact material and a simple motion, or because the traces on Palaeolithic tools were so ambiguous that they could be dismissed as 'unknown' or 'not interpretable'. However, Neolithic assemblages display several types of wear which are well developed and very distinctive, but for which we have no reference in the experimental collections. These traces clearly beg for an interpretation, and thus for new experiments, but it is difficult to imagine what experiments should be carried out and in what way. Ethnographic and ethnohistoric accounts can provide inspiration, but a major drawback of relying too much on these sources forms the danger of only finding what is presently documented. It is perfectly possible that different tasks were performed or that tasks were done in a different way in the past. This 'lack of inspiration' is especially acute for craft activities, because of the complicated and compound nature of the tasks involved.

THE NATURE OF THE DATABASE

In the following, a description will be given of the various craft activities which could be demonstrated on the basis of a use-wear analysis of flint assemblages from different Neolithic cultures in the Netherlands. Use will be made of published reports of other researchers, notably Bienenfeld (1985; 1986; 1989). In some instances Bienenfeld's interpretations were checked on the original artefacts because of new insights into various types of wear traces. The other analyses (Flamman 1990; Schreurs 1988; in press) were done under my supervision. It should be stressed that the following outline is based on only limited data and that it forms part of a continuing project. The samples are not always representative and compatible. This chapter should therefore be considered an exploratory one intended to extend the interpretive possibilities of the use-wear method.

THE EARLY NEOLITHIC

In the southern part of the Netherlands, on the loess-covered hilly landscape of Limburg, a large number of LBK settlements are located, the so-called 'Graetheide' cluster (Bakels 1978). From the approximately thirty sites known here, two have been studied for traces of

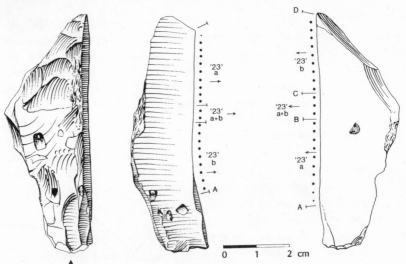

Figure 1. Quartier d'orange from the LBK site of Beek-Molensteeg, displaying location of the two aspects of polish '23'.

wear on flint tools (Elsloo: Flamman 1990; Schreurs 1988 and Beek-Molensteeg: Van Gijn 1990a), while the flint assemblage from the recently excavated site of Geleen-Janskamperveld (Louwe Kooijmans 1991) is presently being studied. Generally speaking, the flint is in mint condition, without traces of post-depositional surface modification. In all three assemblages the large majority of wear traces present are attributable to contact with hide. Most of these traces are located on scrapers, used in a perpendicular (scraping) fashion. Hides were also cut or sliced and, albeit very rarely, pierced. It is remarkable that considerable variation exists within these hide-polishes, probably due to complicated hide-processing techniques practised by the LBK people. Although quite a number of experiments with different processing techniques were executed, we have no experimental equivalents for the entire range of variation. It remains guesswork what this variation means exactly, but it seems beyond doubt that tanning took place on the sites, especially because a certain type of pit demonstrated on a number of LBK sites is best explained as tanning pit (Gronenborn 1989; Van de Velde 1973).

Another type of wear traces that can probably be attributed to craft activity is polish '23' (Van Gijn 1990a: 85). It is observed on *quartiers d'orange*. Technologically speaking it is more appropriate to refer to this tool type as *'debitage en frites'* (Jacques Pélegrin, pers. comm.) and on blades with an obtuse, unretouched edge (Fig. 1). The traces are

A

B

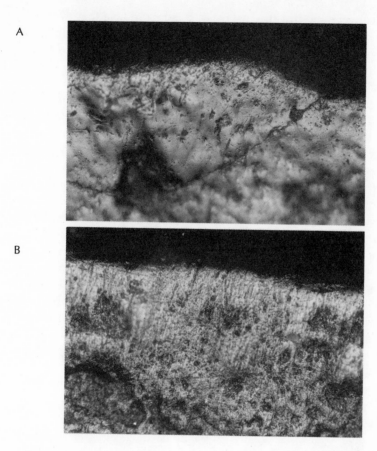

Figure 2. Quartier d'orange from the LBK site of Beek-Molensteeg: A. the smooth polish version and B. the rough polish version, located on what probably formed the contact surface of the tool (both enlarged x 155).

distinctively characteristic, because the two aspects of the edge display different polish attributes. One aspect exhibits a very smooth, highly reflective polish, somewhat reminiscent of reed or well developed antler polish (Fig. 2a). The opposite aspect displays a very rough and matt polish with numerous striations oriented perpendicular to the edge (Fig. 2b). Both versions extend about 2.5 cm along the edge and end quite abruptly. The two polishes are certainly caused by a single instance of use as indicated by one implement, the distal part of which showed the rough version on the ventral and the smooth polish on the dorsal aspect, whereas the proximal part showed the pattern reversed. Clearly, this particular implement was used twice and was turned around between the two use-instances. It is remarkable that every un-retouched edge displaying an obtuse angle of 70–90 degrees and having a regular, sometimes slightly concave shape displays these traces, irrespective of its technological support. This was noted for Elsloo, Beek-Molensteeg, and Geleen-Janskamperveld.

In Belgium the same type of trace was observed on *quartiers d'orange* (Caspar 1985; 1988); it was also seen on a piece from Hienheim, Bavaria (Keeley 1977). It seems, therefore, attributable to a task which formed an integral part of the LBK repertoire. Both Keeley (1977) and Caspar (Cahen et al. 1986: 47) propose that the traces are due to the dehairing of hides while adding mud. I contend that this is not possible (for arguments see Van Gijn 1990a: 85) and that the shredding of some sort of plant fibres, perhaps with the addition of ashes, is the most likely solution. Several experiments were done to attempt to replicate these particular traces, directed at tasks which could have been introduced with the arrival of the LBK and which involved plant material. The first avenue explored was the keeping of bees, an enterprise which requires attention from the exploiters, and thus a certain stability in territory. Ethnohistoric sources mention that bramble branches are preferred for the construction of beehives because juices from its wood repel moths which eat the honeycomb. Prior to the manufacture of the beehives, the thorns should be removed from the branches.

Two experimental *quartiers d'orange* were employed in this task, but only showed a slight resemblance to the prehistoric wear pattern. The experimental implements may have been used too briefly to display the extensive wear traces visible on the archaeological tools. A second possibility which was investigated was the use of limebark. Limebark is frequently used in the production of ropes and threads, whereas the extract from the bark forms an excellent tanning agent (Stambolov 1969). Several flint implements were used for shredding lime bark, but this did not produce extensive polish. The third option studied was the processing of flax (*Linum usitatissimum*). Flax is first grown during the LBK (Bakels 1978; Bakels & Rouselle 1985) and part of the production process, loosening the inner fibres from the putrefied outer stems, could have been performed with an obtuse-angled tool. Again, the resulting polish only bore a superficial resemblance to the archaeological version.

Remarkably enough, Juel Jensen (1988) found similar traces on entirely differently shaped edges, i.e. sharp-angled denticulates, from the Danish early Neolithic. Despite extensive experimental research, she has not been able to unravel the mystery of these traces. She does, however, consider contact with some unspecified plant material the most likely option.

Despite the fact that well over 3000 Bandkeramic flint tools have been studied for traces of wear (Caspar 1988; Flamman 1990; Van Gijn 1990a; Schreurs 1988), traces from the working of bone or antler are rare. This is significant, because bone tools (e.g. combs) are known in LBK contexts, so it would seem that flint tools played no role in their manufacture, an observation which has meaning in terms of cultural preferences. Although sickle blades, interpreted as having functioned for harvesting domesticated cereals, are present in considerable numbers, no artefacts display 'sickle gloss' with a perpendicular directionality; such traces are usually attributed to matting or basketry activities. On the other hand, woodworking seems to have taken place on a considerable scale: coarser flint tools have been used for wedging wood, smaller flakes and blades, sometimes not retouched prior to use, for finely shaping wooden implements.

The use-wear analysis of various Bandkeramic flint assemblages generally points to the presence of a strong correlation between tool type and tool function. Most endscrapers are used on hide and all of the *quartiers d'orange* on polish '23'. Blades, whether retouched or not, seem to constitute a generalised tool. Comparatively, Bandkeramic implements are intensively used, particularly those which are intentionally retouched.

THE MIDDLE NEOLITHIC

Several middle Neolithic flint assemblages have been studied for traces of wear from both inland and coastal sites. The Neolithic Swifterbant sites (Deckers et al. 1980) are located on river dunes in the former IJssel-delta and date from ca 5300 BP. Bienenfeld (1985; 1986) examined the entire Swifterbant-S51 assemblage and sampled S2 and S4. All three sites give a similar spectrum of use-wear traces: silicious plants, bone, hide, and wood, but the interpretation of this spectrum is somewhat problematic. First, Bienenfeld does not discuss the character of the hide-working traces she observed, although ethno-archaeological research shows that a variation of techniques is included in this catch-all term and experiments indicate that, depending on which additives are used, the traces can vary significantly (Van Gijn 1990a; Hayden 1993). Moreover, various stages in the hide-working proces can be carried out in different types of settlement and inferences therefore have implications for questions concerning site typology.

Figure 3. Micrograph of a highly reflective polish, probably from contact with reeds or cat's-tail, seen on a small blade (length 4.7 cm) from Swifterbant S2 (enlarged x100).

Another problem with respect to the Swifterbant use-wear analysis is the interpretation of traces from silicious plants. On several implements, scratches in the polish indicate that the tools were used in a perpendicular fashion, usually interpreted as having functioned for matting or basketry. Bienenfeld does not specify the type of plant, but re-examination of the artefacts shows a very fluid, highly reflective polish which is associated with reeds (*Phragmites*) or cat's-tail (*Lythrum*) (Fig. 3). Experiments have shown that such polishes can be differentiated from the ones resulting from contact with domesticated cereals (Van Gijn 1990a). Bienenfeld also mentions some plant-working tools with parallel scratches which she interprets as cereal-harvesting tools; however, present knowledge would suggest that these tools were not used on cereals but on reeds. Her conclusion that agriculture was practised on the levees of Swifterbant therefore seems somewhat premature (Bienenfeld 1985). Bone-working does not seem to have been an important enterprise at Swifterbant as the number of artefacts showing such traces is small. These traces preserve well and are usually clearly visible, so this low representation cannot be attributed to recovery factors. The absence can, however, be due to the character of the sample which was examined by Bienenfeld: most of the imple-

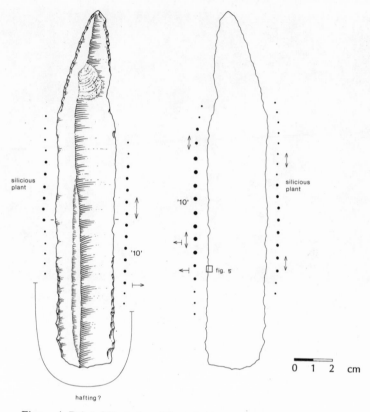

Figure 4. Pointed blade from Hazendonk level 3, showing location of the wear traces (see Fig. 5).

ments studied were retouched tools, whereas other analyses of Neolithic assemblages show that bone working to a large extent is performed with unretouched implements.

The Hazendonk excavations have produced three middle Neolithic levels. The site is situated on a river dune surrounded by peat in the former Rhine/Meuse delta (Louwe Kooijmans 1985). Level 1 is roughly contemporaneous with the levee sites of Swifterbant and yielded only a small number of flint artefacts. Bienenfeld (1986) examined them for traces of use, but most had been affected by natural modifications to such an extent that analysis was impossible. The results from level 2 are equally meagre: one implement displayed traces from contact with plants and was used in a perpendicular motion. From Hazendonk level 3, dating from ca 4900 BP, hide, wood, and bone/antler working were attested. Three plant working implements were found by Bienen-

Figure 5. Pointed blade from Hazendonk level 3 (see Fig. 4), micrograph displaying polish '10' (enlarged x200).

feld, one of which, a large pointed blade made of Rijckholt flint, upon re-examination displayed the same characteristic polish '10' visible on many Michelsberg tools (Figs 4 and 5). Characteristic for polish '10' is the presence of attributes of both a hide-like polish and a sickle-gloss-like polish. Although not resembling 'classic' plant polishes, it is nevertheless likely that polish '10' is caused by plant material (Schreurs in press), but it has not yet been experimentally reproduced. Interestingly enough the contact material responsible for this mysterious polish is worked both in transverse and longitudinal motion, suggesting the tools were used in the processing of raw materials or in the manufacture of objects, rather than in a subsistence activity. The presence of this tool, made of the same raw material as most Michelsberg artefacts and displaying an identical typology and function, indicates contact between the south-east of the Netherlands and the coastal zone during this period.

Brandwijk-Het Kerkhof, also located on a river dune in the former Rhine/Meuse delta, is contemporaneous with Hazendonk 1. Radiocarbon determinations from Brandwijk-Het Kerkhof provide a date around 5300 BP. The site produced a large quantity of flint artefacts and since analysis of the finds is still in progress, the following results are preliminary (Van Gijn & Verbruggen 1991). All the 'show-pieces' are made of Rijckholt flint and, technologically speaking, are similar to those recognised in Michelsberg contexts in the south-east of the Netherlands. The bulk of the material, however, is made from small pebbles and displays less standardised technological features. The standardised Michelsberg scrapers all display hide polish; these scrapers have been used extensively. Several large Rijckholt blades were used as a 'Swiss army knife' for a variety of activities, such as butchering and fish processing. Some also display polish '10', a polish 'type' which seems to be common in Michelsberg flint assemblages. Quite a number of small, blade-like implements made of local river pebbles display polish which can be attributed to contact with reeds or cat's-tail; these tools are used in a perpendicular fashion and can probably be interpreted as having functioned in the preparation of fibres or strips for fishtraps, matting or the like. Basketry was almost certainly made on the spot. The bone awls retrieved all display striations and other wear traces that are consistent with both a piercing and a rotating movement (determination by the author). Perhaps the tools served in manufacturing coiling baskets, to make holes to lace the stitching material.

Yet another craft activity which seems to have taken place at Brand-wijk is the manufacture of bone tools; bone debitage characteristic for the so-called standard metapodium technique (Van den Broeke 1983; Maarleveld 1985) has been retrieved, as well as the final products, bone awls and chisels. However, associated flint implements have not yet been found. Further inland, several middle Neolithic assemblages, attributed to the Michelsberg culture (5500–4800 BP), have been studied. Maastricht-Klinkers, dating from a later phase of the Michels-berg culture, is located on a promontory above the Meuse valley. The majority of the implements appear to have been used, often quite intensively. Hide-working must have been an important activity; the character of the wear traces suggests hide processing rather than the cleaning of fresh hides. Next in importance is light woodwork such as the shaving and cutting of wooden implements and polish '10'. A few implements display traces of bone-working (Schreurs in press). Gassel, located in the eastern Netherlands, is situated on a low, late glacial river dune along the Meuse (Verhart & Louwe Kooijmans 1989). Bienenfeld (1986; 1989) analysed all the retouched artefacts and only found a small number of used edges. Most of the implements display traces of wood-working; considering the morphology of the tools, light woodwork, such as shaving and cutting, seems to predominate. Bienenfeld also found traces of soft plant and hide-working; no men-

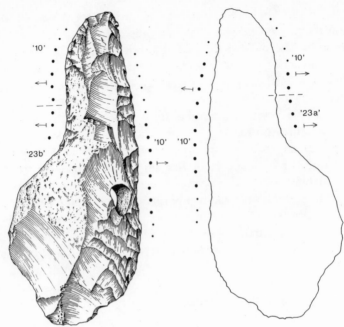

Figure 6. Flint implement from Gassel showing location of wear traces (adapted from Verhart & Louwe Kooijmans 1989: 92).

tion is made of the character of these traces. Because new polish 'types' are lately being recognised, I re-examined one implement reported as a plant-working tool (Fig. 6). The tool displayed intensive use on different contact materials: polish '23' was present on the concave edge, whereas polish '10' appeared on both lateral edges. Both polishes can probably be attributed to plant processing such as fibre-making. Because of these new insights the material from Gassel is currently being re-analysed by Schreurs (Leiden).

The flint from Kraaienberg (Louwe Kooijmans & Verhart 1990), dating from ca 5100 BP, is yet another Michelsberg assemblage currently under investigation. Most tools are made of Rijckholt flint and the wear traces are well developed, indicating that the tools were used quite intensively. Analysis reveals traces of light wood-working (both shaving and cutting motions), polish '10' (also both in longitudinal and perpendicular direction), hide-working, and some bone-working (Schreurs, pers. comm.). If the middle Neolithic flint assemblages are compared, it is clear that the inland sites display a stronger correlation beween tool type and tool function than the coastal ones. At the latter the majority of the implements are produced from rolled pebbles: the implements are much smaller, made in an ad hoc fashion and only lightly used. Only the tools made of Rijckholt flint, appearing at the Hazendonk and at Brandwijk-Het Kerkhof, display relatively heavy use and a stronger correlation between type and function.

THE LATE NEOLITHIC

In the case of the late Neolithic, only flint assemblages from coastal sites, Hekelingen III, Leidschendam, and Vlaardingen, have been studied in detail so far (Van Gijn 1984; 1990a). Contemporary inland sites were considered of insufficient quality to justify a use-wear analysis, either because no provenience was recorded for the artefacts or because they were mixed, making it impossible to include the part of the assemblage which had not been modified into diagnostic types. The three assemblages studied are attributable to the Vlaardingen group, which, together with the Stein group and the Seine-Oise-Marne culture, are considered to be one cultural unit (Louwe Kooijmans 1983).

The assemblage from the site of Hekelingen III was the most intensively studied; Leidschendam yielded a high percentage of abraded artefacts, so that the sample is considerably skewed. Most of the information below derives, therefore, from the analysis of the Hekelingen material. One craft activity which could be demonstrated was the manufacture of awls and chisels from the metatarsal and metacarpal bones of elk and roe deer. Maarleveld (1985) studied the end-products and the bone waste and was able to reconstruct the entire manufacturing process. He also hypothesised about the role and shape of flint implements in this process. Flint tools could play a role in two stages of production: first of all in the deepening of the natural groove on the metapodia and second to saw off the distal end of these bones so that they could be split lengthwise. Experiments were done replicating the manufacture of bone awls and chisels, producing characteristic traces of use. Several prehistoric implements showed identical patterns of wear (Fig. 7). Both the tools to deepen the groove and those employed for sawing the bone were found. It should be noted that the traces were quite frequently located on unretouched tools; suitable edges were selected, rather than shaping a blade or flake into a standardised implement (Fig. 8). Here, clearly, it was possible to reconstruct an entire chain of manufacturing operations.

Another craft activity which could be demonstrated at Hekelingen III was the splitting of soft plants or willows. Most probably, the flint

Figure 7. Micrograph of bonecarving traces from bone-working implements from the late Neolithic site of Hekelingen III (enlarged x200).

implements functioned in the process of basketry making; the surroundings of the site must have abounded with willow and reed (Bakels 1988). Remarkably enough these traces were all located on simple, unretouched flakes, usually with a protrusion suitable for splitting (Fig. 9). Yet another craft activity which could be documented at Hekelingen III was wood-working. Various wooden implements were preserved on the site, such as a yew bow, a paddle, and an axe shaft of maple. Perhaps the flint artefacts served in their maintenance or manufacture. Several borers have been found, some of which displayed traces attributable to contact with soft stone and shell. The boring of shell is suggestive of the making of ornaments on the site. Although both Leidschendam and Vlaardingen may be considered very different from Hekelingen III (cf. Van Gijn 1990b), the character of craft activities is similar: wood, hide, bone/antler, and plant-working. The level of detail, however, is poorer than for Hekelingen III due to the presence of abrasion on the Leidschendam assemblage and a too limited sample from Vlaardingen. In the spirit of the 1970s and early 1980s, it was believed that a 20–30% sample from an assemblage would provide sufficient insight into the variability and quantitative composition of the various activities responsible for the wear traces (cf. Van Gijn 1984). However, I now believe that only studying a sample is

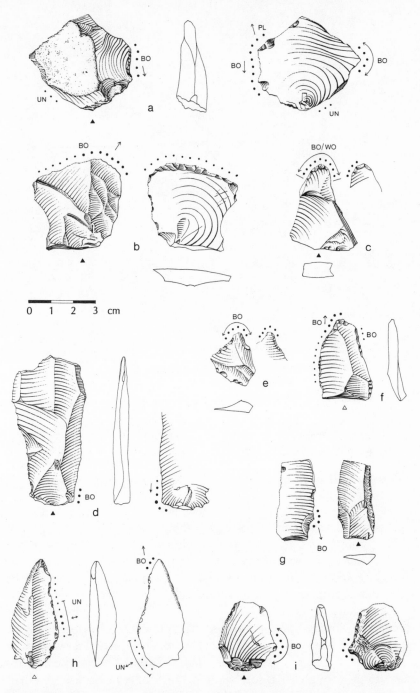

Figure 8. Bone-working implements from the late Neolithic site of Hekelingen III.

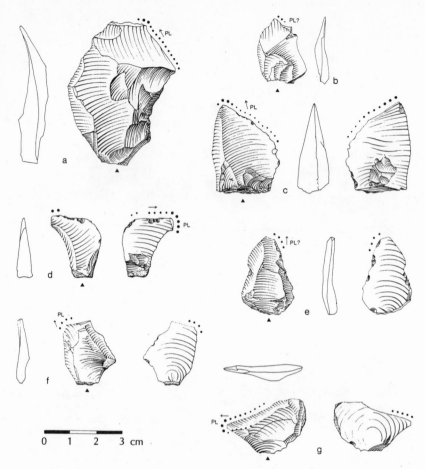

Figure 9. Tools from the late Neolithic site of Hekelingen III, employed in the splitting of plants.

inadequate, because rare tasks are not represented.

It is unfortunate that no contemporaneous assemblages have yet been studied for traces of wear. It is therefore difficult to put into context the results obtained on the Vlaardingen material. This would be especially appropriate as the raw material used at Hekelingen III and Vlaardingen seems to derive from an unknown southern source (determination by L. B. M. Verhart). The presence of southern flint on these coastal sites indicates contact or, more likely, actual movement of 'southerners' (for example, in the context of special-purpose trips). Interestingly enough, at Leidschendam the people made use of rolled pebbles for the production of their tools. It can be argued that Leidschendam was inhabited on a more permanent basis than Hekelingen III (Van Gijn 1990a; 1990b). This interpretation is supported by the fact that the Leidschendam implements exhibit much more wear than those from Hekelingen III. Concerning the relationship between tool type and tool function, this invariably turns out to be a rather loose one in the late Neolithic assemblages studied so far: the functional edge was considered of prime importance rather than the shape of the entire tool.

CONCLUSION

In the preceding pages I have tried to provide an overview of craft activities in the Dutch Neolithic as evidenced by the wear traces on flint implements. I have to admit that a straightforward division between subsistence and craft activities can hardly be made, because many of the above mentioned craft activities were directed at the production of objects related to subsistence, such as fish traps. However, other evidence for craft, such as some of the mysterious 'plant-polishes', may indeed be related to non-subsistence tasks such as fibre-making for clothing.

What does the above overview tell us? First, the way people used stone tools clearly changes from early to late Neolithic and indicates a shift in attitude towards flint as a raw material. In the early Neolithic flint tools are still very standardised (De Grooth 1987) and produced according to a fixed set of rules. There is, moreover, a close relationship between the morphology of the entire tool and the use to which it was put. For example, virtually all the scrapers in Bandkeramic assemblages are used for hide-working. Towards the end of the Neolithic the relationship between type and function becomes a looser one. Instead of being preoccupied with overall shape, people simply selected usable edges. It is remarkable that many craft activities, such as the splitting of plants for basketry or the manufacture of bone awls, were performed with unretouched tools, often small, irregular flakes.

Another change in attitude is presented by the fact that the implements are less intensively used; whereas many LBK scrapers were virtually exhausted by the time they were discarded, this is almost never the case with late Neolithic scrapers. The scrapers from Leidschendam are an exception. The reason for their intensive use must lie in the role of this particular site within the settlement pattern: the place was occupied over a long period of time. This change cannot be explained by an alleged difference in accessibility of suitable raw material.

On the contrary, the LBK people had easy access to good quality Rijck-holt flint; although this may not have been the case towards the end of the Bandkeramic when the amount of imported flint seems to increase and people relied to a greater extent on Valkenburg flint. Yet during the period of the Michelsberg culture the Rijckholt flint mine was in operation. There was no reason to be frugal with flint. If anything, the supply of good quality flint was probably less dependable during the late Neolithic, than during the preceding periods.

What this shift in behaviour towards flint means is difficult to say, especially with respect to the problems of separating stylistic and functional attributes (Sackett 1986). It is obvious, however, that the shape of the total flint implement, and not just the morphology of the functional edge, was significant for early and middle Neolithic societies. For later Neolithic people the functional edge and its characteristics (e.g. edge angle, curvature etc.) were primarily important, regardless of the technological support and its finishing. Could this mean that flint tools were becoming 'more functional' as time went on? Toward the end of the Neolithic and in the succeeding Bronze Age a dichotomy develops between the flint grave-goods, highly standardised and often beautifully finished implements, and the general settlement finds; only a few flint categories from the settlements such as the points, knives, and axes, display an investment of time and effort of the flint knapper. This diminished 'attention' may suggest a different attitude to flint. Another possibility, following Gero's (1991) assumption that women were involved in the production and use of expedient implements, is that women were participating more frequently than before, in activities with flint tools, notably craft activities such as bone awl making. It is especially for such tasks that unretouched implements were used in the late Neolithic context. Evidently, it still served a purpose and there was still a right way of doing things, but this was not determined by the overall shape of the implement. Maybe care and effort were put into other aspects of the material inventory, such as the manufacture of finely retouched grave-goods, like the Sögel points of the Bronze Age, or the shaping and decoration of pottery.

The inventory of craft activities also seems to confirm the idea of two traditions, a Danubian and a Maglemose, within the spatial confines of the Netherlands. Along the coast we find the descendants of the earlier hunter-gatherers, producing artefacts such as fish traps, bone implements, and so forth which reflect traditions going back to the Mesolithic. On the other hand, in the southern and eastern parts of the Netherlands material culture traditions derive from people much further east. In the coastal zones we can observe a continuity through time in the choice of implements. There is an emphasis on easily available rolled flint pebbles for the production of small flakes and blades; these are frequently used without prior retouch. The users selected a proper edge for a task, whereas the remainder of the tool was not considered important. The implements were generally used in an expedient fashion, being rejected upon completion of the task at hand; seldom do we find heavily used tools.

By contrast, flint implements from the inland areas are much more standardised. Instead of haphazard flaking, one adhered to a fixed reduction sequence; moreover, the supports were frequently retouched. There is also a strong correlation between tool type and tool use (see Van Gijn 1990a for examples from Bandkeramic context, Schreurs in press for the Michelsberg situation). Interestingly enough, in the middle Neolithic coastal sites of Brandwijk-Het Kerkhof and the Hazendonk we find standardised Rijckholt implements and tools made from rolled pebbles side by side. The presence of two lithic traditions on one site certainly indicates that contact between the coastal zones and the inland area was established during this period.

We can also observe differences between coastal and inland people in the kind of craft activities carried out. In the coastal zones a continuity in bone-working with flint tools can be observed from the middle to the late Neolithic; it is even highly likely that the techniques employed have their roots in the late Mesolithic. This cannot be substantiated because so far Mesolithic sites are lacking in this area due to the presence of extensive Holocene deposits. The finds dredged from the Bruine Bank and Europoort indicate that the technology of bone working was well developed. Whether the techniques employed in the late Mesolithic are the same as those applied during the Neolithic is as yet impossible to determine. In contrast, LBK communities did not have the sophisticated bone-working technology and only incidentally made use of flint tools for making bone objects. Only with the Michelsberg culture do we start to observe wear traces from bone-working on the flint implements in the south-east of the Netherlands on a more systematic basis.

Another typical coastal activity is the processing of reeds and cat's-tail. Although reeds and other silicious plants could certainly be found in quantity along the streams of the south-east, they were not collected and processed with the aid of flint tools. It may even be that these plants were not used at all, but obviously this cannot be substantiated by lithic research. On the other hand, typical inland activities caused

[347]

polish '10' and '23'. These traces do occur at Brandwijk and the Hazendonk, but only on Rijckholt flint which, of course, is 'imported'.

This chapter intends to contribute to a better understanding of the social identity of the various groups involved in the transformation of society in the course of the Neolithic. Indeed, it could be observed that the patterns of technological choices prevailing in the coastal zones differed from those in the south-eastern part of the Netherlands. Only during the Michelsberg period can we observe a convergence in technological choices from the Hazendonk and Brandwijk, where we have the earliest evidence for contact between the coastal and the inland zones. A crucial, but unfortunately still open, question is whether these sites represent the onset of an acceptance of the 'Neolithic way of life' by coastal people, or whether they reflect the incorporation of the coastal zones into the settlement system of the Michelsberg culture. Nevertheless, it would be tempting to postulate a demise of the Danubian tradition in favour of the Maglemose one. From a lithic point of view, however, the arguments for such a postulation are slight; the appearance of bone-working tools in the Michelsberg period would be one. Complicating the issue are the changes in attitude towards flint taking place through time: in the course of the Neolithic we can observe a breakdown of the links between particular tool types and specific tasks. Separating these changes from synchronic cultural differences is, presently, very difficult. Research on flint assemblages from late Neolithic inland sites is a prerequisite for differentiating between 'the patterns and the processes', at least from a lithic standpoint.

ACKNOWLEDGEMENTS

Jose Schreurs (Institute of Prehistory, Leiden University) provided access to unpublished data. I thank her and Jos Deeben (Archaeological Institute, Amsterdam University) for their comments on an earlier draft of this paper. Henk de Lorm (Institute of Prehistory, Leiden University) drew Figures 1, 7, and 9, Leo Verhart (Rijksmuseum voor Oudheden, Leiden) drew Figures 4 and 6. Jan Pauptit (Institute of Prehistory, Leiden University) printed the photographs.

BIBLIOGRAPHY

Bakels, C. C. 1978. *Four Linearbandkeramik settlements and their environment. A palaeoecological study of Sittard, Stein, Elsloo and Hienheim.* (Analecta Praehistorica Leidensia 11.)

Bakels, C. C. 1988. Hekelingen, a Neolithic site in the swamps of the Maas estuary. In *Der prähistorische Mensch und seine Umwelt. Festschrift fur Udelgard Körber-Grohne*, pp. 155–162. Stuttgart.

Bakels, C. C. & Rouselle, R. 1985. Restes botaniques et agriculture du Néolithique ancien en Belgique et aux Pays-Bas. *Helinium* 25: 37–57.

Bienenfeld, P. F. 1985. Preliminary results from a lithic use-wear study of Swifterbant sites S-51, S-4 and S-2. *Helinium* 25: 194–211.

Bienenfeld, P. F. 1986. Stone Tool Use at Five Neolithic Sites in the Netherlands: a lithic use-wear analysis. Thesis Binghamton.

Bienenfeld, P. F. 1989. Use wear analysis of the Gassel flint assemblage. *Oudheidkundige Mededelingen uit het Rijksmuseum van Oudheden te Leiden* 69: 111–117.

van den Broeke, P. W. 1983. Neolithic bone and antler objects from the Hazendonk near Molenaarsgraaf (prov. South Holland). *Oudheidkundige Mededelingen uit het Rijksmuseum van Oudheden te Leiden* 64: 163–195.

Cahen, D., Caspar, J. P. & Otte, M. 1986. *Industries lithiques danubiennes de Belgique*. Liège (ERAUL, 21).

Caspar, J.-P. 1985. Etude tracéologique de l'industrie de silex du village rubané de Darion. *Bulletin de la Société Royale Belge Anthropologique et Préhistorique* 96: 49–74.

Caspar, J. P. 1988. Contribution a la tracéologie de l'industrie lithique du Néolithique ancien dans l'Europe Nord-Occidentale. Thesis, Louvain-la-Neuve.

Cross, J. R. 1983. Twigs, branches, trees, and forests: problems of scale in lithic analysis. In Moore, J. A. & Keene, A. S. (eds), *Archaeological Hammers and Theories*, pp. 87–106. New York: Academic Press.

Deckers, P. H., de Roever, J. P. & van der Waals, J. D. 1980. Jagers, vissers en boeren in een prehistorisch getijdengebied bij Swifterbant. *ZWO Jaarboek* 111–145.

Flamman, J. 1990. Gebruikssporenanalyse: herkennen, interpreteren en reconstrueren. Een analyse van vuursteenartefacten uit de LBK-nederzetting Elsloo. Leiden, internal report.

Gero, J. M. 1991. Genderlithics: women's roles in stone tool production. In Gero, J. M. & M. W. Conkey (eds), *Engendering Archaeology: Women and Prehistory*, pp. 163–193. Oxford: Basil Blackwell.

van Gijn, A. L. 1984. Preliminary report of the microwear analysis of the flint of Vlaardingen 11, Leidschendam 4 and Voorschoten 17. Amsterdam, internal report.

van Gijn, A. L. 1990a. *The Wear and Tear of Flint. Principles of functional analysis applied to Dutch Neolithic assemblages*. (Analecta Praehistorica Leidensia 22, formerly Leiden University Thesis).

van Gijn, A. L. 1990b. Functional differentiation of late Neolithic settlements in the Dutch coastal area. In Graslund, B. (ed), *The Interpretive Possibilities of Microwear Analysis*, pp. 77–88. Uppsala: Societas Archaeologica Upsaliensis.

van Gijn, A. L. & Verbruggen, M. 1991. *Brandwijk, Het Kerkhof*. Archeologische Kroniek van Holland.

Gronenborn, D. 1989. Neue Überlegungen zur Funktion von Schlitzgruben. *Archäologisches Korrespondenzblatt* 19: 339–343.

de Grooth, M. E. Th. 1987. The organisation of flint tool manufacture in the Dutch Bandkeramik. *Analecta Praehistorica Leidensia* 20: 27–52.

Hayden, B. 1993. Investigating status with hideworking use-wear: a preliminary assessment. In Anderson, P. C., Beyries, S., Otte, M. & Plisson, & H. (eds), *Traces et fonction: les gestes retrouvés*. vol. 1, pp. 119–130. Liège: ERAUL (50).

Ingold, T. 1990. Society, nature and the concept of technology. *Archaeological Review from Cambridge* 9: 5–17.

Juel Jensen, H. 1988. Microdenticulates in the Danish Stone Age: a functional puzzle. In Beyries, S. (ed.), *Industries lithiques; tracéologie et technologie*, pp. 231–252. Oxford: British Archaeological Reports (Int. Ser. 411, vol. 1).

Keeley, L. H. 1977. Beobachtungen über Mikro-Abnutzungsspuren an 14 Klingen von Hienheim. *Analecta Praehistorica Leidensia* 19: 71–72.

Lemonnier, P. 1986. The study of material culture today: toward an anthropology of technical systems. *Journal of Anthropological Archaeology* 5: 147–186.

Lemonnier, P. 1990. Topsy turvy techniques. Remarks on the social representation of techniques. *Archaeological Review from Cambridge* 9: 27–37.

Louwe Kooijmans, L. P. 1983. Tussen SOM en TRB, enige gedachten over het Laat-Neolithicum in Nederland en Belgie. *Bulletin van de Koninklijke Musea voor Kunst en Geschiedenis* 54: 55–67.

Louwe Kooijmans, L. P. 1985. *Sporen in het land*. Amsterdam: Meulenhoff.

Louwe Kooijmans, L. P. 1991. An early Bandkeramic settlement at Geleen-Janskamperveld (Netherlands). *Notae Praehistoricae* 11: 63–65.

Louwe Kooijmans, L. P. & Verhart, L. B. M. 1990. Een middenneolithisch nederzettingsterrein en een kuil van de Stein-groep op de voormalige Kraaienberg bij Linden, Gemeente Beers (N.-Br.). *Oudheidkundige Mededelingen van het Rijksmuseum voor Oudheden te Leiden* 70: 49–108.

Maarleveld, Th. J. 1985. Been en tand als grondstof in de Vlaardingen-cultuur. Leiden, internal report.

Newcomer, M. H., Grace, R. & Unger-Hamilton, R. 1986. Investigating microwear polishes with blind tests. *Journal of Archaeological Science* 13: 203–218.

Newell, R. R. 1973. The postglacial adaptations of the indigenous population of the Northwest European Plain. In Kozlowski, S. K. (ed.), *The Mesolithic in Europe*, pp. 399–440. Warsaw.

Sackett, J. R. 1986. Isochrestism and style: a clarification. *Journal of Anthropological Archaeology* 8: 266–277.

Schreurs, J. 1988. Een gebruikssporen analyse van de vuursteen artefacten uit de Bandkeramische nederzetting te Elsloo. Leiden, internal report.

Schreurs, J. in press. The Michelsberg-site Maastricht-Klinkers: a functional interpretation. *Analecta Praehistorica Leidensia* 25.

Stambolov, T. 1969. Manufacture, deterioration and preservation of leather. A literature survey of theoretical aspects and ancient techniques Amsterdam.

Unrath, G., Owen, L. R., van Gijn, A. L., Moss, E. H. & Plisson, H. 1986. An evaluation of microwear studies: a multi-analyst approach. In Owen, L. R. & G. Unrath (eds), *Technical Aspects of Microwear Studies on Stone Tools*. Tübingen: *Early Man News* 9/10/11, 117–176.

van de Velde, P. 1973. Rituals, skins and Homer: the Danubian 'tan-pits'. *Analecta Praehistorica Leidensia* 6: 50–59.

Verhart L. B. M. & Louwe Kooijmans, L. P. 1989. Een Midden-Neolithische nederzetting bij Gassel, Gemeente Beers (N.-Br.). *Oudheidkundige Mededelingen uit het Rijksmuseum van Oudheden te Leiden* 69: 75–111.

16

The Flint Mines at Rijckholt-Sint Geertruid and Their Socio-economic Interpretation

Marjorie de Grooth

In *recent years* European Neolithic flint mining has been a major topic at several international symposia (Birò 1986; 1987; Bustillo & Ramos Millan 1991; Engelen 1971; 1976; 1981; Séronie-Vivien & Lenoir 1990; Sieveking & Newcomer 1987; Weisgerber et al. 1980). The vast majority of the papers presented at these symposia were devoted to the technical aspects of mining itself, to its geological setting, or to the scientific identification of the types of silex/flint exploited. Considerably less attention was paid to the process of manufacturing tools, to the ways these were distributed or to the socio-economic framework of exploitation.

Although the overall number is relatively small, the few articles which mention organisational and socio-economic aspects of flint mining and tool manufacture tend to revolve around common themes and assumptions. Mining is depicted as a large-scale, highly organised activity, performed by specialists/professionals. The outcrops are considered to be owned and controlled by specialised mining communities, and exploitation is assumed to have been conducted on a year-round basis (or at least for a considerable part of the year). It is also commonly assumed that mining and production were geared towards a maximum output. The manufacture of semi-finished tools was highly standardised, and these products were traded 'ex works' to eager customers, offering among other things essential foodstuffs, pottery, furs, or beads in exchange. This exchange took place in a purely economic context, and the artefacts were of utilitarian value only (Albers & Felder 1980; Borkowski et al. 1991; Bosch 1979; Engelhardt & Binsteiner 1988; Felder & Offenberg 1990; Hubert 1980; Weiner 1986; 1989).

In effect, the majority of existing accounts of European flint mining (be it at Spiennes, the Lousberg, Rijckholt, or Abensberg-Arnhofen and Krzemionki) depict it as a commercial enterprise, strongly resembling the French and English gun-flint industries of the eighteenth and nineteenth centuries. Thus they project onto the past a series of conceptions of the economy that have their roots in modern western culture, superficially antiquated by the use of barter as the exchange mechanism. All these accounts are based exclusively on the interpretation of data from mining sites and do not consider the position of flint mining within a broader socio-cultural framework. Integrated approaches, such as that proposed by Ericson (1984) and practised by Torrence in her study of Mediterranean obsidian industries (1984; 1986), are all but absent. Only rarely are quarrying and the manufacture and use of stone tools seen as dynamic processes involving not only the producers but also the distributors and consumers.

These conceptual problems are highlighted by the marked discrepancy between prevailing archaeological interpretations and the few ethnographic accounts of deep-shaft quarrying and stone tool production in societies with a comparable level of technology and socio-economic integration. For example, in the small sample of New Guinean and Australian Aboriginal societies where quarrying and stone working were ethnographically documented, these were never continuous activities, performed by professionals. The ownership of resources and quarries was extremely varied (de Grooth in press; Torrence 1986). Even where resources were recognised as the property of a special group, outsiders could generally acquire permission to use them, for example by the establishment of an alliance relationship of some sort (Dalton 1981). Moreover, in the societies under consideration, stone tools were seldom produced solely to satisfy practical demands. Rather, production was often driven by the roles that certain objects played in exchange, where patterns of circulation served to mediate kinship ties, socio-political alliances, or ritual obligations. As an alternative to the prevailing 'commercial trading model' (McBryde 1986), I have tried to analyze the production and distribution of flint from the well-known deep shaft-and-gallery mines at Rijckholt with

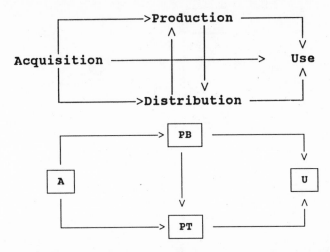

Figure 1. General model for archaeological inferences about prehistoric exchange (after Torrence 1986) (above) and a general model for archaeological inferences about the production of stone tools (below). A: acquisition; PB: production of blanks; PT: production of tools; U: use; arrows indicate possible transport.

the help of a model based on the ethnographic accounts summarised above (a full account of this study can be found in de Grooth 1991).

BUILDING A MODEL FOR EXPLOITATION AND DISTRIBUTION

In this model, prehistoric flint mining and the distribution of mined products are not regarded as autonomous economic activities, but as practices which were fully embedded within kinship, or religious or political relations (Godelier 1986). Equally, it is assumed that the significance of certain flint mine products may have extended beyond their practical application in subsistence, to encompass a variety of social roles (McBryde 1986; McBryde & Harrison 1981). No *a priori* assumptions on the nature of access to resources are made, and the mere presence of deep shafts-and-galleries is not considered 'a *sufficient* criterion from which to infer the existence of a complex economic or socio-political organization' (Torrence 1986: 59). Nor can we take these features as definitive evidence for the operation of large-scale workforces. It is quite likely that the groups involved may have been relatively small, although periodic aggregations in the context of some sort of inter-group gathering should not be ruled out.

The first step is the development of a framework for the drawing of

[353]

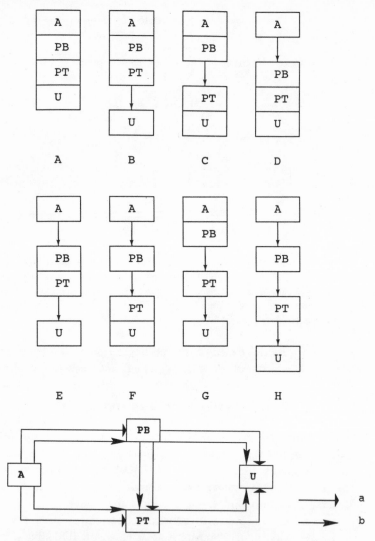

Figure 2. Initial set of specific models for archaeological inferences about the production of stone tools (above) and revised model for archaeological inferences about the acquisition and production of stone tools, distinguishing within-group and between-group transport (below). A: acquisition; PB: production of blanks; PT: production of tools; U: use; a: within-group transport; b: between-group transport.

general inferences concerning the organisation of lithic production and distribution. Robin Torrence's (1986) 'general model for archaeological inferences about prehistoric exchange' provided a suitable starting

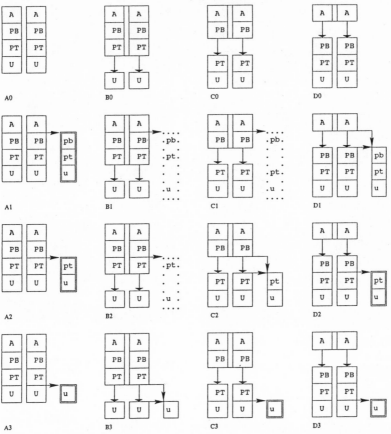

Figure 3. Specific models for the acquisition and production of stone tools, allowing for transport at different stages in the production process, and distinguishing within-group and between-group transport. Double frame: situations where flint assemblages in 'consumer' settlements would differ in quantitave terms from those in 'producer' settlements. Single cadre: situations where only qualitative differences would exist between flint assemblages in 'consumer' and 'producer' settlements. Stippled cadre: ambiguous situations (for general key see Fig. 2).

point (Fig. 1, top). However, in order to obtain more specific models, better suited to present research purposes, a number of modifications were necessary. Firstly, both archaeological and ethnographic data alike show that flint artefacts were often transported not only after the acquisition and first testing of the raw material, or as finished tools, but also halfway through the reduction sequence, i.e. as prepared cores, blanks or rough-outs. Therefore 'production' was subdivided into two

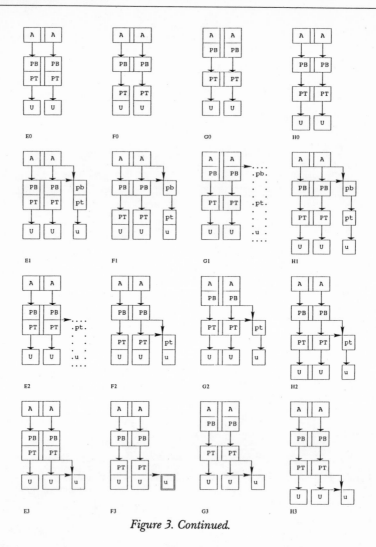

Figure 3. Continued.

separate activities, 'production of blanks' and 'production of finished tools'. 'Transport' was possible after every stage (Fig. 1, bottom).

Secondly, the different spatial relationships between these sets of activities had to be taken into account, giving a total of eight possible combinations (Fig. 2, top). (In model A, the miners live at the quarry site, and perform all activities there. Model D depicts transport of selected, unworked raw material to settlements, where blanks and tools are made and used. etc.) With the exception of F and H all these models can be matched with actual ethnographic or archaeological *distribution patterns* (De Grooth 1994). In this form, however, they cannot be used as heuristic devices to determine the *distribution mechanism*, i.e. to distinguish between direct and indirect supply, or in other terms, between open access to resources and restricted access followed by some form of exchange.

For many researchers this would seem to be a purely academic question. More often than not, we tend to exclude *a priori* the possibility of long-distance expeditions to resources when dealing with sedentary communities, regarding every long-distance transport of goods as evidence of exchange *per se*. This is, however, something that has to be demonstrated rather than assumed as a first principle. As pointed out by Hodder (1984) and Torrence (1986), the act of exchange itself would never result in material remains that could be recovered from the archaeological record, but can at best be inferred indirectly. Therefore, as a final step in modelling, 'distribution' had to be subdivided into two distinct activities, labelled (as neutrally as possible) 'within-group transport' and 'between-group transport' respectively (Fig. 2, bottom). When these two types of transport are added as a possibility after each of the three stages of acquisition and manufacture, each of the main models becomes subdivided into four sub-models, depicting the different moments of between-group transport (Fig. 3). In this set of thirty-two sub-models there are, in essence, no restrictions to the number of participating groups. That is to say, the rights of access to a resource can be shared by a number of groups of 'producers', and these may each supply several groups of 'consumers'.

The M0 version represents the situation without exchange, where all groups participating in the system share open access to the resource. In the M1 sub-models, the between-group transport takes place after the acquisition and first selection of raw material, in the M2 set we find between-group transport after the stage of blank and pre-form production, and in the M3 variant finished tools are transported.

Unfortunately, these models do not serve as an easy-to-use manual, enabling us to detect evidence of restricted access and exchange in our data in an unequivocal manner. Statements about direct versus indirect supply can only be made when all elements in the system are taken into consideration, and when suspected 'producer' and 'consumer' settlements can be compared on equal terms. Even then, the difference between direct and indirect supply would manifest itself only in a few cases as qualitative differences in the flint assemblages of sites with and without open access to resources. There are only a few sub-models where producers and consumers would actually perform different tasks and thus discard different types of rubbish. These situations are highlighted in Figure 3 with double frames.

In other cases, the pattern would be so complicated as to be virtually uninterpretable in archaeological terms (the stippled lines in Fig. 3). Mostly, however, groups with restricted and unrestricted access to sources would execute exactly the same parts of the reduction sequence in their respective settlements and/or workshops, and thus produce exactly the same type of debris (indicated with single frames in Fig. 3). In those cases, any inference about the type of transport would have to be based on the assumption that the supposed suppliers, because of their easier access to resources, worked and used more flint than did the dependent consumers. In other words, it must be assumed that one may regard differences in the abundance of a resource as sufficient evidence for differences in the access to the means of production, and therefore indirectly as evidence for exchange.

Even if one accepts this assumption (as has been done in the models, by indicating the activities of consumers with smaller symbols), one has to make sure that equal standards of recovery apply to all the sites under study (Torrence 1986), or alternatively, one must calibrate the data in such a way that the bias is controlled. In doing so, one must account for differences in excavation and sampling methods, in post-depositional processes, and in former settlement structure or duration and intensity of habitation. Obviously, this kind of standardisation is rather difficult to achieve in archaeological practice.

From the models it is also evident that in many cases of between-group transport one will be unable to decide whether the goods (be it unworked raw material, blanks, rough-outs, or finished tools) were transported directly from the quarry to the user's settlements or via some intermediate location (e.g. the producers' settlements or a 'central place' where systematic – ceremonial? – exchange took place), because these different mechanisms would not leave different traces in archaeological record.

In sum, the models confirm that well-founded interpretations of flint procurement systems cannot be based on the study of a single settlement or extraction point, but must integrate data from different types of sites.

RIJCKHOLT-SINT GEERTRUID

The main information on the mining complex situated between Rijckholt and Sint Geertruid in the Dutch province of Limburg (Fig. 4) was provided through the extensive underground excavations untertaken

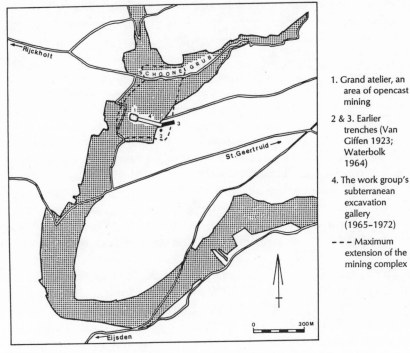

1. Grand atelier, an area of opencast mining

2 & 3. Earlier trenches (Van Giffen 1923; Waterbolk 1964)

4. The work group's subterranean excavation gallery (1965–1972)

− − − Maximum extension of the mining complex

Figure 4. The Rijckholt-Sint Geertruid area (revised from Clason 1971 & Engelen 1980).

between 1964 and 1972 by the 'Work-group for Prehistoric Flint Mining' (initiated by a group of amateur geologists and archaeologists, who were mining engineers by profession), driving a modern tunnel (at their leisure!) for over 150 meters through the mining complex, an achievement only made possible by their professional mining expertise (Bosch 1979; Bosch & Felder 1990; Engelen 1980; Felder 1980). In their subterranean excavation of 3000 square meters seventy-three mines of the deep shaft-and-gallery type were discovered. Owing to the west-east dip of the flint bank, the shafts vary in depth from between two and three metres close to the valley slope in the west to sixteen metres at the eastern limit of the excavation (Bosch 1979). On the basis of the density of shafts in the excavated area it has been estimated that the complete complex consisted of approximately 5000 mines (Bosch & Felder 1990).

Dense concentrations of production waste are found in the topsoil all over the mining complex. They show that robust blades (with an average width of 20–30 mm), massive flake scrapers, and rough-outs

Table 1. Rijckholt Radiocarbon dates (after Bosch & Felder 1990).

GrN 4544	5070 ± 60 BP	(gallery between shaft 3 and 4)
GrN 5549	5000 ± 40 BP	(fill of shaft 23)
GrN 5962	5090 ± 40 BP	(fill of shaft 19)
GrN 9085	5080 ± 45 BP	(fill of shaft 67; floor Grand atelier)
GrN 9058	5065 ± 45 BP	(antler pick shaft 67; floor Grand atelier)

for axes with an oval cross-section were the main types produced on the site. No clear traces of settlements have been discovered at the mining complex itself. Surface scatters of polished flint axes, arrowheads, and other 'domestic' flint implements, as well as querns are known from several sites in the immediate vicinity, but similar find patterns occur on the middle and lower terraces of the river Meuse from at least as far away as Eijsden in the south to Maastricht-Wijck in the north.

The five radio-carbon dates available for the Rijckholt mines cluster around 3800 BC (Table 1). Tools made of mined Rijckholt flint occur, however, not only in settlements assignable to the Michelsberg culture (and its local Dutch facies the Hazendonk group), but also to the subsequent Vlaardingen/Stein/Wartberg complex, indicating that mining activities may have lasted for at least 900, but probably even 1300 years (between 3900 and 2600 BC). This idea is supported by the single sherd recovered from a shaft filling, which belongs to the Stein group (Louwe Kooijmans & Verhart 1990). Artefacts were distributed over a large area, comprising the Limburg Meuse valley, the Dutch Eastern river area, the Rhineland, and even Westphalia and Hesse (Fig. 5). Mined flint was used in the Dutch western river area and the coastal area as well. We are as yet unable to decide whether it originates from Rijckholt or from the Spiennes mine in southern Belgium. These areas, therefore, were not included in the present study.

Given the estimated maximum of 5000 shafts and 1300 years of mining, on average only four shafts a year would have been exploited. As 90–105 person-days were needed to work the average mine, the average yearly work load for mining would have amounted to 360–420 person-days (estimates based on Felder 1980). These figures, of course, reveal nothing about the size of the labour force or the actual time spent on mining. On the one hand we can imagine a three-person team working for 120–140 days (which would mean almost full-time, if we take into account the considerable time needed for artefact manufacture as well). Increasing the number of people involved

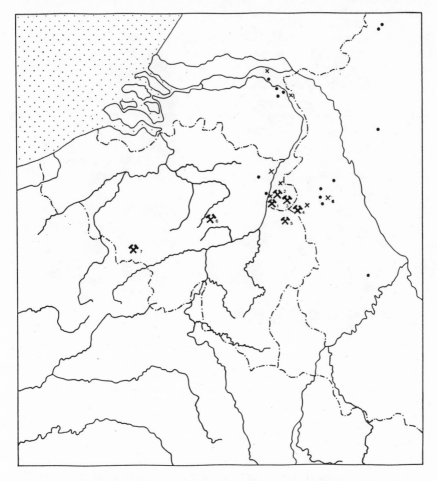

Figure 5. Neolithic flint mines (crossed hammers), Michelsberg/Hazendonk sites with Rijckholt flint (dots) and Vlaardingen/Stein sites with Rijckholt flint (crosses). 1. Rijckholt-Sint Geertruid; 2. Valkenburg; 3. Simpelveld; 4. Lousberg; 5. Rullen; 6. Jandrain-Jandrenouille; 7. Spiennes and Petit Spiennes.

would automatically lead to a corresponding decrease in the amount of time needed. If, for example, four teams worked simultaneously, the job could be done in about a month (either by members of a single large community or by four different groups). On the basis of the data available at the moment, no reliable choice can be made between these possibilities. However, whichever way one looks at it, production certainly need not be regarded as having been large scale.

Figure 6. Two conjoinable parts of a rough-out for a flint axe with an oval cross section broken when nearly finished, from Rijckholt-Sint Geertruid (left) (Collection Bonnefantenmuseum Maastricht) and three conjoinable robust blades of Rijckholt flint, from Linden-Kraaienberg (Collection Rijksmuseum van Oudheden Leiden) (both 1:2).

DISCUSSION

The data on the exploitation and distribution of Rijckholt flint are, generally speaking, compatible with model C. There are no traces of permanent settlement directly connected with the mines. The majority of material was transported from the mines as semi-finished axes (Fig. 6, left) and unretouched flakes and blades to be finished and used elsewhere. No large blade cores and little or no waste by-products are found at the corresponding settlement sites, either in the immediate vicinity or farther afield.

Thus, the organisation differs markedly from that prevailing in Bandkeramik times, where the exploitation all over central and western Europe is best described by model D (in which raw material is only tested at the extraction site, and worked in permanent settlements in the wider region, blades and tools subsequently being distributed over very wide areas. This situation is not restricted to the Rhine/Meuse region (Cahen et al. 1986; De Grooth 1987; Zimmermann 1982; 1991). Similar patterns have been recognised in Bavaria (Engelhardt & Binsteiner 1988; De Grooth 1994; in press), and Poland (Kaczanowska & Lech 1977; Lech 1987; 1989).

The next step in the analysis would be to decide which of the relevant sub-models best fits with the data: C0 (no exchange/open access to mines), C2 (exchange after the production of blanks), or C3 (exchange of finished products). The repeated occurrence of unretouched blades at sites far from the mines, such as Linden-Kraaienberg in the Dutch river area (Louwe Kooijmans & Verhart 1990; Fig. 6, right), shows that goods were certainly not distributed exclusively according to model C3. The choice between the variations C0 and C2 must be based in the first place on a quantitative analysis of flint assemblages in the settlement sites under consideration, searching for a recurring pattern of differences in the relative abundance of mined flint. As most of these sites are known only from surface scatters sampled in different ways by many different archaeologists, it is virtually impossible at present to adjust the data for bias. As a result, it is currently impossible to draw reliable quantitative comparisons between their respective flint assemblages.

An assessment of the general character of settlement structure and subsistence strategies of Michelsberg/Hazendonk and Vlaardingen/Stein people may, however, provide part of the answer on a macroregional level. The available evidence shows that during both the Michelsberg/Hazendonk and the Vlaardingen/Stein periods, different subsistence strategies co-existed. In the Dutch coastal and river regions, many sites are thought to represent periodic visits of people familiar with agriculture, but none the less retaining a partial dependence on the exploitation of wild resources (Van Gijn 1990; Louwe Kooijmans & Verhart 1990). The Michelsberg culture on the sandy soils in the Meuse valley can also be regarded as a relatively mobile society (Wansleeben & Verhart 1990). The same should hold true for the Vlaardingen/Stein sites in this area. Michelsberg habitation in the loess zones of Belgium, Dutch Limburg and the Rhineland is thought to have been fully agricultural in character (Bakels in press; Vermeersch 1987–1988). Its archaeological remains are only seemingly more complete than those of the other regions, because of the presence not only of flint mines but also of a number of large causewayed enclosures, one of them possibly situated eight kilometres to the north-west of Rijckholt, on the other bank of the river Meuse (Disch 1969; 1971–72). There is, however, little evidence for substantial houses, and few traces of local crop cultivation or large-scale grazing are visible in pollen diagrams (Bakels 1993). The Stein group seems to have had a much stronger impact on its environment, as documented by recent pollen evidence from the Maastricht-Randwijck site showing heavy deforestation (Bakels pers. comm.; Bakels et al. in press), but actual traces of habitation are as insubstantial as they are for Michelsberg contexts.

For the enclosures, a number of different functions have been proposed, such as defensive structures controlling resources, corrals, or central places for social or ritual inter-group meetings (Burgess et al. 1988). Although some of them are associated with settlement debris, habitation seems not to have been their primary function. There is no conclusive evidence for year-round habitation (Bakels pers. comm., and in press; Clason 1971; 1981).

Whatever their function, the Michelsberg enclosures clearly indicate that Michelsberg settlements were not always dispersed and that substantial groups came together at least occasionally. Moreover, the people responsible for building them were clearly able to organise large work parties co-operating for a considerable amount of time. In one case, the amount of labour involved was estimated at over 2000 person-hours (Vermeersch 1987–88, 9). This means that one hundred people could have performed this task working continuously for three weeks, and fifty people would have needed at least six weeks to do the job. The earthworks evidently played some kind of central role in Michelsberg society. They seem to reflect a rather strong sense of territoriality (Fleming 1982), a notion supported by the presence of distinct regional pottery styles and subsistence strategies within both the Michelsberg culture and the Vlaardingen/Stein/Wartberg/Seine-Oise-Marne) groups. In such a situation, it would be extremely unlikely that groups not belonging to the regional socio-economic polity would have had unrestricted access to high-quality resources. The reasonable conclusion is that artefacts made from mined Rijckholt flint were distributed by means of between-group transport (in accordance with model C2) on a macro-regional level. It must be stressed, however, that at all times, exchange partners received flint from other sources as well.

As the next step in the analysis, the question of rights of access to the mines has to be studied at the micro-regional level. The data relevant to this question can be summarised in the following points.

1. No indications of permanent settlement were found at the mines themselves.
2. There is no positive evidence of some sort of control over the resources.
3. Production does not appear to have been undertaken on a large-scale basis.
4. While the miners and knappers may certainly be regarded as highly skilled, there is no reason to assume that they were full-time, professional specialists.
5. The settlement debris collected close to the mining area does not differ from material found elsewhere in the region.
6. Assemblages from these settlements reflect the use of a high percentage of local flint which was not derived from the Rijckholt mines; long regular blades are surprisingly rare.
7. The assemblages from many of these settlements contain quite a few polished axes and some blade tools (*Spitzklingen*) of non-local origin.
8. 'Consumers' outside the region obtained artefacts from other sources as well.

In my view these points all argue against the idea of one single community vested with mining rights in either the 'commercial' or the ethnographic sense. They support the alternative interpretation of un-restricted access to the quarries for members of several small com-munities living nearby. These miners did not live permanently at the mines, but settled there periodically in temporary extraction camps. The groups may be conceptualised as having lived within a radius of thirty kilometres, i.e. within a six-hour walking distance of Rijckholt. In other words, it is useful to regard them as groups in whose common home range (Bakels 1978: 5) the source of raw material was situated.

The last two points also suggest that mining at Rijckholt was an intermittent activity, not undertaken for purely economic or practical reasons, and that the exchange of mined products was often directed towards ceremonial/social purposes in a multi-directional network. This exchange almost certainly did not take place at the quarries, and we can only speculate on the role of the causewayed camps. The environment in the loess zones was rather less diversified than that in the river valley and coastal areas further to the north and north-west. Thus we can easily envisage a number of perishable goods that may have travelled to Rijckholt: salt, caviar, smoked herring and eels, seal skins and other furs. I sometimes wonder whether it would not have been primarily the miners that were eager to maintain the exchange networks as a means to obtain highly valued and desirable goods.

In conclusion, I feel the approach presented here will provide a fruit-ful basis for future interpretations, depicting not only the technological but even more the social, ceremonial, and symbolic aspects of mining. That said, we will have to think very carefully about the social context of distribution, considering the possibility that objects changed their meaning after passing from one context to another. Moreover, we must find ways to arrive at an understanding of the symbolic connota-tions of the act of digging deep holes into the earth itself – and so inte-grate the skull deposited without a mandible at the end of one of the galleries (Engelen 1980: 567) into the general picture.

ACKNOWLEDGEMENTS

I would like to thank Funs Horbach for preparing the drawings and Ger Hukkelhoven (Bonnefantenmuseum), Leo Verhart (Rijksmuseum Oudheden) for the photographs, and Diane Webb for improving the English text.

REFERENCES

Albers, H. J. & Felder, W. M. 1980. Die neolithische Abbautechnik vom Typ Aubel auf der Hochfläche der Limburger Kreidetafel als Konsequenz der postoligozänen Bildung einer Feuersteinresiduallagerstätte. In Weis-gerber, G., Slotta, R. & Weiner, J. (eds), *5000 Jahre Feuersteinbergbau. Die Suche nach dem Stahl der Steinzeit*, pp. 67–79. Bochum: Deutsches Bergbau Museum (Veröffentlichungen aus dem Deutschen Bergbau-Museum Bochum 22).

Bakels, C. C. 1978. *Four Linearbandkeramik Settlements and their Environment. A palaeoecological study of Sittard, Stein, Elsloo and Hienheim*. Leiden: Leiden University Press (Analecta Praehistorica Leidensia 11).

Bakels, C. C. in press. Plants and man in Neolithic Belgium. In Cahen, D., Langohr, R. & Van Berg P.-L. (eds), *Peuples agriculteurs de la Belgique préhistorique dans leur cadre naturel*. Bruxelles.

Bakels, C. C., Alkemade, M. J. & Vermeeren, C. E. 1993. Botanische Unter-suchungen in der Rössener Siedlung Maastricht-Randwijck, Nieder-lande. *Archäo-Physika* 13: 35–48.

Birò, K. (ed.) 1986. *Papers Presented to the First International Conference on Pre-historic Flint Mining and Lithic Raw Material Identification in the Carpathian Basin, Budapest-Sümeg, 20–22 May 1986*. Budapest: Magyar Nemzeti Museum.

Birò, K. (ed.) 1987. *Proceedings of the First International Conference on Prehistoric Flint Mining and Lithic Raw Material Identification in the Carpathian Basin, Budapest-Sümeg, 20–22 May 1986*. Budapest: Magyar Nemzeti Museum.

Borkowski, W., Migal, W., Sałaciński, S. & Zalewski, M. 1991. Possibilities of investigating Neolithic flint economies, as exemplified by the banded flint economy. *Antiquity* 65: 607–627.

Bosch, P. W. 1979. A Neolithic flint mine. *Scientific American* 240(6): 126–132.

Bosch, P. W. & Felder, W. M. 1990. Plan of Neolithic flint mines at Rijck-holt-St. Geertruid (The Netherlands). In Séronie-Vivien M.-R. & Lenoir, M. (eds), *Le silex de sa genèse à l'outil. Actes du Ve Colloque international sur le silex (Vth International Flint Symposium), Bordeaux, 17 sept.-2 oct. 1987,* pp. 251–261. Paris (Cahiers du Quaternaire n° 17).

Burgess, C., Topping, P., Mordant C. & Maddison, M. 1988. *Enclosures and Defences in the Neolithic of Western Europe.* Oxford: British Archaeological Reports (IS 403).

Bustillo, M. A. & Ramos Millan, M. 1991. *VI International Flint Symposium, Abstracts, Spain October 1991.* Madrid.

Cahen, D., Caspar J.-P. & Otte, M. 1986. *Industries lithiques danubiennes de Belgique.* Liège (Etudes et Recherches Archéologiques de l'Université de Liège 21).

Clason, A. T. 1971. The Flint-mine workers of Spiennes and Rijckholt-Sint Geertruid and their animals. *Helinium* 11: 3–33.

Clason, A. T. 1981. The flintminer as a farmer, hunter and antler collector. In Engelen, F. H. G. (ed.), *Proceedings of the Third International Symposium on Flint, 24–27 mei 1980 – Maastricht,* pp. 119–126. (Staringia 6).

Dalton, G. 1981. Anthropological models in archaeological perspective. In Hodder, I., Isaac, G. & Hammond, N. (eds), *Pattern of the Past. Studies in honour of David Clarke,* pp. 17–48. Cambridge: Cambridge Univ. Press.

Disch, A. 1969. A.C. Kengen over opgravingen te Caberg-Maastricht 1927–1933. *Jaaroverzicht 1969 Archeologische Werkgemeenschap Limburg,* 31–39.

Disch, A. 1971–1972. Pre- en protohistorische vondsten op de Caberg te Maas-tricht. *Jaaroverzicht 1971–1972 Archeologische Werkgemeenschap Limburg,* 33–48.

Engelen, F. H. G. (ed.) 1971. *First International Symposium on Flint, Maastricht 26–29 April 1969.* Maastricht (Grondboor en Hamer 3).

Engelen, F. H. G. (ed.) 1976. *Proceedings of the Second International Symposium on Flint, 8–11 mei 1975 – Maastricht.* (Staringia 3).

Engelen F. H. G. 1980. NL1 Rijckholt-St. Geertruid, Prov. Limburg. In Weis-gerber, G., Slotta, R. & Weiner, J. (eds), *5000 Jahre Feuersteinbergbau. Die Suche nach dem Stahl der Steinzeit,* pp. 559–567. Bochum: Deutsches Berg-bau Museum (Veröffentlichungen aus dem Deutschen Bergbau-Museum Bochum 22).

Engelen, F. H. G. (ed.) 1981. *Proceedings of the Third International Symposium on Flint, 24–27 mei 1979 – Maastricht.* (Staringia 6).

Engelhardt, B. & Binsteiner, A. 1988. Vorbericht über die Ausgrabungen 1984–1986 im neolithischen Feuerstein Abbaurevier von Arnhofen, Ldkr. Kelheim. *Germania* 66: 1–29.

Ericson, J. E. 1984. Towards the analysis of lithic production systems. In Eric-son, J. E. & Purdy, B. (eds), *Prehistoric Quarries and Lithic Production,* pp. 1–11. Cambridge: Cambridge University Press.

Felder P. J. 1980. Feuersteinbergbau in Rijckholt-St. Geertruid (NL1) und Grime's Graves (GB13) – ein Vergleich. In Weisgerber, G., Slotta, R. & Weiner, J. (eds), *5000 Jahre Feuersteinbergbau. Die Suche nach dem Stahl der Steinzeit,* pp. 120–124. Bochum: Deutsches Bergbau-Museum (Veröffent-lichungen aus dem Deutschen Bergbau-Museum Bochum 22).

Felder, P. J. & Offenberg, G. A. 1990. De vuursteenmijnen van Limburg. *Spiegel Historiael* 25: 360–365.

Fleming, A. 1982. Social boundaries and land boundaries. In Renfrew, C. & Shennan S. (eds), *Ranking, Resource and Exchange*, pp. 52–56. Cambridge: Cambridge University Press.

van Gijn, A. L. 1990. *The Wear and Tear of Flint: principles of functional analysis applied to Dutch Neolithic assemblages.* Leiden: Leiden University Press (Analecta Prehistorica Leidensia 22).

Godelier, M. 1986. *The Mental and the Material.* London and New York: Verso (original French edition, 1984, *L'idéel et le matériel*).

de Grooth, M. E. Th. 1987. The organization of flint tool manufacture in the Dutch Bandkeramik. *Analecta Praehistorica Leidensia* 20: 27–53.

de Grooth, M. E. Th. 1991. Socio-economic aspects of Neolithic flint mining: a preliminary study. *Helinium* 31: 153–190.

de Grooth, M. E. Th. 1994. Die Versorgung mit Silex in der bandkeramischen Siedlung Hienheim Am Weinberg (Ldkr. Kelheim) und die Organisation des Abbaus auf gebündelte Plattenhornsteine im Revier Arnhofen (Ldkr. Kelheim). *Germania* 72: 355–340.

de Grooth, M. E. Th. in press. The system of flint procurement at the Bandkeramik site of Hienheim (Ldkr. Kelheim, Bavaria). In *Proceedings of the Sixth International Symposium on Flint, Madrid October 1991.* Madrid.

Hodder, I. 1984. Archaeology in 1984. *Antiquity* 58: 25–32.

Hubert, F. 1980. Zum Silexbergbau von Spiennes (B1). In Weisgerber, G., Slotta, G. & Weiner, J. (eds), *5000 Jahre Feuersteinbergbau. Die Suche nach dem Stahl der Steinzeit*, pp. 124–141. Bochum: Deutsches Bergbau-Museum (Veröffentlichungen aus dem Deutschen Bergbau-Museum Bochum 22).

Kaczanowska, M. & Lech, J. 1977. The flint industries of Danubian communities north of the Carpathians. *Acta Archaeologica Carpathica* 17: 5–28.

Lech, J. 1987. Danubian raw material distribution patterns in eastern and central Europe. In Sieveking, G. De G. & Newcomer, M. H. (eds), *The Human Uses of Flint and Chert. Proceedings of the fourth international flint symposium held at Brighton Polytechnic 10–15 April 1983*, pp. 241–249. Cambridge: Cambridge University Press.

Lech, J. 1989. A Danubian raw material exchange network: a case study from Bylany. In Rulf, J. (ed.) *Bylany Seminar 1987. Collected Papers*, pp. 111–121. Praha: Archeologicky Ústav SAV.

Louwe Kooijmans, L. P. & Verhart, L. B. M. 1990. Een midden-neolithisch nederzettingsterrein en een kuil van de Stein-groep op de voormalige Kraaienberg bij Linden, gemeente Beers (N.-Br.). *Oudheidkundige Mededelingen uit het Rijksmuseum van Oudheden te Leiden* 70: 49–109.

McBryde, I. 1986. Artefacts, language and social interaction: a case study from south-eastern Australia. In Bailey, G. N. & Callow, P. (eds), *Stone Age Prehistory. Studies in Memory of Charles McBurney*, pp. 76–94. Cambridge: Cambridge University Press.

McBryde, I. & Harrison, G. 1981. Valued good or valuable stone? Considerations of the distribution of greenstone artefacts in south-eastern Australia. In Leach, F. & Davidson, J. (eds), *Archaeological Studies of Pacific Stone Resources*, pp. 183–208. Oxford: British Archaeological Reports (International Series 104).

Séronie-Vivien, M.-R. & Lenoir, M. (eds) 1990. *Le silex de sa genèse à l'outil. Actes du Ve Colloque international sur le silex (Vth International Flint Symposium), Bordeaux, 17 sept. - 2 oct. 1987.* Paris (Cahiers du Quaternaire nᵒ 17).

Sieveking, G. de G. & Newcomer, M. H. (eds) 1987. *The Human Uses of Flint and Chert. Proceedings of the Fourth International Flint Symposium held at Brighton Polytechnic 10–15 April 1983.* Cambridge: Cambridge University Press.

Torrence, R. 1984. Monopoly or direct access? Industrial organization at the Melos obsidian quarries. In Ericson, J. E. & Purdy, B. (eds), *Prehistoric Quarries and Lithic Production*, pp. 49–65. Cambridge: Cambridge University Press.

Torrence, R. 1986. *Production and Exchange of Stone Tools. Prehistoric obsidian in the Aegean.* Cambridge. Cambridge University Press.

Vermeersch, P. M. 1987–1988. Le Michelsberg en Belgique. *Acta Archaeologica Lovaniensia* 26–27: 1–20.

Wansleeben, M. & Verhart, L. B. M. 1990. Meuse Valley Project: the transition from the Mesolithic to the Neolithic in the Dutch Meuse Valley. In Vermeersch, P. M. & Van Peer, P. (eds), *Contributions to the Mesolithic in Europe*, pp. 389–402. Leuven: Leuven University Press.

Weiner, J. 1986. Flint mining and working on the Lousberg in Aachen (North-rhine-Westphalia, Federal Republic of Germany). In Birò, K. (ed.), *Papers Presented to the First International Conference on Prehistoric Flint Mining and Lithic Raw Material Identification in the Carpathian Basin, Budapest-Sümeg, 20–22 May 1986*, pp. 107–122. Budapest: Magyar Nemzeti Museum.

Weiner, J. 1989. 'Stahl der Steinzeit'. Das steinzeitliche Feuersteinbergwerk Lousberg in Aachen. *Das Rheinische Landesmuseum Bonn. Berichte aus der Arbeit des Museums* 3: 36–43.

Weisgerber, G., Slotta, R., & Weiner, J. (eds) 1980. *5000 Jahre Feuersteinbergbau. Die Suche nach dem Stahl der Steinzeit.* Bochum: Deutsches Bergbau Museum (Veröffentlichungen aus dem Deutschen Berbau Museum Bochum 22).

Zimmermann, A. 1982. Zur Organisation der Herstellung von Feuersteinarte-fakten in bandkeramischen Siedlungen. In *Siedlungen der Kultur mit Linearkeramik in Europa, Kolloquium Nové Vozokany 1981*, pp. 319–323. Nitra.

Zimmermann, A. 1991. *Austauschsysteme von Silexartefakten in der Bandkeramik Mitteleuropas.* Frankfurt/Main (Habilitationsschrift).

17

Specialised Production, Diffusion, and Exchange during the Neolithic in Western France: the Example of Polished Stone Axes

Charles-Tanguy Le Roux

The Neolithic in western France spans the majority of the fifth, fourth and third millennia BC, and the name 'Polished Stone Age', given by the first prehistorians, demonstrates the degree to which the period has been identified with the use of ground/polished stone tools. Nowadays, the basis of the definition has significantly changed, following progress in research and an evolution of ideas from definitions of a purely typological nature to criteria now largely derived from socio-economics and human behaviour studies. However, the use of polished stone remains a major element of the material evidence from this period, which saw the emergence of a 'modern mode' of life with agriculture, food production and animal domestication, the development of a well-structured religious way of thinking and complex forms of social organisation.

The discernible archaeological consequences of this social change introduced by agriculture/domestication are many. Amongst other things, they include the development of pottery, weaving, the use of polished stone tools and a relatively sedentary way of life – farmers must be able to look after their cultivated lands – in which we see the beginnings of architecture. Architectural concepts evolved from strictly utilitarian to being loaded with symbolism; in western France one major aspect of this initial 'monumental' expression was the appearance of megaliths which translated the social and spiritual changes of this time into stone, in a spectacular manner.

MAN AND THE AXE

The heavy use of *percussion lancée* is one of the major innovations in the region under consideration during this period; it afforded control of the forest, omnipresent in the post-glacial 'climatic optimum' of temperate Europe. Together with burning, the axe facilitates land clearance, a prerequisite for agriculture. It is also a means of procuring the combustible material necessary for domestic hearths and the means of carrying out the first *art du feu*, that is, ceramics. Finally, the axe (or the adze) supplies the wood which is transformed later in the construction of timber-framed buildings and also in the carpentry involved in the construction of stone-walled houses and the scaffolding, levers, and rollers necessary for the erection of megaliths.

As if naturally, the axe rapidly became loaded with considerable symbolic value: productive and destructive at the same time. We find axes depicted in well-placed positions on Armorican megalithic monuments next to the famous '*idole en écusson*' thought to represent the Neolithic '*grande-déesse-mère*' (great mother goddess). The ancient association of the axe with the lightning bolt is found in numerous folk traditions, such as the Breton *Men-kurun*, which is the heir of a long tradition. This was still well established in the writings of classical authors, for instance, in the 'Dactylotheque' of Marbode, a bishop-poet from Rennes during the eleventh century (Hamy: 1906):

> *Quand l'air s'agite troublé par les vents en furie, quand le tonnerre éclate, horrible, et que l'éclair en feu foudroie les nuées dechirées, alors cette pierre tombe du ciel. Son nom grec est celui même de la foudre puisque c'est dans les lieux seuls où la foudre est tombée que cette pierre, dit-on, peut se rencontrer. De là son nom grec de ceraunie, car ce que nous appelons Fulmen, les Grecs l'ont nommé Keraunon. Ceux qui la portent chastement ne seront point frappés de la foudre; transportés par un navire sur un fleuve ou sur la mer, ils ne seront pas submergés par la tourmente ou atteints par le feu du ciel. Elle fait gagner les procès, elle fait vaincre dans les batailles, elle procure de doux songes et un agréable sommeil.*

The idea that axes were accorded some symbolic significance underlies the term *hache votive* (votive axe) for small artefacts that we cannot imagine having been utilised in the same way as 'true' axes. However,

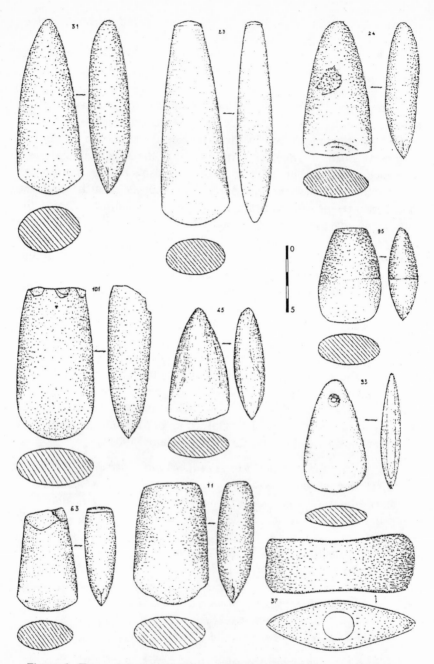

Figure 1. Types of Armorican green stone polished axes (after Le Roux & Lecerf 1980), 23– hache à bouton, *33–* pendant hatchet, *37–* battle axe.

information produced from well-preserved sites demonstrates that worked small pieces had been hafted length-ways like chisels. There has also been a tendency to use the term *hache d'apparat* (ceremonial axes) for all large pieces and/or those which were particularly carefully finished, such as those collected from the great Carnac mounds. A further category that is also worthy of note is the *hache partagée* (divided axe). For a number of years, attention has been directed to work that concentrates on sawing 'fibrolite', a very hard mineral from which nodules are frequently used for the production of polished blades, notably in Brittany where there are several fibrolite outcrops (Giot 1952). One of the most frequent practices attested consists of sawing a piece lengthways into quasi-symmetrical halves, while leaving raw the sawing traces and the break which concludes the operation. Blades treated in this way have been recovered from a variety of contexts, but one exceptional discovery could shed light on this curious practice. Excavations at Gavrinis have recovered four of these miniscule fibrolite axes. Three had been worked in the aforementioned fashion, and two of them appeared to represent the two halves of the same original piece (Le Roux 1985). Also, the parietal art of the Gavrinis monument consists of numerous representations of polished blades, of which several are closely paired. This seems to be illustrating the same phenomena. Tools that are deemed to be of 'normal' size and shape can be shown to be either axes or adzes. We can therefore understand the reasons for prehistorians employing the more practical term 'polished blade' in order not to prejudice the use of the term 'axe' itself.

THE MANUFACTURE OF POLISHED STONE AXES AT PLUSSULIEN . . .

The use of the *percussion lancée* technique in using axes carries with it a number of constraints. To begin with, there is a requirement for hardness, shock-resistance, and a capacity to withstand crushing. At the same time, there is a need for quality material for the processes of knapping, sharpening, and polishing of axes. In addition we should not forget the 'pleasing', aesthetic aspect of a tool loaded with so much symbolic value.

A fine-grain igneous rock from the diabase group, which forms the strong lava flow at the base of the Carboniferous of the Plussulien region (Côtes-d'Armor), seems to provide an excellent compromise between all these more or less contradictory requirements. In terms of the history of research, we should remember that the intensive exploitation of this material, termed 'type A dolerite' was discussed

[373]

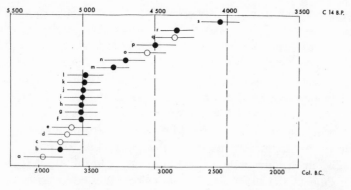

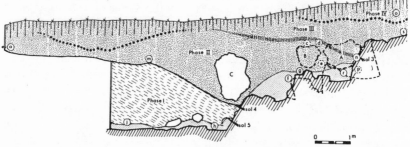

Figure 2. Plussulien (Cotes-d'Armor), type A axe factory. Below: a simplified stratigraphy of the three main phases in the accumulation of artefacts at the foot of the outcrop. Above: a chart of the radiocarbon dates, letters refer to the sampling plots on I (after Delibrias & Le Roux 1975).

'on paper' at the beginning of the 'petrographic studies of polished stone axes in Brittany' (Cogné & Giot 1952), whereas the physical evidence of the outcrop was not revealed until thirteen years later (Le Roux & Giot 1965).

The study of the important factory site that exploited 'type A dolerite' during the fourth and third millennium BC, demonstrated the different complex aspects of the operational sequences (*chaînes opératoires*), which began with the raw material and ended with the finished tool (Le Roux 1975; 1984). Although the first phase of activity is poorly attested, the study revealed methodical exploitation of the source characterised by three major techniques:

1. the extraction of small blocks of good quality rock isolated in a clay matrix in the weathered zone of the outcrop at the very beginning of the fourth millennium BC;
2. the mechanical debitage of the massive rock occurred in various ways, probably when favourable outcrops were ex-

hausted and therefore previous extraction techniques were
no longer possible;
3. the controlled use of 'thermal shock' obtained by heating the
rock face with large fires is attested from the second half of
the third millennium.

In addition to this evidence for stone extraction, the study has also
provided important data on the procedures followed during axe manufacture. Axe-manufacturing processes can be broken down into four
main phases, which vary in detail depending on the type of rock matrix
chosen for manufacture.

1. A rough-out is obtained by knapping with the help of a
hammer stone.
2. The rough-out is then worked in a more refined manner, but
still using a hammer stone until a 'pre-form' is realised.
3. Again, using a hammer stone the definitive shape is obtained
by pecking (*bouchardage*) the edges. This 'pre-axe form' has a
definitive shape but the tool still has a rough surface and its
blade is not yet functional.
4. Finally, the piece is polished and the blade is sharpened.
This last process seems to have occurred widely outside the
source/factory site.

We can estimate that it would have taken about ten hours to produce a tool of medium quality, but more time would have been
needed for the production of more exceptional tools. The total production coming from Plussulien is estimated at several million tools,
which means an average of around ten per day over a period of
twenty centuries during which the site was in use. This may indicate
a dozen full-time workers (or their equivalent part-time) and a demographic support of around a thousand people needed to assure their
subsistence. Taking into consideration the scale of this era, we can then
consider that with an average of one or two inhabitants per square
kilometre, this activity largely regulated, directly or indirectly, the way
of life of the population within a territory of at least twenty kilometres
around the manufacturing sites (Le Roux 1979).

. . . AND THEIR EXPORT

The products of this large-scale activity can be found all over western France and represents more than half of the polished axes discovered in the Armorican peninsula. Diffusion patterns encompass the

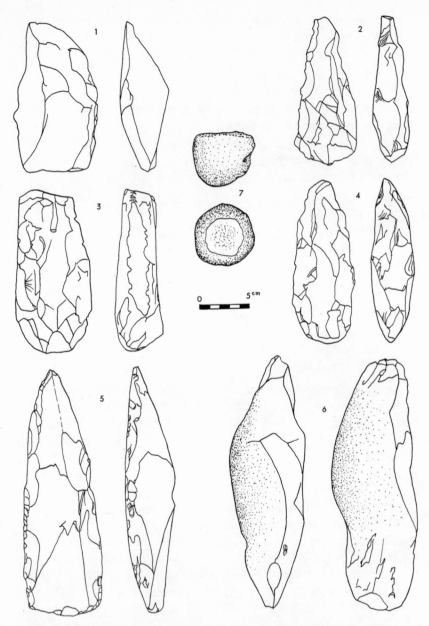

Figure 3. Pieces from the Plussulien factory (all of type A dolerite). 1 and 5 are rough-outs produced from large flakes; 2 and 3 are D on brick-shaped blocks; 4 is a 'knapped axe' ready for picking; 6 is an example of a failure in resorbtion by picking of a knapped mishape; 7 small spheroidal striker.

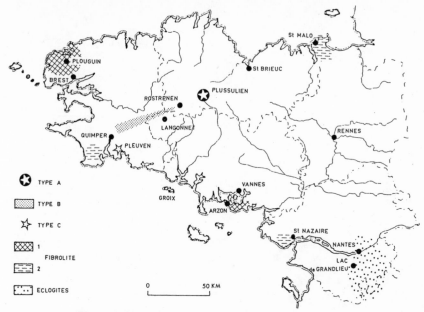

Figure 4. Main rock sources for axe making in Brittany.

Pyrenees, upper Provence, the Rhine valley, Flanders, and five examples have also been found in southern England. Although this last case attests the existence of cross-channel relations during the Neolithic, evidence of material coming the other way – towards western France – has yet to be demonstrated. This kind of diffusion seems to accord particularly well with the general models proposed by Colin Renfrew (1972), particularly 'down-the-line' diffusion, starting from the nuclear zone surrounding the source, within which there is only a slight fall in frequency (*chute de frequence*) due to direct and frequent contact with the producers. This pattern of diffusion corresponds well with the frequency plateau for 'type A': about 50% in the Armorican peninsula with the exception of a peak frequency of 75% observed in the immediate vicinity of the factory.

The rapid fall in frequency at the periphery of the nuclear zone, if interpreted in terms of the basic 'down-the-line' model, is complicated by the existence of two privileged routes or axes: the Atlantic coast to the Gironde and the Loire valley at least to the Loir-et-Cher. In both instances we find characteristics of 'directional trade' with a number of points which seem to play the role of secondary diffusion centres. This is the case in the *Bocage vendéen* (south of the Loire, an area once suspected to be the source of the material) and, as an extreme example,

[377]

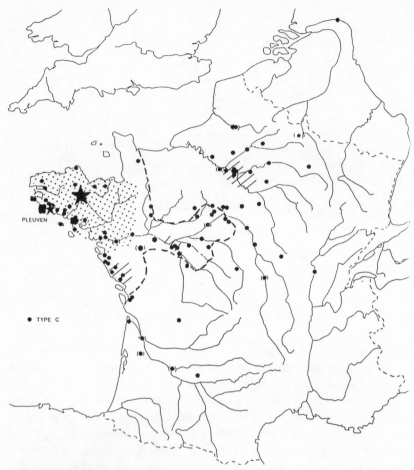

Figure 5. Diffusion of Armorican stone axes. Over 50% of type A are known from the dotted area, over 10% come from between the dotted area and the dashed line, while the hatched areas represent secondary concentrations. Find spots of type C battle axes are represented by black circles.

the site of Machecoul excavated by J. L'Helgouach (1988), where type A represented 69% of the polished material, a higher percentage than at Plussulien, 165 kilometres away. Another centre, more vague but still significant, is located in the Val-de-Loire, in the region of Chinon (Le Roux & Cordier 1974). A third centre is situated in the Paris region, which could have supplied all of the northern Paris basin.

Another point seems to complicate further this model of diffusion in the case of type A dolerite. The factory of Plussulien produced small, but by no means negligible quantities of axes called *haches à bouton* ('button axes'), characterised by a particularly swollen butt. These pieces can be found throughout the area of diffusion of type A, but in variable proportions; some of the concentrations coincide more or less with the secondary centres discussed above (Vendée), other areas yield proportionally more *haches à bouton* than common axes, such as south of the Beauce or north-eastern Armorica. But at the moment we still do not know whether these *haches à bouton* are really semi-deluxe products or if they have a symbolic value, the dispersion of which might be expected to follow particular rules. On the other hand, we have some reason to believe that their manufacture lasted only a rather short time in the third millennium BC. Thus, their diffusion could give us important information concerning exchange processes at this particular time.

The trends attested for type A seem to influence the patterns of diffusion of polished stone tools from other sources in western France, either by a repellent or attractive influence. Another group of dolerite rock, called group B, probably deriving from the Montagnes noires at the limit of the Morbihan and the Côtes d'Armor, spread only to the Atlantic coast, as if rejected because the type A source was located only slightly further away in the north-east. Fibrolite, a material of considerable quality, seems curiously confined to the periphery of its various sources in the peninsula: lower-Leon, the Bigouden area, the Rhuys peninsula, lower-Loire, and the Malouine region (Cogné & Giot 1952). In the Val de Loire and the Paris basin small factories, probably situated in the south-west of Anjou and in the north-west of the Massif Central, exported their material in the same direction of the dominant product, type A (Le Roux et al. 1980).

A particularly interesting case is that of the type C hornblendite, which has its source in Pleuven, south of Quimper (Cogné & Giot 1955). Starting from the south-west of the Armorican coast, a type of diffusion which is almost identical to that of the type A axes, but it concerns a product even more specific than the *haches à bouton*: the majority of the pieces found away from their source, are not normal axes but *haches de combat* (battle axes), *bipennes naviformes* (boat shaped) being the most frequent. That is to say that they are prestige objects, the diffusion of which certainly follows a particular logic, as attested by the contexts in which these axes have been found, frequently during river dredging. It is therefore remarkable that the two distribution patterns are almost identical. On the other hand, these artefacts (about a hundred are known) seem to have been produced during a relatively short period which can be secured at around 3500–2800 BC,

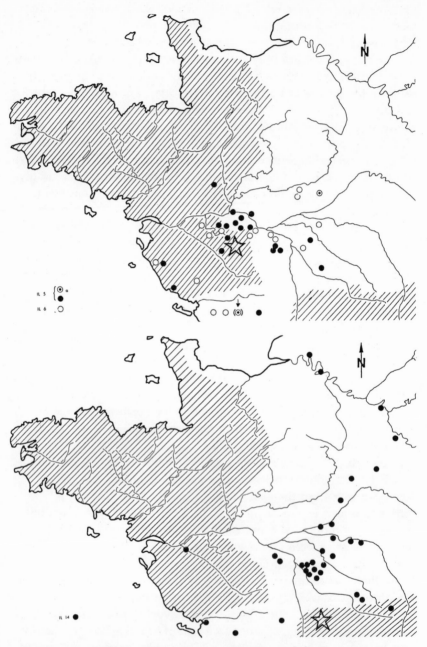

Figure 6. 'Comet-like' diffusion of small petrological groups seemingly influenced by the main stream along the Loire valley. The stars mark the presumable source areas.

thanks to the Peu-Richard stratigraphy from la Sauzaie in Soubize (Charente-Maritime) (Gachina et al. 1975). Distribution maps could therefore give us an instantaneous (if relative) outline of these fluxes during the second half of the third millennium.

IMPORTED AXES

In contrast, flint axes, which were mass produced in Normandy, in the Charentes or in the Bergeracois, in centres equally well structured, exploiting good quality material, have only been found in small quantities in the Armorican peninsula (5 to 6%, with slightly higher frequencies in eastern Brittany). This 'balance of exchange', seemingly tipping in favour of the Armorican products, can be partially explained by the recycling of reworked tools. Broken dolerite axes were no longer useful, they were thrown away and we are likely to find them, whereas flint axes, especially in the Breton region where this material is rare, could be reworked and converted into scrapers or arrowheads, making the original axes no longer recognisable.

Green axes made of sodic pyroxenites from the Alps are distributed along the Mediterranean region as far as Rousillon. They are also frequent further north in Burgundy, but their frequency quickly drops west of Orleans. In Armorica, their presence is infrequent (a few per cent), but this deficiency can be partly explained by two phenomena. *Eclogites* outcrops in the Nantes region probably supplied a certain number of tools, the material of which recalls, on initial observation, the character of Alpine rocks. On the other hand, due to their spectacular appearance, the importance of the well-known jadeite *haches d'apparat* from the large Carnac tumuli, which are the pride of the museums in Vannes and Carnac, is often over-estimated, giving the illusion that there is a relative abundance of this material in Brittany or at least in the Morbihan region.

CONCLUSION: THE UTILITARIAN AND THE AESTHETIC

More than the battle axes, and much more than even the most beautiful type A *haches à bouton*, the extraordinarily large Alpine jadeite Carnac axes reflect a concern with prestige status rather than with practical utility. The 'prestige of the inaccessible', demonstrated by a few objects destined to disappear as funeral offerings after having travelled hundreds of kilometres, occurs at a point which reminds us of the limitations of the information with which prehistorians work and which are only biased and strictly material sources. Evolution through time is even sometimes hard to discern – we saw how difficult it is to distinguish the diffusion of fourth millennium axes from those of the third millennium, and how even the opportunities offered by type C and button axes prove to be rather hazy, the precision of radiocarbon dating having its limitations.

Human, political, symbolic, and emotional factors remain difficult to determine from a purely archaeological perspective. However, common sense suggests that these are determining factors of exchange, sometimes even more than the intrinsic qualities of the range of objects themselves. With the particular case of the type A Armorican axes, it happens that the rather exceptional mechanical properties of the material, its flattering aspect, the possibilities of exploitation, and the range of its diffusion, go together. Conversely, the opposite case exists in the British isles where the success of *porcellanite* (Tievebulliagh, Northern Ireland) owes little to its rather poor geotechnical qualities (Bradley et al. 1992).

A whole ethnological bibliography has been devoted to the production and diffusion of polished stone tools that was routine in the Oceanic world several decades ago and of which there still remain some traces (Blackwood 1964; Dickson 1981; Pétrequin 1988; 1994; etc.). Although it is tempting to search for parallels in order to compensate for the lack of direct information, this remains problematic for the contexts are totally different. The Australian desert or the dense equatorial forest of the mountains of New Guinea have few points in common with post-glacial temperate Europe; their populations are not Neolithic in the ways that we have defined above and they had mastered polishing techniques long before their development in Europe. We are dealing with societies marginalised by their geographical isolation and their highly developed adaptation to very particular and extremely constraining environments, whereas the different European Neolithic groups belonged to innovative cultures, driven by numerous contacts and by the exceptionably favourable natural conditions of the post-glacial climatic optimum.

Another major point to be drawn from this work is that artefacts and mankind must not be confused. There are lots of ways for an object to travel through Europe, rapidly and in large quantities, without necessarily implying that this was tied to the movement of people. Privileged intermediaries, networks and exchange place, as well as systems of inheritance are common elements in many societies and here again we can refer to the various model-types proposed by Renfrew (1972).

Exchange was probably a regular and routine component of life during the Neolithic. What remains to be found are the counterparts (perhaps immaterial and probably both partial and multiple) of the few material objects whose paths we have managed to follow.

Translated by Lesley K. McFadyen and Nelly Y. C. Boyd

BIBLIOGRAPHY

Blackwood, B. 1964. *The Technology of a Modern Stone-Age People in New Guinea.* Oxford: Oxford University Press.

Bradley, R., Meredith, P., Smith, J., & Edmonds, M. 1992. Rock physics and the Neolithic axe trade in Great Britain. *Archaeometry* 34 (2): 223–233.

Cogné, J. & Giot, P.-R. 1952. Étude pétrographique des haches polies de Bretagne. *Bulletin de la Société préhistorique française* 49: 388–395.

Cogné, J. & Giot, P.-R. 1955. Étude pétrographique des haches polies de Bretagne, IV, *Bulletin de la Société préhistorique française* 52: 401–409.

Delibrias, G. & Le Roux, C.-T. 1975. Un exemple d'application des datations radiocarbone à l'interprétation d'une stratigraphie complexe . . . *Bulletin de la société préhistorique française* 72: 78–82.

Dickson, F.-P. 1981 *Australian Stone Hatchets: a Study in Design and Dynamics.* Sydney: Academic press of Australia.

Gachina, J., Gomez, J., & Coffyn, A. 1975. Supplément à l'inventaire des instruments perforés pour les départements de Charente, Charente-maritime et Gironde. *Bulletin de la société préhistorique française* 72: 78–82.

Giot, P.-R. 1952. Le travail de la fibrolite en Armorique. *Bulletin de la société préhistorique française* 49: 395–398.

Le Roux, C.-T. 1975. Il y a plusieurs millenaires . . . fabrication et commerce des haches en pierre polie. *Les dossiers de l'archéologie* 11: 43–55.

Le Roux, C.-T. 1979. Stone axes of Brittany and the Marches. *Stone Axe Studies*, pp. 49–56. London: Council for British Archaeology (Research Report 23).

Le Roux, C.-T. 1984. L'implantation néolithique en Bretagne centrale. *Revue archéologique de l'ouest* 1: 33–54.

Le Roux, C.-T. 1990. La pétro-archéologie des haches polies armoricaine, 40 ans après. *Revue archéologique de l'Ouest*, supplément 2: 345–353.

Le Roux, C.-T. 1996. L'outillage de pierre polie en metadolerite du type A. Production et diffusion au Néolithique dans la France de l'Ouest et au delà (unpublished thesis, Université de Rennes I).

Le Roux, C.-T., Despriée, J., & Leymarios, C. 1980. *Les haches polies du Loir-et-Cher. Étude pétrographique et considérations sur leur diffusion dans les pays de la Loire moyenne et le Sud-Ouest du bassin parisien. Études sur le Néolithique de la Région Centre,* pp. 49–66. Saint-Amand-Montrond: Musée Saint-Vicq.

Le Roux, C.-T. & Giot, P.-R. 1965. Étude pétrographique des haches polies de Bretagne, VI. Découverte des ateliers de la dolérite du type A. *Bulletin de la Société préhistorique française* 62: 128–129.

Le Roux, C.-T. & Lecerf, Y. 1980. Les haches polies de l'arrondissement de Dinan. *Les dossiers du C.E.R.A.A.* 6: 21–44.

L'Helgouach, J. 1988. Le site néolithique final à fosses interrompus des Prises à Machecoul, Loire-atlantique. *Enclosures and Defences in the Neolithic of Western Europe*, pp. 265–273. Oxford: British Archaeological Reports (International Series 403).

Pétrequin, A.-M. & Pétrequin, P. 1988. *Le néolithique des lacs* (cf. pp. 63–94). Paris: Errance.

Pétrequin, P. & Pétrequin, A.-M. 1988. *Ecologie d'un outil: la hache de pierre en Irian-Jaya (Indonésie)*. Valbonne: C.N.R.S. Editions (Monographie du C.R.A.N. n° 12).

Renfrew, C. 1972. Alternative models for exchange and spatial distribution. *Exchange Systems in Prehistory*, pp. 71–90. New York and London: Academic Press.

18

Patterns by Design: Changing Perspectives of Beaker Variation

R. B. Boast

As is the way with publishing, much of what we write may take several years to reach print, and this paper is no exception. I wrote this paper for the conference in 1991 and have not seen much of it until the moment that I had a read of the final proofs. Such an exercise is always shocking, but this paper has seemed to suffer worse for its relatively short age. I would like to believe that this is a good thing, that archaeology has moved on rapidly over the past seven years, working on many of the problems that I raise in this paper and, to a degree, that is the case. However, I must also admit that I now see this paper as an overly optimistic and ambitious work, written at the wrong time.

I continue to support its publication, however, because I feel that there are some important points made about the variability of beaker pots in particular, and variation in general, that are still worth saying. My advice, these seven years later, is to read this paper for its good bits and forgive the excesses as an artefact of age.

Beaker pottery (2300–1600 BC) is one of the most heavily studied prehistoric ceramics in Britain. It has been at the centre of prehistoric typological analysis for the last 70 years (Fox 1923; Mitchell 1934; Childe 1936; Piggott 1963; Clarke 1970; 1976; Lanting and van der Waals 1972; Case 1977), largely due to its fine decoration and foreign origins. The importance of its association with metal has always been realised (Piggott 1963; Lanting and van der Waals 1972: 35; Harrison 1980: 70), as has its association with the re-development of henges and changes in burial tradition (Childe 1940: 101–110; Bradley 1984: 72; Thorpe & Richards 1984). The beaker's distinctive shape, decoration and fabric have helped distinguish and accentuate, almost fetishise, these pots in the early Bronze Age studies across western Europe. The problem remains, however, as to what are the definitive patterns of beaker form and decoration, as well as their role(s) in social practice. What was the social province, or provinces, of beakers within early Bronze Age society and were various forms used to mark these roles?

Traditional beaker typologies (Piggott 1963; Clarke 1970; Lanting and van der Waals 1972; Case 1977) all assume that the changes in form and decoration are taxonomic and indicative of cultural identities – a matter of groups of objects brought by invasion of groups of people and their subsequent modifications through cultural invention. Even less traditional treatments of the 'beaker package' assume some form of passive taxonomy (Clarke 1976; Burgess and Shennan 1976; Miller 1982), of passive objects attached to particular social identities.

Regardless of how the introduction or origin of beakers is explained, archaeology's organisation of beaker formal variation has been based on some form of typology. The *raison d'être* of typology is that of types, definable classes of objects, organised in time. For archaeology, these classes are distinguished by formal attributes and related to each other along some continuous independent scale, usually chronology. Typology removes the objects from the context that produces them and gives them meaning. Because of the strict formalisms of typology, objects can have either an active utilitarian role (the media for adaptation to an environment (Binford 1968; Sackett 1977) or a passive role symbolising social identity (Wiessner 1984). In other words, the object's form is a direct reflection of its role as an intermediary between people and the natural and social environment (Binford 1972: 200; Wobst 1977: 327). The object becomes the fixed entity in the interpretation, the material type is the fixed point in the past. But are archaeological artefacts, and their categories, fixed points? Traditional taxonomy would argue that what defines beakers are their *function*, while the non-functional attributes constitute their *style* (Sackett 1982; Dunnell 1978). This function/style distinction misses the point. The definition of *beakers* are not just determined by their use, but necessarily involves the relationship between certain social activities and a series of appropriate material forms. It is unlikely that beakers were passively appropriated by various fashions or economic necessities, but served to actively signal certain social identities and roles. They simultaneously speak of the object and the individual through a collective material language.

Problems with any formal taxonomies arise once we accept that material objects are produced and used within existing social landscapes that define and structure through references to expectations rather than utility (Giddens 1984: 31–33; Barrett 1987). Practical knowledge, memory, competence, discursive knowledge and contingent purpose, as well as the existing material landscape, all act to develop and maintain the individual material presentations, that is to define what an object looks like and how it is used, and, hence, its identity. The individual artefact that we study is a result of all these factors, as was its place in social practice throughout its period of use. That beakers were probably used as drinking vessels is both apparent and trivial. The significance of beaker form and decoration, that which defined beakers as beakers rather than just pots, is not one of simple identity or rigid functional classes (Rosch 1978; Kempton 1981; Miller 1985; Lakoff 1987), but is one of reference. Reference to both a set of social expectations about the appropriate roles of this object, and an existing set of material conventions manifest in the existing material culture, its active production and the built landscape.

Sørensen (1989: 94) has demonstrated that material objects and their conceptual categories 'participate in creating, evolving and transforming their own context.' In her study of the late Bronze Age of Scandinavia and England, variability of material objects is held to maintain local material tradition. There is access through material form and appearance to this interaction between material and social practices (Sørensen 1989: 94): 'Objects and actions in their relationships are therefore culturally specific since they result from and cause interaction between different levels of social practice. This active aspect of material objects is suggested in part to be reflected by their appearance – and thus to be available for archaeological consideration.' Sørensen argues that because material objects are entwined in social practice, similar references within material categories should be seen as reproductive strategies. From this argument, she builds an analysis that considers changes in bronzes as degrees of relation to common or accepted appearances (ibid.): 'differentiation of the degree of standardisation among objects was therefore used to suggest that the distance from the norm (the general/average) will change the nature of an item's position within the material culture, and through that its social meaning.'

Miller has also offered a comprehensive challenge to the traditional analysis of material culture in archaeology. He challenges the basic premises of the typological debate and finds them without foundation (Miller 1985: 197):

it is assumed that there are relatively unproblematic cultural categories in the living population to which the archaeologist is attempting to approximate. It follows that the problems faced are peculiar to archaeology and the nature of the archaeological record, and therefore that the approaches to be developed are also unique to the discipline.

Rejecting both of these assumptions, Miller argues that the ambiguity and difference within material forms are the consequence of the strategic, though often latent, production of material culture (1985: 201):

> To analyse artefacts as categories is to determine the conditions for the creation of difference and equivalence, and to recognise that distinct objects may be created as representations of identical concepts. It was suggested . . . that pottery as a set of categories should be considered as a pattern with structure, which permitted convention and mutual understanding. . . . Although simplified in this representation, such structure can generate transformations and interpretations of enormous complexity.

Here we see a clear challenge to the traditional role of material form in the explanation of social practice. Classification is not a self-evident demarcation of the material world based on the simple totting up of similarities, even if only in relation to an analytic problem. An object's appearance represents the schemes by which tradition is referenced and challenged. This referencing is not a direct labelling, but a reference that situates the object in relation to a signifying categorical ideal. A reference that proclaims the object's, and its maker's and user's, acceptance of certain appropriate representations, but also its individual character in relation to those conventions. A reference that signals an object's position within a field of references thus marking its position within the material landscape 'and through that its social meaning' (Sørensen 1989: 98).

The usual typological approaches, either monothetic/divisive or polythetic/agglomerative (Sokal and Sneath 1963; Brown 1982), cannot inform on such relationships. This is because they all assume a simplistic similarity, demanding simple gross numbers of shared attributes as the determining criteria (Spaulding 1953; Clarke 1968). In these approaches, categories are determined as fixed, unambiguous and unmovable bounded objects dependent on non-random patterns of shared attributes without concern for any link with practice, reference or intention. The object's role in linking practice into a meaningful social narrative is lost in the semantics of its classification (Ricoeur 1978).

Ethnographic studies and cognitive psychology have demonstrated that, contrary to traditional typological method, the identities of material culture are organised, or categorised, in response to a variety of social constructs and intentions (Berlin & Kay 1969; Rosch 1978; Kempton 1981; Miller 1985). Categorisation of the material world is not a simple assemblage of predefined components, but rather the construction and transformation of material form and design in *relation* to accepted ideals, intentions and already constructed material landscapes. The pot, fresh from the kiln, is not a simple set of emblematic statements with a few individual stylistic foibles thrown in for good measure, but a complete object whose form has been deemed appropriate by its maker for the social practices it is expected to be a part. It must 'make sense' in the social practices it is to take part, but also must define its own identity (or rather that of its owner) in those practices. The object gains its *appropriateness* from sets of categorical structures that are reproduced and maintained by constant referencing in social practices through the objects and narratives present. Cognitive psychology and cognitive anthropology have demonstrated over the last forty years that material identities, categorical structures, are produced and maintained in this way (Wittgenstein 1953; Rosch 1978; Kempton 1981; Miller 1985; Lakoff 1987).

Membership is not constituted by a collection of simple properties, but defined by the individual object's relation to a central idea or 'family resemblance' (Wittgenstein 1953: 66–71). This is not to say that membership becomes relative in a general sense, but that there arises 'degrees of membership' – some members are better examples of the category than others. This aspect of categories, that some members have a more central membership as opposed to the rest of the category, is called 'centrality'. The object, real or ideal, which constitutes the best member of the category is said to be the *prototype* because it embodies the greatest degree of association with the ideal of the category (Rosch 1978). If the criteria for prototypic membership are not necessarily any inherent properties of the objects themselves, but the relative affinity of those objects to a categorical ideal (prototype), this means that the central members of a category are not fixed. The membership of the central, or prototypic, examples of a category can shift depending on the context in which that category is being defined (Kempton 1981).

[389]

Using Wittgenstein's example of gaming with dice, if he was teaching adults 'a game' in a casino, then the dice game would be appropriate and hence sufficiently central to the category in that context. However, in a different context 'Someone says to me: "show the children a game." I teach them gaming with dice, and the other says, "I didn't mean that sort of game." ' (Wittgenstein 1953, 1: 70). Dice is not seen as a central member of what is meant by 'game' in this instance, but there is no question that dicing is a game. All categories, to some degree or another, have such flexibility in their central members by virtue of these *rules of extension*.

Extension and prototype are essential concepts for the understanding of categories in an active social context. The idea that a category consists not of a single uniform group, but prototypic or central members that constitute the categorical meaning, and a series of extended senses based on certain relational principles, creates an image of categories as 'frames of reference' rather than objective entities (Miller 1985: 181–83). These frames can be seen as the potential range of different categorical relationships that are evoked in relation to a prototypic example, thus creating a surface or *gradience* of membership (Kempton 1981; Miller 1985).

Such a description of a category, one that considers prototypic relations structured by extensions creating a membership gradience, requires a method that avoids the usual rigid distinctions of an element-based taxonomy. Boundaries between material groups are less important than the referential structure created by comparing formal elements, design orders, shape, and contextual relation between objects within time and space. It is necessary to rigorously map the topography of similarity and difference within a group of objects so that it may be analysed as a pattern of inter-referencing, rather than simply documenting the group by constructing edges. This is done by mapping the formal variability of a group of objects as a set of multi-level presentations, with each object able to present its 'place' within the surface of potential presentations (Kempton 1981). Presentation refers to the particular configuration of formal elements, design order, and shape. These are not mapped as attributes to be measured apart, but as referential dimensions within a category that situates a particular set of objects in relation one to another. Included in the concept of situation is the object's *place* within the world, its place in time, its place within the social geography, its reference to presentations past and its quotation in presentations future. The formulation of these patterns into a map of related presentations provides the analytical device to present a category's history. Not only a description of individual object's design biographies, but also how these biographies develop as a community.

BRITISH BEAKER VARIABILITY

In a recent study (Boast 1990), I analysed the patterns of form and design on over 800 British beakers. In this study I mapped the continuities and discontinuities of shape, design organisation and design element choice. The result was a series of categorical 'maps' which plotted these similarities and dis-similarities over time and space. The study also analysed fabric types, colours, surface treatments, design methods, features of depositional context, associations, etc., but there is too little space to discuss all these factors, or their full impact, here. These three factors of beaker design (form, design and design elements) will be used to demonstrate what constituted the representation of 'beakerness' and how this representation had changed and developed in Britain throughout the early Bronze Age.

Though the original measurements were completely heuristic, significant patterns of variation were determined through *ordination* (both principal components analysis and correspondence analysis (Greenacre 1984; Shennan 1988: 280–81, 283–86)). These statistical techniques plot the measured variation in a multidimensional space and then define new *latent* variables that correspond to the areas of greatest spread, or greatest variability, within the distribution. This technique allows the definition of a set of variables which correspond most closely with those aspects of form and design that were most frequently reproduced. However, the resulting measurement in the *latent variable* does not furnish a classificatory membership, but only the full range of representations within that variable. In other words, the result does not return a new classification of shape, but a new way of measuring shape – a measurement that reflects the variation within the sample, rather than archaeological conventions of measurement.

What is clear from this analysis (Figs 1–7) is that beakers do not change from one unitary type to another, but vary in different ways within different design factors. For instance, variations in shape can largely be accounted for through three different factors. However, beaker shape does not vary uniformly within these factors (see Figs 1–3), but clear preferences are represented in the distributions. What we see in the distributions of beakers are certain clearly preferred forms with a wide range of alternatives which, while maintaining a

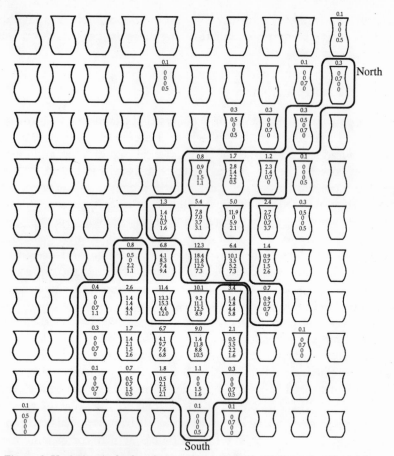

Figure 1. Variation in beaker shape – factor 1. In the X dimension the beakers narrow, while in the Y dimension they get taller. The distribution shows that there are a full range of pots from short-and-wide to tall-and-thin, but that while there are many shorter and thinner pots, there are no taller and wider pots. The numbers on the pots represent percentages by region. The number on top represents the total sample, while the numbers inside the pot (from top to bottom) represent Scotland, Yorkshire, East Anglia and Wessex respectively (see also Figs 2–3).

strong reference to the preferred forms, do not distribute evenly from the 'centre', but differentiate themselves in consistent ways. This categorical pattern is most clearly seen in the differences between the distributions for beakers from Scotland and Yorkshire on the one hand, and East Anglia and Wessex on the other (Fig. 1). In all areas there is a strongly common, or prototypic, set of forms. These are characterised by a height to width ratio of roughly 1.5: 1, an even proportion

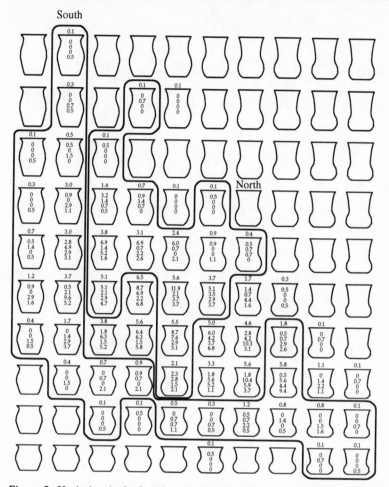

Figure 2. Variation in beaker shape – factor 2. In the X dimension, the belly drops while, in the Y dimension, the beaker gets taller. In this figure, factor 2 (the X dimension) varies in relation to an aspect of factor 1 (variation in height – the Y dimension). The distribution shows a preference for short pots with low bellies extending to tall pots with high bellies.

between the neck-length and the belly-height, and an even proportion between rim-diameter and belly-diameter though favouring a slightly wider rim. Though all regions share this *prototypic* core, there are clear differences between regions in how their pots diverge from this core.

In Scotland and Yorkshire there is a clear preference for beakers that are tall and thin, while in Wessex and East Anglia there is a preference for beakers that are short and slightly wider (Fig. 1). In the north, a narrow range of short- to medium-sized necks is maintained while in

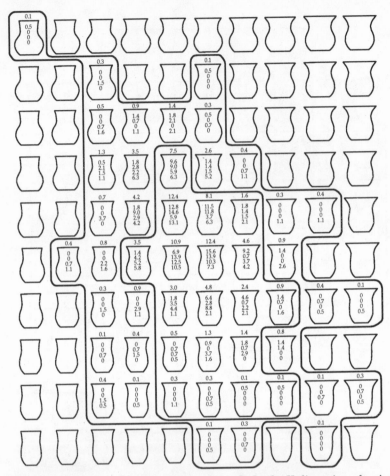

Figure 3. Variation in beaker shape – factor 3. In the X dimension, the rim expands in relation to the pot while, in the Y dimension, the belly expands in relation to the pot. The overall effect of the distribution is from narrow necks with wide bellies to wide necks with narrow bellies.

the south, there is an emphasis on extreme short-necked and long-necked forms (Fig. 2). Finally, while the north maintains fairly proto-typic ratios of rim to belly diameter, the south sees a much greater range of forms from wide-bellied straight necked forms to very wide-rimmed straight-bellied forms (Fig. 3). In summary, the north re-produces generally simple shapes, while the south has a high propor-tion of more extreme forms. However, this difference is maintained in relation to the same set of common forms in all regions.

This categorical pattern, where different regions have different inter-

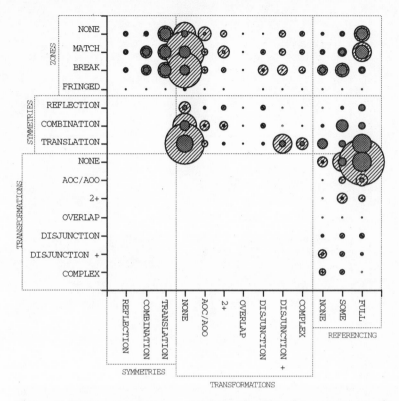

Figure 4. Design organisation – total sample. This figure represents the number of pots which share different pairs of design organisational features. The grey circles represent the proportion of pots which share the two characteristics within each category or pair of features (e.g. symmetries and transformations). The circles with horizontal lines represent the proportion of pots weighted by the size of the category, a slightly more representative measure (see Appendix A for a full discussion of the measurements of design organisation).

pretations of a design tradition rather than different traditions, can also be seen in the design organisation. Generally, the design organisation on British beakers follows a simple strategy. There is a preferred use of transformation, repeated design elements and, when mirror symmetry is used, it is almost always combined with transformation. Zones are used equally either to break or match the symmetric patterns – used either to emphasise or to hide the symmetric design. When there are two or more design patterns on a pot, it is common that the same design elements will be used in both. Finally, though there are several ways to transform, or hide, the design structure, it is most common to not transform the design at all (Fig. 4).

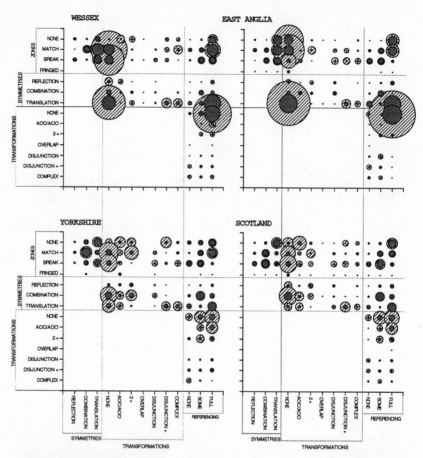

Figure 5. Design organisation – regional samples (see Appendix A for a full discussion of the measurements of design organisation).

Regionally, though these prototypic patterns dominate, we see completely different characters to the design strategies (Fig. 5). Wessex and East Anglia are very similar and both predominantly reflect the simple prototypic design organisations. There is little transformation of design structures, translation is the dominant form of organisation, and the same sets of elements occur together on pots. Scotland and Yorkshire, however, are very different, in that both show a marked diversity in design strategies and display a tradition of more complex design. A high proportion of designs are transformed or hidden in some way, it is more likely that two different designs on the same pot will use quite different elements, and there is a much greater use of mirror symmetry in combination with translation. It is interesting that

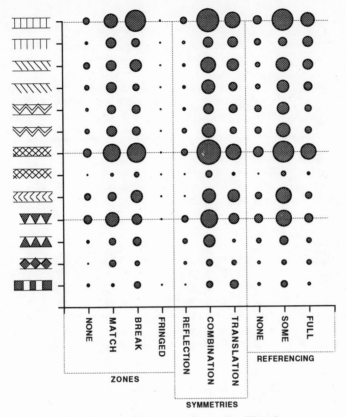

Figure 6. Design element choice – total sample. This figure represents the association of design element choice and design organisation (see Fig. 4).

the different design constituents of form and decorative organisation do not correlate in their regional patterns. In the north, form is relatively simple and conservative while the strategies of design organisation are quite diverse. In the south, it is the strategies of design organisation which are simple and elemental while the diversity is invested in the forms.

This pattern, of the independence of design constituents, is maintained in the selection of design elements. Though the full range of design elements are used commonly in all regions, there is a small relative preference of cross-hatching, ladder designs and triangles (Fig. 6). The only relatively strong distinction that can be seen is that continuous design elements (Cross-hatched, ladders, herring-bone, etc.) are more commonly used than closed design elements (triangles, lozenges, etc.). Regionally, differences in strategy exist, but they are

[397]

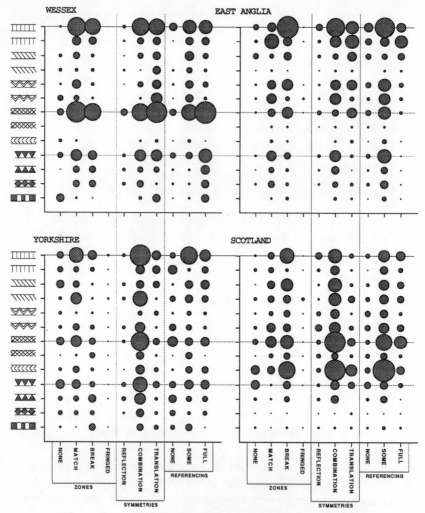

Figure 7. Design element choice – regional samples. This figure represents the association of design element choice and design organisation (see Fig. 4).

quite different from those of the other two design constituents. Wessex's use of design elements is largely prototypic. However, it does not share this pattern with East Anglia, but with Yorkshire (Fig. 7). Yorkshire and Wessex are not the same in their choices of design elements, the use of elements in different design organisations are somewhat different, but the proportional use of elements are very similar. Scotland displays a somewhat different pattern with a strong emphasis on cross-hatching and herring-bone elements and little use of closed design elements. East Anglia, however, is very unusual indeed. Here there is a reliance on a few design elements with ladder designs dominating (though this may be due to the large proportion of rusticated beakers in East Anglia).

Though this represents a different pattern than the simple regional split of the other two design constituents, there does exist one north-south distinction in design element choice. There is a relatively significant increase in the use of both fringed cross-hatching and herring-bone decoration from south to north (Fig. 7). While Wessex has no fringed cross-hatching and little herring-bone decoration, the former has an increasing, though small, usage the further north you go, and the latter is the most common design element in Scotland.

While these show significant results as a *grand scheme*, it must be remembered that these patterns developed and changed over some 700 years. I do not intend to cover the full chronological analysis here (it will be dealt with separately (see Kinnes et al. 1991; Boast forthcoming)), but it is necessary to mention several significant changes in beaker form and design over time. We now know that beakers were made and used in Britain for a long time – from at least 2300 BC to 1600 BC (Kinnes et al. 1991). Preliminary analysis of the new British beaker dates (Kinnes et al. 1991) makes clear that none of the British beaker typologies have much chronological validity (Boast forthcoming). Clarke's typology (1970) looses all of its temporal structure when checked against the new dates, with even the Wessex/middle Rhine beakers spanning some 450 years. Case's simple typology (1977) seems only valid in identifying the *terminus ante quem*, in that earlier forms seem to continue to be made throughout the beaker period. Lanting and van der Waals' (1972) typology also seems only valid in its reflection of the increasing complexity of beaker design over time (though we have seen that this has significant regional variation).

There does seem to be a development in beaker form and design over time which roughly follows the classic typological pattern from early continental forms, to a set of defining regional forms, to a final expansion away from these forms with greater emphasis on extreme designs. However, there is no evidence that any one of these later developments replaced earlier forms. The earlier forms remain with only the diversity of forms expanding, and, as we have seen, expanding within very specific regional strategies distinguished from south to north.

With such a strong north-south distinction in beaker form and design, and increasing complexity of design over time, the question must be asked: was David Clarke (1970) right? He was certainly correct about a north-south distinction in beaker form and design. He was also probably correct that this distinction developed and increased over time (Kinnes et al. 1992; Boast 1995). However, he was also clearly wrong about the classification of the beakers. By collapsing the beaker variability into a series of types, the subtlety and depth of distinction and reference is lost – the subtlety of different local traditions of representation within a category is lost. By creating a set of types out of the complex of design strategies and categorical constraints, the gross differences between Clarke's *types* could only be explained through a number of invasions (Clarke 1970: 272–75). Though Clarke's variety of types and plethora of invasions has been rightly criticised for many good reasons (Lanting and van der Waals 1972; Burgess and Shennan 1976; Miller 1982), no one has challenged the postulate that variation in beaker form, or any other category of material object, is the representation of a few definable types. In the case of British beakers, whether variation is being explained as the normal generation of types over time (Case 1977), or through replacement by invasion (Clarke 1970), or through class emulation (Miller 1982), all ignore the role of reference and intentionality in the design process.

CONCLUSIONS

The analysis of beakers, as presented in this paper, demonstrates that the patterns of decoration and form of the British beakers are far richer than can be captured by a simple set of types. In fact, the pattern of form and decoration on beakers do not correspond to a set of types at all, but represent designs which follow similar rules and maintain common referents. Each pot does not form part of a *type*, but represents one form among many – a single response to a set of categorical restrictions, and expectations, and local historical conditions. By collapsing the variation into a set of types, the significant patterns of reference and transformation (prototype and extension) are lost. We must accept from the onset that beakers do not follow some genealogy through a set of *type species*, each one with a uniform *genotype*, transformed only through some form of *cultural natural selection* into a new *species*. We must accept that material culture is not produced or used in this way. That the inheritance model, on which typology is based, is not appropriate for understanding patterns of material cultural because it necessarily assumes that objects are reproduced in reference to some fixed template.

[400]

By accepting that the form of an artefact is not the result of a simple aggregation of traits, but is a design process where reference is made to known examples, remembered forms, ideals, as well as the competence and social knowledge of the maker, can we begin to unravel the complex of similarities and differences that constitute a diverse material assemblage over time and space. By analysing beaker variability in this way can we begin to understand the beaker's place in its local context of production and use.

These patterns, presented in the categorical maps, beg many questions about beakers and their significance in early Bronze Age society. Beakers come to Britain as an existing category of pot, associated in some way with other material objects and social practices. The traditional associations with metal, with single inhumation and their foreign origins remains unquestioned. It is also clear that once beakers came into Britain they were quickly assimilated into the local social context. There is no evidence that any but a few beakers were made far from where they were used, and the variation in quality of manufacture and design, often quite extreme, suggests that there was competition between producers, with some possibly specialising in the advanced firing techniques required for the finer beaker fabrics. The association between the higher firing temperatures and metal smelting cannot be ignored (Boast 1990). However, even the finest pots were probably being made for local uses.

If beakers are produced locally, how can we account for the overwhelming similarity in form and design, especially in places like Wessex where beakers were made to the same tight constraints for many hundreds of years? Also how do we account for the reproduction, almost to the point of copying, of early beaker forms (e.g. AOC) many hundreds of years apart? And, finally, how do we account for the similarity of design across such a vast area, not just Britain, but across most of western Europe?

We know that at the end of the Neolithic there were many changes in the role and context of the individual and how these roles were distinguished materially (Bradley 1984: 65–67; Thorpe and Richards 1984). Stone axes had already taken on a significance in signalling the identity of their owner that went beyond the local (Edmonds 1995) while the role of the individual was purely maintained in the local context. Through metals (both bronze and gold), beakers and many other objects of personal adornment, competition through public display increased in importance throughout the early Bronze Age. Beakers do not explain these social changes, but are symptomatic of them.

The categorical patterns presented above demonstrate that over time and across regions beaker design is characterised by the subtle change of certain design rules and an increased complexity of form and design. This would indicate that not only are there many beakers around which act as referents, but that the context in which they are used and produced emphasises a strong prototypic ideal. However, the context of use, one where beakers and their owners are somehow 'on display', involves a sense of competition – a context where distinctiveness, largely through complexity of decoration, can develop.

This social context does not require direct knowledge of origins or even direct contact with the original social context within which beakers developed. The context of display and competition was already established in Britain in the late Neolithic. Metal and beakers simply offered a new media through which these practices could develop. Thorpe and Richards (1984) may be right, to some degree, that beakers and metals transformed existing social relations, or at least the ideology that structured those relations (Tilley 1984), but they did not replace them in any direct way. Access to distinctive objects became more widespread and allowed for a diversification or fragmentation of access and, hence, power. If anything distinguishes the early Bronze Age from the Neolithic it is the more dispersed population, the fragmentation of corporate groups and a greater diversity of distinctive objects (Bradley 1984).

Throughout the early Bronze Age there was a vast increase in the number of distinctive objects in circulation. Especially towards the end of the period (1800–1600 BC), many new forms of personal ornament, bronze objects and highly decorated pottery were in use. Many of these were used in, and produced for, the same contexts in which beakers were used (e.g. henges and burials). Specific categories of objects no longer distinguished the social contexts as much as a certain way of displaying relations through material objects did (almost any object). Distinctiveness through distinctive objects increasingly mattered more than the distinctive objects themselves. It was the context of display that was increasingly important rather than the signifying objects.

Under the conditions of increased reference to new materials, categorical structure can shift rapidly (Kempton 1981). The shift is first in the extended senses while the prototype can remain stable for some time (Kempton 1981: 200–201). We see this sort of categorical pattern change in British beakers. The basic prototypic referents in shape, decoration and design remain very stable for a long time. Only at the very end of the period of beaker production does this pattern break down. This is the time when quite radical design forms are used and we see extremes of form including the straight sided handled beakers.

At the end of what is now a very long period of use, beaker design did finally break down. It was through an expansion of choice, an increased use and dominance of extended forms, that the referent increasingly lost its meaning. The prototype did not dissolve into another prototype, nor did an invasion replace it with new more useful commodities. The forces inherent in society used existing material configurations to accommodate changing social needs. The inherent ambiguity of material organisation and use (Geertz 1973) provided the means by which the category was changed and finally replaced. The provision and use of material culture is both the means of its subsistence and destruction.

Distinctions within beakers were not being made along one or two simple dimensions, and do not refer to typic and absolute substitutions over time. A variety of distinctions were constantly being made and maintained within a variety of contexts. Each had its own role to play, and these roles may, or may not, have been orchestrated. Regional traditions, goals, social pressures, local requirements, and proficiency all combined to create the patterns we now observe. Chronology did not determine these patterns, but provided the setting within which the reproduction and transformation of these patterns took place. It is not surprising that chronology is less predicative than the typologies would have us believe. Beaker design patterns, however, suggest that this is in fact the case, and that a fuller accounting of the setting within which these design patterns operated must be made.

ACKNOWLEDGEMENTS

I would like to thank Ian Kinnes for preferential access to the British Museum beaker dates and his many useful comments on this research. I would also like to thank Marie Louise S. Sørensen for keeping me on track and away from the greater flights of fancy. Mostly, though, I would like to thank Mark Edmonds and John Barrett for the many hours of useful discussion and critique. Despite the many influences, the opinions presented in this paper, and the responsibility for them, are wholly my own.

APPENDIX A

Measurement of design organisation

The features recorded are:

1. ZONES which records the degree to which the zones on the pot match or disrupt the symmetric organisation of the elements (none = no zones; match = zones match symmetries; break = zones disrupt or 'break' the symmetries; fringed = zones break an element creating a 'fringe');

2. SYMMETRIES record which symmetric organisation is used on a pot (reflection = mirror symmetry; translation = repeated pattern; combination = a combination of reflection and translation);

3. TRANSFORMATIONS record the level that the symmetric pattern is transformed or hidden (none = simple symmetry; AOC/AOO = all over cord or all over decorated; 2+ = where two symmetric patterns are combined on the same pot; overlap = where two symmetric patterns are combined on the same pot but the patterns overlap; disjunction = where a symmetric pattern is transformed by inserting another element out of sequence; disjunction+ = complex disjunction where two or more elements are inserted; complex = complex design organisations);

4. REFERENCING records the degree to which the same elements used in the design in different roles (none = different elements are used; some = some of the elements match others do not; full = all the elements used match).

REFERENCES

Barrett, J. 1987. Fields of discourse: reconstituting a social archaeology. *Critique of Anthropology* 7: 5–16.

Barrett, J. 1991. The pottery assemblage. In Barrett, J., Bradley, R. & Hall, M. (eds), *Papers on the Archaeology of Cranborne Chase*. Oxford: Oxbow.

Berlin, B. & Kay, P. 1969. *Basic Color Terms: Their Universality and Evolution*. Berkeley: University of California Press.

Binford, L. R. 1968. Archaeological perspectives. In Binford, S. R. and Binford, L. R. (ed.), *New Perspectives in Archaeology*, pp. 1–3. Chicago: Aldine.

Binford, L. R. 1972. *An Archaeological Perspective*. London: Seminar Press.

Boast, R. 1990. The Categorisation and Design Systematics of British Beakers: A Re-examination. Unpublished PhD, Cambridge Univeristy.

Boast, R. 1995. Fine pots, pure pots, and beaker pots. In Kinnes, I. & Varndell, G. (eds), *"Unbaked Urns of Rudely Shape": Essays on British and Irish Pottery for Ian Longworth*, pp. 55–67. Oxford: Oxbow (Monograph 55).

Bradley, R. 1984. *The Social Foundations of Prehistoric Britain*. London: Longman.

Brown, J. 1982. On the structure of artifact typologies. In Whallon, R. and Brown, J. (ed.), *Essays on archaeological typology*, pp. 176–189. New York: Academic Press.

Burgess, C. & Shennan, S. 1976. The beaker phenomenon: some suggestions. In Burgess, C. & Miket, R. (ed.), *Settlement and Economy in the Third and*

Second Millenia B.C., pp. 309–31. Oxford: British Archaeological Reports (33).

Case, H. 1977. The beaker culture in Britain and Ireland. In Mercer, R. (ed.), *Beakers in Britain and Europe*, pp. 71–101. Oxford: British Archaeological Reports (26).

Childe, V. G. 1936. *Man Makes Himself.* London: Collins.

Childe, V. G. 1940. *Prehistoric Communities of the British Isles.* London: Chambers.

Clarke, D. L. 1968. *Analytical archaeology.* London: Methuen.

Clarke, D. L. 1970. *Beaker Pottery of Great Britain and Ireland.* Cambridge: Cambridge University Press.

Clarke, D. L. 1976. The beaker network. In Lanting, J. and van der Waals, J. (ed.), *Glockenbecher Symposium, Oberried 1974*, pp. 459–476. Bussum/Haarlem: Fibula-van Dishoeck.

Dunnell, R. 1978. Style and function: a fundamental dichotomy. *American Antiquity* 43: 192–202.

Edmonds, M. 1995. *Stone Tools and Society: working stone in Neolithic and Bronze Age Britain.* London: Batsford.

Fox, Sir Cyril 1923. *The Archaeology of the Cambridge Region: a topological study of the Bronze, early Iron, Roman and Anglo Saxon Ages, with an introductory note on the Neolithic.* Cambridge: Cambridge University Press.

Geertz, C. 1973. *The Interpretation of Cultures.* New York: Basic Books.

Giddens, A. 1984. *The Constitution of Society.* Cambridge: Polity Press.

Greenacre, M. J. 1984. *Theory and Applications of Correspondence Analysis.* London: Academic Press.

Harrison, R. 1980. *The Beaker Folk: Copper Age Archaeology in Western Europe.* London: Thames and Hudson.

Kempton, W. 1981. *The Folk Classification of Ceramics.* New York: Academic Press.

Kinnes, I., Gibson, A., Ambers. J., Leese, M., & Boast, R. 1991. Radio carbon chronology of British beakers. *Scotish Archaeological Review* 8: 35–68.

Lakoff, G. 1987. *Women, Fire and Dangerous Things.* Chicago: University of Chicago Press.

Lanting, J. & van der Waals, J. 1972. British beakers as seen from the continent: a review article. *Helinium* 12: 20–46.

Miller, D. 1982. Structures and strategies: an aspect of the relationship between social hierarchy and cultural change. In Hodder, I. (ed.), *Symbolic and Structural Archaeology*, pp. 89–98. Cambridge: Cambridge University Press.

Miller, D. 1985. *Artefacts as Categories.* Cambridge: Cambridge Univ. Press.

Mitchell, M. Crichton 1934. A new analysis of the early Bronze Age beaker pottery of Scotland. *Proceedings of the Society of Antiquaries of Scotland* 68: 132–189.

Piggott, S. 1963. Abercromby and after: the beaker cultures in Britain re-examined. In Alcock, L. & Foster, I. (eds), *Culture and Environment: essays in honor of Sir Cyril Fox*, 53–91, London: Routledge and Kegan Paul.

Ricoeur, P. 1978. *The Rule of Metaphor.* Chicago: University of Chicago Press.

Rosch, E. 1978. Principles of categorisation. In Rosch, E. & Lloyd, B. (ed.), *Cognition and Categorization*, pp. 27–48. New Jersey: Lawrence Erlbaum.

Sackett, J. 1977. The meaning of style: a general model. *American Antiquity* 42: 369–380.

Sackett, J. 1982. Approaches to style in lithic archaeology. *Journal of Anthropological Archaeology* 1: 59–112.

Shennan, S. 1988. *Quantifying Archaeology*. Edinburgh: Edinburgh University Press.

Sokal, R. & Sneath, P. 1963. *Principles of Numeric Taxonomy*. San Fransisco: W. H. Freeman.

Sørensen, M. L. S. 1989. Looking at peripheries. The reproduction of material culture in late Bronze Age Scandinavia and England. In Nordstrom, H. & Knape, A. (eds), *Bronze Age Studies*, pp. 63–76. Stockholm: Statens Historiska Museum.

Spaulding, A. C. 1953. Statistical techniques for the discovery of artifact types. *American Antiquity* 18: 305–313.

Thorpe, I. J. & Richards, C. 1984. The decline of ritual authority and the introduction of beakers into Britain. In Bradley, R. & Gardiner, J. (eds), *Neolithic Studies*, 67–84. Oxford: British Archaeological Reports.

Thurnam, J. 1871. On British barrows, especially those of Wiltshire and the adjoining counties. *Archaeologia* 43: 285–552.

Tilley, C. 1984. Ideology and the legitimation of power in the middle Neolithic of southern Sweden. In Miller, D. & Tilley, C. (eds), *Ideology, Power and Prehistory*, pp. 111–146. Cambridge: Cambridge University Press.

Wiessner, P. 1984. Reconsidering the behavioural basis of style. *Journal of Anthropological Archaeology* 3: 190–234.

Wittgenstein, L. 1953. *Philosophical Investigations*. New York: Macmillan.

Wobst, M. 1977. Stylistic behaviour and information exchange. *University of Michigan, Museum of Anthropology Anthropological Papers* 61: 317–342.

19

Understanding the Mesolithic/Neolithic Frontier in the Lower Rhine Basin, 5300–4300 cal. BC

L. P. Louwe Kooijmans

In the study of the Mesolithic-Neolithic transition in northern Europe most attention has been focussed on the problem of explaining *why* this transition took place around ca 4200 cal. BC. This is the 'moment' in which hunter-gatherer societies all over northern Europe, from the British Isles, over the North German Plain toward southern Scandinavia 'suddenly' started to include crop cultivation and animal husbandry in their subsistence package, which by itself is a very remarkable, synchronic process, validating this special attention. Of equal importance, however, is an understanding of the preceding, remarkably long retardation of this transition from the moment when the Bandkeramic communities had established themselves across the full extent of the northern loess zone. I will direct myself to that topic and restrict myself to the western part of the North German Plain: the Lower Rhine basin. Before proposing an explanation of this long 'availability phase', to use the scheme developed by Zvelebil (1986), we must first establish how real this phase is and how it may be grasped archaeologically.

LANDSCAPE ZONES (FIG. 1)

Three major landscape zones are involved. The first comprises a southern zone of loess-covered hills and river terraces north of the low

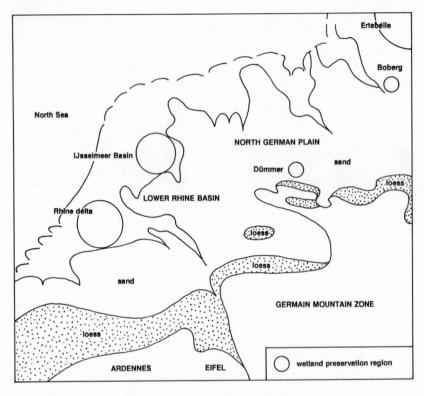

Figure. 1. Outline of the lower Rhine basin with landscape zones and wetland preservation regions for Neolithic sites.

Ardennes-Eifel mountain range. The second is a predominantly flat landscape to the north of the loess, consisting of fluvial, fluvio-glacial and glacial sands, gravels and tills, covered for the greater part by late glacial cover sands. The third zone comprises the extensive Holocene sedimentation district of the Dutch delta. A major research problem in this region is to cope with the extreme differences in archaeological preservation in these three zones. In the loess zone, conditions are favourable for the preservation of soil traces: houseplans, pit fills, enclosures, ditch systems, etc. This is a zone of well-preserved settlement plans and associated assemblages, albeit not for every period (Lüning 1982; Modderman 1985). By contrast, preservation in the sand zone is poor and archaeological information is restricted. There are thousands of surface flint scatters, but few of these have produced pottery or spatial information and many are mixed, disturbed or destroyed as a result of modern agriculture (Louwe Kooijmans & Verhart 1990; Wansleeben & Verhart 1990). In the delta, most Neolithic surfaces are reworked or deeply covered. Consequently sites are restricted in number but very rewarding because of organic preservation and stratigraphy. It is in this zone that the northern communities display high archaeological visibility, but how representative these sites are of a more general situation across zones is a major interpretative problem (Louwe Kooijmans 1987).

Research into the character of the Neolithic in all three zones is currently being undertaken by Leiden University (Louwe Kooijmans 1993b). Settlement excavations have been executed in the loess zone of Bandkeramic, Rössen and Michelsberg sites. An extensive multi-scale geographical analysis has been made of all 6000 Meuse Valley flint assemblages within the southern sand zone (Wansleeben & Verhart 1990) and a systematic geo-archaeological prospection for Neolithic culture layers on the Holocene covered dune slopes has been executed in the delta (Verbruggen in prep.). In addition, large-scale research projects are being undertaken by the other Dutch universities, Belgian and German institutes, all of which adds up to an extensive and rich database.

Taking the large differences in preservation between the three zones into account, one may still consider two opposed communities: those of the loess zone and those of the sands to the north. Such an opposition might be considered highly eco-deterministic. We should, however, realise that the attested settlement systems and palaeo-economy in both zones are indeed different and are linked to divergent natural conditions. The loess zone palaeogeography was one of deciduous forests with a dense canopy and restricted undergrowth, poor in ecological gradients, poor in game, but with a high natural soil fertility: unattractive for hunter-gatherers and well suited to simple hoe agriculture without manuring. The sands of the northern plain were covered by a more open woodland, presumably rich in game, especially in its wetter parts, but with easily exhausted soils on a subsoil of low mineral fertility. Agriculture in this zone would have had to face low yields or to be based on shifting fields or systematic manuring. However, the zone offered good conditions for generalised broad spectrum foragers. In that sense, it seems likely there was a natural foundation to the distinctions that separated the farmers of the loess from the foragers of the sands from the beginning of the Neolithic onward.

What remains as the major focus for research is the nature of interaction between these geographical and cultural zones, and the trajectories of their development. What is clear is that fundamental changes took place in both areas. However, it is difficult to establish the extent to which these developments were autonomous or interrelated. There is clear evidence that contacts between social groups were by no means uncommon, so it is plausible that interaction played an important role in the social and economic transformations that occurred in both zones. Thanks to the settlement excavations of the last few decades, our knowledge of the period has been considerably improved, both for the communities on the loess and for those on the sands. I will first discuss the developments in the loess zone, since these appear to be most prominent, and subsequently reflect on the northern area.

TRANSFORMATIONS IN THE NEOLITHIC OF THE LOESS ZONE (FIG. 2)

So far as we can establish, developments in the loess zone were not gradual but episodic. Periods of structural stability (or very gradual culture change) are interrupted by culture breaks in which many archaeologically observable aspects change simultaneously or within a restricted time span. We can observe changes in pottery styles, flint acquisition and flint artefact styles (basic technology as well as tool kits), materials used in long-distance exchange, major crops, house architecture, and the location and organisation of settlements. Change was profound in such stages, involving all aspects of society, and not restricted to a few 'cultural traits'. A first stage, which largely escapes archaeological observation, is that shortly before 5300 cal. BC, when we think that the local Mesolithic was confronted with intrusive groups using La Hoguette pottery (Lüning, Kloos & Albert 1989. This might well have been the first establishment of an agricultural frontier along a part of the northern loess border.

The second transition encompasses the central European Bandkeramic (LBK) replacing the western La Hoguette. The single La Hoguette site in the region, at Sweikhuizen, differs in a fundamental way from the Bandkeramic villages by its upper terrace edge, gravel subsoil, viewpoint location, 40 m above the valley floor, its lack of soil traces and its modest extent (Modderman 1987). Arguably, La Hoguette has left no identifiable traces in the successive system. However, it could be suggested that we should consider specific western early LBK elements as such: the Y-post setting in the long houses, the poppy seed and the Limburg pottery.

This second transition is followed by a 400-year period of stability, with only internal LBK modifications, but no essential breaks. A major

WARTBERG - STEIN		
first ard?		
deep flint mining		
large, central enclosures		
MICHELSBERG		
BISCHHEIM	CHANGE	4300 cal BC
RÖSSEN		
more positive environmental perception?	STABLE	
more flexible agriculture		
change in all cultural aspects		
GROSSGARTACH	CRISIS	4900 cal BC
population increase		
infilling of territories		
negative environmental perception	STABLE	
rigid and restricted agricultural system		
Southeast European tradition		
BANDKERAMIC	INFLOW	5300 cal BC
Southwestern tradition		
LA HOGUETTE	INFLOW	5400 cal BC?
LATE MESOLITHIC		

Figure. 2. Cultural transformations in the loess zone Neolithic, lower Rhine basin.

process seems to be a population increase that might have been the basis of increasing tensions and of social instability. Northern contacts are reflected in the Meuse valley in a series of ephemeral sites, up to 20 km beyond the loess fringe, probably reflecting LBK use of this zone. LBK adzes are found up to 100 km north of the settled loess area and there are about 100 sites with characteristic LBK arrowheads in the Dutch part of the southern sand zone (de Graaf 1987). There are two possible explanations for these finds: either LBK expeditions far to the north or exchange with the northern European foragers. A remarkable site is Weelde-Paardsdrank, ca 70 km from the nearest known LBK settlement, with a late Mesolithic trapeze industry, including a series of points that can be considered as LBK inspired, but locally made. Some pottery sherds of original technology have, moreover, been found at this site (Huyge & Vermeersch 1982). Similar late Mesolithic assemblages (but without LBK-related points and pottery) have radiocarbon dates up till 5000 cal. BC (Lanting & Mook 1977: 39).

The end of the LBK (around 4900 cal. BC) is marked by transformations documented in greatest detail in the Merzbachtal micro-region of the Aldenhovener Platte, but also clearly evident in the Netherlands. The culture system is completely transformed after a short but distinct epsiode which witnesses earthwork construction and the so-called 'LBK-Grossgartach' horizon (Stehli 1989), the latter developing into (full) Rössen. Changes can be identified in pottery styles and in patterns of flint acquisition, with a shift of emphasis towards the exploitation of the Rullen area. Change can also be detected in settlements, with a move towards very long trapezoidal buildings of more advanced construction, often accompanied by outhouses (Dohrn-Ihmig 1983). Settlements also appear more nucleated, at least in the Merzbachtal, and are often palisaded and loess pits are more localised and restricted in number. Site locations are extended towards the valley floors of the Rhine and Meuse and incidentally into the Eifel valleys and onto the adjacent sands. Cultivated cereals change from predominantly einkorn and emmer wheat to bread wheat and barley (Bakels 1990). Given that there is evidence for basic demographic continuity, these observed changes are difficult to explain. Whatever the case, it seems that the new system worked well, since there again followed a stable period up until ca 4300 cal. BC. Two aspects seem to be especially relevant here. First, the release of the rather rigid Bandkeramic subsistence system in favour, it seems, of a more flexible and adaptive one and, second, the more intense and wider northern contacts. These are reflected not only by the denser and wider spread of various types of perforated adzes, but also by several typical Rössen beakers – some proven to be made of upland clays or loess – on sites at 20 or even 100 km to the north of the nearest loess settlements (Kampffmeyer 1988: 117, fig. 71; Schindler 1962).

The period around 4300 cal. BC is again one of rather fundamental change, but this time not so abrupt and dramatic, albeit the outcome – that is the Michelsberg culture – differs as much from Rössen as Rössen does from LBK. The pottery seems to have lost some of its value as ethnic identifier by the loss of decoration. The production of flint took on 'industrial' characteristics with the appearance of deep mining systems. This is difficult to understand in practical terms alone, particularly since there are no indications of changes in environmental conditions, nor that new tasks were now being performed. These changes in the character of production may have had rather more to do with changes in the values and meanings attached to flint as a raw material for tools. The first polished flint axes were made and the large blades and flakes on which the new macrolithic tools were based were used as long-distance exchange items as far as the lakeside settlements in southern Germany (Willms 1982; pers. comm. Dr H. Schlichtherle, Gaienhofen-Hemmenhofen). Evidence for house plans from this phase is relatively rare. What there is reflects the construction and use of fairly modest (sunken) huts covering not more than 40–60 square metres (compare these with the very large houses of Mairy, northern France (Marolle 1989)). In fact, our archaeological view of the settlement system is dominated by large hill top and valley spur sites, surrounded by palisades and/or wide, flat-based, interrupted ditch systems, that enclose areas of 10–100 ha (Vermeersch 1987/88). These sites are central locations of a type and dimensions unknown before and most probable with a central function for a wide region. These developments can be understood in a number of ways. They suggest that the scale of social units was now greater or more dispersed than it had been in LBK and Rössen times. They may reflect a greater emphasis on corporate identity and the 'communal' rather than on the individual settlement and the *domus* as Hodder puts it (1990).

Our limited evidence demonstrates that all loess societies up until this time were predominantly agrarian (Bogucki 1988: 57). We suppose the introduction of the ard in this phase on the basis of British and Danish evidence, but not on dated plough marks in the Lower Rhine basin, the earliest being those of late Neolithic Bornwird at ca 2900 cal. BC (Fokkens 1982).

THE NORTHERN MESOLITHIC AND ITS TRANSFORMATIONS (FIG. 3)

It remains difficult to identify the northern communities from the centuries after 5000 cal. BC in the thousands of flint assemblages that have been recorded (Wansleeben & Verhart 1990). The evidence must be hidden in mixed and undated assemblages, especially simple mediolithic blade industries with scrapers, some borers and trapezes. Most evidence comes from some wetland sites and non-flint artefacts. The sequence of specific Neolithic elements in this zone starts with the reception of LBK, Grossgartach and, subsequently, Rössen adzes. Local pottery production appears to have started at least as early as

```
3500      MN TRB & VLAARDINGEN

          inflow of mined flint tools

          HAZENDONK 2 & 3              (=NW Michelsberg)
          SWIFTERBANT 3               (= early TRB)

4300      first domesticates & cultigens
          extended broad spectrum economy

          SWIFTERBANT 2               (= classical)

          inflow of Breitkeile        < 300 km
          inflow of beakers           < 100 km

4700      first local pottery
          SWIFTERBANT 1               (= Dümmer 1)

          more intensive use of sand margin
          inflow of durchlochte Schuhleistenkeile   < 200 km


          LBK use of sand margin      < 30 km
          inflow/copies of arrow heads < 100 km
          inflow of adzes             < 150 km

          positive environmental perception

          flexible and broad spectrum foraging system


          North European tradition
>5100     LATE MESOLITHIC
```

Figure. 3. Cultural transformations in the sand zone Neolithic, lower Rhine basin.

4700 cal. BC as shown by evidence from two sites, Dümmer (Stapel 1988; Kampffmeyer 1988) and Bronneger (Kroezenga et al. 1991; Lanting 1992). This is a rather thin-walled, polished and only scarcely decorated ware, with high everted rims and with pointed or round bases. In its forms and technology it is clearly of Rössen inspiration.

A second stage, around 4300 cal. BC, is documented at a series of sites: Bergschenhoek, Hazendonk and other Rhine Delta fossil river dunes tops (so-called *donken*), the Swifterbant cluster, some sites in the north-eastern Polder (esp. P14) and at Dümmer-Hüde 1 (Louwe Kooijmans 1987; Hogestijn 1990). Most sites have evidence for cereal consumption (esp. emmer and barley; van Zeist & Palfrenier 1981; Bakels 1981) and domestic animals, albeit often in low percentages: 5–10% at Hazendonk and Dümmer, 50 % at Swifterbant S3 (Zeiler 1991;

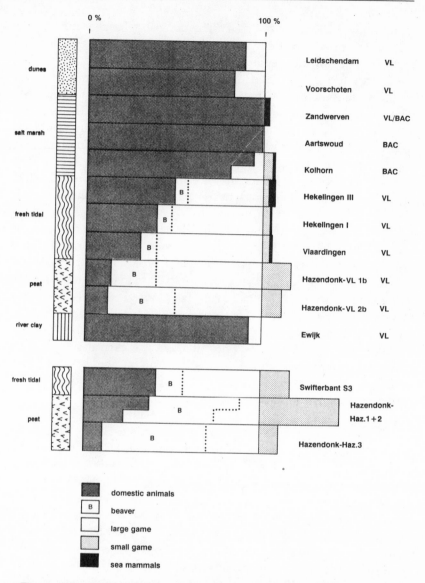

Figure. 4. Bone identifications of three earlier Neolithic (Swifterbant, Michelsberg cultures) and eleven late Neolithic (Vlaardingen Group, Battle Axe culture) assemblages from the Dutch coastal wetlands, arranged according to ecozones. Calculations based on numbers of bones and on large mammals (from beaver upward) being 100%. Note the high proportion of game and the high percentages of beaver and otter in the fresh tidal and peat zone sites, even as late as the 2600 cal. BC late VL assemblage at Hazendonk. Bone composition and site location are the main arguments to conceive some of these sites as (summer) seasonal and others as special activity/extraction sites.

Kampffmeyer 1988: 289 f.; Fig. 4). The domestic: hunted animal ratio will be dependent on site function and so not representative in wider respects. Some of the wetland sites must be considered as short-term camp sites for special task forces and others as seasonal bases for complete households. We have the general impression of a relatively high logistic as well as residential mobility. As such the agrarian aspect of the wetland sites is likely to have been less than that of the (poorly known) upland sites. It is, however, difficult or impossible to guess *how* agricultural (and mobile) these communities might have been. What does it mean, for instance that hardly any upland settlements are known, in contrast to the later TRB phase of the middle Neolithic?

The wetland sites remind one of the Mesolithic in many respects: the flint industry (especially that of Swifterbant S3, Deckers 1979) is mediolithic and has trapezes as the point type. Firm structures are lacking, site dimensions are modest – up to 30 m in diameter – and the living surface shows signs of having been raised with reed or other vegetable matter. Site location along creeks and in peat swamps is, moreover, essentially non-agrarian. We have clear evidence that the supposed broad spectrum food procurement was extended with crops and cattle towards a system that I classify as an *extended broad spectrum economy* (Louwe Kooijmans 1993a). It is, of course, possible that still earlier ceramic sites or earlier evidence for cultigens or domesticates will be found in future research. It is even not improbable that some of the domestic animal bones, identified at Dümmer-Hüde 1 belong to the very beginning of the site around 4700 cal. BC. It is, however, remarkable that the start of the general use of the *donken*, according to recent intensive geoarchaeological prospection, can be dated to ca 4300 cal. BC. This might indicate a moment of rather fundamental change in the overall settlement system and/or the subsistence strategy (Verbruggen in prep.; Louwe Kooijmans 1993b).

There is no doubt that the dominating process in this region has been the subsequent adoption of selected Neolithic cultural traits by indigenous communities. These cultural transformations in the western part of the North European Plain have less in common with the southern Scandinavian Meso-Ertebølle-TRB sequence, than has been suggested up until recently. The Swifterbant-Dümmer complex is different in many aspects from Ertebølle. The western flint industries are completely different; the pottery differs in technology, decoration and there are none of the oval lamps seen in Ertebølle contexts. The closest parallels are to be found on the Rhineland plain in Rössen/

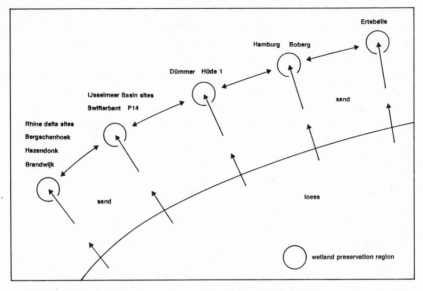

Figure 5. Schematic representation of the N-S and W-E contacts in the North German Plain during the Swifterbant and Ertebølle culture phase.

Bischheim contexts. Researchers now agree that Dümmer, Swifterbant and Hazendonk 1 can be brought together in a separate Western group, with its own characteristics and sequence of development (Kampff-meyer 1988: 337). The differences and similarities of the assemblages within this group and the affinities with southern Scandinavian Erte-bølle can be understood when we refrain from using the culture con-cept and consider each complex in its own right and as a reflection of two contact systems (Fig. 5): the first axis defines traditional west-east contacts. These had existed for millennia between the northern Euro-pean hunter communities, and were responsible for general stylistic similarities of groups as far apart as Swifterbant, Ertebølle and the Pit Comb Ware groups of the Baltic. The second axis lies between the south and the north, reflecting contact and communication between northern communities and adjacent loess margin farmers.

The third phase (ca 4100–3400 cal. BC) witnesses a distinct stylistic divergence between the southern and the northern part of the sand zone, the south having direct links with Michelsberg of the loess. It is at this juncture that we see the first evidence for the development of the western TRB in the north. It may even be appropriate to think in terms of a phase shift in development, with the south in advance of the north. Pottery styles change in the southern region into a new north-western variant of Michelsberg ceramics. These were identified at the Hazendonk and at a series of blown over sand marginal sites. There are also some stylistic relations, especially in the occurrence of carinated bowls, with the British early Neolithic (Louwe Kooijmans 1976: 1980). Another southern trait is its incorporation in the distribution network of artefacts from the Dutch/Belgian flint mines. As a result of this higly diagnostic flint, many sites can be identified, especially in the Meuse valley, but firm indications as to the extent of agrarian activity are lacking. In the Meuse valley project, locational shifts as compared to the late Mesolithic and earlier Neolithic are still under study.

A parallel group has recently been identified in the northern region at site P14 in the north-eastern Polder, with parallels in the phase 2 material of Dümmer-Hüde 1 (ten Anscher in prep.). At both wetland locations there seems to be a continuity of use, similar to the Hazendonk, but upland evidence of any quality is still lacking. In this region the major change seems to be as late as 3400 cal. BC with the introduction of the middle Neolithic TRB Drouwen pottery style and of megalithic collective burial. For the first time, relatively large settlements can be identified. Although subsistence evidence is restricted to pollen and some impressions in pottery, these communities can safely be regarded as fully agrarian, with a (less mobile) settlement system and a social organisation that was distinctly different from those that had existed before.

A STATIC AND A DYNAMIC MODEL (FIGS 6, 7)

We can make a static, descriptive model for the Mesolithic/Neolithic transition of these communities by ordering or grouping our data within a simple chrono-geographical scheme. This framework can then be extended by incorporating synchronic processes and diachronic changes into a rather more dynamic, processual level of interpretation. Two major developments can be identified. The first took the form of a radical cultural transformation, implying a similar social restructuring in the loess zone towards a system that was possibly better adapted to the specific north-western European conditions. It is remarkable that the developments in these early agricultural communities culminate in a system that has much in common with that of the first agricultural societies in other parts of the northern zone, such as Great Britain and southern Scandinavia, where similar enclosed central sites, flint mines and their products and related pottery styles

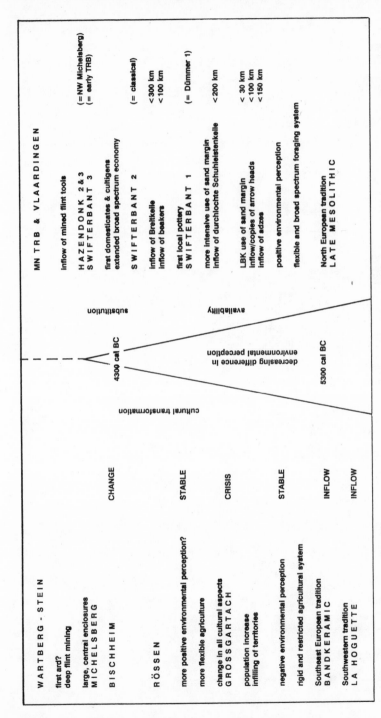

Figure 6. Combination of Figs 2 and 3 in one, correlated scheme, showing converging transformations of two fundamentally different cultural systems over more than 1000 years of increasing interaction, resulting in basically similar societies. Change will have taken place in all cultural spheres. Environmental perception is selected because it seems an archaeologically testable value.

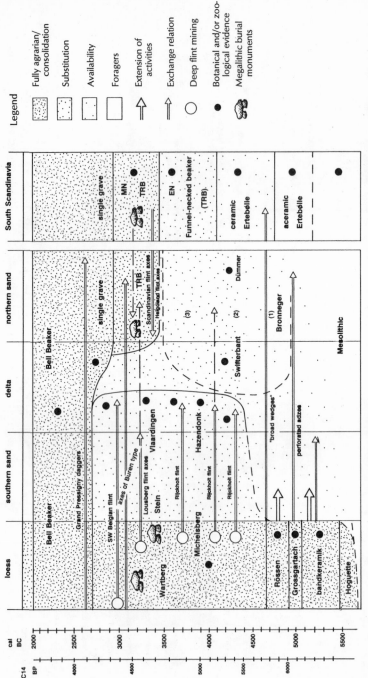

Figure 7. Schematic chronogeographical south-north section of the lower Rhine basin Neolithic showing contacts reflected by long-distance exchange items and locations with evidence on palaeo-economy. Shaded are the zones and stages of Neolithisation according to the model of Zvelebil (1986) as suggested in this paper. Slightly modified after Louwe Kooijmans 1993.

are found. In other words, after a thousand years of development by these agricultural communities a similar situation exists to that amongst foraging communities beyond that region when they increased their reliance upon domesticates. Can we say that a convergence had taken place? That the loess communities had changed to such an extent that at the very least their 'offer' fitted to the 'demands' of the northern communities seems plausible in view of the documented contacts. The Lower Rhine basin, or rather the entire North German Plain, was lagging behind. No enclosures or megaliths are found there at this stage and so this region seems to have been rather outside the mainstream of socio-cultural evolution.

The second development is that of an increased extent and intensity of south to north contacts, as documented in the northern zone. The present evidence points to a slow and gradual process in which various Neolithic elements are added one after the other to a late Mesolithic complex. The major handicap for us is that these northern communities are exclusively represented in wetland contexts. Given the nature of the activities conducted at these sites, it is perhaps unsurprising that they have relatively strong Mesolithic traits. While they may not provide an accurate reflection of the character of the overall system, these sites do demonstrate a long persistence of the old style of life. Another handicap is the restricted and dispersed evidence, implying that most dates must be considered more as a *terminus ante quem* for a certain phenomenon than as a fixed date for its start. New evidence might give earlier starts for most Neolithic traits.

While southern impact on the north is well documented, the reverse is not, at least not directly. This should not surprise us, since the only recognisable Mesolithic elements are microliths. Up until now these have been missing – with some very rare exceptions – in LBK and Rössen contexts (however, see the suggestions for the Belgian Michelsberg by Vermeersch 1984; 1987/88). Documented or not, I am inclined to suppose a reverse north to south information flow in return, and would argue that this played a role in the transformation of societies on the loess. It has been suggested that clearings in the loess zone created a more open landscape, supporting more game which either attracted northern hunters or made additional hunting more profitable for the local farmers. The idea of increased competition between these groups, with the farmers developing transhumant cattle herding beyond the loess and the northern hunters encroaching on the loess and even engaging in cattle raiding is interesting, but difficult to support with archaeological evidence, since large-scale clearings are not attested for the Neolithic in pollen diagrams (Bakels 1992).

It seems that the availability/substitution model gives a reasonable description of the developments in the lower Rhine basin. The sequence begins with a static or stationary frontier that can be considered rather closed for about 400 years. The transformation of the loess societies into Rössen goes together with a restricted opening up of this frontier in the next 500 years or so. Substitution seems to have started ca 4300 cal. BC, but in the south with more subsequent developments than in the north. The region, however, was for some reason apart from the main stream of Neolithisation, as reflected for instance in Great Britain and Denmark.

The economic system reflected in the wetland sites is that of broad spectrum hunting and gathering, to which animal husbandry and crop cultivation were added, a system to be called *extended broad spectrum*. This is more accurate than terms such as 'mixed agriculture' or 'mixed farming', both of which are better used to describe situations in which animal husbandry and arable farming are combined in one integrated system (Louwe Kooijmans 1993a). We have no good view of the character of upland subsistence at this time, but the extended broad spectrum economy persisted at least in the wetlands until the end of the period under review, that is the beginning of the Beaker period, ca 2900 cal. BC. Substitution might have been of shorter duration in the Michelsberg culture of the southern sands, but seems in general to have lasted a considerable time. Added to the cultural arguments mentioned above, this gives us a picture of societies in which Mesolithic hunter-gatherer traditions were maintained long after other groups had changed to fully agrarian subsistence and more complex forms of organisation.

After documenting the archaeology and making a *descriptive* model of changes and patterns, we come to formulate the processes that can be inferred. In this *processual* model interaction, exchange, adoption and acculturation are sufficient to explain the visible transformations. Apart from the initial Neolithic (La Hoguette and Bandkeramic) no migrations or physical expansions are needed. There is enough positive evidence for demographic continuity.

UNDERSTANDING THE TRANSFORMATION PROCESSES: OPPOSED ENVIRONMENTAL PERCEPTIONS

This brings us to the broader problem of explaining the character and timing of the changes outlined above, not least the long retardation of the change towards agriculture in the north. We must realise that this is a difficult realm and that any 'explanation' is ours, reflecting our favourite theory and in its essence untestable. We can only observe that earlier explanations are replaced by new ones, based on more sophisticated theories. In the first instance, we must give significance to the separate roots of both communities. In particular, we need to consider the possibility that they were separated by widely different attitudes and ideologies and, more specifically, by different perceptions of nature and the environment.

The late Mesolithic hunter-gatherers had their roots in the late glacial Federmesser (*Stielspitzen*) and ultimately Hamburgian/Magdalenian hunters of northern and western Europe. They had developed a broad spectrum exploitation of their surrounding environment, which means a full appreciation of its 'gifts', a trust on nature to give food in its yearly cycle, cropping from it and even rigourously exploiting it, and living integrated within it in a flexible way. The Bandkeramic way of life, which was essentially agriculturalist, was derived from the south-east and will have combined ideas and values of south-eastern European groups in an ideology that ultimately had at least some roots in the Near East. So the northern European Mesolithic and the Bandkeramic societies had evolved along separate lines over 8000 years or more. A confrontation took place around 5300 cal. BC. Although Bandkeramic people adjusted to minor differences in the landscape in their site location – terrace edge or stream valley slope – their archaeological remains point to a rather rigid system, lacking appreciation of natural diversity. They selected a stereotypical site location, within narrow limits of geomorphology and soil conditions, essentially created their own micro-environment in the dense primeval forests and practised their specialised food production there. In a sense, they lived with their backs to natural diversity. I might be accused of exaggeration in the qualification of the differences in environmental perception of both societies. I might have said that Bandkeramic communities profited from natural conditions only *in a different way*, but that would have obscured the point I wanted to make here. This major difference between both communities considered here can be supported by archaeological arguments, but will be only one aspect in which both societies differed from each other.

Clarifying our understanding of long-lived relations between foragers and neighbouring farming communities is the current revisionist debate in cultural anthropology that deals with the status of modern hunter-gatherers. Some specialists argue that only few of these can be seen as primary or 'pristine', that is independent in their living from foraging neighbours, like the Australian Aborigines and the Andamans, that live in isolated territories in a geographical sense. Most hunter-gatherers, the Bushmen included, have had historical relations with non-foraging groups, sometimes for centuries. This view is not really new, as pointed out by Lee (1992), but there is a growing awareness of the consequences of this view for evolutionary studies. These 'secondary' or (inter)dependent hunter-gatherers had developed exchange and/or social relations of various kinds – including services in agricultural work – with their non-forager counterparts. These relations appear to be essential for their subsistence and even for their basic existence. The value of the 'commodities from the wild', that is, the role of the hunter-gatherers in the relationship, seems to have been underestimated so far, especially in cases where this input took the form of commercial trade. One might wonder how far these specific symbiotic relations are characteristic for the *present day* generalised foragers, living in environments like the tropical rainforest and (semi-) desert and to what extent these principles can be applied to prehistoric situations, in which ecological choice was hardly restricted. This, however, can be seen as relevant in that the choice not to become incorporated in the differently ('higher') organised societies must be conceived as a matter of free choice and not as a failure or devolution. As Lee argues, many foraging groups seem to have *chosen* for values in the immaterial sphere, for a life at a slower pace, a simpler technology, less inequality and a different sense of human-human and human-land relationships. It is a choice for severe limits in the accumulation of material wealth and the concentration of power, the choice of a specific, more modest way of life in full awareness of the alternatives. This seems to be valid in situations as different as the San-Bantu, the Pygmee-Bantu, or Aboriginal-Western confrontation (Lee 1992; Stiles 1992).

This principle of symbiotic relations and of deliberately refraining from what used to be called 'progress' might very well have been at work in the northern European Mesolithic-Neolithic confrontation. The circulation of items such as stone axes can be seen as the archaeologically visible part of complex relations comparable to those of the modern interdependent forager-farmer systems. Following this line we must be sceptical of the view that the LBK and Rössen adzes had a role as prestige items in the recipient communities, which may have had no need of such objects in view of the supposed very modest stratification. The specific attitude, the differences in perception of nature and in values and ideology in a more general sense may, in my opinion, explain why it took so long before the northern communities changed to agricultural subsistence.

We may ask whether we can understand the long-term substitution phase in the North German Plain in the same perspective. It seems that there was a more gradual and less disruptive change in attitude resulting in semi-agrarian societies that have, as far as I know, few parallels in modern ethnography. Some Amazon Indian groups can be considered as such. Apparently, original choices were made and original solutions found, reconciling foraging and agriculture, that proved successful in the specific environmental setting of this region. We should realise that the plain was less well suited to crop cultivation than the loams of England and the Young Moraine landscape of Denmark. I cannot escape the impression that, apart from the purely social arguments, the ecological setting played a role as well, more specific in the supposed long 'phase of substitution'. Understanding the end of that phase is, however, another theme.

ACKNOWLEDGEMENT

I profited very much from discussions with Wil Roebroeks and Harry Fokkens and from their comments on earlier drafts of this paper.

REFERENCES

ten Anscher, T. in prep. Neolithicum en Bronstijd in de Noordoostpolder. Thesis Amsterdam.

Bakels, C. C. 1981. Neolithic plant remains from the Hazendonk, Province of Zuid-Holland, The Netherlands. *Zeitschrift für Archäologie* 15: 141–149.

Bakels, C. C. 1990: The crops of the Rössen culture: significantly different from their Bandkeramik predecessors – French influence? In Cahen, D. & M. Otte (eds), *Rubané et Cardial*, pp. 83–87. Liège: (Etudes et Recherches Archéologiques de l'Université de Liège 39).

Bakels, C. C. 1992: The botanical shadow of two early Neolithic settlements in Belgium: carbonized seeds and disturbances in a pollen record. *Review of Palaeobotany and Palynology* 73: 1–19.

Bogucki, P. 1988. *Forest Farmers and Stockherders*. Cambridge: Cambridge University Press.

Deckers, P. H. 1979. The Flint Material from Swifterbant, earlier Neolithic of the northern Netherlands. Sites S-2, S-4 and S-51. *Palaeohistoria* 21: 143–180.

Dohrn-Ihmig, M. 1983. *Neolithische Siedlungen der Rössener Kultur in der Niederrheinischen Bucht*. München: C. H. Beck (Materialien zur Algemeine und Vergleichende Archäologie 21).

Fokkens, H. 1982. Late Neolithic occupation near Bornwird (province of Friesland). *Palaeohistoria* 24: 91–113.

van der Graaf, K. 1987. *Inventarisatie en Interpretatie van Vondsten uit de Vroegste Fase van het Neolithicum ten Noorden van de Nederlandse Lössgronden.* Leiden: Essay Institute of Prehistory, Leiden University.

Hodder, I. 1990. *The Domestication of Europe.* Oxford: Basil Blackwell.

Hogestijn, J. W. 1990. From Swifterbant to TRB in the IJssel-Vecht basin – Some Suggestions. In Jankowska, D. (ed.), *Die Trichterbecherkultur, Neue Forschungen und Hypothesen*, pp. 163–180. Poznan: Instytut Prähistorii Uniwersitytetu im Adama Mickiecza w Poznaniu.

Huyge, D. & Vermeersch, P. M. 1982. Late Mesolithic settlement at Weelde – Paardsdrank. In Vermeersch, P. M. (ed.), *Contributions to the Study of the Mesolithic of the Belgian Lowland*, pp. 115-203. (Studia Praehistorica Belgica 1).

Kampffmeyer, U. 1988. *Die Keramik der Siedlung Hüde I am Dümmer, Untersuchungen zur Neolithisierung des Nordwestdeutschen Flachlandes.* Thesis Göttingen.

Kroezenga, P. et al. 1991. Vondsten van de Swifterbantcultuur uit het Voorste Diep bij Bronneger. *Paleoaktueel* 2: 32–36.

Lanting J. N. 1992. Aanvullende ^{14}C-dateringen. *Paleoaktueel* 3: 61–63.

Lanting, J. N. & Mook, W. 1977. *The Pre- and Protohistory of the Netherlands in Terms of Radiocarbon Dates.* Groningen.

Lee, R. B. 1992. Art, science, or politics? The crisis in hunter-gatherer studies. *American Anthropologist* 94: 31–54.

Louwe Kooijmans, L. P. 1976. Local developments in a border land. *Oudheidkundige Mededelingen Leiden* 57: 227–297.

Louwe Kooijmans, L. P. 1980. The middle Neolithic assemblage of Het Vormer near Wijchen and the culture pattern around the southern North Sea, c. 3000 B.C. *Oudheidkundige Mededelingen uit het Rijksmuseum van Oudheden te Leiden* 61: 113–208.

Louwe Kooijmans, L. P. 1987. Neolithic settlement and subsistence in the wetlands of the Rhine/Meuse delta of the Netherlands. In Coles, J. M. & Lawson, A. J. (eds), *European Wetlands in Prehistory*, pp. 227–251. Oxford: Clarendon Press.

Louwe Kooijmans, L. P. 1993a. Wetland exploitation and upland relations of prehistoric communities in the Netherlands. *East Anglian Archaeology* 50: 71–116.

Louwe Kooijmans, L. P. 1993b. The Mesolithic/Neolithic transformation in the Lower Rhine basin. In Bogucki, P. (ed.), *Case Studies in European Prehistory*, pp. 95–145. Boca Raton (FL): CRC Press.

Louwe Kooijmans L. P. & Verhart, L. B. M. 1990. Een Middenneolithisch Nederzettingsterrein en een Kuil van de Stein-groep op de voormalige Kraaienberg bij Linden, gemeente Beers (N.Br.). *Oudheidkundige Mededelingen uit het Rijksmuseum van Oudheden te Leiden* 70: 49–108.

Lüning, J. 1982. Siedlung und Siedlungslandschaft in Bandkeramischer und Rössener Zeit. *Offa* 39: 9–33.

Lüning J., Kloos, U., & Albert, S. 1989. Westliche Nachbarn der Bandkeramischen Kultur: La Hoguette und Limburg. *Germania* 67: 355–393.

Marolle, G. P. 1989. Le village Michelsberg des 'Hautes Chanvières' à Mairy (Ardennes) – étude archéologique. *Gallia Préhistoire* 31: 93–117.

Modderman, P. J. R. 1985. Die Bandkeramik im Graetheidegebiet, Niederländisch-Limburg. *Berichten der Römisch-Germanischen Kommission* 66: 26–121.

Modderman, P. J. R. 1987. Limburger Aardewerk uit Sweikhuizen, Gem. Schinnen, Prov. Limburg. *Analecta Praehistorica Leidensia* 20: 87–93.

Schindler, R. 1962. Rössener Elemente im Boberger Neolithikum. *Germania* 40: 245–255.

Stapel, B. 1988. *Die Geschlagene Steingeräte der Siedlung Hüde I am Dümmer.* Thesis Münster.

Stehli, P. 1989. Merzbachtal – Umwelt und Geschichte einer Bandkeramischen Siedlungskammer. *Germania* 67: 51–76.

Stiles, D. 1992. The hunter-gatherer 'revisionist' debate. *Anthropology Today* 8 (2): 13–17.

Verbruggen, M. in prep. Het Neolithicum op de Donken, een Geologische Prospectie naar Archeologische Lagen rond de Donken in het Nederlandse Rivierengebied. Thesis Leiden.

Vermeersch, P. M. 1984. Du Paléolithique Final au Mésolithique dans le Nord de la Belgique. In Cahen, C. & Haesaerts, P. (eds), *Peuples Chasseurs de la Belgique Préhistorique dans leur Cadre Naturel*, pp. 181–193. Brussels: Patrimoine de l'Institut Royal des Sciences Naturels de Belgique.

Vermeersch, P. M. 1987/88. Le Michelsberg en Belgique. *Acta Archeologica Lovaniensia* 26–27: 1–20.

Wansleeben, M. & Verhart, L. B. M. 1990. The transition from the Mesolithic to the Neolithic in the Dutch Meuse valley. In Vermeersch, P. M. & van Peer, P. (eds), *Contributions to the Mesolithic in Europe*, pp. 389–402. Leuven: (Studia Praehistorica Belgica 5).

Willms, C. 1982. *Zwei Fundplätze der Michelsberger Kultur aus dem Eestlichen Münsterland, Gleichzeitig ein Beitrag zum Neolithischen Silexhandel in Mitteleuropa*. August lax. Hildesheim: (Münstersche Beiträge zur Ur- und Frühgeschichte 12).

Zeiler, J. T. 1991. Hunting and animal husbandry in Neolithic sites in the western and central Netherlands: interaction between man and environment. *Helinium* 31: 60–125.

van Zeist, W. A. & Palfrenier-Vegter, R. M. 1981. Seeds and fruits from the Swifterbant S3 site. *Palaeohistoria* 23: 105–168.

Zvelebil, M. 1986. Mesolithic prelude and Neolithic revolution. In Zvelebil, M. (ed.), *Hunters in Transition*, pp. 5–15. Cambridge: Cambridge University Press.

20

Neolithic Societies and Their Environments in Southern Sweden: a Case Study

Lars Larsson

The year 1982 saw the formal start, and 1988 the end of a multi-disciplinary project under the title 'The cultural landscape during 6000 years. A multidisciplinary study of people and their environment in southernmost Sweden.' It came to be known more commonly as the Ystad project. The aim was to study an area of southern Sweden forming the hinterland of the town of Ystad, in order to describe long-term changes in society and environment, and – as far as possible – to analyse the causes of these changes. An area around the town of Ystad on the southern coast of Scania was chosen for the project (Fig. 1). It comprises the hundreds of Ljunits and Herrestad. Physiographically it can be divided into three zones: the coastal landscape with sandy soils, the outer hummocky landscape with clayey-silty soils, and the inner hummocky landscape with clayey and sandy soils.

A number of different subject areas were already included at the planning stage which started in 1980. The project stated with a general hypothesis, namely, that the agrarian landscape as seen in a long-term perspective is characterised by four phases of expansion in prehistory from the first farming to the Viking Age (Berglund 1969) (Fig. 2). This hypothesis was to be tested by researchers from disciplines such as archaeology, medieval archaeology, history, Quaternary geology, and plant ecology. It was considered particularly important to coordinate and interpret the results of different scientific analyses which had been directed at the study of the human influence on the physical environ-

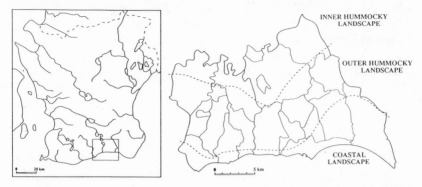

Figure 1. Map of southernmost Sweden (left) and the project area subdivided into three zones (right).

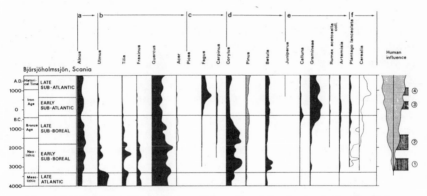

Figure 2. Model for the expansion of the cultural landscape during prehistory according to Berglund (1969).

ment. Expansions as well as phases of stagnation and regression could be noted in two dimensions: in time and/or space with a gradient from the coast to the inner hummocky zone. To analyse these changes, the interdisciplinary research worked on two kinds of studies: *time-vertical studies* mainly of a palaeoecological character; and *time-horizontal* studies focussing on selected periods. Both kinds of studies are of importance for testing the problem of changes. Time-vertical studies deal with landscape changes viewed in a long-term perspective. The time-horizontal studies which were relevant here were:

B1. Expansion following the introduction of agriculture (expansion phase 1), ca 5000 BP (all uncalibrated). This was then followed by a marked decline in plants indicating a cultural landscape during the early part of the middle Neolithic, ca 4500 BP.

[429]

B2. Expansion during the late Neolithic period (expansion phase 2). According to the changes in the cultural landscape postulated by Berglund (1969), this began at the end of the middle Neolithic, ca 4200 BP, but it showed a significant upturn in the late Neolithic, ca 1800 BP, when the true cultural landscape began to make an impact on large parts of the environmental landscape.

The most important research effort was directed towards testing the validity of hypotheses from the point of view of cultural history. To make it possible to combine time-vertical studies with special analyses the entire Neolithic was studied. For practical reasons, however, it was appropriate to retain the division where Mats Larsson dealt with the early phase (M. Larsson 1992) while the author dealt with the later (L. Larsson 1992). The project began at a time of strong influence from ideas associated with the 'new archaeology' and finished during a period under the influence of 'contextual archaeology'. It is also possible to characterise the initial approach to the problems as being influenced by natural determinism, and the work involved in the concluding summary as being influenced by a more cultural-deterministic approach. This continuously changing approach during the project period affected not only the archaeological contributions, but also the dialogue between archaeologists and project members of natural sciences, in particular those in the field of Quaternary biology. This process is made all the more obvious by the fact that the project worked according to a model with a distinct Quaternary geological stamp. The synthesis shows with particular clarity the crucial role of the social environment for the selection principles applied in the utilisation of the physical landscape (Berglund 1991).

An illustration of this point can be seen in the use of the concept of carrying capacity. Although the concept was used, our interest was concentrated upon analysing the social carrying capacity, that is, society's tolerance limits for changes such as population growth, soil erosion, and influence from a wider social environment. It is scarcely likely that people in this area in prehistory would have reached a level where the area was no longer able to feed the population. Large areas were used only marginally right up to the early Middle Ages. The available biomass would have been sufficient. On the other hand, there were changes to the physical environment – some of a natural kind, such as changes in climate, others with social causes, such as erosion. These changes, combined with external social influence put a strain on the society's tolerance level, which meant changes of greater or lesser degree.

The analysis of the remains of features from the project area was also assisted considerably by the fact that the area immediately to the east had already been the subject of a detailed project initially covering the parish of Hagestad, but subsequently extended, producing a picture of the pattern of settlement in south-eastern Scania which is quite unique for the whole of southern Scandinavia (Strömberg 1980). Certain results from the Skateholm project, which was concerned primarily with Mesolithic settlement, were also useful (Larsson 1984; 1988b). Skateholm is situated about five kilometres to the west of the project area.

ASPECTS OF THE SOURCE MATERIAL

Sub-projects B1 and B2 included the cataloguing of find collections. The cataloguing involved both the scrutiny of museum collections and the recording of finds in private collections. The fieldwork involved both surface inspections and archaeological excavations. The former were undertaken on a considerable scale, with the ambition of fully surveying certain selected parishes, to be followed up by a supplementary inspection of those parts of the project area where relics of Stone Age sites might be expected to occur. The result of the field surveying work was to be of critical significance for the choice of places to excavate. The cataloguing revealed a large number of artefacts, mainly axes and daggers. However, very few originated from settlements. Those found in the wetlands came from hoards while others found on dry land might have come from graves.

It is important for an understanding of the social developments presented here to outline some conditions that influenced research and the view of the project area.

1. It must be emphasised that the choice of the investigated area was by no means taken for granted when planning the project. Several other areas in Scania were suggested, including areas in the southwest and north-east of the province. Some of these suggestions were made for archaeological reasons, because the evidence was considered either to be broader or to be more uniformly distributed within each proposed area. The eventual choice of the Ystad area can be explained by the fact that this area was known to offer a much greater potential to Quaternary biology than the other areas suggested (Berglund 1991a).

2. The Ystad area exhibits highly distinctive topographical, geological, and geographical differences within a very restricted area (Berglund 1991b) (Fig. 1). There are areas of flat plain close to the coast. In

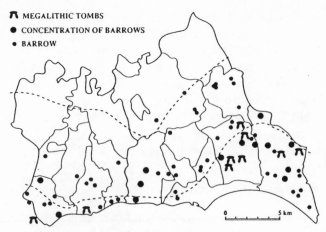

Figure 3. Distribution of megalithic tombs and Bronze Age barrows in the investigated area, in relation to zoning (see Fig. 1).

the eastern part of the project area in particular, this coastal plain is of considerable size. The coastal plain to the far west is the easternmost part of a large plain. An undulating landscape which is rich in clay starts just beyond this, and further in from the coast the undulating landscape has a more varied element of till. In the north-western part of the investigated area is an offshoot of the Romeleåsen ridge – a horst formation. The investigated area also contains two large lakes.

3. The effect of erosion is of great significance for our ability to trace archaeological remains. Cultivation of the soil on the gently rolling sandy plain has caused relatively limited damage. By avoiding deep ploughing, no sterile sand was brought up to the surface here. In the more undulating landscape, on the other hand, cultivation of the soil combined with the effect of surface water has brought about major changes in topography. Material from the top of the hill has been carried down to the foot. Because a significant number of settlement sites were situated at a certain altitude, this effect meant that first the layers containing finds, and then the features which had been dug down into the soil were destroyed. Surface soil has also run down and been deposited at the foot of the hill, causing archaeological remains to be covered by thick erosion layers. Any remains of settlements would thus escape the field survey.

4. To be able to understand the prehistoric situation, one must also have an idea of the situation today as regards visible ancient monuments. In the outer and inner hummocky landscape the spatial distribution of known ancient monuments was sparse (Fig. 3). But there are

Bronze Age barrows located not only on the plain and along the coast, but also at the transition from the plain to the hummocky landscape. In the inner hummocky landscape there are few. Today there is only one surviving megalithic grave, but we know the position of at least five graves from references in written sources and markings on maps from the seventeenth and eighteenth centuries.

5. One practical difficulty encountered both in the field survey and in the excavations was the extremely rapid crop succession practised at the present time, when a considerable proportion of the fields are not covered by growing crops for only short periods of the year. The problem of representativeness also has to do with the fact that considerable tracts of land in certain areas which are rich in archaeological remains, as far as surface finds are concerned, were not accessible because they are under pasture or are military training areas with extensive grass cover.

6. In view of the comparatively limited areas where optimum settlement conditions were encountered, it is not uncommon to find remains from several different periods, relating both to settlement and to burials, in one and the same area. This means that more recent features have influenced earlier features to a greater or lesser degree, and in so doing have made the job of processing the data more difficult. In particular, it gives rise to considerable uncertainty with regard to the interpretation of the layout of the house remains or the choice of charred material for various analyses.

SOCIAL DEVELOPMENT IN THE EARLIEST PART OF THE EARLY NEOLITHIC

The study of the Neolithic has chiefly been concentrated on analysing economic and social issues from the archaeological evidence. The landscape-related studies that were made as a part of the project are the basis for the discussion of changes in economic structure and the pattern of settlement which could be confirmed from the archaeological material. The study in sub-project B1 has concentrated mainly on the changes observed during the early Neolithic (Phase I), on the changes which can be observed during the transition between the early and middle Neolithic, around 4700–4500 BP (Phase II) and on the first part of the middle Neolithic, 4500–4300 BP. The objective was to arrive at an explanatory model which could be applied primarily in south-eastern Scania, but which could also be valid in a more general sense. A particular interest was focussed on the growth of local territories. However, changes in ecology and economy were also examined, in order to provide a background to analyse the factors that lay behind observed changes in the pattern of settlement. The investigations carried out as part of the Ystad project have given us a relatively detailed picture of the settlement pattern. It should, however, be emphasised that this pattern comes out most clearly in the coastal region. As noted above, conditions for archaeological investigation are much worse in the till soils of the hummocky landscape than on the sandy coastal plain.

Although the project concerned Neolithic social developments, the analysis of the introduction of agriculture also required us to have some knowledge of late Mesolithic conditions. The survey work revealed that the lagoon which is now the bog of Öja-Herrestads Mosse in the eastern part of the research area (Fig. 6) was well used in the late Mesolithic. Settlement comprised not only big base camps on promontories and islands in the lagoon but also small sites of a seasonal nature on the beach ridges which arose through sea-level changes and finally almost cut off the lagoon from the sea. Excavations have covered only one site in the lagoon. In this case we can benefit from the findings of the excavations in the former lagoon at Skateholm, about twenty-five kilometres to the west. Here, three large Mesolithic sites combined with cemeteries have been investigated, in an area less than 400 metres long. Other sites can be combined into a settlement pattern where the continuity of the attachment to the lagoon is very clear during the late Mesolithic, that is, ca 6500–5000 BP.

The settlement areas which evidently existed for much of the Neolithic contain remains of sites from early in the early Neolithic. In some areas, such as Öja-Herrestads Mosse, they can be seen as a continuation of the traditional settlement of the late Mesolithic, while in other areas, such as around the estuaries of the small rivers, they can be interpreted as newly established settlements, as at Mossby, where the most interesting site occurs (M. Larsson 1992). This site lies about 400 metres from the present-day coast in the westernmost part of the research area (Fig. 4). Geologically, the area consists essentially of sand. However, an area of heavy clay soils takes over about one hundred metres to the north of the site area. The site area is relatively flat and is situated on the south-facing slope of a plateau, which is about 11 metres above sea level. Extensive areas of boggy ground, which were bays during the early Neolithic, lie to the north and the north-west.

A mechanical excavator was used to strip the topsoil in the area of the two find concentrations which had been identified during the field survey. One of these with an occupation layer consisting of greyish-

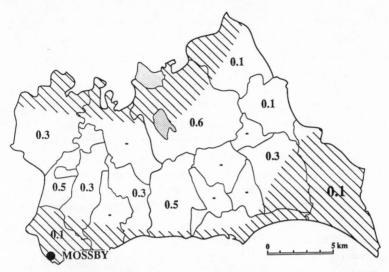

Figure 4. Early Neolithic (phase I) settlement in the Ystad area. The settlement areas are marked by hatching. The figures refer to the number of point-butted flint axes per 100 hectares of cultivated land per parish.

black humus sand is now about 70 square metres but was probably at least twice that size originally. A large number of post-holes were observed; in particular, three stone-lined post-holes and a number of other, smaller post-holes constituted the base for a house that measured 12 metres in length, with a maximum width of 6 metres (M. Larsson 1992: fig. 70). The roof-supporting structure of the house consists of three central posts whose diameter ranges from 40 to 50 cm. Those post-holes which were a part of the wall structure are of much smaller dimensions.

The material yielded by the investigation is relatively comprehensive. Funnel Beakers of different sizes were found. Ear vessels and clay discs are among the other types which have been identified. The overwhelming form of decoration is the corded pattern, and the Funnel Beakers can be attributed to Becker's B-phase. While the number of flint implements is not particularly large, there are fragments of polished, pointed-butted axes included in the assemblage. The similarities with the south-western Scanian Svenstorp group have been emphasised, although there are differences (Larsson & Larsson 1986: 12 f.). Parallels to the Mossby site can be found in the Danish material, in the form of sites belonging to the older Volling group in Jutland and to the Svaleklint group in Zealand (Madsen & Petersen 1984; Ebbesen & Mahler 1980).

A total of five samples for datings were collected; three from carbonised encrusted food residues, and two from carbonised seed barley. The results point to extremely early datings. The three tests performed on incrusted food residues have been dated to between 5238 ± 120 and 5010 ± 110 (Ua-429, Ua-754, Ua-430) BP, and the two performed on carbonised barley to 4925 ± 115 (Ua-755) and 4915 ± 100 (Ua-753) BP. The two oldest dates are the earliest that we have for the early Funnel Beaker culture (TBK) in southern Scandinavia and should be looked upon with certain reservations. The other three fall conveniently within the accepted framework. It is thus quite clear that the Mossby site belongs to the very earliest phase in Scania. Excavations in Zealand in recent years have resulted in the discovery of further house structures of the 'Mossby' type, and ceramic materials have been found which can be dated to the Svaleklint group (Kaul 1988). A similar house surrounding a grave within a long barrow (Rønne 1979) shows a direct relationship between houses for the living and houses for the dead.

Settlement and hoards from the earliest Neolithic – the time of the pointed-butted flint axe – have also been found in the inner hummocky landscape (Fig. 4). The considerable erosion caused by tillage, however, has meant that the evidence consists of flint objects in the plough furrows. Nevertheless, the size of these sites corresponds to those documented in the coastal zone, in other words, only a few hundred square metres, which can be regarded as the space required for one farm unit. On the other hand, the clayey land in the inner hummocky zone was used on a more extensive basis. This can be viewed as a buffer zone between the two other areas (Fig. 4).

In most of the pollen diagrams from the Ystad area, the oldest Neolithic phase is characterised by unstable forest ecosystems with indications of grain cultivation and pasture (Berglund et al. 1991a). From the palaeobotanical point of view, the coastal area during the period has been described as a relatively open forest landscape containing small cultivated areas (Hjelmroos 1985: 48). During phase I we can imagine a system which closely resembled a form of market gardening, with small fields under permanent cultivation (Sherratt 1980: 317). A system of this kind was so well balanced that a number of harvests could be taken within a limited area by using a system of rotation.

THE LATE PART OF THE EARLY NEOLITHIC

The transition from phase I to phase II at the end of the early Neolithic shows a distinct change. New features include the restructuring of the

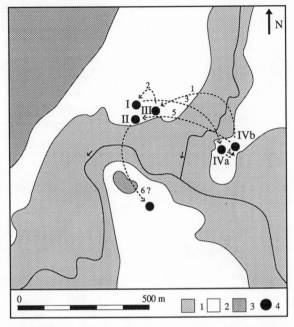

Figure 5. The Kabusa area in the south-eastern part of the research area with the five excavated sites and their chronological and chorological relations (1–6). Legend: 1. area lower than 5 m above sea level; 2. area between 5 and 10 m above sea level; 3. area higher than 10 m above sea level; and 4. site.

pattern of settlement from small, sparsely distributed settlements during phase I to a pattern in which continuous settlement can be observed within certain areas. A clear concentration of settlement can be discerned towards the end of the early Neolithic and during the early part of the middle Neolithic. There is also a tendency for the sites to become somewhat larger. In southern Scania we are dealing primarily with sites of modest size, of up to about 1700–2000 square metres.

Although these changes can be studied in five or six separate areas within the project area, it is at its clearest around the estuary of the river Kabusaån. The area of investigation at Kabusa (Fig. 5) is situated about 1000 metres from the present-day coast in the easternmost part of the research area (Fig. 6). However, during the early and middle Neolithic, the present-day river Kabusaån was a deep bay which extended for a distance of some 1000 metres to the north. The area is flat and consists of light sandy soils with only quite small elements of clay. Topographically the variation in height is between 5 and 10 metres above sea level. The survey took place under favourable condi-

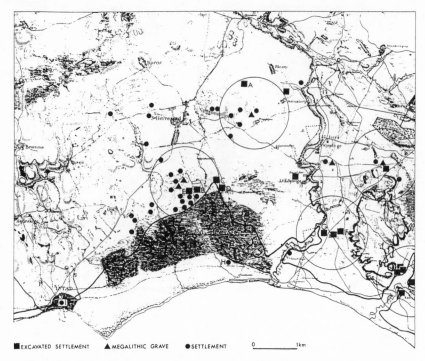

EXCAVATED SETTLEMENT ▲ MEGALITHIC GRAVE ● SETTLEMENT

Figure 6. Extract from the 1812 Scanian Reconnaissance Map (Skånska Re-kognosceringskartan) of the eastern part of the research area with the settlement of the late part of the early Neolithic (phase II) and middle Neolithic A. The filled areas mark water-logged land (from M. Larsson 1992).

tions. A total of twelve sites were found within an area of no more than 1.5 square kilometres, the majority of which could be dated to the early and middle Neolithic. In an area of extremely limited size – at a distance of not more than 450 metres – it is thus possible to follow changes in the settlement for a relatively limited period (M. Larsson 1992).

To judge from the surface finds, most of the concentration of finds indicated small sites covering an area of not more than 200–300 square metres. A considerable quantity of stray finds was recovered, on the basis of which the site could be dated to the early Neolithic, continuing into middle Neolithic III. A total of five sites were investigated; these have been named Kabusa I to IV. Chronologically these sites span the early Neolithic and considerable parts of the middle Neolithic (periods I-III): Kabusa I yielded material, in particular pottery, which permits dating to phase Ia. The site is small, estimated at not more than 600–

800 square metres. It is likely that houses stood on the site, in view of the accumulation of post-holes and the relative abundance of burned clay daub found in the same area. Kabusa II contains significantly more material and can be dated to phase II of the middle Neolithic, primarily on the basis of the pottery. The total area of the site has been estimated at approximately 800 square metres. The remains of at least two houses, consisting of post stains and stone settings, have been identified at the site. Kabusa III is situated not more than about forty metres to the east of Kabusa II. The quantity of material is relatively small, but includes pottery of such a distinctive nature that dating to the later part of the early Neolithic is possible. The estimated area of the site is small, some 600–700 square metres. Kabusa IV is actually two sites. Kabusa IVa is small and has been dated to phase Ia, Kabusa IV to phase Ib, on the other hand, is large and yielded abundant and varied material during the investigation. The chronological span of the site comprises the oldest part of the early Neolithic to the middle Neolithic phase III. The point of main emphasis nevertheless lies in phase I. It was during this period that the site also achieved its greatest extent, which is put at some 1400 square metres.

The number of sites datable to phase II shows an increase over the whole of the Ystad area. The period is characterised not only by a distinct increase in the number of sites, but also by other factors. For instance, the first dolmens in this area were constructed during this period. The only preserved megalithic grave, Trollasten in the parish of Stora Köpinge, has been excavated (Strömberg 1968). The abundant material from this site belongs for the most part to the central periods of the middle Neolithic. One other dolmen has also been investigated. This was a long dolmen with a probable initial stage as a long barrow, which has now disappeared entirely, at Skogsdala, in the parish of Stora Köpinge. The investigation yielded only the impressions of the larger stones which had been a part of the monument (Jakobsson 1986). The pottery finds made here permit the long barrow to be dated to the later part of phase II. There are considerable similarities between the ceramic items recovered from the dolmen and the material from, for example, the Kabusa III site. However, a small settlement was found adjacent to the dolmen. Apart from these excavated examples, three dolmens were located on the basis of old cartographic sources (Tesch 1983: 37; Riddersporre 1992) (Fig. 3). Two of these, situated to the north of the bog Öja-Herrestads Mosse, were clearly of the same type as the Skogsdala long dolmen. Another factor of interest is the increasing use of prestige objects such as copper axes, long thin-butted axes, amber, and perhaps also ceramic items (M. Larsson 1988a: 55; Madsen 1988: 324 ff.; Hårdh 1988: 59 ff.). Hoards with thin-butted flint axes are numerous, and offerings of humans in bogs are also documented.

During phase II we can see the growth of an entirely different system of groupings of sites within certain specific areas (Fig. 6). It is true to say, on the whole, that bays and lagoons were seen as particularly attractive locations for settlement during this period. Osteological investigations of the finds from an excavation of a site – Rävgrav – at another lagoon in the Skateholm area some 25 km to the west nevertheless show that sites located near the coast need not have had direct associations with hunting/fishing, since the bones of cattle, pig and sheep predominate (Larsson 1992).

Many factors are common to all the site concentrations. The soil type is sand. In the northern area, the sites are situated on light soils surrounded by clayey soil. The location of the sites is characterised topographically by their weakly marked height and by their proximity to watercourses. Dolmens are documented in four of the areas. A further common denominator is the small size of the territories. In most cases, the sites in an individual area can be circumscribed by a circle with a diameter of one kilometre (Fig. 6). The sites give the impression of having been of a size suitable for a single family. A local group may have comprised around five or six families with a total population of between forty and sixty persons. Alliances in the form of marriages, for example, may subsequently have been established between these families (Chapman 1988: 32).

A distinct increase in plant species which indicate occupation, and also in the pollen from cereal grains, can be observed in the majority of the southern Scandinavian pollen diagrams, starting in about 4600 BP (Tauber 1971: 128). This provides evidence of a rapidly expanding economy, in which the subsistence economy could no longer be kept within the earlier framework, and in which the broad-leaved deciduous forests had to be utilised in a more effective manner.

THE EARLIEST MIDDLE NEOLITHIC

A clear continuity can be observed between phase II of the early Neolithic and phase I of the middle Neolithic, taking the form of a maintenance of settlement traditions, with small settlements continuing during the period. Dolmens were still being constructed and used during Ia, and it was only during the middle Neolithic Ib that the first passage-tombs were constructed. There are no known passage-tombs in this area today, but they probably did exist.

Whereas the number of known and investigated sites dating from phase II of the early Neolithic and the middle Neolithic I is relatively large in the study area, this is not the case in the following middle Neolithic period, II. It seems that this phase saw a a decline and/or a concentration of settlement. This is a trend which was also observed, for example, on the island of Langeland in Denmark (Skaarup 1985: 363). It is possible to observe a clear continuity in the area, from at least the end of the early Neolithic until the middle of the middle Neolithic, III. The sites were small, at up to ca 1400 square metres, and were inhabited by perhaps eight to ten individuals, in other words, an extended family. This pattern gives an impression of having remained stable throughout the period. However, a clear break occurred in the settlement structure around 4300 BP. Surface finds reveal a renewed expansion towards the heavier soils in the hinterland.

The regeneration phase which can be detected in the pollen diagram at the start of the middle Neolithic can be interpreted in such a way that the forest was transformed into coppiced woodland, and that a system of coppiced woodlands of different ages was growing in an area of light soils. The forests in the surrounding area had also been transformed into a system of coppices of different ages. According to calculations, a system of this kind should have permitted continuous cultivation in the area over a long period. An area of land no greater than about 0.5–0.7 hectares in size would have been needed in order to provide a population of five adults and five children with cereal grain products. The model assumes a proportion of 30% for barley (Olsson 1991a; 1991b).

THE LATE MIDDLE NEOLITHIC

Research within sub-project B2, which covers the late middle Neolithic and late Neolithic, has mostly been geared to studies of the relation between different cultural phenomena and the form of societies and their relation to the cultural landscape. The study of the various material cultures during the middle Neolithic of southern Sweden – the Funnel Beaker culture (TBK), the Pitted ware culture (GRK), and the Battle Axe culture (SYK) – must be examined in the light of a number of different factors. These include chronology, the utilisation of the landscape, and the ideological base of society. It is therefore not fruitful to see southern Scandinavia as a culturally uniform area.

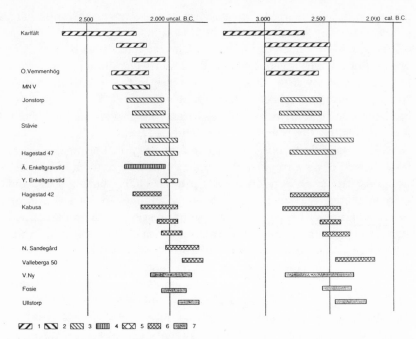

Figure 7. Radiocarbon 14 dates (uncalibrated to the left and calibrated to the right) and intervals from middle Neolithic A and B. Legend: 1. later middle Neolithic A in Scania; 2. middle Neolithic V in Denmark; 3. middle Neolithic V in Scania, 4. early Single Grave culture; 5. late Single Grave culture; 6. sites from the late Battle Axe culture; and 7. graves from the late Battle Axe culture.

In terms of chronology, Danish material places MN V, the latest part of the TRB, within the period 4300–4100 BP (Malmros & Tauber 1977: 81; Davidsen 1978: 170; Tauber 1986: table 1) (Fig. 7). This value can be compared with the mean value of 4130 BP for the Scanian sites with elements of middle Neolithic V character. This difference may indicate that typical elements of this period V existed in Scania for a somewhat longer period than in eastern Zealand. In addition they are present at sites whose material composition differs noticeably from that encountered in the Danish TRB. The Swedish dates for the SYK all originate from features which have been dated to the late part of the culture (Larsson & Larsson 1991; L. Larsson 1992). A variation in the central values from 4000–3800 BP was obtained for these dates. In his detailed study of the SYK, Malmer (1962: fig. 33) concludes that the early phase was slightly shorter than the later phase. This suggests that the SYK was introduced at roughly the same time as the Single Grave culture (EGK) in Denmark, that is, about 4200 BP. In southern

Sweden, the relationship between the early SYK and the late TBK, or elements belonging to it, is more uncertain. The Scanian dates support the assumption that the late TRB in southernmost Sweden could have existed parallel to the early SYK.

With regard to the relationship between the TRB and the Pitted ware culture, the results of a number of investigations have been published in recent years which to a certain extent change our view of these two cultural phenomena. The Pitted ware culture, like the TRB, does not exhibit a uniform combination of artefacts and style. The additional existence of a noticeable difference, not only in the material culture, but also in the economy, has proved to be associated with considerable interpretative problems (Browall 1986: 28 ff.). Certain areas are completely dominated by hunting, fishing, and gathering, whilst animal husbandry and arable farming are well represented in other areas. Clear indications of a mixture of elements from both the TRB and GRK have been documented in the area of southernmost Sweden (Larsson 1982; 1985; Strömberg 1988). North-eastern Jutland and the island of Bornholm also contain similar examples of elements from the late TRB (Rasmussen 1984: 97; Nielsen & Nielsen 1991). Dates from sites with a mixture of artefactual elements have produced values of 4200–4000 BP (Rasmussen 1991: 17 f.; Nielsen & Nielsen 1991: 61 f.). The organic finds indicate a mixed economy, with animal husbandry and arable farming being supplemented by hunting and fishing (Richter 1991). This agrees well with the utilisation of the landscape during the final phase of the Danish TRB (Davidsen 1978: 140 ff.). However, this is a feature for which we have no evidence earlier in the middle Neolithic TRB.

In certain parts of southern Scandinavia, therefore, it is not possible to speak of clearly identified material cultural units. Instead, the finds point towards cultural assimilation between the existing TRB settlement and an expanding Pitted ware culture. This cultural assimilation may have been encouraged by the fact that the two cultures appear to share a common origin. Therefore, the fusion of these population groups was facilitated by similarities in structure and identity. Furthermore, the regional characteristics of the GRK indicate that its social structure was one in which new elements could be readily accommodated. The problem is one of how SYK is to be related to this acculturation. It is difficult in the southern Scandinavian SYK complexes to identify any tradition from the TRB which might reasonably be expected to have existed in the event of a linear change from the late TRB to the early SYK. It is also very important to pay particular atten-

[443]

tion to the study of relationships, not so much from a supra-regional southern Scandinavian perspective, but rather as they relate to a number of regions, in order better to appreciate the nature of cultural and economic relationships. At roughly the same time, then, the southern Swedish TRB was exposed to influence from two sources. One was the Pitted ware culture, which resulted in a considerable process of assimilation. Influence from the SYK did not apparently have any impact on societies with a tradition in the TRB or the GRK. The alternatives here seem to have been either continued existence or disappearance.

Although the finds dating from the SYK are comparatively sparse in terms of ecological facts (Møhl 1962), there is evidence of differences between the forms of farming of the SYK and those of the TBK/GRK (Hjelmquist 1982; 1985; Persson 1982). It is difficult to say whether this reveals a major change in agricultural practice. Site material from these two societies reveals that both wheat and barley were cultivated. As has previously been pointed out, however, significant differences may have existed in social organisation – a factor which may have had major consequences for relations between the societies.

Sites corresponding to the Danish middle Neolithic IV-V occur in the Ystad area, but their number is small. These sites appear to have been of limited extent and were probably widely distributed both within the coastal strip and into the outer hummocky zone (Larsson, L. 1985; 1992). This theory is supported not least by the presence of considerable numbers of late thick-butted axes (type B) (Nielsen 1979). Traces of settlement dating from an early part of the SYK are entirely lacking in southern Scania (Strömberg 1989; Larsson, L. 1992). An important task for the research in the Ystad project was therefore to trace sites from the SYK. Surveys in the Ystad area have now provided evidence of some settlement sites. Those located in the hummocky landscape were, like settlement remains from other parts of the Stone Age, so badly damaged by farming activities that no occupation layers or features were preserved. All that remained were fragments of flint axes, which cannot be used for certain dating to any part of the culture. In the coastal zone, where there has been rather less ploughing, a site from the late SYK was excavated at Kabusa in the easternmost part of the research area (L. Larsson 1992). It had a house structure including a shallow depression. The structure had an almost trapezoidal shape, with a length of 13.5 metres and a width of 7 metres. It shows significant similarities to conditions in sites from the late EGK (Hvass 1977; L. Larsson 1992). A couple of small pits with clay vessels have been interpreted as having a ritual purpose.

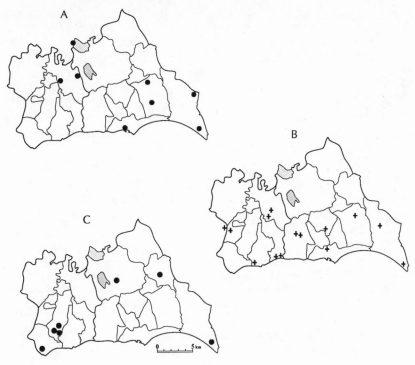

Figure 8. Sites (A), graves (B) and hoards (C) from middle Neolithic B in the project area.

For the purposes of examining the SYK in both its earlier and later phases, graves remain the only adequate basis for the study of settlement distribution. In the Ystad area, at least, the graves are situated in both the hummocky landscape and in the area near the coast (Fig. 8). It should be pointed out that the graves in the hummocky landscape tend to be older than those in the coastal zone in the Ystad area as well as in Scania. The former occupy distinctive locations. In the hummocky landscape the Battle Axe graves sometimes occur in the same locations as the Bronze Age barrows. A possible explanation for this could be that the grave functioning as a social marker had a more important role in the early than in the late SYK. A spread through both the coastal plain and the interior can be traced in the distribution of settlement sites and hoards (Fig. 8). This is a situation which differs markedly from that of the TRB.

This distribution pattern can be interpreted in the following way. An acculturated cultural form of TRB and the GRK existed in the area for a couple of centuries. The representatives of this group used the best

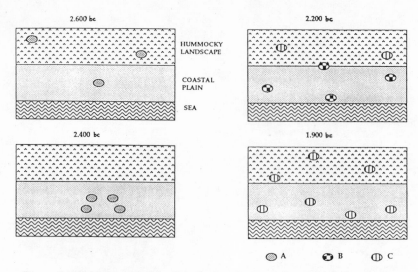

Figure 9. Model for settlement distribution during early and middle Neolithic A-B. 1. sites from Funnel Beaker culture; 2. sites from late middle Neolithic A; and 3. sites from Battle Axe culture. Dates are uncalibrated.

soils adjacent to the coastal plain as well as the outermost parts of the hinterland (Fig. 9). A well-established and thriving community was able to withstand the influence of the new ideology for a couple of centuries. Consequently, the representatives of those who welcomed the new ideological influences were obliged to look for pasture and arable land outside the established settlements. Therefore, new social groups associated with the SYK were established in the hummocky zone peripheral to the traditional areas of settlement. Nevertheless, the SYK proved to be a most vigorous form of social organisation, as a consequence of which, it spread down to the coast and incorporated, with more or less resistance, the traditional areas of settlement.

The data presented here suggest foreign influence in the establishment of the SYK. But what form and scale did this influence take? Was it the immigration of small groups of a missionary character or extensive population movements? There can hardly be any question of large population groups acting independently and taking over the best land, both to feed themselves and to reinforce their ideological seizure of power. In this case there would have been a direct transition from the late TRB to the early SYK, primarily in the coastal region. It is more likely that smaller groups, ambitious to acquire contacts, changed the ideology of existing societies. In some areas, the new immigrants were successful. In certain parts of southern Sweden, for example, in north-eastern Scania, this movement probably experienced a period of un-restricted innovation. However, in parts of western and southern Scania it failed to gain a presence amongst the established cultural districts. Only at a later stage – about two centuries later – did the social order of the SYK spread down into the old settlement districts, taking complete control over them.

The fact that there is no evidence of the initial traces of the SYK in the old districts can be interpreted as indicating marked differences between the structure of social groups. These seem to have been of a sufficient scale to proclude the possibility of assimilation between the new social order and established traditions. This does not necessarily mean that there were fundamental economic differences, as some researchers would have it. What emerges more clearly from an ethno-archaeological viewpoint are those attitudes and systems that structure contacts of a permanent nature, such as marriage. A factor such as the value attached to members of society may be of considerable import-ance in determining whether close contacts occur between two societ-ies. In the case of the EGK, for example, it is felt that one can identify the roles of men and women, with a change in that of men increasing in importance at the expense of that of women (Randsborg 1986: 147 ff.). Marriage between partners from a patrilineal and a matrilineal social system is also very difficult, in spite of great similarities with regard to most socio-ecological factors (Hodder 1982: 153). It has also been noted that family groupings which have a similar economy, and thus make use of the same resources, leading to repeated confronta-tions, prefer to mark their individuality in material culture with, for example, different forms of personal adornment and differing tradi-tions of ornamentation on clay vessels (Hodder 1982: 13 ff.).

An important aspect for any discussion of the transition from middle Neolithic A to B is that the pollen diagrams indicate an increase in human activity during the final part of the middle Neolithic, that is, during the SYK. In previous papers dealing with the expansion phases during prehistoric times, this second expansion phase was taken to represent a time of major change resulting in the rapid establishment of a permanent cultural landscape which had a noticeable influence on the environmental picture (Berglund 1969). The findings of new studies have revealed the dating of this period of steeply increased human activity to be incorrect, and that it should instead be moved to the point of transition between the early and late Bronze Age (Berg-lund et al. 1991a) (Fig. 10).

This means the last part of the middle Neolithic must be reinter-

[447]

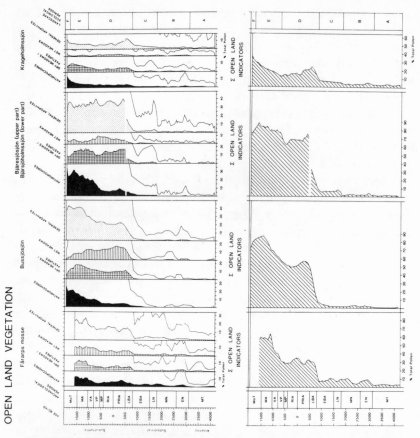

Figure 10. Diagram showing the proportion of non-arboreal (NAP) pollen and fern spores from open land vegetation in total pollen of terrestrial vascular plants in the diagrams from four sites along the transect from coast to inland. Time-scale based on calibrated C 14 values (from Berglund, Malmer & Persson 1991).

preted. According to new interpretations of the pollen analyses, the degree of utilisation has thus not been found to be any greater than during the expansion phase of an early part of the Neolithic period (L. Larsson 1992). Stagnation, or even a regression in the cultural land-scape, can be demonstrated between these comparatively weakly marked periods of expansion. One source-critical factor which might explain the stagnation is that an established area of coppiced wood-land acted as a filter which prevented the distribution of pollen, with an associated decrease in certain species of trees (Göransson 1988; 1991). In this case, any increase in the indications of human influence

[448]

on the landscape could be interpreted as a change associated with a limitation of coppiced woodland. There is, however, no clear evidence of forest clearance in southern Scania to compare with what we see in the diagram from Jutland (Odgaard 1991). It is more like the situation in eastern Denmark, where there are very few features indicating a highly modified cultural landscape (Andersen 1991). In the Ystad area there is, nevertheless, a continuous, albeit limited, element of human impact in the area just inland from the coastal plain.

SOCIAL CHANGE AND THE ROLE OF CATTLE BREEDING

The concentration of settlement which can be confirmed archaeologically to the transition between the early and the middle Neolithic could be associated with a change in the form of production – mainly animal husbandry in addition to a relocation of settlement to the coastal zone. From animal husbandry practised in the vicinity of the settlement during the early Neolithic, the concentration of settlement was eventually to coincide with the introduction of transhumance. The reduction in the importance of pigs and the increase of cattle (Madsen 1982: fig. 17) may be due precisely to the fact that the former species was more difficult to adapt to transhumance while the latter species was well adapted to this form of organisation. A society with a significant element of transhumance may have contributed to the two agricultural processes having taken on divergent forms. Arable farming was practised by the individual farm unit, that is to say, it assumed a more individual character, whereas animal husbandry increasingly took on the appearance of collectivism. It may thus be presumed that the sub-division into arable farming and animal husbandry was related to gender. This is a model with clear parallels in ethnographic evidence. Animal husbandry was a male-dominated occupation in many societies, whereas the cultivation of crops was mainly undertaken by women.

The concentration of settlement which started during the early Neolithic/middle Neolithic transition may have had its distinct advantages. Nevertheless, it resulted in the impoverishment of the land in the long term. The renewed interest in making greater use of sources of livelihood such as fishing and hunting may have arisen from the fact that cereal cultivation was not producing such good yields as it had previously. Throughout the early middle Neolithic with an increased element of tree pollen there is an uninterrupted element of pasture indications in the hinterland of the whole of the

Ystad area (Berglund et al. 1991b; Gaillard & Göransson 1991; Gaillard et al. 1991).

Increasing transhumance in the late TRB met competition for the grazing land, since the element of animal husbandry appears to have been significant in the SYK. Animal husbandry may have been practised in a fashion which corresponds more closely to true nomadism (Kristiansen 1991). Animal husbandry in the SYK may thus have been carried on in a way that broke with the traditional collective form.

With the establishment of the acculturated TBK/GRK, people turned once more to the old sources of livelihood as a possible means of compensating for the fact that areas previously used for transhumance had been taken over by social groups which were part of the SYK. The element of hunting and fishing is indicated by the specific position of the sites, for example, on the shore, together with faunal evidence for the hunting of wild game. Another indication of change is the limited quantity of settlement remains, with regard both to the area covered by the site and to the quantity of finds. It is possible that what we have here are the traces of a certain relocation of settlement. The loss of people to the new cultural phenomenon – the SYK – may also have functioned as an element which exposed traditional society to considerable disruption.

LATE NEOLITHIC

Investigations in the eastern part of the Ystad area have led to the excavation of several late Neolithic sites. These have revealed longhouses with a length of up to 35 metres, with a row of roof-posts. In addition, there are sunken-featured buildings measuring up to 10 metres. An interesting observation is that these house forms do not occur together on the same settlement site. The latter may possibly be a continuous development from house forms in the late SYK. Evidence of this comes from dates obtained from the largest long-house, with values of 2500 BP, which is taken as the boundary between the Neolithic and the Bronze Age. The late SYK saw the start of the development of a social system which was established during the late Neolithic. New crops, notably barley, assumed considerable significance. The importance of sheep probably also increased (Kristiansen 1988: 45). This may be because better use was now being made of the wool by spinning and weaving rather than by plaiting.

The existence of different forms of house and evidence for very large houses (Nielsen & Nielsen 1985) may indicate that society was organised in a somewhat different way than before (Kristiansen 1987: 45). However, excavations and ancient monuments survey indicate that the pattern of settlement which can be traced during the late Neolithic/early Bronze Age does not differ to any appreciable degree from that which existed during an early part of the middle Neolithic. Land use in the old settlement districts remained largely the same, which suggests some agricultural links with the disappearing TRB society. On the other hand, there may have been noticeable changes in social structure and ideology. During the late Neolithic, material deposits in graves provide little evidence for the existence of a clearly hierarchical social structure (Strömberg 1984). Nevertheless, we should note that an emphasis upon the individual can be seen more clearly in the Battle Axe culture than in the late TRB. Moreover, since the distribution of metal artefacts (already established during the Battle Axe culture), could have been of greater significance than is reflected in the find material (Malmer 1988: 94), there is some basis for suggesting a distinct hierarchical subdivision during period II of the Bronze Age.

The natural landscape was not subjected to any greater influences during the late Neolithic than it had been during a late part of the early Neolithic. In the case of some inland pollen diagrams, the presence of plants which point to the existence of a cultural landscape is even less marked than during the early Neolithic (Berglund et al. 1991). Not until ca 3800 BP is there any marked increase in the cultural impact on the landscape in all these areas. This situation is difficult to explain in the light of the reasonable increase in the number of finds on the coast as well as inland. It is probable that a merger of native tradition and new ideas meant that people were able to use the already existing lands, both inland and on the coast, in a more efficient way. The uniform late Neolithic material culture suggests a minimum of conflict, which would also have favoured a rise in population. This could explain why an expansive phase did not leave clearer traces in the physical landscape.

BIBLIOGRAPHY

Andersen, Th. A. 1991. Natural and cultural landscapes since the Ice Age, shown by analyses from small hollows in a forested area in Denmark. *Journal of Danish Archaeology* 8: 188–199.

Berglund, B. E. 1969. Vegetation and human influence in South Scandinavia during prehistoric time. *Oikos* Suppl. 12: 9–28.

Berglund, B. E. (ed.) 1991. *The Cultural Landscape during 6000 Years in Southern Sweden – the Ystad Project.* Copenhagen: Munksgaard (Ecological Bulletins 41).

Berglund, B. E. 1991a. Palaeoecology. In Berglund, B. E. (ed.), *The Cultural*

Landscape during 6000 Years in Southern Sweden – the Ystad Project, pp. 31–35. Copenhagen: Munksgaard (Ecological Bulletins 41).

Berglund, B. E. 1991b. The project area. In Berglund, B. E. (ed.), *The Cultural Landscape during 6000 Years in Southern Sweden – the Ystad Project*, pp. 18–27. Copenhagen: Munksgaard (Ecological Bulletins 41).

Berglund, B. E., Malmer, N., & Persson, T. 1991a. Landscape-ecological aspects of long-term changes in the Ystad area. In Berglund, B. E. (ed.), *The Cultural Landscape during 6000 Years in Southern Sweden – the Ystad Project*, pp. 405–424. Copenhagen: Munksgaard (Ecological Bulletins 41).

Berglund, B. E., Hjelmroos, M., & Kolstrup, E. 1991b. Vegetation and landscape through time. In Berglund, B. E. (ed.), *The Cultural Landscape during 6000 Years in Southern Sweden – the Ystad Project*, pp. 109–112. Copenhagen: Munksgaard (Ecological Bulletins 41).

Browall, H. 1986. *Alvastra pålbyggnad: social och ekonomisk bas.* Stockholm: Institute of Archaeology (Theses and Papers in North-European Archaeology 15).

Chapman, R. 1988. From 'space' to 'place'. A model of dispersed settlement and Neolithic society. In Burgess, C., Topping, P., Mordant, C. & Maddison, M. (eds), *Enclosures and Defences in the Neolithic of Western Europe*, pp. 21–46. Oxford: British Archaeological Report (International Series 403).

Davidsen, K. 1978. *The Final TRB culture in Denmark.* Copenhagen: Institute of Archaeology (Arkæologiske Studier 5).

Ebbesen, K. & Mahler, D. 1980. Virum – Et tidligneolitisk bopladsfund. *Aarbøger for Nordisk Oldkyndighed og Historie* 1979: 11–61.

Gaillard, M.-J. & Gäransson, H. 1991. Vegetation and landscape through time. In Berglund, B. E. (ed.), *The Cultural Landscape during 6000 Years in Southern Sweden – the Ystad Project*, pp. 18–27. Copenhagen: Munksgaard (Ecological Bulletins 41).

Gaillard, M.-J., Olausson, D., & Skansjö, S. 1991. Conclusions. In Berglund, B. E. (ed.), *The Cultural Landscape during 6000 Years in Southern Sweden – the Ystad Project*, pp. 214–219. Copenhagen: Munksgaard (Ecological Bulletins 41).

Göransson, H. 1988. *Neolithic Man and the Forest Environment around Alvastra Pile Dwelling.* Stockholm: Institute of Archaeology (Theses and Papers in North-European Archaeology 20).

Göransson, H. 1991. *Vegetation and Man around Lake Bjärsjöholmssjön during Prehistoric Time.* Lund: Department of Quaternary Geology (Lundqua Report 31).

Hjelmqvist, H. 1982. Economic plants from a middle Neolithic site in Scania. In Larsson, L., A causewayed enclosure and a site with Valby pottery at Stävie, western Scania. *Papers of the Archaeological Institute University of Lund* 1981–1982: 108–113.

Hjelmqvist, H. 1985. Economic plants from two Stone Age settlements in southernmost Scania. In Larsson, L., Karlsfält. A settlement from the early and late Funnel Beaker culture in southern Scania, Sweden. *Acta Archaeologica* 54: 57–63.

Hjelmroos, M. 1985. Vegetation history of Fårarps mosse, South Scania, in the early Subboreal. In Larsson, L., Karlsfält. A Settlement from the early and late Funnel Beaker culture in southern Scania, Sweden. *Acta Archaeologica* 54: 45–50.

Hodder, I. 1982. *Symbols in Action. Ethnoarchaeological studies of material culture.* Cambridge: Cambridge University Press.

Hvass, S. 1977. A house of the Single-grave culture excavated at Vorbasse in central Jutland. *Acta Archaeologica* 48: 219–232.

Hårdh, B. 1988. Coastal connections in the Scanaian middle Neolithic. In Hårdh, B., Larsson, L., Olausson, D. Petré, R. (eds), *Trade and Exchange in Prehistory. Studies in honour of Berta Stjernquist*, pp. 59–70. Lund: Almqvist & Wiksell International (Acta Archaeologica Lundensia 8: 16).

Jacobsson, B. 1986. The Skogsdala dolmen. A long dolmen beneath a Bronze Age burial mound at Skogsdal, South Scania, Sweden. *Papers of the Archaeological Institute University of Lund* 1985–1986: 84–114.

Kaul, F. 1988. Skræppekærgård. Boplads med hus. *Arkælogiske udgravninger i Danmark* 1987, pp. 105–106. København: Det Arkæologiske Nævn.

Kristiansen, K. 1987. From stone to bronze, the evolution of social complexity in northern Europe. In Brumfiel, E. M. & Earle, T. (eds), *Specialization, Exchange and Complex Society*, pp. 31–50. Cambridge: Cambridge University Press.

Kristiansen, K. 1988. Oldtiden o. 4000 f.Kr.-1000 e. Kr. Sten- og bronzealder. In Bjørn, C. (ed.), *Det danske landbrugs historie*, vol. 1, pp. 21–107. København: Landbohistorisk Selskab.

Kristiansen, K. 1991. Prehistoric migrations – the case of the Single Grave and Corded ware cultures. *Journal of Danish Archaeology* 8: 211–225.

Larsson, L. 1982. A causewayed enclosure and a site with Valby pottery at Stävie, western Scania. *Papers of the Archaeological Institute University of Lund* 1981–1982: 65–107.

Larsson, L. 1984. The Skateholm project. A late Mesolithic settlement and cemetery complex at a south Swedish bay. *Papers of the Archaeological Institute University of Lund* 1983–1984: 5–38.

Larsson, L. 1985. Karlsfält. A settlement from the early and late Funnel Beaker culture in southern Scania, Sweden. *Acta Archaeologica* 54: 3–44.

Larsson, L. 1988. The Skateholm project. A late Mesolithic settlement at a south Swedish lagoon. In *The Skateholm Project, I, Man and environment*, pp. 9–19. Lund: Almqvist & Wiksell International (Acta Regiae Societatis Humaniorum Litterarum Lundensis 79).

Larsson, L. 1992. Settlement and environment during the middle Neolithic and late Neolithic. In Larsson, L., Callmer, J. & Stjernquist, B. (eds), *The Archaeology of the Cultural Landscape. Field Work and Research in a South Swedish Rural Region*. Lund: Almqvist & Wiksell International (Acta Archaeologica Lundensia 4: 19) (in print).

Larsson, L. 1992. Neolithic settlement in the Skateholm area, southern Sweden. *Papers of the Archaeological Institute University of Lund* 1991–1992: 5–44.

Larsson, L. 1992. Façade for the dead. A preliminary report on the excavation of a long barrow in southern Scania. *Papers of the Archaeological Institute University of Lund* 1991–1992: 45–56.

Larsson, M. 1988. Exchange and society in the early Neolithic Funnel Beaker society in Scania. In Hårdh, B., Larsson, L., Olausson, D. Petré, R. (eds), *Trade and Exchange in Prehistory. Studies in honour of Berta Stjernquist*, pp. 49–58. Lund: Almqvist & Wiksell International (Acta Archaeologica Lundensia 8: 16).

Larsson, M. 1992. The early and middle Neolithic Funnel Beaker culture in the Ystad Area (Southern Scania). Economic and social change, 3100–2300 BC. In Larsson, L., Callmer, J. & Stjernquist, B. (eds), *The Archaeology of the Cultural Landscape. Field Work and Research in a South Swedish Rural Region*. Lund: Almqvist & Wiksell International (Acta Archaeologica Lundensia 4: 19) (in print).

Larsson, L. & Larsson, M. 1986. Stenåldersundersökningar i Ystadområdet. En presentation av fältverksamhet och bearbetning hösten 1984 – våren 1986. *Ystadiana* 31: 9–78.

Larsson, L. & Larsson, M. 1991. The introduction and establishment of agriculture. In Berglund, B. E. (ed.), *The Cultural Landscape during 6000 Years in Southern Sweden – the Ystad Project*, pp. 315–325. Copenhagen: Munksgaard (Ecological Bulletins 41).

Madsen, T. 1982. Settlement systems of early agricultural societies in East Jutland: a regional study of change. *Journal of Anthropological Archaeology* 1: 197–236.

Madsen, T. 1988. Causewayed enclosures in south Scandinavia. In Burgess, C., Topping, P., Mordant, C., & Maddison, M. (eds), *Enclosures and Defences of Western Europe*, pp. 301–336. Oxford: British Archaeological Reports (403).

Madsen, T. & Petersen, J. E. 1984. Tidligneolitiske anlæg ved Mosegården, Østjylland. Regionale og kronologiske forskele i dansk tidligneolitikum. *Kuml* 1982–83: 61–120.

Malmer, M. P. 1962. *Jungneolithische Studien*. Lund: Liber (Acta Archaeologica Lundensia 8: 2).

Malmer, M. P. 1988. Konstanter och variabler i det förhistoriska samhället. *Fornvännen* 1988 (2): 88–97.

Malmroos, C. & Tauber, H. 1977. Kolstof-14 dateringer af dansk enkeltgravskultur. *Aarbøger* 1975: 78–95.

Møhl, U. 1962. Übersicht über Knochenfunde aus Gräbern der schwedischnorwegischen Streitaxtkultur. In Malmer, M. P. (ed.), *Jungneolithische Studien*, pp. 883–910. Lund: Liber (Acta Archaeologica Lundensia 8: 2).

Nielsen, F. O. & Nielsen, P. O. 1985. Middle and late Neolithic houses at Limensgård, Bornholm. *Journal of Danish Archaeology* 4: 101–114.

Nielsen, F. O. & Nielsen, P. O. 1991. The middle Neolithic settlement at Grødbygård, Bornholm. A local society in times of change. In Jennbert, K., Larsson, L. & Petré, R. & Wyszomirska-Webart, B. (eds), *Regions and Reflections. In Honour of Märta Strömberg*, pp. 51–65. Lund: Almqvist & Wiksell International (Acta Archaeologica Lundensia 8: 20).

Nielsen, P. O. 1979. De tyknakkede flintøksers kronologi. *Aarbøger* 1977: 5–71.

Odgaard, B. 1991. Cultural landscape development through 5500 years at Lake Skånsø, northwestern Jutland as reflected in a regional pollen diagram. *Journal of Danish Archaeology* 8: 200–210.

Olsson, E. G. A. 1991a. Agro-ecosystems from Neolithic time to the present. In Berglund, B. E. (ed.), *The Cultural Landscape during 6000 Years in Southern Sweden – the Ystad Project*, pp. 293–314. Copenhagen: Munksgaard (Ecological Bulletins 41).

Olsson, E. G. A. 1991b. The agro-system of Neolithic farmers at Kabua. In Berglund, B. E. (ed.), *The Cultural Landscape during 6000 Years in Southern Sweden – the Ystad Project*, pp. 117–119. Copenhagen: Munksgaard (Ecological Bulletins 41).

Persson, O. 1982. An osteological analysis of some bones from a settlement at Stävie 4: 1. In Larsson, L. A. (ed.), Causewayed Enclosure and a Site with Valby Pottery at Stävie, Western Scania, p. 114. (Papers of the Archaeological Institute University of Lund 1981–1982).

Randsborg, K. 1986. Women in prehistory: the Danish example. *Acta Archaeologica* 55: 143–154.

Rasmussen, L. 1984. Kainsbakke A47. A settlement structure from the Pitted ware culture. *Journal of Danish Archaeology* 4: 83–98.

Rasmussen, L. 1991. *Kainsbakke. En kystboplads fra yngre stenalder*. Grenaa: Djurslands museum.

Richter, J. 1991. Kainsbakke. Aspects of the palaeoecology of Neolithic man. In Rasmussen, L. (ed.), *Kainsbakke. En kystboplads fra yngre stenalder*, pp. 71–119. Grenaa: Djurslands museum.

Riddersporre, M. 1992. Retrogressive analysis of 18th century landscape – An interdisciplinary approach with archaeological aspects. In Larsson, L., Callmer, J., & Stjernquist, B. (eds), *The Archaeology of the Cultural Landscape. Field Work and Research in a South Swedish Rural Region*. Lund: Almqvist & Wiksell International (Acta Archaeologica Lundensia 4: 19).

Rønne, P. 1979. Høj over høj. *Skalk* 1979 no. 5: 3–9.

Sherratt, A. 1980. Water, social and seasonality in early cereal cultivation. *World Archaeology* 11 (3): 313–341.

Skaarup, J. 1985. *Stenalder på øerne syd fra Fyn*. Rudkøbing: Langeland Museum (Meddelelser fra Langelands Museum).

Strömberg, M. 1968. Der Dolmen Trollasten in St. Köpinge, Schonen. *Acta Archaeologica Lundensia* 8: 7. Lund: Liber.

Strömberg, M. 1980. The Hagestad investigation – A project analysis. *Papers of the Archaeological Institute University of Lund* 1979–1980: 47–60.

Strömberg, M. 1984. Burial traditions in late Neolithic society. Models and results in the Hagestad project. *Papers of the Archaeological Institute University of Lund* 1983–1984: 47–71.

Strömberg, M. 1988. A complex hunting and production area. Problems associated with a group of Neolithic sites to the south of Hagestad. *Papers of the Archaeological Institute University of Lund* 1987–1988: 53–80.

Strömberg, M. 1989. Stridsyxekulturens representation i Hagestadsprojektets arbetsområde. In Larsson, L. (ed.), *Stridsyxekultur i Sydskandinavien*, pp. 77–87. Lund: Institute of Archaeology (University of Lund, Institute of Archaeology Report Series 36).

Tauber, H. 1971. Danske kulstof-14 dateringer af arkæologiske prøver III. *Aarbøger for Nordisk Oldkyndighed og Historie* 1970: 120–142.

Tauber, H. 1986. C14 dateringer af enkeltgravskultur og grubekeramisk kultur i Danmark. In Adamsen, C. & Ebbesen, K. (ed.), *Stridsøksetid i Sydskandinavien*, pp. 196–204. København: Institute of Archeology (Arkæologiske Skrifter 1).

Tesch, S. 1983. *Ystad II. En omlandsstudie*. Stockholm: Riksantikvarieämbetet (Riksantikvarieämbetet Rapport Medeltidsstaden 45).

21

People and Place during the Irish Neolithic: Exploring Social Change in Time and Space

Gabriel Cooney and Eoin Grogan

A 'place'; somewhere to belong, but also something that establishes one's lot and sets aside much to which one doesn't belong.

– Nadine Gordimer, *The Burgher's Daughter*

It is *very easy* in the late twentieth century with its emphasis on location-free technology and instant global communication to forget the importance of time and place in defining social activity and identity in the past. Electronic media erode the specialness or specificity of time and place (Meyrowitz 1985: 125). But time and place do not simply exist in one plane or dimension, they are multi-dimensional and multi-valent (e.g. Glassie 1982: 602–03). In their discussion of time and archaeology, Shanks and Tilley (1987: 128) distinguish 'substantial' time marked by human experience from 'abstract' time which is chronologically measured. Place can also mean different things; in a human context it can be taken to mean both social position and physical location and these may reinforce each other. For example, an individual's physical location during a ceremonial event may indicate and reflect his or her social position (e.g. see Meyrowitz 1985: 5–6). In both these contexts, however, the meaning of place depends on a sense of cultural identity and experience (Tuan 1977: 16–18). The very definition of places in the landscape are the result of human cognition and one can argue that the concept of landscape itself is a cultural one (Daniels & Cosgrove 1988: 1).

With this in mind, it seems reasonable to suggest that Neolithic people in Ireland would have perceived significant differences between the varied spatial, temporal, social and spiritual contexts which provided the totality of their experience. However, this lived experience would also create links between what might initially appear to be unrelated activities. For example a contrast is often made between the sacred and profane, between ceremonial and everyday places and activities (e.g. see discussion in Garwood et al. 1991; de Coppet 1992). A better concept might be to suggest that these are interwoven aspects of life – what is mundane in one context becomes sacred in another. Indeed what makes sacred, ceremonial or ritual activity socially effective is that people can perceive it as having an impact on and relating to their everyday lives (Connerton 1989: 45). The use of similar material items, such as stone axes and pottery, in both everyday and ceremonial contexts would serve to emphasise this linkage. The transformation of everyday activity and performance may become the underpinning symbolism in ritual action. For example, the ordinary act of entering or exiting a house or other structure in a ceremonial context may symbolise entrance into or exit from another world, as in the case of ceremonies in tombs containing the remains of previous generations. These kinds of links and transformations provide resonances between different kinds of human experience, the ordinary and the extraordinary.

In terms of time, ceremonial events may punctuate the seasonal cycle or mark particular stages in a human life in the form of rites of passage. But the rituals accompanying ceremonial events depend for their effectiveness on a sense of timelessness and a perception of stability and permanence (Bloch 1977; Bradley 1991). It is this property that enables ritual to convey a sense of social stability while at the same time it may serve to re-model social relationships and create a new social reality. In looking at cultural change over time we should not be surprised to see that changes in ritual do not necessarily correspond with changes in other aspects of life. It is with these ideas in mind that we should look at the varied contexts we have for Neolithic activity in Ireland.

PEOPLE AND THEIR PLACE IN THE LANDSCAPE

Any detailed analysis of the archaeological evidence might suggest, at least to the archaeologist, a clear contrast between the everyday contexts of human life and those places that were extraordinary – for example where formal ceremonial activity was carried out. While megalithic tombs, certainly in an Irish context, are the most obvious examples of the latter, it is also clear that particular locations within the natural environment, whether unaltered, enhanced or marked, also provided focal points for ritual activity and were perceived of as special. For example, one can point to the use of caves for burial as in the case of the recently discovered site at Annagh, County Limerick (Ó Floinn 1992). Indeed, as Bradley (1993: 22–44) has pointed out, monuments may often be located in places that were already seen as special and be designed to highlight rather than alter or intrude upon a special place. In other cases, less visually obvious locations of ritual or cermonial behaviour, such as flat graves, for example at Clane, Co. Kildare (Ryan 1980), or small enclosures, as at Goodland, Co Antrim (Case 1973) and Armagh (Lynn 1988), may have served to define or enhance the nature of such areas. On a larger scale the ritualisation of the whole landscape – most evident in the case of megalithic cemeteries (Cooney 1990) – was an exceptional aspect of the definition of place in the landscape. However, it should be stressed that the imposition of monumental features onto a landscape was not the sole means of identifying a place or area as special. The accretion of small-scale structures may have served a similar purpose. In the case of megalithic cemeteries, for instance, the development of the form and extent of the cemetery may have evolved over a long period and in turn have come well after the area became known as special (Woodman 1992a: 304).

It is one thing to acknowledge the concept of physically unaltered sacred places, but quite another to identify their locations and meanings archaeologically. Dramatic natural features such as mountain peaks, islands or waterfalls may be suggested as candidates, but in other instances places of major cultural significance may have little visual prominence (Tuan 1977: 162). It seems likely that there were already sacred places in Ireland before the first construction of monuments associated with the Neolithic period. Hunter-gatherer communities had been living in Ireland for well over three thousand years before the beginnings of farming. These Mesolithic people would have had an intimate knowledge of the landscape. In common with hunter-gatherer societies elsewhere, it seems probable that symbolic meanings and historical associations would have been part and parcel of their perception of the landscape (e.g. Brody 1986; Wilson 1988), and that particular places would have been imbued with varying degrees of sacredness. Where might these places have been? One could think of major landmarks or locations with a commanding vista as possibilities. Given the emphasis on fishing for salmonid species and eel in the Irish Mesolithic (Woodman 1978), another possibility would be to focus on the localities in river and lake systems where fishing activities may have been concentrated. In this context the discovery of Mesolithic artefacts in the lithic assemblage from the late Neolithic/Beaker period settlement at Newgrange (Lehane 1983: 142–46, 150–52) raises the question of whether this area was already perceived as a special, sacred one before the Neolithic had begun.

In looking at the Irish Neolithic, the central thesis of this paper is that a sense of place can be seen as a major theme running throughout the period, not only in the sacred sphere but also in the secular realm. The definition of space, or the fixture of elements within it, seems primarily to have been intended to create a sense of permanency in the relationship between the community and the landscape. A concern with inserting and asserting a long-term human presence in the land-scape as part of the natural order was an aspect of *both* secular and sacred life. What made monuments effective was that they could be related to developments in other aspects of life. The image of the monument as a transformation of the earth presented by Bradley (1993) is an apt one. We can cite a number of literal examples of this in the case of Irish megalithic tombs. For example, there is the deliberate creation of the side walls and floor of the tomb at the Linkardstown type site at Ashley Park, Co. Tipperary by splitting the limestone bed-rock (Manning 1985; Fig. 1). At Altdrumman, Co. Tyrone a small portal tomb was placed three metres to the west of, and facing, a rock outcrop (Ó Nualláin 1983: 102) from which the structural stones of the tomb appear to be derived. From any distance away the portal tomb appears to form part of the outcrop, with its roof at the same slope, the combined monument resembling a long cairn.

But of course the earth was altered by other Neolithic activity. The very act of clearing a predominantly forest-covered landscape for agri-cultural purposes would have wrought changes in the land and the creation of field boundaries would have served to emphasise these changes (Cooney 1991). The use of timber for construction purposes would, in the cases of houses, have involved 'domesticating' a visible part of the landscape and different tree species may have also been imbued with special meanings (e.g. O'Sullivan 1990). Wood was also used as the raw material for other acts of transformation: the creation of enclosed settlements, as at Donegore Hill, Co. Antrim (Mallory and Hartwell 1984) and the laying down of trackways across wetland

[459]

Figure 1. Photograph of the tomb at Ashley Park, Co. Tipperary Linkardstown type site, illustrating the splitting of bedrock to provide the passage walls and floor (photograph by Con Manning).

(Raftery 1990). Changing the earth was also an aspect of quarrying to extract the raw materials for lithic production, as in the case of the stepped extraction of flint at Ballygalley Hill (Collins 1978) and the creation of at least two short mining galleries into the porcellanite at Brockley, Rathlin Island, Co. Antrim (Fig. 2).

We associate the monumental with the long term, with remembrance

Figure 2. Photograph of the porcellanite outcrop at Brockley, Rathlin Island, Co. Antrim showing the extraction galleries quarried into the rock.

and something that supercedes purely functional concerns (Bradley 1993: 2; Trigger 1990). Permanency and continuity in the occupation, definition and use of place are clearly evidenced in individual monuments. The long-term use, despite often clear changes in their function and meaning, of megalithic tombs is just one example of this phenomenon. But it is also manifested in the long-term permanence of settlement and habitation sites (see below). Sometimes this can assume the porportions of monumental activity, as for example in the construction and appearance of the extensive coaxial field system at Céide (Behy/ Glenulra), Co. Mayo (Caulfield 1978; 1983; 1988) and the location of the long-term settlement focus on the Knockadoon peninsula on the shores of Lough Gur, Co. Limerick (Ó Ríordáin 1954; Grogan & Eogan 1987).

THE PATTERN OF SETTLEMENT IN THE IRISH NEOLITHIC

In an Irish context we would argue that it is difficult to avoid a general picture of sedentary residence as the principal characteristic of the overall settlement pattern. This interpretation can be contrasted with current views of settlement in the British Neolithic. For example, Thomas suggests that earlier in the Neolithic of southern Britain, the pattern of settlement was largely mobile with similarities to the preceding Mesolithic. By contrast, later in the Neolithic we have increaseed evidence for more sedentary settlement (Thomas 1991: 27–28). In this scenario, the fixed points in the British Neolithic landscape are provided primarily by monuments, such as long barrows, causewayed enclosures and henges. In the case of the Irish evidence our assertion is based on the evidence of the growing number of substantial and clearly permanent Neolithic houses spread throughout the country, with the earliest dates consistently around or shortly before 3000 bc (3800 cal. BC). The latest additions are the houses at Tankardstown, Co. Limerick (Gowen 1988; Gowen & Tarbett 1988), Newtown, Co. Meath (Gowen & Halpin 1992) and Ballygalley, Co. Antrim (Simpson 1993; Simpson et al. 1990).

We can see the house as the context for everyday activity at the family level, and also at community level in the case of clustered settlements. By contrast, a monument such as a megalithic tomb would have been a focus of communal activity at specific times and events. Just as the location of a tomb was carefully chosen, so it was with settlement sites, although the latter might be expected to reflect a more prosaic range of locational factors. Settlements tend to have a relatively prominent location in the immediate landscape, to have a south-facing aspect, a distinct preference for light, well-drained soils, a location overlooking a major source of water and easy access to different types of soil conditions (e.g. Grogan 1988b: 149–50). While we have tended to regard these two places, the home and the tomb, as isolated sets of evidence, it is worth stressing that for people living and dying in the Neolithic they would have been part of the same pattern of life. Of course, one of the interesting aspects in the house/tomb relationship is the number of occasions where a tomb is placed over what was a settlement site or is in a location with potential for settlement (Cooney 1983). Rather than assuming that this is a random happening or that the houses involved must have been non-domestic in nature, it may well be that we are seeing the close links between life and death and, where a tomb is sited over a settlement, as at Ballyglass, Co. Mayo (Ó Nualláin 1972), the transformation of a place from the domain of the living to the dead.

The concept of society as structured in a 'spiralling series of territorial networks' (Smith 1984: 229) is a useful one to employ in widening the discussion about settlement and place as it stresses the idea of human activity spread across the landscape in a complex web of activities of varying intensity and duration. On the domestic front there are three recognisable categories of site with differing implications for people's sense of place. Firstly, there are what could be termed 'maintenance' sites. Here, substantial houses like those discussed above provided the focus for daily life together with the wider elements of habitation such as ancillary buildings and fields. Secondly, there are 'specific activity' sites – less substantial foci associated with shorter-term activity. Their location is usually peripheral to the maintenance sites and they appear to have been used on a seasonal basis with frequent re-use, perhaps for a specific purpose such as hunting, fishing or industrial activity. Examples would include Townleyhall 1 (Liversage 1960) and 2, Co. Louth (Eogan 1963) and the sites on the eastern slopes of Knocknarea, Co. Sligo (Bengtsson & Bergh 1984). Thirdly, there are what appear to be 'transitory' camps. Here there is meagre habitation evidence indicating temporary halting places or places where limited activity took place. An example could be at Lislea, Co. Monaghan (Coffey 1904). Looking at this in terms of a social landscape it can be suggested that people's identity would have been closely tied to their home space, beyond this there were places visited at certain times in the year or for specific purposes and linking these were locations used for brief periods while a group or individuals were in transit. In the category of places used periodically can also be placed monuments or other such places that had a sacred or ceremonial character. These would have been in people's consciousness all the time, perhaps visible in the landscape, but they came to the fore when burials or other rites were undertaken.

The impossibility and artificiality of separating ceremonial from everyday activity can be demonstrated by the evidence from the site of Goodland (Case 1973; Fig. 3). Here at an upland location on a chalk plateau, now covered by blanket bog, there appear to be three phases of use. The presence of *in situ* flint and a large number of pits suggested that flint nodule extraction was undertaken, and two concentrations of debitage mark flint knapping sites. It would appear that primary reduction of flint nodules was carried out, with the final stages taking place after transportation of the material away from the site. But there was also the systematic back-filling of pits and the deliberate and repeated placement of portions of the extracted nodules with other material including deliberately broken pots, porcellanite and quartz around boulders in deposits in the pits and in the ditch which delimited the northern edge of the area of activity. Case (1973:

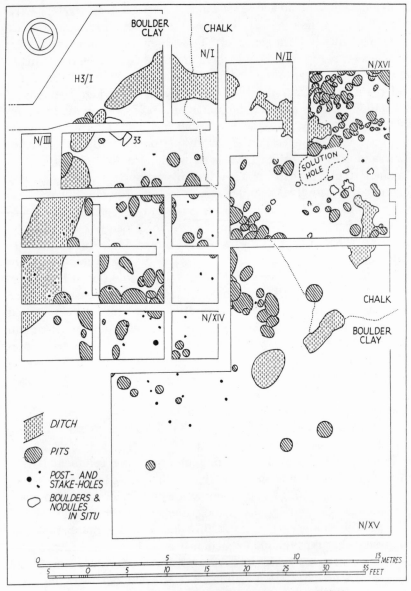

Figure 3. Plan of Goodland, Co. Antrim (from Case 1973).

188–93) suggested that some of this cultural material was brought from settlement sites for ritual disposal but it could have been part and parcel of the on-site industrial activity, and it also resembles the deposition of material which accompanied the placing of human remains

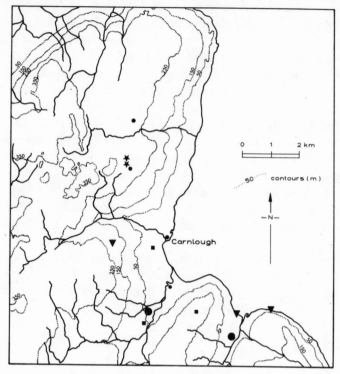

Figure 4. Distribution and different types of Neolithic sites in Glencloy, Co. Antrim (from Woodman 1983). Large circles = possible main settlements; Stars = hollow scraper dominated sites; Squares = end-scraper dominated sites; Triangles = industrial sites; small circles = miscellaneous.

in megalithic tombs. So while Goodland can be viewed as a specialised lithic production site, the evidence for episodes of deliberate deposition suggest that it may have been simultanously a venue for ceremonial activity.

The implication of the ritual and settlement evidence is that there was a sense of social place, of people belonging to a community within a structured social landscape and it was through this social filter that the physical environment would have been perceived and used. The centre of this social landscape was the area around permanent settlement sites and in some areas the megalithic tombs appear to have been placed close to these settlements. Moving out beyond this were places that were visited more occasionally. These more peripheral locations may have had closer associations with concepts of the wild (cf. Hodder 1990). However, there were probably junctures at which these peripheral locations became more central to social life. Evidence to support the presence of this kind of social landscape can be seen in areas where detailed fieldwork has been carried out, as in Glencloy, Co. Antrim (Fig. 4). Here a range of settlement sites in the glen indicates an extensive utilisation of the local environment, from the exploitation of flint on the coast, the location of what appears to be the main settlement focus on the best soils in the area and the occurrence of specialised sites on the uplands above the valley (Woodman 1985: 263). While the spatial constraints of the landscape in many areas did not alter significantly during the course of the Neolithic, the human perception of place was a continuous development. Past activity did not form a passive background but played an active part in the overlaying of new meanings on the landscape. In this sense, the continuity of place may have given a perception of permanency while it also provided a focus for social change. These contrasting but non-contradictory ideas of permanence and change seem to have been expressed in individual ways in different areas. Difficult though their interpretation may be, these patterns can give us insights into the question of regional variability and social change during the Irish Neolithic.

REGIONAL VARIABILITY

One of the interesting aspects of the record for the Irish Neolithic is that there seems to be a degree of uniformity in the settlement and subsistence evidence. There appears to have been a broad spectrum mixed farming system with emphasis on cattle and wheat. The evidence is still relatively meagre and claims for variability in the pattern of subsistence have to be carefully assessed. Thus the suggestion by Woodman (1985: 265) of a contrast between the sedentary life of people in north-western Mayo and the more mobile life-style of groups living in the Carrowmore, Co. Sligo area and the Boyne valley, Co. Meath is based primarily on the survival of field boundaries in the former area, their absence in the two latter regions and the suggestion that passage tomb cemeteries were the focal point of seasonal gatherings rather than integral to the settlement landscape. However, Carrowmore and the Boyne valley are areas that appear to have been in continuous use since the Neolithic. For that reason, prehistoric land divisions are unlikely to have survived and there is little additional evidence to support the concept of a Neolithic settlement pattern based on a high degree of mobility (see discussion in Cooney 1991).

There is a common perception that the dominant element in house design and settlement form was the rectangular, isolated house. However, it can be argued that houses of different forms were in use and that the settlement pattern in any one area probably encompassed a range in the degree of settlement dispersal (see Whittle 1988: 63). Examples of clustered settlements include Lough Gur (Ó Ríordáin 1954; Grogan & Eogan 1987) and Tankardstown, Co. Limerick, and Slieve Breagh, Co. Meath (Herity & Eogan 1977: 49) as well as the possible cases of Mullaghfarna, Carrowkeel, Co. Sligo (Macalister et al. 1912) and Knowth, Co. Meath (Roche 1989; Eogan 1991). Individual farmsteads may be represented at Ballynagilly, Co. Tyrone (ApSimon 1969; 1976) and Newtown, Co. Meath. Architectural styles are also varied; both circular and rectangular structures are known as well as oval and sub-rectangular houses. A clear local style is evidenced at Lough Gur where rectangular and circular houses share common structural details, including the use of stone wall footings flanked by paired posts. The Ballyglass, Ballynagilly, Tankardstown and Newtown rectangular houses demonstrate the existence of a widely distributed tripartite post-and-plank form (Grogan 1988a). The relationship of the rectangular and circular houses is a subject of some debate. In discussing their contemporaneity at Lough Gur, Grogan and Eogan (1987: 469) noted the generally smaller size of the circular houses but indicated that both represented substantial domestic architecture. Bengtsson and Bergh (1984: 314–16) argued that the circular structures on Knocknarea at Carrowmore represented seasonal or specialised sites which were in a peripheral position to the main focus of settlement. Eogan (1991: 114) has suggested that at Knowth there was a switch from rectangular to circular houses associated with a cultural change from a 'western' Neolithic to a passage tomb complex. These different perspectives would certainly suggest a regionally varied attitude to the form of domestic architecture.

The general perception of a contrast between the apparent dominance of megaliths used for select communal burial in the landscapes of the northern half of the country and the use of non-monumental sites for individual burial in the south would appear to be an important illustration of regional variation with wider cultural and social implications. But the situation is more complex than this duality might suggest. Indeed it might be more appropriate to suggest that there was considerable variety in burial practice within regions in Neolithic Ireland. For example, there is considerable variety in megalithic tombs themselves, with four main types and a simple form of chambered tomb now recognised (e.g. Shee Twohig 1990: 9). These overlap spatially and chronologically. Megalithic tombs do, of course, exist in the south (Ó Nualláin 1989: fig. 84) and the Linkardstown tombs in Leinster and Munster can be seen as an adaptation of the megalithic form to commemorate particular individuals. At the end of the Neolithic, megalithic tombs become an important aspect of ritual behaviour and mortuary practice throughout Munster. Kinnes (1992a: 126–27; 1992b: 100–01) has drawn attention to the presence of a non-megalithic component in the megalithic tomb tradition. It also seems likely that non-monumental burial sites occur throughout the country (Ryan 1980: 112–13). That monumental and flat graves were not exclusive of each other is suggested by the evidence at Altanagh, Co. Tyrone where pit burials were recorded at a court tomb (Williams 1986: 70–71). Similarly, several token cremations were deposited in pits and cists at Baurnadomeeny, Co. Tipperary both before, during and after the construction of an unusual wedge tomb (O'Kelly 1960; Cooney 1992). Communal and individual burial were not necessarily separate expressions of the mortuary tradition. For example, in the passage tomb at Tara one of two deposits placed during the construction of the tomb was a pile of cremated bone, representing one individual, in a Carrowkeel pot with a bone/antler pin and beads. This deposit was placed on the ground surface on the outer side of the orthostatic passage and before the insertion of the main multiple cremation deposit in the tomb chamber (see Eogan 1986: 135).

A further overlap in the use of contrasting elements of mortuary ritual is the presence of individual burials within the chambers of megalithic tombs and the apparently collective nature of deposits at non-monumental sites such as Rockbarton ('Caherguillamore'), Co. Limerick (Hunt 1967) and the recently excavated cave burial at Annagh, Co. Limerick (Ó Floinn 1992). At present, then, the evidence offers us a view of the cultural complexity of mortuary practice and related activities which is difficult to resolve into neat regional packages. At the same time, some indications of the likely scale of regional identity in this area of ritual behaviour may be expressed in the extent of the distribution of Linkardstown type tombs and the different styles of court tombs such as dual court tombs in southern Ulster and central and transeptal court tombs in north-western Ireland (Fig. 5).

This impression of regional traditions and broader regularities is borne out by the existence of similar patterns in the material remains over much of the country. This applies especially to pottery but also to flint and stone artefacts, with a discernible pattern of local variation also in evidence. In the distribution patterns of artefacts we can see the

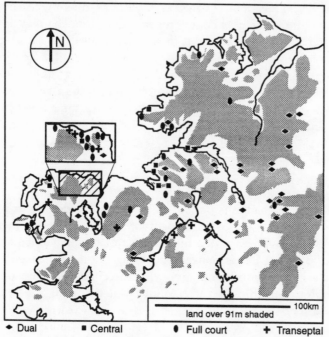

Figure 5. Distribution map of different styles of court tomb in the north-western part of Ireland.

way in which contacts between communities across the country might have formed the basis for a degree of common cultural identity, as expressed for example in the widespread distribution of axes made from porcellanite originating at Tievebulliagh or Brockley, Rathlin Island, Co. Antrim (Sheridan et al. 1992; Mandal pers. comm.). On the other hand, we can point to regional variability in the use of resources. For example, polished flint axes are largely restricted to the north-east of Ireland (Woodman 1992b: 97–98). It is also clear that in different regions of Ireland a range of local lithic sources were used alongside the imports (principally stone axes) from outside the local area (e.g. Cooney 1989).

Similar patterns can be discerned in the ceramic evidence. Research by Cleary (1983) and Sheridan (1989; 1991) on pottery production indicates an emphasis on locally available resources. In a real sense this emphasises the different scales at which people had a sense of place. Attachment to place was dominated by the locale around the settlement where most of the required resources, in this case clay and temper, were obtained. But at the same time, a much wider sense of

[469]

identity would have been evoked and symbolised by the use of similar material culture, such as common ceramic styles. The way in which this material was actively used in a social context may also give insights into an intermediate, regional scale of identity. Examples include regional variation in styles of decorated pottery, as at Lough Gur (Case 1961: 186–96), and differences in the pattern of ceremonial/ formal deposition of similar decorated styles; in some areas in portal tombs and court tombs, in others in Linkardstown burials (Herity 1982).

CHANGES OVER TIME

The process of change is perhaps also easiest to identify in material culture traditions. The development of a series of widespread decorative pottery styles in the middle part of the Neolithic period (ca 2800 bc/ 3500 cal. BC) is an example of this, but it can be seen to occur against a backdrop of continuity with the continuing use of earlier plain styles right through the Neolithic. Alterations in the settlement pattern are not so easily identified. However, increasing evidence for enclosure may indicate a degree of settlement hierarchy and social differentiation which contrasts with the lack of variation on and between sites dated to the early Neolithic. On the ceremonial front, some general changes can be detected. There appears to be a gradual increase in the importance of inhumation, seen for example in the Linkardstown tombs and the later Neolithic individual burials of related traditions. These kinds of changes are sometimes interpreted as indicating a wholesale replacement of one cultural complex by another in Ireland during the course of the Neolithic (e.g. Herity & Eogan 1977). However, given the chronological indications that major elements in these presumed successive phases, such as court tombs to be followed by passage tombs to be followed by single burials, are in fact contemporary (e.g. ApSimon 1986; Brindley & Lanting 1990; Woodman 1992a), a more realistic view suggests that over time society became more diversified at a regional level. Regional identity evolved and was expressed through the choice and use of elements from a general background of an increasingly greater range of material culture. Indeed, the Linkardstown and passage tombs provide an interesting contrast. While the former suggest an increasing focus on the commemoration of specific individuals, apparently within a local setting, the latter appear to reflect an emphasis on specific adult-dominated groups within a larger spatial and social context. Both demonstrate increasing complexity in burial and social behaviour but at different scales. This emphasises the point that rather than one simple trajectory of social change, developments in society over time were regionally varied.

This last point can be best appreciated by contrasting developments at two sites which are crucial for our understanding of the Irish Neolithic: Knowth within the Boyne valley in northern Leinster and Knockadoon within the Lough Gur complex in northern Munster. Eogan (1991) has recently presented a detailed interpretation of the Neolithic sequence at Knowth and Grogan and Eogan (1987: 467–89) in publishing five enclosed sites at Knockadoon, included an updated view, encompassing Ó'Ríordáin's work (1954), on the history of Neolithic settlement on the peninsula. In the first instance, it is striking that both have been referred to as 'islands' which were the scene of intensive Neolithic activity. In many respects, Knockadoon was virtually an island during prehistory (Ó Ríordáin 1954: 448; Grogan & Eogan 1987: 487). Equally, given its location at the western end of the 'Bend of the Boyne', Knowth is situated on an 'island' defined by the course of the river and the very good land between the river and the ridges on which the three main tombs are located (Mitchell 1984: 9–11; Cooney 1991: 130–31).

Perhaps the most notable characteristics of the settlement at Lough Gur (Fig. 6) are the contemporaneity of rectangular and circular houses, the replacement of houses in the same locations on the spine and southern slopes of the peninsula and the growing social differentiation within the settlement over time. Certain of the long-term foci for house construction were enclosed and their inhabitants appear to have had better access to what would have been regarded as non-local, 'prestige' items of ornament (Grogan and Eogan 1987: 470–71). Burial took place on the site and the evidence is dominated by the presence of the inhumed remains of children and adolescents, including a fourteen-year-old youth accompanied by a decorated pot (Ó Ríordáin 1954: 371–72; Grogan & Eogan 1987: 471). Late in the Neolithic, Beaker pottery occurred on the site, but there was little alteration in the settlement structure associated with this new ceramic. In contrast, it appears that in the broader Lough Gur landscape significant changes did occur. The western fringes of the lake became a focus for the construction of embanked stone circles, in particular the Grange Stone Circle (Ó Ríordáin 1951). On the southern side of the lake there was a wedge tomb (Ó Ríordáin and Ó h-Iceadha 1955). In the earlier part of the Bronze Age the lake itself appears to have become less important as a

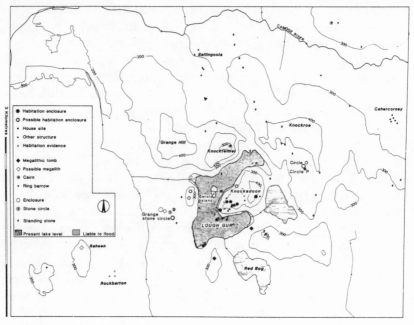

Figure 6. Neolithic settlement evidence at Knockadoon, Lough Gur, Co. Limerick (from Grogan & Eogan 1987).

place for settlement but retained wider significance as a place for the deposition of metal objects (Grogan 1988b: 157).

Knowth offers a number of contrasts to the pattern of contemporary rectangular and circular houses seen at Knockadoon (Fig. 7). Eogan (1991: 107–08) argues that the rectangular houses were in use in an earlier Neolithic phase (P1) and that a group of smaller, circular structures formed a distinct settlement cluster during a later phase (P2, indicated as shaded area). He suggests that these different forms of domestic space are the results of the activities of two distinct and successive cultural groups. The rectangular structures are seen as representing a phase of western Neolithic settlement that was succeeded by a passage tomb phase with tomb construction. In this phase, the building of the circular houses as a domestic settlement was contemporary with at least part of the cemetery construction. This cultural and chronological interpretation is open to alternative views and it should be pointed out that the houses of different architectural design are complementary in a spatial sense, with the rectangular houses lying to the north and west of the circular ones (Eogan 1991: 107). What is interesting is that stratigraphically cutting the large rect-

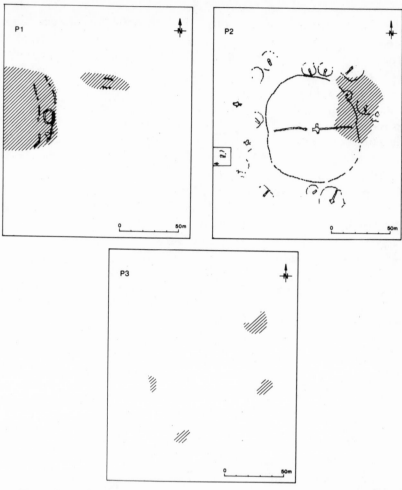

Figure 7. The sequence of Neolithic activity at Knowth, the Boyne Valley, Co. Meath (From Eogan 1991).

angular house on the western side of the site is part of what appears to be a palisaded enclosure, possibly of two phases and probably encompassing an area 100m in diameter. This enclosure phase at Knowth was communal in scale and probably akin to other major enclosed sites such as Lyles Hill (Gibson and Simpson 1989) and Donegore Hill, Co. Antrim. It could be interpreted as representing the kind of social organisation that was to be later reflected in the construction of the main passage tomb at Knowth. The importance of Knowth as a place is not only reflected in these two large-scale structures but also in the accumulation of smaller tombs strategically placed in relation to one another and the large tomb mound. For the ceremonies surrounding the use of these sites we can imagine a large number of people coming from a considerable geographical area. There must have been similar gatherings at Newgrange and Dowth. The Loughcrew passage tomb cemetery lies 40 km to the north-west. A crude index of the region within which people had the closest affinities to events and structures in the Boyne valley would be to suggest that it was the area within twenty kilometres of the Bend of the Boyne (Cooney 1991: 134). The final Neolithic at Knowth is represented by a wooden structure associated with Grooved ware, lying to the east of the entrance to the eastern tomb in the large mound (Eogan & Roche 1994). Later, more domestic activity can be seen in the form of four clusters of material around the main mound (P3) associated with Beaker pottery. Here again, as in the passage tomb phase, we can see the presence of domestic and ceremonial activity. But even more dramatically than Lough Gur, Knowth ceases to be a focus of settlement in the early Bronze Age. It would appear also that the Bend of the Boyne in general became less important as a central social place. As Eogan (1991: 117) puts it, 'Brugh na Bóinne lost its relevance and remained outside the mainstream of cultural developments for close to two millennia.'

It seems then that Knockadoon retained its position as an important local focus of settlement during the Neolithic while Knowth took on a greater significance as a central place for a much larger area. It is the family and local community context that is apparent in the evidence from Lough Gur. At Knowth, a wider social and geographical role is suggested by the features and scale of the settlement and cemetery complex. Thus at Knockadoon what we see over time are growing differences between families within the settlement and communal effort is best seen off-site late in the Neolithic in the construction of monuments such as the wedge tomb and embanked stone circles. What is evident at Knowth is an increase in communal activity culminating in the construction of the enormous passage tomb but continuing into the Beaker period. On the site at Lough Gur we find individual burials, dominated by children and adolescents and these are best seen as being placed in a family rather than communal context. At Knowth, the evidence suggests a greater emphasis upon communal rites and (probably) selective cremation deposits in the tombs.

At the same time, there is a similarity on the two sites in the value placed by people and society on material culture, as shown in the concentration of exotic ornaments on the enclosed sites at Knockadoon and the deposition of a range of material items in the passage tombs with cremated human remains. Indeed, there is a similarity in some of the specific items occurring at both Lough Gur and Knowth, such as porcellanite stone axes and Beaker pottery. This can be parallelled in the architectural forms of the houses – with the use of rectangular and circular houses on both sites. If the transition from rectangular to circular houses suggested by Eogan did occur at Knowth, then it suggests an interesting dichotomy in the cultural specificity of architectural styles in different parts of the country. At the end of the Neolithic, emphasis in both cases appear to be on ceremonies in circular enclosures, like the circular structure at Knowth or the complex of earthen and other enclosures in the Boyne valley (Stout 1991) and embanked stone circles such as the Grange Stone Circle at Lough Gur.

What we seem to see in the Neolithic sequence at both Lough Gur and Knowth is evidence for the long-term importance of place and a similarity in people's domestic style of life, but with marked differences in the way social identity developed over time. Social identity at Knockadoon appears to have been defined on the basis of local differentiation. Social identity at Knowth was vested in the display of communal effort and access to ideas and items from a wide geographical area (Bradley & Chapman 1984; Sheridan 1985/6). People with a common cultural background employed material culture in an active way to create two very different histories of settlement and social development. In the case of Knockadoon, it would seem that it was the immediate, visible and local landscape that would have dominated people's perceptions. At Knowth, the construction of the tombs in particular transformed the perceptual landscape, created new interior spaces, a venue for contemporary ceremonial activity and a backdrop for later action. In the activities undertaken within and outside the tombs we can see a reflection of the wider world to which at least some members of contemporary society would have had access. It is only by appreciating the quite different regional developments and active use of material culture suggested by those histories and by trying to get away from the perception that island-wide contacts and use of similar styles of artefacts can be read as implying island-wide cultural uniformity that we are likely to reach a better understanding of the real character of social change in the Irish Neolithic. That our notions of regional variability and chronological change are as ill defined as set out here might be taken as a comment on the authors, but more seriously it reflects the amount of research still to be done on what is often seen as the best understood period in Irish prehistory.

[475]

ACKNOWLEDGEMENTS

Our thanks to Finola O'Carroll for discussion and her comments on the paper which have greatly added to its value. We are grateful to her also for the quote from Nadine Gordimer. Thanks also to Bernard Guinan for his comments, Steve Mandal for information on the distribution of porcellanite axes and Conleth Mannin for the photograph of Ashley Park. Responsibility for what is said in the paper should of course be placed with the authors!

BIBLIOGRAPHY

Apsimon, A. 1969. An early Neolithic house in Co Tyrone. *Journal of the Royal Society of Antiquaries of Ireland* 99: 165–168.

Apsimon, A. 1976. Ballynagilly at the beginning and end of the Irish Neolithic. In de Laet, S. J. (ed.), *Acculturation and Continuity in Atlantic Europe*, pp. 15–38. Brugge: Dissertationes Archaeologicae Gandenses.

Apsimon, A. 1985/6. Chronological contexts for Irish megalithic tombs. *Journal of Irish Archaeology* 3: 5–15.

Bengtsson, H. & Bergh, S. 1984. The hut sites at Knocknarea North. In Burenhult, G. (ed.), *The Archaeology of Carrowmore: Environmental Archaeology and the Megalithic Tradition at Carrowmore, Co Sligo, Ireland*, pp. 216–318. Stockholm: Institute of Archaeology, University of Stockholm (Theses and Papers in North-European Archaeology 14).

Bloch, M. 1977. The past and the present in the present. *Man* 12: 278–292.

Bradley, R. 1991. Ritual, time and history. *World Archaeology* 23: 209–219.

Bradley, R. 1993. *Altering The Earth*. Edinburgh: Society of Antiquaries of Scotland (Monograph Series 8).

Bradley, R. & Chapman, R. 1984. Passage graves in the European Neolithic: a theory of converging evolution. In Burenhult, G. (ed.), *The Archaeology of Carrowmore: Environmental Archaeology and the Megalithic Tradition at Carrowmore, Co Sligo, Ireland*, pp. 348–356. Stockholm: Institute of Archaeology, University of Stockholm (Theses and Papers in North-European Archaeology 14).

Brindley, A. L. & Lanting, J. N. 1989/90. Radiocarbon dates for Neolithic single burials. *Journal of Irish Archaeology* 5: 1–7.

Brody, H. 1986. *Maps and Dreams*. 2nd edition. London: Faber and Faber.

Case, H. 1961. Irish Neolithic pottery: distribution and sequence. *Proceedings of the Prehistoric Society* 27: 174–233.

Case, H. 1973. A ritual site in north-east Ireland. In Daniel, G. & Kjaerum, P. (eds), *Megalithic Graves and Ritual*, pp. 173–196. Moesgard, Denmark: Jutland Archaeological Society.

Caulfield, S. 1978. Neolithic fields: the Irish evidence. In Bowen, H. C. & Fowler, P. J. (eds), *Early Land Allotment*, pp. 137–144. Oxford: British Archaeological Reports (British Series 48).

Caulfield, S. 1983. The Neolithic settlement of north Connaught. In Reeves-Smith, T. & Hamond, F. (eds), *Landscape Archaeology in Ireland*, pp. 195–215. Oxford: British Archaeological Reports (British Series 116).

Caulfield, S. 1988. *Céide Fields and Belderrig Guide*. Killala: Morrigan Book Co.

Cleary, R. M. 1983. The ceramic assemblage. In O'Kelly, M. J., Cleary, R. M. & Lehane, D., *Newgrange, Co Meath, Ireland: The Late Neolithic/Beaker Period Settlement*, pp. 58–117. Oxford: British Archaeological Reports (International Series 190).

Coffey, G. 1904. Stone celts and a Food Vessel found in the County Monaghan. *Journal of the Royal Society of Antiquaries of Ireland* 34: 271–272.

Collins, A. E. P. 1978. Excavations on Ballygalley Hill, County Antrim. *Ulster Journal of Archaeology* 41: 15–32.

Connerton, P. 1989. *How Societies Remember*. Cambridge: Cambridge University Press.

Cooney, G. 1983. Megalithic tombs in their environmental setting, a settlement perspective. In Reeves-Smith, T. & Hamond, F. (eds), *Landscape Archaeology in Ireland*, pp. 179–194. Oxford: British Archaeological Reports (British Series 116).

Cooney, G. 1989. Stone axes of north Leinster. *Oxford Journal of Archaeology* 8: 145–157.

Cooney, G. 1990. The place of megalithic tomb cemeteries in Ireland. *Antiquity* 64: 741–753.

Cooney, G. 1991. Irish Neolithic landscapes and landuse systems: the implications of field systems. *Rural History* 2 (2): 123–139.

Cooney, G. 1992. Irish Neolithic mortuary practice: Baurnadomeeny reconsidered. *Tipperary Historical Journal* 1992: 223–229.

Daniels, S. & Cosgrove, D. 1988. *The Iconography of Landscape*. Cambridge: Cambridge University Press.

de Coppet, D. (ed.) 1992. *Understanding Rituals*. London: Routledge.

De Valera, R. 1960. The court cairns of Ireland. *Proceedings of the Royal Irish Academy* 60C: 9–140.

Eogan, G. 1963. A Neolithic habitation-site and megalithic tomb in Townleyhall townland, Co Louth. *Journal of the Royal Society of Antiquaries of Ireland* 93: 37–81.

Eogan, G. 1984. *Excavations at Knowth, 1*. Dublin: Royal Irish Academy (Royal Irish Academy Monographs in Archaeology).

Eogan, G. 1986. *Knowth and the Passage Tombs of Ireland*. London: Thames and Hudson.

Eogan, G. 1991. Prehistoric and early historic culture change at Brugh na Bóinne. *Proceedings of the Royal Irish Academy* 91C: 105–132.

Eogan, G. & Roche, H. 1994. A Grooved ware wooden structure at Knowth, Boyne Valley, Ireland. *Antiquity* 68: 322–330.

Garwood, P., Jennings, D., Skeates, R., & Toms, J. (eds) 1991. *Sacred and Profane*. Oxford: Oxford University Committee for Archaeology (Monograph 32).

Gibson, A. M. and Simpson, D. D. A. 1989. Lyles Hill, Toberagnee, Co. Antrim. In Bennett, I. (ed.), *Excavations 1988/9*. Dublin: Wordwell.

Glassie, H. 1982. *Passing the Time: Folklore and History of an Ulster Community*. Dublin: O'Brien Press.

Gowen, M. 1988. *Three Irish Gas Pipelines: New Archaeological Evidence in Munster*. Dublin: Wordwell.

Gowen, M & Halpin, E. 1992. A Neolithic house at Newtown. *Archaeology Ireland* 20: 25–27.

Gowen, M. & Tarbett, C. 1988. A third season at Tankardstown. *Archaeology Ireland* 2 (4): 156.

Grogan, E. 1988a. Possible reconstructions of the (Tankardstown South) house. In Gowen, M. (ed.), *Three Irish Gas Pipelines: New Archaeological Evidence in Munster*, p. 42. Dublin: Wordwell.

Grogan, E. 1988b. The pipeline sites and the prehistory of the Limerick area. In Gowen, M. (ed.), *Three Irish Gas Pipelines: New Archaeological Evidence in Munster*, pp. 148–157. Dublin: Wordwell.

Grogan, E. & Eogan, G. 1987. Lough Gur excavations by Sîan P. Ó Ríordáin: further Neolithic and Beaker habitations on Knockadoon. *Proceedings of the Royal Irish Academy* 87C: 299–506.

Herity, M. 1982. Irish decorated Neolithic pottery. *Proceedings of the Royal Irish Academy* 82C: 247–404.

Herity, M. & Eogan, G. 1977. *Ireland in Prehistory*. London: Routledge Kegan Paul.

Hodder, I. 1990. *The Domestication of Europe*. Oxford: Blackwell.

Hunt, J. 1967. Prehistoric burials at Caherguillamore, Co Limerick. In Rynne, E. (ed.), *North Munster Studies*, pp. 20–42. Limerick: Thomond Archaeological Society.

Kinnes, I. 1992a. Balnagowan and after: the context of non-megalithic mortuary sites in Scotland. In Sharples, N. & Sheridan, A. (eds), *Vessels for the Ancestors*, pp. 83–103. Edinburgh: Edinburgh University Press.

Kinnes, I. 1992b. *Non-Megalithic Long Barrows and Allied Structures in the British Neolithic*. London: British Museum (Occasional Paper 52).

Lehane, D. 1983. The flint work. In O'Kelly, M. J., Cleary, R. M. & Lehane, D., *Newgrange, Co Meath, Ireland: The Late Neolithic/Beaker Period Settlement*, pp. 118–167. Oxford: British Archaeological Reports (International Series 190).

Liversage, G. D. 1960. A Neolithic site at Townleyhall, Co Louth. *Journal of the Royal Society of Antiquaries of Ireland* 90: 49–60.

Lynn, C. J. 1988. Armagh in 3000 BC. In Hamlin, A. & Lynn, C. J. (eds), *Pieces of the Past*, pp. 8–10. Belfast: HMSO.

Macalister, R. A. S., Armstrong, E. C. R., & Praeger, R. Ll. 1912. Report on the Exploration of Bronze-Age Cairns on Carrowkeel Mountain, Co. Sligo. *Proceedings of the Royal Irish Academy* 29C: 311–347.

Mallory, J. P. & Hartwell, B. 1984. Donegore Hill. *Current Archaeology* 8 (9): 271–275.

Manning, C. 1985. A Neolithic burial mound at Ashleypark, Co Tipperary. *Proceedings of the Royal Irish Academy* 85C: 61–100.

Meyrowitz, J. 1985. *No Sense of Place*. New York: Oxford University Press.

Mitchell, G. F. 1984. The landscape. In Eogan, G. (ed.), *Excavations at Knowth*, 1, pp. 9–11. Dublin: Royal Irish Academy (Royal Irish Academy Monographs in Archaeology).

Ó Floinn, R. 1992. A Neolithic cave burial in Limerick. *Archaeology Ireland* 20: 19–21.

O'Kelly, M. J. 1960. A wedge-shaped gallery grave at Baurnadomeeny, Co Tipperary. *Journal of the Cork Historical and Archaeological Society* 65: 85–115.

Ó Nualláin, S. 1972. A Neolithic house at Ballyglass near Ballycastle, Co Mayo. *Journal of the Royal Society of Antiquaries of Ireland* 102: 49–57.

Ó Nualláin, S. 1983. Irish portal tombs: topography, siting and distribution. *Journal of the Royal Society of Antiquaries of Ireland* 113: 75–105.

Ó Nualláin, S. 1989. *Survey of the Megalithic Tombs of Ireland*, vol. 5, Co Sligo. Dublin: Stationery Office.

Ó Ríordáin, S. P. 1951. Lough Gur excavations: the Great Stone Circle (B) in Grange Townland. *Proceedings of the Royal Irish Academy* 54C: 37–74.

Ó Ríordáin, S. P. 1954. Lough Gur Excavations: Neolithic and Bronze Age houses on Knockadoon. *Proceedings of the Royal Irish Academy* 56C: 297–459.

Ó Ríordáin, S. P. & Ó h-Iceadha, G. 1955. Lough Gur excavations: the megalithic tomb. *Journal of the Royal Society of Antiquaries of Ireland* 85: 34–50.

O'Sullivan, A. 1990. Wood in archaeology. *Archaeology Ireland* 4 (2): 69–73.

Raftery, B. 1990. *Trackways Through Time*. Rush, Dublin: Headline Publishing.

Roche, H. 1989. Pre-tomb habitation found at Knowth, Co. Meath, Spring 1989. *Archaeology Ireland* 3 (3): 101–103.

Ryan, M. 1980. Prehistoric burials at Clane, Co Kildare. *Journal of the Kildare Archaeological Society* 16: 108–114.

Shanks, M. & Tilley, C. 1987. *Social Theory and Archaeology*. London: Polity Press.

Shee Twohig, E. 1990. *Irish Megalithic Tombs*. Princes Risborough: Shire Books.

Sheridan, A. 1985/86. Megaliths and megalomania: an account, and interpretation, of the development of passage tombs in Ireland. *Journal of Irish Archaeology* 3: 17–30.

Sheridan, A. 1989. Pottery production in Neolithic Ireland: a petrological and chemical study. In Henderson, J. (ed.), *Scientific Analysis in Archaeology and its Interpretation*, pp. 112–135. Oxford: Oxford University Committee for Archaeology (Monograph 19).

Sheridan, A. 1991. Pottery production in Neolithic and early Bronze Age Ireland: a petrological and chemical study. In Middleton, A. & Freestone, I. (eds), *Recent Developments in Ceramic Petrology*, pp. 305–335. London: British Museum (Occasional Paper 81).

Sheridan, A., Cooney, G., & Grogan, E. 1992. Stone axe studies in Ireland. *Proceedings of the Prehistoric Society* 58: 389–416.

Simpson, D. D. A. 1993. Ballygalley. *Current Archaeology* 134: 60–62.

Simpson, D. D. A., Conway, M. G., & Moore, D. G. 1990. The Neolithic settlement site at Ballygalley, Co. Antrim. Excavations 1989, interim report. *Ulster Journal of Archaeology* 53: 40–49.

Smith, W. J. 1984. Social geography of rural Ireland: inventory and prospect. In Davies, G. L. H. (ed.), *Irish Geography 1934–1984*, pp. 204–236. Dublin: Geographical Society of Ireland.

Stout, G. 1991. Embanked enclosures of the Boyne region. *Proceedings of the Royal Irish Academy* 91C: 245–284.

Thomas, J. 1991. *Rethinking the Neolithic*. Cambridge: Cambridge University Press.

Trigger, B. G. 1990. Monumental architecture: a thermodynamic explanation of symbolic behaviour. *World Archaeology* 22: 119–132.

Tuan, Yi-Fu. 1977. *Space and Place*. Minneapolis. University of Minnesota Press.

Whittle, A. 1988. *Problems in Neolithic Archaeology*. Cambridge: Cambridge University Press.

Williams, B. B. 1986. Excavations at Altanagh, County Tyrone. *Ulster Journal Archaeology* 49: 33–88.

Wilson, P. 1988. *The Domestication of the Human Species*. New Haven: Yale University Press

Woodman, P. C. 1978. *The Mesolithic in Ireland*. Oxford: British Archaeological Reports (British Series 58).

Woodman, P. C. 1983. The Glencloy Project in perspective. In Reeves-Smith, T. & Hamond, F. (eds), *Landscape Archaeology in Ireland*, pp. 25–34. Oxford: British Archaeological Reports (British Series 116).

Woodman, P. C. 1985. Prehistoric settlement and environment. In Edwards, K. J. & Warren, W. P. (eds), *The Quaternary History of Ireland*, pp. 251–278. London: Academic Press.

Woodman, P. C. 1992a. Filling in the spaces in Irish prehistory. *Antiquity* 66: 295–314.

Woodman, P. C. 1992b. Excavations at Mad Mans Window, Glenarm, Co. Antrim: problems of flint exploitation in east Antrim. *Proceedings of the Prehistoric Society* 58: 77–106.

22

From the Collective to the Individual: Some Thoughts about Culture Change in the Third Millennium BC

Harry Fokkens

In this article I will discuss the socio-economic changes that occurred in large parts of Europe at the beginning of the third millennium BC.[1] It is the period in which the Corded ware complex – of which the Dutch Single Grave culture is a branch – replaces the earlier Neolithic cultures in central, northern and north-western Europe. In these areas the most striking transformations are the conclusion of building collective megalithic tombs and the start of a tradition of individual burial underneath barrows, a change in pottery style and the introduction of the plough and the cart (Fokkens 1986; Champion et al. 1984; Sherratt 1981; Van der Waals 1985). Champion et al. also recognise the dispersion of settlements as an element of change, but for the Netherlands that is not a feature. Single Grave settlements do indeed cover a wider variety of landscapes than those of the previous culture groups, but they do not occur in areas that were previously uninhabited.

Often the introduction of the plough is emphasised and explained as an intensification of agrarian production, necessitated by a growing population (following Boserup 1965). However, this explanation implies that almost the whole of Europe became over-populated at the same moment. That is, of course, an untenable position. In the following I will try to make clear that the introduction of plough agriculture may indeed be one of the keys to the explanation of late Neolithic change, but that this was a more or less logical answer to the opening up of the forest landscape; at the same time it had profound impact on the social organisation of Neolithic communities.

A BRIEF DESCRIPTION OF THE DUTCH ARCHAEOLOGICAL SEQUENCE

Since most of the references in this article relate to archaeological data from the Netherlands, especially the northern Netherlands, I will briefly introduce the archaeological sequence for the middle and late Neolithic in the Low Countries. Generally speaking, the Netherlands can be divided into four regions: the northern area, with the Frisian-Drentian boulder clay plateau as the core, the southern pleistocene sand area, the central river area and the western coastal area (also known as the lower Rhine delta). In the last two regions the subsoil is dominated by riverine and coastal deposits with an occasional pleisto-cene sand outcrop. In most prehistoric periods the central river area constitutes – culturally speaking – a transitional region between the southern and northern regions. In the middle Neolithic we find this expressed in the existence of different culture groups in the north, west and south.

In the north, the TRB culture emerges around 3400 BC. There is some discussion about earlier Neolithic habitation in this part of the country. In the deltas and stream valleys of the rivers IJssel and Vecht, local hunting and fishing groups belonging to the Swifterbant culture were present until ca 3800 BC (Hogestijn 1990). They practised farming as well, but on a very small scale and – as far as we know – only near the river valleys and not on the heavily forested boulder-clay plateaux (Fokkens 1991). There are a few indications that late 'survivors' of these Swifterbant culture groups continued to live in the area until 3400 BC, but it is unlikely that these groups of hunters and fishers were responsible for the emergence of the TRB culture in the northern Netherlands. The early material of the Dutch TRB West Group has much in common with the Fuchsberg and Troldeberg phases of the Scandinavian north group and it is suggested that the first farming communities that exploited the Frisian Drentian plateau colonised that area from the north-east (Bakker 1979; Brindley 1988; Madsen 1982; Lanting & Bottema 1991; but see Hogestijn 1990 for a different opinion). On the southern sandy soils, the early Neolithic Michelsberg culture developed into the Seine-Oise-Marne culture, of which the Stein group is the Dutch branch. Here the economy had been pre-dominantly agrarian throughout the Bandkeramik and subsequent Rössen cultures.

In the Rhine delta and the coastal zone, farming was also practised, but only as a subsidiary to the exploitation of the rich coastal environment. Here the Vlaardingen culture dominates the picture until the middle of the third millennium BC. Around 2900 BC this situation of cultural diversity is replaced by the emergence of a seemingly homogeneous Single Grave culture in most parts of the Netherlands. Finds of the TRB culture do not extend south of the river Rhine, but the remains of the Single Grave culture are found also in the southern and western Netherlands. In the delta area the Vlaardingen culture continues its existence, with its main distribution south of the River Rhine. Only during the AOO-phase of the Single Grave culture is Vlaardingen pottery replaced by Single Grave pottery. Around 2400 BC, both cultures are replaced by the Bell Beaker culture – which in the Netherlands is not merely an addition of some cultural elements to existing local groups (Lanting & van der Waals 1976).

MEGALITHIC TOMBS AND EARTHEN BARROWS AS FORMAL DISPOSAL AREAS

One of the most striking elements of change that marks the emergence of the Single Grave culture is the substitution of collective megalithic tombs by barrows with single inhumations and standardised sets of grave gifts. This complex is dominated by cord or otherwise decorated beakers and battle axes. The seemingly explosive spread of cord decorated beakers over large parts of western Europe prompted Childe (1948: 172 ff.) to propose a nomadic nature for the Corded ware people. Although Childe's migration model has been more or less discarded, his interpretation of Corded ware cultures, strengthened by the impressive work of Gimbutas (1965) and by the lack of alternative explanations, continues to influence current work. In the Netherlands, archaeologists have continued to view the emergence of the Single Grave culture as one of the last examples of a migration (cf. Bloemers et al. 1981). In Scandinavia, by contrast, Malmer (1962) has proposed a process of continuous development, although Kristiansen (1989) has recently tried to revive migration as an explanation for the Corded ware complex.

Although this topic has been the subject of much discussion, alternative explanations for the emergence of the Corded ware complex have only rarely been offered. Indeed, most authors avoid making clear statements on the subject. Thomas (1991: 138), for instance, states that these developments are 'the net result of innumerable individual strategies and actions played out over an enormous depth of time.'

[483]

Hodder (1982), Tilley (1984) and Voss (1982) also discuss the transition from the TRB to the Single Grave culture, but none of them really tries to explain the transformations of cultures which they recognise through the analysis of pottery decoration.

In the Netherlands, one of the few authors who has tried to explain the emergence of the Single Grave culture as an indigenous development has been Van der Waals (1985), who based part of his argument on Chapman's concept of formal disposal areas (Chapman 1981). Using Bloch's (1971; 1975) research on Madagascar, Chapman considered megalithic tombs to be burial monuments of corporate groups, who used them to express their formal rights to ancestral land. Van der Waals considered the Single Grave practice of erecting barrows over individual burials as evidence for the disappearance of such formal disposal areas. He interpreted this as a sign of the disintegration of tension on critical resources, notably on land. This was ascribed to the 'revolution of secondary products', especially to the introduction of the plough and the cart (Sherratt 1981; Van der Waals 1985: 6). In his view the ard enabled the reclamation of a wider variety of landscapes, thus making it possible to extend the farming areas. Many authors have used variations on this same hypothesis (cf. Champion et al. 1984).

The problem with Chapman's model, and with Van der Waals' application of it is that it is unclear why barrows should not be considered formal disposal areas just as much as megalithic tombs. These barrows were probably 'curated' and remained visible for many generations. Indeed, many late Neolithic and later barrows are still visible in the landscape today, although the majority have been ploughed over since medieval times. Therefore the categorial distinction between formal and informal disposal proposed by Chapman does not apply to any phase of Dutch prehistory. A second problem with Van der Waals' explanation for late Neolithic culture change is that the primitive plough which was in use until the late Iron Age – the *ard* – is not an instrument that can be used for the reclamation of new areas of forest. It could only be useful in areas that had already been reclaimed and cleared of tree trunks, stones and roots (cf. Boserup 1965; Fowler 1983: 168). In that sense, the ard did not constitute an innovation that resulted in the resolution of tension on land. Rather, one could argue that the opposite was probably the case: in order to use the ard, the land would have had to be more intensively worked than before and thus may have become an even more critical resource.

[484]

MEGALITHIC TOMBS AS CEREMONIAL CENTRES OF CORPORATE GROUPS

In the Low Countries, archaeologists are inclined to believe that mega-lithic tombs (*hunebedden*) served only one purpose: burial. Hardly any-one gives thought to their function as central places or focal points in the social landscape. Where such models have been put forward, they have tended to follow Renfrew's (1973; 1976) view of megalithic tombs as territorial markers. For instance, Harsema postulated a one-to-one relationship for *hunebedden* and settlements (Harsema 1988). He even claims that the Neolithic territorial structure can be compared with the present territorial division of Drenthe (Harsema 1988: 19). This ignores the fact that the *hunebedden* are sometimes found in clusters of two or more close together. It also ignores the distribution of settlement finds of the TRB culture, which occur in a vast region outside the distribu-tion area of the *hunebedden* (Fokkens 1991). The problem here, of course, is that only few of the known settlements of the TRB culture have been excavated. The remainder, a substantial number, are known only from surface collections which have yet to be subjected to systematic analysis. In addition, Bakker's (1982) research demonstrated that the *hunebedden* could not have served as territorial markers in the strict sense of the term. In testing Renfrew's model through the con-struction of Thiessen polygons around the *hunebedden*, Bakker (1982) was able to show a lack of fit between the expectations of the model and archaeological distributions. This is hardly a surprise if one real-ises that the boulders for building the monuments are only found along the eastern and southern borders of the Frisian-Drentian plateau, where they were deposited by the land ice.

An alternative model can be put forward, following Bloch's research in Madagascar (Bloch 1971; 1975). In his analysis of Malagasy mega-lithic tombs and their role in structuring society, Bloch shows that the tombs are connected to corporate groups and signify rights to ancestral land. To their users they represent central places in a myth-ical land, they do not, however, serve as concrete markers in adjoining territories. The members of these corporate groups live dispersed and bury their dead – temporally – near their homes. At certain occasions, however, they rebury the dead in the ancestral tombs, sometimes even after a long journey by car or airplane. This is done at moments of ceremonial feasts centred around the tombs.

Similar ideas may be useful for our understanding of megalithic tombs in the Low Countries. In my opinion the tribal society of the TRB culture was divided into corporate groups, which in origin probably exploited large territories with slash-and-burn or hoe agriculture. The building of a *hunebed* may have marked the arrival of a new group in the area, or the foundation of new 'tomb group' that had separated from existing groups. Folklore and myth placed the tombs in a mythical (ritual) landscape in which the ancestors lived, as in the case of the Malagasy tombs and the Australian songlines (Bloch 1971; Chatwin 1987). The meanings of these tombs were probably transformed over time, as were the rituals and ceremonies carried out in and around them. It is also likely that changes occurred in the conventions that determined who had the right to be buried within these sites. Eventually, some hundred years before the Single Grave culture emerged in the Low Countries, the tradition of building *hunebedden* came to an end. Perhaps this can be taken as indication that fission processes were no longer possible. In any case, it seems that at that time the whole sandy area north of the river Rhine was settled by TRB groups.

ECONOMIC AND SOCIAL CHANGE AFTER 3000 BC

Most authors emphasise the intensification of production, facilitated by the introduction of the ard, as one of the prominent features of social and economic change in the late Neolithic. For the Netherlands, one could argue that further expansion of the TRB groups would have meant entering the habitation areas of the Vlaardingen and Stein groups to the west and the south. That could have been a social reason for an intensification of agricultural practice; in fact I suggested this in an earlier article (Fokkens 1986). Now I feel that emphasising the element of intensification sets us on the wrong interpretative foot. I would rather see the use of the ard as a logical consequence of the opening up of the forest as a result of hundreds of years of continuous hoe agriculture. If the forest is not allowed to regenerate fully, open spaces with low vegetation and shallow but dense root covers will develop (Boserup 1965). In such areas, hoe agriculture becomes less effective. An ard, however, will enable the farmer to break the root cover – possibly after setting fire to the vegetation – and at the same time create a furrow for sowing. It is plausible that in that situation, the plough – having first been introduced several centuries earlier – really became an innovation, adopted at an accelerated pace, when communities became aware of its effectiveness in open spaces.

Once used on a wide scale in the north, the plough was eventually taken up by communities in the Rhine delta. It is probable that slash-and-burn agriculture was seldom practised in this zone; hoes and spades were likely to have been the major tools used to reclaim arable land from the grass covered marshes. If we interpret the beaker as one of the symbols accompanying plough agriculture (see below) this may also explain the seeming expansion of the Single Grave culture and the Corded ware cultures in general.

So far, we have only looked at the economic aspects of the changes that characterise the late Neolithic. However, these developments may have had strong social implications. They may well be responsible for the shift in emphasis from collective to individual burial that marks the transformation of the TRB culture into the Single Grave culture. As I see it, an increased sense of group (i.e., lineage or kin group) owner-ship resulted from the higher labour input in land, cattle and possibly housing (cf. Gilman 1981). Instead of clearing a new part of the forest, or using an old fallow plot, one had to remove tree trunks and possibly fence the arable land. The arable land probably had to be manured since the shorter fallow periods – necessary to prevent re-generation of the vegetation – exhausted the soil. This goes especially for the poor sandy soils in the Netherlands. Oxen were raised for drawing the ard and cattle were kept inside farmsteads or corrals in order to be able to collect manure. The landscape was increasingly domesticated, consolidating the feeling that people owned it.

This development may explain why the traditional corporate groups eventually broke up into more individually oriented, autonomous communities. Instrumental in this process may have been the higher labour input necessary for working the land and raising stock. Even the traditional roles in the domestic domain may have altered due to the changed responsibilities for ploughing and stock raising. Less attention would have been devoted to communal ceremonies centring around the collective tombs. In that sense, the changes were indeed 'the net result of innumerable individual strategies and actions' (Thomas 1991: 138).

The disintegration of the 'tomb groups' was already underway during the later phases of the TRB culture. After 3100 BC new *hune-bedden* were no longer built, flat graves appeared, and the pottery lost its marked TRB decoration, in the Netherlands as well as in Scandi-navia. Probably from that point in time onwards, the ard became more and more accepted, resulting in a revolutionary development around 2900 BC. The introduction of the cart at approximately the same time – also needing oxen as draught animals – may have added to the at-tractiveness of the new economic standards. In time-space geography one would identify this period as the steep part of the logistic curve of

[487]

acceptance, indicating that after a long period of restricted acceptance often a short period of wholesale acceptance follows until the level of saturation is reached (cf. Abler et al. 1972: 144; Hägerstrand 1968).

After 2900 BC people became increasingly focussed on their own kin-groups. In the middle Bronze Age this process had fully crystallised into a stable system, as is demonstrated by the so-called family barrows with a central grave and a number of secondary internments in the barrow. Settlements then consisted of only one or two dispersed homesteads that were rebuilt every twenty to forty years on a different spot in the local territory. The barrows were laid out on fallow plots – as palynological evidence suggests (Casparie & Groenman-Van Waateringe 1980) – and were probably only built for the heads of families or kin groups and their wives (Fokkens 1991; Lohof 1991). Child burials in central graves under a barrow are rare until later in the middle Bronze Age (Lohof 1991). With the movement of settlements, a new location for burying the dead was also chosen, indicating that the supposed connection between land and burials is indeed plausible. Not until the late Bronze Age did larger cemeteries develop, although occasionally clusters of Neolithic or Bronze Age barrows are present. These clusters may indicate settlement movement in rather confined territories where the subsequent kin group elders were buried in each other's vicinity.

Given the fact that both settlement systems and burial practices remained basically unaltered for over a thousand years, one may conclude that the profound changes – seen through the eyes of the twentieth century archaeologist – that took place around 2900 BC were but the symbols of a gradual and accepted culture process. There was no migration or revolution that caused the transformation to the Single Grave culture. There was no change in complexity, as is often suggested, no chiefdoms emerged. The standardised complex of grave gifts of the beaker cultures does not indicate the rise of local elites that controlled critical resources. Of course there are differences between the individual graves, and there certainly will have been persons who during their lifetime acquired wealth and status, using gift exchange and prestige networks to their own and communal ends. However, these positions were not hereditary or institutionalised. In my opinion, the beakers in the graves are nothing more than containers for food or drink, the crockery as opposed to cooking pots. In the Dutch settlements of both the Single Grave and the Bell Beaker cultures, true beakers are found in large numbers. However, beaker pots (rusticated beakers) – also a prominent feature in settlements – are never found in primary graves (only in a few instances they were part of secondary burials). Therefore, the fine beaker ware can be explained as representing the crockery, used at home for meals or for special drinks, and in the graves for supplying the dead with their favourite nourishment. In that sense, more than one beaker in a grave rather signifies good care for the needs of the deceased than a higher status of the dead person in his or her lifetime.

CONCLUSION

The fast spread of the Corded ware complex over northern, western and central Europe was seen as a symbol of social and economic changes which developed rapidly from the beginning of the late Neolithic. The social changes comprise the disintegration of the existing corporate groups into smaller 'land owning' kin groups. The individualisation of society is demonstrated by the emergence of barrow graves, in which a warrior aspect is strikingly present: battle axes, archers gear (bow, arrows, wrist guard, arrow shaft smoother) and dagger signify an emphasis on the warrior status of the male individual. Tribal warfare obviously was an important (new?) aspect in late Neolithic societies.

This element is hardly ever given attention in the analyses of the beaker problem. We are used to speaking of the beaker complex, as a set of grave gifts with a common meaning. This is an oversimplification. The beakers probably should be seen as gifts of the relatives, but the warriors equipment as personal gear, indicating an important quality of the deceased. This quality may not have been related to a prestigious status at all, but rather be connected with the constitution of a person as a valued member of the community. The people standing around the grave probably saw a *man who could defend the community as a warrior*. The beakers signified more of a quality than simply that 'men drink'.

ACKNOWLEDEGMENTS

I want to thank David Fontijn and Daan Raemaekers (Leiden) for reading the text and their constructive criticism.

REFERENCES

Abler, R., Adams, J. S. & Gould, P. 1972. *Spatial Organization: the Geographers View of the World*. London: Prentice/Hall.

Bakker, J. A. 1979. *The TRB Westgroup. Studies in the chronology and geography of the makers of the hunebeds and tiefstich pottery*. Amsterdam: Amsterdam University Press.

Bakker, J. A. 1982. TRB-settlement patterns on the Dutch sandy soils. *Analecta Praehistorica Leidensia* 15: 87–124.

Bloch, M. 1971. *Placing the Dead*. London and New York: Seminar Press.

Bloch, M. 1975. Property and the end of affinity. In Bloch, M. (ed.), *Marxist Analysis and Social Anthropology*, pp. 203–228. London: Malaby Press.

Bloemers, J. H. F., Louwe Kooijmans, L. P. & Sarfatij, H. 1981. *Verleden land*. Amsterdam: Elsevier.

Boserup, E. 1965. *The Conditions of Agricultural Growth: the economics of agrarian change under population pressure*. New York: Aldine.

Brindley, A. L. 1988. The typochronology of TRB West Group pottery. *Palaeohistoria* 28: 93–132.

Casparie, W. A. & Groenman-Van Waateringe, W. 1980. Palynological analyses of Dutch barrows. *Palaeohistoria* 22: 7–65.

Champion, T., Gamble, C., Shennan, S., & Whittle, A. 1984. *Prehistoric Europe*. London: Academic Press.

Chapman, R. 1981. The emergence of formal disposal areas and the 'problem' of megalithic tombs in prehistoric Europe. In Chapman, R., Kinnes, I. & Randsborg, K. (eds), *The Archaeology of Death*, pp. 71–81. Cambridge: Cambridge University Press.

Chatwin, B. 1987. *The Songlines*. New York: Penguin.

Childe, V. G. 1948. *The Dawn of European Civilization*. (4th ed.) London: Routledge & Kegan.

Fokkens, H. 1986. From shifting cultivation to short fallow cultivation: late Neolithic change in the Netherlands reconsidered. In Fokkens, H., Banga, P. M. & Bierma, M. (eds), *Op zoek naar mens en materi'le cultuur*, pp. 5–21. Groningen: Groningen University Press.

Fokkens, H. 1991. Verdrinkend Landschap; archeologisch onderzoek van het westelijk Fries-Drents Plateau 4400 BC tot 500 AD. Dissertation: Groningen.

Fowler, P. J. 1983. *The Farming of Prehistoric Britain*. Cambridge: Cambridge University Press.

Gilman, A. 1981. The development of social stratification in Bronze Age Europe. *Current Anthropology* 22: 1–8, 23.

Gimbutas, M. 1965. *Bronze Age Cultures in Central and Eastern Europe*. Paris: Mouton & Co.

Hägerstrand. T. 1968. *Diffusion of Innovations*. Chicago: University of Chicago Press.

Harsema, O. H. 1988. *Borger ruim 5000 jaar geleden. De Drentse samenleving in Europees perspectief*. ('De Zwerfsteen' – Historisch tijdschrift voor de gemeente Borger) 88/4. (Flint'nhoesreeks 4).

Hodder, I. 1982. Sequences of change in the Dutch Neolithic. In Hodder, I. (ed.), *Symbolic and Structural Archaeology*, pp. 162–177. Cambridge: Cambridge University Press.

Hogestijn, J. W. 1990. From Swifterbant to TRB in the IJssel-Vecht basin – some suggestions. In Jankowska, D. (ed.), *Die Trichterbecherkultur: neue Forschungen und Hypothesen. Material des internationalen Symposiums Dymaczewo, 20–24 september 1988*, vol. 1, pp. 163–180. Poznan: Instytut Prahistorii Uniwersytetu.

Kristiansen, K. 1989. Prehistoric migrations – the case of the Single Grave and Corded ware cultures. *Journal of Danish Archaeology* 8: 211–225.

de Laet, S. J. & Glasbergen, W. 1959. *De voorgeschiedenis van de Lage Landen.* Groningen: Wolters.

Lanting, J. N. & Bottema, S. 1991. Aanwijzingen voor een pre-trechterbeker*landnam* in het Gieterseveentje, gem. Gieten (Dr.). *Paleo-Aktueel* 2.

Lohof, E. 1991. Grafritueel en sociale verandering in de bronstijd van Noord-oost-Nederland. Dissertation, Amsterdam.

Louwe Kooijmans, L. P. 1974. *The Rhine/Meuse Delta. Four studies in its prehistoric occupation and holocene geology.* (Analecta Praehistorica Leidensia 7).

Madsen, T. 1982. Settlement systems of early agricultural societies in East Jutland: a regional study of change. *Journal of Anthropological Archaeology* 1: 197–236.

Malmer, M. P. 1962. *Jungneolithische Studien.* Bonn and Lund: Rudolf Habelt (Acta Archaologica Lundensia 8,2).

Renfrew, C. 1973. Monuments, mobilisation and social organisation in Neolithic Wessex. In Renfrew, C. (ed.), *The Explanation of Culture Change: models in prehistory*, pp. 539–558. London: Duckworth.

Renfrew, C. 1976. Megaliths, territories and populations. In de Laet, S. J. (ed.), *Acculturation and Continuity in Atlantic Europe, papers presented at the IVth Atlantic Colloquium*, pp. 198–220. Brugge: De Tempel (Dissertationes Archaeologicae Gandensis 16).

Shennan, S. J. 1976. Bell beakers and their context in central Europe. In Lanting, J. N. & Van der Waals, J. D. (eds), *Glockenbecher Symposium Oberried 1974*, pp. 231–240. Haarlem: Fibula-Van Dishoeck.

Shennan, S. J. 1982. Ideology, change and the European early Bronze Age. In Hodder, I., Isaac, G. & Hammond, N. (eds), *Pattern of the Past: studies in honour of David Clarke*, pp. 155–161. Cambridge: Cambridge University Press.

Sherratt, A. 1981. Plough and pastoralism: aspects of the secondary products revolution. In Hodder, I., Isaac, G. & Hammond, N. (eds), *Pattern of the Past: studies in the honour of David Clarke*, 261–305. Cambridge: Cambridge University Press.

Thomas, J. 1991. *Rethinking the Neolithic.* Cambridge: Cambridge University Press.

Tilley, C. 1984. Ideology and the legitimation of power in the middle Neolithic of southern Sweden. In Miller, D. & Tilley, C. (eds), *Ideology, Power and Prehistory*, pp. 111–146. Cambridge: Cambridge University Press.

Voss, J. 1982. A study of western TRB social organisation. *Berichten van de Rijksdienst voor het Oudheidkundig Bodemonderzoek* 32: 9–102.

van der Waals, J. D. 1985. Discontinuity, cultural evolution and the historic event. *Proceedings of the Society of Antiquaries of Scotland* 11: 1–14.

23

Funerary and Domestic Domains in the Prehistory of the North-western Iberian Peninsula

Ramón Fábregas and Marisa Ruíz-Gálvez

Ever since the end of the nineteenth century, when research began into the prehistory of the north-western Iberian peninsula (basically defined as the regions of Galicia and Portugal north of the Douro [Fig. 1]), archaeologists' efforts have been concentrated almost obsessively on two types of site: hillforts and tumuli. The special attention given (then and now) to these sites is partly due to their monumental nature and to their imposing presence in the lanscape. In every other way, however, hillforts and tumuli are quite unlike: functionally, the first being fortified settlements, the second funerary constructions; chronologically, hillforts are traditionally ascribed to the Iron Age while tumuli date from the Neolithic; and finally, geographically, in that the tumuli are generally associated with upland areas, whereas the hillforts are more often found on cultivated land, sited on the lower slopes of valleys. Thus we have two very different monumental phenomena in the recent prehistory of the north-west: the tumuli were built at a time when the domestic sphere was practically invisible, and when this became conspicuous in the landscape in the form of fortified settlements, funerary monuments appear to have been absent. In this paper we shall examine and compare the domestic and funerary spheres during the fourth-second millennia (in conventional dates), and try to decipher the socio-cultural dynamics underlying the options presented in the monumental plane by the prehistoric communities

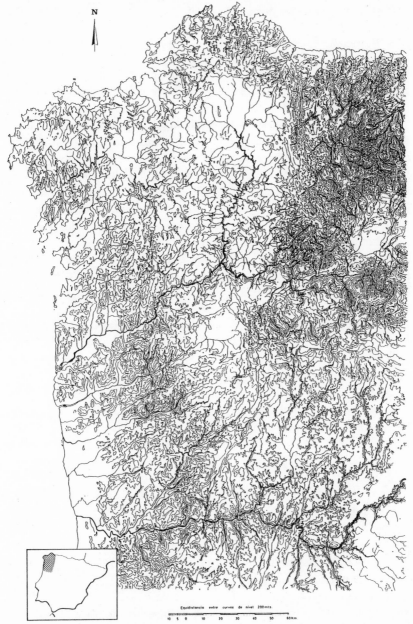

Figure 1. Map of the north-western region of the Iberian peninsula.

that inhabited the north-west between the Neolithic and the late
Bronze Age.

[493]

THE TUMULUS PHENOMENON

The tumuli or *mámoas* of the north-west have attracted the attention of scholars since the study of prehistory began in the area. However, their monumental presence in the landscape had already attracted attention for many generations, and they were a distinctive feature of the peasant world of the historical period. The excavations carried out both in Galicia and in the north of Portugal in the past twenty years have revealed the complexity of a form of tomb that, without achieving the splendour of those of other areas of the Atlantic seaboard, is nevertheless outstanding for the abundance and variety of its manifestations. It developed between the last third of the fourth millennium bc and the beginning of the second, thus extending, broadly speaking, from the middle Neolithic to the beginning of the Bronze Age (Fig. 2).

Although there are certain common features in these funerary sites, such as the existence of some kind of internal stone construction, the feature that gives the tumulus phenomenon unity and cultural coherence is the desire of different communities to make their presence known through monumental funerary constructions in a conspicuous way, displaying a clear desire for an eternal memorial. By building tumuli they affirmed their control over the environment and the domestication of the landscape by using various forms of spatial organisation (Criado & Fábregas 1989; Criado & Fábregas 1994). Initially, towards the last third of the fourth millennium bc, we see the widespread appearance in various areas of earthen tumuli covered with stones and containing a single small dolmen (V. Jorge 1991; Fábregas 1991: 39). There are few grave goods and those found show little variation. Perhaps by the beginning of the third millennium we can see the first signs of increasing complexity in this type of monument, exemplified in the greater variety in internal structure: an elongated ground plan, larger chambers, occasionally decorated with paintings or carvings, a pit instead of the interior stone construction (V. Jorge 1985) and even (at Pena Mosqueira 3) the appearance of an individual burial in a tumulus with no chamber, accompanied by valuable grave goods (Sanches 1987; 1989).

Somewhere before the middle of the third millennium bc we see an important development in megalithic architecture in various parts of the north-west. This development is more common in the coastal areas and at lower altitudes than previously, but should not be seen as an abandonment of upland areas. In certain communities at least, an impulse towards the construction of more monumental passage graves

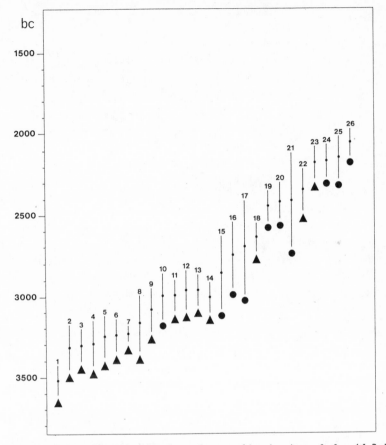

Figure 2. Uncalibrated 14C dates from prehistoric sites of the 4th-3rd millennium: 1. Châ de Parada 4; 2. Furnas 2; 3. Meninas do Crasto 2; 4. Furnas 1; 5. Outeiro de Gregos 3; 6. Chan da Cruz; 7. Monte da Olheira; 8 & 9. Mina do Simâo; 10. Barrocal Alto; 11. Outeiro de Gregos 2; 12. Pena Mosqueira; 13. Châ de Santinhos 2; 14. Châ de Santinhos 1; 15. O Fixón; 16. Castelo de Aguiar; 17. Vinha da Soutilha; 18. Châ de Parada 1; 19. Buraco da Pala; 20. Barrocal Alto; 21. Vinha da Soutilha; 22. Os Campiños 6; 23. Châ de Parada 1; 24. Buraco da Pala; 25. Barrocal Alto; 26. Guidoiro Areoso. Triangles indicate funerary sites, circles domestic sites. Age ranges equivalent to 2 standard deviations. (1–5, 7–9, 11, 13–14 & 18 after Cruz 1988; 12, 19 & 24 after Sanches 1989; 10, 20 & 25 after Sanches 1992; 16–17 & 21 after S. Jorge 1985; 23 after Jorge 1989; 6 & 22 after Fábregas 1988; 15 after García-Lastra 1984; 26 after Rey 1991 and pers. comm.).

can be seen (as at Châ de Parada 1, Dombate). Certain sites are more imposing, not just architecturally, but also in terms of the richness and variety of grave goods. These tombs sometimes have an 'atrium'

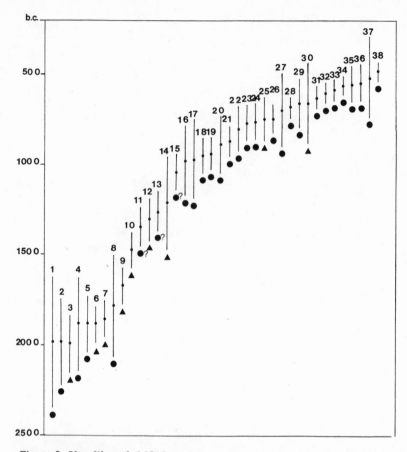

Figure 3. Uncalibrated 14C dates from prehistoric sites of the 2nd-1st millennium: 1. Castelo de Aguiar; 2. Lavapés II; 3. Chã de Parada 1; 4. O Fixón; 5. A Chan de Coiro; 6 and 7. Meninas do Crasto 4; 8. Castelo de Aguiar; 9 & 10. Outeiro de Gregos 1; 11. Tapado da Caldeira; 12. Outeiro de Gregos 5; 13. Tapado da Caldeira; 14. Piedrafita V; 15. Tapado da Caldeira; 16 & 17. Coto da Pena; 18 to 22. São Julião; 23 & 24. Bouça do Frade; 25. Cabritos 1; 26. São Julião; 27. Castro da Graña; 28. Torroso; 29. Castro da Graña; 30. Piedrafita V; 31 to 34. Torroso; 35. Penarrubia; 36. Castrovite; 37. Borneiro; 38. Torroso. Triangles indicate funerary sites, circles domestic sites. Age ranges equivalent to 2 standard deviations. (1, 8, 11, 13, 15 & 23-24 after S. Jorge 1985; 2 after Peña 1984c; 3, 6, 7, 9, 10 & 12 after V. Jorge et al. 1988; 4 & 5 after García-Lastra 1988; 14 & 30 after Blas 1985; 16-22, 26-29, 31-38 after Fábregas & Carballo 1991; 25 after Cruz 1988).

facing the passage, which could have been used for ceremonial purposes. A good example of this change towards greater structural complexity can be seen at the Dombate site itself. This inititially consisted of a simple elongated chamber which was later covered by a larger tumulus holding a passage grave with a small atrium (Bello 1991). At this time, between the late Neolithic and the beginning of the Copper Age, the differences between the types of tomb found in various parts of the north-west become clearer than before, for in some areas large passage graves are scarce or absent, while the simple dolmens or other 'para-megalithic' structures are still found, sometimes of individual use.

In addition to this pattern of increased regional differentiation, an increasing flow or distribution of exotic material culture (such as pottery and stone tools) can also be observed. Once again, this seems to have been more important in coastal areas. These tendencies have also been seen for a similar period in other parts of Atlantic Europe, such as southern England (Bradley 1991 A). The end of the third millennium bc and the early centuries of the second see an accentuation of the process of regional differentiation and an extension of the exchange networks through which such characteristic elements as the Bell Beaker or the first metal items were distributed. While earlier passage graves were reused in some cases, new tumuli, megalithic or otherwise, were also built, displaying a change in architectonic approach: they are smaller and less visible landscape features, which appear to have been used in a more limited, or purely individual way (Criado & Fábregas 1989; Vaquero 1990). Traditionally, these later monuments have been used to mark the end of the tumulus cycle in the north-west at around 1800 bc, roughly coinciding with the appearance of rectangular cists, dug into the ground and containing rich metal grave goods datable to the early Bronze Age. In recent years, however, we have found indications that tumulus burials persisted beyond this date. Radiocarbon dates obtained for cairn-type burials,[1] such as Outeiro de Gregos 1 and 5, and for the chamberless Piedrafita 5 tumulus (Fig. 3), indicate that some funerary monuments were built as late as the later Bronze Age (Jorge et al. 1988; Blas 1985).[2] Although these dates are not without contextual and interpretive problems, both in themselves or due to the complete absence of associated grave goods, we think they may indicate the possibly residual survival of monumental forms of burial in certain parts of the north-west. The occurrence in some tumuli of secondary pits containing a flat-rimmed vessel, a type of pottery that can be assigned to an advanced stage of the Bronze Age (Calo & Sierra 1983; S. Jorge 1988) would strengthen the idea that these monuments still constituted a symbolic point of reference for communities of this period.

SETTLEMENT FROM THE FOURTH TO THE SECOND MILLENNIA

It is a common adage in the archaeology of the north-west that the communities who were more or less contemporary with the megalithic phenomenon died, but never lived, due to the lack of domestic evidence for the period. Until even recently we have had little settlement data for these people or their inmediate predecessors. This is due, apart from any shortcomings in research, to the particular characteristics of the area. The shallow nature of many soils, erosion and the character of occupation often means that we can only talk about 'activity areas'. These are sometimes fairly extensive, but they remain difficult to interpret in functional terms.

There is evidence of a productive economy from at least the fourth millennium bc, shown by the finds of pollen of Cerealia and other sinanthropic species (Vázquez 1988: 331). Territorial analysis carried out in various places show that the tumuli were by preference built on high plateaux in the mountains, sparsely wooded, and with extensive grasslands. Here the soils are light and well drained, so they can be hoed and the slash-and-burn method used, which is not feasible on the heavier, but also more fertile, valley soils (V. Jorge 1991: 207; Criado 1988: 80). However, it is likely that the builders of the first tumuli did not limit themselves to cultivation or stock raising on these plateaux. The lower lands were probably used for hunting and gathering also (V. Jorge 1989: 406).

The application of site-catchment analysis to these funerary sites is pertinent since we have a good indication that there were nearby settlements, revealed by high phosphate content in the soil below the tumuli or the frequent presence of heavy grinding-stones that have been worn out and reused as building material in the tumuli (V. Jorge 1988: 8). Recent research has confirmed these indications with the discovery of stone and pottery items (the latter often decorated, in contrast with an almost exclusively plain pottery among the grave goods) in the proximity of the monuments or even underneath them. Occasionally a structure with a domestic purpose is also found, such as paving stones or post holes (Cleto & Faro 1991: 207; Criado et al. 1991: 150). Other open-air settlements or rocky shelters belonging to the beginning of the third millennium bc display similar characteristics, suggesting a non-permanent type of settlement and an economy that would combine agriculture (and cattle raising?) with gathering, and also the use of predominantly local raw materials (Sanches 1990: 340; 1992: 152).

During the second half of the third millennium we see important changes in the type of settlement in the north-west, although these are not as profound as the changes that can be detected in other areas of the Iberian peninsula, such as the south-east or Portuguese Extremadura (Fig. 2). Domestic sites increase in number and size and are found in a greater variety of geographical areas, from the coast to the plateaux previously occupied. Sometimes, settlements were built in prominent places from which lowland areas used for intensive farming could be watched over. The available evidence endorses the presence of a more developed and diversified economy than in the previous period and a corresponding population increase that would perhaps explain the thrust towards areas less exploited in previous times. Nevertheless, it is important to emphasise the features of continuity: in some settlements (e.g. Buraco da Pala, Barrocal Alto; Sanches 1990, 1992), there are still many elements of late Neolithic material culture (pottery and stone artefacts) and insubstantial dwellings, built of perishable materials and thus scarcely visible in the landscape. However, this lack of architectonic substance is counterbalanced in particular sites in the Chaves region (northern Portugal) by an extraordinary complexity in domestic items such as pots, a very large number of which are decorated (more than 80% in one site) (S. Jorge 1985: 6), something unknown in other domestic contexts of the Iberian Copper Age.

Although data on economic activities are still sparse, it appears that the communities of the second half of the third millennium bc embarked on a process of more intense exploitation of their environment. There is a significant increase in the findings of remains of cereals (wheat or barley), sometimes with evidence of storage, such as in the rock shelter of Buraco da Pala, where legumes (*Vicia faba* L.) have also been recovered, important as animal fodder or human food. Although soil conditions are unfavourable for the preservation of bone, remains of pigs, sheep and goats have been reported from two settlements (S. Jorge 1986: 1099). It seems, therefore, that some elements of what is termed the Secondary Products Revolution (Sherratt 1981; Harrison 1985) occurred at this time, such as the hypothetical use of a light ard, which would have allowed some of the lowlands to be brought into cultivation, and also the use, archaeologically documented, of milk derivates such as cheese or the development of textiles (Sanches 1992: 93 and 152). These communities belonged to exchange networks that extended beyond the purely local area, through which they could obtain scarce raw materials such as flint or variscite more easily than before (Sanches 1989a: 450; S. Jorge 1986: 255) and, by the end of the third millennium, prestige items such as copper, gold and Bell Beaker pottery. Extra-regional contacts, especially with the Copper Age cultures of southern Iberia, can be seen not only in artefacts or raw materials, but also in symbolic aspects, such as the occurrence of the oculus motif, both in pottery and in the schematic painting of this period, and also in certain types of idols (Fábregas 1991a; Sanches 1990).

The outline we have sketched on the basis of the evidence dating from the second half of the third millennium is consistent with a model of communities that led a more sedentary life than before, and were probably seeing the first signs of a internal social differentiation, revealed by the appearance of valuable or prestigious items. Among the questions that remain, however, is the issue of the connection between these domestic sites and the contemporary tumuli, in particular, the differences in their material culture. This is most clearly demonstrated by the pottery assemblages from the two classes of site. These assemblages are often decorated in settlement contexts, but almost exclusively plain in the tumuli. This suggests that either these two types of sites represent different societies with their own traditions or that the divergence is due to strictly functional reasons (S. Jorge 1986: 924). In our opinion, the second thesis would seem more feasible, bearing in mind that decorated pottery has been found from possible late fourth-early third millennium bc settlements under the tumuli but not in the actual tombs. Thus the monumental and funerary/non-monumental and domestic dichotomy, already observed in the middle-late Neolithic, appears to have been maintained in the pre-Bell Beaker Copper Age of the north-west, and reasserted with the expansion of the Bell Beaker (this time present both in domestic and funerary contexts).

THE FUNERARY WORLD BETWEEN THE SECOND AND BEGINNING OF THE FIRST MILLENNIUM BC

The trend towards smaller tumuli and the loss of their commanding position in the landscape, which is visible in the mounds of the later stages of the Copper Age, continues in the subsequent transition to the Bronze Age. This horizon sees the appearance of individual cist burials, some containing rich metal grave goods such as weapons and gold and silver jewellery, which can be linked with the Bell Beaker although the pottery itself is absent (Fig. 4). Although concentrated in

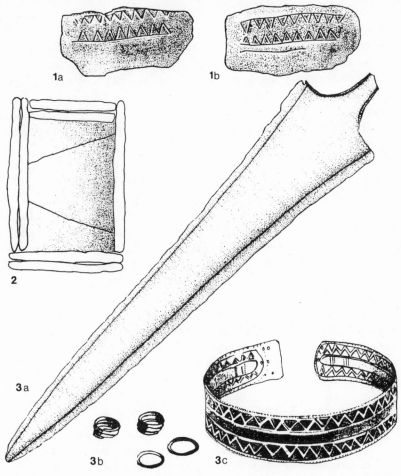

Figure 4. Early Bronze Age cist burials. 1 a-b. decorated slabs of A Insua (Galicia); 2. cist of Chedeiro (Galicia); 3. Grave goods from the cist of Quinta da Agua Branca (N. Portugal): a. copper dagger with silver-like surface, produced by an intentional arsenic-rich alloy; b. gold rings; c. gold diadem. The same features are found in daggers from graves in Carnoët (Briard & Mohen 1974) and Gau-Bickelheim (Hundt 1971) (1 and 2 after Vázquez 1980a; 3a and b after Hernando 1989; 3c after Ruíz-Gálvez).

the north-western corner of the Iberian peninsula, these rich individual burial cists have parallels in the northern Meseta (Delibes 1977), and in other groups of individual tombs beyond our borders, such as those of Wessex I and the first series of Armorican tumuli (Gerloff 1975; Briard 1984).

Without discounting the possibility that some of these burials could be attributed to women or young adults, the richest, containing weapons and jewellery, are undoubtedly masculine in character and it is worth pointing out that while they are rarely discovered as a result of systematic survey and excavation, they seem to be situated in low-land areas that are suitable for agriculture. The fact that many of them (O Cubillón, Lugo; Chedeiro, Orense; Carnota, Corunna; A Insua, Corunna; Taraio, Corunna; Coitemil, Pontevedra; Rodeiro, Ponte-vedra) have been discovered in the course of agricultural work seems to confirm this. Another interesting aspect of these cists is the presence in some of them (A Insua, Coitemil, Rodeiro and perhaps Carnota) of decorated slabs (Vázquez 1980 a & b; 1985–86) (Fig. 4, no. 1 a-b). Un-fortunately the conditions of their discovery make it impossible to determine the exact position of the carvings on the cists. As Vázquez Varela has pointed out (1980a: 37), there seems to be a dichotomy between the carvings on the cists (zig-zags, triangles facing each other, reticula, etc.), motifs rooted in the megalithic tradition, and the carv-ings seen in open-air rock art, unassociated with the funerary world. In at least one case, however, there are grounds for questioning this division. At cist no. 2 at Gandón (Pontevedra), which contained a stone wristguard and a Palmela-type arrow-head (Peña 1985: 81 and pers. comm.), the capstone was made of a large, irregularly shaped slab of granite with five cup-marks on its outside face. The slab seemed to form part of a set of open-air rock carvings from which it had broken off, although it is impossible to know whether this was accidental or intentional. The outside part of the cist appeared to have been en-circled by medium-sized stones driven vertically into the ground. The interesting feature of this example is that, according to the observa-tions of its excavator (ibid., 81), the cist was not originally covered by a tumulus and the surrounding stones protruded from the original soil surface, implying that the capstone with the cup-marks would also have been visible.

This is not an isolated instance, since similar phenomena have been reported in northern Britain, where elements of open-air rock art have been broken off and incorporated face down on tombs (Bradley 1992). However, the circumstances are somewhat different in our case, because the traditional megalithic motifs are found, as in the tumuli, inside the tomb, but the fragment of petroglyph seems to have been in-tentionally placed in order to be seen. The excavation also produced two grinding-stones which may have been associated with a possible settlement (of limited extent and duration) situated close to the site, which may explain the small pottery sherds incorporated in the earth fill of the tomb.

The patterns seen at this site can be considered in relation to the broader scheme outlined above. Some of the elements of the 'Secondary Products Revolution' appear to have been introduced in the middle of the third millennium and this apparently permitted the colonisation of new territories and some degree of demographic increase, as indicated by the settlement of heavier lowland soils and the greater number of habitats now known. However, the evidence for limited duration of settlement, as seen in the settlement associated with the Gandón cists, and the practice of slash-and-burn cultivation may reflect a mobile economy, in which hunting and gathering still played a significant part. Perhaps then, the incorporation of some elements of rock art into the funerary world in the lowland areas was a ritualistic attempt, as in the British case (Bradley 1992a; 1992b), by a population that periodically moved from one area to another to incorporate the landscape of the uplands and their resources. The placement of these carved stones in external and visible positions may indicate the importance of the upland landscape for the Galician communities of the earlier Bronze Age. It suggests that they still conceived of the lowlands in terms of landscape and not just land.

None of these cist burials can be dated exactly. The parallel occurrence of some items with those of Wessex or Armorica merely suggests similar dates for the north-west and their Atlantic neighbours, i.e. the beginning of the second millennium (in conventional dates) without being able to determine whether or not they survive until the middle of that millennium. The haphazard circumstances of their discovery also prevent any social interpretation, and although it would seem they were generally inhumations, in some cases (as at Gandón 1), the cremation of an individual without grave goods is recorded (Peña pers. comm.). Burials under tumuli must have continued at the same time (e.g. Outeiro de Gregos 1 or Meninas do Crasto 4) and perhaps marginally, in cave burials, although here the evidence is not so clear (Sanches 1992).

From the middle of the second millennium bc funerary information becomes rather more rare. It is possible that monumental tombs remained in use, as indicated by controversial radiocarbon dates of certain tumuli that have no stone chamber or grave goods (see Fig. 3). As we noted above, this may indicate that traditional concepts of landscape and ritual practice could have survived in marginal areas into the late second millennium. However, we have no reliable data on burials, and those we do have are ambiguous, as in the case of Tapado da Caldeira (S. Jorge 1980; 1981; 1985), or come from old and un-systematic excavations. A good example of this is the case of alleged inhumations in trapezoidal tombs made of schist slabs. Although the acid soils of the north-west do not favour the preservation of bones, only one has a recorded inhumed body (Ataide & Teixeira 1940; Soeiro 1988). As to the material culture recovered from these tombs, the only definite archaeological and radiocarbon context – the domestic site of Bouça do Frade – (S. Jorge 1988) indicates a late Bronze Age date. There is no way of determining if they could be earlier.

SETTLEMENTS FROM THE SECOND MILLENNIUM BC TO THE END OF THE BRONZE AGE

As with funerary evidence, settlement data are relatively abundant in the transition from the Copper Age to the Bronze Age, and then become gradually more scarce. However, unlike the funerary evid-ence, settlement data once again become abundant from the late Bronze Age onwards and, in contrast to the ambiguity of the former, reflect a definite human presence on the land where it is found (Fig. 3). Curiously, it is generally chronological rather than cultural criteria that determine whether or not these settlements are attributed to the early Bronze Age. There are no significant changes with regard to economy, land use, location or duration of settlements that would make it possible to distinguish the shifting agriculture and gathering economy and incised or impressed pottery sites of the mid-third millennium bc (such as O Regueiriño, A Fontenla and Lavapés I [Pontevedra]: Peña 1984 a, b, & c) from others like Lavapés II, which also had a flimsy occupational structure, shifting agriculture complemented by gather-ing, and incised metopate pottery (Penha) that in settlements in the north of Portugal is dated to the middle of the third millennium bc (S. Jorge 1986: 625). The evidence of in situ copper smelting and, in particular, a suspicious date with high standard deviation (1980±120 bc) are the only criteria that determine its inclusion in the Bronze Age. The same could be said of Bell Beaker sites such as O Fixón and Chan de Armada (Pontevedra) (García Lastra 1984; 1985–86; 1988), O Castro and O Cargadoiro (Corunna) (various authors 1987), or the Os Pericos rock shelter and the open-air site of Morcigueira (Corunna) (Criado & Vázquez 1982), once again placed by chrono-typological rather than cultural criteria, at the beginning of the Bronze Age (Ramil et al. 1990). Something similar happens with some of the sites in the north of Portugal, where it is the radiocarbon dates of the start of the second millennium bc or the presence of Bell Beaker ware which determine their placement in the Copper Age/Bronze Age transition or earlier Bronze Age, despite the few cultural distinctions with previous Copper Age sites (Fig. 3).

From approximately the middle of the second millennium bc or perhaps even earlier, we no longer have settlement information. This pattern continues until the late Bronze Age, at the transition of the second to the first millennium bc (Fig. 3). Even here, when the settlements reappear after a long absence, there is a clear duality in the pattern of human settlement. On one hand, we have places such as Bouça do Frade or Lavra in the north of Portugal (S. Jorge 1988; Sanches 1988), Portecelo, Chan do Carrís or Lamela in Galicia (Cano & Vázquez 1988; Peña 1992a: 377; García Alén 1968), which reflect the survival of an invisible domestic world and mobile and itinerant ways of life, often complemented by gathering. On the other, we see the appearance of hillforts such as Coto da Pena, Baiôes, Sâo Juliâo or Barbudo in northern Portugal (Silva 1986; Martins 1988; 1989) or Torroso in the south of Galicia (Peña 1992b). These sites, with stone buildings and thick stratigraphies, show continuous occupation until the Roman period or even the Middle Ages and a monumental and visible conception of domestic space.

One of the few sites that has been excavated systematically, Bouça do Frade, is probably the best known but by no means the only case, of an open settlement lacking in structures other than storage/rubbish pits, and associated with temporary dwellings that have left no traces, and little or no metal. While the presence of large pottery vessels in some features reflects at least some agricultural practices, the lack of stone dwellings indicates both mobility and instability. Three radiocarbon dates would put the site in the first half of the eighth century bc, making it contemporary with the more permanent hillforts. Dates for these latter sites place them after the tenth century bc (Fig. 3). What is interesting here is that these sites share a series of important features: They are located on the lower slopes, generally dominating good agricultural soils. This can be compared with the upland location, at around 700 m, of places like Bouça do Frade or Lavra. At the same time, they occupy commanding positions for the control of important routes of penetration and communication such as rivers (Coto da Pena, between the rivers Coura and Miño; Sâo Juliâo, on the river Cávado; Barbudo, between the rivers Homen and Cávado; Baiôes, near the river Vouga; Torroso, by the river Louro), or important resources such as tin ores (Baiôes and Coto da Pena). In the case of those few sites for which we have economic information, it seems that gathering coexisted with a sometimes diversified agriculture (Coto da Pena, Baiôes, and Torroso). It is also common to find an abundant presence of metal and even (at Baiôes, Coto da Pena, Torroso) in situ smelting of scrap.

Between the two chronological extremes – the beginning of the second and the beginning of the first millennium bc – there is a temporal hiatus (see Fig. 3) that we cannot fill due to the lack of data and because, in the absence of absolute dating or significant metal items, we do not know how to recognise its characteristic elements, such as pottery. On the other hand, it is very probable that this gap represents an increase in the degree of instability and mobility of populations and thus their inability to maintain the fertility of the lands that they cultivated over long periods. If the great number of places known, many in the lowlands, between the middle of the third and the beginning of the second millennia, reflect the occupation of new lands and a definite demographic increase, the poverty of data now surely indicates a subsequent period of recession.

To this long period of apparent occupational vacuum we should possibly assign many of the 'pit' sites containing pottery and little else, which (as in the case of Bouça do Frade) indicate unstable or limited occupation. Such sites are common in the south of Galicia and northern Portugal. This is the case at O Casal (Pontevedra) (Calo & Sierra 1983; Peña 1992a), where various pits were excavated containing numerous grinding stones, polished axeheads, plain pottery or pottery with incised decoration of limited diagnostic potential. These features were probably connected with temporary huts that have left no traces whatsoever. The same could be said of other sites that are difficult to date, possibly with several phases of occupation, such as Monte Calvo (Gonçalves 1981: 73) or Tapado da Caldeira (S. Jorge 1981: 167) in Portugal.

CONCLUSIONS

In a number of articles, Richard Bradley has offered the persuasive argument that there is an inverse ratio between funerary and settlement evidence between the Neolithic and the end of the Bronze Age in Britain (Bradley 1984; 1990; 1991; 1991b). While the landscape appears to be dominated by the world of the dead for most of the Neolithic and the Bronze Age, this relationship is inverted in the final stages of the latter period, and settlements become the pre-eminent point of reference in a land now permanently inhabited. Despite problems of preservation and gaps in research, a similar pattern can be perceived in the archaeological record of the north-western Iberian peninsula. Here there are two periods of change in the relationship between funerary and habitational spheres, the first more tenuous, the second clearer (Fig. 5) (Ruíz-Gálvez 1991; A). At one extreme we would have, in the words of Criado (1992), a monumentalisation of death as represented by the tumuli. At the other, a fortified landscape in which people's interference with their environment has intensified and has become socialised, with permanent and defended settlements, while funerary structures are now invisible. These two moments are associated with periods of intensified agricultural activity: the Copper Age/Bronze Age transition and the late Bronze Age/Iron Age interface. The phenomena recorded in both periods are not isolated, but repeated in other parts of western Europe.

The first period of agricultural intensification appears to have been connected with the arrival in the north-west of some elements of the 'Secondary Products Revolution' (Sherratt 1981 and 1983; Criado & Fábregas 1989). Elements such as the light ard appear to have enabled greater areas of heavier soils to be cultivated and supported an increase in population. This is shown by the greater number of settlements now found, although they do not appear to be of a permanent nature, and by the presence of some of these settlements and tumuli in the lowlands (Fig. 5). This evidence of agricultural intensification, while restricted to particular areas, can also be found in some parts of Britain during the second half of the third millennium bc, in the later Neolithic (Bradley 1984: 63–65) and it also coincides with data from Brittany indicating possible land enclosures between the end of the Neolithic and the beginning of the Bronze Age. Similarly, the analysis of palaeosoils would indicate that deforestation by slash-and-burn and the cultivation of cereals that began in the Neolithic would have accelerated in the transition to the Bronze Age (Briard 1986; 1987).

This process of agricultural intensification increased the potential for groups to maintain contacts at a regional level. Moreover, as Sherratt (1987) points out, these developments opened Europe in the literal sense of deforestation and in the metaphorical sense of new and wider contacts. These are manifest in the general appearance in western Europe of similar conventions in weapons, drinking, and adornment, the use of gold drinking services and valuable grave goods associated with the adult male. The grave goods of the cists of the north-west of the peninsula appear to be related to this, perhaps most strikingly in

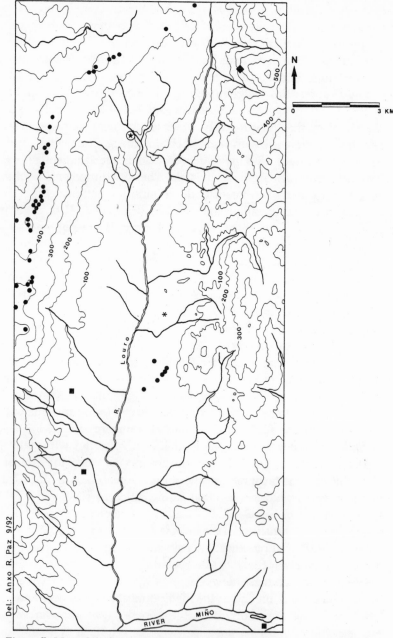

Figure 5. Map of the Louro valley (SW of Galicia) showing the location of different sorts of sites: circles = mounds, lozenge = petroglyph, asterisk = Bronze Age cist, squares = palstave finds or hoards, star = Iron Age hill-fort (after Peña 1992).

the vessels, comb and gold ingots of the treasure of Caldas de Reyes (Pontevedra) (Ruíz-Gálvez 1978; 1991). As with other assemblages, this impressive collection of valuable raw material can be understood as a product of the operation of exchange networks for prestige objects amongst elites, networks which also carried information, knowledge and ideas about technology (Renfrew & Cherry 1986).

This phenomenon did not appear to last, and even before the middle of the second millennium the settlement information (and possibly also the funerary) becomes rare in north-western Iberia and elsewhere. It is no coincidence that the final phase of the earlier Bronze Age is a difficult period to define, both in the Iberian peninsula and in other Atlantic regions. It is very possible that the introduction of a new agrarian technology allowed new lands to be opened up for cultivation, but it did not necessarily help to maintain the fertility of the soil, therefore ensuring the stability of the communities on their land. Perhaps the fact that the man/environment relationship was still more concerned with landscape than land, in the words of Bradley (1984; 1990; 1991; 1991a; 1992a) would justify the maintenance of the concept of monumentality signified by the tumulus until later on in the Bronze Age. Rock art, linked with places of transit or humid basins suitable for hunting or the control of animals also fits this pattern of mobility. [3]

The second period of agricultural intensification, in the late Bronze Age and transition to the Iron Age is more definite and the amount of settlement data increases spectacularly in the north-west, with the exception of Asturias. Two clearly distinguishable patterns emerge at this time. First, there are unstable settlements in which little more than storage/rubbish pits associated with huts in the style of the late Bronze Age habitats of the Spanish northern Meseta are preserved. These contain little or no metal items. Second, there are hillforts, whose stratigraphic and constructional data reflect permanence and stability. Metal is found in them, and there is frequent evidence of 'in situ' smelting. The material culture found in these contexts reflects a concern with weapons, dress, adornment and an emphasis on the communal consumption of food and drink that is common in much of western Europe. The close identification of these themes with the adult male may indicate the appearance of patriarchal systems (Ruíz-Gálvez 1995). In the few cases for which we have paleoeconomic data, there is evidence for a complex agrarian economy, using various types of cereals and legumes and diversified cattle raising. Additional evidence for a change in the traditional relationship between people and their environment, and of the tendency towards permanent settlement and control of land, is found at the hillfort of Torroso. Here, blocks containing rock carvings were reused in the construction of the hillfort (Peña 1992: 42) and this suggests that these designs had lost some of their original significance at a time when people had begun to perceive their surroundings in terms of land rather than landscape (Bradley 1991a; 1991b).

Once again this is not an isolated phenomenon, but a process common to virtually all of Europe, with the advance of certain types of crops from south to north and the generalisation in north-western Europe of the land enclosures of the later Bronze Age (Harding 1989; Barrett et al. 1991). However, we believe certain differences can be perceived between the north-west and other European areas, since the process of emergence of hillforts as a visible indicator of a sedentary and stable population here would not appear to be a consequence of a previous population increase in the area, given the scanty evidence of earlier settlements, but of an external stimulus. The fact that these hillforts were sited to control privileged arteries of communication and important raw materials, the evidence of re-smelting of scrap and the presence in these sites of prestige objects would support this contention (Ruíz-Gálvez 1991; Sherratt 1994). These networks may have also provided the medium through which information and ideas about technology were passed from one region to another, information that enabled a more diversified agrarian economy to develop, capable of sustaining the fertility of the cultivated soil by manuring and/or the use of nitrogen-fixing plants (Ruíz-Gálvez 1994). As a result, stable and permanent settlements would also be possible. It is now the hillfort and not the tumulus which is the visible landmark.

Although it has its strengths, the sequence outlined above is not found in all cases and in all areas. A mobile way of life survived even into the late Bronze Age in places such as Bouça do Frade or Alto da Caldeira, and, with all the reservations that the ambiguity of the information demand, it may be that they are associated with trapezoidal tombs such as those of Sâo Paio das Antas. In neighbouring regions, such as Asturias, the sparse settlement continued almost until the arrival of the Romans. Perhaps that is why it is no coincidence that here, as in other close areas with similar 'habitational vacuums' (Cantabria and the north of Leon), the epigraphic sources and the Roman chroniclers coincide with archaeology in indicating the survival of a matrilineal system and female work in the field (Ruíz-Gálvez 1995). It is also possible that, in these areas at least, the tumuli remained as important features in the landscape for far longer than elsewhere.

ACKNOWLEDGEMENTS

The authors want to express their gratitude to the Ministerio de Asuntos Exteriores de España that awarded each of us with a grant for the travel expenses. The stay in Glasgow of Dr Marisa Ruíz-Gálvez was financed with funds from the DGCIT (Research Project no. PB 900262).

REFERENCES

Ataide, A. & Teixeira, C. 1940. A necrópole e o esqueleto de São Paio de Antas e o problema dos vasos de largo bordo horizontal. *Actas 1er Congresso do Mundo Português*, vol. 1, pp. 669 ff.

Barrett, J., Bradley, R. & Green, N. 1991. *Landscape, Monuments and Society. The Prehistory of Cranborne Chase.* Cambridge.

Bello Dieguez, J. M. 1991. Monumento megalítico de Dombate, Arqueoloxía-Informes, 2, pp. 21–27.

Bello Dieguez, J. M. 1992. Grabados, pinturas e ídolos en Dombate. ¿Grupo de Viseu o grupo Noroccidental?. Aspectos taxonómicos y cronológicos, Seminário O Megalitismo no Centro de Portugal, Mangualde.

de Blas Cortina, M. A. 1985. Piedrafita V. Nuevos aspectos sobre el polimorfismo de las arquitecturas funerarias prehistóricas en el N-N.O. de la Península Ibérica. *Arqueologia* 12: 129–136.

Bradley, R. 1984. *The Social Foundations of Prehistoric Britain.* London: Longman.

Bradley, R. 1990. *The Passage of Arms. An archaeological analysis of prehistoric hoards and votive deposits.* Cambridge: Cambridge University Press.

Bradley, R. 1991. Rock art and the perception of landscape. *Cambridge Archaeological Journal* 1: 77–101.

Bradley, R. 1991a. The pattern of change in British prehistory. In Earle, T. K. (ed.), *Chiefdoms: Power, Economy and Ideology*, pp. 44–70. Cambridge: Cambridge University Press.

Bradley, R. 1991b. Ritual, time and history. *World Archaeology* 23 (2): 209–218 (edited by J. A. J. Gowlett).

Bradley, R. 1992a. Turning the world: rock carvings and the archaeology of death. In Sharples, N. & Sheridan, A. (eds), *Vessels for the Ancestors*, pp. 168–176. Edinburgh, Edinburgh University Press.

Bradley, R. 1992b. Culture and Nature in the British Uplands. Unpublished seminar paper.

Bradley, R., Criado, F. & Fábregas, R. 1994. Rock art research as landscape archaeology: a pilot study in Galicia, north-west Spain. *World Archaeology* 25 (3): 374–390.

Briard, J. 1984. *Les tumulus de l'Armorique.* Paris.

Briard, J. 1986. Paléoenvironnement de l'homme protohistorique de l'Ouest armoricain. *XIe Congrès National des Sociétés Savantes*, pp. 225–234. Poitiers.

Briard, J. 1987. Wessex et Armorique, une révision. Les rélations entre le Continent et les Isles Britaniques à l'Age du Bronze. *Actes du Colloque de Lille, 22ème Congrès Préhistorique de la France*, pp. 77–88.

Briard, J. & Mohen, J. P. 1974. Le tumulus de la fôret de Carnoët à Qimperlé (Finistère). *Antiquités Nationaux* 9: 40–60.

Calo F. & Sierra, X. C. 1983. As oríxenes do castrexo no Bronce Final. In Pereira, G. (ed.), *Estudos de Cultura Castrexa e de Historia Antiga de Galicia*, pp. 19–86. Santiago de Compostela: Universidad de Santiago.

Cano Pan, J. A. & Vazquez Varela, J. M. 1988. Portecelo, un yacimiento de la Edad del Bronce. *Trabalhos de Antropologia e Etnologia* 28: 181–187.

Carballo Arceo, X. & Fabregas Valcarce, R. 1991. Dataciones de Carbono 14 para castros del Noroeste peninsular. *Archivo Español de Arqueología* 64: 244–264.

Cleto, J. A. & Faro, S. 1988. Escavação da mamoa de Igrejinhas. *Arqueologia* 17: 44–57.

Criado Boado, F. 1988. Arqueología del Paisaje y Espacio Megalítico en Galicia. Arqueología Espacial, 12, pp. 61–117.

Criado Boado, F. 1992. Espacio monumental y paisajes prehistóricos en Galicia. In (A. G. H. coord.) *Concepcións Espaciais e Estratexias Territoriais na Hª de Galicia*, pp. 23–54. Santiago de Compostela: Tórculo.

Criado Boado, F. (dir.) 1991. *Arqueología del Paisaje. El área Bocelo-Furelos entre los tiempos paleolíticos y medievales.* Santiago de Compostela: Xunta de Galicia (Arqueoloxía/Investigación 6).

Criado Boado, F. & Fábregas Valcarce, R. 1989. The megalithic phenomenon of NW Spain: Main trends. *Antiquity* 63: 682–696.

Criado Boado, F. & Fábregas Valcarce, R. 1994. Regional patterning among the megaliths of Galicia (NW Spain). *Oxford Journal of Archaeology* 13 (1): 33–47.

Criado Boado, F. & Vazquez Varela, J. M. 1982. *La cerámica campaniforme en Galicia.* Sada.

Delibes de Castro, G. 1977. *La cerámica campaniforme en la Meseta Norte española.* Valladolid (Studia Archaeologica 46).

Fábregas Valcarce, R. 1988. Megalitismo de Galicia. *Trabalhos de Antropologia e Etnologia* 28: 57–73.

Fábregas Valcarce, R. 1991. *Megalitismo del Noroeste de la Península Ibérica. Tipología y secuencia de los materiales líticos.* Madrid: (Colección Aula Abierta 58).

Fábregas Valcarce, R. 1993. Stone figures in passage-graves of Galicia (NW Spain). *XIIth International U.I.S.P.P. Congress, Bratislav (Czecoslovakia), 1991*, vol. 1, pp. 299–304. Nitra: Institute archéologique.

Garcia Alen, A. 1968. Los brazaletes de Lamela (Silleda). *El Museo de Pontevedra* 22: 33–35.

Garcia-Lastra Merino, M. 1984. Primeros resultados de las campañas de excavaciones arqueológicas 1982, en el yacimiento de 'O Fixón' (Hío, Cangas de Morrazo). *Pontevedra Arqueológica* 1: 113–144.

Garcia-Lastra Merino, M. 1985–86. El yacimiento de 'Chan de Armada' (Vilaboa-Pontevedra). Resultados de la excavación arqueológica en 1983. *Pontevedra Arqueológica* 2: 41–64.

Garcia-Lastra Merino, M. 1988. Aportación a la cronología campaniforme del Noroeste. *Trabalhos de Antropologia e Etnologia* 28: 175–179.

Gerloff, S. 1975. *The Early Bronze Age Daggers in Great Britain and a Reconsideration of the Wessex Culture.* München: (Prähistorische Bronzefunde 6).

Gonçalves, A. H. B. 1981. A estação pré-historica de Monte Calvo-Baião. Noticia preliminar. *Arqueologia* 3: 77–87.

Harding, A. 1989. Interpreting the evidence for agricultural change in late Bronze Age in northern Europe. In Nordström, H. A. & Knape, A. (eds), *Bronze Age Studies. Transactions of the British-Scandinavian Colloquium in Stockholm*, pp. 173–181. Stockholm: (Stockholm Historiska Museum Studies 5).

Harrison, R. J. 1985. The 'policultivo ganadero', or the secondary products revolution in Spanish agriculture, 5000–1000 bc. *Proceedings of the Prehistoric Society* 51: 75–102.

Hernando, A. 1989. Inicios de la orfebrería en la Península Ibérica. *Revista de Arqueología*. Extra 4: 32–45.

Jorge, S. O. 1980. A necrópole do Tapado da Caldeira-Baião. *Arqueologia* 2: 36– 44.

Jorge, S. O. 1981. Sondagens arqueolóicas na estação Alto da Caldeira. *Arqueologia* 3: 67–76.

Jorge, S. O. 1985. Datas de carbono 14 para a préhistória recente do Norte de Portugal: Os dados e os problemas. *Arqueologia* 12: 154–183.

Jorge, S. O. 1985a. Povoados da préhistória recente do Norte de Portugal (III° e começos do II° milénios a.C.): Resultados e problemas das escavações dos últimos anos. *Revista da Faculdade de Letras* 2: 297–306.

Jorge, S. O. 1986. *Povoados da Pré-história recente da região de Chaves-V ͣ.P. ͣ de Aguiar*. Porto: Instituto de Arqueologia.

Jorge, S. O. 1988. *O povoado da Bouça do Frade (Baião) no quadro do Bronze Final do Norte de Portugal*. Porto: (Monografías Arqueológicas 3).

Jorge, V. O. 1985. Les tumulus de Chã de Santinhos. *Arqueologia* 12: 98–129.

Jorge, V. O. 1988. Campo arqueológico da Serra da Aboboreira. Arqueologia do concelho de Baião. Resultados de 10 anos de trabalho. *Arqueologia* 17: 5–27.

Jorge, V. O. 1989. Arqueologia social dos sepulcros megalíticos atlánticos: conhecimentos e perspectivas actuais. *Revista da Faculdade de Letras* 6: 365–443.

Jorge, V. O. 1991. *Necrópole pré-histórica da Aboboreira (Distrito do Porto). Uma hipótese de diacronia. Homenagem a Santos Júnior*, pp. 205–208. Lisboa.

Jorge, V. O., Alonso, F. & Delibrias, G. 1988. Novas datas de Carbono 14 para mamoas da Serra da Aboboreira, Arqueologia, 18, pp. 95–99.

Martins, M. 1988. *A Citânia de S. Julião, em Vila Verde*. Braga: (Cadernos de Arqueologia-Monografias 2).

Martins, M. 1989. O Castro de Barbudo, Vila Verde. Braga: (Cadernos de Arqueologia-Monografias 3).

Peña Santos, A. 1984a. Sondeo estratigráfico en el yacimiento de 'O Regueiriño' (Moaña). *Pontevedra Arqueológica* 1: 85–90.

Peña Santos, A. 1984b. Sondeo estratigráfico en el yacimiento de 'A Fontenla' (Moaña). Pontevedra Arqueológica, 1, pp. 91–98.

Peña Santos, A. 1984c. Yacimiento de Lavapés (Cangas de Morrazo, Pontevedra). *Pontevedra Arqueológica* 1: 149–178.

Peña Santos, A. 1985. Las cistas de Gandón (Cangas de Morrazo, Pontevedra). *El Museo de Pontevedra* 39: 79–94.

Peña Santos, A. 1992a. El primer milenio a.C. en el área gallega. Génesis y desarrollo del mundo castreño a la luz de la Arqueología. In Almagro, M. et al. (eds), *Paletnología de la Península Ibérica* 2–3: 373–394.

Peña Santos, A. 1992b. *Castro de Torroso (Mos, Pontevedra)*. Santiago de Compostela: (Arqueoloxía/Memorias 11).

Ramil, P., Aira, M. J., Gonzalez, M. & Criado, F. 1990. Données paléo-botaniques sur la présence des graines de brassicaceae au NO. de la Péninsule Ibérique. *Révue de Paléobiologie* 9 (2): 263–272.

Renfrew, C. & Cherry, J. (eds) 1986. *Peer Polity Interactions and Socio-political Change.* Cambridge: Cambridge University Press.

Ruíz-Gálvez Priego, M. 1978. El tesoro de Caldas de Reyes. *Trabajos de Prehistoria* 35: 173–192.

Ruíz-Gálvez Priego, M. 1991. Songs of a wayfaring lad. Late Bronze Age Atlantic exchange and the building of the regional identity in the West Iberian peninsula. *Oxford Journal of Archaeology* 10 (3): 277–306.

Ruíz-Gálvez Priego, M. 1995. The bartered bride. Goldwork, inheritance and agriculture in the late prehistory of the Iberian peninsula. *Journal of European Archaeology* 2.1: 50–81.

Sanches, M. de J. 1987. A mamoa 3 de Pena Mosqueira. *Arqueologia* 15: 94–115.

Sanches, M. de J. 1988. O povoado da Lavra (Marco de Canaveses). *Arqueologia* 18: 125–134.

Sanches, M. de J. 1989. Cinco datas de C14 para a Pré-história recente do Leste de Tras-os-Montes, *Arqueologia* 19: 113–114.

Sanches, M. de J. 1989a. Breve síntese do povoamento pré-histórico no planalto mirandês. *Revista da Faculdade de Letras* 6: 445–453.

Sanches, M. de J. 1990. Os abrigos com pintura esquemática da Serra dos Passos-Mirandela, no conjunto da arte rupestre desta regiâo. Algumas reflexôes. Revista da Faculdade de Letras, 7, pp. 335–365.

Sanches, M. de J. 1992. *Pré-história recente no planalto mirandês (Leste de Trás-os-Montes).* Porto: (Monografias Arqueológicas 3).

Sherratt, A. 1981. Plough and pastoralism: aspects of the secondary products revolution. In Hodder, I., Isaac, G. & Hammond, N. (eds), *Patterns of the Past. Studies in honour of D. Clarke,* pp. 261–305. Cambridge: Cambridge University Press.

Sherratt, A. 1983. The secondary exploitation of animals in the Old World. *World Archaeology* 15: 90–104.

Sherratt, A. 1987. Cups that cheered. In Waldren, W. & Kennard, R. (eds), *Bell Beakers of the Western Mediterranean,* pp. 81–114. Oxford: British Archaeological Reports (International Series 331, vol. 1).

Sherratt, A. 1994. Core, periphery and margin: perspectives on the Bronze Age. Trade and exchange in prehistory. In Matthers, C. & Stoddart, S. (eds), *Development and Decline in the Mediterranean Bronze Age,* 335–346.. Sheffield: Sheffield University Press.

da Silva, A. C. F. 1986. *A cultura castreja no Noroeste português.* Paços de Ferreira.

Soeiro, T. 1988. A propésito de quatro necrépoles protohistéricas do concelho de Esposende. *Actas do Coloquio Manuel Buenaventura,* pp. 35–47.

Vaquero Lastres, J. 1990. Ríos y tumbas. Sobre el emplazamiento de túmulos en el NW Peninsular. *Trabalhos de Antropologia e Etnologia* 30: 151–168.

Vazquez Varela, J. M. 1980a. Enterramientos en cista de la Edad del Bronce en Galicia. *Pontevedra* 0: 23–40.

Vazquez Varela, J. M. 1980b. Cistas decoradas en Galicia: Una nueva manifestación artística de la Edad del Bronce. *Brigantium* 1: 41–48.

Vazquez Varela, J. M. 1985/86. Nueva cista decorada del Bronce Inicial de Galicia. *Pontevedra Arqueológica* 2: 91–96.

Vazquez Varela, J. M. 1988. El Neolítico en Galicia. In López, P. (ed.), *El Neolítico en España*, pp. 329–335. Madrid.

VV. AA. 1987. *Catalogación de yacimientos prerromanos del Ayuntamiento de Santiago*. Santiago de Compostela: Xunta de Galicia (Arqueoloxía/Investigación 3).

NOTES

1. The term *cairn* does not imply any relationship with the Breton cairns and in the case of the north-west is used to describe tumuli consisting exclusively of stones.

2. Other dates for small paramegalithic tumuli of As Pontes (Corunna) would put its construction towards the twelfth century bc (J. Vaquero Lastres pers. comm.).

3. We have also applied the 'geography of mobility' concept to the location of barrows (Criado & Fábregas 1994). Also we have recently begun to examine the relationship between rock art and the areas of transit in various parts of Galicia (Bradley, Criado, & Fábregas 1994).

24

Centralising Tendencies?
A Re-examination of Social
Evolution in Late Neolithic Orkney

Colin Richards

Given the extraordinary nature and quality of the evidence for Neo-lithic settlement in Orkney, it may seem curious that exactly the same model of social evolution is posited for Orkney as is offered for many other areas of Britain. The main reason for this situation lies in the simple fact that the settlement evidence has been largely ignored in the various interpretations of social change. Indeed, if the settlement evidence of Neolithic Orkney is overlooked, then the *assumed* chronological sequence of collective burial monuments leading on to henge monuments, stone circles and standing stones, appears to follow a similar trajectory to that present in many other areas in Britain.

Just as Vere Gordon Childe affected the way Orcadian Neolithic culture was defined materially, so Colin Renfrew introduced a linear scheme of social evolution which provided a social and temporal order to that material. In 1979, Renfrew published *Investigations in Orkney*, in which a progressive, linear model of social evolution was posited for Neolithic Orkney. The basis or inspiration for the model was derived from two sources: first, a belief in the existence of social 'types' and their ability to graduate into more complex forms (cf. Service 1971). Second, an equation between a particular social 'type' and the scale of monumentality it could achieve. For the model to even appear to work, or be deemed appropriate, a chronological development in scale of public monuments requires to be demonstrated. Once this is estab-

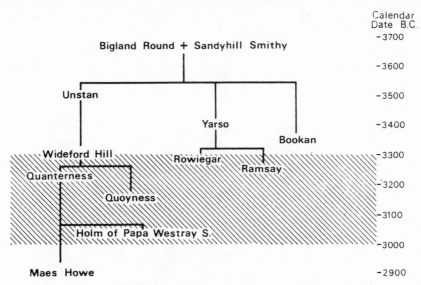

Figure 1. The typology of Orcadian chambered tombs as proposed by Renfrew (after Renfrew 1979).

lished, the corresponding social 'type' can be matched with the expenditure of labour required to build any given monument. Six years earlier, Renfrew (1973) had offered exactly the same model for Neolithic Wessex, and it was just a simple step to transport it to Neolithic Orkney.

For Orkney the basic premises remained the same, with a particular burden on establishing a chronology for monuments exhibiting increased scales of construction. A further dimension of Renfrew's model included the search for group territories. For the island of Rousay, group territories had already been suggested by Childe (1942) in his account of the spatial patterning of the Rousay cairns; an article which perhaps provided the inspiration for Renfrew. Previously developed typologies of Orkney-Cromarty cairns (Henshall 1963; Piggott 1954) suggested a basic chronological order and a reversal of the established Maeshowe typology was easy to achieve through recourse to the simple – complex trajectory of social evolution (Fig. 1) (Renfrew 1979: 211).

Given the association of round-based Unstan pottery with the smaller Orkney-Cromarty cairns, a straightforward evolutionary path was visible with Unstan ware giving way to Grooved ware (Fig. 2). So it was that Renfrew (1979: 208), presented a comprehensive model of social evolution in Neolithic Orkney, where a territorial-based, Unstan

[517]

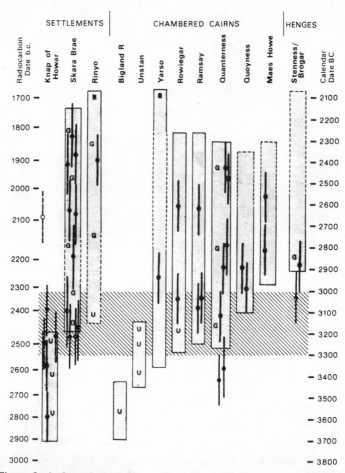

Figure 2. A chronological chart attempting to illustrate the evolutionary sequence of Unstan ware (U) into Grooved ware (G). It is noticeable that some sites have no radiocarbon dates and other dates which do not fit the model are left outside the site 'boxes' (after Renfrew 1979). The dashed area represents the three-century 'transitional' phase (see also Fig. 1).

ware-using, segmentary society developed into a centralised, Grooved-ware-using, chiefdom.

In this scheme, no distinction was made between the different architecture of the chambered tombs; all 'types' were seen as performing the same function: to house all the dead of a corporate group (Hedges 1983: 296). The relatively low labour requirements for construction, when combined with an unsupported notion of communal burial, gave rise to the recognition of a primary egalitarian segmentary society.

Towards the end of the third millennium BC, it is argued, a dramatic increase in labour expenditure, as shown in the construction of the henge monuments Stones of Stenness and the Ring of Brodgar, was seen as representing 'the development of a more centralised society' (Renfrew 1979: 218). Here, social evolution had led to the creation of a 'larger social formation, to which the population of all Mainland may have owed allegiance' (ibid.). For Renfrew, the increase in monumentality was directly related to the ability to mobilise a larger workforce within a situation of increased social complexity; in other words, a function of the emergence of chiefdoms.

Regardless of the elegance or attractiveness of this scheme, it is founded and totally dependent on two basic, but suspect, premises. First, that an equation exists between social types and a scale of monumental construction. Second, the presence in Orkney of a chronological sequence of increasing monumentality.

Although the first premise has been effectively criticised by Richard Bradley (1984: 61–67), and the second, as will be shown later, is dubious, it is interesting that later studies of Neolithic Orkney, while questioning certain elements of detail (cf. Henshall 1985: 110–11; Clarke 1983), continued to accept the basic assumptions of the Renfrew model. For example, in 1982, Hodder (1982: 218–20), outlined a 'contextual analysis' of late Neolithic Orkney. While the emphasis was placed on artefactual and architectural similarities between contexts, the analysis was undertaken within a chronological framework of social change which mirrored that proposed by Renfrew. A more detailed study, again based entirely on the chambered tombs and henge monuments, was undertaken in 1985 by Sharples. Here closer attention was placed on the evidence and rightful criticism was provided of both Renfrew's and Hodder's accounts of late Neolithic Orkney. Ultimately, however, Sharples (1985: 71–72) adheres to the same model of social evolution forwarded by Renfrew and takes the 'massive investment of organised labour' to 'represent the establishment of a central hierarchy within Orkney as a whole.'

All these enquiries, including the original by Renfrew, appear to have been heavily influenced by studies of social evolution and monument typologies in other parts of Britain, particularly Wessex. Renfrew (1973), as noted, had already undertaken a similar analysis of monumental development and social evolution in Neolithic Wessex. Likewise, Hodder (1982: 226) supports the idea of a gradual increase in social complexity through claims that the 'change from local and equivalent communities to some degree of centralisation is supported by evidence from other parts of Britain'. Finally, Sharples (1985: 72) states that 'the method by which this hierarchy achieved dominance involved the control and manipulation of increasingly important rituals which structure social interaction during the late Neolithic throughout Britain.'

Reviewing these separate studies it is clear that Renfrew's view of social evolution has been extremely influential in their formulation. In each case the evolution of society into a hierarchical structure is unquestioningly assumed (see also Hedges 1983). Thus, in virtually every study of the Orcadian Neolithic the same model provides a temporal framework of social change.

At this point we have to consider the validity of claims that late Neolithic Orkney provided the context for growing social complexity and the development of a centralised authority structure. The basic premises of Renfrew's argument are open to question; moreover it should be asked why such a social trajectory of change should occur in Orkney simply because it is apparently detectable elsewhere in Britain during this period (perhaps these ideas also require closer scrutiny).

The main point of evidence, advanced by Renfrew, to substantiate the view of an emerging centralised authority is the construction of larger public works, requiring greater amounts of labour investment, towards the end of the third millennium BC (1979: 218):

> only by the support of the population as a whole, which may have been some 5000 strong, could this investment of labour have been organised. Late Neolithic Orkney thus may have seen, around 2700 bc, the development of a more centralised society, analogous in many ways to the developments taking place in southern Britain at about the same time.

At a later time, Renfrew (1985: 255) attempts to modify his position with the statement, 'this means that we are not necessarily better thinking of distinct stages – an earlier egalitarian phase with chambered cairns and a later, chieftain phase with henge monuments.' He still, nevertheless, maintains the central view of social evolution: 'we can conceive instead of a developing society, in which public ritual was increasingly taking on an important role' (ibid.).

It is clear that the whole notion of a 'developing' society is synonymous with linear social evolution; from simple to complex, from egalitarian to ranked. The foundation of this idea naturally rests on the chronological sequence of monumental construction. But if a closer view is taken of this sequence, it is found that there is no evidence to

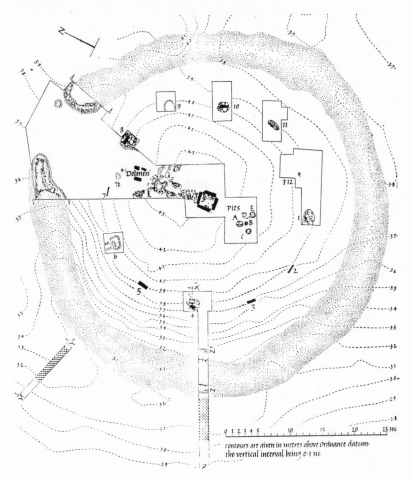

Figure 3. Plan of the Stones of Stenness (after Ritchie 1976).

support the gradual increase in scales of construction envisaged by Renfrew.

In the diagram depicting the chronology of monumental construction (Fig. 1), a clear sequence is proposed running from Wideford Hill – Quanterness/Quoyness – Holm of Papa Westray South – Maeshowe. As may be expected, each of these passage graves requires more labour expenditure in its construction than its predecessor. Whilst Renfrew's diagram correctly orders the increased levels of labour necessary for construction, the equation with a temporal order requires further attention. Of all the passage graves listed by Renfrew, only Quanterness is securely dated (two radiocarbon dates from animal bone of unknown context are available for Quoyness and several dates from the *ditch* at Maeshowe). The primary date from Quanterness is ca 3300–3000 BC, which is considered to correspond with the construction or initial use of the passage grave. This date concurs with the construction and early habitation of the 'villages' at Barnhouse and Skara Brae. Also at this time we see a consistency in the manufacture of Grooved ware ceramics, for instance, the Grooved ware at Quanterness includes a vessel which is identical in design and fabric to those in use at Barnhouse. It is the consistency of this method of decorating Grooved ware which partially defines the earlier 'Grooved ware period' in the mid-third millennium BC (MacSween 1992: 268).

Because henge monuments are clearly a late Neolithic phenomenon in southern Britain, being constructed towards the end of the third millennium BC, such a chronology is assumed to cover all of this type of monument. Of the two definite henge monuments in Orkney, the Ring of Brodgar and the Stones of Stenness (Fig. 3), only the latter has been dated by radiocarbon determinations. A date of 2356±65 bc (SRR 350) was obtained from the second layer, and earliest material deposits, in the ditch. A second date of 2238±70 bc (SRR 351), came from charcoal in the central hearth, which must relate to the final use of this feature. Remembering that the central hearth had been modified on several occasions (Richards 1993: fig. 4.11), this date marks the end of a lengthy history of activity, involving the hearth, at the Stones of Stenness.

The date from the ditch has been seen as representing primary use of the monument, if not its time of construction (e.g. Fraser 1983; Hedges 1983; Sharples 1985; etc.). However, we cannot be sure how long the monument had stood before the animal bone, used as radiocarbon samples, was deposited in the ditch. Of greater significance, however, is the Grooved ware recovered from the same ditch deposit (Fig. 4). Both in method of decoration and surface design it is identical to the majority of decorated Grooved ware from the Barnhouse settlement, which, as noted above, is typical of the earlier 'late Neolithic period'. Here I suggest that the construction and initial use of the Stones of Stenness is actually contemporary with Barnhouse, where the period of occupation is securely dated to circa 3300–2800 BC. Indeed, there is a notable absence at the Stones of Stenness of the later type of Grooved ware that employs applied decoration (cf. Childe 1931: 130; MacSween 1992: 266–67). If, on the basis of the ceramic evidence, we push the construction date of the Stones of Stenness back into the period of

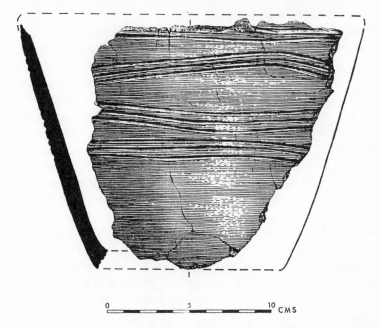

Figure 4. Grooved ware vessel from the Stones of Stenness (after Ritchie 1976).

habitation at Barnhouse, it is found that not only are the henge monument and Quanterness in contemporary use (cf. Ritchie 1985: 129), but there is little to separate their dates of construction. Here then are two monuments, one taking an estimated 40,000 worker hours (Stones of Stenness), the other 6,000 worker hours (Quanterness) (Renfrew 1979: 213–14), being constructed within a short time of each other. Maeshowe, situated in close proximity to the Stones of Stenness and Barnhouse, is estimated to have taken close to 100,000 worker hours to build (ibid.: 214), which dramatically exceeds even the figure for the Stones of Stenness.

Elsewhere I have compared the architecture and sophistication of construction between House 2 at Barnhouse, and the closely situated passage grave of Maeshowe (Richards 1993). Because of this similarity, I would argue that in the absence of reliable radiocarbon dates for the construction of Maeshowe (radiocarbon determinations of 2185±65 bc [SRR 505] and 2020±70 bc [Q1482] were obtained from basal peat in the ditch fill), the two buildings were probably built at approximately the same time. House 2 has radiocarbon determinations of ca 3300–3200 BC for its primary use. In this scheme, Maeshowe is constructed at the same time as the settlement at Barnhouse (including House 2),

Quanterness and the Stones of Stenness.

Thus, there are several contentions which I wish to make. First, Maeshowe and House 2 are contemporary constructions. Second, the Stones of Stenness is built during the life of the Barnhouse settlement. Finally, in this history of construction, the gradual increase in monumentality and labour expenditure suggested by Renfrew does not exist. The corollary of this alternative history of monument construction is of particular significance since it effectively puts all the large constructions into an approximately two-hundred-year time span of public building. Rather than being the results of an evolving 'Grooved ware' society, it appears to coincide with the very appearance of this new 'cultural' repertoire. If this floruit of monumentality occurs at the beginning of the late Neolithic period, how can we account for it and what actually happens throughout the duration of the latter half of the third millennium BC?

Turning now to the archaeological evidence for the late Neolithic period in Orkney, we start from a point of disadvantage since, at approximately 3300–3200 BC, there appears a 'new' assemblage of material culture ranging from Grooved ware ceramics through to domestic and public architecture. We also appear to see the establishment of conglomerate settlement, with villages comprising 10–20 houses. On Mainland these settlements appear to be founded between ca 3300 and 3100 BC. It will be noted that this concurs with the date of construction of Quanterness and perhaps the appearance of passage graves. Thus, at first glance there appears to be a major change occurring in virtually all aspects of the evidence at the end of the fourth millennium BC. This change in material culture may, however, be less of a cleavage than it appears at first sight. Our conception of early Neolithic settlement, in Orkney, is based on the isolated single farmstead, as represented by Knap of Howar, Papa Westray. Indeed, the idea of an early British Neolithic consisting of isolated farmsteads nestling in small woodland clearings is a view shared by many (e.g. Holgate 1988). In light of the more substantial early Neolithic surface lithic scatters discovered on Mainland, by past and present field survey (Rendall 1931; Richards in prep.), the isolated farmstead may be atypical of the majority of earlier Neolithic settlement patterns. Indeed, if the larger surface scatters at Wideford Hill and Deepdale are more representative of early Neolithic settlement on Mainland, then the differences between early and late Neolithic settlement organisation may be less dramatic than previously considered. Moreover, the presence of earlier habitation below the 'Grooved ware' occupation layers at Pool on the island of Sanday (MacSween 1992) and Rinyo on the island of Rousay (Childe & Grant 1947) clearly demonstrates some form of continuity of occupation at *particular* places in Orkney.

Perhaps the main reason why the later Neolithic 'cultural entity' stands distinct is the apparent degree of homogeneity within all aspects of its material culture. For instance, Orcadian Grooved ware was divided into three chronologically ordered categories of decorative technique by V. G. Childe (1931: 130–31) during excavations at Skara Brae. The earliest Grooved ware was decorated by incision and grooves. This characteristic is not confined to Skara Brae, or even Mainland, but, as Anne MacSween (1992: 263–65) has recently noted, is common to all Orcadian Grooved-ware contexts of this period.

Architecture constitutes another medium of remarkable consistency with houses conforming to a uniformity in the principles of spatial organisation (Richards 1990b). This architectural form also characterises passage grave design, hence the identification by Audrey Henshall (1963) of the Maeshowe group. This consistency and uniformity extends to other areas of material culture such as flint technology. Thus, in the mid-third millennium, it can be assumed that there was a common interest in maintaining, through the medium of material culture, a unified self-image of society.

Elsewhere, I (1990b) have discussed the architecture of the late Neolithic Orcadian house in terms of cosmological themes and principles of order. The central pivot of continually changing spatial meaning within the house is the hearth, the *axis mundi*. According to different social situations within the house, different aspects of the cruciform spatial arrangement may be brought into operation. This is promoted in terms of oppositions, for example, back:front and right:left. Thus, within the house the left-hand side of the hearth tends to be an area associated with domestic activities such as food preparation, and it is also the side from which ash is frequently raked (Richards in prep.). Because of a consistent NW-SE orientation of the house, each of the main elements of the interior, the left and right 'beds' and the rear 'dresser' and doorway, is related to a cardinal direction which adheres to the midwinter/ midsummer sunrise and sunset. In this classification we see a fusion of space and time.

The four elements radiating from the central hearth, the rear 'dresser', left and right box 'beds' and the entrance, create the cruciform spatial arrangement which is consistently employed in all houses constructed during the late Neolithic period. However, it is worth noting that in the earlier houses the beds and rear dresser are actually

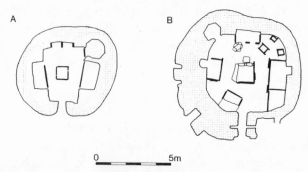

Figure 5. Earlier (a) and later (b) forms of house architecture in late Neolithic Orkney (after Clarke 1976).

recessed into the house wall, thus, the furniture forms part of the main fabric of the house. In the later houses (Fig. 5), while the same elements of furniture are present, they now project into the house interior and are no longer embedded in the house wall.

The apparently minor changes in house architecture witnessed throughout this period need to be emphasised. Initially, the different elements of stone furniture forming a cruciform arrangement are fixed within the basic construction of the house. Later, when this furniture simply projects from the house wall this arrangement becomes more fluid and, while the cruciform structure remains, it is far easier to alter or expand this basic form. The one element which remains fixed and unchanging is the central location of the hearth and the ideas of centrality and concentricity which this position enforces may well be strongly manifest in the spatial organisation of the early villages.

Just as homogeneity has been recognised in Grooved-ware ceramics and house and passage grave architecture, it is suggested that similar principles of order were manifest in settlement or village organisation throughout Mainland, Orkney. If we examine the first phase of settlement at Skara Brae, hints of a similar organisation are present. Because large areas of this early settlement remain unexcavated, only partial reconstruction is possible. Nevertheless, three points may be made.

1. The houses are similar to those at Barnhouse and are free-standing.
2. A large and 'different' building stood in the western area of the settlement.
3. The village organisation may have been concentric with reference to an open central area.

While an exact correspondence in the spatial organisation of settlement may only be inferred between Skara Brae and Barnhouse, in both examples two clear house types are evident: a larger building in the west and smaller houses which form the rest of the village. This organisation recalls a discussion of changing forms of domestic architecture by Duncan (1981: 41), who has noted similar spatial characteristics in societies that maintain collectivistic social relations. This social formation is structured on kin based, age and gender relations, with a fairly stable shared value system and group identity. Individual ambition is discouraged within a situation of fairly low spatial and social mobility. He identifies the inclusion of a single large building, essentially a men's house or cult house, with the more numerous smaller houses which act as shared dwellings by men and women. Women tend to be associated with the house since their work is primarily seen as being based in and around its confines. On the other hand, men spend little time in the house with their work taking them away from the family dwelling. Within such a situation the individual family houses tend not to be embellished and are visually of similar size and appearance.

While not subscribing to ideal types, the description Duncan provides of the form of society which tends to employ such spatial organisation of settlement is very similar to that which I would interpret from the material evidence. It will be noticed that it is also similar to the form of egalitarian segmentary society envisaged by Renfrew (1979: 221). For Renfrew, it was from this form of social organisation that 'a larger social formation[,] to which the population of all Mainland may have owed allegiance' (ibid.: 218), evolved. However, these views of social evolution founder when the histories of the settlements are examined. Indeed, Clarke and Sharples (1985: 69) note that 'while no evidence for the Grooved-ware settlements is fundamentally at variance with the concept of a segmentary society there is as yet nothing from these sites to support the idea of the emergence of a centralising tendency.' Rather than seeing the rise of a central authority and greater social cohesion, I suggest something quite different occurs in late Neolithic Orkney.

It is at this point that the evidence from the 'village' settlements is of special value. It has been argued that the earlier villages were similar in spatial organisation, with free-standing houses concentrically arranged around a central area. Similarly, inside the early house, stone furniture was actually recessed into the wall, forming part of the fabric of the house (Fig. 5). Through time these characteristics vary in several ways. First, settlement organisation changes from the concentric structure to a more conglomerate form. At both Skara Brae and Rinyo the houses decrease in number and become physically conjoined. By implementing such changes settlement organisation alters to a form which can be seen today at Skara Brae. Thus, at the level of settlement organisation, the principles of order based on centrality and con-centricity are no longer present. Also, the architecture of the house changes. The house becomes larger and the interior furniture *projects* from the internal walls, thus it no longer forms part of the actual core fabric of the dwelling and is more easily altered (Fig. 5). This allows internal modification and addition to the cruciform representation.

In all these changes we see a weakening of the cosmologically based principles of order so strongly adhered to in the earlier phase of the late Neolithic period. At Barnhouse, the settlement appears to be abandoned and structure 8 is built. This new construction, despite its large size, demonstrates this 'new' form of architecture. In this altered architecture, it is suggested, we necessarily see changes in both kinship and social practices. The larger interior area of the later house may indicate larger family units and the structural attachment of houses, as seen at Skara Brae, may be a physical manifestation of increased social cohesion, but on an extended family basis. If larger communities fragment into smaller units based on the extended family, then overall we may expect a re-orientation of exchange networks and a narrowing of social contacts.

It is also at precisely this time that we see the subtle changes in material culture. For instance, the decoration on Grooved ware becomes confined to applied techniques. Furthermore, decoration itself becomes restricted to linear motifs. At another level, flint appears to become a limited and restricted resource. This is clearly demonstrated in the later phases of Skara Brae where an inferior chert, which requires heat treatment for its preparation (C. Wickham-Jones pers. comm.), becomes the dominant flaked stone component. At Barn-house, a hoard of large prepared flint nodules is buried in a pit in the floor of structure 8 inner building (Richards in prep.), suggesting that these were precious items. Thus, materials which appear to have been freely available in the earlier period now become scarce, indicating that not only do family groups come to control particular resources, but spheres of contact and exchange become severely curtailed.

For Childe (1931: 97), one of the notable aspects of the material assemblage from Skara Brae was its localised character. Remembering that the majority of his excavations were confined to the later period of settlement, this provides an indication of the lack of contact beyond

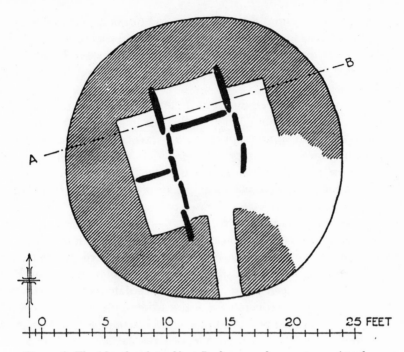

Figure 6. The 'chambered tomb' at Bookan can be seen to consist of a series of cists arranged in a manner which recalls the architecture of the house (after RCAHMS 1946).

Orkney. The two main sources of evidence for such contact in the late Neolithic period comes from the presence of passage grave art on ceramics and inside passage graves, and a number of pieces of Arran pitchstone at Barnhouse (Richards 1990a). Thus, both types of evidence are confined to the *earlier* phase of the late Neolithic period.

As settlement fragments into extended family groups so mortuary practices change. Single inhumation in cists is likely to have followed the changes noted above. I suggest that the anomalous 'chambered tomb' of Bookan can be seen to capture such a movement within its architecture (Fig. 6). Although defined by Davidson & Henshall (1989: 26) as part of the early Orkney-Cromarty series, Bookan, through the use of a series of cists formed by upright slabs similar to 'beds', draws heavily on the spatial representation of the late Neolithic house and I suggest that it dates to this later period. In each of the cists there appear to have been discrete inhumations (ibid.: 104). Where continued burial in passage graves occurs, as at Quanterness, it takes the form of a single inhumation in a pit C (Renfrew 1979: 55). Hence, any element of communality as symbolised (if not actually adhered to in burial) by passage graves now ceases. I would also suggest that this is exactly the time that many passage graves become redundant and are blocked or destroyed, as Sharples (1985) and Henshall (1985: 107–08) have noted.

Finally, with the break-down of a clear progression of monument construction and an examination of changes in house form and settlement organisation, a more appropriate sequence for the late Neolithic can be suggested. From approximately 3300–3000 BC a different cultural repertoire can be discerned in Orkney. Through an architecture heavily influenced by cosmological themes of order we see homologies operating at the level of the house, passage grave, settlement, and landscape. This is suggested to concur with a view of collective social relations, as discussed by Duncan (1981). Interestingly, it is also a time when contacts are identifiable with other areas of north-western Scotland and Ireland. The construction of the Stones of Stenness and Ring of Brodgar can be seen as the work of a corporate social organisation seeking to capture, in concrete form, the order of the social and natural world. Lying centrally within a huge natural bowl in central Mainland, the Stones – like the hearth – serve as a pivotal point around which social landscape was structured (see Richards 1996).

Through time this order changes, as settlement is re-organised, becoming smaller and fragmented, house form and internal architecture alters. Smaller numbers of houses become physically linked to form single units. With this dispersal and the suggested changes in kinship towards a family-based individualistic formation, links beyond Orkney appear to cease. This marks the point when passage graves, symbols of the collective, become redundant and individual burial becomes the norm.

It should be noted, however, that this scenario does not encompass all of Orkney. In peripheral areas, such as South Ronaldsay, older traditions continue even to the extent of a maintenance of Unstan ware. This may explain the fairly late radiocarbon determinations from human skeletal remains associated with Unstan ware ceramics obtained from Isbister. Captured in the architecture of this cairn are the influences of passage grave design (the side cells and side entrance) and a persistent tradition of 'stalled' construction, which is far less obvious or intrusive than at other monuments displaying this architecture. In this respect it is easy to understand the various descriptions of this cairn as unusual (Davidson & Henshall 1989: 4–5) or hybrid (e.g. Hedges 1983: 203) in nature.

To conclude, in the final analysis, Renfrew's scheme of social evolution is difficult to sustain in the face of the archaeological evidence. Instead of an increase in social complexity and the emergence of centralising tendencies we see a change in social relations away from the collective towards individual family groups, which can be traced into the second millennium BC. The monumentality which was supposed to have marked the evolution and emergence of a chiefdom at the end of the late Neolithic period is seen to have occurred at an earlier time, a situation which recalls Bradley's (1984) discussion of monumentality. In short, instead of Renfrew's chiefdom social evolution in late Neolithic Orkney comprised a gradual fragmentation and heterogeneity in 'cultural' form.

The major problem of understanding how an apparently 'new' material assemblage appears in Orkney towards the end of the fourth millennium BC remains obscure (although a new fieldwork project at Stonehall Farm, Firth, Orkney, begun in 1994 may shed more light on this problem). However, the changes, which occur throughout the late Neolithic, begin a period of social fragmentation and isolation which continues into the early Bronze Age and which is destined to last for the next thousand years.

ACKNOWLEDGMENTS

I would like to thank Mark Edmonds, Ian Hodder, Sian Jones, and Lionel Masters who kindly read and commented on this paper in various forms. I would particularly like to thank Colin Renfrew for critical discussion of these ideas over the years.

BIBLIOGRAPHY

Bradley, R. 1984. Studying monuments. In Bradley, R. & Gardiner, J. (eds), *Neolithic Studies*, pp. 61–66. Oxford: British Archaeological Reports (133).

Childe, V. G. 1931. *Skara Brae: a Pictish village in Orkney*. London: Kegan Paul.

Childe, V. G. 1942. The chambered tombs of Rousay. *Antiquaries Journal* 22: 139–142.

Childe, V. G. 1944. *Progress and Archaeology*. London: Watts.

Childe, V. G. & Grant, W. G. 1939. A Stone Age settlement at the Braes of Rinyo, Rousay, Orkney (second report). *Proceedings of the Society of Antiquaries of Scotland* 81: 16–42.

Clarke, D. V. 1983. Rinyo and the Orcadian Neolithic. In O'Connor, A. & Clarke, D. V. (eds), *From the Stone Age to the 'Forty Five: studies presented to R. B. K. Stevenson*, pp. 45–56. Edinburgh: John Donald.

Clarke, D. V. & Sharples, N. 1985. Settlements and subsistence in the third millennium BC. In Renfrew, C. (ed.), *The Prehistory of Orkney*, pp. 54-82. Edinburgh: Edinburgh University Press.

Davidson, J. L. & Henshall, A. S. 1989. *The Chambered Cairns of Orkney*. Edinburgh: Edinburgh University Press.

Duncan, J. S. 1981. *Housing and Identity: cross-cultural perspectives*. London: Croom Helm.

Fraser, D. 1983. *Land and Society in Neolithic Orkney*. Oxford: British Archaeological Reports (British series 117).

Hedges, J. W. 1983. *Isbister: a Chambered Tomb in Orkney*. Oxford: British Archaeological Reports (British series 115).

Henshall, A. S. 1963. *The Chambered Cairns of Scotland*, vol. 1. Edinburgh: Edinburgh University Press.

Henshall, A. S. 1985. The chambered cairns. In Renfrew, C. (ed.), *The Prehistory of Orkney*, pp. 83–117. Edinburgh: Edinburgh University Press.

Hodder, I. 1982. *Symbols in Action: Ethnoarchaeological Studies of Material Culture*. Cambridge: Cambridge University Press.

Holgate, R. 1988. *Neolithic Settlement of the Thames Basin*. Oxford: British Archaeological Reports (British Series 197).

MacSween, A. 1992. Orcadian Grooved ware. In Sharples, N. & Sheridan, A. (eds), *Vessels for the Ancestors: essays on the Neolithic of Britain and Ireland*, pp. 259–271. Edinburgh.

Piggott, S. 1954. *Neolithic Cultures of the British Isles*. Cambridge: Cambridge University Press.

Randall, R. 1931. Notes on a collection of flints from Wideford Hill. *Proceedings of the Orkney Antiquarian Society* 9: 21–24.

Renfrew, C. 1973. Monuments, mobilisation and social organisation in Neolithic Wessex. In Renfrew, C. (ed.), *The Explanation of Culture Change*, pp. 539–558. London: Duckworth.

Renfrew, C. 1979. *Investigations in Orkney*. London: Thames and Hudson.

Renfrew, C. 1985. Epilogue. In Renfrew, C. (ed.), *The Prehistory of Orkney*, pp. 243–262. Edinburgh: Edinburgh University Press.

Richards, C. C. 1990a. The late Neolithic settlement complex at Barnhouse Farm, Stenness, Orkney. In Renfrew, C. (ed.), *The Prehistory of Orkney*, second edition, pp. 305–316. Edinburgh: Edinburgh University Press.

Richards, C. C. 1990b. The late Neolithic house in Orkney. In Samson, R. (ed.), *The Social Archaeology of Houses*, pp. 111–124. Edinburgh: Edinburgh University Press.

Richards, C. C. 1991. Skara Brae: revisiting a Neolithic house in Orkney. In Hanson, W. S. & Slater, E. (eds), *Scottish Archaeology: new perspectives*, pp. 24–43. Aberdeen: Aberdeen University Press.

Richards, C. C. 1993. Monumental choreography: architecture and spatial representation in late Neolithic Orkney. In Tilley, C. (ed.), *Interpretative Archaeology*, pp. 143–178. Oxford: Berg.

Richards, C. C. 1996. Monuments as landscape: creating the centre of the world in late Neolithic Orkney. *World Archaeology* 28 (2): 190–208.

Richards, C. C. in prep. Neolithic Houses of the Living and the Dead: Excavations at Barnhouse, Maeshowe.

Ritchie, J. N. G. 1985. Ritual monuments. In Renfrew, C. (ed.), *The Prehistory of Orkney*, pp. 118–130. Edinburgh: Edinburgh University Press.

Service, E. 1971. *Primitive Social Organistaion* (second edition). New York: Random House.

Sharples, N. 1985. Individual and community: the changing role of megaliths in the Orcadian Neolithic. *Proceedings of the Prehistoric Society* 51: 59–74.